Society for Alleviating
the Miseries of Public
Prisoners, Philadelphia
1787

John Howard
*The State of the Prisons
of England and Wales*
1777

Cesare
Beccaria
*Essay on Crimes
and Punishments*
1764

Jeremy Bentham
*Introduction to the
Principles of Morals
and Legislation*
1789

Transportation to the American
colonies from England ends
1776

U.S. government
under Constitution
goes into effect
1789

Pennsylvania passes
legislation nearly
identical to England's
Penitentiary Act of 1779
1790

Anglican Code
replaces "The
Great Law"
1718

States ratify
Bill of Rights
1791

Establishment of regular
postal service between
London and New England
1721

Boston Tea Party
1773

George Washington
becomes first
president of the
United States
1789

Declaration of
Independence
1776

Establishment
of Mason–
Dixon line
1766

Prohibition on
importation
of slaves
1778

Patent on
cotton gin
1794

Founding of Georgia as a
place for English debtors
and criminals
1733

American Revolution
1775–1781

1700

1800

www.wadsworth.com

wadsworth.com is the World Wide Web site for Wadsworth Publishing Company and is your direct source to dozens of online resources.

At *wadsworth.com* you can find out about supplements, demonstration software, and student resources. You can also send e-mail to many of our authors and preview new publications and exciting new technologies.

wadsworth.com
Changing the way the world learns®

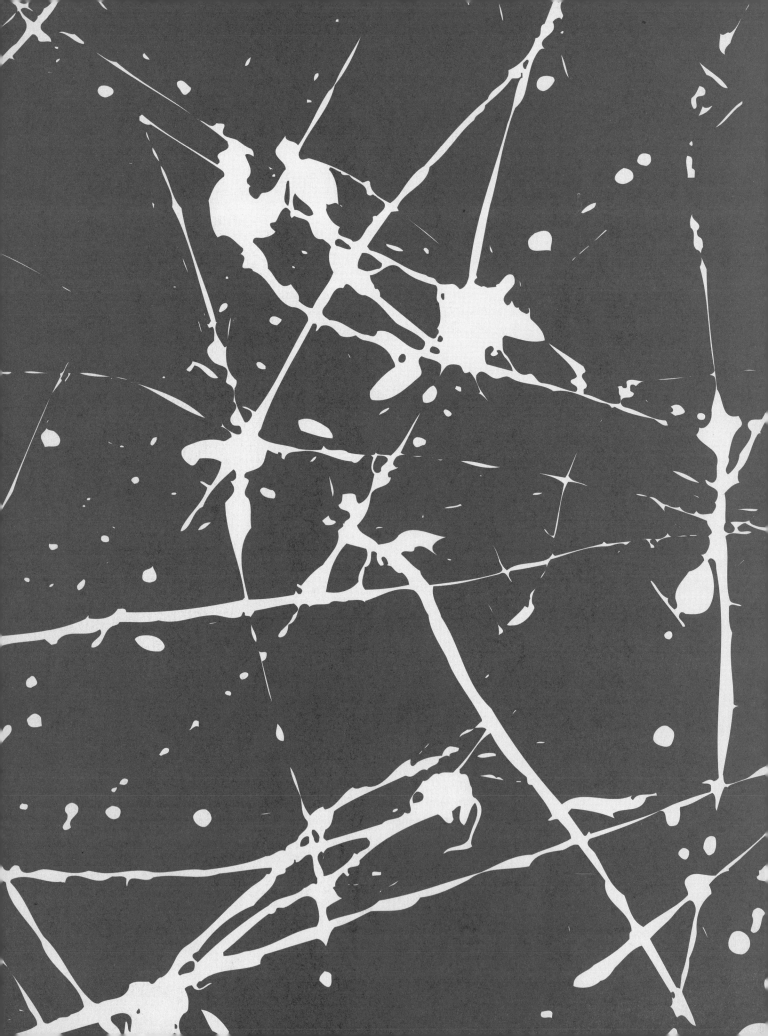

FIFTH EDITION
American Corrections

Todd R. Clear — John Jay College of Criminal Justice

George F. Cole — University of Connecticut

WEST/WADSWORTH

I(T)P® An International Thomson Publishing Company

Belmont, CA ▪ Albany, NY ▪ Boston ▪ Cincinnati ▪ Johannesburg ▪
London ▪ Madrid ▪ Melbourne ▪ Mexico City ▪ New York ▪
Pacific Grove, CA ▪ Scottsdale, AZ ▪ Singapore ▪ Tokyo ▪ Toronto

Executive Editor: Sabra Horne
Senior Developmental Editor: Dan Alpert
Assistant Editor: Shannon Ryan
Editorial Assistant: Ann Tsai
Marketing Manager: Christine Henry
Project Editor: Christal Niederer
Print Buyer: Karen Hunt
Permissions Manager: Bob Kauser

Production: Greg Hubit Bookworks
Designer: rosa + wesley
Photo Editor: Roberta Spieckerman Associates
Copyeditor: Linda Purrington
Cover Design: rosa + wesley
Cover Image: © Lou Jones
Compositor: Thompson Type
Printer: World Color/Versailles

COPYRIGHT © 2000 by Wadsworth Publishing Company
A Division of International Thomson Publishing Inc.
I(T)P® The ITP logo is a registered trademark under license.

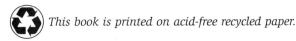 *This book is printed on acid-free recycled paper.*

For permission to use material from this text, contact us:
> web   www.thomsonrights.com
> fax   1–800–730–2215
> phone   1–800–730–2214

Printed in the United States of America
1 2 3 4 5 6 7 8 9 10

Wadsworth Publishing Company
10 Davis Drive
Belmont, CA 94002

International Thomson Editores
Seneca, 53
Colonia Polanco
11560 México D.F. México

International Thomson Publishing Europe
Berkshire House
168-173 High Holborn
London, WC1V 7AA, United Kingdom

International Thomson Publishing Asia
60 Albert Street #15–01
Albert Complex
Singapore 189969

Nelson ITP, Australia
102 Dodds Street
South Melbourne
Victoria 3205 Australia

International Thomson Publishing Japan
Hirakawa-cho Kyowa Building, 3F
2-2-1 Hirakawa-cho, Chiyoda-ku
Tokyo 102, Japan

Nelson Canada
1120 Birchmount Road
Scarborough, Ontario
Canada M1K 5G4

International Thomson Publishing Southern Africa
Building 18, Constantia Square
138 Sixteenth Road, P.O. Box 2459
Halfway House, 1685 South Africa

Library of Congress Cataloging-in-Publication Data

Clear, Todd R.
    American corrections / Todd R. Clear, George F. Cole.
      p.   cm.
    Includes bibliographical references and index.
    ISBN 0–534–52147–9
      1. Corrections—United States.   I. Cole, George F.
    II. Title.
    HV9471.C57 2000
    365'.973—dc21   99-28653

Instructor's Edition: ISBN 0–534–52148–7

Brief Contents

Detailed Contents

Preface

American Corrections was inspired by our shared belief that undergraduates must be exposed to the dynamics of corrections in a manner that captures their attention and encourages them to enter the field. Because corrections is rich in history, is innovative in practice, and is challenged by social problems, it deserves to be taught in both an interesting and an accurate manner. Happily our teaching and research are in different areas of corrections, so each of us was able to focus on the aspects we know best, without forgetting that the other is equally expert and thus qualified to challenge interpretations. Ours has been a pleasurable intellectual and writing experience; we hope that our enthusiasm for our field and the satisfaction we have had in it are reflected in the book.

Corrections is a dynamic and constantly changing field. There have been major changes in American corrections during the past few years. Although crime rates continue to fall, the number of people under correctional supervision has climbed. Pressured by the public to "do something" about crime, political leaders have enacted policies to toughen the punishment of offenders. Laws requiring "truth in sentencing," "three strikes and you're out" policies, sexual offender notification, and chain gangs have been the visible result of public concern. In many states these policies have clogged the courts, crowded prisons and jails, swamped probation and parole caseloads, and tripled correctional costs. Yet increased public and professional attention is being given to research by scholars who have evaluated correctional practices. Many scholars have found these practices wanting and have urged alternatives.

Revision Highlights

As textbook authors we have a responsibility to present current data, coverage of new issues, and descriptions of innovative policies and programs. Toward this end we have completely updated and rewritten this fifth edition on a line-by-line basis. We have been assisted by the comments of an exceptionally knowledgeable team of reviewers who pointed out portions of the text their students found difficult, suggested additional topics, and noted sections that should be dropped. Although the revisions in the fifth edition are too extensive to describe completely here, the following examples illustrate some of the changes that have been made.

New Chapters

Reviewers suggested new chapters to be included in the text. We have followed their advice and added three new chapters.

- *"The Law of Corrections" (Chapter 5)*. This chapter describes the legal rights both of people under supervision and of correctional practitioners.
- *"Corrections for Juveniles" (Chapter 17)*. A key component of corrections is the separate system designed to deal with juvenile offenders.
- *"Community Justice" (Chapter 22)*. The community justice movement has developed innovations to help restore offenders to the community.

New Features

We have always felt that students can learn much from materials that provide real-life examples, examine contemporary issues, or present questions that require thoughtful analysis. To enhance critical learning we have included a number of new features. Several are described here.

- *Comparative Perspective* sections describe aspects of corrections in other countries.
- *Do the Right Thing* sections present ethical dilemmas that often confront correctional practitioners.
- *Workperspectives* written by people in the field are designed to give students a greater appreciation of correctional careers.

The Approach of This Text

In learning about corrections, we believe that students gain a unique understanding of the ways in which social and political forces affect the way organizations and institutions respond to a particular segment of the community. Social values come to the fore in the correctional arena because the criminal sanction reflects those values. In a democracy corrections must operate not only within the framework of law but also within the boundaries set by public opinion. As a public activity corrections is accountable to elected representatives, but it must compete politically with other agencies for resources and "turf."

Two key assumptions about the nature of corrections as a discipline and the best way to analyze correctional practices run throughout the book:

- *Corrections is interdisciplinary.* The academic fields of criminal justice, sociology, psychology, history, law, and political science contribute to our understanding. The cross-fertilization is enriching, yet it requires familiarity with a vast literature. We have structured our text in the interests of coherence.

- *Corrections is a system.* We use the concept of system as a framework for analyzing the relationships among the various parts of corrections and the interactions between correctional professionals and offenders. The main advantage of the system perspective is that it allows dispassionate analysis of correctional practices.

Organization of the Text

As we enter the new millenium, scholars, correctional officials, and political leaders have begun to ask, "Where is corrections headed?" In this fifth edition of *American Corrections,* we explore the context, practices, and special interests of corrections in three major sections. In Part I we describe the historic problems that frame our contemporary experience, by examining the context of the correctional system (Chapter 1), by examining the early history of correctional thought and practice (Chapter 2), by focusing on the distinctive aspects of correctional history in America (Chapter 3), by analyzing current theory and evidence on methods of punishment (Chapter 4), and by surveying the impact of law on corrections (Chapter 5). In Chapter 6, we portray the correctional client: the offender. We consider the offender in relation to criminal legislation, criminal justice processing, and larger societal forces that are associated with crime. Part I is thus a delineation of the underpinnings—the constants—of American corrections: context, history, goals, organizations, and offenders.

In Part II we look at the current state of the major components and practices of the system. The complexity of correctional organization results in fragmentation and ambivalence in correctional services. Jails and other short-term facilities are scrutinized in Chapter 7; probation in the community, by which most offenders are handled, in Chapter 8, and the new focus on intermediate sanctions in Chapter 9. Because imprisonment remains the core symbolic and punitive mechanism of corrections, we examine it in detail. We discuss incarceration (Chapter 10); the prison experience (Chapter 11); incarceration for women (Chapter 12); institutional management (Chapter 13); and educational, industrial, and treatment programs in correctional institutions (Chapter 14). Our perspective is both descriptive and critical, for we hope to raise questions about current incarceration policies. In Chapters 15 and 16, we examine the process of releasing prisoners from incarceration and the ways in which offenders adjust to supervised life in the community. In Chapter 17 (new), we describe the separate system of corrections for juveniles. Thus, in each chapter in Part II we consider closely a functional area of the existing correctional system. We focus on the development, structure, and methods of each area, portraying them in light of the continuing issues described in Part I.

In Part III we analyze those current correctional issues and trends that are of such importance that they deserve individual attention: incarceration trends (Chapter 18); race, ethnicity, and corrections (Chapter 19); the death penalty (Chapter 20); surveillance in the community (Chapter 21); and community justice (Chapter 22). In the Epilogue we conclude by taking both a retrospective view of American corrections and a look toward its future. These chapters are designed to raise questions in the minds of readers so that they can examine and deal with these important issues. An appendix provides career information for students interested in joining the correctional field.

Special Features

Several special features make this introduction to corrections both informative and enjoyable.

1. *Workperspectives:* We asked correctional practitioners to describe their roles, explain how they came to the field, and provide examples of their work practices.

We hope these Workperspectives will help students decide if they want careers in corrections.

2. *Focus sections:* The real-world relevance of the issues discussed in the text is made clear by vivid in-depth accounts by journalists; prisoners, parolees, and their relatives; and corrections workers.

3. *Glossary:* One goal of an introductory course is to familiarize students with the terminology of the field. We have avoided jargon in the text but naturally included terms in common use. Such indispensable words and phrases are set in bold type at their first appearance in the text. A full glossary, with definitions of all terms, is located at the back of the book.

4. *Do the Right Thing:* Correctional workers are often confronted with ethical dilemmas. We present scenarios in which an ethical question arises. You are asked to examine the issues and consider how you would act in such a situation.

5. *Comparative Perspective:* With the move toward more global thinking it is important that we learn more about corrections in other parts of the world. Many chapters of this edition include a Comparative Perspective feature that describes a part of corrections in another country. By learning about others, we learn more about ourselves.

6. *Graphics:* We have created tables and figures that clarify and enliven information so that it can be perceived easily and grasped accurately.

7. *Photographs:* A full program of dynamic photographs is spread throughout the book. These reveal many aspects of corrections that ordinarily are concealed from the public eye.

8. *Careers in corrections:* Because many readers of this book are considering corrections as their profession, we have gathered information in the Appendix to help students guide their decision.

9. *Other student aids:* At the beginning of each chapter is an outline of the topics to be covered; Questions for Inquiry are designed to guide students; at the end of each chapter are a summary, questions for further discussion, and suggestions for further reading.

Instructor's Resources

An extensive package of supplemental aids for a corrections text accompanies this edition. Of most importance are the following items that have been developed to enhance the course and to assist instructors and students.

- *Instructor's Resource Manual with Test Bank*
  A full-fledged Instructor's Resource Manual, backed up by a computerized test bank, has been developed by Pam Hart of Iowa Western Community College.

- *American Corrections Web Site*
  A web site has been designed for *American Corrections* so that students can review materials covered in class, test themselves on text content, and link to other web sites to gain additional information.

- *World-Class Testing Tools*
  A fully integrated collection of test creation, delivery, and classroom management tools featuring all the test items found in the Instructor's Resource Manual. Instructors can generate tests randomly, select specific questions, and write or import their own questions.

In this fifth edition of *American Corrections,* we offer an accurate analysis of contemporary corrections that is based on up-to-date research. We acknowledge the problems with the system, and we hope that our exposition will inspire suggestions for change. We are aware, however, that corrections professionals tend to grasp at one proposed innovation after another. We believe that when human freedom is at stake, policies must reflect research and must be formulated only after their potential effects have been considered carefully. We hope that a new generation of students will decide that a career in corrections is for them. We also hope that they will have a solid understanding of all the aspects of their complex field.

Acknowledgments

In writing this fifth edition of *American Corrections,* we were greatly assisted by people who merit special recognition. Instructors and students who used the fourth edition were most helpful in pointing out its strengths and weaknesses; we took their comments seriously and hope that new readers will find their educational needs met more fully.

We also gratefully acknowledge the valuable contributions of the following reviewers:

Thomas G. Blomberg, Florida State University
Joe Curry, El Paso Community College
Mary Finn, Georgia State University
Pam Hart, Iowa Western Community College
Scott Hedlund, St. Martin's College
Janice Joseph, Richard Stockton College of New Jersey
William Kelly, Auburn University
Joan Petersilia, University of California at Irvine
Greg Pierce, Blue Mountain Community College
Bert Useem, University of New Mexico
Kevin N. Wright, State University of New York, Binghamton

We have also been assisted in writing this edition by a diverse group of associates. Chief among them is Sabra Horne, Criminal Justice Editor, who was supportive of our efforts and kept us on our course. The help of Senior Developmental Editor Dan Alpert was invaluable as we revised the book. The project has benefited much from the attention of Christal Niederer, Project Editor. The talented Gladys Rosa-Mendoza of rosa + wesley designed the interior of the book. Shannon Ryan was invaluable in helping us develop the supplemental aids. Ultimately, however, the full responsibility for the book is ours alone.

Todd R. Clear
tclear@garnet.acns.fsu.edu

George F. Cole
gcole@uconnvm.uconn.edu

FIFTH EDITION
American Corrections

PART ONE

The Correctional Context

To study American corrections, we first need to discuss its social, historical, and political context. For example, what does the term *corrections* mean? How has punishment been used in Europe and the United States to maintain social control? What are the goals of corrections? Part I explores such questions to give the reader (1) a broad, general framework within which to analyze the correctional system and (2) a perspective on the history of corrections within the criminal justice system.

CHAPTER ONE
The Corrections System

The Purpose of Corrections

A Systems Framework for Understanding Corrections
Goals
Interconnectedness
Environment
Feedback
Complexity

The Corrections System Today

Key Issues in Corrections
Managing the Correctional Organization
Working with Offenders
Connecting Corrections and Social Relations

Summary

Twenty-five years ago, most people knew very little about corrections. Prisons were alien "big houses," infused with mystery and located in remote places. The average American had no direct knowledge of "the joint" and no way of learning what it was like. Most people did not even know what probation or parole were, much less have an opinion about their worth.

Since the early 1970s, however, the unprecedented growth in corrections has given the system a high profile. In 1971 the incarceration rate was 96 per 100,000 Americans; by 1997 the rate had mushroomed to 445 per 100,000. Correctional budgets have increased by over 500 percent during that time. Over 3,000 offenders are now on death row, and another 70,000 are serving life sentences.

This growth means that more Americans than ever have direct experience with the corrections system. Counting all its forms—prisons, jails, probation, parole, and community corrections—a total of 5.7 million adults (more than 1 out of every 20 men and 1 out of every 100 women) are now under some form of correctional control. This represents an astounding 2.9 percent of the adult U.S. population. Our incarceration rate is higher than any other nation in the world, except Russia, and is six to ten times higher than incarceration rates in European countries.[1] The extensive growth of the correctional population since 1980 is shown in Figure 1.1.

Surprisingly, correctional population growth has continued throughout the 1990s, although crime rates have been falling since 1992. Many people think correctional population grew in response to this century's growth in crime. So you might think that as crime declines, so would correctional caseloads. But studies of crime rates since the mid-1970s show that the steady increase in prison populations does not match a similar increase in crime.[2] The swelling prison population, despite dropping crime rates, seems to be due to tougher criminal justice policies. If these trends continue, some estimate that in the year 2000 the prison and jail population will exceed 2 million.[3]

The expansion of corrections has been more concentrated in some groups than others. About one-third of all African-American men in their twenties are under some form of correctional control. In some cities, such as Detroit, Baltimore, and Philadelphia, as much as half of this group is under penal supervision. Nearly 7 percent of all African-American men between ages 20 and 40—the age of most fathers—are serving prison terms.

Figure 1.1 Correctional Populations in the United States, 1980–1997

Although the increase in prison populations receives the most publicity, a greater proportion of correctional growth has occurred in probation and parole.

SOURCES: U.S. Department of Justice, Bureau of Justice Statistics, Press Release, August 16, 1998; *Bulletin*, January 1998.

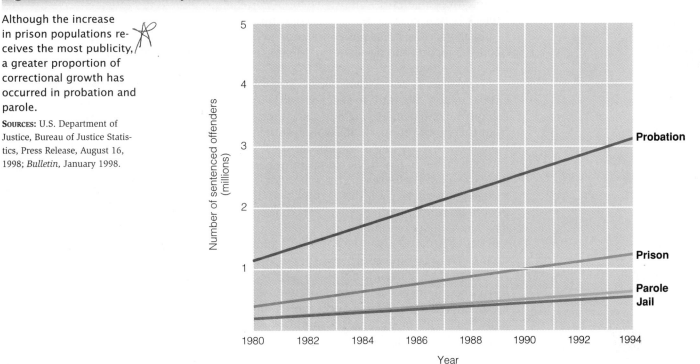

High profile cases such as the death sentence given Timothy McVeigh puts corrections in the public eye. But do these stories accurately portray the system?

So one reason corrections no longer seems as mysterious as it once may have is that today so many more of us experience it directly. Nearly 6 million or so Americans are now in the corrections system, and 900,000 more are convicted of a felony every year. Add the impact on their fathers and mothers, brothers and sisters, aunts and uncles, and husbands, wives, and children. This gives you an idea of how pervasive corrections is today—especially for poor Americans and people of color.

Also, our news media are dominated by crime stories. The O. J. Simpson trial held the nation spellbound for over a year. Americans were similarly fascinated with Susan Smith, convicted in the murder of her children; with Timothy McVeigh, arrested in connection with the terrorist bombing of the Federal Building in Oklahoma City; and "Una-bomber" Theodore Kaczynski, whose trial raised issues of mental competence.

These are just a few of many cases that have shaped recent American thinking about penology. The murder in California of 12-year-old Polly Klaas led to a national crusade for "three strikes" legislation, putting third-time felons away for life. The rape-murder in New Jersey of tiny Megan Kanka by a released sex offender fueled a drive to notify neighborhoods when a convicted sex offender moves in.

For every such story, innumerable other local stories never even make the national press. Read any local newspaper or watch any local nightly news and you will encounter a crime story that raises questions about corrections: Should the offender have been released? Is the sentence severe enough? Should laws for this type of crime be tougher?

In short, corrections has come into the public eye. But are the images we form based on media reports and our own experiences accurate? Do they tell us all we need to know about corrections?

People study corrections because they want to learn more about the problems that rivet attention. We want to see beyond the three-minute news story, to understand what is happening to people caught in the system. And we suspect that what seems so simple from the viewpoint of a politician arguing for a new law or a news reporter telling us today's crime story may in fact be far more complex for the people involved.

One theme in this book is that things are not as simple as they look. New laws and policies seldom achieve exactly what they were intended to, and they often have unintended consequences. In this text we will discuss the fact that most important issues in penology, from the effectiveness of rehabilitation to the impact of the death penalty, have more than one side.

We begin with a seemingly simple question: What is the purpose of corrections? In answering this question, we will engage a pattern that recurs throughout the book. Any important correctional issue is complicated and controversial. The more you learn about a given issue, the more you see layers of truth, so that your first findings are bolstered by evidence and then challenged by further investigation and deeper knowledge. In the end we think you will acknowledge that there are few easy answers, but plenty of intense questions. This chapter focuses on the following Questions for Inquiry.

1. What is the purpose of corrections?
2. What is the meaning and usefulness of a systems framework?
3. What does the corrections system look like today?
4. What are some of the key issues in corrections?

The Purpose of Corrections

It is 11 a.m. in New York City. For several hours, a five-man crew has been picking up trash in a park in the Bronx. Across town on Rikers Island, the view down a corridor of jail cells shows the prisoners' hands, gesturing through the bars as they converse, play cards, share cigarettes—the hands of people doing time. About a thousand miles to the south, almost a hundred inmates sit in isolated cells on Florida's death row. In the same state, a woman on probation reports to a "community control officer." On her ankle she wears an electronic monitoring device that signals the officer if she leaves her home at night. On the other side of the Gulf of Mexico, sunburned Texans in stained work clothes tend crops. Almost due north in Kansas, an inmate grievance committee in a maximum-security prison reviews complaints of guard harassment. Out on the West Coast, in San Francisco, a young man on his way to work checks in with his parole officer and drops off a urine sample at the parole office. All these activities are part of corrections. And all the central actors are offenders.

Punishing people who break society's rules is an unfortunate but necessary part of social life. From the earliest accounts of humankind, punishment has been used as one means of **social control,** of compelling people to behave according to the norms and rules of society. Parents chastise their children when they disobey family rules, groups ostracize individuals who deviate from expected group norms, colleges and universities expel students who cheat, and governments impose sanctions on those who break the criminal laws.

Of the various ways that societies and their members try to control behavior, criminal punishment is the most formal, for crime is perhaps the most serious type of behavior over which a society must gain control.

Thus, in addition to protecting society, corrections helps define the limits of behavior so that everyone in the community understands what is permissible. The nineteenth-century sociologist Emile Durkheim argued that crime is normal and that punishment performs the important function of spotlighting societal rules and values. When a law is broken, citizens express outrage. The deviant thus focuses group feeling. As people unite against the offender, they feel a sense of mutuality or community. Punishing those who violate the law makes people more alert to shared interests and values.

Three basic concepts of Western criminal law—offense, guilt, and punishment—define the purpose and procedures of criminal justice. In the United States, Congress and state legislatures define what conduct is considered criminal. The police, prosecutors, and courts determine the guilt of a person charged with a criminal offense. The post-conviction process then focuses on what should be done with the guilty person.

The central purpose of **corrections** is to carry out the criminal sentence. The term *corrections* usually refers to actions applied to offenders after they have been convicted and implies the action is "corrective," to change these people according to society's needs. Corrections also includes actions applied to people who have been accused—but not yet convicted—of criminal offenses. Such people are often under supervision waiting for action on their cases—sitting in jail, undergoing drug or alcohol treatment, or living in the community on bail.

When most Americans think of corrections, they think of prisons and jails. This belief is strengthened by legislators and the media, which focus much attention on incarceration

social control

Actions and practices of individuals and institutions designed to induce conformity with the norms and rules of society.

corrections

The variety of programs, services, facilities, and organizations responsible for the management of individuals who have been accused or convicted of criminal offenses.

Figure 1.2 Percentage of People in Each Category of Correctional Supervision

Although most people think of corrections as prisons and jails, in fact almost three-quarters of offenders are supervised within the community.

SOURCE: U.S. Department of Justice, Bureau of Justice Statistics, "Nation's Probation and Parole Population Reached New High Last Year," Press Release, August 16, 1998.

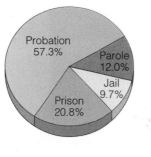

Probation 57.3%
Parole 12.0%
Jail 9.7%
Prison 20.8%

and little on community corrections. As Figure 1.2 shows, however, almost three-quarters of all people under correctional supervision are living in the community on probation or parole.

Corrections thus encompasses all the legal responses of society to some prohibited behavior: the variety of programs, services, facilities, and organizations responsible for managing people accused or convicted of criminal offenses. When criminal justice researchers, officials, and practitioners speak of corrections, they may be referring to any number of programs, processes, and agencies. Correctional activities are performed by public and private organizations; involve federal, state, and local governments; and occur in a variety of community and closed settings. We can speak of corrections as a department of the government, a subfield of the academic discipline of criminal justice, an approach to the treatment of offenders, and a part of the criminal justice system. Corrections is all these things and more.

A Systems Framework for Studying Corrections

system

A complex whole consisting of interdependent parts whose operations are directed toward common goals and influenced by the environment in which they function.

Because it reflects social values, corrections is as complex and challenging as the society in which we live today. Corrections is legal intervention to deter, to rehabilitate, to incapacitate, or simply to punish or achieve retribution. Students need a framework to sort out this complex, multidimensional nature of corrections. In this book we use the concept of the corrections system as a framework for study. A **system** is a complex whole consisting of interdependent parts whose operations are directed toward common goals and influenced by the environment in which they function. Interstate highways, for example, make up a transportation system. The various components of criminal justice—police, prosecutors, courts, corrections—also function as a system.

One of every forty-three Americans is under some form of correctional supervision. Most offenders live among us in the community.

Goals

Corrections is a complicated web of disparate processes that ideally serve the goals of fair punishment and community protection. These twin goals—punishment and protection—both define the purpose of corrections but also serve as criteria by which we evaluate correctional work. Correctional activities make sense when they seem to punish offenders fairly or offer some sense of protection. If people think a correctional practice is unfair or unsafe, that distresses them.

When these two functions of punishment and protection do not correspond, corrections faces goal conflict. For example, people may feel it is fair to release offenders on parole once they have served their sentences, but may be concerned about any threat the parolees pose to the community. Goal conflicts set up conflicts in the way the system operates.

Interconnectedness

Corrections can be viewed as a series of processes: sentencing, classification, supervi-

sion, programming, and revocation, to name but a few. Processes in one part of the corrections system affect, in both large and small ways, processes in the rest of the system.

For example, when a local jail changes its policies on eligibility for work release, the probation caseload will be affected. When a parole agency improves supervision with new drug-screening practices, the increased number of violators uncovered by the new policy will affect jails and prisons within the system. When presentence investigation report writers don't check their facts, poorly reasoned correctional assignments may result.

These processes all affect one another because offenders pass through corrections in a kind of assembly line with return loops. After criminals are convicted, a sentencing selection process determines which offender goes where, and why. This sifting process is itself uncertain and often hard to understand. Most, but not all, violent offenders are sent to prison. Most, but not all, violators of probation or parole rules are given a second chance. Most, but not all, offenders caught committing crimes while supervised by correctional authorities will receive more severe punishment. Figure 1.3 shows examples of interconnections among correctional agencies as they deal with offenders who have been given different sentences.

Figure 1.3 Interconnectedness of Correctional Agencies in Implementing Sentences

Note the number and variety of agencies that deal with these two offenders. Would you expect these agencies to cooperate effectively with one another? Why or why not?

Case 1: Two years probation, drug treatment, and fifty hours of community service.

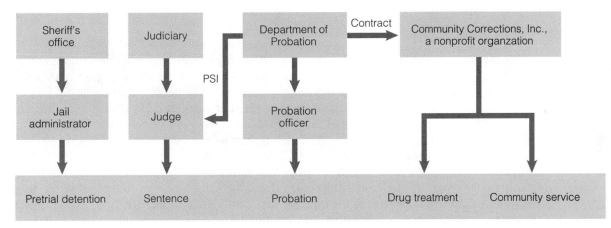

Case 2: Two years incarceration to be followed by community supervision on parole.

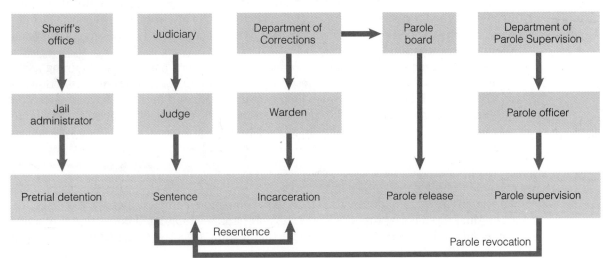

Corrections has links with other criminal justice agencies. The police, sheriff, prosecutor, and judiciary all play roles with regard to correctional clients. What are some of the problems that develop out of these necessary links?

Environment

As they process offenders, correctional agencies must deal with outside forces such as public opinion, fiscal constraints, and the law. Thus, sometimes a given correctional agency will take actions that do not seem best suited to achieving fairness or public protection. At times correctional agencies may seem to work at odds with one another or with other aspects of the criminal justice process.

Corrections has a reciprocal relationship with its environment. That is, correctional practices affect the community, and community values and expectations in turn will affect corrections. For example, if the prison system provides inadequate drug treatment, offenders return to the community with the same drug problems they had when they were locked up. Likewise, when citizens lack confidence in a corrections system, they are unlikely to spend tax dollars on its programs.

Feedback

Systems learn, grow, and improve based on the feedback they receive about their effectiveness. When a system's work is well received by its environment, the system organizes itself to continue functioning this way. When feedback is less positive, the system adapts to improve processes.

Although feedback is crucial for corrections, corrections has trouble obtaining useful feedback. When things go well, the result is the absence of something—no new crimes or no prison riots. It is difficult for people to become aware of things that have not occurred but that might have. In contrast, when corrections fails, everybody knows: The media report new crimes or expose scandals in administration. As a result, corrections systems and their environments tend to overrespond to correctional failure but be less aware of success.

Complexity

As systems grow and mature, they tend to become more complex. Twenty years ago, the traditional three P's—probation, prisons, and parole—dominated correctional practice. Today all kinds of activities come under the heading of corrections, from pretrial drug treatment to electronically monitored home confinement, from work centers where offenders earn money for restitution, to private, nonprofit residential treatment programs.

The complexity of the corrections system is illustrated by the variety of public and private agencies that comprise the corrections system of Philadelphia County, Pennsylvania, as Table 1.1 shows. Note that offenders are supervised by various service agencies operating at different levels of government (state, county, municipal) and in different branches of government (executive, judicial).

The Corrections System Today

The American corrections system today employs more than half a million administrators, psychologists, officers, counselors, social workers, and others. Authorized by the laws of the federal government, fifty states, over three thousand counties, and uncounted municipalities, public and private organizations administer corrections at an average annual cost of over $30 billion.[4]

Corrections consists of many subunits, each with its own functions and responsibilities. These subunits—probation offices, halfway houses, prisons, and others—vary in size, goals, clientele, and organizational structure. Some are government agencies; others are private organizations contracted by government to provide specific services to correctional clients. A probation office is organized differently from a halfway house or a prison, yet all three are part of the corrections system and pursue the goals of corrections. There are, however, important differences among subunits of the same general type. A five-person probation office working closely with one judge in a rural setting,

Table 1.1   The Distribution of Correctional Responsibilities in Philadelphia County, Pennsylvania

Note the various correctional functions performed at different levels of government by different government agencies. What are the correctional agencies of your community?

Correctional Function	Level and Branch of Government	Responsible Agency
Adult Corrections		
Pretrial detention	Municipal/executive	Department of Human Services
Probation supervision	County/courts	Court of Common Pleas
Halfway houses	Municipal/executive	Department of Human Services
Houses of corrections	Municipal/executive	Department of Human Services
County prisons	Municipal/executive	Department of Human Services
State prisons	State/executive	Department of Corrections
County parole	County/executive	Court of Common Pleas
State parole	State/executive	Board of Probation and Parole
Juvenile corrections		
Detention	Municipal/executive	Department of Public Welfare
Probation supervision	County/courts	Court of Common Pleas
Dependent/neglect	State/executive	Department of Human Services
Training schools	State/executive	Department of Public Welfare
Private placements	Private	Many
Juvenile aftercare	State/executive	Department of Public Welfare
Federal corrections		
Probation/parole	Federal/courts	U.S. courts
Incarceration	Federal/executive	Bureau of Prisons

SOURCE: Taken from the 1983 and 1984 annual reports of the responsible agencies.

for example, has an organizational life different from that of the more bureaucratized 100-person probation office in a large metropolitan system. Such organizational variety may help or hinder the system of justice.

federalism

A system of government in which power and responsibilities are divided between a national government and state governments.

The United States operates under **federalism,** a system of government in which power and responsibility are divided between a national government and state governments. All levels of government—national, state, county, and municipal—are involved in one or more aspects of the corrections system. The national government operates a full range of correctional organizations to deal with the people convicted of breaking federal laws; likewise, state and local governments provide corrections for people who have broken their laws. However, most criminal justice and correctional activity takes place at the state level. Only about 2 percent of individuals on probation, 5 percent of those on parole, and 9 percent of those in prison are under federal correctional supervision.

Despite the similarity, from state to state, of behaviors that are labeled criminal, important differences appear among specific definitions of offenses, types and severity of sanctions, and procedures governing establishment of guilt and treatment of offenders. In addition, there are many variations in how corrections is formally organized at the state and local levels. Four state corrections systems—California, Florida, New York, and Texas—handle nearly one-third of all offenders under correctional control in the United States, and each of these four states has developed different organizational configurations to provide corrections (see the Focus box).

prison

An institution for the incarceration of persons convicted of serious crimes, usually felonies.

jail

A facility authorized to hold pretrial detainees and sentenced misdemeanants for periods longer than forty-eight hours. Most jails are administered by county governments; sometimes they are part of the state government.

The extent to which the different levels of government are involved in corrections varies. The scope of the states' criminal laws is much broader than that of federal criminal laws. As a result, only about 200,000 adults are under federal correctional supervision. There are 125 federal **prisons** and 1,375 state prisons. **Jails** are operated mainly by local governments, but in six states they are integrated with the state prison system. As noted in Figure 1.4, criminal justice costs are borne by each level of government, with about 95 percent of correctional costs falling on state and local governments. In most states the agencies of community corrections—probation and intermediate sanctions—are run by the county government and are usually part of the judicial branch. However, in some jurisdictions they are run by the executive branch, and in several states this part of corrections is run by statewide organizations.

That the United States is a representative democracy complicates corrections. Officials are elected; legislatures determine the objectives of the criminal law system and appropriate the resources to carry out those objectives; and political parties channel public opinion to officeholders on such issues as law and order. Over time the goals of correctional policies have shifted. For example, between 1940 and 1970, corrections was oriented toward liberal rehabilitative policies; since about 1970, conservative "get tough" crime control policies have influenced corrections. Questions of crime and justice are thus inescapably public questions, subject to all the pressures and vagaries of the political process.

Clearly corrections encompasses a major commitment on the part of American society to deal with people convicted of criminal law violations. The increase in the number

<u>**Figure 1.4**</u> **Distribution of Justice System Expenditures by Level of Government**

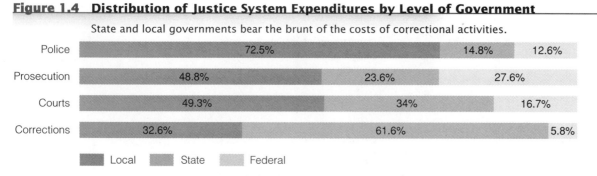

State and local governments bear the brunt of the costs of correctional activities.

Police — 72.5% | 14.8% | 12.6%
Prosecution — 48.8% | 23.6% | 27.6%
Courts — 49.3% | 34% | 16.7%
Corrections — 32.6% | 61.6% | 5.8%

Local   State   Federal

SOURCE: U.S. Department of Justice, Bureau of Justice Statistics, *Bulletin,* September 1993.

FOCUS

The Big Four in Corrections

Four states from four different regions in the United States dominate the correctional scene: California, Texas, New York, and Florida. They account for about 36 percent of all offenders under correctional control (see Table 1 for a breakdown of the key numbers).

California

Not only does California have the largest prison population in the United States, but it also has the second highest rate of growth (after tiny New Hampshire) in number of prisoners since 1983. Much of this growth has been attributed to landmark "get-tough" sentencing reform combined with a gradual increase in the severity of sentences.

The California adult corrections system is administered by the Adult Authority, which is a part of the state executive branch of government. Juvenile institutions are administered by the Youth Authority. Adult and juvenile probation services are provided by the executive branch at the county level and administered by a chief probation officer. A portion of the county probation costs is subsidized by the state, but these subsidies are a smaller part of the budget than in the 1980s. Local taxes pay for jails and probation services, and predictably these services have been hit very hard by funding caps placed on government services. Jails and probation compete with schools and hospitals for scarce funds. One result is that jails are filled to capacity and priority is given to sending prisoners to the state facilities, which are themselves overcrowded (but funded by a different tax base). Probation caseloads have also grown—for example, from 100 per officer a decade ago to over 300 per officer now in Los Angeles County. Californians seem to want to be tough on law violators but not to have to pay for it. The most pressing question in California, especially given the state's huge budget deficit, is how to reconcile these two concerns.

The prospects in California are for increasing numbers of offenders in prisons and jails. Much of this increase will result from new "three strikes" legislation enacted in 1994, which provides longer terms for third-time felons. One study estimates that by 2005 all nonmandated state revenues will be needed to finance corrections.

Florida

The state of Florida is a newcomer to the group of four largest correctional systems. This development is ominous, because the current age profile in Florida represents what the nation as a whole will look like in the year 2010. If Florida is a sign of things to come, corrections in the United States as a whole will continue to grow.

The state of Florida administers all institutional and community-based correctional services regionally, and regional directors have considerable autonomy. The five adult regional administrators report to the secretary of the Department of Corrections and manage all institutional and field services. Juvenile corrections is housed within the Department of Health and Rehabilitative Services and operates in eleven districts. Thus, Florida unifies corrections under the executive branch, with separate adult and juvenile functions.

In 1984, when Florida enacted guidelines to overcome widespread sentencing disparity, institutional admissions skyrocketed. Alarmed, Florida administrators started the Community Control Project, providing close supervision (often with electronic monitoring) to divert offenders from prison. The program is the largest diversion effort in the nation, taking in about a thousand new offenders per month. Florida's prison admissions have been dropping since 1990, but prison populations continue to grow because sentences are longer.

New York

The corrections system in New York was for many decades regarded as innovative. The reformatory was a New York invention, as was modern parole. Today New York is seen as a large, stable, well-administered bureaucracy, but no longer as on the cutting edge.

The Department of Corrections manages adult institutional corrections; the Division of Youth Services manages juvenile institutions and aftercare. Probation is a county function; adult and juvenile services are administered by a single chief probation officer, who is accountable to the county chief executive. The state Division of Probation carries out a coordinating function for probation. The Division of Parole administers both parole release and supervision. New York operates decentralized correctional services with strong state coordination.

As with almost all states, the New York corrections system is overcrowded. Moreover, an added burden is created by New York City corrections, which itself includes jails and prisons. The New York City corrections system is larger than that of many states, and is seriously overcrowded and strapped for funds. This puts pressure on the state operations, because many New York City prisoners are awaiting assignment to state facilities.

In the first half of the 1990s, tightening revenues have raised concern among correctional leaders in New York. As one of his first acts as governor, George Pataki proposed loosening the laws for minor repeat offenders, hoping that would ease pressure on the corrections system. A boot

(continued)

camp program has also shortened incarceration for some drug offenders. Still, experts wonder how the state will deal with the ever-growing numbers of prisoners, especially those from New York City, which faces chronic revenue shortfalls.

Texas

In terms of corrections, Texas earns its reputation of "bigness": More Texans are under correctional control than any other state in the Union. Nearly one in seven of the nation's probationers live in Texas. Recent sentencing laws doubled Texas's prison population in a mere five years.

All adult corrections in Texas are housed under the Department of Criminal Justice, which is supervised by a nine-person board appointed by the governor. This department administers corrections through three separate divisions: institutions, parole supervision, and probation. In addition, the parole board reports to the Board of Criminal Justice. The Institutional Division, in addition to managing all state custodial facilities, monitors the local jails. The Texas Youth Commission handles all juvenile institutions and aftercare. Organized on a county basis,

adult and juvenile probation are run separately by chief probation officers locally appointed by the county judiciary. Standards for both probation functions are established and monitored by state authority. Adult probation is monitored by the Department of Criminal Justice; juvenile probation, by the Juvenile Probation Commission. (There has been a recent effort to bring all juvenile corrections under the umbrella of the Department of Human Services.) Because Texas has over two hundred counties, coordinating the work of these commissions is extremely complicated.

Over the past decade Texas corrections has operated under something of a siege mentality. As a result of a series of lawsuits, Texas prisons have a tight population cap, forcing the rest of the system to be more cautious in incarcerating offenders. Obviously, decision-making fragmentation makes it nearly impossible to develop a coordinated response to the prison overcrowding problem. A federal judge recently threatened to fine the state over $500,000 a day if it failed to comply with court-ordered standards. An emergency legislative session was called, and all parts of the system were pressured to develop responses to control prison crowding.

Table 1   The Big Four by the Numbers

Population	California	Florida	New York	Texas
Prison	153,010	64,703	69,530	136,599
Probation	286,526	237,117	174,406	429,329
Parole	99,578	21,146	57,137	112,594
Jail	69,298	34,183	29,809	55,395

Rank Among 50 states				
Incarceration rate	11	13	22	1
Violent crime rate	7	1	12	14

SOURCES: U.S. Department of Justice, Bureau of Justice Statistics, *Bulletin*, January 1998; Press Release, August 16, 1998.

of offenders under supervision in the past decade has caused a major expansion of correctional facilities, staff, and budgets; some might say that corrections is now a big business.

Spending for corrections has risen more dramatically than for any other state function, jumping more than 400 percent between 1979 and 1995. In 1998, state legislatures increased operating appropriations for corrections by 6.6 percent (excluding construction costs), compared to a 4.1 percent increase for Medicaid and a 5.1 percent increase for higher education.[5] States increasing their correctional appropriations by more than 20 percent included North Dakota (47.1 percent), Missouri (27.5 percent), Montana (21.9 percent), and Arkansas (20.8 percent). Many states now spend more on corrections than on all public higher education. Proband found a correlation between low state expenditures for AFDC (Aid to Families with Dependent Children) and high corrections costs.[6] Figure 1.5 shows how much more correctional costs have grown since 1982 than other justice budgets. Figure 1.6 shows state patterns of correctional budget growth in a single year: 1997 to 1998.

Figure 1.5 Percentage Change in Expenditures for Justice Activities. All Governments, 1982–1993

Among all criminal justice agencies, corrections has had the greatest increase in expenditures expressed in constant 1990 dollars.

SOURCE: U.S. Department of Justice, *Justice Expenditures and Employment Abstracts, 1993* (Washington, DC: U.S. Department of Justice, 1995), p. 42.

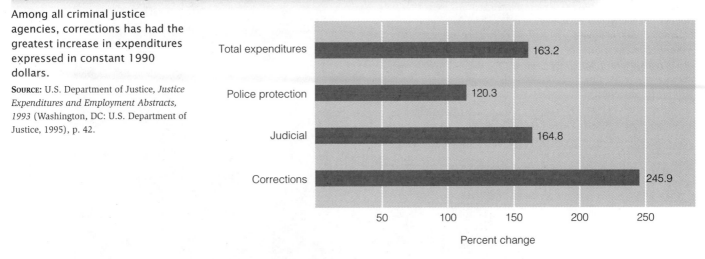

Total expenditures	163.2
Police protection	120.3
Judicial	164.8
Corrections	245.9

Percent change

Figure 1.6 Growth in State Expenditures for Corrections: 1997-1998

In many states, the corrections budget is the fastest-growing part of state government costs.

SOURCE: Stan C. Proband, "State Corrections Budgets Up 5.1 Percent, *Overcrowded Times,* 9, April 1998, p. 2.

WA 2.6 · MT 2.5 · ND 3.5 · MN 0.2 · NH 2.7 · VT 4.6 · ME 1.4
OR 21.9 · ID 1.7 · WY 15.8 · SD 8.5 · WI 4.7 · MI 3.7 · NY −0.5 · MA 7.2 · RI 0.6
NV 7.0 · UT 10.5 · NE 2.5 · IA 8.6 · IL 10.7 · IN 0.8 · OH 13.4 · PA 12.4 · NJ −1.1 · CT 9.5 · DE 7.9
CA 8.1 · CO 5.9 · KS 4.5 · MO 19.0 · WV 5.7 · VA 12.2 · MD −0.1
AZ 11.1 · NM −0.2 · OK 17.2 · AR 10.8 · KY 8.4 · TN 0.9 · NC 8.2 · SC 15.0
TX 5.1 · LA 9.5 · MS 4.4 · AL 1.1 · GA −1.0
AK −1.7 · HI 2.6 · FL 9.0

Key Issues in Corrections

Like all other government services, corrections is buffeted by frequently shifting social and political forces that greatly complicate administration. These forces are also part of what make corrections so interesting to study. In this section we describe some of the controversies, issues, and themes that arise in the study of corrections. These are divided into two main areas: managing the correctional organization and working with offenders.

Managing the Correctional Organization

The ways in which different correctional organizations are managed depend on various factors, including goals, funding, bureaucracy, and interagency coordination.

Goals   The theory inherent in the term *corrections*—the assumption that offenders can be "corrected"—is itself much in dispute. For example, some people believe that it is not

Correctional policies are developed through the political process. Here, Florida representative Johnnie Byrd explains to other legislators a bill requiring parolees to submit to searches.

possible to rehabilitate most offenders, that only social maturation influences most people to abide by the law. Others argue that the penal system should not be concerned with the future behavior of criminals, that the only appropriate response to wrongdoing is punishment. Yet from the end of World War II until the 1970s, the corrective function was so widely accepted that treatment and reform of offenders were virtually the only issues in criminal justice deemed worthy of serious attention.

What goals to emphasize has been a constant question for corrections. Conflict over goals stems precisely from the shifting forces that directly influence corrections. Political ideology, for example, often colors the analysis and development of correctional policy. Liberals believe that corrections should follow one path; conservatives believe in another path. Goals set by conflicting interests do not always mesh.

Thus correctional leaders offer conflicting (or at least divergent) justifications for a given policy in order to maintain an appearance of consensus. A program of private industry employment for prison inmates, for instance, can be commended to liberals as rehabilitative training, to free-enterprise advocates as expansion of the private sector, and to conservatives as a get-tough policy designed to make prisoners pay the costs of their incarceration. Although this tactic helps preserve support for the prison's industrial operations, it also creates managerial problems for correctional leaders because when the program is implemented, the goals of treatment, profit, and punishment may well conflict.

Correctional leaders who state precise objectives risk alienating various important groups or constituencies. Thus they tend to frame goals as vague generalities, such as "to protect the public" or "to rehabilitate offenders." The effects of this vagueness extend well beyond public relations; often it is difficult for correctional staff members to make goal-oriented choices because they are unsure of what the leaders want. This has led some observers to argue that corrections does not work to achieve an overriding goal, but rather seeks to balance stated and unstated goals so that no single goal is sacrificed.

Funding At all political levels, the corrections system is only one of many services operated by government and paid for by tax revenues. Thus corrections must vie for funding, not only with other criminal justice agencies but also with agencies dealing with education, transportation, social welfare, and so on. Per capita spending on all criminal justice activities ranges from less than $100 in West Virginia to more than $400 in Alaska and New York. Table 1.2 shows some of the costs of providing correctional services.

Understandably, corrections does not always get the funding it needs; people may want garbage collected regularly more than they want quality correctional work performed. Recall, too, that corrections is largely invisible until a problem occurs, such as when a parolee commits a heinous crime or a prison riot breaks out. An even greater difficulty stems from the perceived undesirability of those corrected; it is not easy to win larger budgets to help people who have broken the law.

Conflict among the branches and levels of government also creates problems for corrections. Local governments are often responsible for correctional programs for minor offenders; state governments handle longer-term, more serious offenders. Often the two levels vie for operating funds, and each seeks to avoid responsibility for offenders being supervised by the other. Given this fragmentation, correctional services and programs may overlap.

Officials of the executive branch often complain that legislatures enact correctional codes and prescribe operational responsibilities without providing sufficient funds to carry them out. Both branches complain that court rulings set unfair constraints on their ability to handle assigned offenders. In developing and implementing policies, correctional agents must consider not only the sociopolitical environment but also the government setting in which corrections functions.

One result of funding squabbles is that organizational "turf" is often disputed. Most probation offices are attached to the judiciary and funded by county governments. Are they then within the domain of corrections or of the judiciary? Should the sheriff be in charge of transporting offenders from jail to prison, or should the prison administrators be responsible? To what extent should social service agencies become involved with the needs of correctional clients in a halfway house? Should parole officers or the police be responsible for tracking down offenders who have violated the conditions of their release?

Struggles for resources also occur between corrections and related social service agencies. A department of corrections may vie with a department of mental health for funds to set up a drug rehabilitation program; both departments may view the new resources as a way to expand. Such empire-building actions are often taken merely to keep a corrections department strong and viable.

Bureaucracy Michael Lipsky has provided perhaps the most vivid portrait of the problems facing correctional workers. He coined the term **street-level bureaucrats** to refer to

> public service workers who interact directly with citizens in the course of their jobs, [including] teachers, police officers and other law enforcement personnel, social workers, judges, public lawyers and other court officers, health workers and many other public employees who grant access to government programs and provide services within them.[7]

Lipsky's provocative generalizations about street-level bureaucrats apply to virtually all individuals who have face-to-face contact with offenders. They work with inadequate

Table 1.2 What Do Correctional Dollars Buy?

Correctional services are expensive. Compare the average cost for the items listed here with the cost of a college education.

Average Cost ($)	
One adult offender, annually	
In maximum security prison	$19,500
In community-based facility	8,000
On federal community supervision	1,300
On state/local community supervision	643
One unsentenced federal prisoner, per day	
In local jail	$ 36
In halfway house	30
In prison or jail	33
Construction costs per bed	
Maximum-security prison	$80,000
Medium-security prison	53,000
Minimum-security prison	43,000

SOURCES: Adapted from U.S. Department of Justice, Bureau of Justice Statistics, *Report to the Nation on Crime and Justice,* 2nd ed. (Washington, DC: U.S. Government Printing Office, 1988); Edna McConnell Clark Foundation, *Seeking Justice* (New York: Edna McConnell Clark Foundation, 1997).

street-level bureaucrats

Public service workers who interact directly with citizens in the course of their work, granting access to government programs and providing services within them.

resources and face ever-increasing demands. Frequently they are in situations in which they are theoretically obligated to provide higher-quality treatment for their clients than is possible given the associated high costs. Thus street-level bureaucrats soon learn that "with any single client they probably could interact flexibly and responsibly. But if they did this with too many clients, their capacity to respond flexibly would disappear."[8] Probation officers may believe, for example, that they are obliged to find jobs for their probationers, but if they took time to do so they could not provide other services. An officer may genuinely desire to work hard for those probationers who show promise, but not for others. Officers facing these conflicts may become alienated from their clients because they cannot satisfy their clients' needs—it's too frustrating to maintain a working relationship.

Limited resources force administrators of service bureaucracies to carefully monitor the way workers apply their time and energies. Bureaucracies that process people develop categories for their clients, seeking to best use personnel or agency resources and to succeed with some clients, even though they cannot succeed with them all.

Lipsky concluded that a contradiction is inherent in delivering street-level policy through bureaucracy. One person delivering service from one to another suggests human interaction, caring, and responsibility. But delivering service through a bureaucracy suggests detached, inflexible treatment based on limited resources. Conflicting, ambiguous goals, combined with difficulties in measuring work performance, may reduce effectiveness and commitment to the work. Thus the bureaucratic model guarantees that services are delivered only up to a point and that goals are never fully achieved.

Is Lipsky's conclusion too pessimistic or just realistic? Hard to say. Certainly correctional workers and their clients face formidable obstacles. Workers must make daily decisions under conditions of technical uncertainty and sporadic negative feedback; offenders must comply both with legal mandates and with less explicit parameters established by the needs of the correctional organization. Yet bureaucratic worker-client relations have positive benefits. As their time and tasks are more structured, workers have less discretion, and thus less capacity to abuse their positions. Further, limited organizational resources force agencies to clarify their goals and to direct services toward people who most need staff time. And given the extensive power of correctional agencies, conditions in bureaucracies may restrain abuse of state power.

Interagency Coordination   Managing correctional agencies is further complicated because most corrections systems comprise several loosely related organizations that are themselves bureaucracies. Thus decision making is dispersed, and no one person can implement the full range of correctional practices. For example, the sheriff who runs the jail and the probation officer who runs the pretrial release program both are affected by jail crowding and delays in sentencing hearings. Even so, they may resist working together, because each is busily protecting an area of managerial control. Furthermore, line workers in corrections, those in direct contact with offenders, seldom influence organizational policies, even though they are responsible daily for implementing those policies. Corrections itself is unable to determine the type and number of its clients. Others in the criminal justice system, primarily judges, do that, and correctional officials cannot halt or regulate the flow. Thus the efforts of correctional workers are sometimes sporadic, uncoordinated, or inconsistent merely because various bureaucracies are loosely interconnected.

Within the corrections system a great deal of policy is formally interconnected. In some states as many as half or more of all inmates are in prison because they have violated a requirement of probation or parole; in other states, these rule violators are less frequently sent to prison. In other words, the enforcement policies of the supervising agencies largely determine prison intake. Yet in most systems prison authorities have little control over policies for enforcing probation rules. Similarly, a probation officer's caseload is determined by the number of people on probation and the length of their probation terms. Even though officers have a finite amount of time for supervision, they generally have little or no control over their caseloads. As offenders flow through the system—from probation to revocation to prison to work release to parole—one agency determines the workload of the next.

These informal interconnections create an uneasy tension. Agency directors understandably may take steps to protect their piece of the system from encroachment by the rest of the system. Each corrections unit commonly insulates itself from the pressures faced by the other units, because the others often produce unwanted caseload increases. For example, crowded jail conditions may encourage judges to put more offenders on probation. That very isolation makes it more likely that the other units will run into problems resulting from a lack of cooperation, and these problems will haunt all the units when the corrections system as a whole is criticized.

Working with Offenders

"People work" is central to corrections because the raw material of the system consists of people—staff and offenders. In working with offenders, correctional staff must deal with uncertain technologies, engage in exchange relationships with offenders, and follow uncertain correctional strategies.

Professional Versus Nonprofessional Staff   The term *staff* refers to probation officers, correctional officers, counselors, and others who have responsibility for daily management and supervision of offenders. The correctional staff includes both professional and nonprofessional employees. For example, psychologists, counselors, and administrators usually hold at least one college degree. They view themselves as members of various professions, with all the rights that adhere to such callings. They believe they should be able to work without supervision and to make decisions without always consulting rulebooks or guidelines. These professional employees work closely with nonprofessional staff, such as jail or prison correctional officers. The nonprofessional staff frequently have only a high school education, and they function under close, often paramilitary (military-style) supervision, and enforce rules with physical means when necessary. The different perspectives of these two groups and the ways they communicate with one another have caused problems in some types of correctional organizations—for example, conflicts over the best ways to deal with offenders, and distrust of each other's motives and expertise.

technology

A method of applying scientific knowledge to practical purposes in a particular field.

"People work" is central to corrections. Staff must work closely with offenders, using uncertain technologies, engage in exchange relationships, and follow uncertain strategies.

Uncertain Technologies   The term *technology* refers to methods of applying scientific knowledge to practical purposes in a particular field. Yet the technologies of corrections are not as sophisticated as those of, say, engineering, and their subjects—human beings—are far more complex. Methods of effectively dealing with offenders are highly uncertain. Although knowledge of human behavior has developed during the past century, the validity of the various approaches for treating offenders—such as group therapy, behavior modification, and anger management—remains in doubt.

Thus corrections is expected to implement programs of questionable value. Correctional organizations face a serious problem: Not all prison releasees adjust successfully to free society; not all mental health referrals of offenders result in emotional adjustment; not all probationers prove trustworthy. Correctional decisions are prone to error. In fact, correctional organizations may approach the technical problem of human ignorance about humans by seeking to reduce types of error, rather than to eliminate error altogether.

Further, any organization develops routines simply in order to operate. Like most people, workers in correctional organizations want regular and predictable responsibilities. They do not want to venture into uncharted seas where they may make an uninformed decision and then be penalized for it. Uncertainty declines when people reduce operations to routines—patterns that repeat and thus become familiar. Recognizing these routines is essential for understanding corrections.

Exchange   A key facet of corrections is the degree of interdependence between staff and offenders. The unarmed, outnumbered correctional officer assigned to a prison or jail has surprisingly little raw power with which to exact cooperative behavior. Likewise a probation officer can do little with a probationer who resists the officer's influence. Meanwhile the prisoner depends on the work of the correctional officer, and the parolee often feels powerless under supervision. Thus staff and offenders are interdependent; to achieve personal goals, each depends on the other. The officer needs the offender's cooperation to convince superiors that the officer is performing properly; the offender needs the officer's recommendation for favorable termination of parole.

exchange

A mutual transfer of resources based on decisions as to the costs and benefits of alternative actions.

The interdependence of correctional people makes the concept of **exchange** important to understanding their daily world. Exchange occurs when two parties trade promises or concessions that make each person's work easier or more predictable. A probationer, for example, cooperates by reporting regularly and attending an alcohol treatment program; in return, the officer is more likely to overlook incidental, minor violations of probation conditions. Each party's situation is made easier by the voluntary decisions of the other.

Because exchange relations between staff and offenders are very important, they often are subject to informal enforcement. For instance, a rowdy inmate is removed from his cell and placed in solitary until he "settles down" and recognizes officials' authority. A juvenile on probation is arrested and "detained" (locked up) for the weekend while awaiting a hearing on her truancy from school, even though officials have no intention of revoking her probationary status. Conversely, a guard who is hostile or condescending to inmates finds it takes much longer to return prisoners to their cells for the morning count or to quiet down noisy prisoners. Subtle and not-so-subtle pressures unceasingly reinforce the need for keepers and the kept to stay aware of each other's needs.

In sum, correctional transactions almost uniformly involve some aspect of worker–offender contact and interaction. Because staff members and offenders depend on each other to achieve their goals, each person can influence evaluations made by the other. This process must be managed through screening and processing routines, staff training and evaluation programs, and so forth.

Uncertain Correctional Strategies   In the chapters to come, an important theme will be the high uncertainty of choices that correctional workers and managers must make. How does the correctional official organize staff, choose programs, and manage offenders when the consequences of such actions are so ambiguous? Given this uncertainty, organizational theorists say that the correctional environment is unstable and that, as a result, one of management's major concerns is avoiding negative feedback from the community, such as the courts, political leaders, and the public.

Because the effectiveness of correctional strategies in dealing with offenders is so uncertain, organizations often place greater emphasis on secondary technologies in which they have more confidence—the design of a prison's security apparatus, a computer-based offender-tracking system for probation, and so on. But the core work of corrections concerns the interactions of people—staff and offenders—about which uncertainty will always remain, no matter what the technology.

There are two points of interest here. First, offenders obviously are handled in a variety of ways. Who determines what happens to offenders, and how they make this determination, is a key issue in this book. Second, and even more central, corrections gets its "business" not only from the courts but from itself. Policies and practices determine how strictly the rules will be enforced, how dire the consequences will be when they are broken, and how much latitude staff will have in assigning offenders to programs.

Connecting Corrections and Social Relations

All these problems combine to make the field of corrections controversial and therefore engrossing for those who study it. Yet as compelling as these problems may be, they are only a sidelight to the central appeal of the field of corrections. The questions that corrections raises concerning social control are fundamental to defining society and its values. Seemingly every aspect of the field raises questions that concern deeply held values about social relations. For example, what kinds of services and treatment facilities are to be provided to inmates infected with HIV, which leads to AIDS? Should corrections be more concerned with punishing offenders for crimes or with providing programs to help them overcome problems in their lives that contribute to crime? Is placing surveillance devices in people's homes a good idea or an invasion of privacy? Questions of interest to researchers, students, and citizens hardly end here. Crucial public and private controversies lurk at every turn. And you will find you cannot answer the questions inherent in these controversies without reference to your values and those of society.

People who undertake careers in corrections often do so because they find the field an excellent place to express their most cherished values. Probation and parole officers frequently report that their original decision to work in these jobs stemmed from their desire to help people. Correctional officers often report that the aspect of their work they like best is working with people who are in trouble and who want to improve their lives. Administrators report that they value the challenge of building effective policies and helping staff perform their jobs better. All these individuals are saying that the field of corrections helps them be fully involved with public service and social life. Corrections is interesting to them in part because it deals with a core conflict of values in our society—freedom versus social control—and it does so in ways that require people to work together.

Summary

Corrections consists of many programs, services, facilities, and organizations responsible for managing people accused or convicted of crimes. It is complex, because it encompasses broad responsibilities related to the formal responses of society to prohibited behavior.

The concept of the system provides a framework or comprehensive theme for studying corrections. The corrections system is composed of both large and small organizations administered by various levels of government and the private sector. The staff of these organizations are in contact with one another and in direct authority over offenders. In this context they strive to achieve the organizations' complex goals.

Many correctional workers, like others in the human service field, are street-level bureaucrats. They interact with citizens and are in a position to grant access to government programs and to furnish services within those programs. Correctional officials are theoretically obligated to provide high-quality services, but often cannot, because such quality services cost too much. Officials are therefore unable to maintain the standards set for service and must devise strategies to work with limited resources. Moreover, correctional technologies are of uncertain value and offenders have not voluntarily sought the services. Despite these problems, corrections is concerned with basic social values. ■

For Discussion

1. What do you see as some of the advantages and disadvantages of the systems concept of corrections?

2. Corrections is a system in which technologies of uncertain validity are used. What are some of the dangers of using these technologies? What safeguards, if any, should be applied?

3. Assume that the legislature has stipulated that rehabilitation should be the goal of corrections in your state. How might people working in the system displace this goal?

4. What does Lipsky mean by the term "street-level bureaucrat"? Give some examples of how street-level bureaucrats act.

5. Suppose you are commissioner of corrections for your state. Which correctional activities might come within your domain? Which might not?

For Further Reading

Clear, Todd R. *Harm in American Penology: Offenders, Victims, and Their Communities.* Albany: State University of New York Press, 1994. Analyzes the past twenty years of corrections and develops the concept of penal harm.

Cole, George F., and Christopher E. Smith. *The American System of Criminal Justice,* 8th ed. Belmont, CA: Wadsworth, 1998. Introduces the American system of criminal justice.

Flanagan, Timothy J., and Dennis R. Longmire. *Americans View Crime and Justice: A National Public Opinion Survey.* Thousand Oaks, CA: Sage, 1996. Summarizes current public opinion about crime and justice policy, as well as changes in public opinion in recent years.

Garland, David. *Punishment and Modern Society.* Chicago: University of Chicago Press, 1990. Argues that the social meaning of punishment is misunderstood and that we need to discover ways to punish that are more in keeping with our social ideals.

Lauen, Roger. *Positive Approaches to Corrections: Research, Policy and Practice.* Lanham, MD: American Corrections Association, 1997. Analyzes contemporary policy problems in corrections, and suggests policy options supported by the best available research.

Walker, Samuel. *Sense and Nonsense About Crime: A Policy Guide,* 3rd ed. Belmont, CA: Wadsworth, 1997. Examines crime control practices that don't work and those that have some potential for success.

Windlesham, Lord. *Politics, Punishment and Populism.* New York: Oxford University Press, 1998. A study of American politics and crime policies that resulted in the Violent Crime Control and Law Enforcement Act of 1994, done by a former chairman of the Parole Board for England and Wales.

Notes

1. Marc Mauer, *Americans Behind Bars: U.S. and International Use of Incarceration,* 1995 (Washington, DC: The Sentencing Project, June 1997), p. 1.
2. Alfred Blumstein, "U.S. Criminal Justice Conundrum: Rising Prison Populations and Stable Crime Rates," *Crime and Delinquency,* 44(1), January 1998, pp. 127–135.
3. *National Inmate Population of Two Million Projected by 2000* (Washington, DC: The Sentencing Project, July 31, 1998).
4. Jill Rose Smeltz, *Analyzing the Growth of State-Local Corrections Spending* (Albany, NY: Center for Study of the States, July 1995).
5. Stan C. Proband, "State Correctional Budgets up 5.1 Percent in 1998," *Overcrowded Times,* 9, April 1998, 3.
6. Stan C. Proband, "Corrections Costs Lead State Budget Increases in 1995," *Overcrowded Times,* April 1995, p. 1.
7. Michael Lipsky, *Street-Level Bureaucracy* (New York: Russell Sage Foundation, 1980), p. 3.
8. Lipsky, *Street-Level Bureaucracy,* pp. 37–38, 81, 99.

CHAPTER TWO

The Early History
of Correctional
Thought and
Practice

A hush fell over the French courtroom on March 2, 1757, as the chief judge rose to read the sentence on Robert-François Damiens, convicted of trying to assassinate King Louis XV:

> He is to be taken and conveyed in a cart, wearing nothing but a shift, holding a torch of burning wax weighing two pounds; in the said cart to the Place de Greve, where on a scaffold that will be erected there, the flesh will be torn from his breasts, arms, thighs and calves with red-hot pinchers, his right hand, holding the knife with which he committed the said parricide, burnt with sulphur, and, on those places where the flesh will be torn away, poured molten lead, boiling oil, burning resin, wax and sulphur melted together and then his body drawn and quartered by four horses and his limbs and body consumed by fire, reduced to ashes and his ashes thrown to the winds.[1]

Newspaper accounts recorded that Damiens's death was even more horrible than the sentence required. Because the horses were not able to pull him "limb from limb," the executioners resorted to hacking off Damiens's arms and legs. All this occurred while the man was still alive.

What was the point of this punishment? What did the state hope to achieve through this atrocity? Why does this execution seem so horrible to us today? After all, public corporal punishment was the norm for thousands of years, and it was pursued with gusto.

Until the 1800s, throughout Europe and even America punishments were public spectacles. Crowds taunted the condemned as the executioner or sheriff conducted whippings, burnings, pilloryings, and hangings on orders of the king or court. Punishment-as-spectacle was used to control crime and to exhibit the sovereign's power. Yet only a few decades after Damiens's 1757 execution, a major change had taken place in Europe and then the United States. Efforts were now being made to devise a rational, reformative model of criminal sanctions focused on the mind and soul, not the body. With the development of the penitentiary in the 1830s as a place where offenders could reflect on their misdeeds, repent, and prepare for life as crime-free citizens, torture as a public spectacle disappeared. By the 1900s punishments were carried out within prisons or in the community under the supervision of correctional staff who saw themselves not as instruments of suffering but as social workers, managers, and technicians of reform.

Like other social institutions, corrections reflects the vision and concerns of the larger community. For example, in their post–Revolutionary War idealism Americans strongly believed crime could be eliminated from this rich new nation if offenders were isolated from bad influences and encouraged to repent. Similarly, in the early 1900s, inspired by a new faith in the behavioral sciences, penology veered sharply toward a psychological approach to offender rehabilitation. And then, as crime rose in the late 1960s, public opinion demanded another shift in correctional policy, toward greater emphasis on crime control.

Students often wonder why they need to know the history of corrections. They say they are anxious to get right into learning about prisons, probation, and parole. But as historian John Conley notes, understanding the past may help people better evaluate new approaches to corrections. He also says that by understanding the past we can better understand where corrections may be headed in the next century.[2]

In this chapter we examine the broad European antecedents to American correctional thought and practice. In Chapter 3 we continue this historical overview by looking at corrections in the United States from colonial times to the present. Later in the book we discuss the history of such specific correctional practices as prison industry, probation, and parole in greater detail. Let us begin here by examining the correctional practices of earlier times.

Questions
FOR INQUIRY

1. What were the major forms of punishment from the Middle Ages to the American Revolution?

2. What was the Age of Reason, and how did it affect corrections?

3. What was the contribution of Cesare Beccaria and the Classical School?

4. What was the contribution of Jeremy Bentham and the Utilitarians?

5. How did the work of John Howard influence correctional reform?

From the Middle Ages to the American Revolution

cholars point to the Hammurabic Code, developed by the king of Babylon in 1750 B.C. as the first comprehensive statement of prohibited behavior. However, not until the beginning of the European Middle Ages, in the 1200s did forms of legal sanctions appear that are familiar today. Before that time in Europe, responses to crime were viewed as a private affair, with vengeance a duty to be carried out by the person wronged or by a family member. Wrongs were avenged in accordance with the *lex talionis,* or law of retaliation. This principle underlay the laws of Anglo-Saxon society until the time of the Norman Conquest of En-gland in 1066. During the Middle Ages the **secular law** of England and Europe was organized according to the feudal system.[3] In the absence of a strong central government, crimes among neighbors took on the character of war, and the public peace was endangered as feudal lords sought to avenge one another's transgressions. In response, in England by the year 1200 a system of *wergild,* or payment of money as compensation for a wrong, had developed as a way of reducing the frequency of violent blood feuds. During this period the custom of treating offenses as personal matters to be settled by individuals gradually gave way to the view that the peace of society required the public to participate in determining guilt or innocence and in exacting a penalty.

During the Middle Ages various punishments were imposed upon the body of the offender. These punishments were harsh and were used extensively.

   The main emphasis of criminal law thus was on maintaining public order among people of equal status and wealth. Georg Rusche and Otto Kirchheimer describe the procedure:

> *If, in the heat of the moment, or in a state of intoxication, someone committed an offense against decency, accepted morality, or religion, or severely injured or killed his neighbor . . . a solemn gathering of free men would be held to pronounce judgment and make the culprit pay Wergild or do penance so that the vengeance of the injured parties should not develop into blood feud and anarchy.*[4]

Given the parties involved, the main criminal punishments were penance and the payment of fines or restitution. Lower-class offenders without money received physical punishment at the hands of their masters.

   During this same period the church, as the dominant social institution, maintained its own system of ecclesiastical punishments, which had a great impact on society as a whole. Especially during the Inquisition of the 1300s and 1400s, the church zealously punished those who violated its laws. At the same time, it gave refuge from secular prosecution to people who could claim **benefit of clergy.** In time, benefit of clergy was extended to all literate persons.

   In the later Middle Ages, especially during the 1400s and 1500s, governmental authority was extended and the criminal law system more fully developed. With the rise of trade, the breakdown of the feudal order, and the emergence of a middle class, other forms of sanction were applied. In addition to fines, five punishments were common in Europe before the 1800s: galley slavery, imprisonment, transportation, corporal punishment, and death. As we will discuss, each of these punishments had a specific purpose, and the development of each was linked to ongoing social conditions. It is important to recognize that at the time, with no police force or other centralized instruments of order, deterrence was the dominant purpose of the criminal sanction. Thus, before the 1800s it was believed that one of the best ways to maintain order was to intimidate the entire population by publicly punishing offenders.

lex talionis

Law of retaliation; the principle that punishment should correspond in degree and kind to the offense ("an eye for an eye and a tooth for a tooth").

secular law

The law of the civil society as distinguished from church law.

wergild

"Man money"; money paid to relatives of a murdered person or to the victim of a crime to compensate them and to prevent a blood feud.

benefit of clergy

*The right to be tried in an
ecclesiastical court, where
punishments were less
severe than those meted
out by civil courts, given
the religious focus on
penance and salvation.*

Galley Slavery

Galley slavery was the practice of forcing men to row ships. Now popularly identified with ancient Rome or Greece, galley slavery was not formally abolished throughout Europe until the mid-1700s.[5] However, by the 1500s the practice had begun to wane with the advent of heavy sailing ships. At first exclusively for slaves or men captured in battle, galley slavery came to be the lot of some convicts, often as a reprieve from the gallows. According to a 1602 proclamation by Queen Elizabeth I, the galleys were considered more merciful than ordinary civil punishments, even though the oarsmen might remain in chains for life.[6]

Imprisonment

jail

*Until the 1800s a facility
authorized to hold
primarily pretrial
detainees, debtors, and
vagrants. Today jails in the
United States also hold
sentenced misdemeanants.
Most jails are administered
by county governments;
sometimes they are part of
the state government.*

Until the 1800s **jails** were used primarily for the detention of people awaiting trial and for some sentenced political criminals and lower-class people who could not pay their fines or debts. In ancient times offenders were incarcerated in cages, rock quarries, or even in chambers under the Roman Forum while they awaited punishment, but for most offenders imprisonment was not *the* punishment.[7]

Conditions in these prisons were appalling. Men, women, and children, healthy and sick, were locked up together; the strong preyed on the weak, sanitation was nonexistent, and disease was epidemic. Furthermore, authorities made no provision for the inmates' upkeep. Often the warden viewed his job as a business proposition, selling food and accommodations to his charges. The poor thus had to rely for survival on alms brought to them by charitable persons and religious groups.

Attempts to reform prisons began in the 1500s. With the disintegration of feudalism, political power became more centralized and economies began to shift from agriculture to manufacturing. As links to feudal landlords dissolved, the rural poor wandered about the countryside or drifted to the cities. The emphasis of the Protestant Reformation on the importance of hard work and the sinfulness of sloth stirred European reformers to urge that some means be found to provide work for the idle poor. Out of these concerns the **house of correction** or "workhouse" was born.

house of correction

*Detention facility that
combined the major
elements of a workhouse,
poorhouse, and penal
industry by both
disciplining inmates and
setting them to work.*

In 1553 London's Bishop Nicholas Ridley persuaded Edward VI to donate Bridewell Palace as the first house of correction. The facility was not merely a place of detention, as was the jail, but combined the major elements of a workhouse, poorhouse, and penal institution. Whereas jails were thought to promote idleness among the inmates, the house of correction was expected to instill "a habit of industry more conducive to an honest livelihood."[8] The inmates—primarily prostitutes, beggars, minor criminals, and the idle poor—were to be disciplined and set to work. The products made in the house of correction were to be sold on the market, so that the facility would be self-sufficient and not need government subsidy. The term *Bridewell House* came to be used for all versions of the English house of correction.

Institutions similar to the English house of correction appeared in Holland, France, Germany, and Italy. Visiting these places in 1775, the English penal reformer John Howard was impressed by their cleanliness, discipline, and emphasis on rehabilitation through Bible study and regularity of habits. A motto carved over the doorway to one institution succinctly defined the authority of the law with regard to the inmates: "My hand is severe but my intention benevolent." This motto influenced the later development of the penitentiary.

Of the European institutions, the Milan House of Correction, built in 1755, and a similar institution in Ghent, the Maison de Force, built in 1772, attracted particular attention, the latter because of its design. It was an octagonal building surrounding a central yard. Eight long pavilions radiated from the center, allowing the separation of inmates by the seriousness of crime, sex, or status as a member of the noncriminal poor. The prisoners worked in common areas during the day and were segregated at night.

Conditions in England's Bridewells deteriorated as the facilities increasingly housed criminals rather than the poor, the orphaned, and the sick. In the 1700s the labor power provided by the inmates was no longer economically profitable, and the reformative aim of the institution vanished. But as we'll see, elements of the houses of correction were later incorporated in the penitentiary and the industrial prison of the nineteenth century.

Transportation

From ancient times people who have disobeyed the rules of a community have been cast out, or banished. With the breakdown of feudalism and the worsening of economic conditions in 1600s, prisons and houses of correction in England and Europe filled to overflowing. The "New World" represented a convenient place to send French, Spanish, and English offenders from which they would probably not return.[9] For Russians, **transportation** to Siberia often meant death. For a modern example of banishment, see the Focus box.

Bridewell houses were workhouses built throughout England for the employment and housing of offenders. Here prisoners work at the treadwheel while others exercise in the yard of the vagrants' prison.

Initially English prisoners could choose transportation in place of the gallows or the whipping post. With passage of the Vagrancy Act of 1597, transportation became prescribed. By 1606, with the settlement of Virginia, the transportation of convicts to North America became economically important for the colonial companies for whom they labored for the remainder of their sentences. It also helped relieve the overcrowded prisons of England.

Transportation seemed so successful that in 1717 a statute was passed allowing convicts to be given over to private contractors, who then shipped them to the colonies and sold their services. Prisoners who returned to England before their terms expired were to be executed. The Transportation Act of 1718 made transportation the standard penalty for noncapital offenses. From 1718 to 1776 an estimated fifty thousand British convicts were shipped to the American colonies. In 1772 three-fifths of male convicts were transported.[10]

___transportation___

The practice of transplanting offenders from the community to another region or land, often a penal colony.

FOCUS

Teens Banished to Islands After Robbery

They'll have sleeping bags, and tools for cutting firewood and gathering food. But they'll have no way to contact the outside world during a year or more of exile to offshore islands whose only inhabitants are animals, including black bears.

Two 17-year-old Tlingit Indian boys, Adrian Guthrie and Simon Roberts, were banished to separate islands by tribal elders for beating and robbing a pizza delivery man.

It is the first case of a state court referring a criminal case to an American tribal panel for a traditional Indian punishment.

Guthrie and Roberts were held aboard a fishing boat pending their move to the sprawling Alexander Archipelago of hundreds of mountainous islands off the coast of southeastern Alaska. Tribal officials will not disclose their final destinations. . . .

The teenagers pleaded guilty to robbing Tim Shittlesey and beating him with a baseball bat while he was working as a pizza delivery man in Everett, Washington. They stole $47 and a pizza . . . Whittlesey, 25, suffered permanent damage to his hearing and eyesight.

Twelve tribal elders deliberated for three and a half hours before banishing the two for a year to 18 months.

Elder Byron Skinna, Sr., said each boy would be given forks for digging up clams, axes and saws for cutting firewood, and some food to carry them through the first few days. He said they would have sleeping bags and each will build a small shelter, which would be equipped with a wood stove for cooking and heating. . . . They will be checked on periodically, but there will be no way for them to contact the outside world even in case of emergency. . . .

SOURCE: "Two Teens Banished to Islands After Robbery," *The Hartford Courant,* September 4, 1994.

Offenders transported to Australia lived under military rule and were required to work for the Crown. Upon completion of their sentence most remained and helped found a new nation.

hulks

Abandoned ships the English converted to hold convicts during a period of prison crowding between 1776 and 1790.

corporal punishment

Punishment inflicted on the offender's body with whips or other devices that cause pain.

With the onset of the American Revolution, transportation from England temporarily halted. By this time questions also had been raised about the appropriateness of the policy. Some critics argued that it was unjust to send convicts to live in a country where their lives would be easier than at home. But perhaps more importantly, by the beginning of the 1700s American planters had discovered that African slaves were better workers and economically more profitable than English convicts. The importation of black slaves increased dramatically, the prisons of England again became overcrowded, and large numbers of convicts were assigned to live in **hulks** (abandoned ships) along the banks of the Thames.

British transportation began again in 1787, to different locales. Over the next eighty years, 160,000 prisoners were transported from Great Britain and Ireland to New South Wales and other parts of Australia. As historian Robert Hughes explains, "Every convict faced the same social prospects. He or she served the Crown or, on the Crown's behalf, some private person, for a given span of years. Then came a pardon or a ticket-of-leave, either of which permitted him to sell his labor freely and choose his place of work."[11]

However, in 1837 a select committee of Parliament reported that, far from reforming criminals, transportation created thoroughly depraved societies. Critics argued that the Crown was forcing Englishmen to be "slaves until they were judged fit to become peasants."[12] The committee recommended a penitentiary system in which offenders were confined and set to hard labor. This recommendation was only partially adopted; not until 1868 did all transportation from England cease.[13]

Corporal Punishment and Death

Although **corporal punishment** and death have been used throughout history, the sixteenth through eighteenth centuries in Great Britain and Europe were particularly brutal. Because publicity was considered a useful deterrent, punishments were carried out in the market square for all to see. The punishments themselves were harsh: whipping, mutilation, and branding were used extensively, and death was the common penalty for a host of felonies. For example, some 72,000 people were hanged during the reign of Henry VIII (1509–1547), and in the Elizabethan period (1558–1603) vagabonds were strung up in rows of 300–400 at a time.[14] (The modern equivalent would be 15,000–23,000 Americans strung up at once.) Capital punishment could either be a "merciful" instant death (beheading, hanging, garroting, and burying alive), or a prolonged death (burning alive or breaking on the wheel). As Spierenburg notes, prolonged death was practically unknown in England, "although a famous pamphlet of 1701 argued that hanging did not effectively deter potential lawbreakers."[15]

Those criminals who were not executed were subjected to various mutilations—removing a hand or finger, slitting the nostrils, severing an ear, or branding—so that the offenders could be publicly identified. Such mutilation usually made it impossible for the marked individual to find honest employment. In sum, almost every imaginable torture was used in the name of retribution, deterrence, the sovereignty of the authorities, and the public good.

The reasons for the rise in the severity of punishments during this period are unclear but are thought to reflect the expansion of criminal law, the enhanced power of secular authorities, an increase in crime (especially during the eighteenth century), and changes in the economic system. For example, the number of crimes for which the English authorized the death penalty swelled from 50 in 1688 to 160 in 1765 and 225 by 1800. Some of the new statutes made capital crimes of offenses that had previously been treated more leniently, and other laws criminalized certain activities for the first time. But the criminal law, popularly known as the Bloody Code, was less rigid than it seemed; it allowed judicial discretion, and lesser punishments were often given.[16]

London, as well as other cities, doubled in population from 1600 to 1700, although the overall population of England and Wales rose by only 25 percent. As might be expected, the incidence of crime in the cities ballooned, due to the population increases and the accompanying widespread poverty. The rise in the number of prosecutions and convictions may also have represented a response by government and the elite to the threat posed to public order by the suddenly outsized working-class population. As Rusche and Kirchheimer have argued, the rise of capitalism led to economic, rather than penal, considerations as the basis for punishment.[17]

On the Eve of Reform

As noted previously, by the middle of the 1700s England was inflicting capital and corporal punishment extensively, transporting large numbers of convicts overseas, and facing the problem of overcrowded jails and houses of correction; yet crime continued its upward curve. England, the most advanced and powerful country in the world, was ready for correctional reform.

At this stage, economic and social factors, particularly with regard to labor, began to reshape the nature of penal sanctions. Other important influences stemmed from altered political relationships and changes in the power of the church and the organization of secular authority.

Around the same time, the revolutionaries in the American colonies, with their liberal ideas about the relationship between citizen and government and their belief in human perfectibility, were setting the stage for a shift in penal policies.

In view of all these considerations, we can arbitrarily designate 1770 as the eve of a crucial period of correctional reform on both sides of the Atlantic.

The Age of Reason and Correctional Reform

During the 1700s, western scholars and social activists, particularly in England and France, engaged in a sweeping reconception of the nature of society. In this remarkable period, known as **The Enlightenment,** or the **Age of Reason,** traditional assumptions were challenged and replaced by new ideas based on rationalism, the importance of the individual, and the limitations of government. Revolutions occurred in America and France, advances were made in science, and the Industrial Revolution came into full swing.

Until the 1700s European society had been generally static and closed; individuals had their place in a hierarchy of fixed social relationships. The Enlightenment represented a liberal reaction against this feudal and monarchical tradition. The Reformation had already ended the religious monopoly held by the Catholic church, and the writings of such Protestant thinkers as Martin Luther and John Calvin encouraged a new emphasis on individualism and the social contract between government and the governed. The triumph of William of Orange in the Glorious Revolution of 1688 brought increased power to the English Parliament, and the institutions of representative government were strengthened. The 1690 publication of John Locke's two treatises on government further developed the ideas of a liberal society, as did the writings of the French thinkers Montesquieu and Voltaire.

Finally, advances in scientific thinking led to a questioning attitude that emphasized observation, experimentation, and technological development. Sir Isaac Newton argued that the world could be known and reduced to a set of rules. The scientific revolution had a direct impact on social and political thought because it encouraged people to question established institutions, use the power of reason to remake society, and believe that progress would ultimately bring about a just community.

The Enlightenment, or the Age of Reason

The 1700s in England and France, when concepts of liberalism, rationality, equality, and individualism dominated social and political thinking.

What impact did these political and social thinkers of the Enlightenment have on corrections? As we have emphasized, ideas about crime and justice are part of larger philosophical and scientific movements. Because of the ideas that gained currency in the 1700s, people in England and America and in Europe began to rethink such matters as the procedures to be used to determine guilt, the limits on a government's power to punish, the nature of criminal behavior, and the best ways to correct offenders. Specifically they began to reconsider how criminal law should be administered and to redefine the goals and practices of corrections. During this period the classical school of criminology emerged, with its insistence on a rational link between the gravity of the crime and the severity of the punishment. Proponents of the social contract and utilitarian philosophies emphasized limitations on the power of government and the need to erect a system of graduated criminal penalties to deter crime. Further, political liberals and religious groups encouraged reform of the prison system.

The result was a major shift in penal thought and practice. Penal codes were rewritten to emphasize adaptation of punishment to the offender. Correctional practices moved away from inflicting pain on the body of the offender, toward methods that would set the individual on a path of honesty and right living. And the penitentiary developed as an institution in which criminals could be isolated from the temptations of society, reflect on their offenses, and thus be reformed.

Of the many individuals who actively promoted the reform of corrections, three stand out: Cesare Beccaria (1738–1794), the founder of what is now called the classical school of criminological thought; Jeremy Bentham (1748–1832), a leader of reform in England and the developer of a utilitarian approach to crime and punishment; and John Howard (1726–1790), sheriff of Bedfordshire, England, who helped spur changes that resulted in the development of the penitentiary.

Cesare Beccaria and the Classical School

Cesare Beccaria (1738–1794)

Italian scholar who applied the rationalist philosophy of the Enlightenment to the criminal justice system.

The rationalist philosophy of the Enlightenment, with its emphasis on individual rights, was applied to the practices of criminal justice by the Italian scholar, **Cesare Beccaria** in his 1764 book *Essays on Crimes and Punishments*. He argued that the true aim and only justification for punishment is utility: the safety it affords society by preventing crime.[18] Beccaria was particularly concerned with the lack of a rational link between the gravity of given crimes and the severity of punishment. Six principles underlie the reforms Beccaria advocated, principles from which the classical school of criminology emerged:

1. The basis of all social action must be the utilitarian concept of the greatest good for the greatest number of people.
2. Crime must be considered an injury to society, and the only rational measure of crime is the extent of the injury.
3. Prevention of crime is more important than punishment for crimes. To prevent crime, laws must be improved and codified so that citizens can understand and support them.
4. Secret accusations and torture must be abolished. Further, the accused have a right to speedy trials and to humane treatment before trial, as well as every right to bring forward evidence in their behalf.
5. The purpose of punishment is crime deterrence, not social revenge. Certainty and swiftness in punishment, rather than severity, best secure this goal.
6. Imprisonment should be more widely employed, and better physical quarters should be provided, with prisoners classified by age, sex, and degree of criminality.

Beccaria summarized the thinking of those who wanted to rationalize the law: "In order for punishment not to be, in every instance, an act of violence of one or many against a private citizen, it must be essentially public, prompt, necessary, the least possible in the given circumstances, proportionate to the crime, dictated by laws."[19]

Beccaria's ideas took hold especially in France; many of them were incorporated in the French Code of 1791, in which crimes were organized on a scale and a penalty was affixed to each. In the United States James Wilson, the leading legal scholar of the postrevolutionary period, credited Beccaria with having influenced his thinking, notably with regard to the deterrent function of punishment. Through Wilson, Beccaria's principles had an important effect on reform of the penal laws of Pennsylvania, which laid the foundation for the penitentiary movement.[20]

Jeremy Bentham and the "Hedonic Calculus"

Jeremy Bentham, one of the most provocative thinkers and reformers of English criminal law, is best known for his utilitarian theories, often called his "hedonic calculus." Bentham meant it was possible to categorize all human actions and, either through pleasurable (hedonic) incentives or through punishment, to direct individuals to desirable activities. Undergirding this idea was his concept of **utilitarianism,** the doctrine that the aim of all action should be "the greatest happiness of the greatest number." As Bentham noted, an act possesses utility "if it tends to produce benefit, advantage, pleasure, good or happiness . . . or to prevent the happening of mischief, pain, evil or unhappiness to the party whose interest is considered."[21] Thus, according to Bentham, rational people behave in ways that achieve the most pleasure while bringing the least pain; they are constantly calculating the pluses and minuses of potential actions.

Bentham viewed criminals as somewhat childlike or unbalanced, lacking the self-discipline to control their passions by reason. Behavior was not preordained, but rather was an exercise of free will. Thus crime was not sinful but the result of improper calculation. Accordingly the criminal law should be organized so that the offender would derive more pain than pleasure from a wrongful act. Potential offenders, recognizing that legal sanctions were organized according to this scheme, would be deterred from committing antisocial acts.

Bentham sought to reform the criminal laws of England so that they emphasized deterrence and prevention. The goal was not to avenge an illegal act, but to prevent the commission of such an act in the first place. Because excessive punishment was unjustified, the punishment would be no more severe than necessary to deter crime: not "an act of wrath or vengeance," but one of calculation tempered by considerations of the social good and the offender's needs.[22]

Bentham wrote at a time when John Howard, Elizabeth Fry, and others were attempting to reform the English criminal code by reducing corporal punishment and by developing the penitentiary. Bentham sought to end the capriciousness, barbarity, and inconsistency of punishment; to improve the prison system; and to abolish transportation. Like Beccaria he urged that criminal justice follow rules and that punishment focus on rehabilitating the offender.

Bentham developed plans for a penitentiary based on his utilitarian principles. The design of his "panopticon," or "inspection house," called for a circular building with a glass roof and cells on each story around the circumference. This arrangement would permit a prison inspector in the center of the building to keep out of sight of the prisoners yet view their actions through a system of blinds. The panopticon was never constructed in England; one was proposed for France but never adopted, as was one for Ireland. Two panopticon-type prisons actually were constructed in the United States. In 1825 Western State Penitentiary was opened in Pittsburgh, modeled to some extent on Bentham's ideas. The fullest expression of the style was the prison in Stateville, Illinois, where four circular cellhouses were built from 1916 to 1924. Described by an architect as "the most awful receptacle of gloom ever devised and put together with good stone and brick and mortar,"[23] the panopticon was quickly abandoned.

John Howard and the Birth of the Penitentiary

Probably no individual did more for penal reform in England than **John Howard**—county squire, social activist, and sheriff of Bedfordshire. Like many members of the

Jeremy Bentham (1748–1832)

English advocate of utilitarianism in prison management and discipline. Argued for the treatment and reform of prisoners.

utilitarianism

The doctrine that the aim of all action should be the greatest possible balance of pleasure over pain; hence the belief that a punishment inflicted on an offender must achieve enough good to outweigh the pain inflicted.

John Howard (1726–1790)

English prison reformer whose book, The State of the Prisons in England and Wales, *was a major force in passage of the Penitentiary Act of 1779 by the House of Commons.*

John Howard's investigation of conditions in English jails served to rally legislative interest in reform. Howard was a major proponent of the penitentiary.

new merchant class, Howard had a social conscience and was concerned about conditions among the poor. On being appointed high sheriff of Bedfordshire in 1773, he exercised the traditional but usually neglected responsibility of visiting the local prisons and institutions. He was shocked by what he saw, especially when he learned that the jailers received no regular salary but made their living from the prisoners and that many people who had been discharged by the grand jury or acquitted at their trials were still detained because they could not pay their discharge fees.[24]

Howard expanded his inspections to the prisons, hulks, and houses of correction outside his jurisdiction, and then to those in Europe. In England the prisons were overcrowded, discipline was lacking, and sanitation was unheard of—thousands died yearly from disease. Even members of the free community feared "prison fever," for the disease often infected courthouse personnel and others in contact with offenders. At the time, seven years imprisonment was viewed as a de facto penalty of death.

Howard thought that some of the prisons he visited in Belgium, Holland, Germany, and Italy could be copied in England. In particular, he was favorably impressed by separate confinement of inmates at night after their common daytime tasks. Of the Maison de Force in Ghent he wrote, "The convicts were properly lodged–fed–clothed–instructed–worked. The utmost regularity, order, cleanliness prevailed; there was no drunkenness; no riot; no excessive misery; no irons, no starvation."[25]

Howard's descriptions of conditions in English penal institutions horrified the public. Of particular concern was the lack of discipline. After his report to the House of Commons, Howard, along with Sir William Blackstone and William Eden, drafted the Penitentiary Act of 1779, a curious amalgam of traditional and progressive ideas that had a great impact on penology.

The Penitentiary Act originally called for creating houses of hard labor where people convicted of crimes, that would otherwise have earned them a sentence of transportation, would be imprisoned for up to two years. The act was based on four principles set down by Howard: (1) secure and sanitary structure, (2) systematic inspection, (3) abolition of fees, and (4) a reformatory regimen. Prisoners were to be confined in solitary cells at night but were to labor silently in common rooms during the day. The labor was to be "of the hardest and most servile kind, in which Drudgery is chiefly required and where the Work is little liable to be spoiled by Ignorance, Neglect or Obstinancy"—such work as sawing stone, polishing marble, beating hemp, and chopping rags.[26] The legislation further detailed such items as the diet, uniforms, and conditions of hygiene for the prisoners.

Perhaps influenced by his Quaker friends, Howard came to believe that the new penal institution should be a place not merely of industry but also one for contrition and penance. The twofold purpose of the penitentiary was to punish and to reform offenders through solitary confinement between intervals of work, the inculcation of good habits, and religious instruction so that inmates could reflect on their moral duties.

The Penitentiary Act and follow-up legislation passed in 1782 and 1791 attracted political support from a variety of sources. Legalists sought to deter crime; philanthropists wanted to help humanity; conservatives thought products made by convict labor would save money; and pragmatic politicians wanted to solve the disquieting prison situation. Philanthropists and other social reformers believed solitary confinement was the best way to end the evil of inmate association and to allow reflection. Bentham agreed, because he believed the penitentiary would help deter crime by being onerous to but not destructive of the offender.

What Really Motivated Correctional Reform?

But what was behind this era of criminal law reform? Apparently reform was brought about as much by the emergence of the middle class as by the humanistic concerns of the Quakers and individuals like Bentham and Howard. The new industrialists may have been concerned about the existing criminal law because, paradoxically, its harshness was helping some offenders escape punishment: Jurors would not convict people accused of petty property offenses for which death was prescribed. In petitions to Parliament, groups of businessmen complained that their property was not protected if offenders could expect to escape punishment.[27] They wanted swift and certain sanctions, and their demands agreed with the moral indignation of Bentham, Howard, and their fellow reformers.

Traditional scholarship on corrections has emphasized the humanitarian motives of reformers seeking a system of benevolent justice. However, other scholars have focused on the underlying economic or social factors that account for shifts in correctional policies. They do not accept the standard version that such people as Beccaria, Bentham, and Howard were motivated by concern for their fellow humans when they advocated a particular perspective on the problem of criminality. The revisionists suggest, for example, that until 1700 the size of the incarcerated population in England was linked to the economic demand for workers. The penitentiary may thus represent not the product of the humanitarian instincts unleashed by the Enlightenment, but a way to discipline the working class to serve a new industrial society.

Changes were made in England's prisons, and new institutions were constructed along lines suggested by Howard and Bentham, but not until 1842, with the opening of Pentonville in North London, did the penitentiary plan come to fruition. Meanwhile, the concept of the penitentiary had traveled across the ocean to the new American republic, where it developed.

Summary

From the Middle Ages to the American Revolution, corrections consisted primarily of galley slavery, imprisonment, transportation, corporal punishment, and death. But with the Enlightenment in the latter part of the eighteenth century, changes began to be made in penal policy. Rather than stressing physical punishment of the offender, influential thinkers such as Beccaria, Bentham, and Howard sought methods for reforming offenders. These changes were first proposed in Europe and fully developed later in America. ■

For Discussion

1. In what ways have changes in the social, economic, and political environment of society been reflected in correctional policies?
2. How may developments discussed in this chapter have eventually brought about the separation of children from others in the prison system?
3. How have the interests of administrators and the organizations they manage distorted the ideals of penal reformers?
4. Some people believe the history of corrections shows a continuous movement toward more humane treatment of prisoners as society in general has progressed. Do you agree? Why or why not?
5. How may specific underlying social factors have influenced the development of correctional philosophies?

For Further Reading

Foucault, Michel. *Discipline and Punish.* New York: Pantheon, 1977. Describes the transition from a focus on punishment of the body of the offender to the use of the penitentiary to reform the individual.

Hughes, Robert. *The Fatal Shore.* New York: Knopf, 1987. Traces the colonization of New South Wales and the impact of transportation.

Ignatieff, Michael. *A Just Measure of Pain.* New York: Pantheon, 1978. Recounts the coming of penal institutions to England during the latter part of the eighteenth century.

Morris, Norval, and David J. Rothman, eds. *The Oxford History of the Prison.* New York: Oxford University Press, 1995. Fourteen articles by scholars examining the prison from ancient times to the present.

Spierenburg, Pieter. *The Spectacle of Suffering.* New York: Cambridge University Press, 1987. Examines the role of public punishment in preindustrial Europe and its ultimate disappearance by the middle of the nineteenth century.

Notes

1. Michel Foucault, *Discipline and Punish* (New York: Pantheon, 1977), pp. 4, 8.
2. John A. Conley, "A Historian Looks at Corrections," in Todd Clear and George Cole, eds., *American Corrections,* 4th ed. (Belmont, CA: Wadsworth, 1997), pp. 44-45.
3. Pieter Spierenburg, *The Spectacle of Suffering* (New York: Cambridge University Press, 1984), p. 14.
4. Georg Rusche and Otto Kirchheimer, *Punishment and Social Structure* (New York: Russell & Russell, [1939] 1968), p. 9.
5. Pieter Spierenburg, "The Body and the State: Early Modern Europe," in Norval Morris and David J. Rothman, eds., *The Oxford History of the Prison* (New York: Oxford University Press, 1995), p. 75.
6. For a description of the treatment of galley slaves, see George Ives, *A History of Penal Methods* (Montclair, NJ: Patterson Smith, 1970), p. 104.
7. Edward M. Peters, "Prison Before the Prison: The Ancient and Medieval Worlds," in Norval Morris and David J. Rothman, eds., *The Oxford History of the Prison* (New York: Oxford University Press, 1995), pp. 3-47.
8. Adam J. Hirsch, *The Rise of the Penitentiary* (New Haven, CT: Yale University Press, 1992), p. 14.
9. A. Roger Ekirch, *Bound for America: The Transportation of British Convicts to the Colonies 1718–1775* (New York: Oxford University Press, 1987).
10. Spierenburg, "The Body and the State," p. 76.
11. Robert Hughes, *The Fatal Shore* (New York: Knopf, 1987), p. 282.
12. Ibid.
13. Ibid., p. 162.
14. Rusche and Kirchheimer, p. 19.
15. Spierenburg, "The Body and the State," p. 54.
16. Michael Ignatieff, *A Just Measure of Pain* (New York: Pantheon, 1978), p. 27.
17. Rusche and Kircheheimer, p. 96.
18. Mark M. Lanier and Stuart Henry, *Essential Criminology* (Boulder, CO: Westview Press, 1998), p. 67.
19. Harry E. Barnes and Negley K. Teeters, *New Horizons in Criminology* (New York: Prentice-Hall, 1944), p. 461.
20. Francis Edward Devine, "Cesare Beccaria and the Theoretical Foundation of Modern Penal Jurisprudence, *New England Journal of Prison Law,* 7, 1981, p. 8.
21. Gilbert Geis, "Jeremy Bentham," in Herman Mannheim, ed., *Pioneers in Criminology* (Montclair, NJ: Patterson Smith, 1973), p. 54.
22. Ignatieff, p. 27.
23. Geis, p. 65.
24. Anthony Babington, *The English Bastille* (New York: St. Martin's Press, 1971), p. 103.
25. Barnes and Teeters, p. 481.
26. Ignatieff, p. 93.
27. Michael Russigan, "A Reinterpretation of Criminal Law Reform in Nineteenth-Century England," *Journal of Criminal Justice,* 8, 1980, p. 205.

The History of Corrections in America

On October 25, 1829, Charles Williams, an 18-year-old African American from Delaware County, Pennsylvania, began serving a two-year sentence for larceny at the Eastern Penitentiary, located in Cherry Hill outside of Philadelphia. The newly constructed facility was described at the time as "the most imposing in the United States."[1]

Williams was assigned to a cell measuring 12 by 8 by 10 feet with an attached 18-foot-long exercise yard. The cell was furnished with a fold-up metal bedstead, a simple toilet, a wooden stool, a workbench, and eating utensils. Light came from an 8-inch window in the ceiling; the window could be blocked to plunge the cell into darkness as a disciplinary measure.

Charles Williams became prisoner number 1 at Eastern, a model of the separate confinement penitentiary viewed at the time as a great advance in penology. For the two years of his sentence, Williams could expect to be confined to his cell and exercise yard, his only human contact being a weekly visit by the chaplain. Every measure was taken to ensure that the prisoner would not be distracted from his moral rehabilitation. Officials could inspect the interior of the cell through a peephole without the resident knowing. Food was inserted through an opening in the wall designed so that the inmate could not see the guard. Solitary labor, Bible reading, and reflection on his behavior were viewed as the keys to providing the offender with the opportunity to repent.

Few Americans realize that their country gave the world its first penitentiary, an institution created to reform offenders within an environment designed to focus their full attention on their moral rehabilitation. This goal of reform reflected a major shift in correctional thinking. Remember that brutal public punishments such as the dismemberment of Damiens had occurred with some regularity just sixty years before Williams entered Eastern. Thought about both human nature and the purpose of punishment had changed dramatically.

Especially during its formative years, American corrections was greatly influenced by English trends and practices. The work of Cesare Beccaria and the development of the Milan House of Correction had a bearing on penal policies throughout the Western world, but corrections in colonial America followed English ideas and policies. These transatlantic ties have continued over the years, and American correctional institutions and practices also have responded to social and political pressures and developed in decidedly American ways.

In this chapter we survey the historical changes in correctional thought and practices in the United States: We focus on seven periods: the colonial period, the arrival of the penitentiary, the reformatory movement, the progressive movement, the rise of the medical model, the community model, and the crime control model. As we discuss each period, we emphasize the ways in which correctional goals reflected current ideas. We will be examining the following Questions for Inquiry.

Questions FOR INQUIRY

1. What was the importance of "The Great Law"?
2. What were the basic assumptions of supporters of the penitentiary in Pennsylvania and New York?
3. What elements of the Cincinnati Declaration were incorporated in the reformatory?
4. What reforms were advocated by the Progressives?
5. What did advocates of the medical model believe was the nature of criminal behavior and its correction?
6. How did the community model reflect the social and political values of the 1960s and 1970s?
7. What led to the shift to the present crime control model?

The Colonial Period

During the colonial period most Americans lived under laws and practices transferred from England and adapted to local conditions. In New England the Puritans maintained a strict society governed by religious principles well into the middle of the eighteenth century, and they rigorously punished violations of religious

laws. As in England, banishment, corporal punishment, the pillory, and death were the common penalties. In 1682, with the arrival of
William Penn, Pennsylvania adopted "The
Great Law," which was based on humane
Quaker principles and emphasized hard labor
in a house of correction as punishment for most
crimes. Death was reserved for premeditated
murder. The Quaker Code survived until 1718,
when it was replaced by the Anglican Code,
which was already in force in other colonies.
The latter code listed thirteen capital offenses,
with larceny the only felony not punishable by
death. Whipping, branding, mutilation, and
other corporal punishments were prescribed for
other offenses, as were fines. This situation
continued throughout the colonies until the
Revolution.

Until the early 1800s Americans followed the European practice of relying upon punishment that was physically brutal, such as death, flogging and branding. This whipping post and pillory in New Castle, Delaware, continued to be used well into the 19th century.

Unlike the mother country, with its crowded houses of correction, hulks, and jails,
the colonies seldom used institutions for confinement.[2] Instead, banishment from the
community, fines, death, and the other punishments just mentioned were the norm. As
David Rothman writes, the death penalty was common:

> *The New York Supreme Court in the pre-Revolutionary era regularly sentenced crimi-*
> *nals to death, with slightly more than twenty percent of all its penalties capital ones.*
> *When magistrates believed that the fundamental security of the city was in danger, as*
> *in the case of a slave revolt in 1741, the court responded with great severity (burning*
> *to death thirteen of the rebellion's leaders and hanging nineteen others). Even in less*
> *critical times the court had frequent recourse to the scaffold — for those convicted of*
> *pickpocketing, burglary, robbery, counterfeiting, horse stealing, and grand larceny as*
> *well as murder.[3]*

Jails held people awaiting court action or those unable to pay their debts. Only
rarely were convicted offenders jailed for their whole sentences; the stocks, whipping
post, or gallows were the places for punishment. Punishments were public spectacles,
because "rubbing the noses of offenders in the community context was an essential part
of the process of ripping and healing, which criminal justice was supposed to embody."[4]
In keeping with the Calvinist doctrine of predestination, little thought was given to reforming offenders — such people were considered naturally depraved.[5]

The Arrival of the Penitentiary

Until the beginning of the 1800s, America was relatively sparsely populated and predominantly rural. In 1790 the entire population numbered less than 4 million, and no
city had more than 50,000 inhabitants. By 1830 the rural population had more than
doubled and the urban population had more than tripled. Growth was accompanied by
very rapid social and economic changes that affected all aspects of life. Colonial life
had been oriented toward the local community; everyone knew everyone else, neighbors helped one another as needed, and the local clergy and elite maintained social
control. In the nineteenth century, however, social problems could no longer be handled with the help of neighbors. In an increasingly heterogeneous urban and industrial
society, responsibility for the poor, insane, and criminal became the province of the
state and its institutions.

With the Revolution, the ideas of the Enlightenment, as discussed in Chapter 2,
gained currency, and a new concept of criminal punishment came to the fore. This

The penitentiary concept was implemented first in the Walnut Street Jail, Philadelphia, in 1790. A portion of the jail was converted to create an environment based on the assumptions of the penitentiary.

---

penitentiary

An institution intended to isolate prisoners from society and from one another so that they could reflect on their past misdeeds, repent, and thus undergo reformation.

---

correctional philosophy, based on the ideas of Beccaria, Bentham, and Howard, coincided with the ideals of the Declaration of Independence, which took an optimistic view of human nature and a belief in each person's perfectibility.[6] Social progress was thought possible through reforms to match the dictates of "pure reason." Emphasis also shifted from the assumption that deviance was part of human nature, to a view that crime was caused by forces in the environment. The punitive colonial penal system based on retribution thus was held to be incompatible with the idea of human perfectibility.

Reformers argued that if Americans were to become committed to the humane and optimistic ideal of human improvability, they had to remove barbarism and vindictiveness from penal codes and make the prime goal of punishment the reformation of the criminal. Thomas Jefferson and other leaders of the new republic worked to liberalize the harsh penal codes of the colonial period. Pennsylvania led the way with new legislation that sought "'to reclaim rather than destroy,' 'to correct and reform the offenders,' rather than simply to mark or eliminate them."[7] Several states, including Connecticut (1773), Massachusetts (1785), New York (1796), and Pennsylvania (1786), added incarceration at hard labor as an alternative to such public punishments as whippings and the stocks. For example, the Massachusetts State Prison, which opened in 1805, was designed as a workhouse; inmates labored from dawn to dusk making shoes and nails as a means of "destroying [their] 'habit of idleness' and replacing it with a 'habit of industry' more conducive to an honest livelihood."[8]

Incarceration, in the tradition of the English workhouse, developed in the immediate aftermath of the Revolution. The **penitentiary,** as conceptualized by the English reformers and their American Quaker allies, first appeared in 1790, when part of Philadelphia's Walnut Street Jail was converted to allow separate confinement.

The penitentiary differed markedly from the prison, house of correction, and jail. It was conceived as a place where criminal offenders could be isolated from the bad influences of society and from one another so that while engaged in productive labor, they could reflect on their past misdeeds, repent, and be reformed. As the word *penitentiary* indicates, it was hoped that while offenders were being punished, they would become penitent, see the error of their ways, and wish to place themselves on the right path. Then they could reenter the community as useful citizens.

The American penitentiary attracted the world's attention, and the concept was transported back across the Atlantic to be incorporated at Millbank and Pentonville in England and in various other locales in Europe. By 1830 foreign observers were coming to America to see this innovation in penology; they were excited by the changes being made in the United States. For instance, France sent Alexis de Tocqueville and Gustave Auguste de Beaumont, England sent William Crawford, and Prussia sent Nicholas Julius. By the middle of the century, the U.S. penitentiary in its various forms—especially the Pennsylvania and New York systems—had indeed become world famous.

The Pennsylvania System

As in England, Quakers set about to implement their humanistic and religious ideas in the new nation; in Philadelphia their efforts came to fruition. The Quaker philosophy emphasizes that the Inner Light (God's grace) is available to all but must be individually achieved; doing so is directly dependent on the ways in which one behaves in the world. For Quakers penance and silent contemplation were the means to move from the state of sin toward perfection. The penitentiary thus provided a place where individuals, on their own, could be reformed.

Quakers were among the Philadelphia elite who in 1787 formed the reformist Society for Alleviating the Miseries of Public Prisoners. Under the Quaker leadership of Dr. Benjamin Rush and others such as Benjamin Franklin, the society urged replacement of capital and corporal punishment with incarceration. Members had been communicating with John Howard, and their ideals in many ways reflected his.

In 1790 the group was instrumental in passing legislation almost identical to England's Penitentiary Act of 1779. The 1790 law specified that an institution was to be established in which "solitary confinement to hard labour and a total abstinence from spirituous liquors will prove the most effectual means of reforming these unhappy creatures."[9]

To implement the new legislation, the existing three-story Walnut Street Jail in Philadelphia was to be expanded for the solitary confinement of "hardened and atrocious offenders." The plain stone building housed eight cells on each floor and had an attached yard. Each cell was dark and small (only 6 feet long, 8 feet wide, and 9 feet high). From a small grated window high on the outside wall, inmates "could perceive neither heaven nor earth." Inmates were classified by offense: Serious offenders were placed in solitary confinement without labor; the others worked together in shops during the day under a strict rule of silence and were confined separately at night.

When the Walnut Street Jail soon became overcrowded, the legislature approved construction of additional institutions for the state: Western Penitentiary on the outskirts of Pittsburgh and Eastern Penitentiary in Cherry Hill, near Philadelphia. The opening of Eastern in 1829 marked the full development of the penitentiary system based on **separate confinement.** In the years between Walnut Street and Eastern, other states had adopted aspects of the Pennsylvania system. Separate confinement was introduced by Maryland in 1809, by Massachusetts in 1811, by New Jersey in 1820, and by Maine in 1824, but Eastern was the fullest expression of the concept of rehabilitation through separate confinement.

Eastern Penitentiary was designed by John Haviland, an English immigrant and an acquaintance of John Howard. One of the most imposing and expensive public structures of its day, the facility apparently was modeled after the Maison de Force at Ghent. Cell blocks extended from a central hub like the spokes of a wheel. Each prisoner ate, slept, worked, and received religious instruction in his own cell. The inmates did not see peers; in fact, their only human contact was the occasional visit of a clergyman or prison official.[10]

As described by Robert Vaux, one of the original reformers, the Pennsylvania system was based on the following principles:

1. Prisoners would not be treated vengefully, but should be convinced that through hard and selective forms of suffering they could change their lives.
2. Solitary confinement would prevent further corruption inside prison.
3. In isolation, offenders would reflect on their transgressions and repent.
4. Solitary confinement would be punishment because humans are by nature social beings.
5. Solitary confinement would be economical because since prisoners would not need long periods of time to repent, fewer keepers would be needed and the costs of clothing would be lower.[11]

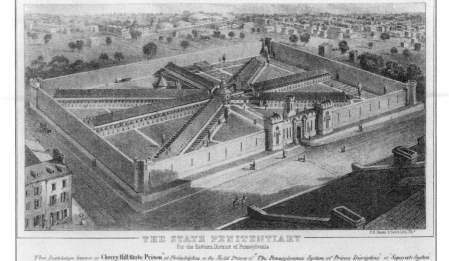

THE STATE PENITENTIARY
For the Eastern District of Pennsylvania

Eastern State Penitentiary located outside of Philadelphia became the model for the Pennsylvania system of "separate" confinement. The building was designed to ensure that each offender was separated from all human contact so that he could reflect upon his misdeeds.

separate confinement

A penitentiary system developed in Pennsylvania in which each inmate was held in isolation from other inmates, with all activities, including craftwork, carried on in the cells.

The Pennsylvania system of separate confinement soon became controversial. In 1831 Tocqueville and Beaumont wrote that "nothing distracts, in Philadelphia, the mind of the convicts from their meditations; and as they are always isolated, the presence of a person who comes to converse with them is the greatest benefit."[12] In contrast, however, after visiting Eastern in 1842, the English novelist Charles Dickens argued that "very few men are capable of estimating the immense amount of torture and agony which this dreadful punishment, prolonged for years, inflicts upon the sufferers." He found the system "cruel and wrong."[13]

Within five years after it opened, Eastern was subjected to the first of several investigations carried out over the years by a judicially appointed board of inspectors. The reports detailed the extent to which the goal of separate confinement was not fully observed, physical punishments were used to maintain discipline, and prisoners suffered mental breakdowns due to the isolation. Separate confinement had declined by the 1860s when crowding required doubling up in each cell, yet it was not abolished in Pennsylvania until 1913.[14]

The New York System

Faced with overcrowded facilities such as Newgate Prison, built in 1797, the New York legislature in 1816 authorized a new state prison in Auburn. Influenced by the reported success of the separate confinement of some prisoners in the Walnut Street Jail, the New York building commission decided that a portion of the new facility should be erected on that model and that an experiment should be undertaken to test its effectiveness. The concept proved a failure, for sickness, insanity, and suicide increased markedly among the prisoners. It was discontinued in 1822, and the governor pardoned those then held in solitary.

congregate system

A penitentiary system developed in Auburn, New York, in which inmates were held in isolation at night but worked with fellow prisoners during the day under a rule of silence.

In 1831 Elam Lynds was installed as the warden at Auburn. Instead of duplicating the complete isolation practiced in Pennsylvania, Lynds worked out a new **congregate system** of prison discipline whereby inmates were held in isolation at night but congregated in workshops during the day. The inmates were forbidden to talk or even to exchange glances while on the job or at meals. Lynds was convinced that convicts were incorrigible and that industrial efficiency should be the overriding purpose of the prison. He instituted a reign of discipline and obedience that included the lockstep and the wearing of prison stripes. Furthermore, he considered it "impossible to govern a large prison without a whip. Those who know human nature from books only may say the contrary."[15]

Whereas inmates of the Pennsylvania penitentiaries worked in their cells, those in New York were employed in workshops both as therapy and as a way to finance the institution. The state negotiated contracts with manufacturers, who then delivered raw materials to the prison for conversion into finished goods. By the 1840s Auburn was producing footwear, barrels, carpets, carpentry tools, harnesses, furniture, and clothing. Thus Auburn and other prisons that adopted the New York system were more concerned with instilling good work habits and thus preventing recidivism (relapse into crime) than with rehabilitating prisoners' character.

Debating the Systems

Throughout this era, the preferred structure of prison systems was hotly debated. Advocates of both the Pennsylvania and the New York plans argued on public platforms and in the nation's periodicals over the best methods of punishment. Underlying the debates were questions about disciplining citizens in a democracy and maintaining conformity to social norms in a society that emphasized individualism. Participants included some of the leading figures of the time. As each state considered new penal construction, it joined the debate.

As often noted, the Quaker method in Pennsylvania (the separate system) aimed to produce honest people, whereas the New York method (the congregate system) sought

It has been said that the Pennsylvania model was oriented primarily toward an earlier religious craft society and that the New York model looked forward to the emerging industrial age.

to mold obedient citizens. Advocates of both systems agreed that offenders must be isolated from society and subjected to disciplined routine. They believed that deviance resulted from pervasive corruption in the community and that institutions such as the family and the church were not effectively countering corrupt influences. Only when offenders were removed from the temptations and influences of society and kept in a silent, disciplined environment could they reflect on their sins and offenses and become useful citizens. The convicts were not inherently depraved; rather, they were the victims of a society that had not protected them from vice.

What divided the two camps was the way in which reformation was to be brought about. Proponents of the New York system maintained that inmates first had to be "broken" and then socialized by means of a rigid discipline of congregate but silent labor. Advocates of Pennsylvania's separate system rejected such harshness and, following Howard, renounced physical punishments and any other form of human degradation. The New Yorkers countered that the silent system cost less, efficiently tapped convict labor, and developed individuals who eventually would be able to return to the community with the discipline necessary for the industrial age. The Pennsylvanians responded that New York had sacrificed the principal goal of the penitentiary (reformation) to the accessory goal (cost-effectiveness) and contended that exploiting inmates through large-scale industry failed to promote the work ethic, but only embittered them.

The Pennsylvania model was predominantly oriented toward an earlier, crafts-oriented, religious society, whereas the New York model looked forward to the emerging industrial age. John Conley has argued that the Pennsylvania model lost out because it embraced an outdated labor system. In contrast, the New York system, as practiced at Auburn, was consistent with the new demands and challenges of factory production, which "would provide the state with a means of exploiting the labor of inmates to defray the expenses of the institution and possibly earn a profit for the state."[16] In this sense Auburn was the forerunner of the industrial prison that was dominant until the rise of organized labor in the twentieth century.

In addition to clarifying some hazy issues in the writings of Bentham and Howard, this debate contributed to decisions in a number of states and in Europe about how penitentiaries should be designed and run. Of the prisons constructed in the United States during this period, the New York style was the overwhelming choice. Most European visitors, however, favored the Pennsylvania model, and the First International Prison Congress, held in 1846 in Germany, endorsed it by a large majority. The separate system was soon incorporated in correctional facilities in Germany, France, Belgium, and Holland. But as prison populations increased in the United States, the Pennsylvania system proved too expensive. In addition, the public became concerned by reports that prisoners were going insane because they could not endure long-term solitary confinement. Yet not until the end of the century did Pennsylvania, the birthplace of the penitentiary, finally convert to the congregate system.

The Reformatory Movement

Unfortunately, ways in which reforms are implemented often do not match the high ideals of social activists. Legislators and governors may be willing to support the espoused goals of change, but putting the ideals into practice requires leadership, money, public support, and innovative administrators. Thus, soon after a given innovation, corrections facilities become overcrowded, discipline becomes lax, programs are abandoned, and charges of official misconduct erupt. The subsequent investigation typically recommends changes that may or may not be implemented—and the cycle continues.

By the mid-1800s, reformers had become disillusioned with the penitentiary. Neither the New York nor the Pennsylvania systems nor any of their imitators had achieved rehabilitation or deterrence. This failure was seen as resulting from poor administration rather than weakness of the basic concept. Within forty years of being built, penitentiaries had become overcrowded, understaffed, and minimally financed. Discipline was lax, brutality was common, and administrators were viewed as corrupt. At Sing Sing Penitentiary in Ossining, New York, in 1870, for example, investigators discovered that "dealers were publicly supplying prisoners with almost anything they could pay for" and that convicts were "playing all sorts of games, reading, scheming, trafficking."[17] The reality was a far cry from the vision of John Howard and Benjamin Rush.

mark system

A system in which offenders are assessed a certain number of points at the time of sentencing based on the severity of their crime. Prisoners could reduce their term and gain release by earning marks through labor, good behavior, and educational achievement.

Across the Atlantic, controversy over penal policy developed that directly influenced American corrections. In England Alexander Maconochie urged the **mark system** of graduated terms of confinement. Penalties would be graded according to the severity of the crime, and offenders would be released from incarceration according to their performance. A certain number of marks would be given at sentencing, and prisoners could reduce the number by voluntary labor, participating in educational and religious programs, and good behavior. Maconochie was arguing for sentences of indeterminate length and a system of rewards. Through these incentives offenders would be reformed so that they could return to society.

Maconochie's ideas were not implemented in England. However, in Ireland in 1854 Sir Walter Crofton adopted practices similar to the mark system that came to be known as the Irish or *intermediate* system. On conviction prisoners spent a period in solitary confinement and then were sent to public work prisons where they could earn marks. When they had enough marks, they were transferred to the intermediate stage, or what today might be called a *halfway house*. The final test was a ticket-of-leave, a conditional release that was the precursor of the modern parole system.[18] Again theory and practice bridged the continents as Maconochie's and Crofton's ideas traveled across the Atlantic.

The reformatory movement emphasized education and training, such as this machine class at Elmira Reformatory in 1898. On the basis of their achievement and conduct offenders moved forward toward release.

Cincinnati, 1870

By 1870 a new generation of American penal reformers had arisen. Among them were Gaylord Hubbell, warden of Sing Sing, who had observed the Irish system in operation; Enoch C. Wines, secretary of the New York Prison Association; Franklin Sanborn, secretary of the Massachusetts State Board of Charities; and Zebulon Brockway, head of Detroit's Michigan House of Correction. Like the Quakers these penologists were motivated by humanitarian concerns, but they also understood how prisons operated.

The National Prison Association (predecessor of the American Correctional Association) and its 1870 meeting in Cincinnati embodied the new spirit of reform. In its famous Declaration of Principles, the association advocated a new design for penology: that prisons should be operated on a philosophy of inmate change, with reformation rewarded by release. Sentences of indeterminate length would replace fixed sentences, and proof of reformation—rather than the mere lapse of time—would be a requirement for a prisoner's release. Classification of prisoners on the basis of character and improvement would encourage the reformation program. Penitentiary practices that had evolved during the first half of the nineteenth century—fixed sentences, the lockstep, rules of silence, and isolation—were now seen as debasing, humiliating, and destructive of initiative.

Given the leadership roles of clergy in the National Prison Association, it is not surprising that, like the activists who had promoted the penitentiary in the 1830s, those gathered at Cincinnati still saw crime as a sort of moral disease that should be treated by efforts at moral regeneration.

Like the Quakers before them, the 1870 reformers looked to institutional life as the way to effect rehabilitation. Inmates would be made into well-adjusted citizens, but the process would take place behind walls. The Cincinnati Declaration could thus in good faith insist that "reformation is a work of time; and a benevolent regard to the good of the criminal himself, as well as to the protection of society, requires that his sentence be long enough for the reformatory process to take effect."[19]

reformatory

An institution for young offenders emphasizing training, a mark system of classification, indeterminate sentences, and parole.

Elmira Reformatory   The first **reformatory** took shape in 1876 at Elmira, New York, when Zebulon Brockway was appointed superintendent. Brockway believed that diagnosis and treatment were the keys to reform and rehabilitation. He questioned each new inmate to explore the social, biological, psychological, and "root cause(s)" of the offender's deviance. An individualized work and education treatment program was then prescribed. Inmates followed a rigid schedule of work during the day, followed by courses in academic, vocational, and moral subjects during the evening. Inmates who did well were released early.[20]

Designed for first-time felons between the ages of 16 and 30, the approach at Elmira incorporated a mark system of classification, indeterminate sentences, and parole. Once the courts had committed an offender to Elmira, the administrators could determine the release date; the only restriction was that the time served could not exceed the maximum prescribed by law for the particular offense.

A three-grade system of classification was linked to the indeterminate sentence. Each offender entered the institution at grade 2, and if the inmate earned nine marks a month for six months by working hard, completing school assignments, and causing no problems, he could be moved up to grade 1—necessary for release. If he failed to cooperate and violated rules of conduct, thus showing indifference to progress and lack of self-control, he would be demoted to grade 3. Only after three months satisfactory behavior could he reembark on the path toward eventual release.[21] In sum, this system placed "the prisoner's fate, as far as possible, in his own hands."[22]

Elmira's proclaimed success at reforming young felons was widely heralded, and over the next several decades its program was emulated in twenty states. Brockway's annual reports claimed that 81 percent of inmates released from Elmira underwent "probable reformation." His optimism was echoed in an article, "How Far May We Abolish Prisons?" that appeared in the journal of the American Social Science Association. The author's answer: "to the degree that we put men into reformatories like Elmira, for it reforms more than 80 percent of those who are sent there."[23] Brockway even weathered an 1893 state investigation into charges of brutality at Elmira, which revealed that the whip and solitary confinement were used there regularly. However, in 1900 he was forced to resign in the face of mounting criticism of his administration.

By 1900 the reformatory movement had spread throughout much of the nation, yet by the outbreak of World War I in 1914, it was already declining. In most institutions the architecture, the attitudes of the guards, and the emphasis on discipline differed little from past orientations. Too often, the educational and rehabilitative efforts took a back seat to the traditional emphasis on punishment. Even Brockway admitted that it was difficult to distinguish between inmates whose attitudes had changed and those who merely lived by prison rules. Being a good prisoner became the way to win parole, but this did not meant that the prisoner had truly changed.

Lasting Reforms

Although the ideals of Wines, Brockway, and the other leaders of the reformatory movement were not realized, these men did make major contributions to American corrections. The indeterminate sentence, inmate classification, rehabilitative programs, and parole were all first developed at Elmira. The Cincinnati Declaration of Principles set goals that inspired prison reformers well into the twentieth century. Still more changes were to come before that, however. In the mid-nineteenth century the United States was entering a period of significant social change. The nation was coming to grips with two forces: the gradual shift of the population from the countryside to the cities and the cultural threat posed by a flood of immigrants. Thus the stage was set for progressive reforms.

The Rise of the Progressives

The first two decades of the 1900s, called the "Age of Reform," set the dominant tone for American social thought and political action until the 1960s.[24] Industrialization, urbanization, technological change, and scientific advancements had revolutionized the American landscape. A group known as Progressives attacked the excesses of this emergent society, especially those of big business, and placed their faith in state action to deal with the social problems of slums, adulterated food, dangerous occupational conditions, vice, and crime.

The Progressives, most of whom came from upper-status backgrounds, were optimistic about the possibility of solving the problems of modern society. They were concerned in particular about conditions in cities, with their large immigrant populations. They believed that civic-minded people could apply the findings of science to social problems, including penology, in ways that would benefit all. Specifically they believed that through individualized treatment criminals could be rehabilitated.

Individualized Treatment and the Positivist School

The Progressive programs, according to David Rothman, can be epitomized in two words: conscience and convenience. The reforms were promoted by benevolent and philanthropic men and women who sought to understand and cure crime through a case-by-case approach. They believed that the reformers of the penitentiary era were wrong in assuming that all deviants were "victims of social disorder" and that the deviants "could all be rehabilitated with a single program, the well-ordered routine" of the prison.[25]

The Progressives thought it necessary to know the life history of each offender and then devise a treatment program specific to that individual. However, to diagnose each criminal, prescribe treatment, and schedule release to the community, correctional administrators had to be given discretion. From this orientation the phrase "treatment according to the needs of the offender" came into vogue, in contrast to "punishment according to the severity of the crime," which had been the hallmark of Beccaria and the reformers of the early 1800s.

Rothman argues that because discretion was required for the day-to-day practice of the new penology, correctional administrators responded favorably to it. The new discretionary authority made it easier for administrators to carry out their daily assignments. He also notes that the Progressives committed to incarceration were instrumental in promoting probation and parole, but supporters of the penitentiary used the requirement of discretion to expand the size of the prison population.

The Progressives had faith that the state would carry out their reforms with justice. In the same way they looked to government programs to secure social justice, they assumed the agents of the state would help offenders. Rothman notes,

> In criminal justice, the issue was not how to protect the offender from the arbitrariness of the state, but how to bring the state more effectively to the aid of the offender. The state was not a behemoth to be chained and fettered, but an agent capable of fulfilling an ambitious program. Thus, a policy that called for the state's exercise of discretionary authority in finely tuned responses was, at its core, Progressive.[26]

As members of the **positivist school,** the Progressives looked to social, economic, biological, and psychological rather than religious or moral explanations for the causes of crime and they applied modern scientific methods to determine the best treatment therapies. Recall that the classical school of Beccaria and Bentham had emphasized a legal approach to the problem, focusing on the act rather than the criminal. In contrast, the scientific positivists school shifted the focus from the criminal act to the offender. By the beginning of the twentieth century, advances in the biological and social sciences provided the framework for the reforms proposed by the Progressives.

Although several theoretical perspectives can be found within the positivist school, most of its practitioners shared three basic assumptions:

1. Criminal behavior is not the result of free will but stems from factors over which the individual has no control: biological characteristics, psychological maladjustments, sociological conditions.
2. Criminals can be treated so that they can lead crime-free lives.
3. Treatment must be focused on the individual and the individual's problem.

positivist school

An approach to criminology and other social sciences based on the assumption that human behavior is a product of biological, economic, psychological, and social factors, and that the scientific method can be applied to ascertain the causes of individual behavior.

Progressive Reforms

Armed with their views about the nature of criminal behavior and the need for state action to reform offenders, the Progressives fought for changes in correctional methods. They pursued two main strategies: (1) improve conditions in social environments that seemed to be breeding grounds for crime and (2) rehabilitate individual offenders. Because they saw crime as primarily an urban problem, concentrated especially among the immigrant lower class, the Progressives sought through political action to bring about changes that would improve ghetto conditions: better public health, landlord-tenant laws, public housing, playgrounds, settlement houses, education. However, because they also believed that criminal behavior varied among individuals, a case-by-case approach was required.[27]

By the 1920s the Progressives had succeeded in getting wide acceptance of four portions of their program: probation, indeterminate sentences, parole, and juvenile courts. These elements had been proposed at the 1870 Cincinnati meeting, but the Progressives and their allies in corrections were instrumental in implementing them throughout the country.

Probation   Probation had its origin in the work of John Augustus in the Boston Police Court in 1841 (see Chapter 8). This alternative to incarceration fitted nicely into the Progressive scheme, for it recognized individual differences and allowed offenders to be treated in the community under supervision. Although Massachusetts passed a probation law in 1878, no other state took the step until 1897, and in 1900 only six states provided for probation. But by 1920 every state permitted probation for juveniles and thirty-three states permitted it for adults. By 1930 the federal government and thirty-six states, including every industrialized state, had adult probation laws on their books. However, probation remained primarily an urban strategy; it never took root in rural or small-town America. The reason may have to do with the cost-effectiveness of the approach in areas where populations are scattered, or perhaps it reflects a different mindset among rural people.

In urban areas problems with staffing, caseload size, and the quality of supervision caused probation to fall short of expectations. Almost no jurisdiction met the 50:1 ratio of clients to supervisors then advocated by penologists. Perhaps more important, probation officers were given an almost impossible task: With very little scientifically based theory to guide their actions, they were expected to keep their charges crime-free. What passed as ways to reform probationers often turned out to be little more than attempts to indoctrinate them with middle-class moral injunctions — work, go to church, keep clean, get ahead, be good — attitudes not consistent with real life in city slums. In addition, politicians sometimes attacked probation as "coddling" criminals. Nevertheless, the system prevailed, in part because it was useful for inducing the guilty plea, then thought necessary to relieve overcrowded courts.[28]

Indeterminate Sentences and Parole   Although the idea of parole release had been developed in Ireland and Australia in the 1850s and Zebulon Brockway had instituted it at Elmira in 1876, not until the mid-1920s did it really catch on in the United States. By then thirty-seven states had indeterminate sentencing laws and forty-four provided for release on parole. Fixed sentences were retained for lesser offenses, but during this period more than three-quarters of convicted offenders whose maximum terms exceeded five years were serving indeterminate sentences.

The sentences were called "indeterminate," but nearly always minimum and maximum terms were set, within which the correctional process of rehabilitation could operate. At no time were state legislatures willing to give correctional officials unbridled authority to decide when (or if) a prisoner could be released. Yet over time legislatures tended to expand the outer limits of sentences. Especially in response to public outcries over crime, politicians often increased the maximum penalties, thus giving wider discretion to parole decision makers.

Like probation, parole expanded greatly during the Progressive period. By the mid-1920s, well over 80 percent of felons sentenced in the major industrialized states left prison via parole. What once had been a way to release deserving offenders in a few reformatories became the means by which the overwhelming majority of inmates returned to the community. As parole expanded, so did public criticism of it, especially when newspapers reported that a particularly heinous crime had been committed by someone released from prison under supervision.[29] Studies conducted in the 1920s and 1930s showed that recidivism was high among parolees and that the purported "diagnostic evaluation" by a parole board usually embodied little more than speculation based on the prejudices of its members.

Although the reforms of the Progressives were much criticized, probation, indeterminate sentences, and parole remain dominant elements of corrections to this day. Perhaps, as Rothman suggests, this is because they provide authority to criminal justice officials and affirm the vitality of the rehabilitative idea.[30] However, these three crucial reforms provided the structure for yet another change in corrections.

The Rise of the Medical Model

Even before psychiatry began to influence American society, the idea that criminals are mentally ill was popular in correctional circles. At the 1870 Cincinnati congress one speaker described a criminal as "a man who has suffered under a disease evinced by the perpetration of a crime, and who may reasonably be held to be under the dominion of such disease until his conduct has afforded very strong presumption not only that he is free from its immediate influence, but that the chances of its recurrence have become exceedingly remote."[31]

Certainly much Progressive reform activity was based on the idea that criminals could be rehabilitated through treatment, but not until the 1930s were serious attempts made to implement what became known as the **medical model** of corrections. Under the banner of the newly prestigious social and behavioral sciences, the emphasis of corrections shifted to treating criminals as people whose social, psychological, or biological deficiencies had caused them to engage in illegal activity.

Rehabilitation as the primary purpose of incarceration took on national legitimacy in 1929, when the new Federal Bureau of Prisons was authorized by Congress to develop institutions that would ensure the proper classification, care, and treatment of offenders. Many states, particularly New Jersey, New York, Illinois, and California, soon fell in line with programs designed to reform through treatment. Most other states and political leaders everywhere adopted at least the rhetoric of rehabilitation, changing statutes to specify that treatment was the goal of their corrections system and that punishment was an outdated concept. Prisons were thus to become something like mental hospitals that would rehabilitate and test the inmate for readiness to reenter society. In many states, however, the medical model was adopted in name only: Departments of prisons became departments of corrections, but the budgets for treatment programs remained about the same.

It is not surprising that corrections moved in the direction of a medical model when it did. In the 1920s the field of social work had gained intellectual legitimacy and professional status; its practitioners were no longer viewed as merely deliverers of charity to the poor. Through the casework approach, social workers attempted to diagnose and help the unfortunate. Psychology also had developed new ways of measuring mental fitness and assessing personality. The theories of Sigmund Freud and Carl Jung dominated American psychiatry, and these approaches began to take their place alongside biological explanations for illness. Advocates of the medical model sought to bring about change through treatment programs, most often with a psychological base. As psychiatrist Karl Menninger observed, criminal acts are "signals of distress, signals of

medical model

A model of corrections based on the assumption that criminal behavior is caused by social, psychological, or biological deficiencies that require treatment.

failure . . . the spasms of struggles and convulsions of a submarginal human being trying to make it in our complex society with inadequate equipment and inadequate
preparation."[32]

Because the essential structural elements of parole, probation, and the indeterminate sentence were already in place in most states, incorporating the medical model
only required adding classification systems to diagnose offenders and treatment programs to cure them. Tests were developed to help psychologists, psychiatrists, and social workers in determining the cause of the inmate's problem and indicating
appropriate treatment. Recognizing that the prison environment would influence the
effectiveness of treatment, supporters of the medical model argued that different types
of institutions should be developed for different types of offenders. Advocates envi-
sioned institutions that not only had differing levels of security but also would be
devoted primarily to vocational training, agricultural work, or psychiatric care. Classification thus became the crucial first step in treatment; the individual was to be differ-
entiated from the masses, and a program of educational, medical, and psychological
care prescribed.

The systems of classification varied greatly from state to state. Generally attempts
were made to differentiate inmates who were likely to benefit from treatment from those
who were not. In some states, recidivists, the feebleminded, and the physically impaired
might get only the "treatment" of custody or labor at a prison farm or industry. In 1937
Wisconsin developed a more extensive classification scheme. Inmates were put into one
of seven exclusively psychiatric groupings:

1. *Mentally deficient: arrested intellectual development,   "feebleminded"*
2. *Mentally defective: inadequate personality, "criminal"*
3. *Mentally diseased: psychotic, "insane"*
4. *Mentally deviate: neurotic, "borderline insane"*
5. *Mentally distorted: inadequate state, "morally aberrant"*
6. *Mentally delayed (minors)*
7. *Atypical or unclassifiable[33]*

Initially the number of psychiatrists and therapeutic treatment programs was limited, but increased sharply after World War II. Group therapy, behavior modification,
shock therapy, individual counseling, psychotherapy, guided group interaction, and
many other approaches all became part of the "new penology." Competing schools of
psychological thought debated the usefulness of these techniques, many of which were
adopted or discarded before their worth had been evaluated. However, the administrative needs of the institution often superseded the treatment needs of the inmate: Prisoners tended to be assigned to the facilities, jobs, and programs that had openings rather
than to those that would provide the prescribed treatment.

Maryland's Patuxent Institution, which opened in 1955, is probably the best example of a prison built on the principles of the medical model. Patuxent was founded to
treat adults given indeterminate sentences and adjudged to be "defective delinquents."
Its administrators had broad authority to control intake, to experiment with a treatment milieu, and to decide when to release "patients." Throughout the period of incarceration, a patient was diagnosed and treated through a variety of programs and
therapies.

By the 1970s, as criticism rose about the lack of success with the medical model,
the Maryland legislature reduced the authority of Patuxent's administrators, especially
with regard to the release decision. By 1991 the legislature had also changed the institution's goal from rehabilitation to remediation—helping inmates overcome such problems as lack of reading skills, poor behavior controls, or substance abuse.[34]

Critics of treatment programs in American prisons pointed out that even during the
1950s, when the medical model was at its zenith, only 5 percent of state correctional
budgets was allocated for rehabilitation. Although states adopted the rhetoric of the
medical model, the institutions were still being run with custody as an overriding goal.

Some people argued that it was impossible to develop the rapport with inmates needed to cure their personality difficulties, and others asserted that custody always took precedence over treatment in the day-to-day running of prisons.

From Medical Model to Community Model

As we have seen, correctional thought and practices are greatly influenced by the social and political values of particular periods. During the 1960s and 1970s, U.S. society experienced the civil rights movement, the War on Poverty, and resistance to the Vietnam War. Americans also challenged governmental institutions dealing with education, mental health, juvenile delinquency, and adult corrections. In 1967 the President's Commission on Law Enforcement and Administration of Justice reported that "crime and delinquency are symptoms of failures and disorganization of the community. . . . The task of corrections, therefore, includes building or rebuilding social ties, obtaining employment and education, securing in the larger senses a place for the offender in the routine functioning of society."[35] This analysis was consistent with the views of advocates of **community corrections,** who felt that the goal of the criminal justice system should be the reintegration of offenders into the community.

Community corrections called for a radical departure from the medical model's emphasis on treatment in prison. Instead, prisons were to be avoided because they were artificial institutions that interfered with the offender's ability to develop a crime-free lifestyle. Proponents argued that corrections should turn away from psychological treatment in favor of programs that would increase offenders' opportunities to become successful citizens. Probation would be the sentence of choice for nonviolent offenders so that they could engage in vocational and educational programs that increased their chances of adjusting to society. For the small portion of offenders who had to be incarcerated, the amount of time in prison would be only a short interval until release on parole. To further the goal of reintegration, correctional workers would serve as advocates for offenders as they dealt with governmental agencies providing employment counseling, medical treatment, and financial assistance.

The reintegration idea was dominant in corrections for about a decade, until the late 1970s. It gave way to a new punitiveness in criminal justice in conjunction with the rebirth of the determinate sentence. Advocates of reintegration claim, as did advocates of previous reforms, that the idea was never adequately tested. Nevertheless, community corrections remains one of the significant ideas and practices in the recent history of corrections.

community corrections

A model of corrections based on the assumption that reintegrating the offender into the community should be the goal of the criminal justice system.

The Crime Control Model: The Pendulum Swings Again

Beginning in the late 1960s, the public became concerned about rising crime rates. At the same time, studies of treatment programs challenged their worth and the Progressive assumption that state officials would exercise discretion in a positive manner. Critics of rehabilitation attacked the indeterminate sentence and parole, urging that treatment be available on a voluntary basis but that it not be tied to release. In addition, proponents of increased crime control called for longer sentences, especially for career criminals and violent offenders.

James Q. Wilson summarized the "new realism" in regard to treatment programs and crime rates when he declared that our efforts to understand and curb the rise in crime have been frustrated by "our optimistic and unrealistic assumptions about human nature."[36] Addressing the fact that the United States experienced an upsurge in crime during the prosperous 1960s and early 1970s, Wilson found it strange that "we should persist in the view that we can find and alleviate the 'causes' of crime, [and] that serious criminals can be rehabilitated."[37]

The Decline of Rehabilitation

According to critics of rehabilitation, its reportedly high recidivism rates prove its ineffectiveness. Probably the most thorough analysis of research data from treatment programs was undertaken by Robert Martinson for the New York State Governor's Special Committee on Criminal Offenders. Using rigorous standards, he surveyed 231 English-language studies of rehabilitation programs in corrections systems. They included such standard rehabilitative programs as educational and vocational training, individual counseling, group counseling, milieu therapy, medical treatment (plastic surgery, drugs), parole, and supervision. Martinson summarized his findings by saying, "With few and isolated exceptions, the rehabilitative efforts that have been reported so far have had no appreciable effect on recidivism."[38]

Critics of the rehabilitation model have also challenged as unwarranted the amount of discretion given to correctional decision makers to tailor the criminal sanction to the needs of each offender. In particular, they have argued that the discretion given to parole boards to release offenders is misplaced because board decisions are more often based on the whims of individual members than on the scientific criteria espoused by the medical model.

The Emergence of Crime Control

crime control model of corrections

A model of corrections based on the assumption that criminal behavior can be controlled by more use of incarceration and other forms of strict supervision.

As the political climate changed in the 1970s and 1980s, and with the crime rate at historic levels, legislators, judges, and officials responded with a renewed emphasis on a **crime control model** of corrections. By 1980 the problem of crime and punishment had become an intense subject for ideological conflict, partisan politics, and legislative action.[39]

The critique of the rehabilitation model led to changes in the sentencing structures of more than half of the states and to the abolition of parole release in many. The new determinate sentencing laws were designed to incarcerate offenders for longer periods of time. In conjunction with other forms of punishment, the thrust of the 1980s was toward crime control through risk containment.

The punitive ethos of the 1980s and 1990s appeared in the emphasis on dealing more strictly with violent offenders and career criminals. It was also reflected in the trend toward intensive supervision of probationers, the detention without bail of accused persons thought to present a danger to the community, reinstitution of the death penalty in thirty-seven states, and the requirement that judges impose mandatory penalties for persons convicted of certain offenses or having extensive criminal records. By the end of the decade, the effect of these "get-tough" policies was evidenced by the record numbers of prisoners, the longer sentences being served, and the size of the probation population. Some observers point to these policies as the reason why the crime rate has begun to fall. Others ask whether the crime control policies have really made a difference given demographic and other changes in the United States. Table 3.1, which traces the history of correctional thought and practices in the United States, highlights the continual shifts in focus.

Where Are We Today?

As the United States enters a new century, the time may be ripe for another look at correctional policy. The language now used in journals of corrections differs markedly from that found on their pages thirty years ago. The optimism that once suffused corrections

Table 3.1 History of Corrections in America

Note the extent to which correctional policies have shifted from one era to the next and are influenced by other societal factors.

				Correctional Model			
	Colonial (1600s–1790s)	Penitentiary (1790s–1860s)	Reformatory (1870s–1890s)	Progressive (1890s–1930s)	Medical (1930s–1960s)	Community (1960s–1970s)	Crime Control (1970s–1990s)
Features	Anglican Code Capital and corporal punishment, fines	Separate confinement Reform of individual Power of isolation and labor Penance Disciplined routine Punishment according to severity of crime	Indeterminate sentences Parole Classification by degree of individual reform Rehabilitative programs Separate treatment for juveniles	Individual case approach Administrative discretion Broader probation and parole Juvenile courts	Rehabilitation as primary focus of incarceration Psychological testing and classification Various types of treatment programs and institutions	Reintegration into community Avoidance of incarceration Vocational and educational programs	Determinate sentences Mandatory sentences Sentencing guidelines Risk management
Philosophical basis	Religious law Doctrine of predestination	Enlightenment, Declaration of Independence Human perfectability and powers of reason Religious penitence Power of reformation Focus on the act Healing power of suffering	NPA Declaration of Principles Crime as moral disease Criminals as "victims of social disorder"	The Age of Reform Positivist school Punishment according to needs of offender Focus on the offender Crime as an urban, immigrant ghetto problem	Biomedical science Psychiatry and psychology Social work practice Crime as signal of personal "distress" or "failure"	Civil rights movement Critique of prisons Small is better	Crime control Rising crime rates Political shift to the right New punitive agenda

has waned. The financial and human costs of the retributive crime control policies of the 1990s are now being scrutinized. Are the costs of incarceration and surveillance justified? Has crime been reduced? Are we safer today? Many researchers think not. As we look to the future, we wonder if there will be a new direction for corrections. If so, what will be its focus?

Summary

Social change is brought about by diverse elements in society that place questions on the political agenda, lobby for new policies, and urge an end to existing practices. The history of correctional thought and practice has been marked by enthusiasm for new approaches, disillusionment with these approaches, and then substitution of yet other tactics. Each reform movement through which American corrections has passed seems to have resulted from the efforts of well-intentioned people working in the name of humanity. As society has changed, so have the assumptions underlying corrections. Regardless of the assumptions, the reformers' ideals were never fully achieved, and the changes they effected often produced unsatisfactory results. In most cases political and bureaucratic influences won out, prisons quickly became poorly managed, and probation and parole cases became too numerous. And always the stone walls of the prisons remained. ■

For Discussion

1. Why do you think the idea of the penitentiary first caught on in the United States?

2. The prison seems to hold continuing fascination in American culture. What other methods might the general public find acceptable as ways to punish offenders?

3. How do you think offenders will be punished in the United States in the future? What philosophical and technical developments would buttress the approaches you foresee?

4. We seem to be constantly driven by images of a "crime free" society. As a result, we adopt drastic solutions as though being "crime free" is possible. Is it?

For Further Reading

Friedman, Lawrence M. *Crime and Punishment in American History.* New York: Basic Books, 1993. An excellent historical overview of the American criminal justice system.

Hindus, Michael S. *Prison and Plantation: Crime, Justice, and Authority in Massachusetts and South Carolina, 1767–1878.* Chapel Hill: University of North Carolina Press, 1980. Shows the differences between corrections in the emerging industrial Northeast and the plantation system of the South.

Pisciotta, Alexander W. *Benevolent Repression: Social Control and the American Reformatory-Prison Movement.* New York: New York University Press, 1994. Argues that reformatories, although dedicated to humane, constructive, and charitable treatment, worked instead to tame and train criminal elements of the working class.

Rothman, David J. *Conscience and Convenience.* Boston: Little, Brown, 1980. Examines Progressive era reforms to individualize treatment for deviants and therefore solve the problems of crime and mental illness.

———. *The Discovery of the Asylum.* Boston: Little, Brown, 1971. Describes changes in the ways Americans treated criminals, the mentally ill, and the poor during the eighteenth and early nineteenth centuries.

Teeters, Negley K., and Shearer, John D. *The Prison at Philadelphia's Cherry Hill.* New York: Columbia University Press, 1957. Tells the history of Eastern Penitentiary, the first correctional facility organized around the concept of separate confinement.

Notes

1. Negley K. Teeters and John D. Shearer, *The Prison at Philadelphia's Cherry Hill* (New York: Columbia University Press, 1957), p. 63.

2. David J. Rothman, "Perfecting the Prison: United States, 1789–1865," in Norval Morris and David J. Rothman, eds., *The Oxford History of the Prison* (New York: Oxford University Press, 1995), p. 112.

3. David J. Rothman, *The Discovery of the Asylum* (Boston: Little, Brown, 1971), p. 51.

4. Lawrence M. Friedman, *Crime and Punishment in American History* (New York: Basic Books, 1993), p. 48.

5. Adam J. Hirsch, *The Rise of the Penitentiary* (New Haven, CT: Yale University Press, 1992), p. 8.

6. Louis P. Masur, *Rights of Execution* (New York: Oxford University Press, 1989), p. 24.

7. Gordon S. Wood, *The Radicalism of the American Revolution* (New York: Knopf, 1992), p. 193.

8. Hirsch, pp. 11-14.

9. Blake McKelvey, *American Prisons* (Montclair, NJ: Patterson Smith, 1977), p. 8.

10. Norman Johnston, *Eastern State Penitentiary: Crucible of Good Intentions* (Philadelphia: Philadelphia Museum of Art, 1994). Eastern State Penitentiary is now a museum open to the public.

11. Thorsten Sellin, "The Origin of the Pennsylvania System of Prison Discipline," *Prison Journal,* 50, Spring/Summer, 1970, pp. 15-17.

12. Gustave de Beaumont and Alexis de Tocqueville, *On the Penitentiary System in the United States and Its Application to France* (Carbondale: Southern Illinois University Press [1833] 1964), p. 146.

13. Charles Dickens, *American Notes,* vol. 1 (London: Chapman & Hall, 1842), p. 238.

14. Teeters and Shearer, ch. 4.

15. Beaumont and Tocqueville, p. 201.

16. John A. Conley, "Prisons, Production, and Profit: Reconsidering the Importance of Prison Industries," *Journal of Social History,* 14, Winter 1980, p. 55.

17. David J. Rothman, *Conscience and Convenience* (Boston: Little, Brown, 1980), p. 18.

18. Elizabeth Eileen Dooley, "Sir William Crofton and the Irish or Intermediate System of Prison Discipline," *New England Journal of Prison Law,* 575, Winter 1981, p. 55.

19. Rothman, *Conscience and Convenience,* p.70.

20. Edgardo Rotman, "The Failure of Reform: United States, 1865–1965," in Norval Morris and David J. Rothman, eds., *The Oxford History of the Prison* (New York: Oxford University Press, 1995), p. 174.

21. Alexander W. Pisciotta, *Benevolent Repression: Social Control and the American Reformatory-Prison Movement* (New York: New York University Press, 1994), p. 20.

22. Pisciotta, p. 41.

23. W. M. F. Round, "How Far May We Abolish Prisons?" *Journal of the American Social Science Association,* 325, 1897, pp. 200-201, as cited in Rothman, *Conscience and Convenience,* p. 55.

24. Richard Hofstader, *The Age of Reform* (New York: Knopf, 1974).

25. Rothman, Conscience and Convenience, p. 5.

26. Ibid., p. 60.

27. Ibid., p. 53.

28. Ibid., p. 99.

29. Rothman, p. 183.

30. Rothman, Conscience and Convenience, p. 99.

31. Quoted in Jessica Mitford, *Kind and Usual Punishment* (New York: Knopf, 1973), p. 96.

32. Karl Menninger, *The Crime of Punishment* (New York: Viking Press, 1969), p. 19.

33. Harry E. Barnes and Negley K. Teeters, *New Horizons in Criminology* (New York: Prentice-Hall, 1944), p. 768.

34. Thomas F. Courtless, "Maryland's Flirtation with Positive Penology: Patuxent Institution: From Cutting Edge Back to the Drawing Board," paper given at the annual meeting of the American Society of Criminology, San Francisco, November 1991.

35. U.S. President's Commission on Law Enforcement and Administration of Justice, *The Challenge of Crime in a Free Society* (Washington, DC: U.S. Government Printing Office, 1967), p. 7.

36. James Q. Wilson, "Lock 'Em Up and Other Thoughts on Crime, "*New York Times Magazine,* March 9, 1982, p.11.

37. Wilson.

38. Robert Martinson, "What Works? Questions and Answers About Prison Reform," *Public Interest,* 35, Spring 1974, p. 22.

39. Michael Tonry, *Sentencing Matters* (New York: Oxford University Press, 1996), p. 3.

The Punishment of Offenders

 ll rise!" The people in the Los Angeles courtroom stand as Judge David Perez of the Superior Court strides from his office and mounts the dais. On this day in 1998, the courtroom is packed with attorneys, reporters, and relatives of Ennis Cosby, son of beloved actor Bill Cosby. Judge Perez is about to sentence Ukrainian-born teenager Mikail Markhasev for killing Ennis in a botched robbery on the side of a dark freeway where he had stopped to change a flat tire. The judge refused a defense request for a new trial; the defense claimed the jury had made up their minds before considering all the evidence. Speaking for the Cosby family, Eric Hanks, Ennis's uncle, delivered an emotional state-

ment recalling the slain Columbia University student as a caring person. He showed photographs of Markhasev smiling throughout the trial, and emphasized that "Our lives are forever changed by this terrible act." Because Markhasev was convicted of committing murder while using a firearm during the attempted robbery, California law required Perez to sentence him to prison for life without the possibility of parole.

As he was led out of the courtroom, Markhasev—a former honor student turned drug addict, gang member, and petty criminal—flashed a smile at his mother and grandmother, who let out gasps when the sentence was announced.

Crucial to every decision in the criminal process is the question "Is it just?" Should Mikail Markhasev have been executed, committed to a mental hospital, given rehabilitative treatment, or imprisoned with the possibility of parole? Did justice serve Markhasev's victims and their families? Was society's need for the maintenance of right conduct supported by the sentence? What rationale governed the punishment?

These types of questions are central to the mission of corrections. In this chapter we examine the goals of corrections, note the various forms of the criminal sanction, and discuss the sentencing process. As we explore these topics, we will examine their links to one another and to the historical and philosophical issues developed in Chapters 2 and 3.

Questions FOR INQUIRY

1. What are the goals of punishment?
2. What are the forms of the criminal sanction?
3. What types of sentences may judges impose?
4. Does the system treat wrongdoers equally?

The Purpose of Corrections

Rationales for punishment are very much influenced by the broad philosophical, political, and social themes of their era. Prevailing ideas about the causes of crime are closely tied to questions of responsibility and hence to the rationale for specific sanctions. As explained in Chapter 2, the ideas of the classical school of criminology, founded by Cesare Beccaria, fitted nicely to the concepts of the Age of Reason, as did Jeremy Bentham's utilitarianism. In the context of the times, "making the punishment fit the crime" was a humanistic advance because it sought to do away with the brutal punishments often inflicted for trivial offenses. With the rise of science and the development of positivist criminology toward the end of the 1800s, new beliefs emerged about criminal responsibility and the desirability of designing punishment to meet the needs of the offender. The positivists considered criminal behavior to be the result of sociological, psychological, or biological factors and therefore directed correctional work toward rehabilitating the offender through treatment.

Mikail Markhasev, convicted of the murder of Ennis Cosby, sits with his attorney listening as his sentence is read. Does life imprisonment without parole serve justice?

Before further examining the goals of the criminal sanction, let's consider what the term *punishment* actually means. Does it encompass all actions taken under law against an offender, or only those that are painful to the offender? Is a person enrolled in a rehabilitation program being punished? These questions must be asked, for in the United States today the punishment is often distinguished from rehabilitation.

Herbert Packer argued that punishment is marked by these three elements:

1. An offense.
2. The infliction of pain because of the commission of the offense.
3. A dominant purpose that is neither to compensate someone injured by the offense nor to better the offender's condition but to prevent further offenses or to inflict what is thought to be deserved pain on the offender.[1]

Note that Packer emphasizes two major goals of criminal punishment: inflicting deserved suffering on evildoers and preventing crime.

Criminal sanctions in the United States have four goals: retribution (deserved punishment), deterrence, incapacitation, and rehabilitation. In Chapter 22 we describe the movement to make restorative and community justice a fifth goal of the criminal sanction. Here, as we discuss each of the four traditional justifications for punishment, bear in mind that although judges often state publicly that their sentencing practices accord with a particular goal, conditions in correctional institutions or the actions of probation officers may be inconsistent with that goal. Thus sentencing and correctional policies may be carried out in such a way that no one goal dominates or, in some cases, that justice itself is not demonstrably served.

Retribution (Deserved Punishment)

retribution

Punishment inflicted on a person who has infringed on the rights of others and so deserves to be penalized. The severity of the sanction should fit the seriousness of the crime.

Retribution is punishment inflicted on a person who has infringed on the rights of others and deserves to be punished. The biblical expression "an eye for an eye, a tooth for a tooth" illustrates the philosophy underlying retribution. Retribution means that those who commit a particular crime should be punished alike, in proportion to the gravity of the offense or to the extent to which others have been made to suffer. Retribution is deserved punishment; offenders must "pay their debts." Retribution focuses on the offense and has no concern for the future acts of the criminal or some utilitarian purpose such as reform or deterrence. Offenders must be penalized for their wrongful acts, simply because fairness and justice require that they be punished.

As discussed in Chapter 2, with the Age of Reason and the development of utilitarian approaches to punishment, the idea of retribution lost much of its influence.

However, some scholars claim that the desire for retribution is a basic human emotion. They maintain that if the state does not provide retributive sanctions to reflect community revulsion at offensive acts, citizens will take the law into their own hands to punish offenders. Under this view, the failure of government to satisfy the people's desire for retribution could produce social chaos. Retribution helps the community emphasize the standards it expects all members to uphold.

This argument may not be valid for all crimes, however. If a rapist is inadequately punished, then the victim's friends, family, and other members of the community may be tempted to exact their own retribution. But what about a young adult smoking marijuana? If the government failed to exact retribution for this offense, would the community really care? The same apathy may hold true with respect to offenders who commit other nonviolent crimes that have a modest impact on society. In these seemingly trivial situations, however, retribution may be useful and necessary to remind the public of the general rules of law and the important values being protected.

Since the 1970s new interest in retribution has arisen as a justification for the criminal sanction. This has occurred largely because people are dissatisfied with the philosophical basis and practical results of rehabilitation. Using the concept of "just deserts or deserved punishment" to define retribution, some theorists argue that a person who infringes on the rights of others deserves to be punished. This approach is based on the philosophical view that punishment is a moral response to harm inflicted on society. In effect, these theorists believe basic morality demands that wrongdoers be punished. Andrew von Hirsch, a leading contemporary writer on punishment, has said that "the sanctioning authority is entitled to choose a response that expresses moral disapproval: namely, punishment."[2] According to von Hirsch and others such as Norval Morris, punishment should be applied only to exact retribution for the wrong inflicted and not primarily to achieve other goals such as deterrence, incapacitation, or rehabilitation.[3]

Deterrence

Many people think of criminal punishment as providing a basis for affecting the future choices and behavior of individuals. Politicians frequently talk about getting tough on crime in order to send a message to would-be criminals. This deterrence approach has its roots in eighteenth-century England among the followers of the utilitarian philosopher Jeremy Bentham (see Chapter 2). He argued that retribution was pointless and unjustified except when pain inflicted was demonstrably more beneficial to society than pain withheld. The presumed benefit of punishment was the prevention of crime. The basic objective of punishment, he said, was to deter potential criminals by the example of the sanctions laid on the guilty.

Modern thinking distinguishes two types of deterrence.[4] **General deterrence** presumes that members of the general public will be deterred by observing the punishments of others and will conclude that the costs of crime outweigh the benefits. For general deterrence to be effective, the public must be constantly reminded about the likelihood and severity of punishment for various acts. They must believe they will be caught, prosecuted, and given a specific punishment if they commit a particular crime. Moreover, the punishment must be severe enough that they will be impressed by the consequences of committing crimes. For example, public hanging was once considered an effective general deterrent.

By contrast, **special deterrence**, also called **specific** or **individual deterrence**, targets the decisions and behavior of offenders who have already been convicted. Under this approach, the amount and kind of punishment are calculated to discourage the criminal from repeating the offense. The punishment must be severe enough to make the criminal say, "The consequences of my crime were too painful. I won't commit that crime again because I don't want to risk being punished again."

general deterrence

Punishment of criminals that is intended to be an example to the general public and to discourage the commission of offenses by others.

special deterrence (specific or individual deterrence)

Punishment inflicted on criminals to discourage them from committing any future crimes.

After two trials, a jury convicted Erik and Lyle Menendez of murdering their parents. Prosecutors said they were motivated by greed for the family's $14-million fortune. Will their life sentence deter others?

Some obvious difficulties trouble the concept of deterrence.[5] Deterrence presumes that all people act rationally and think before they act. Thus deterrence does not account for the many people who commit crimes under the influence of drugs or alcohol, or those whose harmful behavior stems from psychological problems or mental illness. Deterrence also does not account for people who impulsively steal or damage property. In other cases, the low risk of being caught defeats the goal of general or special deterrence. To be "generally deterrent," potential offenders must perceive punishment as relatively fast, certain, and severe. That, of course, is not always the case.

Social science cannot measure the effects of general deterrence; only those who are *not* deterred come to the attention of researchers. A study of the deterrent effects of punishment would have to examine the impact of different forms of the criminal sanction on various potential lawbreakers. How can we ever know how many people—or even if any people—stopped themselves from committing a crime because they were deterred by the prospect of prosecution and punishment? Therefore, although legislators often claim deterrence as a rationale for certain sanctions, we do not really know the extent to which sentencing policies based on deterrence achieve their objectives. Because contemporary American society has shown little ability to reduce crime by imposing increasingly severe sanctions, there is strong reason to question the effectiveness of deterrence for many crimes and criminals. Although deterrence is believed to be a prominent purpose of criminal sanctions, the role it plays and the extent to which sentencing policies can be altered to fulfill its purpose rest on a shaky and complex scientific foundation.[6]

Incapacitation

incapacitation

Depriving an offender of the ability to commit crimes against society, usually by detaining the offender in prison.

The strategy of **incapacitation** assumes that society can remove an offender's capacity to commit further crimes by detention in prison or by execution. Many people express such sentiments when urging that we should "lock 'em up and throw away the key!" In primitive societies, banishment from the community was the usual method of incapacitation. In early America, offenders often agreed to move away or to join the army as an alternative to some other form of punishment. In contemporary America, imprisonment is the usual method of incapacitation. Offenders can be confined within secure institutions and effectively prevented from committing additional harm against society for the duration of their sentence. Capital punishment is the ultimate method of incapacitation.

Any sentence that physically restricts an offender can have an incapacitating effect, even when the underlying purpose of the sentence is retribution, deterrence, or rehabilitation. Sentences based on incapacitation are future oriented. Whereas retribution requires focusing on the harmful act of the offender, incapacitation looks at the offender's potential future actions. If the offender is not likely to commit future crimes, then a severe sentence may be imposed—even for a relatively minor crime.

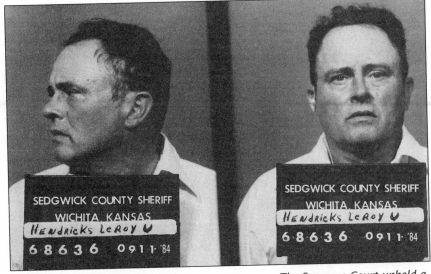

The Supreme Court upheld a Kansas law allowing the extended incapacitation of sex offenders. After child molester Leroy Hendricks completed his prison sentence he was kept behind bars in a mental hospital.

Under the incapacitation theory, for example, a woman who kills her abusive husband as an emotional reaction to his verbal insults and physical assaults could receive a light sentence. As a one-time impulse killer who felt driven to kill by unique circumstances, she is not likely to commit additional crimes. By contrast, someone who shoplifts merchandise from a store and has been convicted of the offense on ten previous occasions may receive a severe sentence. The criminal record and type of crime indicate that he or she will commit additional crimes if released. Thus incapacitation focuses on offenders rather than offenses.

Does it offend your sense of justice that a person could receive a more severe sentence for shoplifting than for manslaughter? This is one basis for criticizing incapacitation. In addition, there are questions about how to determine the length of sentence. Presumably, offenders will not be released until the state is reasonably sure that they will no longer commit crimes. However, can society accurately predict any person's behavior? Moreover, on what grounds can society punish people for anticipated future behavior that cannot be accurately predicted?

In recent years, greater attention has been paid to the concept of **selective incapacitation** whereby offenders who repeat certain kinds of crimes are sentenced to long prison terms. Research suggests that a relatively small number of offenders commit a large number of violent and property crimes.[7] For example, burglars tend to commit many offenses before they are caught. Thus, some argue that these "career criminals" should be locked up for long periods. Such policies could be costly, however. Not only would correctional facilities have to be expanded, but the number of expensive, time-consuming trials might increase if more severe sentences caused fewer repeat offenders to plead guilty. In addition, no one can accurately predict which offenders will in fact commit more crimes on release.

The idea of confining or closely supervising repeat offenders is appealing, yet it involves costs to the criminal justice system. In addition, selective incapacitation raises disturbing moral and ethical questions. Because the theory looks at aggregates—the total harm of a certain type of crime versus the total suffering to be inflicted to reduce its incidence—policymakers may tend to focus on "cost–benefit" comparisons, disregarding serious issues of justice, individual freedom, and civil liberties.

selective incapacitation

Making the best use of expensive and limited prison space by targeting for incarceration those offenders whose incapacity will do the most to reduce crime in society.

Rehabilitation

Rehabilitation is the goal of restoring a convicted offender to a constructive place in society through some form of vocational or educational training or therapy. Many believe that rehabilitation is the most appealing modern justification for the criminal sanction.

rehabilitation

The goal of restoring a convicted offender to a constructive place in society through some form of vocational or educational training or therapy.

Americans want to believe that offenders can be treated and resocialized so they will lead crime-free, productive lives. During the twentieth century, many people have argued that techniques are available to identify and treat the causes of criminal behavior. If the offender's criminal behavior is assumed to result from some social, psychological, or biological imperfection, then treating the disorder becomes the primary goal of corrections.

The goal of rehabilitation is oriented solely toward the offender and does not imply any consistent relationship between the severity of the punishment and the gravity of the crime. People who commit lesser offenses may receive long prison sentences if experts believe that a long period of time is required to successfully rehabilitate them. By contrast, a murderer may win early release by showing signs that the psychological or emotional problems that led to the killing have been corrected.

According to the concept of rehabilitation, offenders are treated, not punished, and will return to society when they are "cured." Consequently, judges should not set a fixed sentence but rather ones with maximum and minimum terms so that parole boards may release inmates when they have been rehabilitated. Such sentences are known as "indeterminate sentences" because no fixed release date is set by the judge. The indeterminate sentence is rationalized by the belief that if prisoners know when they are going to be released, they will not make an effort to engage in the treatment programs prescribed for their rehabilitation. If, however, they know they will be held until cured, they will cooperate with counselors, psychologists, and other professionals seeking to treat their problems.

From the 1940s until the 1970s, the rehabilitative goal was so widely held that treatment and reform of the offender were generally regarded as the only issues worthy of serious attention. People assumed that crime was caused by problems affecting individuals and that modern social sciences had given us the tools to address those problems. During the past twenty-five years, however, the assumptions of the rehabilitation model have been questioned. Studies of rehabilitative programs have challenged the idea that we really know how to cure criminal offenders.[8] Moreover, people no longer take for granted that crime is caused by identifiable, curable problems such as poverty, lack of job skills, low self-esteem, and hostility toward authority. Instead, some scholars argue that we cannot expect to identify the cause of criminal behavior for individual offenders. Morris has argued that coerced in-prison treatment programs not only waste resources but are morally wrong on human rights grounds even if they might be effective in changing behavior.[9]

Clearly, many legislatures, prosecutors, and judges have abandoned the rehabilitation goal in favor of retribution, deterrence, or incapacitation. Yet on the basis of opinion polls, researchers have found public support for rehabilitative programs.[10] Support among prison wardens for rehabilitative programs has also been found.[11]

New Approaches to Punishment

During the past decade many people have called for shifts away from punishment goals that focus either on the offender or the crime. Some have argued that the current goals of the criminal sanction leave out the needs of the crime victim and the community. As Gordon Basemore and Mark Umbreit note, crime has traditionally been viewed as violating the state, but people now recognize that a criminal act also violates the victim and the community.[12] In keeping with the focus on **community justice**—by the police, courts, and corrections—(see Chapter 22), advocates are calling for **restoration** (through restorative justice) to be added to the goals of the criminal sanction.

The restorative justice perspective views crime as more than a violation of penal law. The criminal act also practically and symbolically denies community. It breaks trust among citizens and requires community members to determine how "to contradict the moral message of the crime that the offender is above the law and the victim beneath its reach."[13] Crime victims suffer losses involving damage to property and self that results from the act. Crime also challenges the very essence of community, to the extent that community life depends on a shared sense of trust, fairness, and interdependence.

Critics say that the retributive focus of today's criminal justice system denies the victim's need to be affirmed, and isolates community members from the conflict between

community justice

A model of justice that emphasizes reparation to the victim and the community, approaching crime from a problem-solving perspective, and citizen involvement in crime prevention.

restoration

Punishment designed to repair the damage done to the victim and community by an offender's criminal act.

the offender and the victim. By shifting the focus to restorative justice, sanctions can provide ways for the offender to repair harm to victim and community.

The restorative process involves participation of the offender, the victim, and the community. The offender must take responsibility for the offense, agree to "undo" the harm through restitution, and affirm a willingness to live according to the law. The victim must specify the harm of the offense and the resources necessary to restore the losses suffered, and the victim must lay out the conditions necessary to diminish any fear or resentment toward the offender. The community facilitates the restorative process, emphasizes to the offender the norms of acceptable behavior, provides support to restore the victim, and provides opportunities for the offender to perform reparative tasks for the victim and the community. Finally, it must provide ways for the offender to get the help needed to live in the community crime free.

Criminal Sanctions: A Mixed Bag?

Which should society use: retribution, deterrence, incapacitation, or rehabilitation? Justifications for specific sanctions overlap considerably. A term of imprisonment may be philosophically justified by its primary goal of retribution but also serve the secondary functions of deterrence and incapacitation. General deterrence is such a broad concept that it adapts to the other goals, except possibly rehabilitation.

However, rehabilitation clearly conflicts with the other goals. For example, the deterrent power of incarceration depends primarily on being unpleasant. If incarceration consists mainly of a pleasant rehabilitative experience, its deterrent power is lost. By the same token, the more unpleasant prison life is, the less suitable an environment it is for most rehabilitation programs.

Trial judges carry the heavy burden of fashioning a sentence that accommodates these values in each case. A forger may be sentenced to a long prison term as an example to others, even though this person poses no threat to community safety and probably does not need correctional treatment. The same judge may impose a shorter sentence on a youthful offender who has committed a serious crime yet who may be a good candidate for rehabilitation if quickly reintegrated into society.

To see how these goals might be enacted in real life, consider again the sentencing of Mikail Markhasev for killing Ennis Crosby. Table 4.1 shows various hypothetical sentencing statements the judge *might* have given, depending on prevailing correctional goals. In actuality Judge David Perez spoke directly to Markhasev without extensively explaining the reasons for the punishment.

Table 4.1 Punishment of Mikail Markhasev

At sentencing the judge usually gives reasons for the punishment imposed. Here are possible statements that Judge David Perez *might* have made depending on the goal he wanted to promote.

Goal	Judge's Statement
Retribution	I am imposing this sentence because you deserve to be punished for murdering Ennis Cosby. Your criminal behavior in this case is the basis for your punishment. Justice requires me to impose a sanction that reflects the value the community places on human life.
Deterrence	I am imposing this sentence so that your punishment for killing Ennis Cosby will serve as an example and deter others who may contemplate similar actions. In addition, I hope that the sentence will deter you from ever again committing such an act.
Incapacitation	I am imposing this sentence so that you will be incapacitated and hence unable to kill another during the length of this term. Because you have not committed prior major offenses, selective incapacitation is not warranted.
Rehabilitation	The trial testimony of your psychiatrist and information contained in the presentence report make me believe that aspects of your personality led you to kill. I am therefore imposing this sentence so that you can be treated in ways that will rectify your behavior so you will not kill again.

Forms of the Criminal Sanction

Incarceration, intermediate sanctions, probation, and death are the basic ways the criminal sanction, or punishment, is applied in the United States. Most people think of incarceration as the usual punishment. As a consequence, much of the public equates using alternatives to incarceration, such as probation, with offenders "getting off." However, community-based punishments such as probation and intermediate sanctions are imposed almost three times as often as prison sentences.

Many judges and researchers believe that the sentencing structures in the United States are both too severe and too lenient. That is, many offenders who do not warrant incarceration are sent to prison, and many who should be given more restrictive punishments receive minimal probation supervision. Because sanctions more severe than probation but less severe than incarceration are seldom used, Norval Morris and Michael Tonry have urged greater use of such intermediate sanctions as fines, home confinement, intensive probation supervision, restitution, and community service.[14]

Advocates for more effective sentencing practices increasingly support a range or continuum of punishment options, with graduated levels of supervision and harshness. As Figure 4.1 shows, simple probation lies at one end of this range and traditional incarceration lies at the other. As noted by researchers associated with the Edna McConnell Clark Foundation, "An expanded range of sentencing options gives judges greater latitude to exercise discretion in selecting punishments that more closely fit the circumstances of the crime and the offender."[15] It is argued that by using this type of sentencing scheme, authorities can maintain expensive prison cells for violent offenders. At the same time, less restrictive community-based programs can be used to punish nonviolent offenders.

As we examine the various forms of criminal sanctions, bear in mind that complex problems are associated with applying these legally authorized punishments. Although

Figure 4.1   Escalating Punishments to Fit the Crime

This list includes generalized descriptions of many sentencing options used in jurisdictions across the country.

SOURCE: *Seeking Justice: Crime and Punishment in America* (New York: Edna McConnell Clark Foundation, 1997.), pp. 32–33.

PROBATION

Offender reports to probation officer periodically, depending on the offense, sometimes as frequently as several times a month or as infrequently as once a year.

INTENSIVE SUPERVISION PROBATION

Offender sees probation officer three to five times a week. Probation officer also makes unscheduled visits to offender's home or workplace.

RESTITUTION AND FINES

Used alone or in conjunction with probation or intensive supervision and requires regular payments to crime victims or to the courts.

COMMUNITY SERVICE

Used alone or in conjunction with probation or intensive supervision and requires completion of set number of hours of work in and for the community.

SUBSTANCE ABUSE TREATMENT

Evaluation and referral services provided by private outside agencies and used alone or in conjunction with either simple probation or intensive supervision.

the penal code defines the behaviors considered illegal and specifies the procedures for determining guilt, the legal standards for sentencing—for actually applying the punishment—have not been as well developed. The United States has no common laws of sentencing. Thus judges are given discretion in determining the appropriate sentence within the parameters of the penal code. For a Comparative Perspective, consider the impact of the Canon of Lek, intended to regulate medieval life and still the basis for blood feuds in parts of Albania today.

Incarceration

Imprisonment is the most visible penalty imposed by U.S. courts. Although fewer than 30 percent of people under correctional supervision are in prisons and jails, incarceration remains the standard punishment for violent and serious offenders. Imprisonment is thought to significantly deter crime. However, incarceration is expensive. It also creates problems of reintegrating offenders into society on release.

In the penal code, legislatures stipulate the type of sentences and the amount of prison time that may be imposed for each crime. Three basic sentencing schemes are used: (1) indeterminate sentences, (2) determinate sentences, and (3) mandatory sentences. Each type of sentence makes certain assumptions about the goals of the criminal sanction, and each provides judges with varying degrees of discretion. In addition, an aspect of penal law that affects sentencing is good-time provisions.

Indeterminate Sentences   When the goal of rehabilitation dominated corrections, legislatures enacted **indeterminate** (or *indefinite*) **sentences**. In keeping with the goal of treatment, indeterminate sentencing gives correctional officials and parole boards

indeterminate sentence

A period of incarceration with minimum and maximum terms stipulated, so that parole eligibility depends on the time necessary for treatment; closely associated with the rehabilitation concept.

DAY REPORTING

Clients report to a central location every day where they file a daily schedule with their supervision officer showing how each hour will be spent – at work, in class, at support group meetings, etc.

HOUSE ARREST AND ELECTRONIC MONITORING

Used in conjunction with intensive supervision and restricts offender to home except when at work, school, or treatment.

HALFWAY HOUSE

Residential settings for selected inmates as a supplement to probation for those completing prison programs and for some probation or parole violators. Usually coupled with community service work and/or substance abuse treatment.

BOOT CAMP

Rigorous military-style regimen for younger offenders, designed to accelerate punishment while instilling discipline, often with an educational component.

PRISONS AND JAILS

More serious offenders serve their terms at state or federal prisons, while county jails are usually designed to hold inmates for shorter periods.

COMPARATIVE PERSPECTIVE

Blood Feuds in Albania

Beneath the snow-splashed escarpments that protect northern Albania from the outside world and have left life much as it was centuries ago, the Sylaj family have been cooped up on their homestead for months, too afraid to move.

A blood feud, following precepts laid down in a medieval canon, hangs over the men of the household, including the patriarch, Shaban Sylaj, 99, who welcomes visitors with a two-tooth grin, wisps of ash-colored hair poking from under his skullcap.

Mr. Sylaj's son, Chel, 38, shot and killed another Albanian man in January, and now the dead man's family have the right, under the still-flourishing code, to take revenge. Their target is one of the Sylaj men.

The threat is real. Since the early 1990s, revenge killings have spread among the clans here, where the precepts of Lek Dukagjin, a fifteenth-century chieftain, prize honor and freedom above honesty, and where vengeance is the ruling passion.

Weapons—pistols in the old days, automatic assault rifles now—are valued as much as human life: a man who kills another man and takes his weapon too can be avenged with the taking of two lives.

"Who knows how many people have been killed through revenge?" said Man Mulosmani, 64, a clan leader who is preaching reconciliation rather than retribution. "Countless, countless. People don't want to report killings to the police because then the accused would be protected by the state in prison instead of being available to kill." . . .

Intended to regulate medieval life, the Canon of Lek, as it is known, has been perverted by people to suit their own needs, Mr. Mulosmani said. Now the lawless society floats between the ages-old customs and a state unable to adapt to modernity in the wake of communism.

For example, Fatmir Haklaj, 27, recently resigned as police chief of Tropojo to avenge a family murder and is reported by his former colleagues to have killed, or ordered the killing, of eight men so far for the murder of his brother. His brother was sprayed with nine bullets in January.

The leader of one of the most powerful clans, Mr. Haklaj vowed that he would kill one man for every bullet pumped into his brother's body, his colleagues said. According to Mr. Haklaj's arithmetic, he has one killing to go.

Last week the opposing Hoxe clan, which is accused of killing Mr. Haklaj's brother, were in mourning after burying a relative who they believe was the latest victim of Mr. Haklaj's revenge. The police have stood by, pleading powerlessness. ■

SOURCE: Jane Perlez, "Feuds Rack Albania, Loosed from Communism," *The New York Times*, April 14, 1998, p. A3. © 1998 by The New York Times Company. Reprinted by permission.

significant control over the amount of time a prisoner serves. Penal codes with indeterminate sentencing stipulate a minimum and a maximum amount of time to be served in prison (for example, one to five years, three to ten years, ten to twenty years, one year to life, and so on.) At the time of sentencing, the judge informs the offender about the range of the sentence. The offender also learns that he or she will probably be eligible for parole at some point after the minimum term (minus "good time") has been served. The actual release date is decided by the parole board.

Determinate Sentences   Growing dissatisfaction with the rehabilitative goal and support for the concept of retribution (deserved punishment) led many legislatures to shift to **determinate sentences**. With a determinate sentence, a convicted offender is imprisoned for a specific period of time (for example, two years, five years, ten years). At the end of the term, again minus credited "good time," the prisoner is automatically freed. Thus release is not tied to participation in treatment programs or to a judgment by a parole board on the offender's likelihood of returning to criminal activities.

---

determinate sentence

A fixed period of incarceration imposed by a court; associated with the concept of retribution or deserved punishment.

As states have moved toward determinate structures, some have adopted penal codes that stipulate a specific term for each crime category; others still let the judge choose a range of time to be served. Some states emphasize a determinate **presumptive sentence**; the legislature or often a commission specifies a term based on a time range (for example, fourteen to twenty months) into which most cases should fall. Only in special circumstances should judges deviate from the presumptive sentence. Whichever variant is used, however, the offender theoretically knows at sentencing the amount of time to be served. One result of determinate sentencing is that by reducing the judge's discretion, legislatures have tended to limit sentencing disparities and to ensure that the terms will correspond to those the elected body deems appropriate.[16] However, Pamala Griset argues that with restrictions on judges' discretion, power has shifted to correctional administrators who can make early release decisions.[17]

Mandatory Sentences   Politicians and the public have continued to complain that offenders are released before serving terms that are long enough, and legislatures have responded.[18] All states and the federal government now require **mandatory sentences** (often called mandatory minimum sentences), stipulating some minimum period of incarceration that people convicted of selected crimes must serve. The judge may not consider the circumstances of the offense or the background of the offender, and may not impose nonincarcerative sentences. Mandatory minimum prison terms are most often specified for violent crimes, drug violations, habitual offenders, or crimes in which a firearm was used.

The "three strikes and you're out" laws, now adopted by twenty-three states and the federal government, are examples of mandatory sentencing (see Figure 4.2).[19] Usually passed in a highly charged political context, these laws require that judges sentence offenders with three felony convictions to long prison terms, sometimes to life without parole.[20] In California, where they are broadly used, the laws have had the unintended consequences of clogging the courts, lowering rates of plea bargaining, and causing desperate offenders to violently resist arrest.[21] One study has shown that the law had little impact on the reduction in rates of serious crime or petty theft.[22] Research in Los Angeles has shown that the impact of the law hits African Americans the hardest. During the

presumptive sentence

A sentence for which the legislature or a commission sets a minimum and maximum range of months or years. Judges are to fix the length of the sentence within that range, allowing for special circumstances.

mandatory sentence

A sentence stipulating that some minimum period of incarceration must be served by people convicted of selected crimes, regardless of background or circumstances.

Figure 4.2   States with "Three Strikes" Mandatory Sentencing Laws

From their birth in the legislatures of California and Washington in 1993, "three strikes" mandatory sentencing laws (and their variations) have spread across the country. The laws have had a major impact on corrections in many states.

NOTE: Imposition of the mandatory sentence in the two or three strikes states depends on the circumstances of the crime and the prior record of the offender.

SOURCE: Michael Vitiello, "Three Strikes: Can We Return to Rationality?" *Journal of Criminal Law and Criminology,* 87, Winter 1997, p. 395.

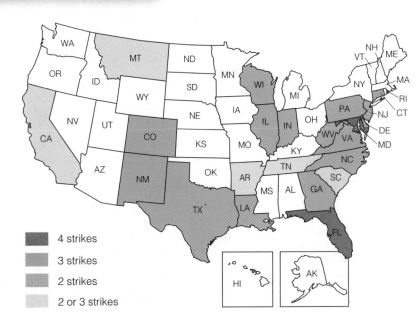

- 4 strikes
- 3 strikes
- 2 strikes
- 2 or 3 strikes

first six months 57 percent of those charged under the three strikes law were African Americans, seventeen times the rate of whites.[23] Although some have argued that these laws unfairly affect nonviolent offenders, one California study reported that 84 percent of a sample of three-strike offenders "had been convicted at least once for a violent crime," as well as an average of five felonies apiece.[24]

Although legislators may assume that mandatory sentences will be imposed and criminal behavior reduced, this intent may be thwarted by the decisions of judges and prosecutors. California prosecutors vary greatly as to whether they charge under the "three strikes" law. Los Angeles and San Diego prosecutors have maximized use of the law; those in Alameda and San Francisco have minimized its use. Regional voter support for the law may account for the disparity.[25]

Is the "three strikes" law making a difference in California? Dickey summarizes the evidence of the impact of the "three strikes" law:[26]

- The law does incapacitate habitual offenders for a long time, but there is no hard evidence that the three-strikes law has had a deterrent effect on crime commission.
- The California law targets repeat felons but captures mostly nonviolent offenders.
- Three-strike defendants decline plea bargains and crowd jails, leading to early release for other offenders.
- More trials strain resources, delay civil actions, increase workloads, and decrease employee safety.
- Wide discretion and racial disparity in applying the law raise questions of legality and fairness.
- Prison problems are exacerbated by demand for space, high costs of building and staffing, safety and health concerns for inmates and employees, and escalation of geriatric inmate health care costs.

The experience of other mandatory sentencing laws suggest the types of impact that three-strike states should expect. For example, when New York imposed tough, mandatory sentences for drug dealers in 1973, these sentences merely raised the stakes so high for the defendant that the prosecutors had to reduce charges to get guilty pleas. Critics say that the impact has been to "pack the prisons, force plea deals and hit small-timers the hardest."[27] Studies of the Michigan Felony Firearms Statute found that, although the law was intended to reduce judicial discretion in sentencing, the result was to transfer wide discretion to the prosecuting attorney.[28] In a study of laws requiring mandatory sentences for crimes in which firearms are used, Thomas Marvell and Carlisle Moody found that such sentences had little influence on either reducing crime or increasing prison populations.[29]

Although many criminal justice scholars believe that mandatory sentences do not achieve their purpose, research conducted on Florida's mandatory minimum sentences does support their effectiveness.[30] The Florida law is designed to ensure that certain offenders are not released early (through good time and other provisions), before a certain portion of their sentence has been served. Eleven categories of offenders — for example, those convicted of capital offenses and of certain drug and firearms offenses, and those labeled habitual offenders — come under the mandatory provisions. These laws have been cited as a major cause of the longer prison terms that have in turn led to increases in the prison population.

good time

A reduction of an inmate's prison sentence, at the discretion of the prison administrator, for good behavior or for participation in vocational, educational, and treatment programs.

The Sentence Versus Actual Time Served   Regardless of judges' discretion, prison sentences imposed may bear little resemblance to the amount of time served. In reality, parole boards in indeterminate sentencing states have broad discretion in release decisions once the offender has served a minimum portion of the sentence. In addition, offenders can have their prison sentence reduced by earning **"good time"** for good behavior, at the discretion of the prison administrator.

All but four states have good-time policies. Days are subtracted from prisoners' minimum or maximum term for good behavior or for participating in various types of vocational, educational, or treatment programs. Correctional officials consider these policies necessary for maintaining institutional order and reducing crowding. The possibility of receiving good-time credit provides an incentive for prisoners to follow institutional rules. Good time is considered by prosecutors and defense attorneys during plea bargaining. In other words, they think about the actual amount of time a particular offender is likely to serve.

Figure 4.3 Estimated Time to Be Served in State Prison, by Offense

Most offenders serve a third or less of their mean sentences. Why is there such a difference between the sentence and actual time served?

SOURCE: U.S. Department of Justice, Bureau of Justice Statistics, *State Court Sentencing of Convicted Felons, 1994* (Washington, DC: U.S. Government Printing Office, 1998), p. 8.

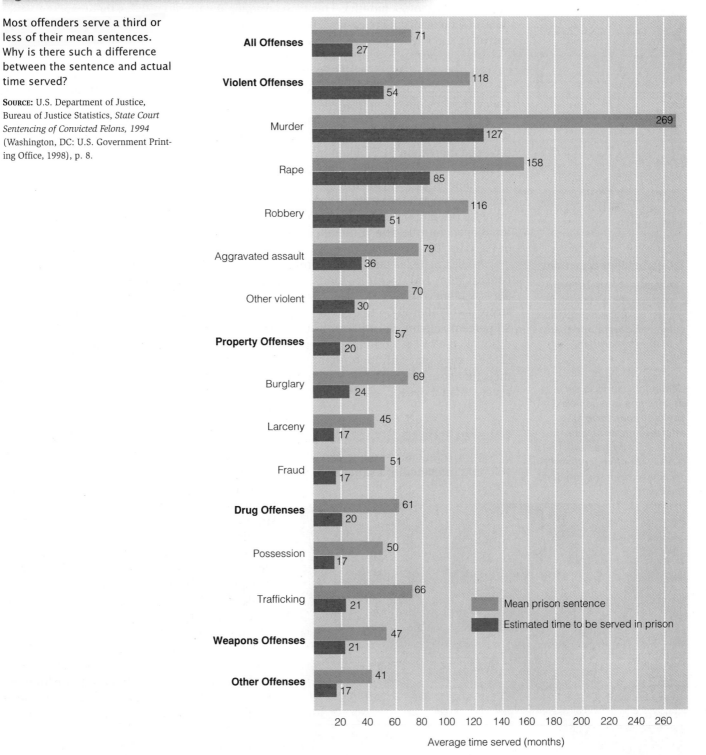

The amount of good time one can earn varies among the states, usually from five to ten days a month. In some states, once ninety days of good time are earned they are "vested"; that is, the credits cannot be taken away as a punishment for misbehavior. Prisoners who then violate the rules risk losing only days not vested.

Judges in the United States often prescribe long periods of incarceration for serious crimes, but good time and parole reduce the amount of time spent in prison. Figure 4.3 shows the estimated time actually served by offenders sent to state prisons versus the mean sentence. Note that the national average for time served is 27 months, or 38 percent of the mean sentence of 71 months. This type of national data often hides the impact of variations in sentencing and releasing laws in individual states. In many states, because of prison crowding and release policies, offenders are serving less than 20 percent of their sentences.

"Truth in Sentencing"   Calls for "truth in sentencing" have arisen when the public has learned that the actual time served is much less than expected. A truth-in-sentencing policy requires offenders to serve a substantial proportion (usually 85 percent for violent crimes) of their prison sentence before being released on parole. Forty states now have some version of a truth-in-sentencing law, and since 1996 the Department of Justice has provided more than $1.3 billion in the incentives grants program.[31] This has become such a "hot," politically attractive idea that the federal government has allocated most of the $10 billion for prison construction, authorized under the 1994 federal crime bill, only to those states that adopt truth in sentencing.[32] Critics maintain that truth in sentencing will increase prison populations at a tremendous cost. Jones and Austin estimate that with the 85 percent rule, the national prison population would rise to 1.6 million by the end of the year 2000 at a cost of $32.5 to $37 billion in construction and operating costs.[33]

Studies in Texas and Illinois project major increases in the prison population, new construction, and operating funds. If Texas imposed the 85 percent rule for only *aggravated* violent offenses, it would need to add 30,600 beds, costing $980 million to construct and $510 million to operate. In Illinois a statute has been proposed to impose the 85 percent rule on *all* inmates. If it passes, the prison population will double at an additional cost of $4.6 billion in operating costs and $1.5 billion in construction costs.[34] Clear argues that although inmates may currently be serving a smaller proportion of their time, they are actually serving sentences about as severe, and in some cases more severe, than a decade ago.[35]

Intermediate Sanctions

Prison crowding and the low levels of probation supervision have spurred interest in developing **intermediate sanctions**, punishments less severe and costly than prison, but more restrictive than traditional probation.[36] Intermediate sanctions provide a variety of restrictions on freedom such as monetary sanctions, home confinement, intensive probation supervision, restitution, community service, boot camp, and forfeiture. According to estimates, if murderers and rapists, plus those previously incarcerated, and those with a prior sentence for violence were excluded from consideration for intermediate punishments, then 29 percent of those now bound for prison would be sanctioned in the community.[37]

In advocating intermediate punishments, Morris and Tonry stipulate that these sanctions should not be used in isolation but rather in combination to reflect the severity of the offense, the characteristics of the offender, and the needs of the community. In addition, inter-

---

intermediate sanctions

A variety of punishments that are more restrictive than traditional probation but less severe and costly than incarceration.

Community service, such as assisting in a homeless shelter, is one form of intermediate punishment. Advocates of these sanctions stress that offenders need to recognize responsibility for their acts.

mediate punishments must be supported and enforced by mechanisms that take seriously any breach of the conditions of the sentence. Too often criminal justice agencies have devoted few resources to enforcing nonincarcerative sentences. If the law does not fulfill its promises, offenders may feel they have "beaten" the system, resulting in a meaningless punishment. Citizens who see the system's ineffectiveness may develop the attitude that nothing works and that stiffer sentences are needed. Intermediate sanctions are discussed fully in Chapter 9.

Probation

The most frequently applied criminal sanction is **probation**, whereby an offender serves a sentence under supervision in the community. Nearly 60 percent of adults under correctional supervision are on probation. We discuss this sanction more fully in Chapter 8; here it is important to note that probation is designed to maintain supervision of offenders while they try to straighten out their lives. Probation is a judicial act, granted by the grace of the state rather than extended as a right, and conditions specify how an offender must behave throughout the length of the sentence. Probationers may be ordered to undergo regular drug tests, abide by curfews, enroll in educational programs or remain employed, stay away from certain parts of town, and meet regularly with probation officers. If the offender does not meet the conditions of probation, the supervising officer recommends to the court that the probation be revoked and that the rest of the sentence be served in prison. Probation may also be revoked if the person commits a new crime.

Although probationers serve their sentences in the community, the sanction is often tied to incarceration. In some jurisdictions, the court is authorized to modify an offender's prison sentence, after a portion is served, by changing it to probation. This pattern is often referred to as **shock probation** (or *split probation*): After a period of incarceration (the "shock"), an offender is released and resentenced to probation. An offender on probation may be required to spend intermittent periods, such as weekends or nights, in jail. Whatever the specific terms of the probationary sentence, it emphasizes guidance and supervision in the community.

Probation is generally advocated as a way of rehabilitating offenders whose crimes are less serious or whose past records are clean. It is seen as less expensive and more effective than imprisonment, which may embitter youthful or first-time offenders and mix them with hardened criminals so that they learn more sophisticated criminal techniques.

Death

Although other western democracies abolished the death penalty years ago, the United States continues to use it. Before the late 1960s capital punishment was regularly imposed and carried out. Amid debates about the constitutionality of the death penalty and with public opinion polls showing increasing opposition to it, the U.S. Supreme Court suspended its use from 1968 to 1976.[38] Eventually, however, the Court decided that capital punishment does not violate the Eighth Amendment's prohibition on

probation

A sentence allowing the offender to serve the sanctions imposed by the court while living in the community under supervision.

shock probation

A sentence in which the offender is released after a short incarceration and resentenced to probation.

Death by hanging was the method of execution used in most states well into the twentieth century. Although executions were usually shielded from the general public by the time of the Civil War, officials often allowed some observers to be present.

cruel and unusual punishments. In 1977 executions resumed as a majority of states began, once again, to sentence murderers to death.

The number of people facing the death penalty has increased dramatically in the past decade, as Figure 4.4 reveals. Over 3,500 people are now awaiting execution in thirty-five of thirty-eight death penalty states. Two-thirds of those on death row are in the South, mostly in Texas, Georgia, Alabama, and Florida. Is this situation the result of the appeals process or of the lack of will on the part of political leaders and a society that is perhaps uncertain about the taking of human life? The death penalty may have more significance as a political symbol than as a deterrent to crime. Is it possible that in the future the United States will join the other industrial democracies and stop executing criminals? These are important questions, and in Chapter 20 we discuss the death penalty more fully.

Forms and Goals of Sanctions

The various forms of criminal sanction are designed to serve various purposes, as listed in Table 4.2. Note that incarceration, intermediate sanctions, probation, and death can each be used to achieve one or more punishment goals. As you examine the sentencing process, notice how judges use their discretion to set the punishment within the provisions of the law and the characteristics of the offender.

The Sentencing Process

Now that we have reviewed the goals and forms of the criminal sanction, let us take a close look at the process for deciding the punishment to be imposed. Regardless of how and where the decision has been made—misdemeanor court or felony court, plea bargain or adversarial context, bench or jury trial—judges have the responsibility for imposing sentences.

Sentencing is often difficult and is often not just a matter of applying clear-cut principles to individual cases. In one case, a judge may decide to sentence a forger to prison as an example to others, although he is no threat to community safety and probably

Figure 4.4   People Under Sentence of Death and Persons Executed, 1953–1999

Since 1976 about 250 new offenders have been added to death row each year, yet the number of executions has never been greater than thirty-eight. What explains this situation?

SOURCES: NAACP Legal Defense and Education Fund, *Death Row, USA*, Winter, 1998 (mimeographed report); Death Penalty Information Center (web site *http://www.essential.org/dpic/*).

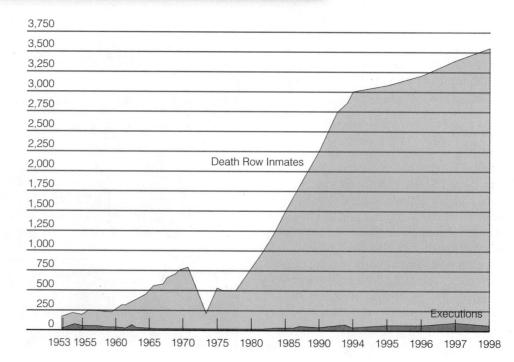

does not need rehabilitative treatment. In another case, the judge may impose a light sentence on a youthful offender who, although having committed a serious crime, may be a good risk for rehabilitation if he or she can be moved quickly back into society.

Legislatures establish the penal codes that set forth the sentences that judges may impose. These laws generally give judges wide powers of discretion with regard to sentencing. They may combine various forms of punishment to tailor the sanction to

Table 4.2 The Punishment of Offenders

The goals of the criminal sanction are carried out in a variety of ways depending on the provisions of the law, the offenders' characteristics, and the judge's discretion. To achieve punishment objectives, judges may impose sentences that combine several forms.

FORM OF SANCTION	DESCRIPTION	PURPOSES
Incarceration	Imprisonment.	
Indeterminate sentence	Specifies a maximum and minimum length of time to be served.	Incapacitation, deterrence, rehabilitation.
Determinate sentence	Specifies a certain length of time to be served.	Retribution, deterrence, incapacitation.
Mandatory sentence	Specifies a minimum amount of time for given crimes that must be served.	Incapacitation, deterrence.
Good time	Subtracts days from an inmate's sentence because of good behavior or participation in prison programs.	Rewards behavior, relieves prison crowding, helps maintain prison discipline.
Intermediate sanctions	Punishment for those requiring sanctions more restrictive than probation but less restrictive than prison.	Retribution, deterrence.
Administered by the judiciary		
Fine	Money paid to state by offender.	Retribution, deterrence.
Restitution	Money paid to victim by offender.	Retribution, deterrence.
Forfeiture	Seizure by the state of property illegally obtained or acquired with resources illegally obtained.	Retribution, deterrence.
Administered in the community		
Community service	Requires offender to perform work for the community.	Retribution, deterrence.
Home confinement	Requires offender to stay in home during certain times.	Retribution, deterrence, incapacitation.
Intensive probation, supervision	Requires strict and frequent reporting to probation officer.	Retribution, deterrence, incapacitation.
Administered institutionally		
Boot camp/shock incarceration	Short-term institutional sentence emphasizing physical development and discipline, followed by probation.	Retribution, deterrence, rehabilitation.
Probation	Allows offender to serve a sentence in the community under supervision.	Retribution, incapacitation, rehabilitation.
Death	Execution.	Incapacitation, deterrence, retribution.

The sentence imposed by the judge can be viewed as the beginning of corrections. What punishment would you give Mary Kay Latourneau after she pleaded guilty to child rape for having sex with a 13-year-old student and having his child? What if the offender was a male and the student a female?

the offender. The judge may stipulate, for example, that the prison terms for two charges are to run either concurrently (at the same time) or consecutively (one after the other) or that all or part of the period of imprisonment may be suspended. In other situations, the offender may be given a combination of a suspended prison term, probation, and a fine. Judges may also suspend a sentence as long as the offender stays out of trouble, makes restitution, or seeks medical treatment. The judge may also delay imposing any sentence but retain power to set penalties at a later date if the offender misbehaves.

When a judge gazes at a defendant and pronounces sentence, what thinking has gone into his or her decision? Within the discretion allowed by the code, various elements in the sentencing process influence the decisions of judges. In the Focus box Judge Robert Satter tells us some of the difficulties of sentencing. Let us look at several of the factors that social scientists believe influence the sentencing process: (1) the administrative context of the courts, (2) the attitudes and values of judges, (3) the presentence report, and (4) sentencing guidelines.

The Administrative Context

Judges are very much influenced by the administrative context within which they impose sentences. As a result, we can see differences between, say, the assembly-line style of justice allocated in the misdemeanor courts and the more formal proceedings found in felony courts.

Misdemeanor Court: Assembly-Line Justice   Misdemeanor or lower courts possess limited jurisdiction because they cannot normally impose prison sentences of less than one year. These courts hear about 90 percent of criminal cases. Whereas felony cases are processed in lower courts only for arraignments and preliminary hearings, misdemeanor cases are processed completely in the lower courts, normally through dismissals or guilty pleas. Only a minority of cases adjudicated in lower courts end in jail sentences; most cases result in fines, probation, community service, and/or restitution.

Most lower courts are overloaded and allot minimal time to each case. Judicial decisions here are mass-produced, because actors in the system share three assumptions. First, any person appearing before the court is guilty, because the police and prosecution have presumably filtered doubtful cases out. Second, the vast majority of defendants will plead guilty. Third, those charged with minor offenses will be processed in volume, with dozens of cases being decided in rapid succession within a single hour. The citation will be read by the clerk, a guilty plea entered, and the sentence pronounced by the judge for one defendant after another.

Defendants whose cases are processed through the lower-court assembly line may seem to receive little or no punishment. However, people who get caught in the criminal justice system experience other punishments whether or not they are ultimately convicted. A person who is arrested but then released at some point in the process still incurs various tangible and intangible costs. Time spent in jail awaiting trial, the cost of a bail bond, and days of work lost have an immediate tangible impact. Poor people may

FOCUS

A Trial Judge at Work: Judge Robert Satter

I am never more conscious of striving to balance the scales of justice than when I am sentencing the convicted. On one scale is society, violated by a crime, on the other is the defendant, fallible, but nonetheless human.

As a trial judge I am faced with the insistent task of sentencing a particular defendant who never fails to assert his own individuality. I hear each cry out, in the words of Thomas Wolfe, "Does not this wonderful and unique I, that never was before and never will be again; this I of tender favor, beloved of the gods, come before the Eye of Judgment and always plead exception?"

In my early years on the bench, I presided mainly over misdemeanors. . . . Because they are not so serious, I could be more creative, or even experimental, in sentencing.

When sparing a defendant from going to jail, I often imposed conditions related to the crime or the underlying cause of the crime. Young boys charged with destroying public property might be required to spend several Saturdays weeding the flower beds in the town green. A man charged with exposing himself in public might be required to obtain psychiatric treatment. If a husband was accused of beating his wife for the first time, I would get the court family relations officer to counsel the couple. When a crime stemmed from alcoholism, I would order that the offender attend Alcoholics Anonymous.

Later in my career when I came to hear felony cases, I found to my surprise that sentencing for minor crimes is more difficult than sentencing for serious ones. The decision for misdemeanors is whether to incarcerate; that is the hard one. The decision for felonies is the number of years in the state prison; that is much easier. But sometimes even felony cases present the dilemma of whether to imprison or not to imprison.

George Edwards was tried before me for sexual assault, first degree. The victim, Barbara Babson, was a personable woman in her late twenties and a junior executive in an insurance company. She described on the stand what had happened to her:

I was returning to my Hartford apartment with two armloads of groceries. As I entered the elevator, a man followed me. He seemed vaguely familiar but I couldn't quite place him. When I reached my floor and started to open my door, I noticed him behind me. He offered to hold my bags. God, I knew right then I was making a mistake. He pushed me into the apartment and slammed the door. He said, "Don't you know me? I work at Travelers with you." Then I remembered him in the cafeteria and I remembered him once staring at me. Now I could feel his eyes roving over my body, and I heard him say, "I want to screw you." He said it so calmly at first, I didn't believe him. I tried to talk him out of it.

When he grabbed my neck, I began to cry and then to scream. His grip tightened, and that really scared me. He forced me into the bedroom, made me take off my clothes. "Then," she sobbed, "he pushed my legs apart and entered me."

"What happened next?" the state's attorney asked.

"He told me he was going to wait in the next room, and if I tried to leave he would kill me. I found some cardboard, wrote HELP! on them, and put them in my window. But nobody came. Eventually I got up the courage to open the door, and he had left. I immediately called the police."

Edwards's lawyer cross-examined her vigorously, dragging her through the intimate details of her sex life. Then he tried to get her to admit that she had willingly participated in sex with the defendant. Through it all, she maintained her poise. She left the stand with her version of the crime intact.

Edwards took the stand in his own defense. A tall man with bushy hair, he was wearing baggy trousers and a rumpled shirt. In a low voice he testified that the woman had always smiled at him at work. He had learned her name and address and gone to her apartment house that day. When he offered to help her with her bundles, she invited him into her apartment. She was very nice and very willing to have sex. He denied using force.

I did not believe him. I could not conceive that Miss Babson would have called the police, pressed the charges, and relived the horrors of the experience on the stand if the crime had not been committed as she testified. The jury did not believe him either. They readily returned a verdict of guilty.

First-degree sexual assault is a class B felony punishable by a maximum of twenty years in the state prison. If I had sentenced Edwards then, I would have sent him to prison for many years. But sentencing could take place only after a presentence report had been prepared by a probation officer.

It revealed that Edwards was thirty-one years old, born of a black father and white mother. He had graduated from high school and had an associate's degree from a community college. He had served in Vietnam, where he had been decorated with the Purple Heart for wounds in action and the Bronze Star for bravery under fire. After the army, Edwards had worked successfully as a coordinator of youth programs in the inner city of Hartford. Simultaneously he had taken computer courses. At the time of the crime, he was a computer programmer at Travelers Insurance Company. Edwards was separated

(continued)

from his wife and child, and fellow employees had recently noticed a personality change in him; he seemed withdrawn, depressed, and sometimes confused. His only criminal offense was a disorderly conduct charge three months before the crime, which had not been prosecuted.

I gazed out the window of my chambers and reflected. What should be my sentence?

Before the rescheduled date, I had weighed the factors, made up my mind, and lived with my decision for several days. In serious criminal cases I do not like to make snap judgment from the bench. I may sometimes allow myself to be persuaded by the lawyers' arguments to reduce a preconceived sentence, but never to raise it.

I nod to the state's attorney to begin. He asks to have Miss Babson speak first. She comes forward to the counsel table. "That man," she says, pointing to Edwards, "did a horrible thing. He should be severely punished not only for what he did to me, but for what he could do to other women. I am furious at him. As far as I am concerned, Judge, I hope you lock him up and throw away the key."

She abruptly stops and sits down. The state's attorney deliberately pauses to let her words sink in before he stands up. Speaking with less emotion but equal determination, he says,

This was a vicious crime. There are not many more serious than rape. The defendant cynically tried to put the blame on the victim. But it didn't wash. She has been damaged in the most fundamental way. And the defendant doesn't show the slightest remorse. I urge the maximum punishment of twenty years in prison.

Edwards's lawyer starts off by mentioning his client's splendid Vietnam war record and his lack of a criminal record. Then he goes on, "George and his wife have begun living together again with their child, and they are trying to pick up the pieces of their lives. More important," the lawyer continues, "George started seeing a psychiatrist six weeks ago."

The lawyer concludes, "If you will give George a suspended sentence, Your Honor, and make a condition of probation that he stay in treatment, he won't be before this court again. George Edwards is a good risk."

even lose their jobs or be evicted from their homes if they fail to work and pay their bills for even a few days. For most people, simply being arrested is a devastating experience. It is impossible to measure the psychic and social price of being stigmatized, separated from family, and deprived of freedom.[39]

Felony Courts Felony cases are processed and offenders are sentenced in courts of general jurisdiction. Because of the seriousness of these crimes, the atmosphere is more formal and generally lacks the chaotic, assembly-line environment of misdemeanor courts. Caseloads can affect how much time is devoted to individual cases. Sentencing decisions are ultimately shaped, in part, by the relationships, negotiations, and agreements among the prosecutor, defense attorney, and judge.

Table 4.3 shows the types of felony sentences imposed as related to the conviction offense. It must be emphasized that these outcomes are for felony sentences; misdemeanor sentences result in much greater use of probation and much less use of incarceration.

Attitudes and Values of Judges

All lawyers recognize that judges differ from one another in their sentencing decisions. The differences can be explained in part by the conflicting goals of criminal justice, administrative pressures, and the influence of community values. Judges' sentencing decisions also depend on their own attitudes toward the law, toward a particular crime, or toward a type of offender.

Judges are products of different backgrounds and have different social values. Martin Levin's now classic study of the criminal courts of Pittsburgh and Minneapolis showed the influence of judges' values on sentencing behavior. He found that Pittsburgh judges, all of whom came from humble backgrounds, exhibited a greater empathy toward defendants than did judges in Minneapolis, who tended to come from upper-class backgrounds. The Pittsburgh judges tried to make decisions that

I look at Edwards. "Do you have anything you want to say, Mr. Edwards?"

The question takes him by surprise. Gathering his thoughts, he says with emotion, "I'm sorry for what I did, Judge. I'm sorry for Barbara, and I understand how she feels. I'm sorry for my wife. I'm . . ." His voice trails off.

I gaze out the courtroom window struggling for the words to express my sentence. I am always conscious that the same sentence can be given in a way that arouses grudging acceptance or deep hostility.

Mr. Edwards, you have committed a serious crime. I am not going to punish you to set an example for others, because you should not be held responsible for the incidence of crime in our society. I am going to punish you because, as a mature person, you must pay a price for your offense. The state's attorney asks for twenty years because of the gravity of the crime. Your attorney asks for a suspended sentence because you are attempting to deal with whatever within you caused you to commit the

crime. Both make valid arguments. I am partially adopting both recommendations. I herewith sentence you to state prison for six years.

Edwards wilts. His wife gasps. I continue.

However, I am suspending execution after four years. I am placing you on probation for the two-year balance of your term on the condition that you continue in psychiatric treatment until discharged by your doctor. The state is entitled to punish you for the crime that you have committed and the harm you have done. You are entitled to leniency for what I discern to be the sincere effort you are making to help yourself.

Edwards turns to his wife, who rushes up to embrace him. Miss Babson nods to me, not angrily, I think. She walks out of the courtroom and back into her life. As I rise at the bench, a sheriff is leading Edwards down the stairwell to the lockup.

Source: Robert Satter, *Doing Justice: A Trial Judge at Work* (New York: Simon & Schuster, 1990), pp. 170–181. Copyright © 1990 by Robert Satter. Reprinted by permission of the author.

Table 4.3 Types of Felony Sentences Imposed by State Courts

Note that although we often equate a felony conviction with a sentence to prison, almost a third of felony offenders are given probation.

Most Serious Conviction Offense	Prison	Jail	Probation
All Offenses	45%	26%	29%
Violent Offenses	62	20	18
Murder	95	2	3
Rape	71	17	12
Robbery	77	11	12
Aggravated Assault	48	27	25
Other Violent	45	30	25
Property Offenses	42	26	32
Burglary	53	22	25
Larceny	38	28	34
Fraud	32	28	40
Drug Offenses	42	27	31
Possession	34	32	34
Trafficking	48	23	29
Weapons Offenses	42	27	31
Other Offenses	36	30	34

Source: U.S. Department of Justice, Bureau of Justice Statistics, *State Court Sentencing of Convicted Felons, 1994* (Washington, DC: U.S. Government Printing Office, 1998), p. 5.

they believed would help straighten out the troubled defendants' lives, the Minneapolis judges were more inclined to follow the law precisely and to emphasize society's need for protection from crime.[40]

It is widely assumed that judges are predisposed to treating female offenders less severely than men. But research on sentencing in Pennsylvania suggests that judges are concerned not only with an offender's prior record and level of involvement in the crime, but also such practical considerations as the responsibility for children, pregnancy, and availability of prison space.[41] Kathleen Daly and Rebecca Bordt found that gender effects are more likely to be found for felony offenses, those prosecuted in urban courts, and in the decision to incarcerate rather than in the length of sentence.[42]

The Presentence Report

presentence report

Report prepared by a probation officer, who investigates a convicted offender's background to help the judge select an appropriate sentence.

Even though sentencing is the judge's responsibility, the **presentence report** has become an important ingredient in the judicial mix. Usually a probation officer investigates the convicted person's background, criminal record, job status, and mental condition to suggest a sentence in the interests of both the offender and society. Although the primary purpose of the presentence report is to help the judge select the sentence, it also helps in classifying probationers, prisoners, and parolees with respect to treatment planning and risk assessment. In the reports, the probation officer makes judgments about what information to include and what conclusions to draw from that information. In some states, however, probation officers present only factual material to the judge and make no sentencing recommendation. The probation officer need not follow evidentiary rules and may include hearsay statements as well as firsthand information. An example of a presentence report is found in Chapter 8.

Although presentence reports are represented as diagnostic evaluations, critics point out that they are not scientific and often reflect stereotypes. John Rosecrance has argued that in actual practice the presentence report primarily serves to maintain the myth of individualized justice. He found that the present offense and the prior criminal record determine the probation officer's final sentencing recommendation.[43] He learned that officers begin by reviewing the case and typing the defendant as one who should fit into a particular sentencing category. Their investigations are then conducted mainly to gather further information to buttress their early decision.

The presentence report is one means by which judges ease the strain of decision making. The report lets judges shift partial responsibility to the probation department. Because a substantial number of sentencing alternatives are open to judges, they often rely on the report for guidance. But two questions often arise: (1) Should judges rely so much on the presentence report? and (2) Does the time spent preparing it represent the best use of probation officers' time?

Sentencing Guidelines

sentencing guidelines

An instrument developed for judges that indicates the usual sanctions given previously to particular offenses.

Since the 1980s **sentencing guidelines** have been established in the federal courts, seventeen states, and are being developed in five other states.[44] Guidelines are designed to indicate to judges the expected sanction for particular types of offenses. They are intended to limit the sentencing discretion of judges and to reduce disparity among sentences given for similar offenses. Although statutes provide a variety of sentencing options for particular crimes, guidelines point the judge to more specific actions that *should* be taken. The range of sentencing options provided for most offenses allows for the seriousness of the crime and the criminal history of an offender.[45] Intermediate sanctions have been incorporated into some state guidelines.[46]

Legislatures — and in some states and the federal government, commissions — construct sentencing guidelines as a grid of two scores.[47] As Table 4.4 shows, one dimension relates to the seriousness of the offense, and the other to the likelihood of offender recidivism. The offender score is obtained by totaling the points allocated to such fac-

Table 4.4 Minnesota Sentencing Guidelines Grid (Presumptive Sentence Length in Months, Effective August 1, 1994)

The italicized numbers within the grid denote the range within which a judge may punish without the sentence being deemed a departure. The criminal history score is computed by adding one point for each prior felony conviction, one-half point for each prior gross misdemeanor conviction, and a quarter of a point for each prior misdemeanor conviction.

LESS SERIOUS ←————————————→ MORE SERIOUS

CRIMINAL HISTORY SCORE

	0	1	2	3	4	5	6 or more
Sale of simulated controlled substance	12	12	12	13	15	17	19 *18–20*
Theft-related crimes ($2,500 or less) Check forgery ($200–$2,500)	12	12	13	15	17	19	21 *20–22*
Theft crimes ($2,500 or less)	12	13	15	17	19 *18–20*	22 *21–23*	25 *24–26*
Non-residential burglary Theft crimes (over $2,500)	12	15	18	21	25 *24–26*	32 *30–34*	41 *37–45*
Residential burglary Simple robbery	18	25	27	30 *29–31*	38 *36–40*	46 *43–49*	54 *50–58*
Criminal sexual conduct, second degree	21	26	30	34 *33–35*	44 *42–46*	54 *50–58*	65 *60–70*
Aggravated robbery	48 *44–52*	58 *54–62*	68 *64–72*	78 *74–82*	88 *84–92*	98 *94–102*	108 *104–112*
Criminal sexual conduct, first degree Assault, first degree	86 *81–91*	98 *93–103*	110 *105–115*	122 *117–127*	134 *129–139*	146 *141–151*	158 *153–163*
Murder, third degree Murder, second degree (felony murder)	150 *144–156*	165 *159–171*	180 *174–186*	195 *189–201*	210 *204–216*	225 *219–231*	240 *234–24*
Murder, second degree (with intent)	306 *299–313*	326 *319–333*	346 *339–353*	366 *359–373*	386 *379–383*	406 *399–413*	426 *419–433*

LESS SERIOUS / MORE SERIOUS

▭ At the discretion of the judge, up to a year in jail and/or other nonjail sanctions can be imposed instead of prison sentences as conditions of probation for most of these offenses. If prison is imposed, the presumptive sentence is the number of months shown.

▭ Presumptive commitment to state prison for all offenses.

NOTE: First-degree murder is excluded from the guidelines by law and is punished by life imprisonment.

SOURCES: *Seeking Justice: Crime and Punishment in America* (New York: Edna McConnell Clark Foundation, 1995).

tors as the number of juvenile, adult misdemeanor, and adult felony convictions; the number of times incarcerated; the status of the accused at the time of the last offense, whether on probation or parole or escaped from confinement; and employment status or educational achievement. Judges look at the grid to see what sentence should be imposed on a particular offender who has committed a specific offense. Judges may go outside of the guidelines if aggravating or mitigating circumstances exist, however, they must provide a written explanation of their reasons for doing so.[48]

Sentencing guidelines are expected to be reviewed and modified periodically so that recent decisions will be included. Since guidelines are constructed on the basis of past sentences, some critics argue that because the guidelines reflect only what has happened,

Politics and Sentencing: The Case of Crack Cocaine

In 1986 the American public first heard about a potent new form of cocaine called crack. Crack was reputed to be extremely addictive and cheaper than the powdered form of cocaine. The media spread the fear that crack not only was the drug of choice in the ghetto but was being used by middle-class, suburban Americans. To address this new peril, Congress rushed through a new anticrime bill before the fall 1986 election. The new law specified that conviction for possession or distribution of 5 grams of crack cocaine would mean a mandatory five-year sentence with no parole. Unnoticed at the time was the fact that the crack penalty equaled a 100:1 ratio, compared with conviction for possession or distribution of the more expensive powdered cocaine. In other words, before a cocaine user or seller received a five-year sentence, he or she would have to possess 500 grams of the powdered substance.

Of the 90,000 federal prisoners, 14,000 are serving sentences for crack cocaine offenses. A study of 1993 convictions showed that 88.3 percent of these offenders were African American, 7.1 percent Hispanic, and 4.1 percent white. Of those convicted of powdered cocaine offenses, 32 percent were white, 27.4 percent African American, and 39.3 percent Hispanic.

The disparity between punishments for crack and powdered cocaine offenders has become a major issue for African Americans. In 1991 the Minnesota Supreme Court ruled that a state law treating crack more harshly was unlawfully discriminatory against African Americans. Several federal judges have issued similar rulings.

After studying the issue of racial disparity, the U.S. Sentencing Commission recommended that the legal distinction be dropped and that the penalties be calibrated the same way at the 100:1 ratio (100 grams of crack or powdered cocaine equals one year in prison). However, Congress and the Clinton administration rejected this recommendation. As Scott Wallace, head of the National Legal Aid and Defender Association has noted, it would be difficult for lawmakers to make the change as they head into an election year.

Source: *Newsweek*, November 6, 1995, p. 81; *The New York Times*, October 24, 1995, p. A18.

they do not reform sentencing. Others question the choice of characteristics included in the offender scale and charge that some are used to mask racial criteria.[49] However, as Terance Miethe and Charles Moore note, the Minnesota guidelines have resulted in sentences that are "more uniform, more predictable, and more socioeconomically neutral than before the guidelines."[50] These findings are supported in research conducted in Minnesota by Lisa Stolzenberg and Steward J. D'Alessio. They found, compared to preguideline decisions, an 18 percent reduction in disparity for the prison/no prison outcome and a 60 percent reduction in disparity of length of prison sentences.[51]

Sentencing guidelines have led to the development of a rich body of appellate case law.[52] Until the advent of guidelines the right of defendants or prosecutors to appeal the terms of a sentence was limited. Challenges of judicial interpretations of the guidelines have now increased so that a common law of sentencing is developing. For example, Chapper and Hanson have found that whereas in 1975 virtually all appeals challenged only the conviction, today sentencing issues may be the sole or primary basis in about half of the cases appealed.[53]

Although guidelines have been found to make sentences more uniform, many judges object to having their discretion limited in this manner.[54] In particular, many scholars and judges view the U.S. Sentencing Commission guidelines as impossibly complex, politically motivated, and unduly harsh.[55] Research by Celesta Albonetti found disparity in the sentencing of drug offenders based on gender, race, and ethnicity.[56] Michael Tonry has called them "the most disliked sentencing reform initiative in the United States in this century."[57] However, Peter Rossi and Richard Berk found a fair amount of agreement between the sentences prescribed in the guidelines and those desired by the general public.[58]

Who Gets the Harshest Punishment?

The prison population in most states contain a higher proportion of African-American and Hispanic-American men than is found in the general population. Women are less represented than men in prisons and jails.[59] Poor people are more likely to be convicted of crimes than those with higher incomes. Are these disparities a result of the prejudicial attitudes of judges, police officers, and prosecutors? Are poor people more liable to commit crimes that elicit a strong response from society? Are enforcement resources distributed so that certain groups are subject to closer scrutiny than other groups?

Charges of racial discrimination have been leveled at all stages of the criminal justice process, however, much of the harshest criticism has focused on judges' sentencing decisions. Some argue that African Americans and Hispanics receive much harsher sentences than do whites who commit the same crimes. These critics say that American judges are mainly white men and use their sentencing discretion inappropriately.[60] Other scholars contend that sentencing decisions are not racially motivated.[61]

A central question is whether gender, racial, ethnic, and class **sentence disparity** is the result of discrimination. Sentence disparities occur when widely divergent penalties are imposed on offenders with similar backgrounds who have committed the same offense, with no discernible or reasonable justification. Discrimination occurs when criminal justice officials either directly or indirectly treat someone differently because of their race, ethnicity, gender, or class. The fact that African Americans and Hispanics receive harsher punishments than do whites may reflect sentencing disparity, because minorities may commit more serious crimes than do whites. However, if officials single out members of these groups for harsh punishment because of their race or ethnicity, that is discrimination.

Racial disparities in criminal justice are often explained in one of three ways: (1) African Americans and Hispanics commit more crimes; (2) the criminal justice system is racist, with the result that people of color are treated more harshly; or (3) the criminal justice system expresses the racism found in society as a whole.[62] Research on these questions is inconclusive (see Chapter 19). Some studies have shown that members of racial minorities and the poor are treated more harshly by the system; other research has been unable to demonstrate a direct link between harshness of sentence and race or social class.[63] Laws dealing with possession and sale of crack cocaine raise interesting questions as to sentencing disparity and racial discrimination (see the Focus box).

Another serious dilemma for the criminal justice system concerns people who are falsely convicted and sentenced. Whereas much public concern is expressed over those who "beat the system" and go free, comparatively little attention is paid to those who are innocent, yet convicted. Each year several cases of convicted but innocent people come to national attention. For example, Randall Dale Adams, whose story was portrayed in the movie *The Thin Blue Line*, had his murder conviction overturned after he had spent twelve years on death row. Likewise, Kevin Byrd was released and pardoned after serving twelve years in a Texas prison for a rape that DNA tests showed he had not committed.[64]

How prevalent are such miscarriages of justice? It has been estimated that about 1 percent of felony convictions are in error.[65] Eyewitness error, unethical conduct by police and prosecutors, community pressure, false accusations, inadequacy of counsel, and plea-bargaining pressures are usually cited as contributing to wrongful convictions. Not only is the real criminal presumably still free in such cases, but the standards of our society are damaged when an innocent person has been wrongfully convicted.

sentence disparity

Divergence in the lengths and types of sentences imposed for the same crime or for crimes of comparable seriousness when no reasonable justification can be discerned.

Leaving the Kankakee County Courthouse, Illinois, after the state dropped murder charges are Joe Burrows and his wife, Shari. Burrows spent eight years on death row for the murder of an 88-year-old farmer before new evidence overturned his conviction.

Summary

The goals of retribution, deterrence, incapacitation, and rehabilitation may be viewed as distinct, but they overlap in many areas. Rehabilitation appears to be the one goal requiring the creation of distinctive sentencing, correctional, and releasing structures.

Punishment may take a variety of forms, but public attention is focused on incarceration. Only a small proportion of adult offenders go to prison; most receive fines or probation.

Although many of the actions taken by criminal justice officials from the time of arrest to a plea or verdict are based on assumptions about the ultimate sanction, sentencing may be viewed as the beginning of the postconviction and corrections process. Sentencing specifies the sanction and fixes the punishment that the state imposes on the offender.

The attitudes and background of the judge, the administrative context of decision making, the presentence report, and the agreed-on plea bargain strongly influence the actual sentence handed down. One problem with sentencing in the United States is that disparities exist in the severity of punishment accorded offenders who have committed the same crime. The campaign to shift the goal of the criminal sanction away from rehabilitation to deserved punishment has resulted in widespread legislation to reduce the discretion of judges and parole boards by instituting determinate sentences.

Efforts at reform alert us to various aspects of the corrections system. Policies are not merely the outcomes of decisions made by correctional officials; they have their basis in laws passed by legislatures, whose members are attuned to public opinion and political pressures. Through the political process of compromise, laws may incorporate elements unanticipated by the promoters of reform. ■

For Discussion

1. What should be the dominant goal of the criminal sanction? Why?

2. What are the prospects for rehabilitating offenders? Given this assessment, how should the corrections system be structured?

3. How much discretion should judges and parole board members have in administering the criminal sanction? What justifies the latitude currently given these individuals?

4. Suppose you are a state legislator. What considerations will influence your vote on the process by which criminal sanctions are set?

5. Is selective incapacitation a good idea? What are the implications of the concept for crime control? for due process?

For Further Reading

Bennett, William J., John J. DiIulio, Jr., and John P. Walters. *Body Count*. New York: Simon & Schuster, 1996. A conservative view of the problem of violent crime in America and what to do about it. Argues that the root cause of crime is moral poverty.

Gaylin, Willard. *The Killing of Bonnie Garland*, rev. ed. New York: Simon & Schuster, 1997. Tells the story of the murder of a Yale student by her boyfriend and the reaction of the criminal justice system to the crime. Raises important questions about the goals of the criminal sanction and the role of the victim in the process.

Satter, Robert. *Doing Justice: A Trial Judge at Work*. New York: Simon & Schuster, 1990. Gives one judge's view of his daily caseload and the factors influencing the decisions.

Shichor, David, and Dale K. Sechrest, eds. *Three Strikes and You're Out: Vengeance as Public Policy*. Thousand Oaks, CA: Sage, 1996). An excellent collection of articles on the history, implementation, impact, and special issues of such laws.

Tonry, Michael. *Sentencing Matters*. New York: Oxford University Press, 1996. Examination of sentencing reforms over the past quarter century; critiques of the just deserts model, sentencing guidelines, and mandatory penalties.

von Hirsch, Andrew. *Doing Justice*. New York: Hill & Wang, 1976. Represents the best statement of the "just deserts" model, with recommendations for implementing it.

Zimring, Franklin E., and Gordon Hawkins. *Incapacitation*. New York: Oxford University Press, 1995. Examines the theoretical issues surrounding incapacitation and its use to justify imprisonment today.

Notes

1. Herbert L. Packer, *The Limits of the Criminal Sanction* (Stanford, CA: Stanford University Press, 1968), pp. 33–34.

2. Andrew von Hirsch, *Doing Justice* (New York: Hill & Wang, 1976), p. 49.

3. Norval Morris, "Punishment, Desert, and Rehabilitation," *Equal Justice Under Law*, U.S. Department of Justice, Bicentennial Lecture Series (Washington, DC: U.S. Government Printing Office, 1977), pp. 137–167.

4. Mark C. Stafford and Mark Warr, "A Reconceptualization of General and Specific Deterrence," *Journal of Research in Crime and Delinquency*, 30, May 1993, p. 123.

5. Ibid.

6. Daniel S. Nagin, "Criminal Deterrence Research at the Outset of the Twenty-First Century," in Michael Tonry, ed., *Crime and Justice: A Review of Research*, vol. 23 (Chicago: University of Chicago Press, 1998), pp. 1–42.

7. Todd R. Clear, *Harm in American Penology* (Albany: State University of New York Press, 1994), p. 103.

8. Robert Martinson, "What Works? Questions and Answers About Prison Reform," *The Public Interest*, Spring 1974, p. 25.

9. Morris.

10. Richard C. McCorkle, "Research Note: Punish and Rehabilitate? Public Attitudes Toward Six Common Crimes," *Crime and Delinquency*, 39, April 1993, p. 240; Brandon K. Applegate, Francis T. Cullen, and Bonnie S. Fisher, "Public Support for Correctional Treatment: The Continuing Appeal of the Rehabilitative Ideal," *The Prison Journal*, 77, September 1997, pp. 237–258.

11. Francis T. Cullen, Edward J. Latessa, Velmer S. Burton, Jr., and Lucien X. Lombardo, "The Correctional Orientation of Prison Wardens: Is the Rehabilitative Ideal Supported?" *Criminology*, 31, February 1993, pp. 69–92.

12. Gordon Bazemore and Mark S. Umbreit, *Balanced and Restorative Justice: Program Summary* (Washington, DC: Office of Juvenile Justice and Delinquency Prevention, 1994), foreword.

13. Todd R. Clear and David R. Karp, *Community Justice: Preventing Crime and Achieving Justice* (Washington, DC: National Institute of Justice, in press).

14. Norval Morris and Michel Tonry, *Between Prison and Probation: Intermediate Punishments in a Rational Sentencing System* (New York: Oxford University Press, 1990).

15. *Seeking Justice: Crime and Punishment in America* (New York: Edna McConnell Clark Foundation, n.d.), pp. 32–33.

16. Pamala L. Griset, "Determinate Sentencing and the High Cost of Overblown Rhetoric: The New York Experience," *Crime and Delinquency*, 40, October 1994, p. 552. Griset argues that the determinate sentencing model is flawed.

17. Pamala L. Griset, "Determinate Sentencing and Administrative Discretion over Time Served in Prison: A Case Study of Florida," *Crime and Delinquency*, 42 January 1996, p. 127.

18. Although public opinion polls show high support for mandatory sentences in the abstract, support quickly diminishes when the questions present particular circumstances. See Brandon K. Applegate, Francis T. Cullen, Michael G. Turner, and Jody L. Sundt, "Assessing Public Support for Three-Strikes-and-You're-Out Laws: Global versus Specific Attitudes," *Crime and Delinquency*, 42, October 1996, pp. 517–534.

19. Michael G. Turner, Jody L. Stundt, Brandon K. Applegate, and Francis T. Cullen, "Three Strikes and You're Out Legislation: A National Assessment," *Federal Probation*, September 1995, pp. 16–18; Michael Vitiello, "Three Strikes: Can We Return to Rationality?" *Journal of Criminal Law and Criminology*, 87, Winter 1997, p. 395.

20. Michael Vitiello, pp. 395–463.

21. Walter J. Dickey, "The Impact of 'Three Strikes and You're Out' Laws: What Have We Learned?" *Corrections Management Quarterly*, 1, Fall 1997, pp. 55-64.

22. Lisa Stolzenberg and Stewart J. D'Alessio, "Three Strikes and You're Out": The Impact of California's New Mandatory Sentencing Law on Serious Crime Rates," *Crime and Delinquency*, 43, October, 1997, p. 457.

23. Vincent Schiraldi and Michael Godfrey, "Racial Disparities in the Charging of Los Angeles County's Third 'Strike' Cases," *In Brief* (San Francisco: California Center on Juvenile and Criminal Justice), October 1994, pp. 1–4.

24. *Sacramento Bee*, March 31, 1996, A1ff. See also William J. Bennett, John J. DiIulio, Jr., and John P. Walters, *Body Count* (New York: Simon & Schuster, 1996), pp. 97–98.

25. Ibid., p. 58.

26. Ibid., p. 62.

27. Christopher S. Wren, *The New York Times*, January 18, 1998, p. A1.

28. Timothy S. Bynum, "Prosecutorial Discretion and the Implementation of a Legislative Mandate," in Merry Morash, ed., *Implementing Criminal Justice Policies* (Beverly Hills, CA: Sage, 1982).

29. Thomas B. Marvell and Carlisle E. Moody, "The Impact of Enhanced Prison Terms for Felonies Committed with Guns," *Criminology*, 33, May 1995, pp. 247–281.

30. Florida Department of Corrections, *Mandatory Minimum Sentences in Florida: Past Trends and Future Implications* (Tallahassee: State of Florida, February 11, 1991).

31. Fox Butterfield, "Inmates Serving More Time, Justice Department Reports," *The New York Times*, January 11, 1999, p. A106; U.S. Department of Justice, Bureau of Justice Statistics, "State Sentencing Law Changes Linked to Increasing Time Served in State Prisons," Press Release, January 10, 1999, p. 1.

32. Steven R. Donziger, *The Real War on Crime: The Report of the National Criminal Justice Commission* (New York: Harper Perennial, 1996), p. 24.

33. M. A. Jones and James Austin, "The 1995 NCCD National Prison Population Forecast: The Cost of Truth-in-Sentencing Laws," *NCCD Focus* (Washington, DC: National Council on Crime and Delinquency, July 1995).

34. James Austin, "The Impact of Truth in Sentencing on Prison Classification Systems," *Correctional Management Quarterly,* Spring 1997, pp. 54–55.

35. Todd Clear, "Mis-truths in Sentencing," *Perspectives,* 20, Spring 1996, pp. 12–13.

36. Morris and Tonry.

37. Joan Petersilia and Susan Turner, "The Potential of Intermediate Sanctions," *State Government,* March–April, 1989), p. 65.

38. T. J. Keil and Gennaro F. Vito, "Fear of Crime and Attitudes Toward Capital Punishment: A Structural Equations Model," *Justice Quarterly,* 8, December 1991, p. 447.

39. Malcolm M. Feeley, *The Process Is the Punishment* (New York: Russell Sage Foundation, 1979).

40. George F. Cole and Marc G. Gertz, eds., *The Criminal Justice System: Politics and Policies,* 7th ed. (Belmont, CA: Wadsworth, 1998), pp. 331–351.

41. Darrell Steffensmeier, John Kramer, and Cathy Streifel, "Gender and Imprisonment Decisions," *Criminology,* 31, 1993, p. 411.

42. Kathleen Daly and Rebecca L. Bordt, "Sex Effects and Sentencing: An Analysis of the Statistical Literature," *Justice Quarterly,* 12, March 1995, pp. 141–175.

43. John Rosecrance, "Maintaining the Myth of Individualized Justice: Probation Presentence Reports," *Justice Quarterly,* 5, June 1988, p. 235.

44. Richard S. Frase, "State Sentencing Guidelines: Still Going Strong," *Judicature,* 78, (January–February 1995, p. 173.

45. Julian V. Roberts, "The Role of Criminal Record in the Sentencing Process," Michael Tonry, ed., *Crime and Justice: A Review of Research,* vol. 22 (Chicago: University of Chicago Press, 1997), pp. 303–362.

46. Michael Tonry, "Intermediate Sanctions in Sentencing Guidelines," in Michael Tonry, ed., *Crime and Justice: A Review of Research,* vol. 23 (Chicago: University of Chicago Press, 1998), pp. 199–253.

47. Michael Tonry, "Sentencing Commissions and Their Guidelines," in Michael Tonry, ed., *Crime and Justice,* vol. 17 (Chicago: University of Chicago Press, 1993), pp. 140–141.

48. John H. Kramer and Jeffrey T. Ulmer, "Sentencing Disparity and Departures from Guidelines," *Justice Quarterly,* 13, March 1996, p. 81.

49. Joan Petersilia and Susan Turner, "Guideline-Based Justice Prediction and Racial Minorities," in Norval Morris and Michael Tonry, eds. *Crime and Justice,* vol. 15 (Chicago: University of Chicago Press, 1987), pp. 151–181.

50. Thomas D. Miethe and Clarence Moore, "Sentencing Guidelines: Their Effects in Minnesota," *Research in Brief* (Washington, DC: National Institute of Justice, 1989).

51. Lisa Stolzenberg and Steward J. D'Alessio, "Sentencing and Unwarranted Disparity: An Empirical Assessment of the Long-Term Impact of Sentencing Guidelines in Minnesota," *Criminology,* 32, 1994, p. 301.

52. Richard S. Frase, "Sentencing Principles in Theory and Practice," in Michael Tonry, ed., *Crime and Justice: A Review of Research,* vol. 22(Chicago: University of Chicago Press, 1997), p. 398.

53. Joy A. Chapper and Roger A. Hanson, "Managing the Criminal Appeals Process," *State Court Journal,* 12, 1988, p. 4; Roger A. Hanson, *Time on Appeal* (Williamsburg, VA: National Center for State Courts, 1996), p. 56.

54. Jack B. Weinstein, "A Trial Judge's Second Impression of the Federal Sentencing Guidelines," *Southern California Law Review,* 66, 1992, p. 357.

55. David J. Rothman, "The Crime of Punishment," *New York Review of Books,* February 17, 1994, pp. 34–38. See also a series of articles critical of the guidelines and the U.S. Sentencing Commission, in *The Washington Post,* October 6–10, 1996.

56. Celesta A. Albonetti, "Sentencing under the Federal Sentencing Guidelines: Effects of Defendant Characteristics, Guilty Pleas, and Departures on Sentencing Outcomes for Drug Offenses, 1991–1992," *Law and Society Review,* 31, 1997, pp. 789–820.

57. Tonry, "Sentencing Commissions," p. 138.

58. Peter H. Rossi and Richrad A. Berk, *Just Punishments: Federal Guidelines and Public Views Compared* (New York: Aldine DeGruyter, 1997).

59. Kathleen Daly and Michael Tonry, "Gender, Race, and Sentencing," in Michael Tonry, ed., *Crime and Justice: A Review of Research,* vol. 22 (Chicago: University of Chicago Press, 1997), pp. 201–252.

60. See, for example, Coramae Richey Mann, *Unequal Justice: A Question of Color* (Bloomington: Indiana University Press, 1993).

61. William Wilbanks, *The Myth of a Racist Criminal Justice System* (Pacific Grove, CA: Brooks/Cole, 1987).

62. Samuel Walker, Cassia Spohn, and Miriam DeLone, *The Color of Justice* (Belmont, CA: Wadsworth, 1996), p. 153.

63. Ibid., p. 154.

64. *The New York Times,* October 9, 1997, p. A18.

65. C. Ronald Huff and Arye Rattner, "Convicted but Innocent: False Positives and the Criminal Justice Process," in Joseph E. Scott and Travis Hirschi, eds., *Controversial Issues in Crime and Justice* (Newbury Park, CA: Sage, 1988), p. 130.

The Law of Corrections

During the early morning hours of October 30, 1983, Keith Hudson, an inmate at the State Penitentiary, Angola, Louisiana, was washing clothes in his cell toilet. Jack McMillian, a correctional officer, came to the cell, used racially abusive language, and told Hudson to stop flushing the toilet and go to sleep. Believing that he was doing nothing wrong, Hudson kept doing his laundry. An argument ensued. McMillian, assisted by officers Marvin Woods and Arthur Mezo, seized Hudson, placed him in handcuffs and shackles, and walked him toward the prison's administrative lockdown area, known as the "dungeon." Hudson later testified that on the way McMillian pushed him up against the wall and punched him in the mouth, eyes, chest, and stomach while Woods held him in place and kicked and punched him from behind.

"Hold him," McMillian told Woods. "Let me knock his gold teeth out."

As Hudson was being assaulted, Officer Mezo, the supervisor on duty, is alleged to have said, "Don't have too much fun!" The pummeling split Hudson's lip, broke his dental plate, and left him "bleeding and swelling about the body."

Keith Hudson sued the three correctional officers in the federal district court, alleging that his rights under the Eighth Amendment's prohibition of cruel and unusual punishments had been violated. The judge found for Hudson and awarded him $800. However, the U.S. Court of Appeals for the Fifth Circuit reversed this decision, holding that the Eighth Amendment did not apply because Hudson's injuries were minor and no medical attention was required.

Hudson appealed that decision to the U.S. Supreme Court. In a seven-to-two decision, the Court agreed with the inmate. Writing for the majority, Justice Sandra Day O'Connor said, "When prison officials maliciously and sadistically use force to cause harm, contemporary standards of decency always are violated. This is true whether or not significant injury is evident."[1]

For many Americans the idea that a prisoner can sue correctional officials over constitutional rights seems absurd. They believe that criminals do not have the same rights as free citizens. Until the 1960s, courts agreed. This belief was well stated by a Virginia judge in *Riffin v. Commonwealth* (1871): "The prisoner has, as a consequence of his crime, not only forfeited his liberty, but all his personal rights except which the law in its humanity accords to him. He is for the time being the slave of the state."[2]

But since the late 1960s federal and state courts have become increasingly involved in correctional matters. Although much correctional law concerns claims by inmates that their rights have been violated, judges have also upheld the due process rights of probationers and parolees. In some jurisdictions the courts have declared entire correctional systems to be operating in ways that violate the Constitution. Courts have also ruled on claims by correctional personnel regarding employment discrimination, affirmative action, collective bargaining, and liability for job-related actions.

In part, the judiciary's increased involvement must be credited to the civil rights movement of the 1960s, as well as to efforts since the end of World War II to fundamentally democratize American society. Paralleling the movements to bring nonwhite minorities, women, children, gays, the handicapped, the aged, and mental patients into the societal mainstream, the movement toward advancing the rights of offenders has been an "effort to redefine the status (moral, political, as well as legal) of offenders in a democratic society."[3]

Since the 1960s, prisoners such as Keith Hudson have been able to sue state officials for violations of their civil rights. To facilitate these actions the Supreme Court ordered that prisoners have access to law libraries.

Correctional law has also gained importance as the numbers of offenders under supervision and correctional personnel have grown. As emphasized in Chapter 1, more than 6 million adults and juveniles receive correctional supervision from more than 500,000 administrators and officers, at a cost of more than $30 billion a year. Because corrections programs affect the lives of an astounding 2.9 percent of U.S. adults, it is especially important that legal rules guide correctional practices.

In this chapter we examine the legal foundations of correctional law, analyze the constitutional rights of offenders, and explore the rights and liabilities of correctional personnel.

Questions FOR INQUIRY

1. What foundations support the legal rights of people under correctional supervision?
2. What has been the role of the U.S. Supreme Court in interpreting correctional law?
3. What are the constitutional rights of prisoners?
4. What alternatives to litigation are available?
5. How does law affect corrections personnel?

The Foundations Of Correctional Law

Four foundations support the legal rights of people under correctional supervision: (1) constitutions, (2) statutes, (3) case law, and (4) regulations. Most correctional litigation has involved rights claimed under the U.S. Constitution. State constitutions generally parallel the U.S. Constitution but sometimes confer other rights. Legislatures are of course free to grant additional rights to offenders and to authorize corrections departments to adopt regulations that recognize the rights.

Constitutions

Constitutions contain basic principles and procedural safeguards. Constitutions describe the institutions (legislature, judiciary, and executive), the powers of government, and the rights of individuals. Constitutional rights are basic protections that individuals have against improper limitations of their freedom. For example, the first ten amendments to the U.S. Constitution, together known as the Bill of Rights, provide protection against government actions that would violate basic rights and liberties. Several have a direct bearing on corrections, because they uphold freedom of religion, association, and speech; limit unreasonable searches and seizures; require due process; and prohibit cruel and unusual punishment.

constitution

Fundamental law contained in state or federal document that provides a design of government and lists basic rights for individuals.

States have their own constitutions, which parallel the U.S. Constitution and contain protections against state and local governments. During the early 1960s the U.S. Supreme Court decided to require state governments to respect most of the rights listed in the Bill of Rights. Before that time the Bill of Rights protected citizens only against actions of the federal government. As a result of Supreme Court decisions, the power of all government officials is limited by the U.S. Constitution and their own state constitution.

The courts of each state are empowered to declare correctional conditions and practices in violation of either the state or the federal constitution. Although most state constitutions do not give offenders any greater rights than those granted by the U.S. Constitution, some do. For example, a California court has ruled that electronic surveillance of prisoners violates the privacy guarantees of state statutes; an Oregon court has ruled that the state constitutional guarantee against "unnecessary rigor" in correctional

The Supreme Court of the United States has the final word on questions concerning interpretations of the Constitution. During the 1970s, the Court ended the "hands off" policy and greatly extended the rights of prisoners.

practices provides grounds to stop certain genital searches.[4] These rulings would have been unlikely if the cases had been brought in the federal courts.

Constitutional rights are not completely lost when a person is convicted of a crime. However, the courts have emphasized that some rights may be limited when legitimate governmental interests outweigh them and when the restriction is reasonably related to those interests. The courts have recognized three specific interests as justifying some restrictions on the constitutional rights of prisoners: (1) maintaining institutional order, (2) maintaining institutional security, and (3) rehabilitating inmates. Thus the courts must ask, on a case-by-case basis, Are proposed restrictions reasonably related to preserve these interests? Later in this chapter we discuss specific amendments to the U.S. Constitution and decisions of the U.S. Supreme Court as they relate to prisoners' rights.

Statutes

statute

Law created by the people's elected representatives in legislatures.

Statutes are laws passed by legislatures at all levels of government. At the top level, the U.S. Congress is responsible for statutes dealing with problems concerning the entire country. Thus, laws passed by Congress define federal crimes and punishments, allocate funds for criminal justice agencies of the national government, and authorize programs in pursuit of criminal justice policies. Each state legislature enacts laws that govern the acts of its governments (state and local) and individuals within their borders, and appropriates funds for state agencies such as corrections. Statutes defining criminal behavior can be found in the penal codes of the national and state governments.

Statutes are written in more specific terms than are found in constitutions. Courts are frequently asked to interpret the meaning of the terms and to rule on the legislature's intention when the statute was passed. For example, in 1998 the Supreme Court was asked to rule whether the Americans with Disabilities Act of 1990 applied to state prisoners. The act prohibits discrimination against disabled people by all agencies of the federal, state, and local governments. The case, brought by a Pennsylvania offender, was opposed by most states on the grounds that governments should not have to make special provisions for disabled prisoners. In a unanimous decision the court said that "The statute's language unmistakably includes state prisons and prisoners within its coverage."[5]

State legislatures are free to grant specific rights to inmates beyond those conferred by the state constitutions or the U.S. Constitution. Some state statutes have been held to create "liberty interests" that cannot be denied without due process of law. Some states also have enacted "right-to-treatment" legislation and other statutes that charge correctional officials with particular duties. Prisoners may sue officials who fail to fulfill their statutory duties and obligations. If such claims are upheld, inmates may be entitled to collect monetary damages from the responsible officials and/or to receive a court ruling ordering a practice stopped.

Case Law

Court decisions, often called **case law,** are a third foundation of correctional law. The United States operates under a common law system in which judges create law or modify existing law when they rule in specific cases. In deciding the cases presented to them, American judges are guided by constitutional provisions, statutes, and decisions in other cases. These prior rulings, also known as **precedent,** establish legal principles used in making decisions on similar cases. When such a case arises, the judge looks to the principles arising from earlier rulings and applies them to the case being decided. The judges' ability to adjust legal principles when new kinds of situations arise make the common law, or case law, flexible so as to respond to changes in society.

As we have noted, constitutions often have phrases that lack clear, definite meanings, for example, the Eighth Amendment's phrase "cruel and unusual punishment." Thus in some cases judges must interpret its meaning. For example, in a Florida case (*Ford v. Wainwright,* 1986) the U.S. Supreme Court was asked to consider whether it was cruel and unusual punishment to execute an offender who became mentally ill while incarcerated. In his opinion for the Court, Justice Thurgood Marshall concluded that the Eighth Amendment prohibits the state from executing a prisoner who is insane. He said that in common law executing an insane person has little retributive value, no deterrence value, and simply offends humanity.[6] He also said that Florida's procedures for determining a prisoner's sanity were inadequate.

With this decision, *Ford v. Wainwright* became a precedent (and part of case law) that judges are to use when the execution of a mentally ill death row inmate is challenged. The decision also alerts states that they should not have sanity determination procedures similar to Florida's.

Regulations

Regulations are rules made by federal, state, and local administrative agencies. The legislature, president, or governor gives agencies the power to make detailed regulations governing specific policy areas such as health, safety, and the environment.

A department of corrections may create regulations for questions as to the personal items prisoners may have in their cells, when prisoners can have visitors, how searches are to be carried out, and the ways that disciplinary procedures will be conducted. Often these regulations are challenged in court. For example, weekend visiting hours in some prisons are regulated so that half the inmates are eligible for a visit on Saturday and the other half on Sunday. This is justified because of the great numbers who swamp the visiting area on weekends. However, the regulation might be challenged by people who for religious reasons cannot travel on the designated day.

Regulations are a form of law that guides the behavior of correctional officials. They are often the basis of legal actions filed by prisoners and correctional employees. It may be claimed that the regulations violate constitutional protections or statutes. The claims may also allege that officials are not following the regulations.

case law

Legal rules produced by judges' decisions.

precedent

Legal rules created in judges' decisions that serve to guide the decisions of other judges in subsequent similar cases.

regulation

Legal rules, usually set by an agency of the executive branch, designed to implement in detail policies of that agency.

Correctional Law and the U.S. Supreme Court

For most of American history, the Bill of Rights was interpreted as protecting individuals only from acts of the national government. These important constitutional rights were viewed as having no bearing on cases where citizens felt unjustly abused by state and local laws. This meant that the Bill of Rights had little influence over criminal justice, because the vast majority of cases are in state courts and corrections systems.

The Fourteenth Amendment, ratified in 1868, barred states from violating people's rights to due process and equal protection of the law. But not until the 1920s did the Court begin to name specific rights that the Fourteenth Amendment protected from infringement by states. Only during the 1960s under the leadership of Chief Justice Earl Warren did the Court begin to require that state officials abide by the specific provisions of the Bill of Rights.

hands-off policy

A judicial policy of noninterference in the internal administration of prisons.

Prior to the 1960s, courts held a **hands-off policy** with respect to corrections. Judges in some states applied their states' constitutions to correct abuses in jails and prisons. However, most judges followed the belief of the Virginia judge in *Ruffin v. Commonwealth* (1871) that prisoners did not have rights.[7] In addition, judges argued that the separation of powers among the three branches of government prevented them from interfering in the operations of any executive agency. Judges supposed that because they were not penologists, their intervention in the internal administration of prisons would disrupt discipline.

The End of the Hands-Off Policy

The end of the hands-off policy was signaled by the U.S. Supreme Court decision in *Cooper v. Pate* (1964), which states that prisoners in state and local institutions are entitled to the protections of the Civil Rights Act of 1871 (referred to here as Section 1983) state prisoners were *persons* whose rights are protected by the Constitution.[8] The justices ruled that a prisoner could sue a warden or other official under Title 42, United States Code, Section 1983 (42 U.S.C. 1983), which imposes **civil liability** on any person who deprives another of constitutional rights. It allows suits against state officials to be heard in the federal courts.[9] Because of *Cooper v. Pate,* the federal courts now recognize that prisoners may sue state officials over such things as brutality by guards, inadequate nutrition and medical care, theft of personal property, and the denial of basic rights.[10] At the time, the federal courts were considered more likely than state courts to rule in the prisoner's favor.[11] As Jacobs points out, "Just by opening a forum in which prisoners' grievances could be heard, the federal courts destroyed the custodian's absolute power and the prisoners' isolation from the larger society. And the litigation in itself heightened prisoners' consciousness and politicized them."[12]

civil liability

Responsibility for the provision of monetary or other compensation awarded to a plaintiff in a civil action.

habeas corpus

A writ (judicial order) requesting that a person holding another person produce the prisoner and give reasons to justify continued confinement.

Although Section 1983 is the most commonly used legal action to challenge prison and jail conditions, inmates may also seek relief filing a **habeas corpus** petition. In this ancient legal writ, a prisoner (or pretrial detainee) asks a court to examine the legality of his or her imprisonment and asks for release from illegal confinement. In recent years the U.S. Supreme Court has issued several decisions limiting opportunities for prisoners to file habeas corpus petitions. In 1996 Congress passed the Antiterrorism Act, which included a provision imposing a one-year limit, from the time of conviction, to file a federal habeas petition.

In 1997, almost 19,000 habeas corpus petitions were filed in federal courts compared to almost 42,000 Section 1983 cases.[13] Remember that prisoners filing habeas petitions are asking to be released from illegally imposed confinement, whereas the Section 1983 civil rights cases are seeking improvements in prison conditions, return of property, or compensation for abuse by officers (see Figure 5.1). But merely filing a case in court does not mean that it will be heard. Hanson and Daley found that 74 percent of Section 1983 cases were dismissed because the plaintiff had not followed the court's rules or because there

Figure 5.1 Issues in Section 1983 Lawsuits

Most suits filed by state prisoners in the federal courts deal with issues affecting only the plaintiff rather than all prisoners as a class.

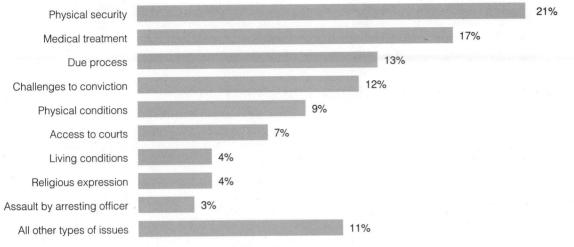

Physical security	21%
Medical treatment	17%
Due process	13%
Challenges to conviction	12%
Physical conditions	9%
Access to courts	7%
Living conditions	4%
Religious expression	4%
Assault by arresting officer	3%
All other types of issues	11%

SOURCE: Roger A. Hanson and Henry W. K. Daley, *Challenging the Conditions of Prisons and Jails: A Report on Section 1983 Litigation* (Washington, DC: Bureau of Justice Statistics, 1995), p. 17.

was no evidence of a constitutional rights violation. Ultimately only 2 percent of the cases went to trial, and only half were decided in favor of the prisoner.[14]

After *Cooper v. Pate,* the amount of prisoner-initiated litigation skyrocketed. The number of suits brought by state prisoners in federal courts alone rose from 218 in 1966 to 41,952 in 1996.[15] Additional cases, of course, are filed in state courts, arguing infringement of rights guaranteed by the constitutions and laws of the various states.

Access to the Courts

The increase in filings was encouraged by U.S. Supreme Court decisions that eased prisoners' access to the courts. Until the 1970s many states limited communications between prisoners and their attorneys, prohibited jailhouse lawyers, and did not provide prison law libraries. These limitations were imposed on the grounds of institutional security, but prisoners need access to the courts to make sure officials follow the law.

The leading case on access to courts is *Johnson v. Avery* (1969).[16] Johnson, a Tennessee inmate, was disciplined for violating a regulation prohibiting one inmate from helping another inmate with legal matters. The Supreme Court ruled that prisoners are entitled to receive legal assistance from other prisoners unless alternative resources are provided to help prepare necessary legal documents. However, the Court said that the prison could impose reasonable regulations on "jailhouse lawyers" in keeping with the need for order and security.

In a second case, *Bounds v. Smith* (1977), the Supreme Court extended the principle of prisoner access by addressing the question of law libraries. North Carolina had libraries in only seven of its seventy-seven prisons. Inmates could be transported to a library for one day of legal research. The Court ruled this inadequate, stating that "the fundamental constitutional right of access to the courts requires prison authorities to assist inmates in the preparation and filing of meaningful legal papers by providing prisoners with adequate law libraries or adequate legal assistance from persons trained in the law."[17]

But does the mere presence of a law library satisfy inmates' constitutional rights of access to courts? What did the Court in *Bounds* mean by "adequate" legal assistance?

The Supreme Court addressed these questions in the 1996 case of *Lewis v. Casey*.[18] A lower federal court had held that the Arizona Department of Corrections was not providing adequate legal assistance to inmates. This lower court ordered more training for library staff, updating of legal materials, photocopying services, better access to the library, and so forth. In its ruling, the Court said that *Bounds* did not create an abstract, free-standing right to a law library or legal assistance but that inmates must show that the inadequacy of the library hindered efforts to pursue a legal claim.

The Prisoners' Rights Movement

As an outgrowth of the Civil Rights Movement organizations such as the Legal Defense and Education Fund of the NAACP (National Association for the Advancement of Colored People), and the National Prison Project of the American Civil Liberties Union (ACLU) became concerned about prisoners' rights. In the liberal political climate, many groups placed legal protections for inmates high on their political agendas. It was no longer unheard-of for prisoners to sue wardens or commissioners of corrections. Efforts such as those of Keith Hudson often resulted in major changes in the law (see Focus box).

The first successful prisoners' rights cases involved the most excessive prison abuses: brutality and inhuman physical conditions. In 1967, for example, the Supreme Court invalidated a Florida inmate's confession of rioting made after he had been thrown naked into a "barren cage," filthy with human excrement, and kept there for thirty-five days.[19] A federal district court in 1971 declared the notorious Cummins Farm Unit of the Arkansas State Prison (depicted in the Hollywood film *Brubaker*) to be in violation of the Eighth Amendment. In that case the judge noting that Arkansas State Prison operations, which relied on trusties for security and housed inmates in barracks, leaving them open to "frequent assaults, murder, rape, and homosexual conduct," were unconstitutional.[20]

By the end of the 1970s, federal judges had imposed changes on prisons and jails in nearly every state. In addition, important court decisions required due process in probation and parole. By 1990 most of the worst abuses had been corrected and judges stopped expanding the number and nature of prisoners' rights.

Over the past three decades prisoners have pursued rights guaranteed in the U.S. Constitution by filing Section 1983 petitions (42 U.S.C. 1983) in the federal courts. They have asserted that civil rights found in the Bill of Rights have been violated. Now let's examine the case law that has evolved as the Supreme Court has considered these claims.

Constitutional Rights of Prisoners

The rights applicable to inmates are essentially summarized in a handful of phrases in four of the amendments to the U.S. Constitution. Three of these—the First, Fourth, and Eighth Amendments—are part of the Bill of Rights. The last, the Fourteenth Amendment, became effective in 1868. In this section we present the text of those amendments and discuss rights under them in some detail.

It is important to recognize that constitutional rights are not absolute and may conflict with the broader needs of society. Courts must examine government rules to distinguish rules that infringe on protected behavior from those that govern behavior. Not until 1987 did the Supreme Court fully address these boundaries with regard to prisoners' rights. Lacking guidance from above, "lower courts developed a number of contradictory tests to resolve these cases."[21]

Some lower courts have held rules that conflict with First Amendment protections to be unconstitutional unless they were the **least restrictive method** of dealing with

least restrictive methods

Means of ensuring a legitimate state interest (such as security) that impose fewer limits to prisoners' rights than alternative means of securing that end.

FOCUS

From a Lonely Prison Cell, an Inmate Wins an Important Victory

Somewhere in the bowels of Camp J of the Louisiana State Penitentiary at Angola, not far from where three guards kicked, punched, and pummeled him . . . , prisoner No. 91888, Keith J. Hudson, may be savoring something few lawyers anywhere have known in recent years: He took a civil liberties case to the Supreme Court of the United States, and won.

By a vote of 7 to 2, the Justices agreed with Mr. Hudson that prison beatings can be unconstitutionally "cruel and unusual" even if they "result only in split lips and bloody noses rather than concussions and broken bones." . . .

For the 32-year-old Mr. Hudson, the ruling was the culmination of nine years of legal work, in which he read precedents from the law books brought to his cell by prison messengers, and hunted and pecked his legal briefs on a portable typewriter. Mr. Hudson, serving a 20-year sentence for armed robbery, could not argue his case personally; that case was handled by Alvin Bronstein of the American Civil Liberties Union's national prison project.

In a handful of homemade documents, written in a patois of street talk and legalese, Mr. Hudson offered his version of events in the early morning of October 30, 1983.(See chapter opening.)

The pummeling split his lip, broke his dental plate, and left him "bleeding and swelling about the face and bruised about the body," Mr. Hudson wrote in a typewritten account dotted with misspellings, typos, fractured grammar and uneven margins. He said he quickly filed a complaint seeking "fifty thousand dollars" in damages and an order "to prohibit further crulity (sic) to myself and other inmates housed in Camp J."

At a hearing, Mr. Hudson produced and questioned two corroborating witnesses, cited his rights under the First, Eighth, and Fourteenth Amendments to the Constitution, recounted the guards' racist, crude, curse-ridden comments, and told the judge that he had suffered "not only mental and physical anguish but a permanent psychological scar for life."

Convinced, the judge awarded Mr. Hudson $800 in damages. But a three-judge panel of the Federal Court of Appeals for the Fifth Circuit reversed the decision. The judges concluded that the force the guards used was unreasonable, excessive, unnecessary, wanton—and constitutional. Mr. Hudson asked the Supreme Court to review the case.

In his typewritten petition, he contended that the appellate judges had misread the Constitution. "This ruling falls short, because of its negligence in also considering the 'mental injury' sustained, which is more significant than physical damage," he argued. The Court resoundingly agreed.

SOURCE: David Margolick, "At the Bar," *The New York Times,* March 6, 1992, p. B8. © 1992 by The New York Times Company. Reprinted by permission.

---

an institutional problem. For example, a court struck down the punishment of inmates for writing inflammatory political tracts because officials could merely have confiscated the material.[22] Other courts have stated that a right may be limited if it interferes with a **compelling state interest** such as the goal of maintaining security. A rule prohibiting receipt of nude photographs of wives and girlfriends was found unconstitutional. The court ruled that the right to receive such photographs was protected; however, because other inmates might be aroused by the sight of them, a rule against their display would have been proper as a security measure.[23] Limitations on the receipt of certain publications have also been upheld on the grounds that they present a **"clear and present danger"** to the security of a prison, or to the rehabilitation of prisoners.[24]

Because courts were using different methods to distinguish constitutional from unconstitutional policies, the Supreme Court needed to set a standard. The Court first enunciated guidance for the lower courts in *Turner v. Safley* (1987), upholding a Missouri ban on correspondence between inmates in different correctional institutions. Writing for a five-to-four majority, Justice O'Connor said such a regulation was valid only if "reasonably related to legitimate penological interests."[25] She specified the four elements of the **rational basis test:**

compelling state interest

An interest of the state that must take precedence over rights guaranteed by the First Amendment.

"clear and present danger"

Any threat to security or to the safety of individuals that is so obvious and compelling that the need to counter it overrides the guarantees of the First Amendment.

rational basis test

Requires that a regulation provide a reasonable, rational method of advancing a legitimate institutional goal.

1. There must be a rational connection between the regulation and the legitimate interest put forward to justify it.
2. Alternative means of exercising the right must remain open to prison inmates.
3. The regulation must have only a minimal impact on correctional officers and other inmates.
4. A less restrictive alternative must be available.

This test is the current standard for analyzing not only prisoners' First Amendment claims but other constitutional claims as well.[26]

The First Amendment

Amendment I: Congress shall make no law respecting an establishment of religion, or prohibiting the free exercise thereof; or abridging the freedom of speech, or of the press; or the right of the people peaceably to assemble, and to petition the government for a redress of grievances.

Since the 1940s, the Supreme Court has maintained that the First Amendment holds a special position in the Bill of Rights because it guarantees freedoms essential in a democracy. Because this amendment has a preferred position, it is not surprising that some early prisoners' rights cases concerned rights it protects: access to reading materials, noncensorship of mail, and freedom of religious practice. Table 5.1 shows some of the more significant cases decided under this amendment.

Speech   Since the 1970s courts have extended the rights of freedom of speech and expression to prisoners, requiring correctional administrators to show why these rights must be restricted. For example, in 1974 the Supreme Court ruled that censorship of mail was permissible only when officials could demonstrate a compelling governmental interest in maintaining security.[27] The result has been a marked increase in communications among inmates and the outside world. As discussed earlier, however, the decision in *Turner v. Safley* allowed Missouri to ban correspondence among inmates at other institutions as a means of combating prison gangs and communicating escape plans.[28]

The right of free speech also includes access to publications. Prisoners generally receive books and magazines directly from the publisher or as separate mailings from family and friends. The Federal Bureau of Prisons had regulations authorizing wardens to reject incoming publications considered detrimental to security, good order, institutional discipline, or that might facilitate criminal activity. These regulations were upheld in *Thornburgh v. Abbott* (1989).[29] The Court said that publications did not have the same First Amendment protections as personal correspondence and that the regulations were justified on security grounds.

Religion   The First Amendment prevents Congress from making laws respecting the establishment of religion or prohibiting its free exercise. Cases concerning the free exercise of religion have caused the judiciary some problems, especially when the practice in question may interfere with prison routine and the maintenance of order.

The first amendment to the Constitution provides for the free exercise of religion. The Black Muslims have been a major factor in forcing correctional administrators to recognize that right.

Table 5.1   Selected Interpretations of the First Amendment as Applied to Prisoners

The Supreme Court has made numerous decisions affecting prisoners' rights to freedom of speech and expression and freedom of religion.

Case	Decision
Freedom of Speech Cases	
Procunier v. Martinez (1974)	Censorship of mail is permitted only to the extent necessary to maintain prison security.
Turner v. Safley (1987)	Inmates do not have a right to receive mail from one another, and this mail can be banned if "reasonably related to legitimate penological interests."
Thornburgh v. Abbott (1989)	Rules permitting wardens to reject incoming publications deemed detrimental to the security, good order, and discipline are constitutional.
Freedom of Religion Cases	
Fulwood v. Clemmer (1962)	The Muslim faith must be recognized as a religion, and officials may not restrict members from holding services.
Gittlemacker v. Prasse (1970)	The state must give inmates the opportunity to practice their religion but is not required to provide a member of the clergy.
Cruz v. Beto (1972)	Prisoners who hold other unconventional beliefs may not be denied the opportunity to practice their religion.
Kahane v. Carlson (1975)	Orthodox Jewish inmates have the right to a diet consistent with their religious beliefs unless the government can show cause why it cannot be provided.
Theriault v. Carlson (1977)	The First Amendment does not protect so-called religions that are obvious shams, that tend to mock established institutions, and whose members lack religious sincerity.
O'Lone v. Estate of Shabazz (1987)	The rights of Muslim prisoners are not violated when work assignments make it impossible for them to attend religious services if no alternative exists.

The growth of the Black Muslim religion in prisons set the stage for lawsuits demanding that this group be granted the same privileges as other faiths (special diets, access to clergy and religious publications, and opportunities for group worship). In the 1960s many wardens believed the Muslims were a radical political group posing as a religion. They did not grant them the benefits extended to people who practiced conventional religions.

In an early case (*Fulwood v. Clemmer*, 1962), a federal court ruled that officials must recognize the Black Muslims as a religion and allow them to hold worship services as do inmates of other faiths. It did not accept the view that the Muslims posed a "clear and present danger."[30] In another religion case (*Cruz v. Beto*, 1972), the justices declared that a Buddhist prisoner must be given reasonable opportunities to practice his faith, like those given fellow prisoners belonging to religions more commonly practiced in the United States.[31]

However, in *O'Lone v. Estate of Shabazz* (1987), the court ruled that a Muslim's rights to freely exercise his religion were not violated by prison officials who would not alter his work schedule so that he could attend Friday afternoon Jumu'ah services.[32] Shabazz's assignment took him outside the prison, and officials claimed that returning him for services would create a security risk. The justices ruled that the policy was related to a legitimate penological interest.

Muslim, Orthodox Jewish, Native American, and other prisoners have gained some of the rights considered necessary for practicing their religions. Court decisions have upheld prisoners' right to be served meals consistent with religious dietary laws, to correspond with religious leaders and possess religious literature, to wear a beard if one's beliefs require, and to assemble for services. In sum, members of religious minorities have broken new legal ground on First Amendment issues.

That religious freedom is a continuing issue — witness the Religious Freedom Restoration Act passed by Congress and signed into law by President Clinton in 1993.[33] This legislation was developed in response to a 1990 Supreme Court decision, unrelated to corrections, upholding denial of unemployment compensation to two drug treatment counselors dismissed for using peyote during a Native American religious ceremony.[34] Religious leaders immediately became concerned that the Court had weakened First Amendment protections for believers. A broad coalition of groups pressured Congress to restore the requirement that the government must show a compelling interest before it can limit the free exercise of religion. Congress supported the act even though certain legislators wanted to exclude prisoners from its protections. The act might have been used to undermine the *Turner* and *Shabazz* decisions.[35] In 1997, however, the Supreme Court declared that Congress did not have the authority to enact such legislation (*City of Boerne v. Flores*). Nevertheless, legislatures can probably pass such laws for their own states. Whether states will exempt prisoners from their laws is an interesting question.

The Fourth Amendment

Amendment IV: The right of the people to be secure in their persons, houses, papers, and effects, against unreasonable searches and seizures, shall not be violated, and no warrants shall issue but on probable cause, supported by oath or affirmation, and particularly describing the place to be searched, and the people or things to be seized.

On entering a correctional institution, prisoners surrender most of their rights under the Fourth Amendment. The amendment prohibits only "unreasonable" searches and seizures, but courts have not been active in extending such protections to prisoners. Thus regulations viewed as reasonable to maintain security and order in an institution may be justified. For example, the decision in *Hudson v. Palmer* (1984) allowed officials to search cells and confiscate any materials found there.[36]

Table 5.2 outlines some of the U.S. Supreme Court's Fourth Amendment opinions. They reveal the fine balance between the right to privacy and institutional need. Body searches have been harder for administrators to justify than cell searches, for example, but the Court has upheld them when they have been governed by a clear policy demonstrably related to a legitimate institutional need and not conducted with the intent to humiliate or degrade.[37] Courts have ruled that staff members of one sex may not supervise inmates of the opposite sex during bathing, use of the toilet, or strip searches.[38] Here the inconvenience of ensuring that the officer is of the same sex as the inmate does not justify the intrusion. Yet the authority of female guards to "pat down" male prisoners, excluding the genital area, has been upheld.[39]

The most intrusive personal searches involve body examinations. Officials may require a "digital [by finger] examination" of the inmate's body openings, an x-ray, or the forced taking of a laxative if officers believe the offender has secreted contraband. In general, courts have favored the security and safety interests of prison officials when dealing with search and seizure. Only the most intrusive physical searches have come under scrutiny and must be justified on the grounds that officers suspected contraband.

The Eighth Amendment

Amendment VIII: Excessive bail shall not be required, nor excessive fines imposed, nor cruel and unusual punishments inflicted.

The Constitution's prohibition of cruel and unusual punishments has been tied to prisoners' need for decent treatment and minimal health standards. Three principal tests have been applied by the courts under the Eighth Amendment to determine whether conditions are unconstitutional: (1) whether the punishment shocks the general conscience of a civilized society, (2) whether the punishment is unnecessarily cruel, and (3) whether the punishment goes beyond legitimate penal aims. Some of the major Eighth Amendment cases are summarized in Table 5.3.

Federal courts have ruled that although some aspects of prison life may be acceptable, the combination of various factors — the **totality of conditions** — may be such that life in the institution may constitute cruel and unusual punishment. This concept developed with the 1976 decision in *Pugh v. Locke.* Here federal district court Judge Frank M. Johnson, Jr., found that "the evidence . . . establishes that prison conditions

totality of conditions

The aggregate of circumstances in a correctional facility that, when considered as a whole, may violate the protections guaranteed by the Eighth Amendment, even though such guarantees are not violated by any single condition in the institution.

Table 5.2   Selected Interpretations of the Fourth Amendment as Applied to Prisoners

The Supreme Court has often considered the question of unreasonable searches and seizures.

Case	Decision
Bell v. Wolfish (1979)	Strip searches, including searches of body cavities after contact visits, may be carried out when the need for such searches outweighs the personal rights invaded.
Lee v. Downs (1981)	Staff members of one sex may not supervise inmates of the opposite sex in toilet and shower areas even if providing a staff member of the same sex is inconvenient to the administration.
U.S. v. Hitchcock (1972)	A warrantless search of a cell is not unreasonable, and documentary evidence found there is not subject to suppression in court. It is not reasonable to expect a prison cell to be accorded the same level of privacy as a home or automobile.
Hudson v. Palmer (1984)	Officials may search cells without a warrant and seize materials found there.

Table 5.3   Selected Interpretations of the Eighth Amendment as Applied to Prisoners

The Supreme Court is called on to determine whether correctional actions constitute cruel and unusual punishment.

Case	Decision
Ruiz v. Estelle (1975)	Conditions of confinement in the Texas prison system are unconstitutional.
Estelle v. Gamble (1976)	Deliberate indifference to serious medical needs of prisoners constitutes the unnecessary and wanton infliction of pain, and thus violates the Eighth Amendment.
Rhodes v. Chapman (1981)	Double-celling and crowding do not necessarily constitute cruel and unusual punishment. It must be shown that the conditions involve "wanton and unnecessary infliction of pain" and are "grossly disproportionate" to the severity of the crime warranting imprisonment.
Whitley v. Albers (1986)	A prisoner shot in the leg during a riot does not suffer cruel and unusual punishment if the action was taken in good faith to maintain discipline rather than for the mere purpose of causing harm.
Wilson v. Seiter (1991)	Prisoners must not only prove that prison conditions are objectively cruel and unusual but also show that they exist because of the deliberate indifference of officials.

[in Alabama] are so debilitating that they necessarily deprive inmates of any opportunity to rehabilitate themselves or even maintain skills already possessed."[40]

When courts have found brutality, unsanitary facilities, overcrowding, and inadequate food, judges have used the Eighth Amendment to order sweeping changes and, in some cases, even to take over administration of entire prisons or corrections systems. In these cases judges have ordered wardens to follow specific procedures and to spend money on certain improvements.

In several dramatic cases, prison conditions were shown to be so bad that judges have demanded such changes.[41] In *Ruiz v. Estelle* (1980), the court ordered the Texas prison system to address unconstitutional conditions. Judicial supervision of the system continued for a decade, finally ending in 1990. The impact of these reforms on the social structure of the prison are described more fully in the following Focus box.

In *Hutto v. Finney* (1978) the Supreme Court upheld a lower court's decision that confinement in Arkansas's segregation cells for more than thirty days was cruel and unusual punishment. In that decision the Court also summarized three principles with regard to the Eighth Amendment:

1. Courts should consider the totality of conditions of confinement.
2. Courts should specify in remedial orders each factor that contributed to the violation and that required a change in order to remove the unconstitutionality.
3. Where appropriate, courts should enunciate specific minimum standards that, if met, would remedy the total constitutional violation.[42]

FOCUS   The Impact of *Ruiz v. Estelle*

In December 1980 William W. Justice, federal judge for the Eastern District of Texas, issued a sweeping decree against the Texas Department of Corrections. He ordered prison officials to address a host of unconstitutional conditions, including overcrowding, unnecessary use of force by personnel, inadequate numbers of guards, poor health care practices, and a building-tender system that let some inmates control other inmates.

Eastham is a large maximum security institution housing recidivists (repeat offenders) over age 25 who have been in prison three or more times. It is tightly managed and has been the depository for troublemakers from other Texas prisons. To help with these hard-core criminals, the staff relied on a select group of inmates known as *building tenders (BTs)*. Co-opting the BTs with special privileges, officials used them and their assistants, the turnkeys, to handle the rank-and-file inmates.

In May 1982, Texas signed a consent decree, agreeing to dismantle the building tender system by January 1983. BTs were reassigned to ordinary prison jobs; stripped of their power, status, and duties; and moved to separate cell blocks for their protection. At the same time Eastham received 141 new officers, almost doubling the guard force, to help pick up the slack. These reforms were substantial and set off a series of shifts that fundamentally altered the guard and inmate societies.

Removing the BTs and turnkeys, restricting guards' unofficial use of force, and instituting a prisoner discipline system that emphasized due process, fairness, and rights, severely strained the traditional social structure of Eastham. Major upheavals took place in interpersonal relations between guards and inmates, in the organization of inmate society, and in the guard subculture and work roles.

Guards and Inmates

Ordinary inmates had formerly been subject to an all-encompassing, totalitarian system in which they were "dictated to, exploited, and kept in submission." But in the new relationship between keepers and kept, inmates challenged the authority of correctional officers and behaved in more confrontational and hostile ways. In response to verbal and other assaults on their authority, the guards cited inmates for breaking the rules. A number of factors changed the relationship between guards and inmates as a result, including the fact that there are now more guards, restrictions on guards mean physical reprisals are not feared, the guards no longer have BTs to act as intermediaries, and social distance between guards and prisoners has diminished. The last factor is important because one result of the civil rights movement is that prisoners were no longer viewed as "nonpersons." Inmates have rights

The Court has indicated that unless extreme conditions are found, the courts must defer to correctional officials and legislators. Yet the federal courts have intervened in states where institutional conditions or specific aspects of their operation have been found to violate the Eighth Amendment.

Of particular concern to correctional officials have been court orders requiring an end to overcrowding that violates the Eighth Amendment. For example, the courts have stated that cells must afford each inmate at least 60 square feet of floor space. However, in *Rhodes v. Chapman* (1981) the Supreme Court upheld that double-bunking (two inmates in a cell designed for one) in Ohio did not constitute a condition of cruel and unusual punishment.[43] To prove violation of the Eighth Amendment, the Court noted, it must be shown that the punishment either "inflicts unnecessary or wanton pain [or is] grossly disproportionate to the severity of the crime warranting punishment." Unless the conditions in the Ohio prison were "deplorable" or "sordid," the Court declared, the courts should defer to correctional authorities.[44]

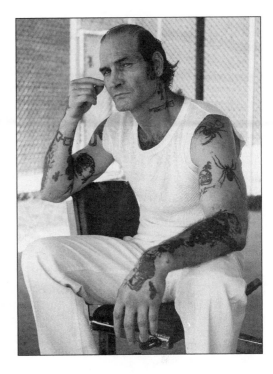

Until Ruiz v. Estelle, *the staff in many Texas prisons relied on a select group of inmates known as "building tenders" (BTs) to handle the rank-and-file. These BTs had extensive power over their fellow inmates.*

and may invoke due process rules to challenge decisions of guards and other officials. "Although the guards ultimately control the prison, they must now negotiate, compromise, or overlook many difficulties with inmates within the everyday control system."

Reorganization Within the Inmate Society

Purging the BT-turnkey system created a power vacuum characterized by uncertainty. One outcome was a rise in the amount of inmate–inmate violence. In the past, the BTs had helped to settle disputes among inmates; after the reform these conflicts more often led to violence in which weapons were used. Violent self-help became a social necessity. As personal violence escalated, so did inmate gang activities. Gang members knew that if they were threatened, assaulted, or robbed, they had to have help from others. For nongang prisoners, heightened personal insecurity meant that they had to rely on themselves and avoid contact with inmates known for their toughness.

Guard Subculture and Work Role

The court-imposed reforms upset the foundations of the guard subculture and work role. The guards' world of work is no longer well ordered, predictable, or rewarding. One aspect of the change has been that rank-and-file guards fear the inmates more. On removal of the BTs, guards took

cell block duty for the first time, in close contact with inmates. Most guards were new to prison work, so they hesitated to enforce order. Many officers believed that because they could not physically punish inmates and their supervisors did not back them up, it was better not to enforce the rules at all. They thought that their authority had been undermined and that the new disciplinary process was frustrating. Many preferred simply to look the other way.

The court-ordered reforms brought Eastham's operations more into line with constitutional requirements of fairness and due process but disrupted an ongoing social system. Before the *Ruiz* decision the administration had run the prison on the basis of paternalism, coercion, dominance, and fear. Guards exercised much discretion over inmates, and used BTs to help maintain order and provide information. During the transition to a new bureaucratic and legal order, levels of violence and personal insecurity increased. Authority eroded, relations between inmates and officers became combative, and inmate gangs developed to provide security and autonomy for members.

Judicial supervision of the Texas prison system as a result of this case lasted for a decade and ended on March 31, 1990. And an overriding question still remains: Can a prison be administered in ways that conform to the requirements of fairness and due process yet maintain security for the inmates and staff?

Source: Adapted from James W. Marquart and Ben M. Crouch, "Judicial Reform and Prisoner Control: The Impact of *Ruiz v. Estelle* on a Texas Penitentiary," *Law and Society Review,* 19, 1985, pp. 557–586.

The Fourteenth Amendment

Amendment XIV: All persons born or naturalized in the United States, and subject to the jurisdiction thereof, are citizens of the United States and of the state wherein they reside. No state shall make or enforce any law which shall abridge the privileges or immunities of citizens of the United States; nor shall any state deprive any person of life, liberty, or property without due process of law, nor deny to any person within its jurisdiction the equal protection of the laws.

One word and two clauses of the Fourteenth Amendment are relevant to the question of prisoners' rights. The relevant word is *state,* which is found in several clauses of the Fourteenth Amendment. Remember that by the 1970s the Supreme Court had ruled that through the Fourteenth Amendment, the Bill of Rights restricts state governments.

procedural due process clause

The constitutional guarantee that no agent or instrumentality of government will use any procedures to arrest, prosecute, try, or punish any person other than by those procedures prescribed by law.

The first important clause concerns procedural due process. **Procedural due process** requires that all people must be treated fairly and justly by government officials and that decisions must be made according to procedures prescribed by law. Prisoners have filed claims based on the due process clause when they believe that state statutes or administrative procedures have not been followed regarding, for example, parole release, intraprison transfers, transfers to administrative segregation, and disciplinary hearings.

The **equal protection** clause is the second important clause with respect to prisoners. Claims that prisoners have been denied equal protection of the law are based on claims of racial, gender, or religious discrimination.

equal protection clause

The constitutional guarantee that the law will be applied equally to all persons, without regard for such individual characteristics as gender, race, and religion.

Due Process in Prison Discipline   Administrators have the discretion to discipline inmates who break institutional rules. Until the 1960s disciplinary procedures could be exercised without challenge, because the prisoner was physically confined, lacked communication with the outside, and was legally in the hands of the state. In addition, formal rules of prison conduct either did not exist or were vague. For example, disrespect toward a correctional officer was an infraction, but the characteristics of "disrespect" were not defined. The word of the correctional officer was accepted, and the inmate had little opportunity to challenge the charges.

In a series of decisions in the 1970s, the Supreme Court began to insist that the most sensitive of institutional decisions—the decisions by which inmates are sent to solitary confinement and the methods by which good-time credit may be taken away because of misconduct—must follow procedural due process.

The 1974 case of *Wolff v. McDonnell* extended certain due process rights.[45] The Supreme Court specified that when a prisoner faces serious disciplinary action that may result in the withdrawal of good time or segregation, the state must follow certain minimal procedures that conform to the guarantee of due process:

1. The prisoner must be given twenty-four-hour written notice of the charges.
2. The prisoner has the right to present witnesses and documentary evidence in defense against the charges.
3. The prisoner has the right to a hearing before an impartial body.
4. The prisoner has the right to receive a written statement from that body concerning the outcome of the hearing.

However, the Court also recognized the special conditions of incarceration and stated that prisoners do not have the right to cross-examine witnesses and that the evidence presented by the offender may not be unduly hazardous to institutional safety or correctional goals. [46]

As a result of the Supreme Court's decisions, some of which are outlined in Table 5.4, most prisons have established rules that provide some elements of due process in disciplinary proceedings. In many institutions a disciplinary committee receives charges, conducts hearings, and decides guilt and punishment. Such committees are usually made up of administrative personnel, but sometimes inmates or citizens from the out-

Table 5.4 Selected Interpretations of the Fourteenth Amendment as Applied to Prisoners

The Supreme Court has ruled concerning procedural due process and equal protection.

Case	Decision
Wolff v. McDonnell (1974)	The basic elements of procedural due process must be present when decisions are made concerning the disciplining of an inmate.
Baxter v. Palmigiano (1976)	Although due process must be accorded, an inmate has no right to counsel in a disciplinary hearing.
Vitek v. Jones (1980)	The involuntary transfer of a prisoner to a mental hospital requires a hearing and other minimal elements of due process such as notice and the availability of counsel.
Sandin v. Conner (1995)	Transfer to disciplinary segregation is not the type of atypical, significant deprivation of liberty that requires due process protections as outlined in *Wolff*.

side are included. Even with these protections, prisoners are still powerless and may risk further punishment if they challenge the warden's decisions too vigorously.

Equal Protection   In 1968 the Supreme Court firmly established that racial discrimination may not be official policy within prison walls.[47] Segregation can be justified only as a temporary expedient during periods when violence between races is demonstrably imminent. Equal protection claims have also been upheld in relation to religious freedoms and access to reading materials of interest to racial minorities. For instance, cases brought by members of the Black Muslim religion, discussed previously, concerned both the First Amendment right to religious freedom and the Fourteenth Amendment right to equal protection.

The most recent cases concerning equal protection deal with issues concerning female offenders. Although the U.S. Supreme Court has yet to rule, state and lower federal courts have considered a number of cases. In *Pargo v. Elliott* (1995), Iowa female inmates argued that their equal protection rights were violated because programs and services were not at the same level as those provided male inmates. The court ruled that because of differences and needs, identical treatment is not required for men and women. It concluded that there was no evidence of "invidious discrimination." In the next few years the U.S. Supreme Court is likely to consider equal protection for female prisoners.

A Change in Judicial Direction

During its early years, the prisoners' rights movement won noteworthy victories. As noted, the Supreme Court's decision in *Cooper v. Pate* (1964) allowed prisoners to sue state officials in the federal courts when their constitutional rights had been denied. But not until 1974, in *Wolff v. McDonnell,* did the Court provide "the kind of clarion statement that could serve as a rallying call for prisoners' rights advocates."[48] In that case Justice Byron White, speaking for the Court, wrote,

> *Lawful imprisonment necessarily makes unavailable many rights and privileges of the ordinary citizen, a retraction justified by the considerations underlying our penal system. . . . But though his rights may be diminished by the needs and exigencies of the institutional environment, a prisoner is not wholly stripped of constitutional protections when he is imprisoned for crime.*[49]

This language, and that contained in the Court's decisions in several subsequent cases, gave prisoners' rights advocates the feeling that the Supreme Court was backing their efforts.

During the last twenty years, the Supreme Court has been less supportive of expanding prisoners' rights, and a few decisions reflect a retreat. In *Bell v. Wolfish* (1979), the Court asked if the particular restrictions under question were intended as punishment or as an "incident of some other legitimate governmental purpose." The justices also seemed at great pains to say that "Prison administrators ...should be accorded wide-ranging deference in the adoption and executing of policies."[50] This ruling was followed by *Rhodes v. Chapman* (1981), in which the Court held that to prove an Eighth Amendment violation, the inmate must show the punishment was unnecessary or out of proportion to the prison rule violation. Again, the justices said that in most cases the court should defer to correctional authorities.[51]

The emergence of the doctrine that "due deference" must be given to administrators to run their prisons has struck some observers as a return to the hands-off doctrine.[52] Yet the justices seem to distinguish between the two doctrines, expressing a willingness to hear cases involving substantive rights issues but being unwilling to intervene in problems of administration. This distinction is explained in a 1985 federal circuit court opinion:

> In the great majority of cases it would be sheer folly for society to deny prison officials discretion to act in accordance with their professional judgment. At the same time it would be an abrogation of our responsibility as judges to assume such judgments (or, more precisely, to reassume) a "hands-off" posture, requiring categorical acquiescence in such judgments.[53]

The concept of deliberate indifference surfaced in *Daniels v. Williams* (1986). Here the Court said that an inmate could sue for damages only if officials had inflicted injury intentionally or deliberately.[54] This reasoning was extended in *Wilson v. Seiter* (1991), where the Court ruled that a prisoner's conditions of confinement are not unconstitutional unless it can be shown that administrators had acted with "deliberate indifference" to basic human needs.[55] The opinion cites *Estelle v. Gamble* (1976) and *Whitley v. Alpers* (1986) as other Eighth Amendment cases requiring a showing of correctional officials' motives to prove a constitutional violation.[56]

Many scholars believe that the "deliberate indifference" requirement indicates a shift from objective criteria (proof that the inmate suffered conditions protected by the Eighth Amendment) to subjective criteria (the state of mind of correctional officials, namely deliberate indifference) in determining whether prison conditions are unconstitutional.[57] Other scholars believe the impact of *Wilson* will not be great.[58]

That the pace of prisoners' rights cases may be slowed even further is indicated by *McCleskey v. Zant* (1991), which limits access to the federal courts. Here the Court ruled that all habeas corpus claims must be raised in the initial petition.[59] Also, in *Colman v. Thompson* (1991) it stated that a habeas petition should not be considered even when attorney error resulted in violations of state procedural rules.[60] Thus, although prisoners have a right to access to the courts via law libraries and the help of fellow inmates, in reality access has diminished, especially for prisoners who lack counsel and are likely to be tripped up by the stricter procedural rules.

Today the pace of civil rights litigation, compared to the 1970s under the Warren and Burger courts, has definitely slowed. Litigation by prisoners continues, but victories are less frequent. Apparently, having carved out a portion of the Bill of Rights applicable to prisoners, the justices are not interested in expanding that area.

In 1996, Congress passed the Prisoner Litigation Reform Act, limiting the authority of federal judges to interfere in the operations of correctional institutions. To stem the number of Section 1983 cases, this act made it difficult for prisoners to file cases without paying court fees, a problem for most inmates. Since the Act was passed there has been a drop in Section 1983 filings.[61]

Although the Supreme Court and Congress have cooled off toward prisoners' claims, the lower federal courts and many state courts continue to support judicial intervention to uphold civil rights. A return to a strict hands-off policy seems highly unlikely, but the courts are giving greater deference to prison administrators.

Impact of the Prisoners' Rights Movement

The prisoners' rights movement can be credited with general changes in American corrections since the late 1970s.[62] The most obvious are improved institutional conditions and administrative practices. Law libraries and legal assistance are now generally available, communication with the outside is easier, religious practices are protected, inmate complaint procedures have been developed, and due process requirements are emphasized. Prisoners in solitary confinement undoubtedly suffer less neglect than before. Although overcrowding is still a major problem, many conditions have much improved and the more brutalizing elements of prison life have diminished.[63]

Individual cases may have made only a dent in correctional bureaucracies, but over time real changes have occurred. The prisoners' rights movement has clearly influenced correctional officials. The threat of lawsuits and public exposure has placed many in the correctional bureaucracy on guard. On the one hand, it can be argued that this wariness has merely further bureaucratized corrections, requiring staff to prepare extensive and time-consuming documentation of their actions to protect themselves from lawsuits. On the other hand, judicial intervention has forced corrections to rethink existing procedures and organizational structures. As part of the wider changes in the "new corrections," new administrators, increased funding, reformulated policies, and improved management procedures were, at least in part, influenced by the prisoners' rights movement.

Extending constitutional rights to prisoners has by no means been a speedy process, and the courts have addressed only limited areas of the law. The impact of these decisions on the actual behavior of correctional officials has not yet been measured, but evidence suggests that court decisions have had a broad effect. Wardens and the subordinates may now be refraining from traditional disciplinary actions that might result in judicial intervention. In sum, after 200 years of judicial neglect of the conditions under which prisoners are held, courts have begun to look more closely at the situation of the incarcerated.

Alternatives to Litigation

Although many prisoners do have legitimate claims, correctional specialists, judges, and even litigators are questioning the suitability of lawsuits as the only means to resolve such claims. Each year more than 42,000 state prisoners petition the federal courts to halt certain correctional practices or to seek monetary awards for damages. The courts deem many of these suits frivolous and dismiss them for failure to state legitimate claims. Among the remainder only a few are decided in ways that affect anyone but the litigant.

Litigation is a cumbersome, costly, and often ineffective way to handle such claims. Except for class action and isolated individual grievances, most prisoner cases resemble disputes settled in small claims courts. As former Chief Justice Burger has said, "Federal judges should not be dealing with prisoner complaints which, although important to a prisoner, are so minor that any well-run institution should be able to resolve them fairly without resort to federal judges."[64]

Still another problem is that, although most suits that prisoners file under 42 U.S.C. 1983 are dismissed before trial, the remaining cases force correctional officials to spend time and resources in litigation, to face the possibility of being sued personally, and to risk the erosion of their leadership. Correctional administrators have charged that much prisoner litigation is designed merely to hassle them.[65]

From the prisoner's perspective litigation may be neither effective nor satisfying. Most prisoners face three problems: (1) they generally lack legal representation, (2) constitutional standards are difficult to meet, and (3) even if a suit succeeds, changes in policies or financial compensation may be slow in coming.

Legal assistance attorneys are often able to "nip a problem in the bud" before it develops into a major controversy.

Four alternatives to litigation have been incorporated in the corrections systems of various states: (1) inmate grievance procedures, (2) an ombudsman, (3) mediation, and (4) legal assistance. All are designed to solve problems before the inmate feels compelled to file suit, but mediation and legal assistance also may be invoked after a suit has been initiated.

Inmate Grievance Procedures

Although informal procedures for hearing inmates' complaints have existed for many years, only since the mid-1970s have formal grievance mechanisms been widely used. All states and the Federal Bureau of Prisons now have grievance procedures.

A three-step inmate grievance process is used in most corrections systems. A staff member or committee in each institution usually receives complaints, investigates them, and makes decisions. If the prisoner is dissatisfied with the outcome, the case may then be appealed to the warden and ultimately to the commissioner of corrections.

Reports indicate that some grievances are more easily resolved than others. For example, many inmates complain they are not receiving proper medical treatment, but because medical personnel can usually document the treatment provided, such complaints normally subside. The many complaints of lost personal property are another matter. Most involve items deposited at the reception center at the time of arrival, but not transferred with the prisoner to another institution. Staff members often cannot account for missing property, and the process for receiving compensation for property lost or damaged can be complicated. Probably the most difficult situation to resolve is alleged brutality by a guard. Such a complaint virtually always comes down to the inmate's word against the officer's, because staff members rarely will testify against each other.

The inmate grievance procedure is useful for defusing tensions in correctional facilities. It is also a useful management tool. By attentively monitoring the complaint process, a warden can discern patterns of inmate discontent and act to prevent more serious problems from developing.

ombudsman

A public official who investigates complaints against government officials and recommends corrective measures.

mediation

Intervention in a dispute by a third party to whom the parties in conflict submit their differences for resolution and whose decision (in the correctional setting) is binding on both parties.

The Ombudsman

Ombudsman programs (which originated in Sweden) are the second most common dispute resolution mechanism in corrections and have been used successfully throughout the United States for more than a decade. An ombudsman is a public official with full authority to investigate citizens' complaints against government officials.

Ombudsman programs are successful if inmates have quick and easy access to the office. When inmates respect ombudsmen, their advice may help reduce the number of frivolous claims; when they see merit in claims, they can try to convince authorities it would be in their interest to resolve the matters out of court.

Mediation

Mediation is a consensual and voluntary process in which a neutral third party helps the disputants reconcile their differences. The informality of the process contrasts with complex, cumbersome courtroom procedures. Proponents point out that in the mediation process straightforward questions can be asked so that underlying issues may be explored. This feature is of special advantage to prisoners, most of whom would not have legal counsel if they took their cases to court. Mediation is particularly effective when the essence of a complaint is not a conflict of abstract principles, but an administrative problem requiring an administrative solution. However, it has not lived up to its potential in the correctional arena because in many cases neither party seems willing to be bound by the decision.

Legal Assistance

As noted previously, the Supreme Court has emphasized that prisoners must have access to legal resources so that they may seek postconviction relief.[66] Since the early 1970s several legal assistance mechanisms have been developed in correctional institutions, including providing staff attorneys to help inmates with legal problems, inmate ("jailhouse") lawyers, and law school clinics.

Providing legal assistance may seem counterproductive if the goal of correctional administrators is to avoid litigation, but lawyers do more than simply help prisoners file suits. They also advise their clients as to the legal merits of their complaints and thus are in a position to discourage frivolous suits. Further, counsel can help determine the underlying issues of a complaint and therefore can frame questions in terms that will be understood by other people who have legal training.

Law and Community Corrections

Although public attention and most correctional law concerns prisons and jails, less than one-third of adults under supervision are incarcerated; two-thirds live in the community on probation and parole. However, as with prisoners, offenders in the community are not without rights and courts have addressed issues concerning due process and searches and seizures.

As discussed in Chapter 4, probation is a type of community sentence whereas parolees are offenders released to community supervision after spending a portion of their sentence in prison. Probation is imposed by a judge and is administered by probation officers. Parole is usually granted by a parole board and is administered by parole officers. Eligibility for parole is stated in the law, as are the release criteria. Even in states with determinate sentencing and mandatory release, parolees are supervised for a specified length of time.

There is no *right* to parole. In *Greenholtz v. Inmates of the Nebraska Penal and Correction Complex* (1979), the U.S. Supreme Court made it clear that the state grants release on parole and that there is no right to be conditionally released before expiration of a sentence.[67] Supporting the authority of parole and pardons boards, the Court ruled in *Connecticut Board of Pardons v. Dumschat* (1981) that an inmate did not have a right to a hearing before the board. The Court also ruled that although Dumschat claimed he had some expectation of receiving a commutation because 85 to 90 percent of lifers had been released, there was no legal basis for this contention.[68]

Constitutional Rights of Probationers and Parolees

While living in the community as probationers or parolees, offenders must live according to conditions specified at the time of their sentencing or parole release. If these conditions are violated community supervision may be revoked and the offender sent to prison for the rest of the sentence. But does this mean probationers and parolees do not enjoy the constitutional rights of ordinary citizens? As Justice Scalia has said, "It is always true of probationers (as we have said it to be true of parolees) that they do not

Convicted child rapist
Michael P. Nickerson listens
during a hearing to revoke
his parole in Brockton
(Mass.) Superior Court.
Three weeks after being
released from prison, he was
found carrying a knife and
hanging around with two
teenage boys.

enjoy 'the absolute liberty to which every citizen is entitled, but only . . . conditional liberty properly dependent on observation of special restrictions.'"[69]

The conditions placed on probationers and parolees may interfere with their constitutional rights. The conditions typically limit the right of free association by restricting offenders from contact with their crime partners or victims. But courts have struck down conditions preventing parolees from giving public speeches and receiving publications. The case of *Griffin v. Wisconsin* (1987) is a good example of the clash between the Bill of Rights and community corrections.[70] Learning that Griffin might have a gun, probation officers searched his apartment without a warrant. The Supreme Court noted the practical problems of obtaining a search warrant while the probationer was under supervision. The Court said the probation agency must be able to act before the offender damaged himself or society. In Griffin's case the Court felt that the agency had satisfied the Fourth Amendment's reasonableness requirement.

In a 1998 case, *Pennsylvania Board of Probation v. Scott,* a closely divided Court ruled that evidence that would be barred by the exclusionary rule from use by the prosecution in a criminal trial, can be used in parole revocation hearings.[71] Officers, without a search warrant, found guns in the home of a paroled murderer who was barred from owning weapons. The Court upheld revocation of the offender's probation.

Revocation of Probation and Parole

When probationers or parolees do not obey their conditions of release they may be sent to prison. As fully discussed in Chapters 8 and 16, if the offender commits another crime parole or probation will likely be revoked. For minor violations of the conditions (such as missing an AA meeting), the supervising officer has discretion as to whether to ask for revocation.

The Supreme Court has addressed the question of due process revocation. In the case of *Morrissey v. Brewer* (1972), the Court held that a parolee who faces revocation must be given due process with a prompt informal inquiry before an impartial hearing officer. However, the Court distinguished the requirements of such a proceeding from the normal requirements of a criminal trial. For example, attorneys are not involved. The Court required a two-step revocation hearing process. In the first stage, a hearing officer determines whether there is probable cause that a violation has occurred. The parolees have the right to be notified of the charges against them, to know the evidence against them, to be allowed to speak on their own behalf, to present witnesses, and to confront the witnesses against them. In the second stage, the revocation hearing, the parolee must receive a notice of charges and the evidence of the violation disclosed.

The parolee may cross-examine witnesses. The hearing body determines if the violation is sufficiently severe to warrant revocation. It must give the parolee a written statement outlining the evidence and giving reasons for the decision.

In the following year the Supreme Court applied the *Morrissey* procedures to probation revocation proceedings in *Gagnon v. Scarpelli* (1973). But in *Gagnon* the Court also looked at the question of the right to counsel. It ruled that there was no absolute requirement but that in some cases probationers and parolees might request counsel, which should be allowed on a case-by-case basis depending on the complexity of the issues, mitigating circumstances, and the competence of the offender.

Law and Corrections Personnel

Just as law governs relationships among corrections personnel, inmates, probationers, and parolees, laws and regulations also define relationships between administrators and their staff. With the exception of those working for private, nonprofit organizations, most corrections personnel are public employees. Two aspects of corrections work merit consideration. First, as public employees all corrections workers are governed by civil service rules and regulations. Second, correctional clients may sue state officials using Section 1983 of the United States Code. We now need to examine the liability of corrections personnel with regard to these suits.

Civil Service Laws

From the time a public employee is recruited until he or she leaves public service, civil service rules and regulations govern the work environment. Civil service laws set the procedures for hiring, promoting, assigning, disciplining, and firing public employees. Public employees are protected from arbitrary actions by their supervisors by these laws. Workplace rules also develop through collective bargaining agreements between unions and the government. Where corrections personnel are able to join unions, the bargaining process develops rules concerning assignments, working conditions, and grievance procedures. These agreements have the force of law.

Like their counterparts in the private sector, government employees are protected from discrimination. With the Civil Rights Act of 1964, Congress prohibited discrimination in employment based on race, gender, national origin, and religion. Subsequent federal legislation prohibits discrimination against people with disabilities (Americans with Disabilities Act) and age discrimination (Age Discrimination in Employment Act). States have their own antidiscrimination laws. All these laws have increased the number of minorities and women who work in corrections.

Unlike many public employees, people who work in corrections are in a difficult position. Offenders have not chosen to be incarcerated or supervised in the community. They thus do not look on correctional personnel as offering them assistance.

Corrections employees must assert authority to control the behavior of people who have shown they lack self-control or have little regard for society's rules. Whether in prison, in a probationer's home, or on the street, this responsibility creates pressures and difficult—sometimes dangerous—situations.

Corrections personnel also face pressures from their supervisors. They are monitored by supervisors who may not always appreciate the quick decisions that must be made on the "front line." If they expect to succeed in their jobs and gain promotions, they must carry out their duties in a professional manner that will please their supervisors.

Liability of Correctional Personnel

In *Cooper v. Pate* (1964) the Supreme Court said that Section 1983—the federal civil rights statute—provides a means for prisoners, but also probationers and parolees, to bring lawsuits against corrections officials. The statute says that "any person" who deprives others of their constitutional rights while acting under the authority of law may be liable in a lawsuit.[72]

In subsequent decisions the Court further clarified the meaning of Section 1983. In *Monell v. Department of Social Services for the City of New York* (1978), the Court said that individual officers and the agency may be sued when a person's civil rights are violated by the agency's "customs and usages." If an individual can show that harm was caused by employees whose wrongful acts were the result of these "customs, practices, and policies, including poor training and supervision," then the employees can be sued.[73]

In Section 1983 litigation, corrections employees may be sued as individuals in their personal capacity, as opposed to their official capacity as a state employee. Usually attorneys for the state will defend the case and most states will assume responsibility for any financial damages awarded the plaintiff. However, if the court finds the employee to have acted intentionally or maliciously or to have committed a criminal act against a client, he or she may be responsible for paying the legal defense costs and the damages that the jury awards.

How should the corrections workers protect themselves from civil rights suits? Clair Cripe, former general counsel, Federal Bureau of Prisons, suggests five rules for corrections employees.[74] First, follow agency policies and the instructions of supervisors. By following policies the staff member will be in step with the professional expectations of the agency's management. From a legal standpoint the employee should follow the policies to ensure compliance with legal standards and avoid liability from a lawsuit. The second rule is to obtain good training. Staff need to know the areas of their performance in which there are the greatest exposure to liability. Third, become familiar with the law directly affecting the job. This is true whatever the specialty—casework, security, health care, probation, parole, or institutional programs. To ensure a good defense when being sued, Cripe suggests a fourth rule—find a good mentor. Although correctional workers receive formal training, on the job they gain much knowledge of how things "really" work. As he says, "Be patient, learn from the good and respected workers around you." Finally, keep good records. If you are called to testify at a trial or grievance hearing, good records are invaluable.

Although huge financial settlements make headlines and the number of Section 1983 filings are large, few cases come to trial and very few corrections employees must personally pay financial awards to plaintiffs. However, no correctional employee wants to be involved in such legal situations. Not only are they time-consuming and emotionally draining, but the mere fact of being sued can seriously damage a professional career.

Summary

Until the 1960s the courts were not concerned with the administration of prisons and the rights of inmates. With the civil rights movement and the extension of due process rights by the U.S. Supreme Court, prisoners and their supporters pushed to secure rights for inmates. After prisoners' rights advocates won initial successes with regard to portions of the First Amendment, the courts also required that other amendments govern prison conditions.

The foundations of offenders' rights are the U.S. Constitution, the constitution of the state in which the institution is located, statutes, case law, and regulations. In particular, the First, Fourth, Eighth, and Fourteenth Amendments to the U.S. Constitution have been important bases for the extension of rights.

Litigation is not always the best way to secure the rights of prisoners and to correct institutional conditions. Many lawsuits brought by prisoners have been dismissed as frivolous, improperly drafted, outside the court's jurisdiction, and filed in quest of solutions that are difficult to implement. Alternatives to litigation, including inmate grievance procedures, ombudsmen, mediation, and legal assistance, now have a place in most corrections systems.

Although much law in the correctional setting focuses on prisons, probationers and parolees also have rights. However, under certain circumstances the rights of free citizens may be limited for offenders in the community. In several decisions the Supreme Court has ruled that elements of due process must be part of any revocation process.

Law also governs relations between corrections personnel and their supervisors. Civil service rules stipulate the procedures that govern most aspects of public employment. Corrections personnel need to be aware of their liability in the workplace and follow rules to protect them from actions that may bring on a lawsuit.

As basic rights have been extended to offenders, the past three decades often have been turbulent. The courts have insisted that fundamentally unfair practices be abolished, and judges have exerted their influence to change corrections systems. Many correctional officials have opposed some of these moves, yet most now agree that the impact has generally been positive. ∎

For Discussion

1. After the courts abandoned the hands-off policy, what problems did correctional administrators encounter?

2. What difficulties might you, as a correctional officer, foresee in attempting to run your unit of the institution while at the same time upholding the legal rights of the prisoners?

3. Suppose that you are a prison warden. What if a group of prisoners calling themselves the "Sons of the Purple Flower" and claiming to be a religious organization requested a special diet and permission to chant when the moon is full as part of their First Amendment rights? How would you determine whether you must grant these requests?

4. What can a correctional employee do to reduce the potential for lawsuits contesting conditions of confinement?

For Further Reading

Carroll, Leo. *Lawful Order: A Case Study of Correctional Crisis and Reform.* New York: Garland, 1998. Examination of the Rhode Island prison system over a twenty-five-year period, focusing on the impact of *Palmigiano v. Garrahy.*

Cripe, Clair A. *Legal Aspects of Corrections Management.* Gaithersburg, MD: Aspen, 1997. An excellent text geared primarily to correctional administrators.

DiIulio, John J., Jr., ed. *Courts, Corrections, and the Constitution.* New York: Oxford University Press, 1990. Contains a collection of essays that examine the capacity of judges to intervene in ways that improve the quality of life behind bars.

Martin, Steve J., and Ekland-Olson, Sheldon. *Texas Prisons: The Walls Came Tumbling Down.* Austin: Texas Monthly Press, 1987. Recounts the history of the Texas prison system, focusing on the rise of the writ-writers, the case of *Ruiz v. Estelle,* and the impact of Judge William Justice's decision.

Mushlin, Michael B. *Rights of Prisoners.* 2nd ed. Colorado Springs, CO: Shepard's/McGraw-Hill, 1993. Provides an excellent overview of prisoners' rights law. 2 vols.

Smith, Christopher E. *Law and Contemporary Corrections.* Belmont, CA: Wadsworth, 1999.

Notes

1. Hudson v. McMillian, 503 U.S. 1 (1992).
2. *Riffin v. Commonwealth,* 62 Va. 790 (1871).
3. James B. Jacobs, *New Perspectives on Prisons and Imprisonment* (Ithaca, NY: Cornell University Press, 1983), p. 35.
4. *Sterling v. Cupp,* 290 Ore. 611, 625 P.2d 123 (1981); *Delancie v. Superior Court of San Mateo County,* 31 Cal.3d 865 (1982).
5. *Pennsylvania v. Yeskey,* No. 97-634 (1998).
6. *Ford v. Wainwright,* 477 U.S. 399 (1986)

7. *Ruffin v. Commonwealth*, 62 Va. 790 (1871)

8. *Cooper v. Pate*, 378 U.S. 546 (1964).

9. References are often made to Section 1983 petitions. These are petitions filed in federal courts by state prisoners in which they seek civil damages from public officials (usually correctional officers) for violating their constitutional rights.

10. Note that federal prisoners cannot use Section 1983 to bring suits charging federal officials of violating their constitutional rights. But the Supreme Court in *Bivens v. Six Unknown Federal Narcotics Agents*, 403 U.S. 388 (1971) and later cases has allowed federal prisoners to sue federal officials. Thus federal prisoners bring "Bivens suits," and not Section 1983 actions.

11. Clair A. Cripe, *Legal Aspects of Corrections Management* (Gaithersburg, MD: Aspen, 1997), p. 53.

12. Jacobs, *New Perspectives*, p. 37.

13. Fred Cheesman, II, Roger A. Hanson, and Brian J. Ostrom, "To Augur Well: Future Prison Population and Prisoner Litigation," paper presented at the Federal Judicial Center, Washington, DC, May 20, 1998.

14. Roger A. Hanson and Henry W. K. Daley, *Challenging the Conditions of Prisons and Jails: A Report on Section 1983 Ligitation* (Washington, DC: Bureau of Justice Statistics, 1995).

15. Cheesman, Hanson, and Ostrom.

16. *Johnson v. Avery*, 393 U.S. 413 (1967).

17. *Bounds v. Smith*, 430 U.S. 817 (1977).

18. *Lewis v. Casey*, 64, U.S.L.W 4587 (1996).

19. *Brooks v. Florida*, 389 U.S. 413 (1967).

20. *Holt v. Sarver*, 442 F.2d 308 (8th Cir. 1971).

21. Michael Mushlin, *Rights of Prisoners*, 2nd ed. (Colorado Springs, CO: Shepard's/McGraw-Hill, 1993), p. 257.

22. *Brown v. Wainwright*, 419 F.2d 1308 (5th Cir. 1969).

23. *Pepperling v. Crist*, 678 F.2d 787 (9th Cir. 1982). However, the U.S. Court of Appeals for the Seventh Circuit, in *Trapnell v. Riggsbuy*, 622 F.2d 290 (7th Cir. 1980), found absolute prohibition a "narrowly drawn and carefully limited response to a valid security problem."

24. *Sostre v. Otis*, 330 F.Supp. 941 (S.D.N.Y. 1971).

25. *Turner v. Safley*, 482 U.S. 78 (1987).

26. John McLaren, "Prisoners' Rights: The Pendulum Swings," in Joycelyn M. Pollock, ed., *Prisons: Today and Tomorrow* (Gaithersburg, MD: Aspen, 1997), p. 357. See also *O'Lone v. Estate of Shabazz*, 107 S.Ct. 2400 (1987).

27. *Procunier v. Martinez*, 416 U.S. 396 (1974).

28. *Turner v. Safley*.

29. *Thornburgh v. Abbott*, 490 U.S. 401 (1989).

30. *Fulwood v. Clemmer*, 206 F.Supp. 370 (D.C. Cir. 1962).

31. *Cruz v. Beto*, 450 U.S. 319 (1972).

32. *O'Lone v. Estate of Shabazz*, 482 U.S. 342 (1987).

33. 2000bb.

34. *Employment Division of Oregon v. Smith*, 494 U.S. 872 (1990).

35. Jack E. Call and Charles Samarkos, "RFRA: Which Test Is Best?" *Corrections Today*, 58, April 1996, pp. 136–142.

36. *Hudson v. Palmer*, 468 U.S. 517 (1984).

37. *Smith v. Fairman*, 678 F.2d 52 (7th Cir. 1982).

38. *Lee v. Downs*, 641 F.2d 1117 (4th Cir. 1981).

39. *Smith v. Fairman*.

40. *Pubh v. Locke*, 406 F.2d 318 (1976).

41. Bradley S. Chilton, *Prisons Under the Gavel: The Federal Court Takeover of Georgia Prisons* (Columbus: Ohio State University Press, 1991).

42. *Hutto v. Finney*, 98 S.Ct.2565 (1978).

43. *Rhodes v. Chapman*, 452 U.S. 337 (1981).

44. Ibid.

45. *Wolff v. McDonnell*, 418 U.S. 539 (1974).

46. Ibid.

47. *Lee v. Washington*, 390 U.S. 333 (1968).

48. Jacobs, p. 42.

49. *Wolff v. McDonnell*, 418 U.S. 539 (1974).

50. *Bell v. Wolfish*, 441 U.S. 520 (1979).

51. *Rhodes v. Chapman*.

52. Charles H. Jones, "Recent Trends in Corrections and Prisoners' Rights Law," in Clayton A. Hartjen and Edward E. Rhine, eds., *Correctional Theory and Practice* (Chicago: Nelson Hall, 1992), p. 119.

53. *Abdul Wali v. Coughlin*, 754 F.2d 1015 (2nd Cir. 1985).

54. *Daniels v. Williams*, 474 U.S. 327 (1986).

55. *Wilson v. Seiter*, 111 S.Ct. 2321 (1991).

56. *Estelle v. Gamble*, 429 U.S. 97 (1976); *Whitley v. Albers*, 475 U.S. 312 (1986).

57. Christer E. Smith, "Justice Antonin Scalia and Criminal Justice Cases," *Kentucky Law Journal*, 81, 1991–1992, p. 207.

58. Jack E. Call, "Prison Overcrowding Cases in the Aftermath of Wilson v. Seiter," *The Prison Journal,* 75, September 1995, pp. 390–405.

59. *McCleskey v. Zant,* 111 S.Ct. 1454 (1991).

60. *Colman v. Thompson,* 111 S.Ct. 2546 (1991).

61. Cheesman, Hanson, and Ostrom.

62. Malcolm M. Feeley and Roger A. Hanson, "The Impact of Judicial Intervention on Prisons and Jails: A Framework of Analysis and a Review of the Literature," in John J. DiIulio, Jr., ed., *Courts, Corrections, and the Constitution* (New York: Oxford University Press, 1990), p. 12.

63. James B. Jacobs, "Judicial Impact on Prison Reform," in Thomas G. Blomberg and Stanley Cohen, eds., *Punishment and Social Control* (New York: Aldine DeGruyter, 1995), pp. 63–76.

64. Warren E. Burger, "Chief Justice Burger Issues Year-End Report," *American Bar Association Journal,* 62, 1976, pp. 189–190.

65. Jeffrey H. Maahs and Rolando V. del Carmen, "Curtailing Frivolous Section 1983 Inmate Litigation: Laws, Practices, and Proposals," *Federal Probation,* 59, December 1995, pp. 53–61.

66. *Johnson v. Avery,* 393 U.S. 499 (1969).

67. *Greenholtz v. Inmates of the Nebraska Penal and Correction Complex,* 442 U.S. 1 (1979).

68. *Connecticut Board of Pardons v. Dumschat,* 452 U.S. 458 (1981).

69. *Griffin v. Wisconsin, 483 U.S. 868 (1987).*

70. *Griffin v. Wisconsin.*

71. *Pennsylvania Board of Probation v. Scott,* No. 97-581 (1998)

72. *Cooper v. Pate,* 378 U.S. 546 (1964).

73. *Monell v. Department of Social Services for the City of New York,* 436 U.S. 658 (1978).

74. Clair A. Cripe, *Legal Aspects of Corrections Management* (Gaithersburg, MD: Aspen, 1997), pp. 75–77.

The Correctional Client

C hances are, someone in this class with you, studying corrections, has been incarcerated. In fact, it is likely that more than one of your class members has been to jail, probably just an overnight stay for some public order infraction or another. Perhaps one of your fellow students has been to prison as well and has now joined you in studying the system that once held him — or less likely, her — captive. It may strike us as odd to think that someone we see almost every day might have been locked behind bars, but statistics tell us that in any group of 30 or so young adults, probably at least one has been locked up, typically for a minor offense. As noted in Chapter 1, about 3 percent of all adults in the United States are currently under some form of correctional control. The group is large, and extends into all kinds of households, neighborhoods, and social groups.

Still, the idea that one of "us" might be under correctional authority can be unsettling. We are used to thinking of offenders as somehow different from "normal" citizens, so when we encounter someone who has been imprisoned, we wonder both about how that person ended up in jail, and also about our preconceptions of offenders. Who are offenders? What gets them into trouble? What should we think of them?

Actually, anyone can get into trouble. So one answer to the question "What are offenders like?" is that they can be like any of us. Yet when we look at offenders as a group, we see that while they come from every walk of life, in fact the powerful and wealthy rarely encounter the criminal justice system. The typical client of the criminal justice system is a young, minority male from a poor neighborhood. For example, African Americans make up less than one-seventh of the U.S. population but nearly half of the accused and convicted people in the justice system. Males comprise one-half of the general population but as much as nine-tenths of the justice system population. Half of those entering state prisons are between 18 and 27 years old.[1]

In this chapter we examine why correctional clients, as a group, seem to differ so markedly from the general population. The reasons are not clear, but they generally have to do with the selection process that determines who gets charged, prosecuted, and convicted. Exactly how this selection process produces the subjects for corrections is a matter of some controversy. We will address the following Questions for Inquiry.

Questions FOR INQUIRY

1. What factors influence the offender selection system?
2. What are the characteristics of the offenders who are under correctional supervision?
3. What is the purpose of offender classification?
4. How are offenders classified?

Selection for the Corrections System

The nature of the process leading up to conviction may make it seem as if becoming a correctional subject is quite difficult — as if corrections had to be "broken into," like a career. In fact, there is some truth to that idea. As Figure 6.1 shows, the criminal justice system operates as a large offender selection bureaucracy, removing some clients at each stage and passing others on to the next decision point.

The filter begins with the decision that street crimes — committed disproportionately by the underprivileged — warrant more attention from police than do corporate or white-collar crimes committed by the middle and upper classes. When people with "stakes" in the community, such as homeowners and those with good jobs, are arrested, they are likely to be released pending trial, under the theory they will appear to face the charges because they have a lot to lose if they don't show up. People without jobs or property are more likely to be held in custody to make sure they will not flee.

Figure 6.1 Percentage of People Arrested, and Imprisoned, for Offenses in Twelve Categories

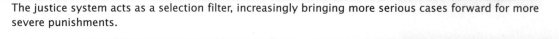

The justice system acts as a selection filter, increasingly bringing more serious cases forward for more severe punishments.

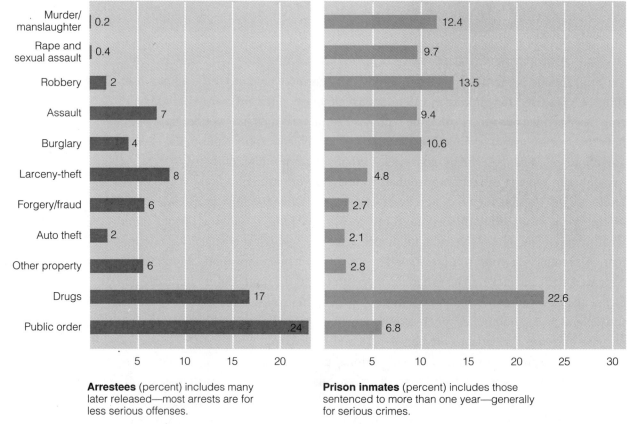

Arrestees (percent) includes many later released—most arrests are for less serious offenses.

Prison inmates (percent) includes those sentenced to more than one year—generally for serious crimes.

Source: U.S. Department of Justice, Bureau of Justice Statistics, *Bulletin*, January, 1998; Federal Bureau of Investigation, *Crime in the United States, 1994* (Washington, DC: U.S. Government Printing Office, 1995).

Obviously, indigent defendants also lack money to post bail, which helps secure attendance at court hearings.

Once a person is convicted, the judge bases the sentence partly on the defendant's previous criminal history. Those accused of serious crimes and those who have had previous contact with the court are more likely than petty offenders or first-timers to receive terms of incarceration. Thus the defendant who has been free on bail can be portrayed to the court as a solid citizen, someone for whom a jail term would be a severe personal disruption. The pretrial detainee, by contrast, often appears in court wearing dingy jail garb, looking for all the world like a person for whom being locked up would not much disrupt life.

In sum, costly jail space tends to be reserved for people who show little connection to the community, and prisons are filled with those who commit serious street crimes or have longer criminal histories. By default, through its everyday policies, the criminal justice bureaucracy concentrates on poor, young men, many of whom are men of color.

If these policies seem defensible and reasonable—and few people advocate that we abandon them—then they must also be seen as a double-edged sword: People unfortunate enough to have few resources and to have had prior contacts with the justice system are generally treated more harshly. The result is a correctional population that differs significantly from the general population. The distinctiveness of the correctional population is not lost on the inmates themselves. They recognize that many other offenders' charges were dropped or reduced and theirs were not, that other offenders could avoid the full penalties of the law by tapping resources they did not have. Herein lies one of the significant consequences of the filtering process in criminal justice: Despite their guilt, many offenders feel unjustly treated in comparison with others. Perhaps not surprisingly, these offenders are often not easy to manage in the correctional setting.

The obvious contrast between prison populations and the general community also leads some critics to view prisons as a mechanism for social control of minorities and the lower classes. Historical studies of American corrections have shown that in earlier eras members of the newest immigrant groups filled the prisons out of proportion to their numbers in the general population. Although since the Civil War African Americans have consistently made up the largest group in southern prisons, elsewhere the largest group has changed over time: first Germans, Irish, and Italians, and now African Americans and Hispanics. This idea of ethnic succession is not entirely consistent with more contemporary research, but our prisons and jails undeniably hold disproportionate numbers of poor, disadvantaged, and minority citizens.

However, even if many correctional clients share characteristics of social class, race, and sex, they also have important differences. In the sections that follow, we classify correctional clients according to some of those differences, and discuss the implications of such classifications for correctional programming.

Types of Offenders and Their Problems

In some respects every offender assigned to corrections is unique; no two are exactly alike. Thus, in referring to "types" of offenders, we may group individuals because they share an important characteristic (such as type of offense) even when they differ in some other vital characteristic (such as prior record, social class, or intelligence). Any attempt to describe groups of offenders reflects a decision to generalize about people while potentially sacrificing individualism.

When groups of offenders are discussed, this point is too often forgotten. We tend to talk about "sex offenders" or "professional criminals" as though they all behaved in the past (and will behave in the future) in the same way. This approach simplifies policymaking and correctional programming, but bears little resemblance to reality. Therein lies the peril of grouping offenders: We forget that the grouping is done only to enable correctional officials to take action and may inevitably distort portraits of individual offenders.

To be honest, then, our discussion of criminal categories will contain disputable statements about groups of offenders with whom corrections must work. Keep this in mind as you read about types of offenders. Whether situational offender or career criminal or elderly offender, some individuals will fit in a group nicely; others are more difficult to place; and all individuals within a group will vary in some respects. The groupings are made for our convenience, to help us understand the types of people corrections manages and the ways in which their characteristics influence the work of corrections.

The Situational Offender

Most people convicted of a felony are not arrested again. Some studies estimate that this is true for 80 percent of first-time offenders. Of course, some undoubtedly commit further felonies and are simply never caught again, but most do not commit a second felony. The person who enters the corrections system having committed what appears to be a one-time offense is called a **situational offender.** Martin Haskell and Lewis Yablonsky describe this type of offender as one who (1) confronted a problem requiring action, (2) took action that violated the criminal law, (3) was caught and given the status of criminal, and (4) until the time of the offense, was committed to the normative system of our society and was indistinguishable from other people.[2] Thus the situational offender "made a mistake" and "paid a debt to society" for that mistake (see the "Susan's Story" Focus box).

situational offender

A person who in a particular set of circumstances has violated the law but who is not given to criminal behavior in normal circumstances and is unlikely to repeat the offense.

F⦿CUS

Susan's Story

On October 25, 1994, Susan Smith released the brake on her maroon Mazda Protege and watched as it rolled into John D. Long Lake and took six endless minutes to sink, drowning her two sons, Michael (age 3 years) and Alex (age 14 months), who were strapped into their car seats inside. She then flagged down a passing motorist and told a panicky, concocted story claiming she had been carjacked and her children kidnapped by a young black male. In front of the television cameras, with her estranged husband David by her side, she tearfully pleaded for the return of the children unharmed.

Nine days later Susan Smith confessed to the murders. Stunned Americans asked themselves how a mother could kill her own babies so cold-heartedly.

There is no easy answer to the question. Susan Smith is a situational offender, but her situation, and the circumstances leading to her crime, are complicated and tragic. No single fact explains her actions, of course, but when the totality of her life is presented, a picture emerges of a weak woman who had been victimized most of her life and who sought desperately to cling to a lover who rejected her because of her children.

The list of calamities befalling Susan Smith is devastating. Her father committed suicide when she was 6 years old, only a month after her parents' divorce. By the time she was 15, she was a victim again, repeatedly sexually molested by her stepfather, Beverly Russell, a pillar of the small town of Union, South Carolina, and a seemingly exemplary member of the Christian Coalition. When the abuse was discovered, Susan's mother seemed to blame Susan for the crime and chose not to prosecute. After a brief interval the sexual assaults resumed, and they continued into Susan's early twenties, even after she was married to David Smith and bore their two children.

The marriage was no haven either, and it ended after three years under accusations of infidelity by both parties. In the time between her marital separation and the murders of her children, Susan had a series of sexual encounters, including an affair with a steady boyfriend named Tom Findlay and with Tom's father, who also happened to be Susan's boss.

When Tom broke off their affair, saying he did not want to raise another man's children, Susan's desperate need for love and fear of losing it must have erupted into a compulsion that ended in the frenzied decision to take her children's lives.

After hearing testimony about Susan's pitiful life, a jury sentenced her to life in prison without parole. We may be appalled by her act, but we cannot help but feel pity for the string of events that led her to it.

The situational offender presents many problems for corrections. First, the crime is usually a serious, violent crime (often murder or aggravated assault), and the offender usually knew the victim well (often a spouse or other family member). For such a crime, a severe punishment is thought appropriate. Even though only an extremely small percentage of murderers commit murder again, fear of the situational offender, together with outrage at the offense, often results in lengthy incarceration.

Yet once the situational offender begins the sentence, there is little for corrections to do. The person typically has a positive orientation toward accepted social values, a solid work history, and good basic employment skills. The prognosis for successful readjustment while on parole is extremely high. However, other than help in adjusting to the life crisis of imprisonment, few positive programming options exist for the situational offender. Managing the time served by these essentially adjusted offenders is thus troublesome for corrections because few positive actions can be taken. Although situational offenders may participate in programs as a means of self-improvement, their time in prison is mainly a matter of simply serving the sentence.

Moreover, with prison crowding, it is precisely the situational offenders whom correctional officials and parole boards believe are most appropriate for early release, because they pose very little threat to the public. The space they vacate can house far more serious criminals. Deciding to grant early release to a situational offender opens the corrections system to criticism, however. Citizens inevitably react against what they may see as coddling and a failure of justice. Furthermore, the one situational offender out of twenty who murders again can destroy the careers of the officials who allowed parole.[3] Therefore situational offenders often remain in prison while other felons, those who actually represent more threat to society but less threat to corrections, are released.

The Career Criminal

One of the most slippery concepts in the classification of offenders is the so-called **career criminal.** When criminologist Walter Reckless first developed the idea of the career criminal, he had in mind a specific set of attributes:

1. Crime is his way of earning a living, his main occupation.
2. He develops technical skills useful to the commission of his crimes.
3. He started as a delinquent child and progressed toward criminality.
4. He expects to do some time in prison as a "cost" of doing this type of work.
5. He is psychologically normal.[4]

Reckless attributed these characteristics to a small, more or less undifferentiated group of offenders who worked at crime, including organized crime figures, white-collar criminals, and professional criminals who worked continuously at an illegal occupation (see the "Archie's Story" Focus box). However, given research ranging from studies of a group of men born in Philadelphia in 1958 to interviews with convicted and imprisoned adults in California, Texas, and Michigan, scholars have concluded that a small group of active criminals commits a majority of all crimes.[5] This led to a significant shift in thinking about career criminals. Instead of applying the term to someone whose work is crime, policymakers began to use it to refer to any offender with several convictions or arrests. Thus a person with as few as three or four convictions now is commonly labeled a "career criminal." This may seem a bit odd to most of us; we would hardly call our own jobs a career if we had been seen at work only three or four times.

Of course, many individuals who are repeatedly convicted actually do admit to more crimes, sometimes many more than the handful for which they are being punished. Peter Greenwood's famous study of robbers, for example, found that as many as half of those with multiple convictions for robbery admitted to having committed a large number of robberies for which they were not caught.[6] Undeniably this small minority made something of a career out of that crime. Still, many repeaters—almost half of Greenwood's sample, for example—are not high-rate offenders. That is, the mere existence of multiple convictions does not mean that the person is working at crime as a career as Reckless defined it; the person may simply be a frequent offender (have committed several crimes in the past few years) who shifts from one type of crime to another.

Why, then, this recent trend to paint the picture of the career criminal with such a broad brush? The answer has to do partly with political pressures. With the devaluation

Susan Smith confessed to the murder by drowning of her sons. The situation and the circumstances leading to this crime are complicated and tragic.

career criminal

A person who sees crime as a way of earning a living, who has numerous contacts with the criminal justice system over time, and who may view the criminal sanction as a normal part of life.

Archie's Story

Archie left home at age 13 and traveled around the country as a transient, sometimes supporting himself as a truck driver. Archie claims to have committed about five hundred burglaries, five hundred auto thefts, and five robberies before his eighteenth birthday. Of them, he was arrested for only one robbery. As he was not convicted, however, he has no juvenile record. Even in this early phase of his criminal career, Archie was quite sophisticated in his MO (modus operandi, method of operating). He used theatrical makeup to disguise himself for his burglaries and robberies, including contact lenses of various colors. He recalls being fairly violent and obsessed about his small size. He injured one of his robbery victims when the man tried to resist.

Archie's first incarceration did not come until his mid-thirties. For this conviction he served several years in a California prison. Although his rap sheet shows nine arrests for drug violations and petty theft, the only serious prison time he served before his present term was for an auto theft conviction.

Before his first incarceration, Archie was employed much of the time, but his main source of income was crime. His wife was a heroin addict. Between his eighteenth birthday and his first incarceration, he estimates that he committed about one hundred grand thefts, one hundred burglaries, and twelve robberies. His average take per robbery was about $2,500. He was never arrested for any of these crimes. He used the loot mainly to support his wife's drug habit and for partying.

The main targets of Archie's robberies were savings and loan banks or payroll offices. His MO was to disguise himself in full theatrical makeup and to enter the savings and loan carrying a sawed-off shotgun, which he would point at a young female employee.

The main targets of Archie's burglaries were pawnshops or businesses. His few residential burglaries were at private homes where an informer had told him a valuable collection or large sums of money were kept. His typical MO was to make the acquaintance of the prospective victim and gain access to his home to learn where the valuables were kept. Within a month after befriending the victim, Archie would burglarize his house. He also performed insurance fraud burglaries in which the "victim" would indicate the articles he wanted stolen. Archie would burglarize the house at a prearranged time, stealing the articles that had been specified and selling them to a fence. The fence would profit, Archie would profit, and the insurance company would reimburse the victim for the items stolen.

Archie reports having shot victims when they tried to resist, in both burglaries and robberies. He also mentions having retaliated against two heroin addicts who were friends of his wife and who apparently had tried to kill him. Archie says that both were seriously injured. Archie relates that his first conviction and incarceration occurred because his wife informed on him when he was trying to stop her from using drugs.

After release from the first incarceration, in his late thirties, Archie remained on the street about five years before being incarcerated for his present term. During this period he committed only four robberies, at large stores or markets, and they yielded very large amounts of money. As in his earlier years, he engaged in elaborate planning for each crime. Archie was convicted by a jury on two counts of armed robbery with a prior felony conviction, and he is serving two concurrent sentences of five-to-life; he is also serving two consecutive five-to-life sentences for use of a firearm in these robberies.

Source: Joan Petersilia, Peter W. Greenwood, and Marvin Lavin, *Criminal Careers of Habitual Felons* (Washington, DC: U.S. Government Printing Office, 1978), pp. 100–101.

of rehabilitation in the 1970s came renewed confidence in incapacitation as the appropriate correctional course. But if incapacitation was the political catchword, what group would be the target? Previous studies had unearthed so few career criminals that this notion was not promising for crime control hardliners. Yet if the career criminal concept could be expanded to include virtually all multiple repeaters, then the target group for this newly popular policy would be large indeed.

Corrections has borne the cost of this conceptual shift. Much as in the case of violent situational criminals, pressure has grown to keep repeaters in prison longer to prevent them from pursuing their predatory "careers." Yet these criteria result in nonprofessional but intermittent offenders being misclassified as career criminals. One result is serious prison overcrowding.

Without question our prisons hold some career criminals—professional offenders committed to lives of crime. But we must examine the accuracy of the overall label and recognize that any decision to classify offenders has social and political significance.

The Sex Offender

Although a wide array of legislation regulates sexual conduct in most jurisdictions, corrections commonly deals with three basic types of **sex offenders**: (1) rapists (sexual assaulters), (2) child molesters (pedophiles), and (3) to a lesser extent, prostitutes. Each subclass of sex offender has a variety of economic, psychological, and situational motivations, and for each the correctional response is deeply influenced by prevailing public opinion about the crimes themselves. Unfortunately, the treatment of sex offenders has not been successful in most cases.[7] This has led to legislative efforts to require prison sentences for rapists and child molesters, and in some states laws requiring public notification when they are paroled.

The Rapist   With the resurgence of feminism in the 1960s and 1970s, the justice system's response to rape became a major political issue. Indeed, to discuss rape under the heading of "sex offenses" is to risk ignoring that it is primarily an act of violence against women. In her classic study *Against Our Will*, Susan Brownmiller persuasively argued that rape needs to be reconceptualized; it is not a sex crime but a brutal personal assault: "To a woman the definition of rape is fairly simple. . . . A deliberate violation of emotional, physical and rational integrity and . . . [a] hostile, degrading act of violence. . . ."[8] When rape is placed where it truly belongs, within the context of modern criminal violence and not within the purview of archaic masculine codes, the crime retains its unique dimensions, taking its place with armed robbery and aggravated assault. The link between lethal violence and sexual assault is illustrated by the fact that about half of all murders of women committed by acquaintances and two-thirds of those by strangers occurred in the process of sexual assaults.[9]

The widespread recognition that rape is not sexually motivated, but represents a physical intrusion fueled by a desire for violent coercion, led to two broad shifts in criminal justice. The first was a move to redefine the crime of "rape" as a gender-neutral "sexual assault" or even as a special case of the general crime of assault. The second was a trend toward harsher treatment of convicted rapists.

The sexual assaulter presents particular difficulties for correctional management. The truly violent sex offender may well be a security risk inside the prison, for the same irrational attitudes and unpredictable behavior patterns may occur during incarceration. It is more likely, however, that the rapist will become a target for inmate violence. In the prisoner subculture "crazies," including many rapists, are near the bottom of the pecking order. Such offenders commonly are subjected to humiliating physical and sexual attacks as a form of inmate domination. Thus, whether unpredictably violent or predictably vulnerable to attack, the incarcerated sexual assaulter is a security risk.

The Child Molester   Few offenses are so uniformly reviled or have so great a stigma attached to the act as child molestation. However, only in recent years, with more open discussion of sexual issues, has significant scholarly attention been given to convicted child molesters.

The picture of the child molester that emerges from various studies is more tragic than disgusting (see the "Nevin's Story" Focus box). Estimates are that as many as 90 percent of child molesters were themselves molested as children, and studies show that sex offenders are about twice as likely as other offenders to report being sexually victimized as a child.[10] Child molestation is a complex crime involving many factors; it ordinarily stems from deep feelings of personal inadequacy on the part of the offender. As many as 20 percent of child molesters are over 50 years old, and many cases involve

sex offender

A person who has committed a sexual act prohibited by law, such as rape, child molestation, or prostitution, for economic, psychological, and even situational reasons.

Nevin's Story

For as long as he can remember, Nevin has relived in his dreams the experience of being forced to have oral sex with a man when he was about 5 years old. Now, at the age of 49 and serving a five- to ten-year term for sexual assault of a 10-year-old boy, Nevin has confronted correctional authorities in Connecticut with a problem. He has filed a lawsuit to force the state to provide treatment for him after his release from the maximum-security prison in Somers. He has no money to pay for treatment, and he says flatly that he will never be able to resist the attraction he feels toward young boys.

Nevin's criminal record stretches back thirty-five years. He has been in and out of prisons in Connecticut, New York, and Pennsylvania for all but five of those years. He estimates that he has sexually assaulted about a thousand boys during his lifetime, and he has said that he has never had any difficulty finding willing partners. "I hang out where the prostitutes hang out, and they [boys] approach me. That solves the problem. I walk down Forty-Second Street in New York City, and in fifteen minutes I have five kids asking if they can go home with me, because I'm known as that type of person." Nevin prefers dark-haired, dark-skinned youngsters and says that he has paid various fees. "I'd pay twenty dollars. I'd pay fifty cents."

Pedophilia, preference for children as sexual objects, is an extremely difficult abnormality to cure. Psychologists believe pedophiles are generally sane and in all other respects are good citizens, but they cannot control this one aspect of their lives. Sexual aversion therapy has been used in some cases. At the Somers Prison it was used until 1975, when it was stopped as a result of a lawsuit filed by child molesters who said that they were being denied pa-

role release unless they underwent the treatment. The technique involved the application of electric shocks to the genital area when photographs of nude children were flashed on a screen. Injections of Depo-Provera are also being used with some pedophiles at the Sexual Disorders Clinic at Johns Hopkins University Hospital, Baltimore. The drug blunts the male sexual drive, and success has been reported when its use is accompanied by therapy. Depo-Provera, however, is not approved for use in the prison setting.

Nevin has written to the Superior Court asking for treatment on release. The Department of Correction says it has given him treatment, cannot hold him longer than his sentence, and cannot provide treatment after release. Should Nevin be able to prove that the state has an obligation to provide treatment, providing that treatment would be up to another state agency, such as the Department of Mental Health.

Nevin acknowledges he has a responsibility "not to engage in this type of behavior." Nevin is more concerned with the rights of the boys he fears will become his next victims than he is with the protection of his own rights. In his letter to the court he wrote, "I believe it is time we consider the rights of the people to be safe in their homes and to be secure in the knowledge that their children can go to school safely without being molested."

Because he is sane, Nevin cannot be involuntarily committed to a state mental hospital. What should be done? What of the pedophiles who are not so concerned about their problem as Nevin is?

Source: Adapted from *The Hartford Courant*, October 12–14, 1984. Reprinted by permission.

ambivalent feelings of attachment between adults and children that gradually become converted into sexual contact.

Many victims of molestation are confused by the crime and feel guilty about it because their emotional attachment to their molesters is quite real. They usually are aware that the act is "wrong" or "bad." And if the act arouses pleasurable feelings, the situation is further complicated.

The child molester is often the most despised offender in court and in prison. An incarcerated molester is almost certain to be the target of repeated threats, actual violence, and routine hostility from other prisoners. Moreover, because most prison systems have very little treatment options for molesters, this offender's experience in prison typically is quite bleak. As a result some states have to set aside special institutions or cell blocks for molesters in order to ensure their safety.

The Prostitute Prostitution is more an economic than a sexual crime; that is, it is an illegal business transaction between a service provider and a customer. Public opinion about prostitution is ambivalent; public policy seems to fluctuate between "reform" legislation designed to legalize and regulate prostitution and wholesale police roundups of hookers and pimps to "clean up" the streets. The current AIDS epidemic has fueled renewed concern that prostitutes are major transmission agents for the disease. In response some courts have ordered infected prostitutes to refrain from practicing their trade. In any event, prostitution exists (even flourishes) in virtually every section of the country, and when prostitutes or their pimps are punished, the sentence generally is probation.

Because prostitution is an economic crime, correctional caseworkers are forced to find a substitute vocation for offenders. This is not easy, for many prostitutes lack education and other marketable skills, and many are addicted to drugs. Further, many have little desire to change their lifestyle. Because prostitution is more a public nuisance than a public threat, caseworkers are likely to accord such cases low priority, as are the courts and prosecutors. Therefore prostitution is a crime that often receives marginal enforcement of laws and indifferent punishment.

The Substance Abuser

Substance abuse and addiction has a fundamental influence on the nature of the correctional population. As noted by the National Center on Addiction and Substance Abuse, as America enters the twenty-first century, crime and alcohol and drug abuse are joined at the hip. They found that four out of five jail and prison inmates "had been high when they committed their crimes, had stolen to support their habit or had a history of drug and alcohol abuse that led them to commit crime."[11]

The criminal law typically distinguishes between the use of illegal drugs and the illegal use of alcohol. In the case of drugs, any unauthorized possession of a controlled substance is prohibited. Laws against mere possession of some drugs are so strict that in the federal system as well as many states, prison terms are mandatory for these offenders. In contrast, possession of alcohol is prohibited only for minors. The criminal justice system becomes involved in alcohol offenders' lives primarily because of their conduct under the influence of alcohol. The difference between these two types of offenders is important for correctional policy, so we discuss them separately.

The Drug Abuser   Our culture is a drug-using culture, from aspirin and caffeine to marijuana and cocaine. Not surprisingly, then, substance abuse figures prominently in criminal behavior (see the "Mary Lou's Story" Focus box). A national survey of state prison inmates found that over half (54 percent) of those serving time for violent offenses admitted they were under the influence of an illegal drug when they committed the crime. This survey also found that nearly one in four of all inmates in local jails are there for drug crimes.[12] In over one-third of all violent criminal victimizations, the victim perceives the offender as under the influence of drugs or alcohol.[13] As Figure 6.2 shows, from 42 to 79 percent of offenders arrested in twenty-three U.S. cities tested positive for an illegal drug at the time of their arrest.[14]

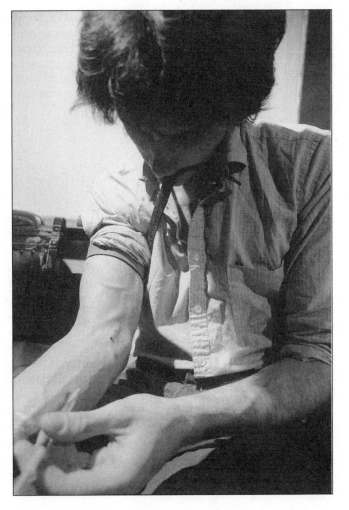

The drug abuser poses both treatment and management problems for corrections.

FOCUS   Mary Lou's Story

Mary Lou looks much older than her 25 years. She was brought up in Chicago in a family of six children, and the only income was her mother's monthly welfare check. She is now approaching the time of her release from prison after serving a sentence for driving the getaway car involved in the armed robbery of a drugstore.

A school dropout at 16, Mary Lou met Frankie, a flashy dude who seemed to have money to spend, yet was always on the street. Soon she was doing drugs with Frankie, and even though her girlfriends warned her that he was a junkie and a pimp, she moved into his apartment; by then she had graduated to heroin. During their first weeks together they were high much of the time—sleeping through the morning, getting a fix, then cruising the streets in Frankie's Oldsmobile, dropping in at bars and apartments to visit what seemed like an endless number of his friends.

When Frankie's money ran low, he told Mary Lou she was going to have to "hustle" if she expected to live with him. She told him she wouldn't and moved in with a girlfriend. Within a day she was feeling so bad that she had to borrow money for a fix. Faced with her habit and an empty pocketbook, Mary Lou hustled. She turned two tricks the first night, but her second customer beat her up. Shaken by the experience and hurting for heroin, she returned to the only person she thought could help her—Frankie. He was not happy to see her because another girl

had already taken her place, but he agreed to help if she would hustle for him. During the next six months she was able to make enough money to retain Frankie's protection and to support her habit.

With the onset of winter, the streets of Chicago turned cold, and the supply of heroin on the streets suddenly tightened in response to a strong law enforcement effort. By this time both Mary Lou and Frankie were heavy users. After two frantic days of trying to find affordable heroin, Frankie decided to rob a drugstore. In a haze Mary Lou drove him to the store, parked in an alley, and waited while Frankie, armed with a gun, entered the store. Within minutes he came dashing back, a burglar alarm blaring in his wake. Mary Lou gunned the Olds down the alley and into the street, where it struck another car. Frankie jumped out and ran off. A stunned Mary Lou just sat behind the wheel while a crowd formed and an officer arrived to investigate the accident.

It took little detective work for the police to link the collision to the robbery. They arrested Frankie back at his apartment and took him to the station house for booking. Mary Lou was already there when he was brought in. Held in the Cook County Jail awaiting court action, she endured agonizing withdrawal from heroin.

At the suggestion of her public defender, Mary Lou pleaded guilty to a reduced charge of abetting an armed robbery and was sentenced to a three- to five-year term.

---

drug abuser

A person whose use of illegal chemical substances disrupts normal living patterns to the extent that social problems develop, often leading to criminal behavior.

The **drug abuser** presents both treatment and management problems for corrections. The offender may have been convicted for possession or sale of drugs or for some other offense committed as a result of their use. Thus correctional personnel must address the effects of drug dependency while the client is in detention, on probation, in prison, or on parole. The drug abuser also represents a potential control problem for correctional staff because of a high likelihood of rearrest.

The street addict's life is structured by the need to get money to support the habit, and that need often leads to property crime. Studies of the relationship between drugs and crime have found that although much of the money for supporting a drug habit may be legitimately obtained, a high proportion of drug users admit engaging in income-generating crimes. Even if an addict supports only a small fraction of the habit's cost through crime, this can translate into large amounts of crime.

Habits costing $50–$150 a day are not uncommon. Because stolen goods are fenced at much less than their market value, an addict must steal goods worth several times the cost of the drug just to support the habit. Figure 6.3 shows some of the crimes committed to support a drug habit. Robbery is more directly lucrative than theft but also more chancy: There is always a risk of violence, and the victim may have little cash.

Figure 6.2 Drug Use by Booked Arrestees in Twenty-Three U.S. Cities

A large proportion of felony arrestees are under the influence of drugs at the time of their arrest.

Source: U.S. Department of Justice, National Institute of Justice, *ADAM: 1997 Annual Report on Adult and Juvenile Arrestees* (Washington, DC: U.S. Government Printing Office, 1998).

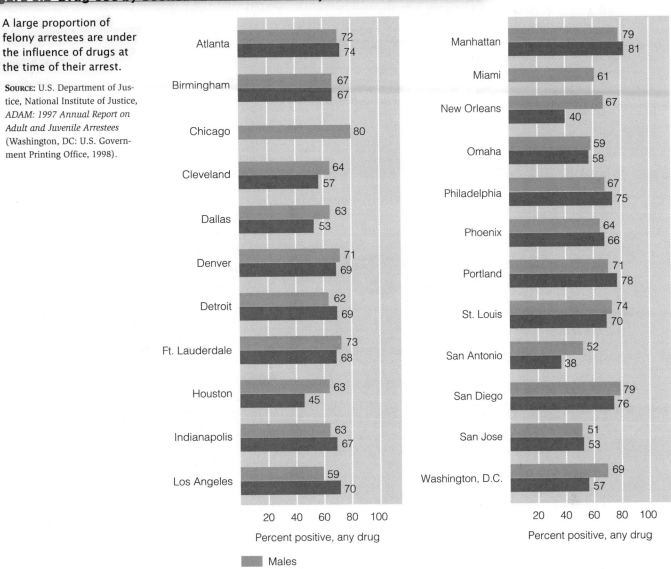

Treatment programs for people who compulsively or habitually use drugs do not have high success rates, and some are controversial. As the social movement against heroin grew in the 1950s and 1960s, support for clinical treatment of addiction also grew, and special drug treatment facilities were opened to house addicts as a special population of incarcerated offenders. Civil commitment procedures were often used to send convicted offenders to such facilities, where their incarceration term frequently exceeded what they would otherwise have received. Evaluations of these programs showed dismal results. For example, the first long-term follow-up of 100 releasees from one program found only 10 instances of five or more consecutive years of abstinence following hospitalization.[15]

Thus substance abusers represent a serious dilemma for corrections. By definition their behavior is compulsive and likely to be repeated. Although the mere act of drug abuse is not considered a serious offense, the collateral acts of predatory crime and violence are considered very serious.

Figure 6.3 Percentage of Convicted Jail Inmates Who Committed Their Offenses to Support a Drug Habit

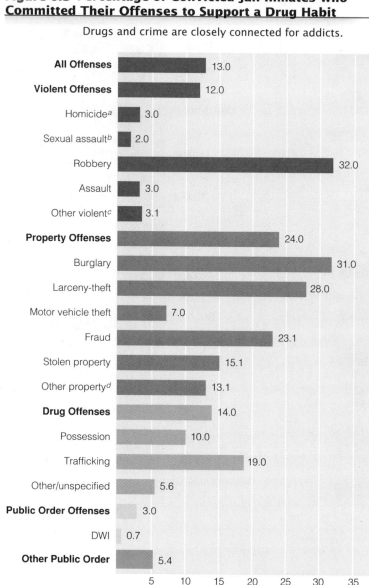

Drugs and crime are closely connected for addicts.

Offense	Percent
All Offenses	13.0
Violent Offenses	12.0
Homicide[a]	3.0
Sexual assault[b]	2.0
Robbery	32.0
Assault	3.0
Other violent[c]	3.1
Property Offenses	24.0
Burglary	31.0
Larceny-theft	28.0
Motor vehicle theft	7.0
Fraud	23.1
Stolen property	15.1
Other property[d]	13.1
Drug Offenses	14.0
Possession	10.0
Trafficking	19.0
Other/unspecified	5.6
Public Order Offenses	3.0
DWI	0.7
Other Public Order	5.4

Percent convicted inmates

[a] Includes murder, nonnegligent manslaughter, and negligent manslaughter
[b] Includes rape
[c] Includes kidnapping
[d] Includes arson

Source: Office of Justice Programs, *Drugs and Crime* (Washington, DC: U.S. Department of Justice, September 1994), p. 8.

alcohol abuser

A person whose use of alcohol is difficult to control, disrupting normal living patterns and frequently leading to violations of the law while under the influence of alcohol or in attempting to secure it.

Since the 1980s federal policies have sought to combat drug abuse by providing tougher criminal sanctions. Punishments for drug possession and sales were made considerably harsher, especially in the federal courts, where sentences of ten years or longer became routine.[16] There was also a renewed emphasis on treatment for drug addiction, and some of these prison-based programs had better results than the earlier civil commitment programs. Yet most experts believe the dual-track strategy of punishment and treatment has not yet appreciably lowered drug abuse among citizens and offenders.

The Alcohol Abuser   Unlike marijuana, heroin, and other controlled substances, alcohol is widely available and relatively inexpensive, and its consumption is an integral part of life in the United States. Only when alcohol leads to problems such as unemployment, family disorganization, and crime does society become concerned (see the "Bill's Story" Focus box).

The **alcohol abuser's** problem translates into crime much less directly than that of the drug user. Because alcohol is legal for adults, no criminal subculture surrounds its use. Where many addicts must engage in a criminal act just to get the drug of their choice, the alcoholic need only go to the corner store. However, alcoholics may produce far more disastrous consequences than heroin addicts do. According to estimates, alcohol use contributes to almost 100,000 deaths annually, five times the total number of homicides reported to the police. Moreover, many automobile injuries and personal offenses are at least partly caused by intoxication. Alcohol use impairs coordination and judgment, reduces inhibitions, and confuses understanding; criminal acts can easily follow. Thus a drunk's drive home may become vehicular homicide, a domestic dispute may become aggravated assault, a political debate or quarrel over money may become disorderly conduct, and a night of drinking may lead to burglary or auto theft.

Although research on alcoholic offenders has focused on the incarcerated, these offenders appear in other correctional environments as well. Like drug abusers, alcoholics present problems for probation officers, community treatment providers, and parole officers. Because some alcoholics become assaultive when they drink, dealing with them is neither pleasant nor safe.

Other problems are also related to the treatment of alcohol abusers. To some extent the problems stem from Americans' generally ambivalent attitude toward alcohol use—it is seen as recreational behavior rather than deviance. Consequently treatment programs seem to work best when they focus on getting people to recognize the nature of their own patterns of alcohol use rather than on alcohol use per se. This is one reason why the program of Alcoholics Anonymous (AA) has consistently proved the most suc-

FOCUS Bill's Story

Bill Gunderson is only 39 years old but he looks 60. His eyes are sunken; his face is bony, pockmarked, and stubbly. He is bundled up in layer on layer of clothing, topped by a grease-stained, military-green overcoat. His hair, clotted in bunches and standing out all over his head, combines with his physique to give him the appearance of a scarecrow. On this day in late December, Gunderson is stumbling among the crowd of affluent holiday shoppers on King Street in Alexandria, Virginia, looking for handouts and having little success. They can immediately tell that he is drunk.

Being drunk is Gunderson's normal state. Because he has no home, he is often drunk in public and has been arrested repeatedly on this charge since he arrived in Alexandria two months before. "The cops pick me up whenever I get too drunk, not because they want to," Gunderson says. "A couple of times they just took my bottle and poured it on the street. But usually they pick me up. It's for my own health, I reckon."

After his first arrest, Gunderson was driven directly to the city's detoxification center, a six-bed facility designed to relieve some of the burden on the Alexandria Correctional Center. "They gave me a bed, let me take a shower, and gave me some coffee," Gunderson says. But after a few hours he began to go into withdrawal, and because the detox center is not staffed or equipped to administer sedatives to ease the pain, Gunderson left in search of the only relief he knows—another bottle of wine. "I was shaking so bad, but the only thing they told me was, 'Hey, you gotta go through it.'"

The second time Gunderson was arrested, the detox center refused to admit him and the police took him to jail. Every time after that—Gunderson guesses it has happened 16 times in a month and a half—he has gone straight to jail. He is always released after a few hours and told to appear later for trial. Gunderson says he has never appeared in court and has no intention of doing so. "They don't care," he says with a toothless grin. "Why should they?"

Sheriff Michael Norris of Alexandria admits that the police do not track down drunks like Gunderson for court appearances. The offense is punishable only by a $10 fine, and no matter what the police do, they are likely to pick up the same offender on the same charge a few days later. "It's just a merry-go-round," Sheriff Norris says.

Source: D. Whitford, "Despite Decriminalization, Drunks Still Clog Our Nation's Jails," *Corrections Magazine*, April 1983, p. 31. Reprinted by permission of the Edna McConnell Clark Foundation.

cessful of alcohol treatment methods: It provides intensive peer support to help people face their own personal inability to manage alcohol use.

Despite its general success, AA may be of limited usefulness to criminal offenders, many of whom come from lower social classes that appear less responsive to AA's middle-class orientation. Moreover, AA views itself as a strictly voluntary treatment program; individuals must want to help themselves to subscribe to it. This characteristic often clashes with the coercive nature of treatment in corrections, which may require attendance at AA meetings as a condition of the sentence. The poor fit between AA's voluntary peer group structure and the involuntariness of corrections may explain why studies find these programs somewhat ineffective with offenders convicted of public drunkenness.

The Mentally Ill Offender

Alex Ocasio, inmate no. 91A9788, held in New York's Stormville maximum-security prison, is a paranoid schizophrenic who not only hears voices that aren't there but must endure the taunts of other inmates who call him "bug" for the medication ("bug juice") that he and many other mentally ill prisoners must drink every night. Ocasio, serving time for robbery, is one of an estimated 10,000 mentally ill prisoners held in the New York system alone.[17] Nationwide, it is estimated that 10 percent of all prisoners suffer from schizophrenia, manic depression, or major depression.[18]

Should mentally ill offenders be placed in prisons, or in mental hospitals? Andrew Goldman, 29, accused of pushing Kendra Webdate to her death under a subway train, has been receiving psychiatric care since he was 16.

___

mentally ill offender

A "disturbed" person whose criminal behavior may be traced to diminished or otherwise abnormal capacity to think or reason as a result of psychological or neurological disturbance.

Few images disturb people more than that of the "crazy," violence-prone criminal whose acts seem random, senseless, or even "psychopathic." To understand such people better, others often roughly classify them as "disturbed" or **mentally ill offenders** — people whose rational processes do not seem to operate in normal ways (see the "Johnnie's Story" Focus box). Mentally ill offenders are less able to think realistically about their conduct, including criminal conduct. Psychopaths are mentally ill, but there are many kinds of mental illness. Not all mentally ill offenders are violent or psychopathic — recent studies show that only 3 percent of the violent behavior in the United States is attributable to mental disorder, and people with mental illness are more likely to be victims of crime than perpetrators of violence.[19] Yet those citizens whose mental disorders translate into criminality present significant problems for corrections.[20]

Recently people have come to recognize that the classification of most violent offenders as "mentally ill" is both an overgeneralization and a social issue. For one thing, not all violent offenders are demonstrably mentally ill. For another, the decision to apply the label "sick" (which the term *psychopath* or *sociopath* implies, *-path* meaning ill person) makes the person seem somehow less whole and makes it easier to justify extreme correctional measures.

There is some overlap between what we described as the career criminal and the so-called psychopath. Both engage in frequent criminal activity. The intended distinction between them is made clear in the original description of the psychopath: "an asocial, aggressive, highly impulsive person, who feels little or no guilt and is unable to form lasting bonds of affection with other human beings."[21] Thus the psychopath lacks attachment to people or rules, whereas a career criminal is motivated by economic gain. However, in practice this distinction is problematic because it presumes knowledge of another person's private thoughts. Who can prove that another individual never feels love, affection, or guilt and should therefore be labeled psychopathic? Who can prove that the same individual may not also be motivated by material gain?

The central problem with the mental health model of criminality is that the mind cannot be observed; a person's inner feelings and thoughts can only be inferred from behavior. When we see people behaving in outrageous or bizarre ways, we are tempted to infer that their mind or emotions work in strange ways. We call these people "sick" or "emotionally ill" even when there is no evidence of an illness, in the sense of the flu or any other physical disease. In earlier times deities, witches, and instincts were considered to cause a variety of odd or criminal behaviors. As Thomas Szasz has argued, today we use the term mental illness to explain behaviors we do not understand, even if the behavior is not caused by a "disease of the brain."[22]

Our need to explain some criminal behavior as "mental illness" can easily lead us to overgeneralize and ascribe mental illness to all criminals. The National Commission on the Causes and Prevention of Violence recognized the problem when it concluded that (1) the popular idea that the mentally ill are overrepresented in the population of violent criminals is not supported by research evidence, and (2) people identified as mentally ill generally pose no greater risk of committing violent crimes than does the population as a whole.[23]

This conclusion underscores the problem for corrections represented by mentally ill offenders: Their mental illness is often a separate issue from their criminality, and deal-

FOCUS Johnnie's Story

Johnnie Baxstrom was a black male, born on August 12, 1918, in Greensboro, North Carolina. He quit school when he was seventeen, while he was in the eleventh grade. As described by his hospital notes, throughout his childhood "he had what he termed 'fainting headaches.'" He said it felt as though someone were beating on the side of his temple and that he would black out in school. He was hospitalized from May 29, 1956, to June 8, 1956, for head injury. Diagnosis: "Idiopathic Epilepsy and residuals from Bilateral Subdural Hematoma, following skull fracture."

Baxstrom had a very irregular job record showing that he worked only for short times at a variety of unskilled positions. He did have a good military record; he entered the armed forces in September 1943 and received an honorable discharge in March 1946. He was married three times.

Baxstrom's criminal record is a lengthy list of drinking and property offenses. However, his first offense did not occur until he was thirty, which was two years after his getting out of the military service and while he was living with his second wife. He was charged with assaulting a female with a dangerous weapon, but the case was never disposed of in the courts. Again in 1950, he was arrested on two counts of assault and one of larceny in Baltimore. . . . He was found not guilty of all charges. His first conviction occurred six months later. He received a twelve-month sentence on the road gang for an "affray assault on a female." Over the next few years, Baxstrom appears to have taken up a wandering lifestyle involving no work. Between 1951 and 1958, when he was sentenced to Attica, Baxstrom was arrested twelve times ...for such things as trespassing on Southern Railway property, drunkenness, vagrancy, disorderly conduct, intoxication, and one time for robbery for which he received and served a one-year sentence in the Maryland House of Corrections.

On October 21, 1958, Baxstrom was arrested in Rochester, New York, for attacking a police officer with an ice pick. According to hospital records, he stabbed the officer in the face, forehead, and collarbone. . . . Apparently Baxstrom was drinking in a bar where he got into a fight with another patron. During the fight Baxstrom pulled a knife or ice pick and stabbed the other combatant. This other combatant turned out to be a police officer in civilian clothes. For this act, he received a two-and-a-half- to three-year sentence. The conviction was for assault, second-degree. He was admitted to Attica State Prison.

While in Attica, Baxstrom was reported to "often have epileptic fits during which he was aggressive, assaultive toward guards and inmates. He also used obscene language." Because of this, he was transferred to Dannemora.

SOURCE: H. J. Steadman and J. J. Cocozza, *Careers of the Criminally Insane* (Lexington, MA: Lexington Books, 1974), pp. 43–45. Reprinted by permission.

ing with their criminality may not require treatment of their mental illness. In other words, the fact that a person has mental or emotional problems and is an offender does not necessarily mean that he or she will continue to offend until the mental or emotional problems are resolved.

The general public links mental illness, crime, and the insanity defense because of a handful of highly publicized trials, such as that of John Hinckley, the would-be assassin of Ronald Reagan. But only about 8 percent of convicted or accused persons in mental hospitals are there because they were found not guilty by reason of insanity. Another 6 percent are in hospitals because they have been judged mentally disordered sex offenders, and 32 percent have been found incompetent to stand trial. The largest group (54 percent), and the group of greatest concern to corrections, consists of offenders who became mentally ill after having been imprisoned.[24]

Why do some offenders become mentally ill while serving their terms? We must recognize that incarceration is stressful, even for the emotionally strong. Prisoners lose contact with families and other sources of emotional support. Often they feel humiliated by being convicted and sentenced to prison. Then they must face the strains of prison life, which are often augmented by unsafe and burdensome prison conditions. For some prisoners the strain proves too much; they lose their emotional stability.

Institutional care for mentally ill offenders has paralleled historical shifts in corrections. There were early efforts to separate the mentally ill from other incarcerated offenders, but not until 1859 was the first institution built specially for such people, the New York State Lunatic Asylum for Insane Convicts, opened near Auburn Prison. The facility held both convicted and unconvicted patients, and it later received patients judicially transferred from civil hospitals.

Today all states have either separate facilities for mentally ill criminals or sections of mental hospitals reserved for them. In some states these institutions are under the control of the department of corrections, and in others the department of mental health.

deinstitutionalization

The release of mental patients from mental hospitals and their return to the community.

In the coming decade corrections will face an increased number of mentally ill clients. Much of the increase is related to a major policy shift in the mental health field: **deinstitutionalization.** With the availability of drugs that inhibit aberrant behavior, it became possible to release a multitude of mental patients to the community. Unfortunately, under- or even unsupervised former patients often fail to take their medication and then commit deviant or criminal acts. Typically these are relatively minor offenses related to public order or larceny, but they may be assaultive as well. Because the acts are minor, mentally ill offenders generally receive treatment from correctional personnel while awaiting disposition of their cases or from probation officers working cooperatively with mental health workers.

The Mentally Handicapped Offender

The 43-year-old man entered the Dunkin' Donuts shop, approached the counter, and demanded, "All your money and a dozen doughnuts." With his finger pointed inside his pocket, he announced that he had a gun and would use it. When the police arrived, they found the man standing outside the shop eating the doughnuts—just as they had found him after several previous holdups. The man's name is Eddie; he has an IQ of 61. He has served prison sentences for this type of offense, but almost immediately upon release he commits another such crime.

Ron, a thirty-three-year-old man who functions at the level of a ten-year-old, was sentenced to a five-year prison term for bank robbery. He was easily identified by the police because he signed his name on the note he gave to the teller demanding money.

Charlie, who has an IQ of 85, set fire to a trash barrel in the hallway of his apartment building. A psychotic woman tenant, panicked by the smoke, jumped out of the window and was killed by the fall. Charlie is awaiting trial for murder.

mentally handicapped offender

A person whose limited mental development prevents adjustment to the rules of society.

These cases point to another problematic type of person for the correctional system: the **mentally handicapped offender.** An estimated 2 percent of the U.S. population are mentally handicapped or developmentally disabled (having IQs below 70). Among the incarcerated population about 5 percent (50,000) are in this category, and countless others are on probation or under juvenile care. In California alone, correctional agencies handle 22,000 adults and juveniles who are classified as mentally retarded.[25]

Like other Americans mentally handicapped people commit crimes, but there is no proven link between their disability and a propensity for criminal behavior. Their criminality may result from the fact that they do not know how to obtain what they want without breaking the law (see the "Donald's Story" Focus box). It may also result from the fact that they are easily duped by persons who think deviant behavior is a joke or who use them to illicitly secure something for themselves. Mentally handicapped people also are disproportionately poor, so if they need or want something, they may commit a crime to get it. And because they cannot think quickly, they get caught more often than other criminals do.

The majority of the offenses committed by mentally handicapped people are classified as property or public order crimes. This is not to say that they do not also commit serious violent crimes; among the incarcerated a higher proportion of mentally handicapped offenders than others have been convicted of homicide and other crimes against persons.

FOCUS

Donald's Story

Donald stole to survive. Often he took food from grocery stores. Sometimes he broke into diners to cook meals for himself in the middle of the night.

"I'd never break into anybody's house," Donald said. "That would be wrong. People have to work too hard for their money. I only break into stores." He doesn't understand that when he steals from businesses, he hurts the people who own them. He is mentally retarded.

Donald, whose IQ is in the 60s (100 is normal), spent most of his life in Ladd School, Rhode Island's institution for the retarded. In 1967, when he was twenty-four years old, he was released and given a job washing dishes in an East Greenwich, Rhode Island, restaurant.

"It wasn't enough money," said Donald. "It was only $30 a week. If I paid for my room, I couldn't eat. So I quit. I had to survive somehow, so I would go out and steal. I didn't know how to do no job."

Asked why he didn't go on welfare, he replied, "I didn't know about that stuff. Nobody ever told me anything about it. It's hard to get on welfare. You have to write stuff on papers."

Arrests came one after the other, Donald's court records show. One was for breaking into a diner and stealing thirty-five cents.

At one point, Donald found a job at a Providence laundry and for a few months the break-ins stopped.

"All I did was fold clothes from the dryer," he recalled. "There was me and another guy. Then they decided one person could do it, and they got rid of my helper. I got scared. I couldn't do it alone. So I just quit."

So it was back to the break-ins.

Donald often got caught and was continually before the courts. But the judges never knew what to do with him; Rhode Island has no program for retarded offenders. Sometimes they put him on probation, and on several occasions they sent him to the state mental hospital for observation.

But no one helped Donald get a job. Finally, the judges lost patience and started sending Donald to prison. He has served at least three prison sentences, although court records are unclear and Donald is not sure there were not more. He is not good with numbers. When asked, he didn't know his age, which is thirty-seven.

On July 30, 1978, police records show that Donald was out of prison again. At 10:02 that night, a burglar alarm went off at a Providence factory building. Police found Donald hiding behind a door with a glass cutter in his pocket. As usual, Donald confessed. "I felt like getting some money," he told police. "I didn't know where to get it. Then I tried to get it in there."

A sympathetic judge put Donald on probation on the condition that he voluntarily live at the state mental hospital until a better arrangement could be made for him. Since then, Donald hasn't done any stealing. "Don't need to," he said. "I eat for free now."

Every weekday, after breakfast at the mental hospital, Donald takes the bus to downtown Providence and walks the streets looking for a job. He's been doing it for more than a year now, without success.

"If only I can get a job, maybe I can get out of the hospital," he said. "But I can't read and write. I can't do the forms. They ask you where you live. I live in a nuthouse. They ask about your last job." . . .

What's his future? "I don't know," he said. "I don't want to steal no more. It ain't worth it. I wish when I got in trouble a cop had shot me. So I wouldn't have to do it no more."

SOURCE: B. DeSilva, "Donald's Story," *Corrections Magazine,* August 1980, p. 27. Reprinted by permission of the Edna McConnell Clark Foundation.

Deinstitutionalization has been a recent focus of programs to deal with mentally handicapped individuals. Like the mentally ill, the mentally handicapped have been returned to the community, where they are expected to live, work, and care for themselves with minimal supervision. Because they have difficulty adjusting to the rules of the community, they often come to the attention of the criminal justice system.

What can corrections do for or with this special category of offender? Obviously the usual routines of probation, diversion, incarceration, and community service will not work. Mentally handicapped individuals typically are not comfortable with change, are difficult to employ outside of sheltered workshops, and are not likely to improve significantly in terms of mental condition or social habits. And so they violate probation or break prison rules and are further penalized. While incarcerated, they are often the butts of practical jokes and exploited as scapegoats or sexual objects. Recent litigation has called attention to the fact that these offenders require special programs, and the Americans with Disabilities Act (ADA) provides federal oversight to local correctional programs for those suffering from mental disabilities.

Some observers believe that mentally handicapped offenders are less criminals than misfits who lack training in how to live in a complex society; they belong not in prison but in a treatment facility where they could learn rudimentary survival skills. Criminal justice practitioners often argue that mentally handicapped offenders constitute a mental health problem, but because they have committed crimes, mental health agencies do not want them. Thus they are shunned by both camps and get little help from either.

The Offender with AIDS

For the foreseeable future, human immunodeficiency virus (HIV—and its full-blown symptomatic stage, acquired immune deficiency syndrome (AIDS)—is going to have a major impact on American corrections. In 1995 over 5,000 verified offenders had AIDS and more than 27,000 were HIV positive, in U.S. prisons and jails—twelve times higher than the regular U.S. population. That year over 1000 inmates died of AIDS, the biggest single cause of death.[26] Because many HIV-infected inmates are undiagnosed, these numbers underestimate the scope of the problem.

The offender who is ill with AIDS—or even simply carrying the virus—confronts probation and parole officers with a number of problems. For jail and prison administrators, the problems are mainly policy issues concerning the people under their supervision. Institutional administrators must develop policies covering such matters as ways to prevent disease transmission, housing those infected, and medical care for inmates who have the full range of symptoms found in the end stage of AIDS. In determining what actions should be taken, administrators have found that a host of legal, political, budgetary, and attitudinal factors limit their ability to make the best decisions (see the "Mike's Story" Focus box).

Prevention   AIDS is a communicable disease that occurs when the human immune defenses are broken down by the HIV virus and the body becomes unable to combat infections. The virus is transmitted in contaminated blood and semen, primarily by needle sharing related to intravenous drug use and by sexual activity. HIV is difficult to transmit, and scientific evidence shows that it is not passed on through casual contact.

A key way to prevent AIDS transmission is knowledge about the virus. If people don't understand how the virus is transmitted and how to prevent transmission, they run a higher risk of acquiring and transmitting the disease. Researchers have found that people in the "free world" who represent the "feeder population" for correctional institutions—young, poor, undereducated, minority males—know very little about AIDS.[27]

Preventing the spread of AIDS is also made difficult because there is a long incubation period between time of infection with HIV and the first outward symptoms. Thus carriers may engage in unsafe drug taking and sex without knowing they are infecting others. Although the overwhelming number of infected offenders were infected with HIV before they were incarcerated, transmission within the institution remains a problem.

In most prisons educational programs now inform staff and inmates about the disease and how it spreads. Some observers have suggested that hypodermic needles and condoms be made available to prisoners so that if they do engage in intravenous drug taking and homosexual behavior, they will be protected. However, because these behaviors violate prison rules, administrators are reluctant to legitimize them. The policy of testing all residents and new inmates for the HIV antibody has been widely debated. Figure 6.4 shows the testing policies of state correctional systems. Opponents of systemwide testing argue that there is no evidence of higher transmission rates in prisons than in the free community, and thus no reason to screen. Further, because it is allegedly

FOCUS Mike's Story

On July 15, 1986, at 9:30 A.M., Mike Camargo lay in his hospital bed in the prison ward of Bellevue Hospital in New York City. Camargo was a pretrial detainee accused of selling drugs to an undercover police officer the previous summer. When he was conscious, he felt sharp, stabbing pains in his arms and feet. He could hardly move, much less sit up. Camargo was told that he suffered from pneumonia and toxoplasmosis.

Six weeks later he was transferred to an intensive care unit of the hospital. He had gone into shock because the bacteria growing in his brain deprived his nervous system of necessary oxygen. His inability to breathe was also caused by other bacteria clogging his heart valves. Mike Camargo's life had been spent in petty crime as a small-time drug dealer. The cops had caught him more than once, and he had served several sentences. Now he was dying of AIDS.

On December 8, Camargo's presence was required for a court appearance before Justice Sheindlin of the Supreme Court of New York in the Bronx. Dr. Jonathan Cohn, Camargo's attending physician at Bellevue Hospital, was subpoenaed by Camargo's lawyer to explain the defendant's absence. Cohn was placed under oath, and he then graphically explained to the court why he believed Camargo's deteriorating condition made producing the prisoner, much less continued prosecution, futile.

Over the prosecutor's objection, the court granted the defendant's motion to dismiss in the interest of justice. Justice Sheindlin explained to the prosecutor that although the defendant was a recidivist, it was doubtful he could be regarded as a threat to the safety or welfare of society. To impose incarceration on this minor drug dealer would be absurd given his imminent death. Further, the court noted that no sentence would compare with the many diseases now attacking the defendant.

The typical AIDS prisoner is much like Mike Camargo: He was in his early thirties. He was an intravenous drug user who had been incarcerated for a drug-related crime. And he died of AIDS-related pneumonia.

SOURCE: Adapted from Patricia Raburn, "Prisoners with AIDS: The Use of Electronic Processing," *Criminal Law Bulletin*, May–June 1988, pp. 213–214. Reprinted by permission. Copyright © 1988 by Warren, Gorham & Lamont Inc., 210 South Street, Boston, MA 02111.

Figure 6.4 HIV Testing Policies in State Correctional Systems, 1995

All states provide for HIV testing on request or medical referral, but most states augment this with routine testing under other circumstances.

SOURCE: U.S., Department of Justice, Bureau of Justice Statistics, *Bulletin*, August 1997, p. 7.

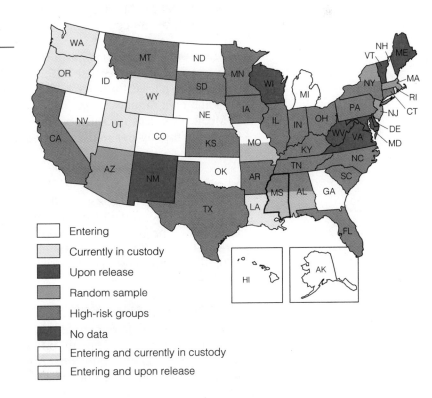

- Entering
- Currently in custody
- Upon release
- Random sample
- High-risk groups
- No data
- Entering and currently in custody
- Entering and upon release

impossible to keep test results confidential, infected individuals will be stigmatized while incarcerated and discriminated against in insurance, housing, and employment upon release. Finally, policies have been developed to ensure that correctional personnel and inmates do not become infected while handling blood or body fluids in their duties. Using protective coverings, avoiding needle injuries, and taking care in handling diseased bodies have all become standard operating procedure.

Housing   If inmates are found to be HIV-positive or to have AIDS, what should be done? When they do become ill, unquestionably they should be cared for in a medical facility. But what about inmates who test positive yet may not become ill for several years? Should they be housed in a segregated facility or remain in the general population? Should they be protected from the hostility of other inmates and staff?

Correctional administrators have selected among various housing options, depending on such factors as the number of infected inmates in a given population and the availability and cost of separate facilities. A survey of corrections systems sponsored by the National Institution of Justice found that most systems segregate inmates with AIDS but keep asymptotic HIV carriers in the general population.[28] On a case-by-case basis most administrators segregate prisoners who display high-risk behavior, who need protection, or whose medical condition calls for separate housing.

In some systems HIV-infected people are kept in the general population but given special treatment to reduce the possibility that they will transmit HIV to others. For example, in Nebraska and New Hampshire they are assigned single cells; in Nevada and Texas they are housed together in double cells. These policies have been criticized at some institutions because making particular cell arrangements for HIV-infected inmates announces their condition to staff and other inmates.

When inmates exhibit AIDS-related symptoms, they are usually confined in a hospital or infirmary setting. In some states (New Jersey among them), such inmates are placed in a hospital in the community; in other states (California among them), they are placed in correctional medical facilities. In states with a large number of prisoners carrying the virus, segregated housing is the policy, even when they show no symptoms of AIDS. California, for example, now houses all HIV-infected inmates in a wing of the Correctional Medical Facility at Vacaville to prevent transmission and to most effectively provide medical and counseling services to the group.

Medical Care   Corrections has a legal responsibility to furnish medical care to persons under its supervision. Because AIDS patients experience serious psychological problems in addition to physical problems, they require counseling and support services for themselves and their families.

Medical services for AIDS patients are costly; ranging from an estimated $50,000 to $145,000 annually per patient; for each New York City inmate, the cost of extended acute medical care could run as high as $300,000.[29] States with a large number of HIV-positive and AIDS-infected prisoners are facing costs that could easily constitute a major portion of their entire correctional budget.

The release of inmates with AIDS after they complete their sentences also raises difficult issues. On humanitarian grounds it might be argued that executive clemency or parole should be granted so that AIDS patients do not spend their last days in prison, yet there is a moral—and probably a legal—obligation to ensure that they are not simply "dumped" on the streets.

The Elderly Offender

Crime—at least predatory street crime—is the province of young men more than any other group. In visiting a prison, one is usually struck by the predominant numbers of young men, especially minorities. America's prison population has traditionally been young and poor, but in recent years it has been aging. In 1997 U.S. prisons held 37,342 offenders over 55 years old, a more than 50 percent increase in the elderly population of three years prior.[30]

The prison population is growing older for two reasons. First, the U.S. population in general is aging, so the overall citizenry is becoming older. Second, and more importantly, sentencing practices are changing. Consecutive lengthy sentences for heinous crimes, long mandatory minimum sentences, and life sentences without parole mean that more men who enter prison will spend most or all the rest of their life behind bars.

The prison population of elderly can be divided into three general groups. Most elderly offenders were young when they first entered prison facing very long terms for particularly serious crimes such as murder or brutal sexual assault (see the "Grant's Story" Focus box). A few enter prison in their old age for the first time, usually convicted either of financial crimes such as embezzlement or sexual assaults such as molestation or pedophilia. Finally, there are the experienced committed criminals, those who have been in prison before (usually more than once) but who are returning on yet another conviction. Obviously, then, elderly offenders vary in terms of criminal history and prison sophistication, but they also differ significantly from their younger peers.

An increasing portion of persons under correctional supervision are elderly. In some states their numbers have grown to such a degree that nursing home wings have been added to prisons. How should these offenders be treated?

FOCUS Grant's Story

Grant Cooper knows he lives in prison, but there are days when he cannot remember why. His crimes flit in and out of his memory like flies through a hole in a screen door, so that sometimes his mind and conscience are blank and clean.

He used to be a drinker and a drifter who had no control over his rage. In 1978, in an argument with a man in a bread line at the Forgotten Man Ministry in Birmingham, Alabama, his hand automatically slid into his pants pocket for a knife.

He cut the man so quick and deep that he died before his body slipped to the floor. Mr. Cooper had killed before, in 1936 and in 1954, so the judge gave him life. Back then, before he needed help to go to the bathroom, Mr. Cooper

was a dangerous man. Now he is 77, and since his stroke in 1993 he mostly just lies in his narrow bunk at the Hamilton Prison for the Aged and Infirm, a blue blanket hiding the tubes that run out of his bony body. Sometimes the other inmates put him in a wheelchair and park him in the sun. . . .

Mr. Cooper travels only in his mind. "I don't know if they'll ever set me free," he said, looking up from his bed, a pair of black-framed glasses sitting crooked on his face.

"I don't know. I don't reckon so."

Some days, if he forgets enough, he already is.

SOURCE: Rick Bragg, "Where Alabama Inmates Fade into Old Age," *The New York Times*, November 1, 1995, pp. A1, A18. Copyright © 1995 by The New York Times Company. Reprinted by permission.

The most obvious difference has to do with health. Aging prisoners have more trouble handling the physical strains of prison life than do the younger inmates, and they usually need increased medical care. Elderly offenders also have different social interests. Whereas younger inmates enjoy physical sports and competitive recreation, older inmates, like older men on the outside, may prefer solitude and less strenuous interaction.[31] These differences between elderly prisoners and the rank-and-file inmate translate into significantly greater per-inmate operating costs for the former, due to the need for special health, recreation, and housing services: one year's incarceration for an inmate over 60 years old costs $69,000, more than three times the overall average costs per inmate.[32]

Even though many elderly inmates have committed quite serious crimes, studies indicate that age reduces the chance that the prisoner will violate prison rules. Older prisoners often are more stable and dependable than their youthful counterparts, and they frequently occupy positions of trust within the prison. On release these inmates typically pose little risk to the public.

The adjustment problem facing most elderly offenders has to do with the way extended prison terms tend to institutionalize them. When a person spends many years in prison, the routines of the prison become debilitating. The prison regime controls all of the inmate's time and takes away most personal autonomy and decision making. After years of being told what to do almost every waking hour, it becomes difficult for a person to relearn how to make even the simplest decisions.

With prison space a valuable resource, many correctional administrators believe that elderly offenders should be released to the community so that their cells may be reallocated to those young offenders still able to commit serious crimes. Columnist George Will has endorsed programs such as POPS (Project for Older Prisoners), founded in New Orleans, which advocates and assists the release of elderly prisoners unlikely to return to crime.[33]

The Long-Term Offender

More prisoners serve long sentences in the United States than in any other Western nation (see the "Michael's Story" Focus box). Whereas the average first-time offender serves about twenty-two months, an estimated 11–15 percent of all prisoners—well over 100,000 inmates nationwide—will serve more than seven years in prison.[34] About 9 percent of all prisoners are serving life sentences, and another 24 percent are serving sentences of over twenty-five years. These long-term prisoners are often the same people who will become elderly inside prison walls, with all the attendant problems just discussed.

There is no one standard way that a long-term prisoner reacts to the time in prison. Studies show substantial differences in the way the long-termer responds, with some prisoners but not others experiencing severe stress, depression, and other health problems.[35] When severe emotional stress occurs, it tends to take place earlier rather than later in the sentence.

Long-term prisoners are not generally seen as control problems—they are charged with disciplinary infractions about half as often as short-term inmates—but they do present a management problem for prison administrators. Program managers have to find ways of making prison life livable for those who are going to be there a long time. According to Timothy Flanagan, one of the foremost authorities on long-term inmates, this involves three main principles: (1) maximizing opportunities for the inmate to exercise choice in living circumstances, (2) creating opportunities for meaningful living, and (3) helping the inmate maintain contact with the outside world.[36]

Classifying Offenders: Key Issues

Our descriptions of the categories of offenders should make it clear that several factors frustrate attempts to classify correctional clients. Problems center on overlap and ambi-

Michael's Story

Just after his twenty-fourth birthday, Michael Santos was sentenced to forty-five years in prison on nonviolent continuing criminal enterprise charges for his participation in cocaine trafficking. Under U.S. Sentencing Commission guidelines, which are expressly designed to deal harshly with drug dealers, Santos will serve at least 85 percent of the sentence: over thirty-eight years. He will be in his sixties when he is released.

Michael Santos's case illustrates a growing trend in American corrections—prisoners serving long terms. His sentence is an almost unimaginable length of time. For many of you reading this book, it is more than two times your current age. What must it mean to a man in his twenties to hear a judge impose such a sentence? How can a person face it?

In a recent scholarly paper on the topic, Santos mused on some of the dread and distress he felt facing his future: "Would my life be reduced to a prison registration number, being counted periodically as I waited for paint to peel off prison walls and years to pass away?"

Long-term prisoners must confront three main areas of concern. First, there is the inevitable shock, dismay, and sense of injustice on hearing the sentence pronounced. Even when lawyers have prepared the defendant for the worst, something ruinous occurs when the judge reads the sentence aloud. And even when the crime has been particularly heinous, disbelief and angry disheartenment accompanies the hearing of the penalty, as though in some way it is disconnected from the crime itself.

Second, there is the problem of personal loss. Santos realized that the long term was "likely to rip apart my relationships." He had married only a few months before his arrest, and he had little hope that the marriage could survive the fissure of imprisonment. But even if the marriage did not end, he had to wonder about what its quality would be—its intimacy and its potential for meaningful family life with no children and restricted contact. No matter how much love was present, it seemed woefully inadequate to overcome the abyss of forty-five years in prison.

Whenever Santos wondered about the future, he had countless other inmates' stories to advise him of the possibilities: mates who had long since abandoned them in painful, often acrimonious splits; children who themselves felt deserted by their fathers, an accusation nearly impossible to dispute from behind the prison wall. Even the salvaged relationships seem strained and unappealing.

Third, there is the challenge of finding meaningful ways to while away the interminable hours among society's outcasts. Like most long-term prisoners Santos spent the first years involved in legal wrangles, trying to overturn his conviction or obtain clemency. But after these initial years, "an ocean of depression swallowed me." The biggest battle is simply how to cope, how to escape the inviting sinkhole of hopelessness.

Michael Santos has now served eight years of his forty-five-year term. He fights every day for self-respect and for his future. To give his prison time meaning, he has completed bachelor's and master's degrees. He has continued to write, publishing on topics of correctional policy and administration. And he battles the system—against desperate odds—to get his sentence reduced. But in the end he struggles with hopelessness: "The coming of the Messiah," he protests, "seems closer than my release from prison."

SOURCE: Adapted from Michael G. Santos, "Facing Long-Term Imprisonment," in Timothy J. Flanagan, ed., *Long-Term Confinement: Policy, Science and Correctional Practice* (Thousand Oaks, CA: Sage, 1995), pp. 36-40.

guity in classification, the programmatic needs of corrections, behavioral probabilities, sociopolitical pressures, and individual distinctions.

Overlap and Ambiguity in Offender Classifications

Some sex offenders may also be alcoholics; some situational offenders may have emotional problems (perhaps even stemming from their new status as offender); some career criminals may be addicts. A classification system that has so much overlap cannot give correctional decision makers much guidance as to appropriate treatment. Should an addicted multiple burglar be treated as a career criminal or as an addict?

To combat ambiguities in classification, correctional administrators have started using **classification systems,** which apply a specific set of objective criteria to all inmates in order to arrive at an appropriate classification. The objective criteria usually

classification systems

Specific sets of objective criteria, such as offense history, previous experience in the justice system, and substance abuse patterns, applied to all inmates to determine an appropriate classification.

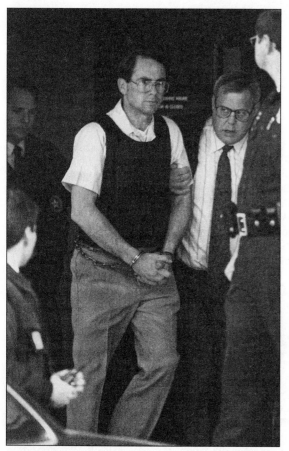

What level of custody and what type of programs should be given to Terry Nichols, convicted of conspiracy and manslaughter in connection with the Oklahoma City Federal Building bombing?

include such factors as current and prior offense histories, previous experiences in the justice system, and substance abuse patterns. By using objective criteria, these systems reduce the unreliability of the offender's classification, and by limiting the criteria to a few relevant facts, overlap is avoided.

Offense Classifications and Correctional Programming

Some critics have argued that the most important requirement for any correctional classification system is that it should improve our ability to manage and treat offenders effectively. If the categories described leave many correctional programming decisions unresolved, of what use are they? When one considers offenders, the normal temptation is to ask first what the person's crime is and then what the person's criminal history is. The nine classes of offenders we have described probably constitute 80 percent or more of the felony offenders managed by corrections, yet in each case the category is so broad that it leaves unanswered the important question, How shall this offender be managed? Broad categories may be useful for portraying the nature of offenders, but much narrower and more precise classification systems are required for the programmatic needs of corrections. In particular, corrections must be able to identify the offender's potential risk to correctional security and to the community.

Behavioral Probabilities in Classification

Human behavior may be impossible to predict, but we can certainly make educated guesses about a person's likely future behaviors. Thus a five-time check forger is likely to commit a similar offense again, just as a first-time offender is unlikely to do so. We know, of course, that the check forger may stop offending after the fifth time, just as the first-time offender may continue. But, on average, our educated guesses will more often than not be right. This is often thought of as a probabilistic approach to classification.

Recent classification systems have included probabilistic concepts. Officials try to see what offender characteristics are associated with reinvolvement in crime. The approach is similar to that used by automobile insurance companies, whose actuaries recognize that even though many teenagers do not have accidents, teenagers as a group have much higher accident rates than adult drivers. Therefore teenagers pay higher premiums, because they represent a greater risk.

Similarly offenders who have characteristics associated with higher risk can be classified as more likely to pose a threat and so can be required to pay a penological "premium": higher bail or no bail, closer supervision on probation or parole, tighter security in institutions, and so on. Therefore, even though most offenders will not commit more offenses, probabilistic classification serves the action needs of corrections.

Sociopolitical Pressures and Classification

One of the most frustrating aspects of offender classification is that the public response to crime frequently makes classification an emotionally charged issue. As a result, in managing offenders corrections is often forced to respond to changing public demands. Each group of offenders we described has been subjected to intense public hostility. In the 1940s and 1950s, for instance, public outrage over narcotics use led to stiff penalties for their sale and the establishment of addiction hospitals across the United States. In the 1950s and 1960s public concern with the "psychopath" led to the establishment of long-term treatment facilities just for the "dangerous" offender, such as Maryland's famous Patuxent Institution. More recently attention has focused on "high-rate" offenders, and policies have sought to selectively or collectively incapacitate them.

In each case public alarm about crime has produced new labeling patterns in the criminal justice system, with special handling mandated for all those who fit the label. The difficulty is that the labels are often broadly applied (partly because of the overlap in any classification system) and the handling is ordinarily more severe than necessary. Those who object to the frequent "reform" movements in corrections recognize that misapplying labels can do great harm. Yet in many instances the accuracy of the label and the appropriateness of the new offender management method for which the label calls are of little concern to correctional policymakers, who face the more severe problem of responding to the public demand for "action" to "crack down" on one type of crime or another. The problem is more political than penological.

Distinctions in the Criteria for Classifying Offenders

We all classify people around us. We think, *John is a Democrat, Nancy is a nice person, Tim is untrustworthy,* and so on. We realize these terms do not fully describe the persons but serve only as rough labels that help us gauge how they may behave or think in a given situation. In reality we know that sometimes John may sound like a Republican, Nancy may be grumpy, and Tim may keep his word. A person's behavior may be characterized by certain tendencies, but it is seldom fixed.

Given the variability of human behavior, offender classification must be seen as a rough way of grouping people. It is equally important to be precise about the criteria used for grouping. Three general kinds of criteria are used to classify offenders:

1. Offense criteria classify offenders as to the seriousness of the crime committed.
2. Risk criteria classify offenders as to the probability of future criminal conduct.
3. Program criteria classify offenders as to the nature of correctional treatment appropriate to the person's needs and situation.

These criteria do not lead to the same correctional consequences. Many offenders who committed serious crimes are not likely to do so again; many offenders who have few treatment needs still represent a risk to the community; and so on. Thus corrections systems need to apply a range of classification systems to determine the most appropriate way to manage any given offender.

Summary

A selection process filters certain kinds of cases out of the criminal justice system, so that offenders constitute a subgroup of people who may differ from the general population. Offenders are more likely to be minority men in their late teens or early twenties, from lower socioeconomic backgrounds, and lacking education and/or job skills.

The composition of the correctional population has a direct impact on corrections and its ability to achieve its goals. Because many offenders are undereducated, underskilled, and ill prepared for legitimate lifestyles, programs have been developed to correct these deficiencies.

The corrections population includes nine basic categories of offenders: the situational offender, the career criminal, the sex offender, the substance abuser (drugs and alcohol), the mentally ill offender, the mentally handicapped offender, the offenders with AIDS, the elderly offender, and the long-term offender. Each group has distinctive characteristics and problems related to offense situations and basic needs. When you understand these differences, you can see it is impossible to talk of "the offender" as if all criminals were similar.

Offender classification is influenced by the public's response to certain crimes at particular times. Public attitudes target certain groups for more severe or specialized punishment, and corrections must respond to this concern. ■

For Discussion

1. Is the process by which correctional clients are selected discriminatory? What might be done to reduce actual or perceived discrimination?
2. In what ways does the classification of correctional clients reflect the fragmentation of corrections?
3. What role should public opinion play in categorizing various offenders for the purpose of punishing them?
4. Is classifying offenders according to the probability of future criminal conduct a good idea? What are the dangers of the practice? What are its advantages?
5. What policy recommendations would you make with regard to the way career criminals are handled?

For Further Reading

Flanagan, Timothy, ed. *Long-Term Imprisonment: Policy, Science and Correctional Practice.* Thousand Oaks, CA: Sage, 1995. Provides a selection of papers and studies on offenders who serve long sentences.

Hobbs, Richard. *Bad Business.* New York: Oxford University Press, 1995. Studies professional criminals using interviews to understand their motivations for crime and methods of work.

McCarthy, Belinda, and Langworthy, Robert. *Older Offenders.* New York: Praeger, 1988. Summarizes studies of the needs and problems of elderly offenders.

Schwartz, Barbara K., and Cellini, Henry P. *The Sex Offender: Corrections, Treatment, and Legal Practice.* Kingston, NJ: Civil Research Institute, 1995. Collects papers dealing with all aspects of sex offenders in corrections, from psychodynamics to treatment and management in the community.

Van Voorhis, Patricia. *Psychological Classification of the Adult Prison Inmate.* Albany, NY: University of Albany, 1994. Provides a comprehensive discussion of several techniques for classifying offenders according to psychological profiles, risk profiles, and other attributes.

Notes

1. James Austin and John Irwin, *It's About Time: America's Imprisonment Binge* (Belmont, CA: Wadsworth, 1997).
2. Martin R. Haskell and Lewis Yablonsky, *Criminology: Crime and Criminality* (Chicago: Rand McNally, 1974), p. 264.
3. Patrick A. Langan and Mark A. Cuniff, *Recidivism of Felons on Probation, 1986–89* (Washington, DC: Bureau of Justice Statistics, 1992), p. 6.
4. Walter C. Reckless, *The Crime Problem* (New York: Appleton-Century-Crofts, 1961), pp. 153–177.
5. Alfred Blumstein, Jacqueline Cohen, Jeffrey Roth, and Christy Visher, *Criminal Careers and "Career Criminals"* (Washington, DC: National Academy of Sciences, 1986).
6. Peter Greenwood, *Selective Incapacitation* (Santa Monica, CA: Rand Corporation, 1982).
7. *The New Yorker,* March 7, 1994, p. 6.
8. Susan Brownmiller, *Against Our Will: Men, Women, and Rape* (New York: Simon & Schuster, 1975), pp. 376–377.
9. Lawrence A. Greenfeld, *Sex Offenses and Offenders: An Analysis of Data on Rape and Sexual Assault* (Washington, DC: U.S. Department of Justice, Bureau of Justice Statistics, February 1997).
10. Lawrence A. Greenfeld, *Sex Offenses and Offenders* (Washington, DC: Bureau of Justice Statistics, U.S. Department of Justice, February 1997), p. 23.
11. *Behind Bars: Substance Abuse and America's Prison Population* (New York: National Center on Addiction and Substance Abuse, 1997); *The New York Times,* January 9, 1998, p. A1.
12. U.S. Department of Justice, Bureau of Justice Statistics, *Special Report,* April 1998, p. 3.
13. Lawrence A. Greenfeld, *Alcohol and Crime: An Analysis of National Data on the Prevalence of Alcohol Involvement in Crime* (Washington, DC: U.S. Department of Justice, 1998), p. 9.
14. National Institute of Justice, *ADAM: 1997 Annual Report on Adult and Juvenile Arrestees* (Washington, DC: U.S. Department of Justice, July 1998), p. 2.
15. George E. Vaillant, "A 20-Year Follow-up of New York Narcotic Addicts," *Archives of General Psychiatry,* 29, August 1973 pp. 237–241.
16. Kit R. Van Stelle, Elizabeth Mauser, and D. Paul Moberg, "Recidivism to the Criminal Justice System of Substance-Abusing Offenders Diverted into Treatment," *Crime and Delinquency,* 40(2), April 1994, pp. 175–196.

17. *The New York Times,* April 13, 1995, p. A1.

18. Fox Butterfield, "Prisons Replace Hospitals for Mentally Ill," *The New York Times,* March 5, 1998, p. A1.

19. John Monahan, *Mental Illness and Violent Crime, National Institute of Justice Research in Preview* (Washington, DC: U.S. Department of Justice, October 1996).

20. Robert D. Hare, "Psychopathy: A Clinical Construct Whose Time Has Come," *Criminal Justice and Behavior,* 23(1), March 1996, pp. 25–54.

21. William McCord and Joan McCord, *The Psychopath* (New York: Van Nostrand, 1964), p. 2.

22. Thomas S. Szasz, *Law, Liberty, and Psychiatry* (New York: Macmillan, 1963), p. 12.

23. National Commission on the Causes and Prevention of Violence, *Crimes of Violence* (Washington, DC: U.S. Government Printing Office, 1969), p. 444.

24. U.S. Department of Justice, Bureau of Justice Statistics, *Report to the Nation on Crime and Justice* (Washington, DC: U.S. Government Printing Office, 1983), p. 68.

25. Joan Petersilia, "Justice for All? Offenders with Mental Retardation and the Criminal Justice System," *The Prison Journal,* 77(4), December 1997, pp. 358–380.

26. U.S. Department of Justice, Bureau of Justice Statistics, *Bulletin,* August 1997.

27. Dorothy E. Merianos, James W. Marquart, and Kelly Damphousse, "Examining HIV-Related Knowledge Among Adults and Its Consequences for Institutionalized Populations," *Correctional Management Quarterly,* 1, Fall 1997, pp. 84–87.

28. Theodore M. Hammett, *AIDS in Correctional Facilities: Issues and Options,* 3rd ed., publication of U.S. Department of Justice, National Institute of Justice (Washington, DC: U.S. Government Printing Office, 1988), pp. 82–84.

29. Susan Darst Williams, "Corrections' New Balancing Act: AIDS," *Corrections Compendium,* 11, August 1987, p. 1.

30. Darrell K. Galliard and Allen J. Beck, *Prisoners in 1997, Bureau of Justice Statistics Bulletin* (Washington, DC: U.S. Department of Justice, August 1998), p. 10.

31. Michael J. Sabath, "Factors Affecting the Adjustment of Elderly Inmates to Prison," in Belinda McCarthy and Robert Langworthy, eds., *Older Offenders* (New York: Praeger, 1988), p. 185.

32. *Seeking Justice: Crime and Punishment in America* (New York: Edna McConnell-Clark Foundation, 1997, p. 9.

33. *Newsweek,* July 20, 1998, p. 70.

34. Timothy J. Flanagan, "An American Portrait of Long-Term Imprisonment," in Timothy J. Flanagan, ed., *Long-Term Imprisonment: Policy, Science, and Correctional Practice* (Thousand Oaks, CA: Sage, 1995), pp. 10–21.

35. James Bonta and Paul Gendreau, "Reexamining the Cruel and Unusual Punishment of Prison Life," *Law and Human Behavior,* 14(4), 1990, pp. 347–372.

36. Timothy J. Flanagan, "Adaptation and Adjustment Among Long-Term Prisoners," *The Federal Prisons Journal,* 2(2), Spring 1991, pp. 45–51.

Correctional Practices

Part 2 deals with the heart of corrections. Here we

examine the different correctional practices as they

relate to the major institutions of community

corrections and incarceration. As you read each

chapter, consider how you would act if you found

yourself in the position of either offender or officer.

CHAPTER SEVEN

Jails: Detention and Short-Term Incarceration

San Francisco's jails are overcrowded — as are almost all jails in the big cities of America. A few years ago Sheriff Michael Hennessey decided to try a new idea: He sought to house fifty prisoners in the Pontiac Hotel, a transient hotel south of Market Street, a low-income area bordering the business district. Specially selected "low-risk" prisoners would be removed from the jail to the hotel, where they and others in the neighborhood would have access to a variety of social services. The idea seemed to have merit, and the overall cost would be much cheaper than jail.

There was only one hitch: Most of the hotel's neighbors objected. One anxious resident worried that the program would worsen "alcohol and drug problems on a street already deluged with both." Another asked, "Why does everything get pushed off here, to the armpit of the city?" To get his innovative program going, the sheriff would have to disregard the objections of people whose votes he needed to stay in office—an act of grave political risk.[1]

Jails are not very popular, whatever neighborhood they are in. They are a strange correctional hybrid: part detention center for people awaiting trial, part penal institution for sentenced misdemeanants, part refuge for social misfits taken off the streets. Jails hold men, women, and juveniles of all colors who have been accused of violating the law. Jails are the traditional dumping ground not only for criminals but also for petty hustlers, derelicts, junkies, prostitutes, the mentally ill, and disturbers of the peace, mainly from the poorer sections of cities. Thus jail's functions include those of the workhouse of the past.

Students interested in improving corrections during their future careers could find no area in more obvious need of reform than this country's jails. Among the institutions and programs of the corrections system, jail is the one most neglected by scholars and officials and least known to the public. Uniformly jam-packed and frequently brutalizing, jails almost never enhance life. Many criminal justice researchers agree that of all correctional agencies, jails are the oldest, most numerous, most criticized, and most stubbornly resistant to reform.

Jails are in such a state of decline that the estimated cost to bring them up to acceptable standards far exceeds what the nation can afford, at least in the foreseeable future. More than a decade ago the price tag for jail construction and renovation was estimated to be more than half a billion dollars, and that figure covered improvements in only about 10 percent of existing facilities.[2] Today conditions in jails are even worse because sentenced felons are being held there while awaiting vacancies in overcrowded state prisons. Therefore scholars, administrators, policymakers, and elected officials agree that using jail for any offender should be avoided whenever possible. Yet jail represents nearly all Americans' initial contact with corrections. For many people, this will be their only time in a correctional institution, and the impression it leaves will greatly influence their views of the criminal justice system.

With an estimated 13 million jail admissions per year, more people directly experience jails than experience prisons, mental hospitals, and halfway houses combined.[3] Even if we consider the fact that some portion of this total is admitted more than once, probably at least 6 to 7 million people are detained at some time during the year.

In this chapter we examine problems of operating jails and how some individuals avoid pretrial detention. We also raise questions about the role of corrections in this type of facility, where prisoners generally sit idle, without access to treatment and rehabilitative programs. We will focus on the following Questions for Inquiry.

Questions FOR INQUIRY

1. What is the nature of the contemporary jail?
2. What is the purpose of pretrial detention, and what problems does it pose?
3. What problems do sentenced inmates present to jail managers?
4. What alternatives to incarceration are available?
5. What are some of the issues in jail management?
6. What is the future of the jail?

The Contemporary Jail: Entrance to the System

Jails are the entryway to corrections. They house both accused individuals awaiting trial and sentenced offenders, usually serving one-year terms or less. People appealing sentences are often held in jail as well, as are those awaiting transfer to other jurisdictions. Nationally, almost 600,000 people are in jail on any one day, as Figure 7.1 shows.

Some people argue that jails lie outside corrections. For one thing, they claim that most of the nation's 3,300 jails are really a part of law enforcement, because sheriffs administer them. For another, they note that sentenced offenders make up only about half of the jail population and that pretrial detainees, who comprise most of the other half, should not fall within the scope of correctional responsibility. Finally, they suggest that, because most jails have neither treatment nor rehabilitative programs, they should be excluded from corrections.

We believe jails are an important part of corrections and demonstrate many complexities of the system. Administered by locally elected officials, jails are buffeted by the local politics of taxation, party patronage, and law enforcement. Jail practices also affect probation, parole, and prison policies.

Jails are perhaps the most frustrating component of corrections for people who want to apply treatment efforts to help offenders. Of the enormous numbers of people in jail, many need a helping hand. But the unceasing human flow usually does not allow time for such help—nor are the resources available in most instances.

Origins and Evolution

Jails in the United States are direct descendants of feudal practices in twelfth-century England. At that time an officer of the crown, the *reeve*, was appointed in each shire (what

Figure 7.1 Adult Male and Female Jail Inmates in the United States

Jails serve a number of purposes and hold both convicted offenders and pretrial detainees.

Convicted
Males (210,600)
Female (24,700)

Unconvicted
Males (288,200)
Female (34,600)

Source: U.S. Department of Justice, Bureau of Justice Statistics, *Bulletin,* January 1998.

we call a *county*) to collect taxes, keep the peace, and operate the *gaol* (jail). Among other duties the *shire reeve* (from which the word *sheriff* evolved) caught and held in custody, until a formal court hearing determined guilt or innocence, people accused of breaking the king's law. With the development of the workhouse in the sixteenth century, the sheriff took on added responsibilities for vagrants and the unemployed who were sent there. The sheriff made a living by collecting fees from inmates and by hiring out prison labor.

English settlers brought these traditions and institutions with them to the American colonies. After the American Revolution, law enforcement officials — particularly sheriffs and constables — were elected by the local community, but the functions of the jail remained unchanged. Jails were used to detain accused persons awaiting trial, as well as to shelter misfits who could not be taken care of by their families, churches, or other groups.

The American jail has been called the ultimate ghetto because most of the 600,000 people in jails are poor. They are held in jail awaiting disposition of their cases, serving sentences of under one year, or awaiting transfer to state prison.

The jails often were in the sheriffs' homes and were run like the sheriffs' households. Detainees were free to dress as they wished and to contribute their own food and necessities. The historian David Rothman notes, "So long as they did not cost the town money, inmates could make living arrangements as pleasant and homelike as they wished."[4] Local revenues paid room and board for detainees who could not make independent contributions.

In the 1800s the jail began to change in response to the penitentiary movement. Jails retained their pretrial detention function but also became facilities for offenders serving short terms, as well as for vagrants, debtors, beggars, prostitutes, and the mentally ill. Although the fee system survived, other changes took place. The juvenile reformatory movement and the creation of hospitals for the criminally insane during the latter part of the nineteenth century siphoned off some former jail inhabitants. The development of probation also removed some offenders, as did adult reformatories and state farms. And inmates now were segregated by sex. However, even with these innovations, the overwhelming majority of accused and convicted misdemeanants were held in jail.

Population Characteristics

Not until 1978 was a complete nationwide census of jails conducted by the Bureau of the Census for the Bureau of Justice Statistics. Repeated every five years by local officials, the census collects information on inmates in jails that hold people beyond arraignment (usually more than forty-eight hours). Excluded from the count are persons in federal and state-administered facilities. An annual survey of the top one-third largest jails, which hold about 75 percent of the inmate population, supplements these five-year nationwide counts.

The 1997 National Jail Census shows that about 90 percent of inmates are men, most are under 30 years old, a little more than half are white, and most have very low incomes.[5] The demographic characteristics of the jail population differ from those of the national population in many ways: People in jail are younger and disproportionately African American, and most are unmarried (see Figure 7.2).

As with prisons, jail populations vary from region to region and from state to state. The proportion of a state's population in jail, known as the *jail rate,* is high in the West and South (see Figure 7.3). In many states where prisons are filled to capacity, sentenced felons sit in jails awaiting transfer.

Figure 7.2 Characteristics of Adult Jail Inmates in U.S. Jails

Compared with the American population as a whole, jails are disproportionately inhabited by men, minorities, the poorly educated, and those with low income.

SOURCE: U.S. Department of Justice, Bureau of Justice Statistics, *Special Report*, April 1998.

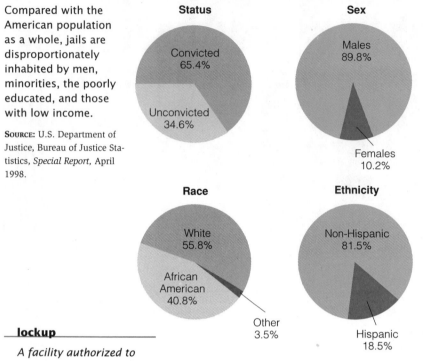

Status

Convicted 65.4%

Unconvicted 34.6%

Sex

Males 89.8%

Females 10.2%

Race

White 55.8%

African American 40.8%

Other 3.5%

Ethnicity

Non-Hispanic 81.5%

Hispanic 18.5%

lockup

A facility authorized to hold people before court appearance for periods of up to forty-eight hours. Most lockups (also called drunk tanks or holding tanks) are administered by local police agencies.

One of the most troubling trends in jails is the increasing rate of incarceration for African Americans. Figure 7.4 shows the changes in these rates since 1983; most of the increase in jail population over the past decade has been due to a more than doubling of the number of African Americans in jails. As we discuss in Chapter 18, this trend applies to all of corrections, not just jails.

Administration

Of the 3,300 jails in the United States, 2,700 have a county-level jurisdiction, and most are administered by an elected sheriff. An additional 600 or so municipal jails are in operation. Only in six states — Alaska, Connecticut, Delaware, Hawaii, Rhode Island, and Vermont — are jails for adults administered by state government. There are also an estimated 13,500 police **lockups** (or drunk tanks) and similar holding facilities authorized to detain people for up to forty-eight hours. The Federal Bureau of Prisons has only four detention facilities (in New York, Chicago, San Diego, and Florence, Arizona), and thus it contracts with local governments to hold more than a thousand people awaiting trial or sentence.

The capacity of jails varies greatly. The twenty-five largest jurisdictions hold almost 30 percent of the nation's jailed inmates. The two jurisdictions with the most inmates,

Figure 7.3 People Incarcerated in Local Jails per 100,000 Population, by State

What accounts for the fact that incarceration rates in jails differ from state to state?

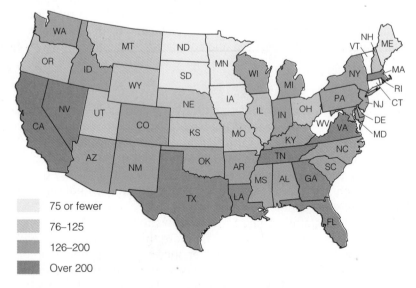

75 or fewer

76–125

126–200

Over 200

NOTE: Five states — Connecticut, Rhode Island, Vermont, West Virginia, and Hawaii — have integrated jail-prison systems; therefore information for these states is not given.

SOURCE: U.S. Department of Justice, Bureau of Justice Statistics, *Bulletin* (Washington, DC: U.S. Government Printing Office, April 1995), pp. 2–3.

Figure 7.4 Incarceration Rates for African American and White Jail Inmates, 1983–1997

What can explain the phenomenal increase in the incarceration rate of African Americans?

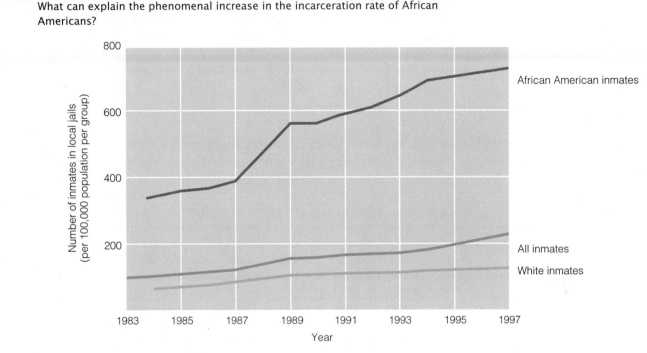

SOURCE: U.S. Department of Justice, Bureau of Justice Statistics, *Bulletin* (Washington, DC: U.S. Government Printing Office, January 1998), p. 8.

Los Angeles County and New York City, together hold approximately 39,000 inmates in multiple jails, or 7 percent of the national total. The Los Angeles County Men's Central Jail alone holds more than 6,000 people, but most jails are much smaller, with 67 percent holding fewer than 50 people.[6] However, these small facilities are dwindling in number because of new jail construction and the creation of regional, multicounty facilities.

As facilities to detain accused persons awaiting trial, jails customarily have been run by law enforcement agencies. We might reasonably expect that the agency that arrests and transports defendants to court should also administer the facility that holds them. Typically, however, neither sheriffs nor deputies have much interest in corrections. They often think of themselves as police officers and of the jail as merely an extension of their law enforcement activities. In some major cities municipal departments of correction, rather than the police, manage the jails.

Many experts argue that jails have outgrown police administration. Jails no longer are simply holding places but now represent one of the primary correctional facilities in the criminal justice system. In fact, much correctional work is directed toward jail inmates. Probation officers conduct presentence investigations in jails, alcohol and drug abusers receive treatment in many facilities, and inmates perform community service or work toward reintegration out of some facilities. Therefore the effective administration of jails requires skills in offender management and rehabilitation that are not generally included in law enforcement training. This point was well made over twenty-five years ago by the President's Commission on Law Enforcement and Administration of Justice: "The basic police mission of apprehending offenders usually leaves little time, commitment, or expertise for the development of rehabilitative programs, although notable exceptions demonstrate that jails can indeed be settings for correctional treatment."[7]

Good management practices may not always overcome several problems that face jail administrators. One problem is that some jails cannot send their prisoners to state facilities after they are sentenced. Many state prisons are so crowded that they refuse to accept sentenced offenders until space becomes available. In fact, over 27,000 offenders remained in local jails in 1995 as they awaited openings in prisons.[8]

Another problem is that many jails are still budgeted under a **fee system**, whereby the costs of housing, food, and services are averaged and a standard amount (say, $10 per day per prisoner) is remitted to the sheriff's department. This creates an incentive for poor jails: inadequate food, services, and prisoner support. Often the sheriff uses money saved on housing prisoners to augment the kinds of law enforcement services that attract public support and are therefore helpful at the polls.

fee system

A system by which jail operations are funded by a set amount paid for each prisoner held per day.

The Influence of Local Politics

Because of the close links between jail administration and local politics, fiscal pressures and political conservatism have a powerful effect on jails. Fiscally sound measures often are ignored because of political pressures. For example, pretrial release programs are cost efficient and a proven means of reducing institutional crowding, yet the public's fear of crime often makes the programs politically infeasible. Conversely political pressures may support expanded use of jail confinement for misdemeanant offenders or probation violators (particularly when crime is a potent electoral issue), but funds often are lacking to expand or upgrade the jail's capacity to handle additional offenders. The jail is a crime control service but also a drain on revenues. The tension between these two public interests is often expressed in local-level debates over capital expenditures for jail construction. Because revenues often are insufficient, many jails are overcrowded and cannot house all the inmates assigned to their supervision, and some are released or placed in other facilities.

It is very hard to wrest control of local facilities away from a politically sensitive office such as that of sheriff or police chief. The more than 362,000 jail-related jobs constitute a large block of political patronage for elected officials to distribute to political supporters. Political appointees will spend most of their time on the jail, but during political campaigns they hustle votes and money for their bosses. Even when jail employees are civil servants, political considerations can be a factor in hiring and promotion. Few politicians willingly surrender control over such a potential political force as the jail. So change is slow.

Regional Jails

Most local jails are located away from major population centers, and many may hold as few as thirty people. Even though the state may provide a portion of their operating funds, the smaller jails lack essential services such as medical care that must be provided no matter how few people may need them.

A recent trend designed to remedy these problems has been toward regionalization: the creation of combined municipal–county or multicounty jails. This multijurisdictional or **regional jail**, fiscally sound though it may be, has been slow to catch on because several interest groups are negatively affected by it. Local political and correctional leaders do not want to give up their autonomy or their control over patronage jobs, and reformers often object to moving inmates away from their communities. Finally, citizens oppose having regional jails "in their backyard," as did the San Franciscans described at the beginning of this chapter.

regional jail

Facility operated under a joint agreement by two or more governmental units, with a jail board drawn from representatives of the participating jurisdictions and having varying authority over policy, budget, operations, and personnel.

Pretrial Detention

Imagine that you have been arrested by the police and accused of a crime. Probably you were handcuffed, read your rights, and taken to the station for booking. You are frightened and have a hundred questions, but the police treat you as if your fears were irrelevant to their work. You may be angry with yourself for what you have done. You may be frustrated that you cannot seem to control the flow of procedure: fingerprints, mug shots, long waits while detectives and prosecutors discuss you without acknowledging your presence. Slowly you begin to understand you have acquired a new status: accused offender.

Then you are taken to the detention section of the jail. If it is an advanced facility, you are placed in a holding room for an intake interview. There your situation is explained to you, you are asked questions about your background that will help determine how best to manage you while you are in jail, and you are told what you can expect next. If, however, you are in one of many jails with no formal intake procedure, you are simply put in the holding tank. If you are a male, several strangers likely will be in the cell with you, men whose stories you do not know and whose behavior you cannot predict. If you are a female, you probably will be by yourself. In either case, once the guard leaves, you are on your own behind bars, and the full extent of your situation begins to sink in. This can be an especially trying period for some detainees who are thrust into a hostile and threatening environment, as discussed in Do the Right Thing.

Russell Henderson, Aaron McKinney, and Chastity Pasley wait to be arraigned in Laramie, Wyoming, for the death of Matthew Shepard, a gay student who was beaten, burned, and tied to a fence like a scarecrow.

D O   T H E   Right   T H I N G

Ted Bliss entered the office of Dick Steele, Warden of the Montville County Jail.

"Dick, we can't put Josh Welch into the general population, he'll be eaten alive! With the Latin Kings and the CRIPS trying to impress each other, that young white kid is going to be jail meat."

"I know, Ted, but what can we do? The place is crowded, I can't separate by race or by gang. This is no hotel where someone gets his own room and special services. We've got one 30-man dorm for the detainees, and twenty beds in the other wing for those under sentence. I know he's going to have trouble, but he is just going to have to work it out himself."

"But you could put him over in the sentenced wing. There's a bed there and those guys are less aggressive. It's these young gang members just off the street who try to impress each other by being so macho. They really put the pressure on the new boys."

"I know, but we can't make exceptions."

Does Warden Steele have an ethical obligation to protect Josh Welch? Should Officer Bliss continue to pressure for a policy exception? What would you do if you were Ted Bliss? ■

In such circumstances, many people panic. In fact, the hours immediately following arrest are often a time of crisis, due to the sense of vulnerability and hopelessness, the fear of lost freedom, and the sheer terror. During 1993, 36 percent of deaths that occurred in jail were suicides.[9] Not surprisingly, most of these suicides happened within the first six to ten hours after lockup, and most psychotic episodes occur during or just after jail intake.

The crisis nature of arrest and detention can be exacerbated by other factors. Often the arrestee is intoxicated or on drugs, a state that may have contributed to the crime for which the person is being held. Sometimes the criminal behavior stems from an emotional instability that may worsen in detention. Especially for young offenders, the oppressive reality can trigger debilitating depression. Unquestionably one of the most crucial times for arrestees is the period immediately following arrest (see the Focus box).

FOCUS   Rite of Passage

Between the booking desk and the holding tank, the corridor is a fluorescent tunnel, rank with the smell of vomit and old piss. The jailer keeps behind me, walking slow, his boot heels clicking ominously on the gray linoleum. He stops at the last door, slips his key into the lock. The heavy iron grinds open and my whole body goes rigid. For a moment I want to drop the towel and plastic mattress, turn and run. But I don't. I hesitate for a moment and then allow him, with one fat hand, to shove me into the smoky dimness of the holding tank.

The door slams and I blink my eyes twice against the dirty light, straining to see through the shadows. The tank might be a dozen feet across, windowless, the ceiling light screened with an iron grillwork and a shredded towel that reads Santa Cruz County Jail. Below it, covering the iron bunks and the floor between them, are a half dozen men, each glancing up to look me over. I turn to the closest man, a heavyset guy with greasy hair and a Harley Davidson tee shirt, and ask what I should do with my mattress. "It's my first time in jail," I announce. "They just booked me in."

He looks back without speaking, his expression suggesting a vague annoyance. He stares, his face hard, and I stare back, a slow chill forming at the base of my spine. "Will you check this one out?" he says to the man at his right.

The other man, a skinny guy with elaborate dragons tattooed on both arms, answers with a trace of derision. "Looks like another fish, don't he? Don't he look like a fish, fellas?"

"He's a pretty one though," says a Chicano over in the corner. "Long hair, nice buns. . . ."

When they laugh, my whole body tenses and I edge backward, retreating until the bars of the cell push against my back, ice-cold. For a second I consider yelling for the guard—the fat cop who booked me in, read me my Miranda rights, made me strip naked and spread my ass, joking about the fun I'd have in the holding tank. Remembering the hostility in his voice, I decide against yelling. Instead, I move with my mattress still dragging into the center of the tank. The others arrange themselves around me as if preparing for an inquisition. Each of their expressions is curious or hostile, indifferent or angry. Looking them over, I wonder suddenly what it is I've done.

I don't ask them that though, afraid of what they'd say. I keep silent, listening while the silence grows and becomes painful: the kind of silence that might precede an execution, the silence of a gas chamber.

From the sink on the back wall I can hear a faucet dripping, each drop a small explosion. Out in the hall I can hear someone's laughter, a cop maybe, oblivious to anything going on inside. I look again at the faces: the stocky man in the Harley shirt, the skinny guy with the dragon arms, two Chicanos in white tee shirts, a black man wearing sunglasses, a few others lost in shadows along the far wall. I examine each face for a sign of recognition, a potential ally or supporter. Each expression though is blank, mute, closed. I could be in jail in Turkey or Morocco, some place where another language was spoken.

When the tattooed man spits something near my foot, every nerve in my body convulses. I look away sharply, aware that my fear has given me away, has become visible here under the dirty light.

"Why don't you tell us what you're in here for?" begins the one in the Harley shirt. His voice is cold and mocking. Before I can answer, a second voice, dripping venom, joins the first.

"He's probably in for sniffin' bicycle seats," snaps the skinny guy, his tattoos livid in the dim light.

"That, or staying out past curfew," laughs the man in the dark glasses. He flips a cigarette butt past my leg and adds, "I don't know why they put him with us adults."

Becoming impatient, the one in the Harley shirt shifts on his bunk, his voice rising. "You gonna tell us about your beef, kid, what you're in here for? Or do you have something to hide?"

I make myself look him in the eye, my face level with his. "I'm in for drugs," I answer, wondering if I should have lied, told him kidnapping or robbery. "I'm in for possession." I say it again for emphasis, though my voice is shaking now like my hands.

"Possession of what, oregano?" cracks the biker. A moment ago, walking into the tank, I thought the biker might be on my side, a source of support. His voice now is without sympathy, sarcastic, unrelenting.

"Possession of marijuana." I hear my voice waver, crack, slip out of control.

"How much marijuana?"

I wet my lips, stalling, then continue. "A pound and a half. Colombian weed." I emphasize the word *Colombian*, as if it might impress one of them, as if I were speaking to potential buyers.

"A pound and a half of weed isn't shit. It ain't nothin'—except to a kid. And say, does your mommy and daddy know you're down here in jail?"

"My parents are dead." They aren't, but I say they are, hoping to buy time, wanting them to ease up. The fear is rising like warm lava up my spine.

"Poor baby. All alone with us criminals. Who do you got to bail you out of here?"

Nobody, I think, or nobody close enough to go my bond. A year ago, a few hundred miles from here, there was a girl, Susan, who I might have called. For a while we'd thought we loved each other. Drugs were the thing we'd argued about. We argued and she told me I'd end up here, busted, that I'd have nobody to turn to. My parents had sided with her, making the same prediction. It had been a year since I'd seen any of them. I wasn't even sure of their phone numbers, whether they'd accept my call.

"C'mon, hot shit, talk up," taunts the biker. "Think you're big time? Big-time dealer? Think you're pretty hot shit?"

I want to say nothing, deny that I'm scared of them. I can't though, and they know it. With that realization I can feel my chest constrict—as if the walls of the tank were closing in, like the cell was becoming smaller. I can feel my heart pounding like a fist against my ribs. Abruptly I think back to the place where I was busted, the highway where I'd been hitchhiking: a black strip of asphalt rising over a slope of mountains, the sky above the high peaks a crystalline blue, and above them sunlight like lemon meringue over everything. How could I have imagined there'd be a sheriff's car cruising that highway, that I'd be stopped and frisked?

The man with the tattoos breaks the silence. "You know you'll probably get prison time for that much weed. Maybe years, a nickel or so. Think you can handle that? Think you'll like doing time?"

"I'm not going to consider it until I know—"

"Look on the bright side of that, though," interrupts the one in sunglasses. "When you hit the joint, you'll make somebody a fine kid. Anybody as young and pretty as you will be real popular with all those men."

I ignore the insinuation, trying not to think about the penitentiary. I remember instead the beauty of the mountains, the western desert rolling out to the horizon. Against the ugliness of their voices, the shadowy iron of the holding tank, the memory becomes vivid, nearly exquisite.

The one in the biker shirt resumes. "How you think you'll like that? Being somebody's kid? Somebody's punk? Some lifer that ain't had no real woman in ten years?"

I leer back at him. I try to appear indifferent.

With each insult I can feel something tightening in my chest, winding there like a spring. My hands have begun to sweat and I realize suddenly that I've been holding my mattress the whole time, my arm going gradually numb. I let the mattress fall, watching as it strikes the foot of the Chicano who's been yelling the loudest.

He jerks back as if he's been slapped, exaggerating the effect of my action. "You trying to break my foot with that mattress? You *loco*? You tryin' to start something?" Turning to the other he shouts: "Did you all see that? This guy threw a mattress on me! I think he wants a fight."

"I saw it," yells the Harley shirt, wanting a confrontation. "He's trying to provoke you, Martinez. He's looking to start something."

"No, he ain't," someone in back yells. "He's too *puta.*"

"What about it, kid?" demands the man with the dragon tattoo. "You too scared to fight? You rather turn puta than fight Martinez?"

"Or maybe you'd enjoy that," chants the black man. "Maybe you got some girl in you. Maybe you'd like Martinez to rip you off. You'd make it sweet to him, wouldn't you, Martinez?"

In response, the Mexican pushes closer. "I'd make it real nice, just like I'd do a woman. And I wouldn't have to raise a finger, would I? Huh, *gringo?*" He inches closer, breathing hard, rocking on the balls of his feet.

"Answer him, kid," demands the biker. "You gonna fight him or not?"

"What's it gonna be, kid?" yells an old man in back, someone who hasn't spoken until now. "You better hurt him—or get hurt yourself. Come out of here a sissy."

They take turns screaming ultimatums, each one trying to outdo the others. In front of me, Martinez prances back and forth like a prizefighter, as if he'd been preparing all his life for this moment. When he levels his fists in anticipation, the others go wild.

"Can I get a wager on this?" yells the biker. "I'll bet a pack of Camel filters on Martinez."

"I'll double that," calls the man with the dragon tattoo. "I'll bet you breakfast and dinner."

Someone else shouts louder. "I'll go two packs of smokes and four meals. But I want a knockout. I want to see some blood."

The skinny man near the toilet, his voice like ice, yells over all of them. "You're wasting our time, kid. You gonna defend yourself? You gonna fight the man—or get your ass kicked?"

Fight him for what? I want to tell them this is pointless, that we have no reason to fight. The man called Martinez has nothing against me and I've done nothing to harm him. I want to remind them we're in this tank together.

The Mexican's first jab catches me off guard, a warning, his fist floating slowly past my jaw. He feints twice with short jabs, baiting me to fight, teasing me. He swings again with his right, the fist coming closer, and then dances back, turning to the others for encouragement.

The biker yells first: "You've cut him enough slack, Martinez. Let him have it."

The black in sunglasses: "Down him, Martinez."

The tattooed man, his voice rabid: "He's a punk. He's got it coming."

Their voices run together now, a scramble of noise demanding blood. Watching Martinez's fists, their rapid movement, I feel myself going dizzy. I raise my hands in fear, wanting to protect my eyes and mouth, wanting just to get through this. When the Mexican spits on my cheek, I'm not sure at first what it is. I hesitate, glancing around uncertainly.

(continued)

"He spit in your god-damn face, kid. How'd you like that?"

"You're a sissy if you take that."

"*Puta!*"

When he spits again, something tightens and then snaps in my chest: my fear becoming rage, something primitive that precludes reason. I watch my fists fly at him. Once, twice, again. I swing like I want to kill him, every muscle in my body rigid. I swing like my life depends on it. Wanting his blood on my hands, wanting to see him go down. And wanting them to shut up, all of them, and leave me alone. I swing like a machine, not sure whether I'm hurting him or not.

When someone's arms lock around my shoulders, forcing my own arms in against my chest, I know I've had it. The man's standing behind me, his arms like steel bands around my own body. I yell that this isn't fair, then feel my legs go weak and buckle, caving in beneath me, my body slipping heavily to the floor. Lying motionless on the concrete, I look up at the circle of faces gathered above. When Martinez extends his hand again I cringe in terror, expecting to be knocked unconscious.

"Grab my hand," he says, his voice neutral as he lifts me awkwardly from the floor. "The fight's over. No *puta.*"

"You did all right," states the biker, patting my back with one big hand. "You fought back."

"You stood up to him," says the black man.

"You done all right," admits another. "You need to work on that right hook though . . ."

Their arms around my shoulders, we walk together to one of the benches. I listen as each one tells me his name, and then I announce mine. Taking turns, we relate our stories. How we got busted, why we shouldn't have been, how we're going to beat our cases. A.J., the biker, rolls me a cigarette and we smoke it together like old comrades. Later, we're playing poker when someone turns to the door, says abruptly: "Shut up—there's someone walking in the hall, a fish maybe. Get ready."

We wait together then, one group, none of us daring to speak, each anxious for the next new prisoner to appear at the door, hoping for a very young one, somebody scared, each of us hungry for the ritual to begin again.

Source: Adapted from M. Knoll, "Rite of Passage," *Greenfield Review*, 11, Winter–Spring 1984, pp. 121–127. Reprinted by permission.

Detainees differ in their need for help during this period. Those under the influence of mind-altering substances need time to overcome the effects; others need to be left alone; still others need communication and advice. Jails lack the programmatic flexibility to accommodate the range of needs. However, the early confinement period also represents a mental health opportunity, because an individual in crisis is most likely to respond positively to efforts at help. Unfortunately the jail is not ordinarily well suited to provide aid in the first hours of detention. Elaborate mental health measures are not feasible, nor are they necessarily required. But even simple human contact—conversation with correctional staff, involvement in some activity, communication about what the detainee is likely to be experiencing—frequently is enough to reduce many initial anxieties.

Special Problems of Detainees

Beyond the initial crisis of being arrested and jailed, serious problems arise for many people who are detained for an extended period. As we will discuss, the most significant are mental health problems, substance dependency, medical needs, and legal problems. Because so many jail inmates have these problems, jails often have been referred to as the social agency of last resort. In the Workperspective, Marylin Chandler describes her career and some of the problems she faces.

Mental Health Problems   Growing attention is being paid to the mental health of arrestees whose behavior, while not seriously criminal, is socially bizarre—those who are only partially clothed, who speak gibberish or talk loudly to themselves, who make hostile gestures, and so on. These people, whose behavior is unpredictable and to some extent uncontrollable, formerly were transported to mental institutions where they could be treated. But with the nationwide deinstitutionalization movement, they have become outpatients of society, and they often spend time in jail instead of receiving the psychiatric treatment they once might have. Studies show that up to one-fourth of jail inmates have

Marilyn Chandler Ford

WORKPERSPECTIVE

**Assistant Corrections Director,
Volusia County, Florida**

Although my early educational interests foreshadowed my later career, my jobs have spanned varying aspects of criminal justice.

I was an undergraduate at the State University of New York at Buffalo during the student demonstrations and riots against the Vietnam War. Student debate focused on the role of government and the agents of social control—particularly the police. At this time I took my first sociology course and encountered readings on deviance. The instructor offered a "ride along" experience with the Buffalo police. A year later the nation's attention became fixed on the prisoner riots at Attica, not far away.

My own fascination with corrections was whetted. I took courses on corrections and ended up majoring in social work. My first full-time job was as a youth counselor-outreach worker, while I pursued a master's degree at SUNY-Albany. By the close of my first semester of graduate work I knew that my thirst for knowledge about criminal justice was barely quenched. I wanted to learn as much as I could, but I still thought I would return to the field as a practitioner or become a researcher in a criminal justice agency. I didn't do either—right away.

After teaching for a short time in a small liberal arts college and completing my doctorate, I relocated to Florida, where I joined the Department of Corrections as a probation officer. In Florida, the DOC administers felony probation and parole while misdemeanant probation is carried out at the local or county level. Probation officers must be state certified, so shortly after beginning the job I completed three months at the academy. As a probation officer I carried a caseload of 120–130 people and completed presentence investigations for the court.

After nine months, I was hired by Volusia County to conduct research and to coordinate the jail's information and automation needs. At this time the jail had a serious problem of crowding. My research focused on the dynamics of crowding and was designed to help decision makers respond to the rising jail population. This project was crucial, because a construction program to alleviate inmate crowding would not relieve the immediate problem.

Jail administrators do not control how many or who arrives at their doorstep. And similarly, they do not control who or how many people get released. In a jail, inmates require rooms (cells) with linens, bathroom facilities, meals, and some type of recreation or leisure activities.

There must also be standardized check-in and check-out procedures to ensure an accurate count of occupants.

Another challenge was developing the jail's information processing system. Many jails maintain manual record systems or have automated only recently. Over a ten-year period a majority of jail records and processes of the Volusia County Jail were automated. Databases for planning purposes were crafted and "on demand" reports may now be generated to understand the inmate population and assess the impacts of potential policy changes.

Eventually I was placed in charge of the booking office, the "gatekeeper" for the institution. People may not enter custody until the paperwork is reviewed and found to meet legal standards, and inmates may not be released without the proper authority. Staff must be familiar with arrest reports, court documents, bond collection and surrender procedures, out-of-county detainers, and extradition and first appearance processes. Work in the booking office is fast paced and high stress. Its impact and responsibilities are enormous. Problem resolution was a key part of my duties—clarifying and disentangling paperwork and conflicting court orders.

Nearly two years later I took charge of the jail's Program Services Division. The primary functions of this division including classifying inmates and coordinating inmate programs. We use an objective classification instrument to refer inmates to programs. Much of my time is spent coordinating and developing the educational, substance abuse, domestic violence, HIV/AIDS, life skills, and religious programs, conducted primarily by volunteers. I serve on several community boards to keep informed about local social services and national policy incentives. I thus can pass on to my staff information about postrelease resources.

In my current position as assistant corrections director, I'm still responsible for inmate programs but also have duties that cross security and program lines. I review disciplinary board actions and approve whether a loss or gain of good time is appropriate. In these capacities I exercise a good deal of discretion. Although departmental policy is the foundation for handling inmates, as supervisor and final reviewing authority, I need to examine whether sufficient reasons exist to deviate from policy. Factors include the inmate's good conduct in the institution, the effect of the decision on staff and institutional order, whether the situation is likely to apply to a number of inmates, and the legal principles set forth in court cases, state statutes, and professional accreditation policies. ■

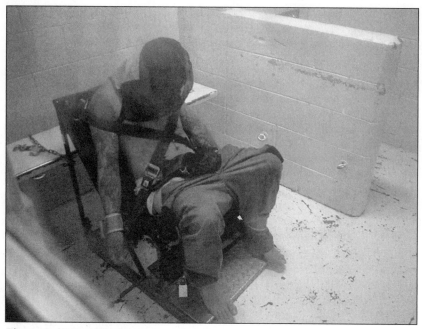

The period immediately after arrest and detention is a time of stress. Some detainees must be restrained and placed under a suicide watch.

mental health problems requiring psychiatric services, and as many as half are seriously depressed and in need of treatment.[10]

Observers say the number of inmates considered mentally ill is increasing. However, police have few alternatives to confinement for people who behave oddly or self-destructively, even if they are more nuisances than criminal. Moreover, unstable people often respond to the stress of jail with emotional outbursts and irrational behavior. Jails not only draw from but add to the ranks of the mentally disturbed.

Most jails lack resources to provide care for mentally ill offenders. Three-fourths of all jails have no rehabilitative staff, and among the remainder the vast majority of rehabilitative personnel lack training to deal with severe cases of mental and emotional stress, particularly when threats of self-injury are involved. Consequently mentally disturbed inmates often languish in jails, where they are abused by other inmates, misunderstood by correctional workers, and untreated by professional personnel.

The news is not all bad, however; some positive steps have been taken to divert the mentally ill from jail. Many jails screen new arrivals for mental health problems, with specially trained counselors interviewing and evaluating pretrial detainees.[11] Inmates with mental health problems are usually referred to local social service agencies for treatment and may be diverted from criminal prosecution in order for treatment to proceed.[12]

Substance Dependency   Depending on the locality, from just under 40 percent to nearly 80 percent of arrestees test positive for drug use at the time of arrest.[13] Many are drug dependent. The most dramatic problems posed by offenders' drug abuse occur during withdrawal, when the addict's body reacts to the loss of the substance on which it has grown dependent. Both alcoholics and drug addicts suffer withdrawal, but it is especially painful for the latter group and may last as long as a week. Addicts may attempt suicide to escape the pains of withdrawal, and a higher percentage of drug addicts than nonaddicts succeed in the attempt. Early identification of the drug addict thus is a high priority in urban jails, for withdrawal symptoms can be assuaged by methadone maintenance or release to an addiction treatment facility. Despite the short stays of inmates in jails, specialized treatment programs designed especially for jails have shown some success.[14]

Every jail regularly houses alcoholic offenders, many of whom, during the initial hours of confinement, are physically sick, hallucinating, and paranoid. These symptoms tend to be viewed as inconveniences rather than as conditions requiring treatment. Few jails provide any real form of treatment, and treatment by outside agencies is often just as rare because agencies prefer voluntary clients to offenders.

Since the first detoxification center in the United States was established in St. Louis in 1966, the national trend has been toward treating public drunkenness as more of a medical than a criminal problem. These detox centers are quasi-voluntary facilities for recidivist inebriates, many of whom have no other place to go. The centers provide shelter, medical care, food, clothing, and counseling for residents, most of whom are taken there by police.

Medical Needs   Detainees have many medical needs, ranging from minor scrapes and bruises sustained during arrest and booking, to major injuries sustained during the crime and its aftermath. To these injuries can be added the routine health deficiencies of any lower-class citizens: infections, poor nutrition, lack of dental care, and so forth. Even so, over three-quarters of U.S. jails neither contain medical facilities nor offer sound medical services.

Today the most pressing medical issue in jails relates to the offender with AIDS, estimated at over 2 percent of jailed inmates nationally.[15] As noted in Chapter 6, jail officials should be in a position to provide certain treatments for arrestees with AIDS, and all correctional workers should take standard precautions around these offenders. The main problems have to do with staff training, because many jail employees have misconceptions about how AIDS is spread, which can lead to mishandling of AIDS-infected inmates.

Legal Needs   Pretrial detainees are people, and they need access to legal assistance to cope with it. In the emotionally stressful postarrest period, suspects need information about what will happen prior to their trial. They also need legal help in securing release through bail or diversion. If release is not possible, they must have help in preparing their case, negotiating with the prosecutor about charges, or directing the attorney to people who may provide an alibi or exonerating evidence. Not surprisingly, research consistently shows that people locked up in jail until trial are at a disadvantage in preparing their defense.

People in jail are likely to need a public defender, an appointed counsel, or an attorney provided by contract. Unfortunately, because they must process large numbers of cases for relatively small fees, criminal defense attorneys cannot spend much time locating witnesses, conducting investigative interviews, and preparing testimony. So for many detainees these essential defense plans are only partially pursued.

Detainees can expect to spend long periods of time without seeing an attorney. In fact, most have only one or two hurried conversations with their attorneys before they appear in court. To add insult to injury, detainees are brought to court in shackles and jail-issue clothing, in dramatic contrast to well-groomed defendants who have been able to remain free. Detainees once employed have long since been fired. In short, detainees have relatively dim prospects.

Pretrial Detainees' Rights   Unlike prisoners, pretrial detainees have not been convicted of the crimes for which they are being held. Technically they are innocent, yet they are detained under some of the worst conditions of incarceration. In the 1970s several courts reasoned that such people should suffer no more restrictions than are necessary to ensure their presence at trial and that legal protections for detainees should exceed those of sentenced prisoners.

However, in 1979 the U.S. Supreme Court overruled the lower courts by limiting pretrial detainees' rights. As discussed in Chapter 5, the Court in *Bell v. Wolfish* ruled that conditions can be created to make certain that detainees are available for trial and that administrative practices designed to manage jails and to maintain security and order are constitutional.[16] The justices said that restrictions other than those that ensure court appearance may legitimately be imposed on detainees and that when jail security, discipline, and order are at stake, detainees may be treated like other prisoners.

Release from Detention

One of the most startling facts about U.S. jails is that about half of their occupants are awaiting trial. For many, this pretrial detention will last a long time: The average delay between arrest and trial is six months or more in many states. In urban jails the wait is often longer, because of heavy court backlogs. Remarkably, despite the constitutional right to a speedy trial, in some court systems defendants can expect to languish in jail for up to a year or more before their cases come to trial. In some countries, especially those in eastern Europe, the pretrial detention period can last *years,* as described in the Comparative Perspective.

COMPARATIVE
PERSPECTIVE

Pretrial Detention in Russia

Prisoners almost always swear they are not guilty. In Russian pretrial detention centers, many inmates insist that they no longer care about proving their innocence.

"At first, all I wanted was a fair trial," Pyotr Kuznetsov, 51, said in a dank and stinking cell of Matrosskaya Tishina, one of Moscow's largest and most infamous detention centers.

He said he had been arrested and brutally beaten, for stealing less than $5 and had already spent 10 months behind bars awaiting trial. His lice-ridden 18th-century cell, built for 30, currently warehouses more than 100 men. The inmates share beds, sleeping in three shifts.

"All I want now is to get out of here, even to a labor camp," Mr. Kuznetsov said. "I've been in prison before, and it is not as bad as this."

Perhaps the most terrifying aspect of the Russian penal system is pretrial detention. Close to 300,000 people awaiting trial are now in jail. There, a death sentence stalks people who have not yet been convicted of a crime.

Unprotected from the TB epidemic (as many as 50 percent of Russian prisoners are believed to be infected) and other infectious diseases, many detainees end up spending two, three, and even four years awaiting their day in court in cells as packed as a rush-hour subway car.

The Russian legal system is so tortuous that people can find themselves detained for months or years even on minor charges. Prosecutors are legally required to complete a criminal investigation within two years, but there is no time limits for judges, who can

keep a suspect waiting for trial indefinit
The average stay in detention is 10 months

In Soviet times, bail was dismissed as capitalist folly. Today, bail is legal, bu remains a novelty, granted to less than 2 cent of the country's accused—usually to sters who have ready cash and connections compliant judge.

Russian courts operate on the European quisitorial model rather than the American versarial system, putting an additional st on overloaded judges and narrowing the def dants' chances.

"Under our system, it is much harder t quit than find a person guilty," Sergei Pa a judge in a Moscow appeals court, explain "Less than 1 percent of all cases end in a acquittal, and that is because before a ju can acquit, he must do a huge amount of wo that is not done by the police: requesting formation, soliciting expert testimony, et

The fact that time served before trial subtracted from convicted prisons' sentenc can hardly be viewed as justice, Judge Pas said. "The predetention centers are a far worse punishment than prison," he said. Pr ons and labor camps in Russia are grim, bu they are not nearly as overcrowded.

In a report on torture in Russia, Amnes International said that "torture and ill-treatment occur at all stages of detention imprisonment," but noted that it was most often reported in pretrial detention.

"Its main purpose appears to be to inti date detainees and obtain confessions," th report said. Confessions, more than eviden are a major part of criminal investigation Russia. ∎

SOURCE: Alessandra Stanley, "Russians Lament the Crime of Punishment," *The New York Times*, January 1, 1998, p. A1. © 1998 The New York Tim Company. Reprinted by permission.

The hardship of pretrial detention exerts pressure on defendants to waive their rights and plead guilty. Further, as we have seen, it undermines their defense. And delay, often a useful defense tactic because it can weaken the prosecutor's case, imposes a further penalty on the detained defendant.

Small wonder, then, that in recent years there has been a major emphasis on programs to facilitate the release of offenders awaiting trial. Rates of pretrial release have gradually grown from less than 50 percent in the early 1960s to nearly 90 percent in many of today's largest urban areas. Even so, jail overcrowding is accelerating the development of new mechanisms for pretrial release, one of the simplest ways to reduce a jail's population. Innovative alternatives to the traditional bail system have enabled police departments to sustain high volumes of arrests, even when local jails are severely overcrowded and under court order to reduce daily populations.

In Russia, pretrial detention averages 10 months. Fewer than 2 percent of arrestees are given bail. In the Matrosskaya Tishina Detention Center in Moscow, 5,000 prisoners await trial in a Dickensian world of squalor, disease, and lice.

The Bail Problem

When someone is arrested for a crime, the court primarily is concerned that that person appear at the appointed time to face charges. Judges traditionally have responded to this need by requiring that the person post **bail,** normally ranging from $1,000 to $25,000 (although higher amounts may be required), to be forfeited if the accused fails to appear.

Defendants have two principal ways to make bail. They may post the full amount to the court, where it is held until the case is decided. Or they may pay a set fee to a **bondsman,** who posts the amount with the court; the fee varies, depending on the jurisdiction.

Dissatisfaction with the bail process stems from several factors. First, many defendants are practically indigent and cannot afford bail. A survey of 88,120 pretrial detainees found that of the 87 percent whose bail had been set, 94 percent were incarcerated simply because they could not afford bail or even a bondsman's fee.[17] Second, money is a weak incentive for appearance in court in many cases, because the people who can afford bail are the ones most likely to appear at trial without the threat of its forfeiture. Perhaps the most disquieting factor is that human freedom can be had for a price. Imprisoning people merely because they are too poor to pay for their release seems antithetical to our cultural ideals and our concept of justice.

Alternatives to Traditional Bail

To avoid the problems of bail, some jurisdictions have increased the use of citations and summonses. For nonserious offenses police can give the accused a "ticket" specifying a court appearance date and thus avoid having to take the accused into custody. Experiments with this approach indicate that it effectively reduces demands for short-term detention space.

By far the most successful programs have been those that allow defendants to be released solely on their promise to appear at trial, a practice known as **release on recognizance (ROR).** ROR programs assume that ties to the community (residence, family, employment) give people an incentive to keep their promise to appear and to retain their status in the community.

ROR defendants frequently have higher appearance rates than defendants freed through various bail programs, lower rearrest rates, and higher rates of sentences to probation rather than prison. ROR programs have demonstrated clearly that the vast majority of accused people can be safely released into the community on their promise to return for trial. Loss of bail is an unnecessary threat. The rate of willful failure to appear in most jurisdictions is normally less than 5 percent.

bail

An amount of money specified by a judge to be posted as a condition for pretrial release to ensure the appearance of the accused in court.

bondsman

An independent businessperson who provides bail money for a fee, usually 5–10 percent of the total.

release on recognizance (ROR)

Pretrial release granted on the defendant's promise to appear in court because the judge believes the defendant's ties in the community are sufficient to guarantee appearance.

preventive detention

Detention of an accused person in jail to protect the community from crimes the accused is considered likely to commit if set free pending trial.

Preventive Detention   The heightened public concern about crime over the past two decades has led to a political movement to prevent pretrial release, especially release on bail. With preventive detention defendants who are regarded as dangerous or likely to commit crimes while awaiting trial are kept in jail for society's protection. In 1984, the Comprehensive Crime Control Act authorized the holding of an allegedly dangerous defendant without bail if the judge finds that no conditions of release would ensure the defendant's appearance at trial and at the same time ensure the safety of the community.

The notion of the need for protection from accused criminals has been subjected to sustained analysis. Many scholars believe that holding in custody a person who has not been convicted of committing a crime but who someone thinks might commit a crime violates the due process provisions of the Constitution. Others argue that the practice is impractical and potentially nefarious. In reality, less than 16 percent of all defendants who are released pending trial are arrested for another crime before trial, and less than half of those are eventually convicted of the new crime.[18]

Political pressure to incorporate public safety concerns into release decisions has become so strong that well over half of the states have laws allowing preventive detention. The U.S. Supreme Court, in *Schall v. Martin* (1984) and *United States v. Salerno* (1987), approved preventive detention practices.[19]

pretrial diversion

An alternative to adjudication in which the defendant agrees to conditions set by the prosecutor (for example, counseling or drug rehabilitation) in exchange for withdrawal of charges.

Pretrial Diversion   As an alternative to adjudication, **pretrial diversion** had its genesis in the belief that formal processing of people through the criminal justice system is not always beneficial. Each of the three main reasons advanced in its support has provoked controversy:

1. Many offenders' crimes are caused by special problems—vagrancy, alcoholism, emotional distress—that cannot be managed effectively through the criminal justice system.
2. The stigma attached to formal criminal labeling often works against rehabilitation and promotes an unnecessarily harsh penalty for a relatively minor offense.
3. Diversion is cheaper than criminal justice processing.

For the most part correctional leaders agree that jails can do very little for inmates who have mental, emotional, or alcohol-related problems. For such people social programs are more suitable than jails. There is less agreement about appropriate treatment for those whose problems are less clearly beyond their own control—for example, unemployed and unskilled youths, multiple drug users, and episodic offenders, to name a few. Their marginal criminality may stem primarily from their disadvantaged status, and their status can be seen at least partly as their own fault. Diversion from the criminal justice system is controversial, because to some critics these people seem to be "getting off easy." Yet the rationale of diverting them is attractive. The jail sanction does little to alter their disadvantaged status; indeed, the stigma of a conviction often decreases their chances of becoming productive citizens. A more enlightened policy would deflect them from criminal justice processes and instead put them into reparations programs. That is, in fact, the precise aim of most pretrial diversion.

widening the net

Increasing the scope of corrections by applying a diversion program to people charged with offenses less serious than those of the people the program was originally intended to serve.

The mixed success of pretrial diversion programs highlights a persistent problem of criminal justice reform. Innovations designed to reduce the overall intrusiveness of the system, no matter how well intentioned, often backfire and instead expand its capacity for social control. The process, called **"widening the net,"** occurs when a new program is applied to less serious offenders than those for whom it was originally designed; rather than focusing on the more serious offenders, it increases the scope of corrections. If pretrial diversion programs are to meet their objectives, they must be applied to offenders who otherwise would be treated more harshly. This is not easy to accomplish, because many criminal justice system officials distrust programs that are more lenient or more oriented to community service than their current practices.

The Sentenced Jail Inmate

The sentenced jail inmate presents special difficulties for the correctional administrator, mainly because of the short duration of the term and the limitations of the jail's physical plant. By definition, jail terms are short—typically thirty to ninety days for a misdemeanor. Less common are terms of six months to a year, which may be imposed to ensure that the offender serves the full term, rather than possibly gain early release from a crowded state prison. In many cases the sentence ultimately imposed is "time served," because the judge believes that the time already spent in pretrial detention—when by law the person was presumed innocent—is sufficient, or more than sufficient, punishment for the offense committed. The real punishment is not the sentence, but rather the impact on the offender of the unpleasant, costly, and harmful conditions of life behind bars from arrest up to case disposition. In short, the process is the punishment.

In many states, prisons are so crowded that offenders are backed up in county jails awaiting transfer. These inmates in the Franklin County, North Carolina, jail have little to do but wait for prison space to open up.

Of those sentenced to additional jail time, misdemeanants constitute the forgotten component of local criminal justice operations. Their short terms make treatment difficult. Most have not graduated from high school, and many are illiterate; yet educational programming is unlikely to yield results in such short time periods, especially with adults. For example, offenders can rarely earn a high school equivalency diploma in one or two months, and prospects for continued education after release are dim. Similar impracticalities are inherent in job training programs, which may require twenty-five to thirty weeks to complete. In addition, job placement prospects are spotty for the former inmate, who may not even have the help of a parole or probation officer in looking for work. Treatment programs for the mentally ill, the emotionally disturbed, and alcoholics and drug addicts suffer from the same time constraints. Treatment programs run in jails tend to be based on more short-term psychotherapeutic approaches, such as group therapy, transactional analysis, reality therapy, and contingency contracting (see Chapter 14).

The jail facility also limits program opportunities. Jobs within the institution are few, and most inmates have no real work. Those assigned to work details find the labor menial and monotonous: janitorial, kitchen, and laundry tasks. Still, they are lucky; the vast majority of inmates simply languish in small cells. Recreational options may consist of a small library of donated books, a Ping-Pong table, and a few card tables; few jails have basketball courts, weight rooms, and the like. And whatever the resources, recreational time is carefully rationed. Contact with friends and relatives is the only thing that sustains many prisoners in jail, but visiting hours often are limited to a few minutes each week.

In sum, with isolated exceptions jail time is the worst kind of time to serve as a correctional client. For corrections jail is an expensive and largely ineffective proposition—a revolving door that leads nowhere.

Issues in Jail Management

American jails are faced with numerous problems, many of them age-old: lack of programs, poor financial resources, antiquated facilities, and so on. But five issues related to jail management are particularly important: legal liability, jail standards, personnel matters, jail crowding, and the jail facility itself.

Legal Liability

As discussed in Chapter 5, jail employees may be legally liable for their actions (42 U.S.C. 1983). Whenever a governmental official (such as a correctional officer) uses his or her authority to deprive a citizen of civil rights, the victim can sue the official to halt the violation and to collect damages (both actual and punitive) and recoup legal costs. Supervisors (including wardens) also may be liable for actions of staff members—even if they were not aware of those actions—if it can be shown that they should have been aware. Lack of funds does not excuse an administrator from liability for failing to train staff sufficiently or to provide basic, constitutionally required custodial arrangements. Local governments that administer the jails are also liable for injurious conduct.

Many people believe that court decisions awarding civil judgments under the act are an open invitation for prisoners to sue, and sue they do. Prisoners have litigated just about every conceivable aspect of the conditions of incarceration, from hours of recreation to quality of food. The most successful suits have been those showing that an employee's action has contributed to a situation that harmed a prisoner.

The threat of litigation has forced jails to develop basic humane practices for managing offenders. Civil damages and legal fees of more than $1 million have been awarded often enough to draw the attention of sheriffs, jail managers, and local government officials. Budgets for jails have been increased to reflect the additional costs of developing training programs, classification procedures, and managerial policies to prevent liability actions.

Jail Standards

One of the best ways to reduce litigation is to develop specific standards for routine jail operation practices and procedures. Standards are important for at least three reasons. First, they indicate proactive criteria for jail management, which helps eliminate the "Monday morning quarterback" (rehashed in hindsight) aspect of much litigation. If jails are following standard procedures, they cannot be held as accountable for problems inmates experience during incarceration. Second, standards provide a basis by which administrators can evaluate staff performance: They need merely ask whether staff are complying with operational standards. Third, standards facilitate planning and evaluation of jail programs by giving program managers a target to consider in their work.

However, authorities are uncertain about the best way to design and implement jail standards. Some experts argue that standards should be binding. Generally this means that an oversight agency will have responsibility for visiting each jail in the state and determining whether its programs are consistent with the standards. Jails that fail to comply with standards are given a deadline by which to meet them. If they do not, they may be fined—or even closed down.

Other experts argue that jails differ so much in size and needs and so many of them suffer from underfunding and inadequate facilities, that holding all jails accountable for meeting the same inflexible standards is unreasonable. These experts push for voluntary guidelines by which program goals for jail operations would be set by groups such as the American Correctional Association and monitored by teams of professionals.

The bottom line is that if jail administrators do not implement standard practices, the courts will intervene. Even new jails are not immune to this problem: In the late 1980s jails commonly came under court orders soon after opening, and sometimes even before opening.

Personnel Matters

Local correctional workers are among the most poorly trained, least-educated, and worst-paid employees in the criminal justice system. Many take custodial positions on a temporary basis while awaiting an opening in the ranks of the sheriff's law enforcement officers. Of the approximately 165,500 jail employees noted in the last census, about 72 percent performed direct custody functions, 13 percent were clerical and maintenance workers, 7 percent were professionals, and 1 percent were in education.[20]

Personnel problems facing jail administrators stem from several factors, but the primary source is probably a combination of low pay and poor working conditions. Local correctional workers earn substantially less than firefighters and police officers in the same jurisdiction. And whenever these correctional workers can, they leave for better-paying jobs with less stressful working conditions. Many correctional employees, however, have only limited education and do not fare well in competition for better positions, so they must stay where they are.

The poor working conditions in most jails are further exacerbated by understaffing. Jails are twenty-four-hour operations. Assuming that the typical jurisdiction has a forty-hour workweek with normal holidays and leave time, nearly five full-time employees are required to fill one position around the clock. The national ratio of inmates to jail custodial employees is about 5 to 1, or over 25 to 1 for "full-time" posts. In essence, each jail employee must be able to control twenty-five inmates or more, which helps account for the common practice of simply locking the doors and leaving inmates in their cells all day.

Not surprisingly, local correctional workers are often an unhappy bunch. Turnover is extraordinarily high, with many jails reporting complete staff turnover every two or three years. The effects are disastrous. No matter what the level of staffing, proper security must be maintained in the jail, so there is pressure to move new employees directly into the ranks, despite the fact that training at a state academy may last thirty to sixty days—and classes may not start for several months. The dilemma is obvious and has prompted the National Jail Center of the National Institute of Corrections in Boulder, Colorado, to make the training of jail staff instructors a high national priority. This strategy seeks to increase the number of qualified trainers for jail workers so that no new employee lacks the necessary preparation for the assignment. At best, however, this is a stopgap measure. In the long run society must improve pay rates and working conditions to make jail employment more attractive.

Jail Crowding

The number of people confined in jails reached nearly crisis proportions in the early 1990s. The jail population, which remained fairly stable during the 1970s, more than doubled between 1983 and 1993. Much of this crowding stems from the fact that jails are expected to handle a wide range of people, including drug addicts, the mentally ill, and alcoholics. Further, more than 150 jails have been forced to close as a result of litigation, and ten times that number are operating under court orders.

Recently jail crowding has worsened for yet another reason: The state corrections system does not immediately accept sentenced offenders who should be serving time in prisons but for whom there is no space. This situation has led to problems for sheriffs and jail administrators. One sheriff in Arkansas brought inmates to the state penitentiary, chained them to the fence, and tried to leave them there; state officials armed with shotguns and a court order made him take the inmates back. Judges frustrated with prison crowding may also sentence to jail low-level offenders who would otherwise go to prison.[21]

Jail administrators know that crowding can produce problems in jail management.[22] Cells intended to hold one or two people are holding three, four, even five inmates. It is not uncommon for prisoners to sleep in hallways, with or without mattresses. Direct and immediate consequences of overcrowding are violence, rape, and a variety of health problems. In addition, some evidence indicates that prolonged exposure to seriously crowded conditions reduces the life expectancy of inmates. Certainly tempers flare in close quarters, and the vulnerable inmate becomes a more likely victim. And remember: Many of the people subjected to these conditions have not yet been tried and must be presumed to be innocent.

There are many possible solutions to jail crowding. Two center on people detained before trial: (1) increasing the availability of release options, such as ROR and

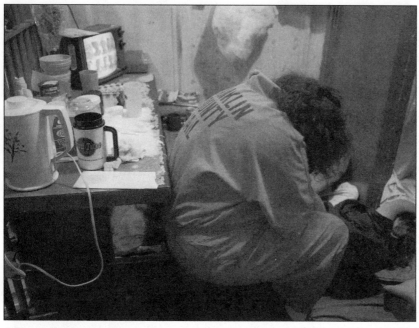

Jail crowding has meant that many pretrial detainees must await their trials in close quarters, without recreation facilities or programs.

supervised release, and (2) speeding up trials. Other ameliorative measures are directed toward people serving time and include work release sentences, which at least relieve crowding for part of the day. Yet less than half of all jails currently have some form of work release programs, and barely a third have provisions for weekend sentences.

Oddly, building new jails—or increasing the capacity of existing facilities—apparently has little effect on the problem of crowding. Instead, policies regarding the use of jails, combined with crime rates in the jurisdiction served by the jails, seem to determine the amount of crowding. In a study of a national sample of jails, wide variations were found among jurisdictions in patterns of jail usage, controlling for population served. Some jails were heavily used, others less so. The most crowded jails tended to be those housing "pass-through" populations—arrestees and detainees—and these tended to be larger facilities as well.[23] This may explain the common phenomenon of new jails with expanded capacities opening, only to suffer renewed conditions of crowding. The solution to crowding is not so much jail capacity as it is jail policy.

The Jail Facility

According to a survey of sheriffs, almost 30 percent of all jail cells are at least fifty years old, despite an unprecedented construction boom to replace old facilities. Jails are expensive structures, costing as much as $100,000 per cell to build—and perhaps $200,000 per cell when financing is taken into consideration. But running a physically outmoded jail can be more expensive still. In some states inmates are being required to help pay for those costs (see the Focus box).

As recently as 1983, even such basic items as radios and television sets were lacking in over half of all jails. With idle time, poor physical security, and little or no program space, prisoners are often cheek to jowl, day in and day out. Crowded cells make for threatening environments that may translate into potentially costly lawsuits. Often the only way to counteract poor security in older jails is to hire extra staff. For these reasons and others, many jurisdictions have turned toward what is called the **new-generation jail.** This jail is both a design and a set of programs that attempts to use the physical plant to improve the staff's ability to manage and interact with the inmate population and to provide services. Three general concepts are employed: podular design, interaction space, and personal space.

The **podular unit** (the term is derived from *pod* and *modular*) is a living area for a group of inmates that defines a post or a watch. The podular unit replaces the old cell blocks. Twelve to twenty-five individual cells are organized into a unit (the pod) that serves as something like a self-contained minijail. Typically the cell doors open into a common living area where the inmates of the pod are allowed to congregate.

The new-generation jail tends to reinforce interaction of various sorts. For example, inmates have greater freedom to interact socially and recreationally, and correctional staff are in direct physical contact with them throughout the day, in what is called the **direct supervision** approach. In older jails bars and doors separate correctional officers from inmates; the new-generation jail places them in the same rooms with inmates. The

new-generation jail

A facility of podular architectural design and management policies that emphasizes interaction of inmates and staff and provision of services.

podular unit

Self-contained living areas, for twelve to twenty-four inmates, composed of individual cells for privacy and open areas for social interaction. "New-generation jails" are made up of two or more pods.

direct supervision

A method of correctional supervision in which staff members have direct physical interaction with inmates throughout the day.

FOCUS
Jail Inmates Pay for Jail Time . . . in Cash!

In the old days in England, inmates in gaol used to pay the keeper for their board. The system led to abuses, in which gaol keepers favored some prisoners over others, and even made a profit on their charges. Those who could not afford to pay for their keep got whatever dregs the keeper felt obligated to provide. Reformers long ago ended the practice, apparently thinking that jail keepers ought to provide for their inmates regardless of their ability to pay.

But now, in Florida, the idea that prisoners should pay for the cost of their care has received a rebirth: The Broward County Sheriff's office has started charging each of its inmates $2 per day for "room and board."

The new plan is part of a "co-pay" system for prisoners in the local jails. A new Florida statute empowers local facilities to charge inmates a "fair portion" of their daily subsistence costs. After a review of inmates' commissary accounts, which averaged $60 or more for over 60% of the inmates (the rest had nothing or next to nothing), the jail administrators determined that it would be "fair" to charge a $2 daily fee and a $10, one-time admissions fee.

Predictably, the local public defender's office objected. It argued the fee was not only vindictive, but was unconstitutional and discriminatory. But the jail administrators pressed forward with their plan, undaunted. Each inmate was assessed for "ability to pay," and every inmate was given an opportunity to appeal the system. On August 15, 1996, the jail started automatically deducting $2 every day from the commissary account of every inmate determined "able to pay."

Equally predictably, inmates began manipulating the system, getting money added into their commissary accounts just before their monthly purchases of goods, then keeping their balances below the indigence standard for the remainder of the time, to avoid the $2 deduction. An unintended by-product of the new policy was that inmates reduced their commissary purchases, and more inmates requested "indigence kits"—basic provisions for those without commissary funds—instead of commissary purchase rights. At the outset of the program, 85% of the prisoners were determined "indigent," and the number has remained high.

In the first fiscal quarter of the program, $203,463 have been raised in inmate per-diem fees.

In addition to the per-diem, the jail has implemented an inmate co-pay plan for use of health care facilities in the jail to defray inmate health system costs of $10.5 million a year. Again, applied only to those "able to pay," the co-pay system ranges from $3 for a nurse sick call to $15 for the attention of a specialist such as a gynecologist. It has resulted both in a reduction in requests for health care and a total of $37,167 in the first 4 months of co-payments.

To date, the amounts collected represent but a tiny percentage of the annual operation and health costs for the jail, and nobody projects they will ever amount to much more than that. But public reaction has been reported as positive.

SOURCE: Susan W. Campbell, "Room with a View, at a Price," *American Jails*, March 1997, pp. 37–44.

inmates are also given personal space, and may stay in their individual cells to pursue their own interests when they wish. They may even have keys to their own quarters within the pod. The new structure has several advantages over older jails. First, its economics are flexible. When jail populations are low, whole pods can be temporarily shut down, saving personnel and operational costs. Second, minimum standards for recreation time and nonlockup time can be met routinely without costly construction or renovation. Third, supervising staff is less demanding, for staff have greater autonomy to manage their pods. Finally, research indicates that new-generation jails are as much as 20 percent cheaper to construct, and they provide more effective inmate security and supervision.[24]

The greatest advantages, however, are programmatic. In larger jails, pods can serve specialized offender groups who share a need, such as for remedial educational services, or who for any reason (for example, AIDS, gang affiliation, or offense type) need

The new-generation jails, like this one in Manchester, New Hampshire, are designed to increase the interaction of inmates with correctional officers. How might this type of jail influence your work as a correctional officer?

to be segregated from the rest of the jail population. Thus the needs of the inmate can become a more significant factor in the nature of the confinement.

Placing correctional staff in closer contact with inmates also has benefits. Prisoners often show symptoms of depression or behave disruptively due to stress or the emotional strain of confinement; this can become more troublesome without appropriate staff response. When correctional officers are physically closer to inmates, they can more readily become aware of feelings or behavior that may require attention. Further, the physical structure potentially can moderate staff–inmate conflict. By getting to know one another better, staff and inmates can learn to live on easier terms with one another. Thus, in the long run the new-generation jail can help overcome the correctional officer's traditional alienation from inmates and break down the false stereotypes fostered by alienation. The officer in proximity to inmates learns to rely on communication skills and judgment rather than force in controlling the inmate population.

In the 1980s prison administrators became enamored of the tight management approaches that criminologist John DiIulio advocated (see Chapter 13). DiIulio's "control model" emphasizes running prisons safely and securely. The control model asserts that a prison manager's first priority is to exert total control over the prison population at all times. This control is achieved by isolating prisoners as much as possible and limiting interpersonal contact. However, research on the new-generation jail has called his ideas into question, at least as concerns the jail. Studies show that an alternative "employee investment" approach, in which staff and inmates are seen as resources to be developed rather than problems to be controlled, is more successful in achieving the results DiIulio sought with his control model. This is one reason that many experts now agree that the direct supervision jail is the best route toward improved staff morale, reduced staff sick leave, reduced injury to staff and inmates — and even reduced maintenance costs.[25]

Despite its advantages, all is not well with the new-generation jail. For one thing, it is hard to sell the concept to a public that underestimates the painfulness of the jail experience and sees the new system as a means of coddling offenders. That more than half jail inmates typically have *not* yet been convicted of a crime, does not dampen the public's desire for harsh punishment of offenders. Jail administrators need to inform political decision makers about the fiscal and programmatic advantages of the new jail.

A second problem is more troubling: Many new jails become outmoded between the planning stage and completion of construction. Legal standards may change, creating new requirements for cell space, recreation space, visitation areas, and the like. Inadequate attention may have been given to possible programmatic needs. Often the very existence of a new jail leads to such an enthusiastic response by judges and other criminal justice officials that the new facility quickly becomes crowded.

Finally, the number of cells that should be built into a new jail is controversial. Planners often argue that new jails need to be more spacious than old jails to accommodate growing numbers of offenders. Architects pleading for large jails often use projections of burgeoning jail populations to support expansion. Critics respond that jail populations grow to meet available capacity, and they cite numerous new jails of doubled capacities that became overcrowded the day they opened. The need, they say, is for both policies to keep jail populations under control and facilities to house those populations.

The Future of the Jail

Few governmental functions in the United States are under assault from as many camps as the jail. Reform groups call for more humane jail conditions; the media expose jails as cruel, crowded, and counterproductive; inmates sue their keepers for mistreatment, often successfully; and experts describe jails as failures.

In some respects the jail's importance to the criminal justice system has seldom been greater than it is today. With many prisons more crowded than they are legally permitted to be, jails have become a backup resource for managing the many offenders for whom the state lacks space. As local governments experiment with ways to improve the credibility of the criminal justice system, solutions seem inevitably to involve the jail—for work release, for enforcing court orders for probationers, for new laws against drunkenness, and for other initiatives. Local decision makers have more control over jails and jail policy than over facilities operated by state correctional agencies.

Perhaps because of the jail's centrality, two general trends—if they continue—bode well for its future. First, many jurisdictions have renovated or replaced jail facilities since the early 1970s. The overwhelming difficulties associated with decrepit physical plants are at least partially overcome by this new construction. Second, many jurisdictions are joining together to build and maintain a single jail to serve their collective needs. Although political problems abound in such an arrangement—politicians resist giving up authority over jail budgets—this movement seems to be gaining adherents.

Summary

As the entryway to the corrections system, the jail holds a mixed and changing population. Sentenced offenders make up only about half of the jail population; the rest are pretrial detainees. In urban areas the jail holds people with long criminal histories alongside alcohol and drug abusers and released mental patients.

Jail operation is generally a county responsibility. The jail administrator thus is subject to local political pressures. In most jurisdictions jails are poorly funded and the facilities are inadequate for the functions they are expected to serve.

People awaiting trial in jail are those who are unable to obtain their release on bail or by some other pretrial release mechanism. Many of these people have alcohol- or drug-abuse problems and must suffer the pangs of withdrawal in jail with minimal medical assistance. In recent years a variety of release mechanisms have been developed as alternatives to traditional bail. Citations and summonses and release on recognizance are among the new approaches.

Most jails incarcerate sentenced offenders for periods of no more than one year. For these misdemeanants, alternatives to jail have been developed, including community service, work release, intensive supervision probation, and home detention.

Jail administrators and staffs must be aware of current issues that affect their performance. The prisoners' rights movement, for example, has raised the question of the legal liability of jail officials. Personnel problems stemming from low pay and poor working conditions require constant attention. The problem of jail crowding, caused in part by prison crowding, results in heightened costs and tension.

The new-generation jail has been designed as a secure environment that allows for interaction of staff and inmates while providing personal space. Although these facilities are controversial, the advantages they offer to administrators, staff, and inmates have won them many adherents. ■

For Discussion

1. How does local politics affect jail administration? Should political influence be as extensive as it is? Does it help or hinder good corrections?
2. What special problems and needs do jail detainees have? Why? What problems do these needs pose for jail administrators?
3. What are the pros and cons of preventive detention? How may it affect crime control? Due process?
4. How would you balance tensions between jail management and public safety?
5. What are some problems you would expect to encounter if you were in charge of providing rehabilitative programs in a jail?

For Further Reading

Braly, Malcolm. *Felony Tank*. New York: Pocket Books, 1976. Describes life in pretrial detention from a fictional perspective.

Goldfarb, Ronald. *Jails: The Ultimate Ghetto*. Garden City, NY: Doubleday, 1975. Presents a powerful critique of the American jail.

Irwin, John. *The Jail*. Berkeley: University of California Press, 1985. Describes the jail experience and inmates' reaction to it.

Kerle, Kenneth E. *American Jails: Looking to the Future*. Boston: Butterworth-Heinemann, 1998. Provides a contemporary analysis of problems facing jails and analyzes potential for jail reform.

Moynahan, J. M., and Stewart, Earle K. *The American Jail: Its Development and Growth*. Chicago: Nelson-Hall, 1980. Provides a critical history of jails in the United States.

Thompson, Joel A., and Mays, G. Larry, eds. *American Jails: Public Policy Issues*. Chicago: Nelson-Hall, 1991. Provides a series of papers on contemporary jail issues.

Notes

1. Gerald D. Adams, "Sixth Street Jail Proposed," *San Francisco Examiner*, January 7, 1993, pp. B4–5.
2. Richard Allinson, "Crisis in the Jails," *Corrections Magazine*, 8, April 1982, p. 20.
3. U.S. Department of Justice, Bureau of Justice Statistics, *Bulletin* (Washington, DC: U.S. Government Printing Office, April 1995), p. 13.
4. David Rothman, *Discovery of the Asylum* (Boston: Little, Brown, 1971), p. 56.
5. U.S. Department of Justice, Bureau of Justice Statistics, *Special Report* (Washington, DC: U.S. Government Printing Office, April 1998).
6. U.S. Department of Justice, Bureau of Justice Statistics, *Bulletin* (Washington, DC: U.S. Government Printing Office, January 1998), p. 8.
7. President's Commission on Law Enforcement and the Administration of Justice, Task Force Report: Corrections (Washington, DC: U.S. Government Printing Office, 1967), p. 79.
8. U.S. Department of Justice, Bureau of Justice Statistics, *Sourcebook of Criminal Justice Statistics* (Washington, DC: U.S. Government Printing Office, 1997), p. 514.
9. U.S. Department of Justice, *Bulletin,* (Washington, DC: U.S. Government Printing Office, January 1998), p. 11.

10. Jeanette M. Jerrell and Richard Komisaruk, "Public Policy Issues in the Delivery of Mental Health Services in a Jail Setting," in Joel A. Thompson and G. Larry Mays, eds., *American Jails: Public Policy Issues* (Chicago: Nelson-Hall, 1991), pp. 100–115.
11. Suzanne M. Morris, Henry J. Steadman, and Bonita M. Veysey, "Mental Health Services in United States Jails: A Survey of Innovative Practices," 24(1), March 1997, pp. 3–19.
12. National Coalition for Jail Reform, (Washington, DC: National Coalition for Jail Reform).
13. U.S. Department of Justice, National Institute of Justice, *ADAM: 1997 Annual Report on Adult and Juvenile Arrestees* (July, 1998), pp. 2–3.
14. James Swartz, Arthur J. Lurigio, and Scott A. Slomka, "The Impact of IMPACT: An Assessment of a Jail-Based Treatment Program," *Crime and Delinquency*, 42(4), October 1996.
15. U.S. Department of Justice, Bureau of Justice Statistics, *HIV in Prisons and Jails, 1995* (Washington, DC: U.S. Government Printing Office, August 1997), p. 1.
16. *Bell v. Wolfish*, 441 U.S. 520 (1979).
17. Wayne Welsh, "Changes in Arrest Policies as a Result of Court Orders Against County Jails," *Justice Quarterly*, 10(1), March 1993.
18. Mary A. Toborg, *Pretrial Release: A National Evaluation of Practices and Outcomes* (Washington, DC: U.S. Department of Justice, 1981), p. 6.
19. *Schall v. Martin*, 467 U.S. 253 (1984); *United States v. Salerno*, 481 U.S. 739 (1987).
20. U.S. Department of Justice, *Bulletin*, (Washington, DC: U.S. Government Printing Office, January 1998), p. 9.
21. Stewart J. D'Allessio and Lisa Stolzenberg, "The Impact of Sentencing Guidelines on Jail Incarceration in Minnesota," *Criminology*, 33(2), 1995, p. 283.
22. Patrick Kinkade, Matthew Leone, and Scott Semond, "The Consequences of Jail Crowding," *Crime and Delinquency*, 41(1), January 1995, 150–161.
23. John M. Klofas, "Disaggregating Jail Use: Variety and Change in Local Corrections over a Ten-Year Period," in Joel A. Thompson and G. Larry Mays, eds., *American Jails: Public Policy Issues* (Chicago: Nelson-Hall, 1991), pp. 40–58.
24. Jay Farbstein, Dennis Liebert, and Herbert Sigurdson, *Assets of Podular Direct-Supervision Jails* (Washington, DC: National Institute of Justice, February 1996).
25. Mary K. Stohr, Nicholas P. Lovrich, Jr., Ben A. Menke, and Linda Zupan, "Staff Management in Correctional Institutions: Comparing DiIulio's 'Control Model' and 'Employee Investment Model' Outcomes in Five Jails," *Justice Quarterly*, 11(3), September 1994, pp. 93–95.

CHAPTER EIGHT
Probation

The History and Development of Probation
Benefit of Clergy
Judicial Reprieve
Recognizance
The Modernization of Probation

The Organization of Probation Today
Should Probation Be Centralized or Decentralized?
Who Should Administer Probation?
Should Probation Be Combined with Parole?

The Dual Role of Probation: Investigation and Supervision

The Investigative Role of Probation
Contents of the PSI
Recommendations of the PSI
Disclosure of the PSI
Private PSIs

The Supervisory Role of Probation
The Officer
The Offender
The Bureaucracy

The Effectiveness of Supervision
Case Management Systems
Specialized Supervision Programs

Revocation and Termination of Probation

Probation in the Coming Decade

Summary

he New York City Probation Department faces a problem. Despite a caseload of over 44,000 probationers, or almost 200 per probation officer, the
city budget office has advised the department that over the next three years
probation must absorb an unprecedented budget cut. Because the budget
mostly pays for probation officers, their number will have to be reduced.
Faced with this crisis, probation officials have undertaken what The *New York Times*
has called "a bold experiment." The new approach calls for a two-tier system of supervision: Violent offenders will be seen in lengthy group sessions designed to deal with
the attitudes that lead to violence; nonviolent offenders will not see a probation officer,
but rather will report electronically to banklike ATM machines that use laser techniques
to read fingerprints.[1]

This proposal speaks volumes about modern probation. Instead of dealing with
petty offenders, today's probation departments are increasingly called on to deal with
tough, even violent offenders. Yet they are asked to handle this more difficult work load
under decreasing levels of funding for staff. In New York City, probation officials are trying to forge a new way out of this dilemma. If the experiment works, probation in New
York and other big cities will never be the same.

Most people would say that probation needs to change. Although few citizens or
political leaders give it much respect, it is by far the most extensively used form of corrections in the United States. Over half of all adults under correctional authority are
serving probation sentences. In 1997 this figure represented almost 3.2 million people,
or nearly two and one-half times the number of adults in felony prisons and double the
number of adults in all penal institutions combined.[2] Even though escalating prison
growth gets the public's attention, since 1985 the U.S. probation population has actually
grown even faster than the incarcerated population.

Despite the wide use of probation, it is frequently given short shrift by media critics, who tend to portray it as "a slap on the wrist." This notion is so widespread that a
well-known scholarly work on correctional policy once referred to probation as "a
kind of standing joke."[3] These views sharply contrast with official policies. For example, government devoted over a quarter of a billion dollars in federal funds to improve
and expand probation in the past decade alone, and supervision in the community is
being used as the sanction for more and more offenders. Further, advocates of intermediate sanctions point to probation as the base on which more severe punishments
can be built.

What is the reality of probation? How effective is it? How important is it today? In
this chapter we describe the function of probation in corrections and review numerous
studies of probation supervision and court services. Although in today's correctional environment probation is increasingly coupled with a variety of intermediate sanctions, in

this chapter we consider traditional probation services (intermediate sanctions are covered in Chapter 8). Our review demonstrates that, as in most other areas of corrections, probation agencies work amid social and political ambivalence about punishment. This ambivalence, together with uncertainty about treatment methods, leaves probation in a quandary: We ordinarily rely heavily on it in sentencing offenders, but we show limited confidence in its corrective capacities. Our study is framed by the following Questions for Inquiry:

Questions FOR INQUIRY

1. What is the history and development of probation?
2. How is probation organized today?
3. What are the dual roles of probation?
4. How can the supervision of probationers be more effective?
5. What are the procedures for revoking probation?
6. What will be the thrust of probation in the coming decade?

The History and Development of Probation

P robation is the practice of giving an offender the chance to remain within the community and demonstrate a willingness to abide by its laws, rather than being imprisoned. In this country probation began with the innovative work of John Augustus, a Boston bootmaker who was the first **to stand bail** for defendants under authority of the Boston Police Court in 1841. But the roots of probation lie in earlier attempts, primarily in England, to mitigate the harshness of the criminal law.

to stand bail

The practice, by a private citizen, of posting bail for a defendant and promising to make certain that the defendant will appear for trial.

Benefit of Clergy

From the 1200s until the practice was abolished by statute in 1827, people accused of serious offenses in England could appeal to the judge for leniency by reading in court the text of Psalm 54. The original purpose of this "benefit of clergy" was to protect people under church authority, such as monks and nuns, from the awesome punitive power of the king's law. Because this benefit was gradually extended to protect ordinary citizens from capital punishment—the predominant sanction for serious offenses under English law in those days—Psalm 54 came to be known as the "neck verse."

Originally the invocation of Psalm 54 required that the person be able to read, and thus it discriminated in favor of the upper social classes. Eventually common thugs memorized the verse so they could pretend to read it before the court and thus avail themselves of its protection. Consequently judges became more arbitrary in granting the benefit.

For a short period the benefit of clergy was practiced in the United States, but it fell into disrepute because of its unequal application and baffling legal character. Criticisms once leveled against it—arbitrariness and invidious favoritism—are often directed today at probation. Probation's detractors assert that the cynical penance of the privileged and socially advantaged affords them a leniency denied to lower-class and less reputable offenders.

It was in the Boston Police Court that John Augustus convinced Judge Peter Oxenbridge Thatcher to place an offender on probation.

Judicial Reprieve

Legal statutes often are based on an image of the offender as evil or dangerous. In reality, however, most offenders are more or less ordinary people whose problems or circumstances have led to confrontations with the law. Judges have long understood the need for leniency with some offenders and thus have regularly deflected the full punitive force of the law.

In nineteenth-century England a common law practice called **judicial reprieve** became widespread. If a convicted offender requested, the judge could suspend either the imposition or execution of a sentence for a specified length of time, on condition of good behavior by the offender. At the end of that time, the offender could apply to the Crown for a pardon.

In the United States judicial reprieve took a different form and led to a series of legal controversies. Rather than limiting the duration of the reprieve, many judges suspended imposition of punishment as long as the offender's behavior remained satisfactory. The idea was that the reprieved offender who remained crime free need not fear the power of the court; the offender who committed another crime, however, was subject to punishment for both crimes.

In 1916 the U.S. Supreme Court declared discretionary use of such indefinite reprieves unconstitutional.[4] The Court recognized the occasional need to suspend a sentence temporarily because of appeals and other circumstances, but it found that indefinite suspension impinged on the powers of the legislative and executive branches to write and enforce laws. With this decision, the practices of probation became subject to the states' penal codes.

Even today an uneasy balance exists between legislatures and the judiciary regarding selective mitigation of the harshness of the law. Although the judiciary seeks discretion to avoid imposing full sentences specified by law on all defendants, legislatures increasingly pass mandatory penalties that make probation unavailable to certain offenders. The innovation of judicial reprieve, which essentially forgave offenders on condition of good behavior, no longer seems a legitimate sentencing alternative.

Recognizance

In a search for alternative means to exercise leniency in sentencing, early nineteenth-century judges began to experiment with extralegal forms of release. Much of this innovation occurred among the Massachusetts judiciary, whose influence on modern probation was enormous.

One of the most famous trailblazers was Boston Municipal Court Judge Peter Oxenbridge Thatcher, the originator of the practice of **recognizance.** In 1830 Thatcher sentenced Jerusha Chase "upon her own recognizance for her appearance in this court whenever she was called for."[5] In 1837 Massachusetts made recognizance with monetary sureties into law. What made recognizance important was the implied supervision of the court—the fact that the whereabouts and actions of the offender were subject to court involvement.

The main thrust of both reprieve and recognizance was to humanize the criminal law and mitigate its harshness. The practices foreshadowed the move toward individualized punishment that would dominate corrections a century later. The major justifications for probation—the need for flexibility in sentencing and for individualized punishment—already had strong support. Yet an institutionalized way of performing recognizance functions was still needed.

This formalization of court leniency is the main contribution of John Augustus (1785–1859), recognized as the first probation officer. Because his philanthropic activities made Augustus a frequent observer in the Boston Police Court, the judge was willing to defer sentencing a man charged with being a common drunkard and release him into Augustus's custody. At the end of a three-week probationary period, the man convinced the judge that he had reformed and therefore received a nominal fine.

Not only was Augustus the first person to use the term *probation,* but he developed the ideas of the presentence investigation, supervision conditions, social casework, reports to the court, and revocation of probation. He was careful to screen his cases "to ascertain whether the prisoners were promising subjects for probation, and to this end

judicial reprieve

A practice under English common law whereby a judge might suspend imposition or execution of a sentence on condition of good behavior on the part of the offender.

recognizance

A formally recorded obligation to perform some act (such as keep the peace, pay a debt, or appear in court when called) entered by a judge to permit an offender to live in the community, often on posting a sum of money as surety, which is forfeited by nonperformance.

it was necessary to take into consideration the previous character of the person, his age, and the influences by which he would in future be likely to be surrounded."[6] His supervision methods were analogous to casework strategies: He gained offenders' confidence and friendship and, by helping them get a job or aiding their families in various ways, he helped them reform.

The Modernization of Probation

The probation concept eventually extended to every state and federal jurisdiction. In the course of its development, the field underwent a curious split. The legacy of Augustus and his followers was a humanitarian orientation that focused on reformation. In contrast, the new probation officers were drawn largely from the law enforcement community—retired sheriffs and policemen—whose orientation they shared.

The strain between the so-called law enforcer role of probation, which emphasizes surveillance of the offender and close controls on behavior, and the social worker role, which emphasizes provision of supportive services to meet offenders' needs, continues today—with no resolution in sight. Advocates of the law enforcement model argue that conditions for community control must be realistic, individualized, and enforceable. Proponents of the social work model believe that supervision must include treatment to help the offender become a worthwhile citizen. Each view has dominated at one time or another in the past half-century.

In the 1940s leaders in probation and other correctional branches began to embrace ideas from psychology about personality and human development. Probation began to emphasize a medical model, with rehabilitation as its overriding goal. This new focus moved probation work—or at least its rhetoric—into the realm of the professions. Although psychiatric methods probably were never fully implemented by even a small number of probation departments, the ideas underlying the approach certainly dominated the professional literature.

The orientation toward a medical model remained strong through the 1960s, when the reintegration model came to the fore. This model assumed that crime is a product of poverty, racism, unemployment, unequal opportunities, and other social factors. Probation was seen as a central correctional method because it was the primary existing means of working with the offender in the problem context—the offender's community. Methods of probation began to change from direct service (by psychological counseling) to service brokerage: After their needs were assessed, clients were put in touch with appropriate community service agencies. The reintegrative approach was heralded by government studies, and federal funds were shifted to community-based correctional agencies (discussed in Chapter 9), including probation agencies.

In the latter part of the 1970s, thinking about probation changed again. Now the goals of rehabilitation and reintegration have given way to an orientation widely referred to as *risk management*. The goal here is to minimize the probability that an offender will commit a new offense, especially by applying tight controls over the probationer's activities and maintaining careful surveillance. Risk management combines values of the just deserts model of the criminal sanction with the commonly accepted idea that the community deserves protection.

One of the main ways probation has changed in the 1990s is that it no longer is exclusively a sentence imposed in lieu of incarceration. (See Table 8.1.) Other sentencing arrangements include the following:

1. *Split sentence:* The court specifies a period of incarceration, to be followed by a period of probation.
2. *Modification of sentence:* The original sentencing court reconsiders an offender's prison sentence within a limited time frame and modifies it to probation.
3. *Shock incarceration:* An offender sentenced to incarceration is released after a period of confinement (the shock) and resentenced to probation.
4. *Intermittent incarceration:* An offender on probation spends weekends or nights in a local jail.

Table 8.1 Type of Sentence for Adult Probationers

More serious offenders often have "split sentences" requiring a period of incarceration prior to probation supervision.

Type of Sentence	Total	Severity of Offense Felony	Misdemeanor
Probation Only	49.8%	45.7%	54.8%
Probation and Incarceration[a]	50.2	54.3	45.2
Jail	37.3	36.5	38.3
Prison	15.3	20.6	9.3
Number of Probationers	2,571,605	1,470,814	974,029

[a]Sums to more than total because some probationers were sentenced to both jail and prison.

SOURCE: U.S. Department of Justice, Bureau of Justice Statistics, *Bulletin*, December 1997, p. 6.

Clearly probation practices reflect current social forces. For instance, the emphasis on psychiatric social work was a natural outcome of the conceptualization of corrections as reformative, a vision held by religious and social reformers of the day. The reintegration movement represented a shift away from imprisonment toward more direct services, such as job training and education. This approach was consistent with President Lyndon Johnson's vision of the Great Society, which would make equal opportunities available for all citizens and would eliminate discrimination, poverty, and injustice. When the Great Society failed to materialize, attention turned to the fundamental responsibility of a society to protect its citizens from crime. Thus the recent emphasis on risk management is an outgrowth of widespread public demands that the justice system be streamlined and that it focus on reducing crime. Many see combining probation with periods of incarceration as a way to make it "tougher" and more effective against crime. For a somewhat different orientation, see the Comparative Perspective on Probation in England.

Today, there has been a growing interest in probation's role as a part of "community justice." The term community justice refers to a philosophy that emphasizes reparation to the victim and the community, problem-solving strategies instead of adversarial procedures, and seeks to increase citizen involvement in crime prevention.[7] By breaking away from the traditional bureaucratic practices, community justice advocates hope to develop a more flexible and responsive form of local justice initiatives—and many see probation as leading the way. The community justice concept is discussed in detail in Chapter 22.

The Organization of Probation Today

Probation originated in a court, and the first probation agencies were units of the judicial branches of city and county governments, primarily in the eastern United States. As the idea of probation caught on and moved westward, variations in its organization were attempted. Probation has been placed in the executive branch, it has been subjected to statewide unification, and it has been consolidated with parole. Figure 8.1 shows the seven jurisdictional patterns of probation organization nationwide.

Three general issues are involved in the organization of probation: (1) whether it should be centralized or decentralized, (2) whether it should be administered by the judiciary or the executive branch, and (3) whether it should be combined with parole services.

Should Probation Be Centralized or Decentralized?

The centralization issue concerns the location of authority to administer probation services. Proponents of decentralization argue that an agency administered by a city or county instead of a state is smaller, more flexible, and better able to respond to the

COMPARATIVE PERSPECTIVE

Probation in England

Although many correctional practices such as the penitentiary were first proposed in England, probation in its modern form is an American creation that was later adopted by the "mother country." Of special interest is the local nature of English probation and the provision of hostels and day training centers to help probationers. But unlike the United States the percentage of offenders sentenced to probation is relatively low. English judges seem to use probation primarily when they believe that the supervision and assistance of a probation officer will have a real impact on the offender.

In England the Probation and After Care Department of the national government administers noninstitutional programs. But the fifty-six local probation committees, composed of magistrates (nonpaid judges of the lowest criminal courts) and local citizens, exercise a great deal of control. They select the probation officers, pay their salaries, and review their work. The committees, as part of local government, are also responsible for providing the necessary facilities, including the hostels and day training centers. If a nonprofit organization is assisting local probation, the committee pays for these services. Local government is responsible for providing the funds to run the probation service in its area.

In the past, probation officers were not required to meet specific educational and training standards; in fact, many were volunteers. Today, the Central Council of Education and Training in Social Work controls the selection and training process. In recent years there has been a considerable influx of new probation officers holding university degrees. These people viewed themselves not as mere officers of the court, but rather as a professional class of social workers allied more frequently with their clients than with the court.

It appeared for a time that the probation service would be exclusively populated by these professionals, but increased caseloads and a recognition that lay volunteers would enhance the work of the service has led to a return to using volunteers.

Probation orders contain some standard conditions, such as maintaining good behavior, keeping in touch with the probation officer, and notifying the officer of a change in address. As in the United States, a court may impose additional requirement which include specifying the place of residence, requiring medical or psychiatric treatment, and prohibiting association with certain people or the frequenting of specific places.

When the court decides it is necessary to specify a probationer's place of residence, or if the person does not have a fixed address, he or she may be ordered to live in a probation hostel. Hostels are run either by a voluntary group or by the probation department and are designed to give the offender a place to live while working in the community. Group treatment and other rehabilitative services are often available in the hostel. Courts may also require day attendance at a training center to help a probationer acquire basic job skills.

In recent years some have criticized the classification of people sent to hostels and day centers. Hostels were originally designed to help improve employment skills of probationers. As the prison system has tried to cope with crowding, parolees have been sent to live in hostels. High rates of unemployment have made it difficult to help these people find work. In addition, many parolees need special services to help them adjust to the community. Finally, the number of offenders who suffer drug and alcohol abuse disrupts the facilities because the behavior of these individuals is somewhat unpredictable. ■

SOURCE: Adapted from Richard J. Terrill, *World Criminal Justice Systems*, 2nd ed. (Cincinnati, OH: Anderson, 1992), pp. 68–70.

WORK PERSPECTIVE

Robin Osterhaven

**Chief Probation Officer,
State District Court, Lansing, Michigan**

As a freshman at Michigan State University, I enrolled in "Introduction to Criminal Justice." One of our speakers was a former felon. He had been in prison and was rehabilitated. His story so impressed me that I declared criminal justice as my major.

During my junior and senior years I did volunteer work to learn about jobs in corrections. I volunteered as a clerical worker at the county jail, helped with arts and crafts at the juvenile facility, and supervised recreation activities in a halfway house for young adult offenders. In my senior year I accepted an internship with a pretrial diversion program in the local prosecutor's office. I interviewed people charged with nonviolent crimes and recommended whether they should be accepted into the diversion program. Diversion consisted of payment of fees, community services, and minimal supervision in lieu of prosecution. My internship supervisor recommended me for a full-time position as a juvenile probation officer, but I declined because I would have had to move to a different city.

After graduation I worked in jobs outside of criminal justice for four years in my hometown. When I decided to look for work elsewhere, a friend told me about an advertised position for a probation officer in another part of the state. I applied and was hired. As a probation officer for more than a decade, I have learned much about the job and about myself.

I recommend that students interested in criminal justice professions develop good communication skills; do volunteer work and internships to gain experience; and be outgoing, firm, and forthright in working with other people. Employment opportunities often arise from personal contacts, including those developed in student internships.

As a district court probation officer in Michigan, I work with adults age 17 and over, convicted of misdemeanors. The majority involve drinking and driving, or assaultive behaviors. I conduct presentencing interviews and background investigations to formulate sentence recommendations. Each report is submitted to the judge and read by the defendant and defense attorney. As regular probation officer, I used to supervise a caseload of 200. As a supervisor I now have a smaller caseload. I also conduct probation violation hearings. Much of my work involves people with substance abuse problems. As chief probation officer, I supervise employees and student interns, prepare the annual budget, and evaluate our policies and practices.

Probation work involves many difficult discretionary decisions. For example, I may have to recommend a sentence for two cases—both 22-year-old women, unemployed and convicted of shoplifting. Both women have no prior arrest history, and the items taken were valued at less than $100. One stole baby clothes for her infant, and the other stole a pair of designer jeans for herself. What would you recommend? probation or jail time?

I look at many factors in making sentencing recommendations. I examine the offenders' prior arrest and conviction history. I look at their driving record. Are they irresponsible drivers? Do they pay their traffic tickets and paper in court? Obviously, I also consider the seriousness of the offense and whether they injured a victim. I am interested in whether they show regret and remorse about their actions. I look for their expressed willingness to seek counseling, participate in Alcoholics Anonymous, and obey probation conditions. I check to see whether they followed through when given opportunities to be on probation in the past. I also evaluate the general circumstances of their lives to see the extent they will need or benefit from probation supervision. The judge ultimately determines the sentence recommendation to the judge and includes my consideration of these factors. ■

unique problems of the community. Because decentralized probation draws its support from the community and from its city or county governments, it can offer more appropriate supervision for its clients and make better use of existing community resources.

In contrast, centralization places authority for a state's probation activities in a single statewide administrative body. Proponents of this approach assert that local probation has been characterized by a lack of professionalism and a tendency to follow

Figure 8.1 The Seven Jurisdictional Arrangements for Probation, by State

The organization of probation varies depending on the traditions and politics of state and local governments.

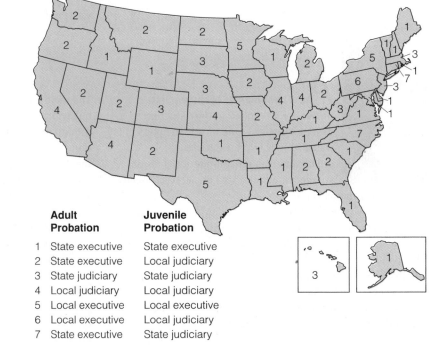

	Adult Probation	Juvenile Probation
1	State executive	State executive
2	State executive	Local judiciary
3	State judiciary	State judiciary
4	Local judiciary	Local judiciary
5	Local executive	Local executive
6	Local executive	Local judiciary
7	State executive	State judiciary

SOURCE: American Correctional Association, *ACA Directory 1995* (College Park, MD: American Correctional Association, 1995).

Probation officers work closely with judges, especially regarding sentencing options. In many jurisdictions judges want to know the progress of the offenders being supervised.

outdated practices. State agencies, they argue, are larger, can train staff to take a variety of roles, and can implement broader programs with greater equality in supervision and services.

Who Should Administer Probation?

Though the recent trend has been away from judicially administered probation, many observers (especially those who seek greater accountability in probation) believe that the probation function rightfully belongs under the judiciary. The usual claim is that under judicial administration probation is more responsive to the desires of the sentencing judge, who is more likely to scrutinize supervision when it is performed by judicial employees. Also, probation officers' morale is believed to be higher when they work closely with judges.

Proponents of placing probation under the executive branch argue that the judiciary is ill prepared to manage a human services operation. To coordinate and upgrade the quality of a human services operation such as probation requires the full attention of professional public administrators. It is argued that placing probation under the executive branch would result in better allocation of probation services, increased interaction and administrative coordination between corrections and allied human services, increased access to the legislature and the budgeting process, and more appropriate service priorities.

Should Probation Be Combined with Parole?

Probation and parole are analogous services in that both supervise offenders who are serving portions of their sentences in the community. Indeed, the growth in use of split sentences and shock probation means that probation often begins after a jail or even prison term—just as with parole.

Because of these similarities, many states have combined probation and parole functions into a single agency, which promotes more efficient hiring and training practices. Arguably the professionalization of community supervision officers also is promoted by such comprehensive community correctional approaches.

There are, however, subtle but important distinctions between probationers and parolees that some experts suggest are hard to sustain in a unified system. Probation clients ordinarily are less deeply involved in criminal lifestyles, and parole clients always face serious problems in reentering the community after longer incarceration (see Chapter 16). These differences call for different handling, which some people believe can best be done by separate agencies.

No solution to the problem of how to organize probation is at hand. Rather than searching for a single "best" way to organize probation, it may be more fruitful to look at how criminal justice services generally operate in a state or region. In jurisdictions with a tradition of strong local government, decentralized probation under the executive branch may be the best alternative. In states that typically have provided services through centralized, large-scale bureaucracies, perhaps probation should be a part of such services. Likewise, a strong judiciary with a history of administrative competence may be the optimal site for probation authority.

The Dual Role of Probation: Investigation and Supervision

Probation officers have traditionally performed two major functions: investigation and supervision. Investigation involves preparation of a **presentence investigation (PSI)** for the judge to use in sentencing an offender. Typically the court orders the PSI after the offender's conviction (often on a guilty plea). A date is set for sentencing the offender, and in the interim the probation officer conducts the investigation and prepares the PSI. The PSI process typically begins with an interview of the newly convicted offender to obtain basic background information. The probation officer then seeks to verify, clarify, and explore the information derived (or omitted) from the initial interview. The final PSI document summarizes the officer's findings, evaluates the offender, and often recommends a sentence.

Supervision begins once an offender is sentenced to probation. Supervision policies and practices vary greatly from agency to agency but generally involve three steps:

1. The probation officer establishes a relationship with the offender and defines the roles of officer and offender.
2. The officer and offender establish supervision goals to help the offender comply with conditions established by the court (often directed at helping the offender confront significant needs or problems in his or her life).

presentence investigation (PSI)

An investigation and summary report of the background of a convicted offender, prepared to help the judge decide on an appropriate sentence.

3. On the basis of the offender's response to supervision, the officer decides how to terminate probation. Options include early termination because of satisfactory adjustment, termination because the sentence has expired, or revocation because of a new conviction or violation of probation conditions set by the judge or probation officer.

Investigation and supervision are divergent functions. In investigating clients and preparing PSIs, the probation officer is working primarily with other human service professionals—teachers, officials, psychologists, and so forth. In addition, the officer may build a sense of partnership with the judge: Both parties seek the best sentence and therefore value useful, accurate information on which to base the disposition. These relationships may reinforce the self-esteem of the officer. Supervision, by contrast, is fraught with uncertainty and error. There are no standard solutions to the problems faced by most probation clients, and officers' daily interactions with them, many of whom are troubled and hard to manage, may provide little sense of accomplishment. Further, supervision seldom yields a tangible product; instead, work consists of a series of tasks loosely connected to possible rehabilitation.

This difference between the two functions often puts informal pressure on probation officers to give investigation a higher priority than supervision. The quality of the investigation is more visible to superiors than the quality of supervision. As a result, producing a sound, professionally appealing PSI can seem more important than serving the offender described in the PSI.

To circumvent this problem, large probation departments often assign some officers only to supervision and others only to investigation—an approach that contains some obvious efficiencies but inefficiencies as well. For example, the supervising officer must learn much of the information that the presentence officer has already discovered. Similarly, when probationers are convicted of new offenses, it would be easier for the supervising officer to write a PSI, given his or her familiarity with the case. Ironically, specialization does not necessarily protect the supervision function. Frequently the best staff members are assigned to the PSI units, and top priority is given to maintaining an adequate PSI workforce, even under unwieldy supervision caseloads.

Nevertheless, it is much easier to manage a probation system whose workers are specialized. Presentence officers can more easily be held accountable for the timeliness and accuracy of their PSIs. Supervising officers can be monitored more effectively to ensure that their work conforms with agency policies. Therefore the trend is toward specialization of these functions, almost as if they were two different jobs.

The Investigative Role of Probation

As noted earlier, the primary purpose of the presentence investigation is to help the judge select an appropriate sentence for the offender. Its secondary purposes include helping with the eventual classification decisions regarding probation, incarceration, and parole that the offender may encounter; aiding in treatment planning and parole decisions; and serving as a document for systematic research.

The PSI also is important to the sentencing process because no uniformly accepted guidelines or rationales for sentencing exist. Individual judges, even in the same court system, may vary in how they weight factors in the case. The PSI must therefore be comprehensive enough to meet the information needs of judges with a variety of sentencing perspectives.

The rehabilitative goal requires assessment of the offender's treatment needs. The consensus is that imprisonment has limited rehabilitative value, so in practice a commitment to rehabilitation poses two questions: (1) Does the offender have special problems, circumstances, or needs that led to the criminal behavior? and (2) Can these problems be overcome by community services for offenders combined with careful supervision to prevent further criminal involvement?

The increasingly popular goal of community protection leads to other questions. With risk management in mind, the probation officer assesses the likelihood that the offender will continue criminal behavior if allowed to remain in the community. Estimates of risk are based on degree of prior criminal involvement, stability of the offender's lifestyle, and pattern of prior adjustment to correctional treatment.

In practice, two circumstances constrain the influence of the PSI in sentencing. Because goals are unclear, judges often seek some balance between rehabilitation and risk management. Rather than pursue a single value in sentencing, judges ordinarily ask a more complicated question: If this offender is not a risk to the community, is there some rehabilitative reason to keep him or her in the community—a reason strong enough to overcome the objection that probation tends to depreciate the seriousness of the offense?

The second constraint is plea bargaining. When the sentence has already been proposed in the process of negotiation between the prosecutor and the defense attorney, the role of the PSI is altered. It no longer serves as the basis of the judge's decision, but instead is used to determine whether the negotiated agreement is appropriate. To counter this problem, some probation officials argue that PSIs should be written before the defendant's initial plea. Although support exists for this innovation, it is unclear whether in the long run pre–plea bargain PSIs would be feasible for most cases.[8]

Contents of the PSI

For many years the ideal PSI was thought to be a lengthy narrative description of the offense and offender, culminating in a sentence recommendation and justification (see the Focus box). Early manuals for the writing of PSIs stressed length and breadth of coverage. Now, however, people are questioning the assumption that more is better. Although long PSIs may make for interesting reading and be relatively satisfying to prepare, information theory suggests that shorter PSIs are not necessarily less useful. This theory is supported by the experiences of probation officers who have seen judges skim through long PSIs, search for a few pertinent items, and then read the sentencing recommendation.

The recent trend has been toward a shortened, directed, and standardized PSI format. This approach may seem less professional, but in practice it places even greater responsibility on the probation officer. Early in the investigative process, the officer will probably develop an idea of the disposition that fits the case. This disposition is then constantly tested against new data on the offender as the investigation continues. Should something call into question the original tentative judgment, the officer reviews the entire case. A detailed PSI is occasionally necessary, but usually the officer's summary of the key factors contains the information most significant to the judge. The process requires more skill than the longer PSI, but it can be considerably more efficient.

The PSI's validity and reliability are related to the amount of information. Probation officers improve validity by verification: Before they put information into the PSI, they cross-check it with some other source for accuracy. For example, if during the PSI interview the offender says he or she has no drinking problem, the investigator questions the offender's family, friends, and employer before writing "No apparent problem" in the PSI. Officers improve reliability by avoiding drawing vague conclusions about the case. For instance, rather than describe the offender simply as "immature" (a term subject to various interpretations and thus of doubtful reliability), the PSI writer might describe specific observed behaviors that suggest immaturity: poor work attendance, not understanding the seriousness of the offense, and so forth.

The "victims' rights" movement of the 1970s included a drive to have the PSI reflect not just the offender's circumstances but also the impact of the crime on the victim. Called **victim impact statements,** this new section of the standard PSI requires the probation officer to interview the victim and determine, in the victim's own words, the

victim impact statements

Descriptions in PSIs of the costs of the crime for the victim, including emotional and financial losses.

FOCUS   Presentence Investigation Report

Date: May 13, 1997
Name: Matthew Martin
Address: Metropolis, Jefferson
County: Jefferson
Court Number: 1775-1
Offense: Burglary I
Class: Felony A
Custody Status: Jail
Maximum Penalty: 20 years/$2,500
Detainers or Pending Charges: None known
Judge: Wilson Morgan
D.A.: Paula Harrison
Counsel: David Acorn
Plea: Not Guilty
Verdict: Guilty
Birth Date: 8/19/73
Height: 5'11"
Eyes: Brown
Age: 25
Weight: 198
Hair: Red
Race: White
Sex: Male
Marital Status: Single
Education: 3 years college
Citizenship: U.S.A.
Employment Status: Temporary leave
Concerned Agencies: None known
Place of Birth: Delta, Louisiana
Marks: Tattoo, right arm: "Born to Raise Hell"
No. of Dependents: None

Report Submitted by: Leslie Blue

Jefferson County Probation Department
State of Jefferson

The Honorable Wilson Morgan
May 13, 1997

Jefferson County Circuit Court
Court Number 1775-1
10 Main Avenue
Metropolis, Jefferson 99999
Dear Judge Morgan:

The following is the presentence report on Matthew Martin that you ordered on April 15, 1997.

Offense Summary

On February 13, 1997, Jefferson Police arrested Matthew Martin at the scene of a burglary. He was subsequently charged with Burglary I. On April 15, 1997, Jefferson County Circuit Court Jury found Mr. Martin guilty of the charge. He is in custody and sentencing is set for May 20, 1997, at 9 A.M.

Plea Bargain/Negotiations and Stipulations

N.A.

Official Version

On February 13, 1997, at approximately 7:09 P.M. Jefferson Police responded to a silent alarm at Petcare Animal Clinic, located at 17 Maybelle Dr. On arrival, the responding officers discovered Mr. Martin and Arthur James on the roof of the building. Mr. Martin had a pair of gloves, a screwdriver, and a pocketknife. The defendant refused to answer any questions without his attorney present. Mr. Martin and Mr. James were taken into custody.

Further investigation revealed that entry was made through a plastic-covered window. The plastic was cut away from the window frame. Drawers and cabinets had been rummaged through, a wooden box had been pried open, and numerous burnt matches were found on the floor.

During an interview, Mr. Martin reported that he burglarized the veterinarian clinic to obtain records on his cat. He explained that he had brought his cat to the clinic a couple of weeks ago and did not have the money to pay the bill. It was his intention to remove the records on his cat, but he found the bookkeeping system to be very extensive and he was unable to find the file. He admitted to gaining entry by cutting the plastic on the window but refused to answer any further questioning. The police confirmed the fact that Mr. Martin's cat was treated at the Petcare Animal Clinic from 2/2/97 to 2/4/97.

Defendant's Version

Mr. Martin admitted to breaking into the animal clinic, but explained that he became "petrified" and decided to leave the building. At that point, the police came and he stated that he lay down and waited for them. The defendant related that he had been unemployed and was behind in rent. His cat acquired a respiratory disease and he took her to the veterinarian. Mr. Martin indicated that he gave the clinic $10 and was to pay them $40 at a later date. One evening, he and Mr. James were sitting around "chewing the fat" and he came up with the idea to break in the office and get the records. He admitted to entering the animal clinic by ripping the plastic-covered window.

Mr. Martin expressed his remorse and stated, "I don't blame anyone but myself." He related that he did not take the stand at his court hearing upon his attorney's suggestion and feels that this may jeopardize his position at the time of sentencing.

Accomplices/Codefendants

Criminal Circuit Court records indicate that on 4/10/97 Judge Carey issued a bench warrant for Mr. James's arrest. As of 5/8/97, the Court had not received a return of services.

Victim's Statement/Damages

Dale Rector, the receptionist at Petcare Animal Clinic, reported that although the office was badly vandalized, no items were noted to be missing with the exception of a screwdriver.

Prior Record

Conviction Summary
Juvenile:
1. 11/3/86: Metropolis, Jefferson—Incorrigible, Beyond Parental Control—Committed to Danville School for Boys.
2. 6/27/86: Metropolis, Jefferson—Child Molesting—Returned to Danville School for Boys. The defendant had a 5-year-old girl's clothes off and was fondling her genitals.
3. 8/29/88: Metropolis, Jefferson—Runaway, Burglary I— Returned to Danville School for Boys.
Mr. Martin had run away from Danville and committed burglary.
4. 4/5/89: Bequinta, California—Carrying a Concealed Weapon and Runaway—Returned to School for Boys. Mr. Martin went to California and was picked up by police for carrying a concealed weapon.
Adult:
1. 1/5/92: Metropolis, Jefferson—Resisting Arrest, Theft II—The defendant indicated that he received ten days County Jail time.
2. 2/11/95: Metropolis, Jefferson—Burglary I—Pled guilty to Burglary II, sentenced to five years jail. Records reveal that Mr. Martin broke into the Rialto Theater, took $900 and flew to Texas with the stolen money.
3. 3/15/94: Metropolis, Jefferson—Sodomy I—The defendant was sentenced to ten years jail to run concurrently with item number 2. The defendant engaged in sexual intercourse with a seven-year-old boy while he was released on recognizance for his burglary charge.
4. 3/25/94: Metropolis, Jefferson—Theft II, Menacing with a Knife. The defendant was found guilty of Theft II and sentenced to nine days County Jail time.
5. 2/13/97: Metropolis, Jefferson—Burglary I—Present offense, disposition pending.

Arrests Not Resulting in Conviction

Juvenile:
1. 5/9/87: Metropolis, Jefferson—Vandalism and Burglary in a School—Disposition unknown.
2. 12/26/87: Metropolis, Jefferson—Shoplifting—No complaint.
3. 1/21/88: Metropolis, Jefferson—Unauthorized Use of a Vehicle—Released.
Adult:
1. 2/12/92: Metropolis, Jefferson—Theft II—Dismissed.
2. 10/26/93: Metropolis, Jefferson—Schedule IV Drug Possession—No misdemeanor complaint.

Driving Record

Division of Motor Vehicle records reveal that Mr. Martin's driver's license is currently invalid. His license was suspended for Failure to Appear at a Hearing. He incurred citations for Expired Registration, No Driver's License, and Failure to Obey Traffic Control Device.

Prior Parole, Probation, and Institutional Performance

Mr. Martin was committed to Danville School for Boys 11/3/86 for Incorrigibility and Beyond Parental Control. During the five years he spent at Danville School for Boys, he had at least two runaways and incurred new charges each time.

Mr. Martin was received at Jefferson State Correctional Institution on 4/11/94 and again on 6/27/94, for a period of five years and ten years concurrent on charges of Burglary II and Sodomy I. He was paroled to Washington County on 10/5/95 with conditions. On 2/13/96, his parole officer, Larry Prouse, submitted a special report to the Parole Board informing them that Mr. Martin was arrested and charged with Theft II. The charges were later dismissed. The defendant's parole was continued on February 28, 1996. The defendant had been receiving mental health treatment with Dr. Cathart. Through Dr. Cathart's recommendation, Mr. Martin reported to the State Hospital on 3/8/96. The hospital would not admit the defendant, and he was subsequently referred to the Division of Mental Health. During his parole supervision he was enrolled as a student at Metropolis Community College.

On 3/25/96, Mr. Martin was again arrested. He was charged with Theft II and Menacing with a Knife. A special report was again submitted by his probation officer, and Mr. Martin's parole program evaluation was considered as "poor." Washington County detectives indicated that Mr. Martin was involved in at least twenty-five burglaries and thefts in Lincoln and Washington counties. His former parole officer, Larry Prouse, recommends that Mr. Martin be sent back to the penitentiary. While Mr. Martin was incarcerated, he was involved in the sex offender group. Dr. Williams, psychiatrist, indicated that Mr. Martin "has learned some insight, and through some college classes in psychology and sexual education and school, he has learned that he is pretty much like everyone else except for his acting out with pedophilia. Apparently he has made a great deal of growth in this institution, especially in the last eight months."

Family History

Father: Bernard Martin died in 1977 from chronic alcoholism. The defendant related that his father was in the United States Army for twenty-eight years.
Stepfather: Willie Olsen, age unknown, is currently unemployed. The defendant related that his stepfather and his mother had been living together since 1982 and were divorced only recently.
Mother: Bernice Olsen, 51, lives in Delbarten, Jefferson, and is employed as a waitress. The defendant indicated

that she and his natural father were divorced when he was very young.

Sister: Lucy Daly, 30, lives in Wilson, Jefferson. She is employed as a secretary. She is divorced and has three children.

Sister: Dettie Conwald, 28, also lives in Wilson, Jefferson. She is a housewife and has a part-time job with a dentist. She is married and has three children.

Brother: Barry Martin, 27, lives in Jefferson; address and employment are unknown to the defendant. The defendant related that his brother is married and has one child.

Brother: David Martin, 20, lives in Metropolis, Jefferson. The defendant related that he is employed as a painter, is single, and has no children.

Stepsister: Melissa Olsen, 12, lives with her mother in Wilson, Jefferson. She attends junior high school.

The Defendant: Matthew Martin was born to the union of Bernard Martin and Bernice Cathwall in Delta, Louisiana, on August 19, 1975. His parents were divorced when he was approximately 5 years old, and the defendant remained with his mother. The defendant's mother married Willie Olsen when the defendant was 12 years old. His stepfather was described as a "strict disciplinarian" and his mother as an "extremely permissive, indulgent person." Correctional files indicate that Mr. Martin's deviant behavior began at age 12. State Prison files report that Mr. Martin had been kidnapped and sexually molested for three days when he was 6 years old. The defendant related that this "messed up" his sexual orientations since that time. He indicated that he does not remember this episode, which he learned of from his psychologist.

Mr. Martin moved to Metropolis in 1977 and indicates that he has lived within the area in various residences since that time.

Marital History
Mr. Martin has never been married.

Education
The defendant reports that he has received forty-four college credit hours, being registered in educational courses at Jefferson State Prison and college courses at Metropolis Community College subsequent to his release. He relates that he was enrolled in General Studies courses. He related that, prior to his college credits, he received his high school diploma while incarcerated at State Prison.

Health
Physical: The defendant related that his physical health is good and that he suffers from no handicaps. He stated that he is allergic to penicillin.

Mental: A psychiatric evaluation stated, "He does not appear to be psychologically ill, only anxious, and has a grossly immoral character." Another psychological report indicated that "Matthew does not belong in Danville School for Boys. He is certainly much more a candidate for State Hospital." Mr. Martin was involved in the Sexual Offenders Program while incarcerated. He related that his psychologists gave him a "clean bill of health." He related that he saw Dr. Cathart for nine months while he was incarcerated and two months subsequent to his release. Dr.

Cathart believes that Mr. Martin no longer needs mental health treatment.

Alcohol: The defendant related that he began alcohol consumption at the age of 17. He related that he drinks once a week "at the most." He stated that he has never had an alcohol problem and has never received any alcohol abuse counseling.

Drugs: The defendant related that he began experimenting with drugs at the age of 17. He indicated that he received drug abuse counseling while he was incarcerated and explained that his attorney told him to admit to a drug abuse problem to get him into a treatment program. He indicated that this did not work out the way he wanted it, because he had no drug abuse problem. Mr. Martin denies any current usage of illicit drugs.

Employment
October 15, 1995, to Present (approximately two and one-half years, intermittently)—Paint Contractor. The defendant related that he and his brother-in-law are painting subcontractors. He related that when he is working he earns $5 per hour working 55 hours a week. We were unable to verify employment information at the time of this writing. His parole officer related that this job was only part-time and described it as "fishy."

October 1994 to October 1995—Nurse's Aide. His employer indicated that he was employed as a nurse's aide, earning $3.25 per hour. The defendant indicated that he quit subsequent to being accused of stealing a purse. Employment verification was made on 5/11/97.

Military Service
Mr. Martin has never been in the military.

Financial Condition
Mr. Martin reported that his income averages between $400 and $600 per month. He related that he pays $250 per month in rent and $80 per month in utilities. He indicated that he has no car and stated that he has no other assets nor outstanding debts.

Current Situation
Mr. Martin lives by himself but also spends a great deal of time with his girlfriend, Sheila Vettor. He says that they are considering marriage but that the prospect is unsettling to him. He reports he has few regular friends.

Psychological Evaluation
This 25-year-old white male was interviewed and administered a battery of psychological tests in the Jefferson County Jail on May 12, 1997. During the psychological evaluation, he was initially somewhat sleepy, distracted, and wary. As the interview progressed, Mr. Martin became quite articulate, intelligent, and extraordinarily alert.

There is a high level of vigilance and distrust in this man's overt behavior that is highly suggestive of underlying emotional or psychological problems. This perhaps is exemplified by the fact that Mr. Martin refused to complete any formal psychological tests presented to him by this examiner. He said he didn't trust psychologists and he didn't trust the criminal justice system; he believes the type of questions and procedures that psychologists offered were stupid and of little value. He said he had taken many psychological tests in the past, and no one ever seemed to give him any help following these tests. He insisted that it was a waste of time.

Mr. Martin went on to say that he really didn't care what happened as the result of his refusing to take the tests. He noted, "I'm unique. I don't want to be categorized. I just want to be left alone. I never want to see another cop or another judge or another psychologist again. I hate tests. I am a unique individual. People may believe I am institutionalized. I am not institutionalized. I am not a criminal. Lots of things have changed in my life. I have stayed out of trouble for three years. I have a girlfriend. I don't hang around with the same kind of people I used to. I have taken all of the psychological tests before, and I refuse to be categorized."

Mr. Martin also indicated that he received an extended amount of psychotherapy from Dr. Cathart regarding some underlying sexual problems, and he signed a release indicating that I could talk to Dr. Cathart about his treatment. I was unable to reach Dr. Cathart before dictating this report.

Mr. Martin was able to discuss some of his history. He explained that he was born in Delta, Louisiana, but traveled all over the country because his father was in the service. In 1977 (age 2) he came to Metropolis. He reported that he had a "nervous breakdown" in 1986 or 1987 when he was at Danville. According to his account, he was told by a staff member that he would never again return home. In response, he became extremely hysterical. Despite injections of tranquilizing medication, staff was unable to calm him, so he was transferred to the State Hospital,

where he spent some time. Mr. Martin also openly admitted that he spent much of a five-year sentence in the State Prison as the result of a burglary and sodomy conviction. He noted that while there, he participated in their sex offender program for about a year and then followed up with about four months of psychotherapy with Dr. Williams in the community.

This examiner's impression is that Mr. Martin is a stubborn, control-avoidant, and paranoid individual. It was also indicated that he probably has above-average intellectual abilities and he has taught himself to be highly tuned to the slightest intrusion on his sense of independence and autonomy. Even though some of his suspicions and distrust of the mental health and criminal justice system may be justified, he seems unable to escape from the sweeping generalization that everybody that he meets is going to assume a persecutory role. He did indicate that he had a considerable amount of trust in Dr. Cathart and that he would allow Dr. Cathart to report openly regarding his course in treatment.

Mr. Martin is the type of person who tends to provoke the most unsympathetic types of sentiments from people in the criminal justice system. As long as he remains in the system, neither he nor the system will have much relief from that antagonism. In many ways, Mr. Martin's desired outcome of being free from contact with the system is the most desirable one for the system as well. Unfortunately, the way in which he goes about trying to avoid the system is highly ineffective.

Diagnosis: Borderline personality
Prognosis: Guarded

Case Supervision Plan
Supervising Officer: Leslie Blue   **Client's Name: Matthew Martin**

Date: 6/12/97
Supervision Level _X_ Intensive ____ Regular ____ Minimal ____

Client's Supervision Objectives	Target Date	Resource
1. To obtain full-time employment	6/30/00	Probation Officer; Metropolis Employment Center
2. To enroll in college on a part-time basis; at least one course per semester	9/1/97	Probation Officer; Metropolis Junior College
3. To have no contact with Arthur James while on probation	N.A.	Probation Officer
4. To discuss with girlfriend the nature of their relationship in order to clarify whether to marry	N.A.	Metropolis Community Mental Health Center

Special Conditions:
1. Probationer will seek and cooperate with mental health treatment.
2. Probationer will make $500 restitution to victim.

damage caused by the crime. Victims' advocates claimed that adding these statements to the PSI would let the judge better appraise the seriousness of the crime and choose a sentence that best served both offender and victim. Critics worried that the judge would be unfairly prejudiced by articulate victims and those who overestimated their true losses. However, studies have shown that the addition of victim impact statements to PSIs "neither increased officials' consideration of harm to victims nor resulted in generally harsher sentencing decisions."[9]

Recommendations of the PSI

The recommendation is a controversial aspect of the PSI because a person without authority to sentence the offender is nevertheless suggesting what the sentence should be. For this reason not all probation systems include a recommendation in the PSI. Yet there is a well-established tradition of sentence recommendations by nonjudicial court actors; normally the judge solicits recommendations from the defense and prosecution, as well as the probation officer. But what the probation officer says may carry extra weight because presumably it is an unbiased evaluation of the offender based on thorough research by someone who understands the usefulness of probation and is familiar with community resources. These considerations may explain why judges so often follow the recommendations in the PSI.

Statistics show consistently that PSI recommendations and judicial sentences agree in 70–90 percent or more of cases. Of course, it is hard to know whether judges are following the officers' advice or whether the officers' experience has given them the ability to anticipate the sentences that the judges would have chosen anyway.

If the reason for the congruence between a probation officer's recommendations and the sentences imposed is the judge's confidence in the officer's analysis, then that confidence may be misplaced. One of the few evaluations of this issue found that "in only a few instances did the offenders they recommended for probation behave significantly better than those they recommended for prison."[10] Perhaps, the study speculated, this prognostic inaccuracy arose because officers did not have time to verify information reported in the PSI, because of their heavy caseloads.

The recommendation may be most useful when a plea-bargaining agreement includes a sentence. In such cases the PSI is a critical check on the acceptability of the negotiated settlement, permitting the judge to determine whether any factors in the offense or in the offender's background might indicate that the agreement should be rejected.

Disclosure of the PSI

Given the importance of the PSI to the sentencing decision, one would think the defendant would have a right to see it. After all, it may contain irrelevant or inaccurate information that the defense would want to dispute at the sentencing hearing. Nevertheless, in many states the defense does not receive a copy of the report. The case most often cited in this regard is *Williams v. New York* (1949), in which the judge imposed a death sentence on the basis of evidence in the confidential PSI despite the jury's recommendation of a life sentence.[11] The Supreme Court upheld the judge's decision to deny the defense access to the report, although without such access the defense was incapable of challenging its contents at the sentencing hearing.

Cases, state law, and general practice since 1949 have reduced the original restrictive impact of *Williams.* It is common policy to prohibit PSI writers from referring to illegally seized evidence that was excluded from a trial, and legislation in many states requires full disclosure of the PSI. Elsewhere, a common policy is to "cleanse" the report and then disclose it. Cleansing involves deleting two kinds of statements: (1) confidential comments from a private citizen that, if known to the offender, might endanger the citizen, and (2) clinical statements or evaluations that, if disclosed, might be damaging to the offender. Moreover, many judges allow the defense to present a written challenge to any disclosed contents of the PSI.

Private PSIs

Private investigative firms have recently begun to provide judges with PSIs. These firms work in one of two ways. Some contract with defendants to conduct comprehensive background checks and suggest to judges creative sentencing options as alternatives to incarceration. In this approach, often called **client-specific planning,** the firm serves as an advocate for the defendant at the sentencing stage. Other firms contract directly with the court to provide a neutral PSI in lieu of the report traditionally prepared by a probation officer.

Privately conducted PSIs have sparked controversy. Because the defendant pays for the client-specific planning, many people view it as an unfair advantage for upper- and middle-class offenders, who can afford the special consideration the advocacy report provides. Often the white-collar offender can make the best case for creative sentences. (For instance, Richard Nixon's convicted former aide John Ehrlichman offered to do free legal work with Native Americans instead of going to prison; but his suggestion was rejected.) These concerns are well taken; as advocates of private PSIs point out, their reports often result in less severe sentences for their clients.

The neutral PSI also raises serious issues. Proponents claim that private investigators do what the probation department does—only better. Yet critics question whether private firms ought to be involved in the quasi-judicial function of recommending sentences. Moreover, the liability of private investigators for the accuracy and relevance of the information they provide in this context is unclear. Finally, private PSIs contracted for by the court likely cost taxpayers more than do the traditional alternative.

client-specific planning

Process by which private investigative firms contract with convicted offenders to conduct comprehensive background checks and suggest to judges creative sentencing options as alternatives to incarceration.

The Supervisory Role of Probation

Offenders placed on probation supervision come from a mix of backgrounds, and the charges against them represent a range of seriousness. Compared to inmates in prison and jail, probationers are more likely to be white and slightly more likely to be female (see Table 8.2). Of the 3.2 million offenders on probation, about one in six were convicted of a violent offense, and another two in six were consisted of a property offense. Half have at least one conviction before they were arrested on the charge leading to probation. The variety of offenders requires a range of supervision strategies.

Just as there are no universally accepted standards for the investigation of offenders by probation officers, neither are there universally accepted standards for their supervision. Indeed, both probation officers and clients generally enjoy wide latitude. To show how this latitude is exercised in practice, we will describe the three major elements of supervision: the officer, the offender, and the bureaucracy.

Table 8.2 Ethnicity and Sex of Probationers and Prisoners

Probationers are more likely to be white and female than offenders who are confined in prison or jail.

	Race			Sex	
	White	African American and Hispanic	Other	Male	Female
Probation	58.3	39.2	2.4	79.1	20.9
Prison	47.9	49.4	2.7	93.6	6.4
Jail	37.3	59.3	3.5	89.8	10.2

SOURCE: U.S. Department of Justice, Bureau of Justice Statistics, *Bulletin,* August 1998; *Bulletin,* December 1997; *Bulletin,* April 1998.

Offenders sentenced to probation are told to report to their officer on a given date. During this initial interview the officer spells out the rules under which the probationer is to live and assess his or her housing and employment situation.

power

The ability to force a person to do something he or she does not want to do.

authority

The ability to influence a person's actions in a desired direction without resorting to force.

The Officer

The probation officer faces role conflict in virtually every aspect of the job. Most of this conflict has its genesis in the uneasy combination of two responsibilities: (1) enforcing the law and (2) helping the offender. Although the responsibilities sometimes may be fairly compatible, just as often they are not.

The chief conflict between the officer's two roles arises from the use of power and authority. In human relations, these terms have very specific meanings. **Power** is the ability to force a person to do something he or she does not want to do. **Authority** is the ability to influence a person's actions in a desired direction without resorting to force. Thus a person who chooses to exercise power in a relationship can almost always be shown to lack authority.

The problem of power and authority is a thorny one for probation officers. Officers are expected to exercise the power of law in controlling offenders under their supervision. This is one reason that in many jurisdictions probation officers are legally classified as "peace officers," with the power of arrest. Yet the actual power of the role is less than it seems: Short of exercising their formal power to arrest or detain probationers, probation officers normally can do little to force compliance with the law. And the powers of arrest and revocation are themselves carefully constrained by case law and statutes.

The lack of substantive power explains why probation officers rely heavily on their authority in supervising offenders: It is a more efficient and ultimately more effective tool. The techniques of authority in probation are like those in social casework, but many people question their applicability in a role permeated by the power of law. They point out that the principles of social work have long been based on the concept of self-determination, which lets clients decide the nature, goals, and duration of the intervention—a condition not always feasible in the probation setting.

Despite such skepticism professionals have tried to develop an understanding of how probation officers might use authority as a positive tool. It is useful to think about three different types of authority used by probation officers in their work:

1. Irrational authority is based solely on power.
2. Rational authority derives from the officer's competence in deciding on the best approach to take.
3. Psychological authority, the most influential type, reflects acceptance by both client and officer of each other's interest in jointly determined goals and strategies of supervision.

The most effective probation officers combine all three types of authority, rather than resorting to the formal power of the role. As Charles Newman, one of the earliest writers on professional probation, put it:

> *One of the first major accomplishments of treatment comes about when the offender becomes aware, both intellectually and emotionally, that the officer represents not only authority with the power to enforce certain restraints and restrictions but that [the officer] is also able to offer material, social and psychological adjustment aids.*[12]

This concept is difficult to execute and often complicated. The officer is attempting to gain the offender's trust and confidence so that, guided by a measure of rational or (even better) psychological authority, the offender will change lifestyle patterns that tend to promote involvement in crime. Yet both parties know that the officer can wield raw power should the offender falter. Often the message is simply, "Let me help you—or else!" This kind of mixed message leads to manipulation by both officer and probationer and may make the supervision relationship seem inconsistent.

In response to the complicated nature of their authority, probation officers often define their role in very simplistic terms, as if choosing between two incompatible sets of values: protecting the public versus helping offenders, enforcing the law versus doing social work, and so on. But such simplistic classification does not resolve the ambiguities of the probation officer's job. The officer frequently is given only vague guidelines for supervision; as a result, approaches to clients can indeed be inconsistent, and wide disparities exist.

These disparities can complicate the job because probation officers are now held accountable for any abridgment of the community's safety resulting from acts of commission or omission in performing their duties. In practice, this means they must make reasonable efforts to monitor the behavior of clients and to exercise caution with those whose backgrounds make them potential risks to the community. The most famous case that established this principle involved a probationer convicted of sexual assault. His probation officer helped him get a job as a maintenance worker in an apartment complex, giving him access to keys to various apartments. In placing the probationer, the officer withheld his client's past record from the employer. The probationer sexually assaulted several apartment residents, who later sued the probation officer for covering up the probationer's record. The court decided in favor of the victims, ruling that probation officers indeed are liable for their conduct as government employees.[13]

The liability of probation officers (and parole officers as well) is a new area of law, not yet well formulated. Its chief significance is that operational procedures in probation become even more important. To defend against possible allegations of misconduct, probation officers must now more than ever document in writing their handling of clients so that they can meet a potential challenge to the reasonableness of their actions.

The Offender

The offender's response to supervision strongly influences the overall effectiveness of probation. Some offenders respond favorably to probation and get along well with their probation officers; others are resentful or resistant. The probationer influences the potential effectiveness of probation by deciding how much and in which ways to cooperate with the probation officer.

The offender's response to probation depends in part on his or her perception of the officer's power as the supervision relationship progresses. Most probationers believe they have little effect on the supervision process. Although probation officers' real power is limited by law and bureaucracy, offenders may see the officer as occupying a commanding role. Officers decide on the style of supervision—whether relatively supportive or controlling—and offenders have little direct influence on even this decision. Therefore probationers often perceive themselves as relatively powerless in the face of potentially arbitrary decisions by the officers.

Not surprisingly, then, probationers commonly resent their status, even when most people think they should be grateful for "another chance." Many probation officers try to blunt the indignity by involving the probationer in determining the goals and strategies of supervision. Rather than simply requiring the offender to seek assistance, the officer brings the client into a problem-solving process. Such strategies are aimed at reducing the perceived discrepancy between the power of the officer and the powerlessness of the client.

The Bureaucracy

Ultimately all supervision activities take place in the context of a bureaucratic organization, which imposes both formal and informal constraints. Formal constraints are the

standard conditions

Constraints imposed on all probationers, including reporting to the probation office, reporting any change of address, remaining employed, and not leaving the jurisdiction without permission.

punitive conditions

Constraints imposed on some probationers to increase the restrictiveness or painfulness of probation, including fines, community service, and restitution.

treatment conditions

Constraints imposed on some probationers to force them to deal with a significant problem or need, such as substance abuse.

"legal conditions" of probation, whether standard, punitive, or treatment; these are set by the court or written into law. **Standard conditions,** imposed on all probationers, include such requirements as reporting to the probation office, notifying the agency of any change of address, remaining gainfully employed, and not leaving the jurisdiction without permission. **Punitive conditions,** including fines, community service, and some forms of restitution, are designed to increase the restrictiveness or painfulness of probation. A punitive condition is usually established to reflect the seriousness of the offense. **Treatment conditions** are imposed to force the probationer to deal with a significant problem or need, such as substance abuse. Figure 8.2 summarizes some of the conditions that may be imposed on offenders. An offender who fails to comply with a condition is usually subject to incarceration; thus one main purpose of the officer's supervision is to enforce compliance with the conditions.

Until recently most probation agencies had to enforce large numbers of conditions of all types, perhaps because the sentencing judges believed that the more conditions they imposed, the greater the control over the offender. In fact, the reverse is often true: With numerous conditions, some quite meaningful to the offender and others not at all meaningful, the credibility of all the conditions is reduced. If the offender disobeys a trivial condition, the probation officer may well choose to look the other way, leading the probationer to wonder if *any* conditions will be enforced. Moreover, scattershot conditions cloud the supervision rationale and the officer's authority to assist the client.

The formal constraints imposed by the organizational policy often pale before the informal constraints imposed by bureaucratic pressures. Three such pressures are (1) case control, (2) case management structure, and (3) competence.

Case control pressures emerge because judges, prosecutors, administrators, and community members all expect probation officers somehow to "make" probationers abide by the conditions and legal requirements of probation. But the officer can do little to "make" the offender cooperate, for real power (such as the threat of revocation) may be limited. Consequently officers are forced to rely on their discretion and individual su-

Figure 8.2 Special Conditions Imposed on Probationers

The problems probationers bring to the probation system vary from one jurisdiction to the next, as do the resulting conditions of probation.

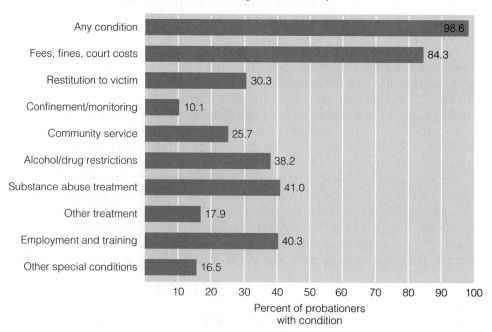

SOURCE: U.S. Department of Justice, Bureau of Justice Statistics, *Bulletin*, December 1997, p. 7.

pervision style, often minimizing or deliberately ignoring formal requirements in order to persuade the offender to cooperate.

Similarly, the often large caseloads that bureaucracies generate and the unpredictability of the job produce a need for case management structure (see Figure 8.3). This is achieved by means of paperwork documenting the officer's activities on cases and by such routines as scheduled reporting days (when offenders come for office visits) and field days (when officers make home visits). But the demands of the caseload do not always correspond to the case management routines, nor do documented activities always lead to positive results. And so the management of work through regular schedules and operating procedures limits the officer's creativity and intensity and the overall responsiveness of the supervision effort.

The pressure for competence that a correctional bureaucracy exerts can be demoralizing for probation staff. Officers simply cannot manage all their cases effectively — there is no surefire approach to take with offenders. At best, the officer is faced with a variety of approaches that may or may not work. Add the fact that the officer typically receives little feedback about successes but much about failures, and the result is an unintentional but systematic attack on the officer's sense of competence. Many officers react with cynical, defensive stances: Probationers cannot be changed unless they want to be; probationers are losers; and so forth. When several probation officers within an office develop this kind of cynicism, their negativism can pollute the whole working atmosphere.

In sum, probation supervision is best understood as a complex interaction between officers (who vary in style, knowledge, and philosophy) and offenders (who vary in responsiveness and need for supervision) in a bureaucratic organization that imposes significant formal and informal constraints on the work.

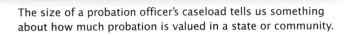

Figure 8.3 Probation Officer's Caseload Size, by State

The size of a probation officer's caseload tells us something about how much probation is valued in a state or community.

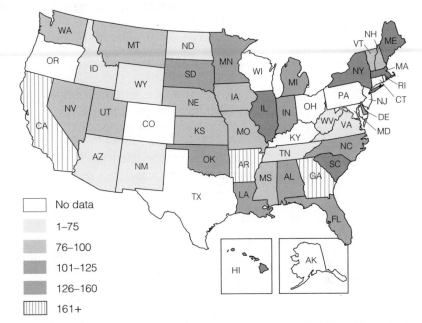

No data
1–75
76–100
101–125
126–160
161+

SOURCE: U.S. Department of Justice, Bureau of Justice Statistics, *Sourcebook of Criminal Justice Statistics* (Washington, DC: U.S. Department of Justice, 1995), p. 87.

The Effectiveness of Supervision

In light of such complexity, the effectiveness of probation supervision is difficult to assess. It depends on several factors: the skills of the officer, the availability of services such as employment counseling or drug treatment, and the needs and motives of the probationer. Much also depends on how the client responds to the probation officer. Some researchers believe that the best way to improve effectiveness is for the officer to tailor the supervision style to take advantage of offenders' different responses to being on probation. In a widely used model of community supervision, Gary Arling and Ken Lerner have described four general supervision strategies probation officers might use, based on the offender's current circumstances:

1. Selective intervention strategies can help probationers cope with the temporary situational crisis that led to involvement in crime.

2. Environmental structure strategies try to develop daily living skills and promote prosocial activities such as helping people associate less with other criminals.
3. Casework/control strategies seek to overcome serious instability, particularly in emotional, personal, and substance abuse areas.
4. Limit-setting strategies allow close monitoring of probation conditions and assertive enforcement of supervision requirements.[14]

This classification scheme underscores the importance of selecting appropriate ways to handle probationers. Consider, for example, how ineffective a supportive, nonaggressive selective intervention approach would be with an offender who needs the control implied by a limit-setting strategy.

For many years experts believed that reducing probation officers' caseloads could make supervision more effective. They reasoned that smaller caseloads would let officers devote more attention to each case, improving services. Frequently cited standards called for caseloads of thirty-five to fifty, although such figures had never been justified by empirical study. During the 1960s and 1970s, dozens of experiments were conducted to find the optimal caseload. Yet subsequent reviews of those studies showed that caseload reduction alone did not significantly reduce recidivism in adult probationers.

Why don't smaller caseloads improve supervision effectiveness? Perhaps the assumption that "more supervision is better supervision" is too simplistic, overlooking the significant elements of supervision. Many factors—including the overall supervision experience, classification of offenders, officers' competence, treatment types, and policies of the probation agency— affect effectiveness more than does caseload.

Case Management Systems

Case management systems have been developed to focus the supervision effort of probation officers on client problems, which are identified using a standardized assessment of probationer risks and needs. In 1980 the National Institute of Corrections (a division of the Federal Bureau of Prisons) developed what it called a "model system" of case management. This model has five principal components—statistical risk assessment, systematic needs assessment, contact supervision standards, case planning, and workload accounting—each designed to increase the effectiveness of probation supervision.

1. *Statistical risk assessment:* Because fully accurate predictions are impossible, there is pressure to assess risk conservatively—to consider the client a risk even when the evidence is ambiguous. This tendency toward overprediction (estimating that a person's chance of being arrested is greater than it actually is) means officers will spend time with probationers who really need very little supervision. The use of statistically developed risk assessment instruments reduces overprediction and improves the accuracy of risk classifications.
2. *Systematic needs assessments:* Subjective assessments of clients' needs often suffer from the probation officer's lack of information and even biases. Systematic needs assessment, which requires evaluation of the probationer according to a list of potential needs areas, is a more comprehensive way to determine what problems the probation officer should address.
3. *Contact supervision standards:* Probation officers have an understandable tendency to avoid "problem" clients and spend more time with the ones who cooperate. Ideally, however, more time should be focused on those who pose the greatest risk and have the greatest needs. Based on the needs assessments, offenders are classified into supervision "levels." Each level has a minimum supervision contact requirement, with the highest-risk or -need offenders receiving the most supervision.
4. *Case planning:* The broad discretion given probation officers to supervise their clients leads to idiosyncrasies in approaches. When a probation officer must put the

supervision plan in writing, the result is likely to be a better fit between the client's problems and the officer's supervision strategy. In addition, the officer's work is more easily evaluated.

5. *Workload accounting:* Because different cases have varying supervision needs, simply counting cases can misrepresent the overall workload of an agency. A better system for staffing the agency involves time studies that estimate the number of staff needed to carry out supervision.

This five-part model has enjoyed widespread support from probation and parole administrators. In just over ten years, it has come to be considered standard practice in virtually every large probation agency in the United States, as well as being adopted in a number of other countries.

Structured case management systems also help probation staff determine more reliably which clients need intensive supervision, special services, or traditional probation monitoring. Research suggests that when all three components of the system are used in combination, probation can become more effective.

The results of an evaluation conducted in Texas of this kind of system are shown in Figure 8.4. The study compared jurisdictions using the new system with jurisdictions using traditional probation. The structured case management system had lower revocation rates, especially for higher-risk cases. This finding suggests that the key to effective supervision does lie in differential supervision: giving some offenders more intensive supervision, and others less, and targeting the supervision effort to precise services and objectives for higher-risk probationers.

Specialized Supervision Programs

The needs of probationers vary dramatically. Sex offenders require different supervision strategies from those needed by cocaine addicts; mentally ill offenders must be handled differently from embezzlers. However, because caseloads often exceed 100 probationers per officer, officers cannot realistically be expected to tailor supervision to fit each case. Thus the emphasis recently has been on grouping probationers with similar problems into a single caseload (see Figure 8.5). This specialization allows the probation officer

Figure 8.4 Revocation Rates for Various Levels of Risk for Probationers Receiving Structured Case Management System, or Case Management Clients (CMCs) and Those Not Receiving the Structured System (non-CMCs)

Structured case management systems work better—especially for high-risk clients.

SOURCE: Adapted from Greg Markley and Michael Eisenberg, "Something Works in Community Supervision," *Federal Probation,* 51(4), 1987, pp. 28–32.

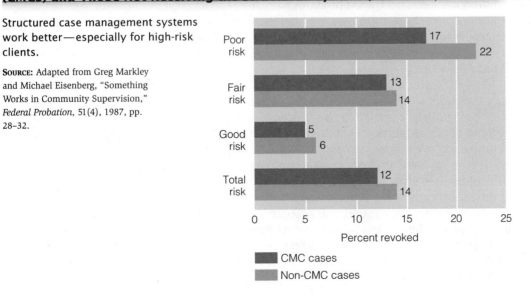

Figure 8.5 Participation of Adult Probationers in Special Supervision Programs

Most probationers participate in at last one special program related to the problems that led to their criminality.

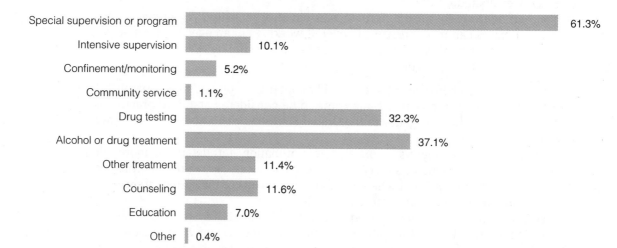

SOURCE: U.S. Department of Justice, Bureau of Justice Statistics, *Special Report*, December 1997, p. 9.

to develop more expertise in handling that problem, and it promotes a concentrated supervision effort.

Studies show that this approach has promise. For example, employment counseling programs and support services improve employment possibilities, and specialized treatment for sex offenders on probation has reduced their recidivism.[15] In general, targeted, specialized services have been found to be more effective than traditional services.

Recent interest in the problem of substance abuse has increased the attention given to offenders on probation who have problems with drugs and alcohol. Several specialized programs have been tried to combat the use of drugs by probationers. These programs typically take advantage of new techniques for drug surveillance and treatment. **Urinalysis** determines if an offender is using drugs. **Antabuse,** a drug that stimulates nausea when combined with alcohol, is used to inhibit drinking. **Methadone,** a drug that reduces craving for heroin, spares addicts from painful withdrawal symptoms. These approaches are often combined with close surveillance to reinforce abstinence during probation (see the Focus box).

Another new specialized program pairs the probation officer more closely with street police officers. Officers who work in tandem with the police are often given caseloads of especially tough probationers. The police liaison allows for more effective searches and arrests and lets probation officers take advantage of information available to the police about probationers.

The difficulty with specialized supervision programs is what to do with the "ordinary" offender who is slated for traditional services. Often probation officers regard "regular" probation as a less attractive function, and conflict among the specialized units can become a serious management problem. As a consequence, specialized service programs in probation, even when successful, require extensive managerial support.

However, there are very good reasons to believe that specialization of supervision will continue to grow in popularity. One reason has to do with an increasing recognition of the seriousness of the problems faced by probationers and parolees. In a 1995 sample of probationers, it was found that 40 percent were under the influence of alcohol at the time of their offense, and 14 percent had been using illegal drugs.[16] Statistics such as these point to the importance of providing treatment in specialized programs for probationers whose problems with drugs or alcohol lead to repeat criminality and pave the road for revocation.

urinalysis

Technique used to determine whether someone is using drugs.

Antabuse

A drug that, when combined with alcohol, causes violent nausea; it is used to control a person's drinking.

methadone

A drug that reduces the craving for heroin; it is used to spare addicts from painful withdrawal symptoms.

F🔍CUS Dealing with the Drug Offender

*D*rug-involved offenders present problems and opportunities to probation. The problem is that many such offenders lead disorganized lives and consequently have trouble abiding by even the simplest rules of probation, such as reporting and remaining employed. The opportunity is that getting a drug offender to stay off drugs is one of the most effective ways to prevent crime.

There is no easy way to help drug-involved offenders stay clean. In developing a training program regarding the supervision of drug offenders, the American Probation and Parole Association identified several "principles" in supervising drug offenders:

1. *Use urine tests to confirm behavior.* Effective supervision is impossible unless the probation officer knows reliably whether the probationer is truly "clean." Drug testing—more frequent early in the sentence and gradually tailing off—is the best way to know the truth.
2. *Know the pharmacology of drugs.* Different drugs have different effects. Knowing those effects can help in the early identification of relapse, and can help the officer understand the sometimes erratic behavior of the probationer.
3. *Expect "slips," especially at first.* Recovery from drug addiction is a lifelong process. Almost no one who is truly addicted walks away from drugs the first time. The probation officer needs to be prepared for "slips," even in the most motivated client.
4. *Have realistic goals.* Abstinence is the right goal, but it is more reasonable to aim the supervision strategy a bit lower: reduce the duration of "slips" and increase the time between them.
5. *Have a graduated program of enforcement sanctions.* When a client fails, don't start with prison as a first response. Instead, begin with a rapid response (say, a curfew) and gradually escalate the severity if the failures continue. Save prison or jail as a last resort.

Source: Todd R. Clear, Val B. Clear, and Anthony Braga, "Intermediate Sanctions for Drug Offenders," *The Prison Journal*, Summer 1993.

Revocation and Termination of Probation

Probation status ends in one of two ways: (1) The person successfully completes the period of probation or (2) the person misbehaves and probationary status is revoked. Revocation can result from a new arrest or conviction or from a rules violation—the probationer has failed to comply with a condition of probation. Rules violations that result in revocations are referred to as **technical violations.**

Revocations for technical violations are somewhat controversial, because behaviors that are not ordinarily illegal—changing one's residence without permission, failing to attend a therapy program, neglecting to report to the probation office, and so forth—can result in incarceration. Some years ago probation revocation was common whenever probationers were uncooperative or resistant to supervision. Today probation is revoked when the rules violation is persistent or poses a threat to the community. Otherwise, rules violations are handled by other means.

Although patterns vary across the country, the most common reason for a revocation is a new offense by the probationer. Sometimes the court will await conviction on the new offense before revoking probation, but if the offense is serious enough, probation is immediately revoked. In such cases a technical violation is alleged, even though the real basis for revocation is the new offense.

According to most studies of probation revocation, from one-fifth to one-third of probationers fail to abide by the terms of their probation.[17] A widely publicized Rand Corporation study, however, which found much higher rates of violation, resulted in a sense of concern on the part of probation administrators. The Rand researchers

Providing direct supervision of drug offenders has become a dangerous task for probation officers. Here, the probation officer has police assistance in bringing a client to court for revocation.

technical violation

The probationer's failure to abide by the rules and conditions of probation (specified by the judge), resulting in revocation probation.

studied a sample of probationers from two urban California counties who had been placed on probation for FBI Index crimes, following them for forty months. More than one-third had been reincarcerated for technical violations or new offenses, 65 percent had been arrested for a felony or misdemeanor, and 51 percent were convicted of a crime. Many of these probation "failures" remained on probation after their convictions, even though the crimes were often serious. This study found that once a person is placed on probation, serious misbehavior does not necessarily result in removal from the community.[18]

The overall results of the Rand study have been supported by other follow-up studies of probationers. A three-year follow-up of over 12,000 Texas probationers found that one-third of that group ended up revoked and back in prison.[19] A similar study of a national sample of probationers found that 36 percent were incarcerated before successfully completing their terms.[20]

Replications of this type of follow-up study outside of "big-corrections states" such as California and Texas have found somewhat lower levels of serious misbehavior by probationers. One recent study suggests that probation supervision may have quite marked effects on some offenders' criminality: A sample of probationers in three Virginia probation districts followed for a year and interviewed repeatedly about their criminal activity reported a three-quarters drop in most types of crime after being placed on probation.[21]

Perhaps probation works well in some areas, but less well in others, partly depending on the nature of the person placed on probation. As it turns out, the kind of person placed on probation varies dramatically from place to place. One study of felony sentencing found that rates of probation sentences for robbers varied among fourteen cities from a low of less than 1 percent to a high of 13 percent, and probation sentences varied from 2 to 40 percent.[22] Probation agencies that supervise more serious offenders can be expected to have higher rates of revocation. In locations where probationers have serious criminal histories, some probation departments have begun to collaborate with police departments to improve the public safety effectiveness of both agencies.[23]

Because revocation of probation is a serious change in the offender's status, the courts have ruled that the offender has several due process rights in the revocation procedure. The major case governing probationers was *Mempa v. Rhay*, decided by the U.S. Supreme Court in 1967.[24] The suspension of Jerry Mempa's sentence for the offense of joyriding had been revoked after he admitted to involvement in burglaries while on probation for the joyriding offense. The court ruled that sentences could not be imposed after probation revocation without an attorney to represent the offender.

In a later decision the Supreme Court further clarified revocation procedures.[25] The approved practice is to handle the revocation in three stages:

1. *Preliminary hearing (sometimes waived):* The facts of the arrest are reviewed to determine if there is probable cause that a violation has occurred.
2. *Hearing:* The facts of the allegation are heard and decided. The probation department presents the evidence to support the allegation, and the probationer has an opportunity to refute the evidence. Specifically the probationer has the right to see written notice of the charges and the disclosure of evidence of the violation, to testify and to present witnesses and evidence to contradict the allegations, to cross-examine adversarial witnesses, to be heard by a neutral and detached officer, and to review a written statement of findings. Unless unusual grounds exist to deny counsel, the probationer also has a right to an attorney.
3. *Sentencing:* With an attorney present the judge decides whether to impose a term of incarceration and, if so, the duration of the term. This stage is more than a technicality, because after a minor violation, probation is often reinstated with greater restrictions.

For those who successfully complete probation, the sentence is terminated. Ordinarily the probationer is then a completely free citizen again, without obligation to the court or to the probation department. But supervision often confronts the probation officer with difficult ethical questions.

DO THE Right THING

As you look over the Recommendation for Revocation Report sent to you by Officer Sawyer, you are struck by the low-level technical violations used to justify sending James Ferguson, a minor drug offender, to prison. Sawyer cites Ferguson's failure to attend all the drug treatment sessions, to complete his community service, to pay a $500 fine. You call Sawyer in to discuss the report.

"Bill, I've looked over your report on Ferguson and I'm wondering what's going on here. Why isn't he fulfilling the conditions of his probation?"

"I'm really not sure, but it seems he just doesn't want to meet the conditions. I think he's got a bad attitude, and I don't like the guys he hangs around with. He's always mouthing off about the 'system' and says I'm on his case for no reason."

"Well, let's look at your report. You say that he works for Capital Services cleaning offices downtown from midnight till 8 A.M. yet has to go to the drug programs three mornings a week and put in 10 hours a week at the Salvation Army Thrift Store. Is it that he isn't trying or does he have an impossible situation?"

"I think he could do it if he tried, but also, I think he's selling cocaine again. Perhaps he needs to get a taste of prison."

"That may be true, but do you really want to revoke his probation?"

What's going on here? Is Sawyer recommending revocation because of Ferguson's attitude and the suspicion that he is selling drugs again? Do the technical violations warrant prison? ■

Probation in the Coming Decade

As we enter the new century, there is evidence of dramatic changes in probation, as noted in the Workperspective. Traditional probation caseloads are growing well beyond reasonable management, with 200- and even 300-person caseloads no longer unusual. In many locales traditional probation has experienced "a massive deterioration in supervision due to loss of staff and budget and a heavy increase of cases."[26] Yet the importance of probation for public safety has never been greater: it was estimated that up to 17 percent of felony arrests in one sample of large urban counties were of people who were on probation at the time of their alleged offense.[27] As a result of the renewed emphasis on public safety, many agencies also experienced a resurgence of intensive and structured supervision for selected offenders (see Chapter 9).[28]

This leaves us with two increasingly divergent paths for probation in the future. One is largely a paper exercise. Whatever services are provided will be done through brokerage: The probation officer serves as a referral agent, involving the probationer in single-focus community service agencies (such as drug treatment programs) that work with a variety of community clients, not just with offenders. The remaining probationers — a minority of all offenders, to be sure — will be watched closely and will receive first-rate supervision and control from highly trained professionals working with reasonable levels of funding and programmatic support.[29] The use of brokerage is not necessarily a bad idea. Proponents argue that persons with special skills in any problem area can provide treatment superior to what a generalist can offer and that communities ought to be providing such assistance to offenders. Yet community agencies are not always quick to offer services to offenders; they prefer to work with voluntary clients, not those who avail themselves of services only under threat of the law.

WORKPERSPECTIVE Norman Helber

**Chief Probation Officer,
Maricopa County, Arizona**

Since that first day in 1841 when John Augustus looked for a better way of working with criminals, probation has continued to grow. What was once known as an "alternative to incarceration" is now the number one sentencing option used by judges all across America.

During the last twenty years probation has gone through some major changes, from an emphasis on rehabilitation to one of surveillance, and eventually to a concentration on risk management. Probation now finds itself on the brink of what could be another major directional change. More and more jurisdictions are indicating that probation must take responsibility for the desired behavioral changes in probationers.

In a pubic opinion survey, residents of Arizona were asked whether they would favor "giving nonviolent offenders probation or home arrest instead of prison." This question was answered favorably by 72 percent, in a state considered extremely conservative. The public wants probation to work. The public supports the message of hope that probation brings to its community. Being a chief probation officer is being in a position to fill a real societal need.

Probation administrators are also changing the way they want to be evaluated. Most of the time—and in most studies cited in this chapter—probation's effectiveness is determined by rearrest rates: High rates are seen as a sign of ineffective supervision. Yet administrators know that high rearrest rates can also mean that staff is watching high-risk clients vigilantly, something most citizens would applaud. From this viewpoint recidivism rates are not the sole outcome criterion for a probation department. Instead, some feel probation should also be evaluated by a series of "performance indicators" that better reveal whether probation is doing its job. These indicators include numbers of community service projects performed by probationers, the amount of probation fees and restitution collected, days free of drug use, employment rates, and taxes paid.[30] However, detractors claim that even if these performance indicators are high, the public is interested in crime as a bottom line—and that means recidivism rates matter most.

In many respects, then, probation finds itself at a crossroads. Although its credibility is probably as low as it has ever been, its workload is growing dramatically and, in view of the crowding in prisons and jails, will probably continue to do so. Under the strain of this workload and on-again, off-again public support, probation faces a serious challenge: Can its methods of supervision and service be adapted successfully to high-risk offenders? Many innovations are being attempted, but it is unclear whether such new programs actually improve probation or detract from it. Certainly they expand the variety of probation sanctions, making them more applicable to more offenders. But do they strengthen the mainstream functions of probation—investigation and supervision? These functions must be improved for probation to succeed in its current challenge.

Summary

Probation is the most extensively used sanction: About two-thirds of all adults under correctional supervision are on probation. Probation can be combined with incarceration or other punishments, such as fines, restitution, and community service. It allows offenders to serve terms imposed by the court in the community under supervision.

Although probation in the United States began with the work of John Augustus in 1841, previous attempts had been made to mitigate the harshness of criminal law through benefit of clergy, judicial reprieve, and recognizance.

Three controversial issues with regard to the organization of probation are whether it should be centralized or decentralized, whether it should be administered by the judiciary or the executive branch, and whether it should be combined with parole services.

Probation officers serve two major functions: investigation and supervision. The presentence investigation helps judges determine the appropriate punishment for the offender. The extensiveness of the investigation varies; the trend is toward short reports that focus on the potential risk to society. Such organizational problems as unclear sentencing goals, plea bargaining, and heavy workloads limit the influence of the PSI on the sentencing decision.

The probation officer, required both to enforce the law and to help the offender, faces role conflict in virtually every aspect of the job. Because officers lack substantive power, they must rely heavily on their authority in supervising offenders. The offender's response to supervision greatly influences the nature and effectiveness of the relationship with the officer, as does the fact that all supervision activities take place in the context of the probation bureaucracy.

Probation may be revoked as the result of a new arrest or for violation of the conditions of community supervision. Most research reports that about a third of probationers do not complete probation successfully. A recent study in California, however, indicated a much higher rate. ■

For Discussion

1. How does the use of probation affect the corrections system? Why is it used so extensively?
2. How does the presentence investigation report contribute to the dispersion of accountability for the sentence that is imposed?
3. How could the investigative and supervisory functions of probation be most effectively organized? What would the judges in your area say about your proposal? What would the department of corrections say?
4. Given the two major tasks of probation, how should officers spend their time? How do they actually spend their time?
5. Why might some probationers be kept in the community after a technical violation, rather than having their probation revoked?

For Further Reading

Clear, Todd R., and O'Leary, Vincent. *Controlling the Offender in the Community*. Lexington, MA: Lexington Books, 1981. Presents the argument for risk management methods in probation.

Ditton, Jason, and Ford, Roslyn. *The Reality of Probation: A Formal Ethnography of Process and Practice*. London: Avebury Press, 1995. Uses interviews with judges, probation officers, and probationers to paint a picture of the operations of the probation system.

Duffee, David, and McGarrell, Edward. *Community Corrections: A Community Field Approach*. Cincinnati: Anderson, 1990. Takes a theoretical approach to probation, focusing on the forces that surround it.

Petersilia, Joan, and Turner, Susan. *Granting Felons Probation: Public Risks and Alternatives*. Santa Monica, CA: Rand, 1985. Recounts the results of a study of probation for serious offenders in California.

Vass, Anthony A. *Alternatives to Prison: Punishment Custody and the Community*. Newbury Park, CA: Sage, 1990. Gives an up-to-date critique of imprisonment and defense of probation.

Notes

1. *The New York Times,* February 14, 1993, p. A20. See also Marc Renzema, "Reporting Kiosks: A Logical Idea Meets Resistance," *The Journal of Offender Monitoring,* 11, Summer 1998, pp. 13–14.
2. Darrell K. Gillard and Allen J. Beck, *Prison and Jail Inmates at Midyear 1997,* Bureau of Justice Statistics Bulletin (Washington, DC: U.S. Department of Justice, January 1998); and *Nation's Probation and Parole Population Reached New High Last Year,* Bureau of Justice Statistics News Release (Washington, DC: U.S. Department of Justice, August 16, 1998).
3. Robert Martinson, "California Research at the Crossroads," *Crime and Delinquency,* 22, April 1976, p. 191.
4. *Ex parte United States,* 242 U.S. 27 (1916); often referred to as *Killits.*
5. John Augustus, *First Probation Officer* (New York: Probation Association, 1939), p. 26. First published as *John Augustus, A Report of the Labors of John Augustus, for the Last Ten Years, in Aid of the Unfortunate* (Boston: Wright & Hasty, 1852).
6. Augustus, p. 34.
7. Todd R. Clear and David R. Karp, "Community Justice: An Essay," *Corrections Management Quarterly,* 2(3), Summer 1998, pp. 49–60.
8. Mark M. Lanier and Cloud Miller, "Attitudes and Practices of Federal Probation Officers Toward Pre-Plea/Trial Investigative Report Policy," *Crime and Delinquency,* 4(3), July 1995, pp. 364–377.
9. Robert C. Davis and Barbara E. Smith, "The Effects of Victim Impact Statements on Sentencing Decisions: A Test in an Urban Setting," *Justice Quarterly,* 11(3), September 1994, pp. 453–470.
10. Joan Petersilia, Susan Turner, James Kahan, and Joyce Peterson, *Granting Felons Probation: Public Risks and Alternatives* (Santa Monica, CA: Rand, 1985), pp. 39, 41.
11. *Williams v. New York,* 337 U.S. 241 (1949).
12. Charles L. Newman, "Concepts of Treatment in Probation and Parole Supervision," *Federal Probation,* March 25, 1961, p. 38.
13. *Rieser v. District of Columbia,* 21 Cr.L. 2503 (1977).
14. Gary Arling and Ken Lerner, Client Management Classification (Washington, D.C.: National Institute of Corrections, 1980).
15. *This Works! Community Sanctions and Services for Special Offenders* (Lacrosse, WI: International Association of Residential and Community Corrections, 1994).
16. Christopher J. Mumola and Thomas P. Bonczar, "Substance Abuse and Treatment of Adults on Probation, 1995," Bureau of Justice Statistics Special Report (Washington, DC: U.S. Department of Justice, March 1998), p. 1.
17. Michael Geerken and Hennessey D. Hayes, "Probation and Parole: Public Risks and the Future of Incarceration Alternatives," *Criminology,* 31(4), November 1993, pp. 549–564.
18. Petersilia et al., *Granting Felons Probation,* p. 39.
19. Bill Bryan, *Recidivism of Offenders in Community Corrections: The Record So Far,* Austin, TX: Criminal Justice Policy Council, May 1996.
20. Joan Petersilia, "Probation in the United States," in Michael Tonry, ed., *Crime and Justice: A Review of Research,* vol. 22. Chicago: University of Chicago, 1997, pp. 149–200.
21. Michael Geerken and Hennessey D. Hayes, "Probation and Parole: Public Risks and the Future of Incarceration Alternatives," *Criminology* 31(4) November 1993, pp. 549–564.
22. Stephen Klein, Patricia Ebener, Allan Abrahamse, and Nore Fitzgerald, *Predicting Criminal Justice Outcome: Measuring What Matters* (Santa Monica: Rand, 1991).
23. Richard Faulkner, "Community Policing and Community Corrections," *Perspectives,* Summer 1997, p. 10.
24. *Mempa v. Rhay,* 389 U.S. 128 (1967).
25. *Gagnon v. Scarpelli,* 411 U.S. 778 (1973).
26. Edwin Lemert, "Visions of Social Control: Probation Reconsidered," *Crime and Delinquency,* 39(4), October 1993, pp. 447–461.
27. Brian A. Reaves and Pheny Z. Smith, *Felony Defendants in Large Urban Counties, 1992* (Washington, DC: Bureau of Justice Statistics, U.S. Department of Justice, 1995).
28. Joan Petersilia, "A Crime Control Rationale for Reinvesting in Community Corrections," *The Prison Journal,* 75(4), 1995, pp. 479–496.
29. James M. Byrne, "The Future of Probation and the New Intermediate Sanctions," *Crime and Delinquency,* 36, 1990, pp. 6–14.
30. Harry N. Boone and Betsy Fulton, *Results-Driven Management: Implementing Performance-Based Measures in Community Corrections* (Lexington, KY: American Probation and Parole Association, 1995).

CHAPTER NINE

Intermediate Sanctions and Community Corrections

Put yourself in the judge's shoes. When you are getting ready to impose a sentence, how adequate are the available choices?

It is easy to think about the best way to sentence offenders whose crimes and backgrounds place them on the extremes. Imposing a prison term on a murderer, a rapist, or someone who engages in gratuitous violence makes sense to just about everyone. And for the first-time offender whose crime is neither violent nor unusual, and who has a solid link to the community such as a good job, most of us would feel comfortable with a probation term. But the cases you will face will seldom be violent crimes, and the true first-time, nonviolent felon will also be unusual. The far more likely case will have complexities that make choosing a sentence a problem.

Usually the offense you must consider is not the first crime in which the defendant has been involved. Probation or some other sanction has been tried before, and it may have worked well for a while, but the person now returns to stand before the bench, ready for another judgment. The crime will be serious enough, of course, but not alarming: The person was caught once again using drugs, or was implicated in another theft, or was caught with an illegal handgun, or got drunk and got in a fight. Yet under what circumstances would you want to try another term of probation? What message does that send?

However, a prison term makes little sense. At nearly $20,000 a year in taxpayer costs, the 18 months or so your sentence will require—$30,000—seem a bit expensive in view of the minor costs of the crime itself. And what will prison accomplish? You have seen plenty of cases fresh from incarceration, seemingly damaged by the experience, standing in front of you with glazed eyes, having pled guilty to yet another crime. What will prison teach the average case?

There are other considerations. The typical, middle-range case standing before you has dependents—a spouse and children—and you wonder what will happen to them, what they will think, after you reject their pleas not to send their father-husband-son-brother away. Will your lack of consideration of their interests embitter them toward the court, the law? It doesn't help that they all seem to be poor—too often, people of color—and face hard enough times as it is. If you send to prison the felon standing before you, you will make a hard life harder for some innocents who deserve better and pile disadvantages onto a person who started life out with one strike against him or her.

What about the victims? They always seem to want the toughest penalty the law provides, but you know that sending offenders to prison will gain them little. Most victims, in your experience, leave court feeling alienated from justice, whether you grant probation or give them a maximum penalty. And they all face the uphill battle of recovering from the emotional and practical costs of crime, a battle for which your sentence has limited meaning.

You look into the eyes of the self-admitted, repeat, second-rate felon, and search for something: remorse, or a promise to reform. If you could wave a magic wand, the person standing before you would feel immense contrition and would promise to pay the victim restitution, make reparation to the community, get into a treatment program, get a job, etc., etc. These are all routes you hope for when you impose a probation term, but with probation officer caseloads in excess of 100, what can you realistically expect?

You wish you had some choice between probation and prison—some intermediate sanction. As you mentally express this desire, you join thousands of other judges in feeling dispirited about the traditional sentencing options available for the vast majority of cases. As Norval Morris and Michael Tonry note, "Prison is used excessively; probation is used even more excessively; between the two is a near vacuum of purposive and enforced punishments."[1]

In this chapter we analyze nonprobation programs designed to keep offenders in local community corrections instead of prisons. We begin by discussing what might be called the modern intermediate sanctions movement. We will address this topic by seeking answers to the following Questions for Inquiry.

Questions FOR INQUIRY

1. What is the rationale for intermediate sanctions?
2. What is the continuum-of-sanctions concept?
3. What are some of the problems associated with intermediate sanctions?
4. What are the various types of intermediate sanctions?
5. What strategies can be used to make intermediate sanctions work?
6. What is the future of intermediate sanctions and community corrections?

The Case for Intermediate Sanctions

The rationale for correctional strategies between probation and imprisonment includes three related ideas: (1) imprisonment is too restrictive for many offenders, (2) traditional probation doesn't work with most offenders, and (3) justice is well served by having options in between. Now let's explore these arguments in more detail.

Unnecessary Imprisonment

Americans have traditionally tended to equate prison with punishment. When an offender is sentenced to something other than prison, many people are tempted to think that he or she "got off"; when an offender receives a short prison sentence, many think he or she "got a break." Yet to treat prison as the primary means of punishment is wrong on two grounds.

First, most sanctions in Western democracies do not involve imprisonment. In the United States probation is the most common sanction: For every offender in prison or jail three are on probation or parole.

In Europe this is even more true. Germany, for example, imposes fines as a sole sanction on two-thirds of its property offenders; in England the figure approaches half.[2] Community service is the preferred sanction for most property offenders in England.[3] Sweden, the Netherlands, France, Austria—and virtually every other European Common Market country—use other sanctions than prison

Wichita, Kansas, Judge Richard Shull sentences a drug offender. With a range of intermediate sanctions, judges are able to tailor the sentence to the particular needs of the offender and the community.

far more than incarceration. Because nonprison sanctions are a worldwide phenomenon, it makes little sense to think of them as nonpunishment.

The second reason to question prison as a punishment is that it is simply not very effective. We expect punishment to teach the offender something and divert him or her from a life of crime, but evidence shows this does not happen for many offenders. One study suggests that only 44 percent of all prison releases successfully complete their parole term, compared to 66 percent who complete their probation terms.[4] In short, prison punishes but does not educate.

If prison is neither the most common nor the most effective sanction, why does it dominate our thinking on punishment? Perhaps it is time to recognize that corrections can and should develop nonincarcerative sanctions that fill the gap between prison and probation.

Limitations of Probation

As we said in Chapter 8, probation is probably ineffective with serious offenders. Caseloads are too large to allow meaningful probation supervision. Because probation officers handle 100 or more offenders at a time, the average probationer gets maybe fifteen minutes of contact per week, hardly meaningful supervision. Further, in many cases what happens between the probation officer and the offender is not very relevant to the latter's problems. The probation officer may check the person's pay stubs and take a urine sample to test for drug use. But in the limited time available, little may happen to help the probationer achieve a change in lifestyle.

Intermediate sanctions can improve traditional probation supervision in two ways. First, they often can intensify supervision. Second, they can provide specialized programs better suited to address the offender's needs.

Improvements in Justice

Judges sometimes complain that their sentencing choices are too limited. They say they confront an offender whose crime does not warrant prison, but for whom probation seems inadequate. Developing an array of sanctions between these two extremes lets judges better match the sentence to the crime. Similarly, when an offender breaks probation or parole rules, some response is needed to maintain the credibility of the rules. But sending the rule violator to prison for behavior that is not otherwise criminal seems unwarranted.

Finally, intermediate sanctions allow a closer tailoring of the punishment to the offender's situation. Many offenders can be adequately punished by a fine. Others may be required to complete a drug treatment program. Still others can be confined to home for a while. In sum, intermediate sanctions, tailored to fit the offender's circumstances, may be more just. This may be one reason why public opinion surveys so consistently find support for intermediate sanctions as alternatives to prison and traditional probation.[5]

The Continuum-of-Sanctions Concept

continuum of sanctions

A range of correctional management strategies based on the degree of intrusiveness and control over the offender, along which an offender is moved based on his or her response to correctional programs.

Intermediate sanctions fit the concept of the continuum of sanctions. The term **continuum of sanctions** refers to a range of punishments that vary in intrusiveness and control as shown in Figure 9.1. Probation plus a fine or community service may be appropriate for minor offenses, whereas six weeks of boot camp followed by intensive probation supervision may be right for serious crimes.

The continuum-of-sanctions concept also incorporates a range of correctional management strategies that vary in intrusiveness and control. Delaware's sentencing accountability approach, presented in Table 9.1, illustrates this idea. Offenders are initially assigned to a level based on the seriousness of their offense and their prior

Figure 9.1 Continuum of Sanctions

Judges may use a range of intermediate sanctions, from those in which the offender requires a low level of control to those in which the offender requires a high level of control.

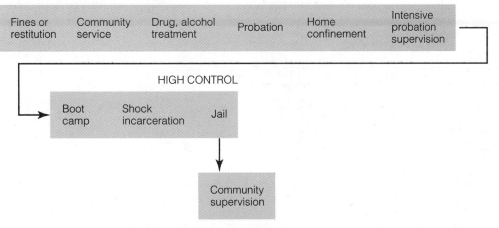

record. They then may move to a less restrictive or a more restrictive level, depending on their conduct and their response to supervision. Under this model all offenders are graded based on the seriousness of the current offense and the perceived risk of a new offense. Their movement through the corrections system depends on how well they do at each level.

Many jurisdictions have developed a continuum of sanctions, and its advantages now seem plain. First, it increases the corrections system's flexibility. As jails and prisons become more crowded, selected offenders can be moved to less restrictive options. For instance, jailed inmates can be placed in work release programs. Second, it allows more responsive management of individual offenders. For example, if a person on regular probation is not reporting, a brief home confinement can be followed by a return to probation. Finally, it costs less.

The continuum-of-sanctions idea is flexible enough to operate at both state and county levels. Further, it can be either codified into law or operated as a practice agreed to by the various agencies responsible for corrections. For instance, in Maricopa County, Arizona, the combined resources of multiple agencies—the jail, treatment centers, and probation—are used to develop the punishment system along a continuum of sanctions. This meets the same aims as Delaware's sentencing accountability system, but is not a part of penal law, nor is it operated by a single state agency.

Problems with Intermediate Sanctions

Despite the growing range of available alternatives, all is not well with the intermediate sanctions movement. Problems arise in selecting which agencies operate the process and which offenders receive the sanctions. Further, intermediate sanctions often inappropriately "widen the net."

Selecting Agencies

Administrators of such traditional correctional agencies as jails, prisons, probation, and parole often argue that they should also administer intermediate sanctions. They claim to have the staff and the experience to design new programs for special offender

Table 9.1 Sentencing Accountability System of Delaware

In Delaware offenders are assigned to a correctional accountability level based on their current offense and their prior record.

	Accountability Level			
Restrictions	**I** **0–100**	**II** **101–200**	**III** **201–300**	**IV** **301–400**
Mobility in the community	100% (unrestricted)	100% (unrestricted)	90% (restricted 0–10 hours/week)	80% (restricted 10–30 hours/week)
Amount of supervision	None	Written report monthly	1–2 face-to-face/month, 1–2 weekly phone contact	3–6 face-to-face/month, weekly phone contact
Privileges withheld or special conditions	(100%) same as prior offense conviction	(100%) same as prior conviction	1–2 privileges withheld	1–4 privileges withheld
Financial obligations	Fine/costs/may be applied (0–2 day fine)	Fine/costs/restitution/probation/supervisory fee may be applied (1–3 day fine)	Same as II (increase probation fee by $5–10/month) (2–4 day fine)	Same as III (increase probation fee by $5–10/month) (3–5 day fine)
Examples[a]	$50 fine/court costs; 6 months unsupervised probation	$50 fine/restitution/court costs; 6 months supervised probation; $10/month fee; written report	Fine/costs/restitution; 1 year probation; weekend community service; no drinking	Weekend community service or mandatory treatment, 5 hours/day; $30/month probation fee; no drinking; no out-of-state trips

[a]These are examples only—many other scenarios could be constructed meeting the requirements of each level.

SOURCE: Norval Morris and Michael Tonry, *Between Prison and Probation: Intermediate Punishments in a Rational Sentencing System* (New York: Oxford University Press, 1990), pp. 66–67. Copyright © 1990 Oxford University Press, Inc. Reprinted with permission.

subgroups, and they suggest that to maintain program coherence, they ought to operate all correctional processes. Critics counter that intermediate sanctions programs should be run by new agencies, both public and private. Because traditional correctional organizations must give highest priority to traditional operations, it is argued, they cannot give adequate attention or support to midrange alternatives. However, other critics believe that intermediate sanctions programs inevitably will be controlled by the currently dominant probation and prison systems — especially because these systems need intermediate sanctions to resolve swollen caseloads and overcrowded facilities.

Selecting Offenders

A second issue has to do with selecting appropriate offenders for alternative programs. One school of thought emphasizes selection by seriousness of offense; the other concentrates on the offender's problems. A focus on the offense usually eliminates some crime categories from consideration for intermediate sanctions. Many argue that violent or drug-marketing offenses are so abhorrent that a nonincarcerative program is not appropriate. Yet these offenders are often best able to adjust to these programs. Moreover,

Accountability Level

V 401–500	VI 501–600	VII 601–700	VIII 701–800	IX 801–900	X 901–1000
60% (restricted 30–40 hours/week)	30% (restricted 50–100 hours/week)	20% (restricted 100–140 hours/week)	10% (90% of time restricted)	0% (incarcerated)	0% (incarcerated)
2–6 face-to-face/week, daily phone, weekly written reports;	Daily phone, daily face-to-face, weekly written reports;	Daily on-site supervision, 8–16 hours/day	Daily on-site supervision, 24 hours/day	Daily on-site supervision, 24 hours/day	Daily on-site supervision, 24 hours/day
1–7 privileges withheld	1–10 withheld	1–12 withheld	5–15 withheld	15–19 withheld	20 or more withheld
Same as IV (pay partial cost of food/lodging/supervisory fee) (4–7 day fine)	Same as V (8–10 day fine)	Same as V (11–12 day fine)	Fine/costs/restitution payable upon release to VII or lower (12–15 day fine)	Same as VIII	Same as VIII
Mandatory rehabilitation skills program, 8 hours/day; restitution; probation fee of $40/month; no drinking curfew	Work release; pay partial cost of room/board/restitution; no kitchen privileges outside mealtime; no drinking; no sex; weekends home	Residential treatment program; pay partial program costs; limited privileges	Minimum security prison	Medium security prison	Maximum security prison

to the degree that these programs are needed to reduce prison overcrowding, they must include more serious offenders.

In practice, both the crime and the criminal are considered. Certain offenses are so serious that the public would not long tolerate intermediate punishments for them (even though there are many instances of successful community-based control of murderers and other serious offenders). At the same time, judges want programs to respond to the needs of the offenders they sentence.

Underlying this issue is the thorny problem of **stakes.** The concept of stakes is easily illustrated. Most of us would be willing to bet $1 on a one-in-ten chance of winning $10, yet few of us would be willing to bet $1,000 on a one-in-ten chance of winning $10,000. The odds are the same, but we stand to lose so much more in the second case. Similarly, officials who administer intermediate sanctions programs often are unwilling to accept offenders convicted of serious crimes, particularly violent crimes, even though the chances of the offenders' successfully completing a program may be quite good. If those offenders commit additional serious crimes, the damage to the community and—through negative publicity—to the corrections system can be substantial. With some offenders the stakes are simply too high, regardless of the amount of risk.

stakes

The potential losses to victims and to the system if offenders fail; stakes include injury from violent crimes and public pressure resulting from negative publicity.

Widening the Net

A third major problem with selecting offenders for intermediate sanctions is that of widening the net. In some ways this problem is potentially the most damaging, because it strikes at the very core of the intermediate sanctions concept. Critics argue that instead of reducing the control exerted over offenders' lives, the new programs actually have increased it. You can readily see how this might occur. With the existence of an alternative at each possible point in the system, the decision maker can select a more intrusive option than ordinarily would have been imposed. Community service, for instance, can be added to probation; shock incarceration can be added to a straight probation term.

Available evidence reveals that implementing intermediate sanctions has had these consequences:

1. *Wider nets:* The reforms increase the proportion of people in society whose behavior is regulated or controlled by the state.
2. *Stronger nets:* The reforms augment the state's capacity to control people by intensifying the state's intervention powers.
3. *Different nets:* The reforms create new jurisdictional authority or transfer it from one agency or control system to another.

Varieties of Intermediate Sanctions

There are many different types of intermediate sanctions; only the main types will be discussed here. How the various programs relate to one another depends on the jurisdiction running them. For example, one county may use intensive supervision in lieu of a jail sentence; another may use it for probation violators. We have organized our description of intermediate sanctions according to which agencies administer them—the judiciary, probation departments, or correctional departments.

Sanctions Administered Primarily by the Judiciary

The demand for intermediate sanctions often comes from judges dissatisfied with other sentencing options. In courts that have managerial authority over probation, this discontent has translated into new probation programs (described later in this section). Other courts have sought to expand their sentencing options by relying more on other programs within their control, such as pretrial diversion, forfeiture, fines, community service, and restitution. These programs primarily aim to reduce trial caseload, especially focusing on less serious offenders who ought not to tie up the court system; the programs also seek to impose meaningful sanctions without incarceration.

Pretrial Diversion The functions of pretrial diversion, especially as a jail alternative, were examined in Chapter 7. Because courts have extremely broad discretion in the pretrial phase of adjudication, some have sought to apply this discretion to a broader range of offenders.

Pretrial diversion programs typically target petty drug offenders. A new strategy in Wayne County (Detroit), Michigan, exemplifies this practice. First-time arrestees for drug possession are "fast-tracked" into drug treatment programs within twenty-four hours of arrest. They are promised that if they successfully complete the drug treatment program, the charges against them will be dropped. This kind of treatment-based diversion program depends on cooperation between court and prosecution. Judges indicate willingness to delay trial if prosecutors are willing to eventually drop charges against less serious offenders who change their lives.

Fines According to estimates, over $1 billion in fines is collected annually in the United States. Yet compared with other Western democracies, the United States makes little use of fines as the sole punishment for crimes more serious than motor vehicle violations.

Instead, fines typically are used with other sanctions, such as probation and incarceration. For example, it is not unusual for a judge to impose two years' probation and a $500 fine.

Many judges cite the difficulty of enforcing and collecting fines as the reason they do not make greater use of this punishment. They note that offenders tend to be poor, and many judges fear that fines would be paid from the proceeds of additional illegal acts. Other judges are concerned that relying on fines as an alternative to incarceration would let affluent offenders "buy" their way out of jail while forcing the poor to serve time.

In Europe fines are used extensively, are enforced, and are normally the sole sanction for a wide range of crimes. The amounts are geared to both the severity of the offense and the resources of the offender. To deal with the concern that fines exact a heavier toll on the poor than on the wealthy, Sweden and Germany have developed the **day fine,** which takes into account, by basing the penalty on offenders' income, the differing economic circumstances of offenders who have committed the same crime. (See the Comparative Perspective.) Thus the total penalty — the degree of punishment — should place an equivalent economic burden on offenders of differing means who are convicted of similar offenses. For example, a person making $36,500 a year and sentenced to ten units of punishment would pay $3,650; a person making $3,650 and receiving the same penalty would pay $365. The day fine concept currently is being

day fine

A criminal penalty based on the amount of income an offender earns in a day's work.

COMPARATIVE
PERSPECTIVE

Day Fines in Germany: Could the Concept Work Here?

Modern implementation of fines related to the income of the offender began with creation of the day fine system in Finland in 1921, followed by its development in Sweden (1931) and Denmark (1939). The Federal Republic of Germany instituted day fines in 1975. Since then there has been a major change in punishments, so that now more than 80 percent of those convicted receive a fine-alone sentence.

Judges determine the amount of the day fine through a two-stage process. First, judges relate the crime to offense guidelines, which have established the minimum and maximum number of day fine units for each offense. For example, according to the guidelines, theft may be punished by a day fine within the range of 10 to 50 units. Judges choose the number of units by considering the culpability of the offender and by examining the offender's motivation and the circumstances surrounding the crime. Second, the value of these units is determined. The German day fine is calculated as the cost of a day of freedom: the amount of income an offender would have forfeited if incarcerated for a day. One day fine unit is equal to the offender's average net daily income (considering salary, pensions, welfare benefits, interests, and so on), without deductions for family maintenance, as long as the offender and his or her dependents have a minimal standard of living. Finally, the law calls for publishing the

number of units and their value for each day fine set by the court so that the sentencing judgment is publicly known.

For example, say a judge faces two defendants, separately convicted of theft. One defendant is a truck driver who earns an average of DM100 per day and the other is a business manager whose earnings average DM300 per day. The judge decides that according to the guidelines, the circumstances of the theft and the criminal record of each offender are the same. He decides that each should be assessed 40 day fine units. Multiplying these units by the average daily income for each, the truck driver's fine is DM4,000 and the manager's fine is DM12,000.

Since the day fine system was introduced in Germany the use of fines has increased and short-term incarceration has decreased. The size of fines has also increased, showing that affluent offenders are now being punished at levels corresponding to their wealth. Fines for poor offenders have remained low. These fines have not increased the default rate.

Some Americans believe day fines would be more equitable than the current system of low fines for all regardless of wealth. Others believe that to levy higher fines against rich people than poor people is unjust, because the wealthy person is being penalized for working hard for a high income. What do you think? ▪

adapted to the U.S. system and has been tested in five jurisdictions in Arizona, Connecticut, Iowa, New York, and Washington.

Forfeiture With passage of the Racketeer Influence and Corrupt Organizations Act (RICO) and the Continuing Criminal Enterprise Act (CCE) in 1970, Congress resurrected **forfeiture,** a criminal sanction that had lain dormant since the American Revolution. Through amendments in 1984 and 1986, Congress improved ways to implement the forfeiture provisions of the law.[6] Similar laws are now found in a number of states, particularly with respect to controlled substances and organized crime.

Forfeiture, in which the government seizes property derived from or used in criminal activity, can take both civil and criminal forms. Under civil law, property used in criminal activity (for example, equipment to manufacture illegal drugs, automobiles, boats) can be seized without a finding of guilt. Under criminal law, forfeiture is imposed as a consequence of conviction and requires that the offender relinquish various assets related to the crime. These assets can be quite considerable. For example, in 1990 state and federal officials confiscated an estimated $1 billion worth of assets from drug dealers.

However, forfeiture is controversial. Critics argue that confiscating property without a court hearing violates citizens' constitutional rights. In 1993 the U.S. Supreme Court restricted the use of summary forfeiture. Now the growth in this form of sanction has waned.[7]

Community Service and Restitution Community service and restitution have been among judges' options for years, but relatively few judges have used them as exclusive sanctions. Recently, with prisons overcrowded and judges searching for efficient sentencing options, interest in these sanctions has increased.

A **community service** condition requires the offender to provide a specified number of hours of free labor in some public service, such as street cleaning, repair of run-down housing, or hospital volunteer work. A **restitution condition** establishes a sum of money that must be paid by the offender either to the victim or to a public fund for crime victims.

Both alternatives rest on the assumption that the offender can atone for his or her offense with a personal or financial contribution to the victim or to society. They have been called *reparative alternatives*, because they seek to repair in part some of the harm done. Such approaches have become popular because they force the offender to make a positive contribution to offset the damage, and thus satisfy a common public desire that offenders not "get away" with their crimes. They also are touted as ways to reduce correctional overcrowding.

The evidence on the effectiveness of these programs is mixed. Most studies seem to find that without such programs the vast majority of offenders who were ordered to provide community service and restitution would have been punished with a traditional probation sentence — which bodes poorly for community service as a real solution for correctional crowding.[8] Nor have community service and restitution programs proved especially effective at reducing the criminal behavior of their participants; in fact, they seem to have somewhat higher failure rates than do the regular supervision cases. Yet

forfeiture

Seizure by the government of property and other assets derived from or used in criminal activity.

community service

Compensating for injury to society by performing service in the community.

restitution

Compensation for financial, physical, or emotional loss caused by an offender, in the form of either payment of money to the victim or work at a service project in the community, as stipulated by the court.

Convicted of misdemeanor assault for spray-painting the faces of teenagers he caught painting graffiti, Mike Quintana was fined and sentenced to 40 hours of community service. Here he works off some of those hours painting over graffiti in southwest Denver.

offenders subjected to fines and restitution report that they experience these sanctions as both punitive and rehabilitative.[9]

In sum, community service and restitution show that simply implementing a so-called alternative does not always achieve the aims of intermediate sanctions. Careful attention must be paid to selecting appropriate offenders in order not to widen the net. And judicial decision making must be controlled to ensure that people who enter the programs are those who otherwise would have been incarcerated.

Sanctions Administered in the Community

One basic argument for intermediate sanctions is that probation, as traditionally practiced, is inadequate for large numbers of offenders. Probation leaders have responded to this criticism by developing new intermediate sanctions programs and expanding old ones. New programs often rely on increases in surveillance and control. Old programs often are revamped to become more efficient and expanded to fit more probationers.

Probation Day Reporting (Treatment) Centers As prisons became more and more crowded, judges grew reluctant to incarcerate probation violators except when the violation involved a new crime. As a result, probationers in some jurisdictions came to realize that they could disregard probation rules with relative impunity. Probation administrators found that the lack of credibility with clients severely hampered their effectiveness.

The solution seemed to be development of probation-run enforcement programs. For example, Georgia has experimented with **probation centers,** where persistent probation violators reside for short periods. Massachusetts and New York City have instituted **day reporting centers,** where violators attend day-long intervention and treatment sessions. Minnesota and other states have established **restitution centers,** where those who fall behind in restitution are sent to make payments on their debt.

All these forms of centers are usually referred to as day reporting centers, and they are modeled after an innovation developed in Great Britain in the 1970s.[10] In the United States these facilities vary widely, but all provide a credible option for probation agencies to enforce conditions when prisons are overcrowded. Most day reporting centers incorporate a mix of common correctional methods. For example, some provide a treatment regime comparable to a halfway house—but without the problems of siting a residential facility. Others "provide contact levels equal to or greater than intensive supervision programs, in effect, creating a community equivalent to confinement."[11]

So far, there are few outcome evaluations of these programs. One study of New York City's program found that its stiff eligibility requirements resulted in very small numbers of cases entering the program, a problem common to newly established intermediate sanctions programs.[12] A recent evaluation of a jail-run day reporting center in Cook County (Chicago) found that jail pretrial detention fell, and program participants had lower levels of drug use and absconding, but because participants were carefully screened before acceptance, applicability may be limited to low-risk cases.[13]

Day reporting centers are growing in popularity faster than the evidence concerning their effectiveness—by 1995, 115 day reporting centers were already operating, in 22 states.[14] The real test of these programs will involve two issues: (1) How much do they improve probation's credibility as a sanction, and (2) How well do they combat jail and prison crowding? These questions remain unanswered.

Intensive Supervision Intensive supervision probation (ISP) programs have sprung up around the country, and they seem ideally suited to the pressures facing corrections today. Because ISP programs target offenders who are subject to incarceration, they should help alleviate crowding; because they involve strict and close supervision, they respond to community pressures to control offenders.

What constitutes intensive supervision? Even the most ambitious programs require only once-a-day meetings between officers and offenders. Such meetings, which may

probation center
Residential facility where persistent probation violators are sent for short periods.

day reporting center
Facility where probation violators attend day-long intervention and treatment sessions.

restitution center
Facility where probationers who fall behind in restitution are sent to make payments on their debt.

last ten minutes or less, can never occupy more than a minuscule portion of the offender's waking hours. So, no matter how intensive the supervision, substantial trust must still be placed in the probationer.

Early evaluations of ISP programs in Georgia, New York, and Texas found that intensive supervision can reduce rearrest rates. Nevertheless, these programs were not received without controversy. For one thing, the low number of rearrests came at a cost. All evaluations of intensive supervision found that, probably because of the closer contact, probation officers uncovered more rules violations than in regular probation. Therefore ISP programs often had higher technical failure rates than regular probation, even though their probationers had fewer arrests.

This was precisely what Rand researchers found in a series of important experiments testing ISP effectiveness. Offenders in the California counties were randomly assigned to either ISP or regular probation. Results indicated no differences in overall arrest rates but substantial differences in probation failure rates. ISP clients did much worse under the stricter rules—possibly because ISP makes detecting rules violations easier.[15] In sum, these programs not only failed to reduce crime but actually cost the public more than if the programs had not been started in the first place.

Despite questions about the effectiveness of ISP, the approach has enjoyed wide support from correctional administrators, judges, and even prosecutors. The close supervision has revitalized the reputation of probation in the criminal justice system. It has also demonstrated probation's ability to enforce strict rules, ensure employment, support treatment programs, and so forth. Given the positive public relations, ISP likely is here to stay.

Even as intensive supervision may satisfy public demands for control measures, however, probationers continue to need various forms of assistance. Many offenders are buffeted by serious personal problems—unemployment, emotional and family crises, substance abuse—that cannot be addressed effectively without service or treatment. Therefore officers still have to juggle the roles of helper and controller. On paper the conflicts between these roles in ISP programs may seem less extreme, but in practice they may well continue and perhaps be exacerbated by the mixed messages of the programs.

home confinement

Terms of incarceration that offenders serve in their own homes.

Home Confinement With **home confinement** offenders are sentenced to incarceration, but serve those terms in their own homes. Variations are possible. For instance, after a time some offenders might be allowed to go to work or simply to leave home for restricted periods of the day; others might be allowed to maintain employment for their entire sentence. Whatever the details, the concept revolves around using the offender's residence as the place of punishment.

On the surface, the idea of home confinement is appealing. It costs the state nothing to house the offender; the offender pays for lodging, subsistence, and often even the cost of an electronic monitor. More importantly, significant community ties can be maintained—to family, friends (restricted visitation is ordinarily allowed), employers, and community groups. The punishment is more visible to the community than if the offender were sent to prison. In a sense the goals of reintegration, deterrence, and financial responsibility are served simultaneously. Studies find that large majorities of citizens, for such reasons, favor home confinement as a sanction for some nonviolent offenders.[16]

Evaluations of home confinement provide a few impressions of how the program works. One survey concluded that "most offenders placed in home confinement appear to be more similar to incarcerated offenders than to probationers and [it] does genuinely divert from incarceration at least half, and sometimes a much higher proportion, of those who receive it."[17] Anecdotal evidence suggests the effectiveness of home confinement seems to wear off after a few months; it is increasingly difficult to enforce detention conditions as the sentence rounds into its second half-year. (This should come as no surprise: The impact of imprisonment on offenders seems to stabilize after about the same length of time.) The program seems best suited to low-risk offenders who have relatively stable residences.

Electronic Monitoring One of the most popular new approaches to probation supervision is surveillance by electronic monitors. **Electronic monitoring** is ordinarily combined with and used to enforce home confinement. The number of offenders currently being monitored is difficult to reliably estimate because the equipment manufacturers consider this privileged information. However, the best estimates are that about 70,000 people are being monitored at any given time.[18]

Two basic types of electronic monitoring devices exist. Passive monitors respond only to inquiries; most commonly, the offender receives an automated telephone call from the probation office and is told to place the device on a receiver attached to the phone. Active devices send continuous signals that are picked up by a receiver; the receiver computer notes any break in the signal.

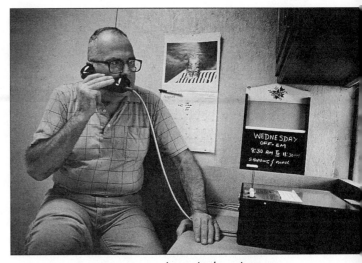

Larry Ingles, given a one-year sentence of home confinement for DWI, answers his electronic monitoring call. Failure to answer the telephone within three minutes may result in revocation of probation.

Advocates of these systems point out that they are cheaper than incarceration (especially because the offender often pays to use the system) and tougher than probation. They are also more humane than prison or jail, because offenders keep their jobs and stay with their families. In addition, probation officers are free to address the offenders' needs. Supporters of electronic monitoring can point to recent studies showing that Florida's community control offenders did not have higher rearrest rates than similar offenders sentenced to prison[19] and that a program targeting drunk drivers did not have a higher technical violation rate than regular probation for the same type of offender.[20] Other observers are more skeptical, however. They point out that only offenders who own telephones and can afford the $25–$100 per week these systems cost to rent are eligible. In addition, confinement to the home is no guarantee that crimes will not occur. Many crimes—child abuse, drug sales, and assaults, to name a few—commonly occur in offenders' residences.

Moreover, the reliability of these devices recently has become an issue. Some offenders have figured out how to remove the monitors without detection; others have been arrested at the scene of a crime—even though the monitoring system indicated they were safely at home. They can also intrude on the privacy of the family and be unduly stressful for the offender and his or her family (see the Focus box).

Despite these drawbacks, the use of electronic monitoring likely will continue to increase, and technological advances will continue. Recently, "global positioning systems" have become more feasible using satellite tracking devices to monitor offenders' whereabouts. These new approaches provide twenty-four-hour verification of an offender's exact location.[21] (See Chapter 21 for a description.)

electronic monitoring

Probation supervision technique, ordinarily combined with home confinement, that uses electronic devices to maintain surveillance on offenders.

Sanctions Administered in Institutions and the Community

Because they have been the hardest hit by problems of overcrowding, correctional agencies have had to develop intermediate sanctions to manage the burgeoning load of offenders. Some correctional agencies rely on electronic monitoring to support an early release program, but shock incarceration and boot camps are the two most common responses to overcrowding.

Shock Incarceration The fact that the deterrent effect of incarceration wears off after a very short term of imprisonment has led to experimentation with **shock incarceration.** The offender is sentenced to a jail or prison term; then, after the offender has served thirty to ninety days, the judge reduces the sentence. The assumption is that the offender will find the jail experience so distasteful that he or she will be more motivated to "stay clean."

Shock incarceration is controversial. Its critics argue that it combines the undesirable aspects of both probation and imprisonment. Offenders who are incarcerated lose

shock incarceration

A short period of incarceration (the "shock"), followed by a sentence reduction.

FOCUS   Jail Moves into Probationer's Home

J ay Match fidgets. He paces the floor, sits for a while at a kitchen table to flip the pages of a textbook for electrical contractors, walks back out into his living room.

In a corner near the telephone sits a black box about the size of an attaché case. The box is Mr. Match's jailer. In a classic way, the prisoner has come to hate his jailer.

It has been two weeks since Mr. Match was placed under three-month house confinement by a county judge. A three-ounce transmitter strapped to his leg above the ankle emits a radio signal every thirty-five seconds.

The electronic innards of the black box in the corner monitor the signals and report Mr. Match's movements over the telephone to a computer miles away in the offices of Pride Inc., a company that charges chronic misdemeanor defendants like Mr. Match a substantial fee for the right to be supervised at home.

Pride Inc. is a nonprofit private concern that in a few years has pioneered private supervising of traffic and misdemeanor probation cases. Like a medieval jailer, the monitor tells the IBM-PC computer downtown in electronic pulses the equivalent of "all is well; the prisoner is not in violation."

Law enforcement officials are monitoring the company to see how well it manages a program that allows chronic misdemeanor and traffic offenders to stay out of jail and how it does other probation work.

Company Is Also Counselor

Most of the probationers, of whom there were more than 9,000 last year, are required to report in person to Pride

Inc.'s offices on a regular basis for conferences with the concern's counselors. In the past, these duties were administered by local or state agencies.

Electronically monitored in-house confinement as an alternative to jail operates like a program in which the prisoner is released to work. But these offenders spend a sentence confined at home with time off during the day to go to a place of employment. It also allows single parents, like Mr. Match, to remain at home with their children rather than having to place them elsewhere.

Mr. Match's adjustment to nighttime and weekend confinement had not been as easy as he thought it would be. By the end of the first week, he said, he was studying ways to dismantle the monitoring equipment without being caught. . . .

The puzzle sometimes keeps Mr. Match awake late at night when his jailer automatically dials the computer, making soft internal clicks and whirs in the black box.

"I hear that box kick in and I feel like tearing it from the wall," he said with a faint smile, newly mindful that iron bars do not a prison make.

SOURCE: Adapted from J. Nordheimer, "Jail Moves into Probationer's Home," *The New York Times*, February 15, 1985. Copyright © 1985 by The New York Times Company. Reprinted by permission.

---

their jobs, have their community relationships disrupted, acquire the label of convict, and are exposed to the brutalizing experiences of the institution. Further, the release to probation reinforces the idea that the system is arbitrary in decision making and that probation is a "break" rather than a truly individualized supervision program. It is hard to see how such treatment can avoid demeaning and embittering offenders. Many studies of shock incarceration confirmed this idea, finding no improvement in recidivism rates. But interest has remained high, leading to a new form of the shock technique, called boot camps.

boot camp

A physically rigorous, disciplined, and demanding regimen emphasizing conditioning, education, and job training. Designed for young offenders.

Boot Camps One variation on shock incarceration is the **boot camp.** With boot camp, offenders serve a short institutional sentence and then are put through a rigorous, paramilitary regimen designed to develop discipline and respect for authority. The daily routine includes strenuous workouts, marches, drills, and hard physical labor.

Proponents of boot camp argue that many young offenders get involved in crime because they lack self-respect and are unable to order their lives. Consequently the boot camp model targets young first offenders who seem to be embarking on a path to sustained criminality.

Evaluations show that these offenders may improve in self-esteem. But critics of boot camps argue that military-style physical training and the harshness of the boot camp experience do little to overcome problems that get inner-city youths in trouble with the law. In fact, follow-ups of boot camp graduates show they do no better than other offenders after release from the program.[22] This fact led California officials in 1997 to close the only boot camp in that state—at San Quentin.[23]

Studies show that only boot camps that are carefully designed, target the right offenders, and give them rehabilitative services are likely to save money and reduce recidivism.[24] Too many boot camps overemphasize the value of discipline, to the detriment of the graduates. In fact, in Maricopa County a special group had to be set up for boot camp graduates because their failure rates were so high after leaving the program.

Do boot camps work? There is no firm answer. Perhaps job training and education would be more beneficial than physical training. The intentionally harsh tactics of boot camp are brutal, especially for impressionable young offenders. Nevertheless, the approach has proved very popular with a public that is searching for new ways to handle offenders.

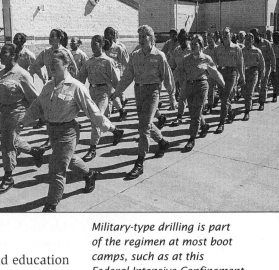

Military-type drilling is part of the regimen at most boot camps, such as at this Federal Intensive Confinement Center for Women in Bryan, Texas. Evaluations of boot camps have faded the initial optimism about this approach.

Making Intermediate Sanctions Work

Intermediate sanctions have been in use too briefly to allow complete evaluation of effectiveness. Of the hundreds of such programs attempted since the mid-1980s, few have been studied, and even fewer evaluated. Summaries note frequent failures to achieve stated goals, but that certainly does not mean the idea should be abandoned.

One evaluation problem is that intermediate sanctions often profess lofty goals such as improving justice, saving money, and preventing crime. Any correctional strategy that can produce these results surely deserves broad support. Yet the limited record on intermediate sanctions suggests that these goals are not always accomplished. If intermediate sanctions are to work, they must be carefully planned and implemented—and even then, obstacles must be overcome if the sanctions are to be effective. Issues these programs must resolve to reach their potential include sentencing philosophies and practices, offender selection criteria, and surveillance and control methods.[25]

Sentencing Issues

The most important issue in intermediate sanctions concerns sentencing philosophy and practice. In recent years sentencing philosophy has increasingly emphasized deserved punishment: Similar offenses deserve penalties of similar severity. Because intermediate sanctions fall between imprisonment and probation, they could potentially increase the number of midrange severe punishments and thus improve justice.

Yet advocates of deserved punishment argue that it is not clear how intermediate sanctions compare with either prison or probation in terms of severity, nor how they compare with one another. For example, placing one offender on intensive probation while ordering another to pay a heavy fine may violate the equal punishment rationale of just deserts.

When intermediate sanctions are used to reduce prison crowding, the issue becomes even murkier. Using intermediate sanctions as sentencing alternatives for some

principle of interchangeability

The idea that different forms of intermediate sanctions can be calibrated to make them equivalent as punishments despite their differences in approach.

offenders may raise serious concerns about equity. Is it fair for some offenders to receive prison while others receive the intermediate sanction?

For intermediate sanctions to be effective, agencies must develop exchange rates consistent with the **principle of interchangeability** so that one form can be substituted for or added to another form. For example, two weeks of jail might be considered as equal to thirty days of intermittent confinement or two months of home confinement or 100 hours of community service or one month's salary.

Advocates say that in terms of intrusiveness a short prison sentence can be roughly equivalent to some intensive supervision programs or residential drug treatment and that various forms of intermediate sanctions can be made roughly equivalent to one another. Studies of intensive supervision support this contention. For instance, one study reported that some offenders would rather be in prison than placed on tough intermediate sanctions.[26] A Texas study found that "75 percent of a sample of offenders rated one or more intermediate sanctions as more severe than an incarcerative sanction."[27] Thus intermediate sanctions can be designed that equate with incarceration in terms of intrusion and therefore do not violate principles of deserved punishment. Yet these studies are troubling in that they find substantial differences across racial groups in preferring prison to intermediate sanctions. Blacks and Hispanics are more likely than whites to rate prison as preferable—raising a concern that widespread adoption of intermediate sanctions may further exacerbate racial disproportions in prison populations.[28]

In practice, some observers have tried to structure this interchangeability by describing punishment in terms of units: A month in prison might count as thirty units; a month on intensive supervision might count as ten. Thus a year on ISP would be about the same as a four-month prison stay. To date, no one has designed a full system of interchangeability, although both the federal sentencing guidelines and those in Oregon embrace the punishment units concept. In the future we likely will see attempts to create interchangeability based on equivalence in punishments.

Selection of Offenders

If intermediate sanctions are to work, they must be reserved for appropriate offenders, which in turn depends on a given program's goals. No matter what the program's goals are, however, intermediate sanctions must be made available regardless of race, sex, or age.

The Target Group Intermediate sanctions have two general goals: (1) to serve as a less costly alternative to prison and (2) to serve as a more effective alternative to probation. To meet these two goals, intermediate sanctions managers search for appropriate offenders for their staff to supervise—often a difficult task.

Prison alternatives are designed for offenders who would otherwise be sentenced to prison. But how can we be certain that an offender given an alternative sanction would have otherwise been sentenced to prison? In most jurisdictions a person who is sentenced to probation is legally eligible for a prison sentence. Research shows that even though many offenders sentenced to intermediate sanctions are eligible for prison, most—if not all—actually would have been placed on probation instead. Yet plenty of prison-bound offenders seem appropriate candidates for intermediate sanctions: One study of those entering California prisons found that as many as a fourth would have been suitable for intermediate sanctions.[29]

Because of judges' reluctance to divert offenders from prison, many intermediate sanctions programs billed as prison alternatives actually serve as probation alternatives. As an example, consider boot camp programs, which are usually restricted to first-time property offenders ages 16 to 25. Boot camp, then, cannot be considered an effective prison alternative, because young, first-time property offenders seldom go to prison.

Probation alternatives (often called *probation enhancements*) face a similar problem. Theoretically they should be restricted to the highest-risk offenders on probation—

those needing the most surveillance and control. Typically, however, the conservatism inherent in new programs means that the true high-risk cases are made ineligible for the program.

Clearly, when intermediate sanctions are applied to the wrong target group, they cannot achieve their goals. When prison alternatives are applied to nonprison cases, they cannot save money. When probation enhancement programs are provided to low-risk clients, they cannot reduce much crime.

One solution is to use intermediate sanctions as backups for clients who fail on regular probation or parole. This practice would increase the probability that the target group was composed of high-risk, prison-bound offenders.

Problems of Bias Race, sex, and/or age bias is a concern anywhere in the justice system, but particularly for intermediate sanctions. Because getting sentenced to an intermediate sanction generally is a matter of official (usually judicial) discretion, the concern is that white, middle-class offenders will receive less harsh treatment than will other groups. In fact, nonwhites are more likely to remain incarcerated rather than receive alternative sanctions, and minorities are more likely to be subjected to tougher supervision instead of regular probation.

Alternative sanctions also tend to be designed for men, not women. Of course, men make up over 80 percent of the correctional population, but the patently unfair result may be that special programs are available only to men. Moreover, the design of intermediate sanctions, which is often based on tough supervision, is challenged by some experts on female offenders. They are concerned that such tough measures may be inappropriate for many women offenders, whose problems require more emphasis on social services.

The solution to problems of bias is neither obvious nor uncontroversial. Most observers recognize that some discretion is necessary in placing offenders in specialized programs. They believe that without the confidence of program officials, offenders are likely to fail. Thus automatic eligibility for these programs may not be a good idea. It may be necessary to recognize the potential for bias and to control it by designing programs especially for women, making certain to take cultural factors into account in selecting offenders.

Surveillance and Control

Intermediate sanctions have, for the most part, been developed during a period in which correctional policy has been enmeshed in the politics of "getting tough on crime." Not surprisingly, then, most alternatives tend to emphasize, at least in public relations, their toughness. Boot camps are described as providing no-nonsense discipline; intensive supervision expressly incorporates surveillance and control as primary strategies. Certainly this rhetoric is useful in obtaining public support for the programs. But do the programs themselves benefit from being so unabashedly tough?

Growing evidence indicates that the tough aspects of intermediate sanctions may not be totally positive. As we've seen when both the requirements of supervision and the surveillance of offenders are increased, more violations are detected and more probationers face revocation of probation. Whether it is in the interest of the system to increase detection of violations by upgrading the supervision standards and their enforcement—by being tough—is an open question. If this tough approach has no impact on crime, but instead merely costs more money (through the need to process more violators), what is the benefit?

In many jurisdictions, violators are a serious management problem. For example, in Oregon over 60 percent of new prison admissions are probation or parole violators, many of whom have not been accused of a new crime.[30] In other states, such as California and New York, if the rate of violations could be reduced, the costs of the equivalent of an entire prison's population could be saved. Identified violations have been increased by both more stringent enforcement and improved surveillance, especially drug testing. Some people wonder whether the benefits of these changes have outweighed the costs.

The New Corrections Professional

Without doubt intermediate sanctions have changed the work of corrections professionals. The long-standing choice between prison and probation has been expanded to include community and residential options that run from tough, surveillance-oriented operations to supportive, treatment-based programs. The kinds of professionals needed to staff these programs vary from recent college graduates to experienced and well-trained mental health clinicians. (See the Workperspective.) Central to this growth, however, are two major shifts in the working environment of the new corrections professional.

First, nongovernmental organizations have emerged to administer community corrections programs. Hundreds of nonprofit agencies, such as Connecticut Halfway

WORKPERSPECTIVE Lisa A. Zimmer

Chemical Dependency Counselor, Residential Treatment Program for Convicted Offenders, Cincinnati, Ohio

I hold a bachelor's degree in journalism from Northwestern University. After eleven years in public relations, I knew I wanted to find a career that made a greater contribution to society, even if it meant a smaller salary. I went back to earn a master's degree in social work at the University of Kentucky. During my graduate program I worked for two semesters at a hospital providing psychiatric emergency services. Most of my patients had substance abuse problems that contributed to their mental problems. To learn more about substance abuse I served in treatment programs for offenders with this problem.

I now work for an agency that contracts with the county to provide substance abuse treatment in a residential facility for people serving misdemeanor jail sentences. The clients live in two large dormitory rooms that can house fifty men. Security is maintained by county correctional officers. Judges may ask that specific offenders with chemical dependency problems be considered for our program. If they are selected, and complete the 90- to 120-day treatment program, they are usually released by the judge to two years of probation. While on probation, they must continue treatment. I know that the prospect of early release, rather than a genuine desire to address substance abuse problems, is the primary motivation for many of my clients.

Chemical dependency treatment is sorely needed in the corrections environment. Our treatment involves individual and group counseling. In group sessions, counselors encourage clients to share thoughts and experiences, ana-

lyze their problems together, and confront one another about avoiding important personal issues. Special group meetings deal with certain problems, such as alcohol, drug, or assaultive behavior.

I am a social worker by training and by philosophy. As such, I am an advocate for my clients. However, I am not opposed to penalties for crimes they have committed—I bear a responsibility to the public, too. However, we don't have a "crystal ball" to tell us how our clients will behave in the future. The possibility always exists that someone released from the program will commit additional crimes with tragic consequences, so I do not take my responsibilities lightly.

I make decisions on a daily basis about how to counsel clients and facilitate their group discussions. I also must make more difficult decisions, such as recommending that a client return to jail if he is not making genuine efforts to participate in the program or is violating rules. This is a particularly difficult decision when I am told that one client has threatened another client—grounds for a return to jail to serve out the sentence. If I have conflicting versions of events, whom should I believe? I always look for additional evidence, such as witnesses or others who have been threatened by the same person. The last thing I would want is to send someone back if he did nothing wrong. On the other hand, I bear responsibility for the safety of clients and staff and for the success of the program. Thus a decision may have to be made—one that will cause someone to serve months in jail—based on our best judgment, even if we cannot know with absolute certainty exactly what happened.

Houses, Inc. (see the Focus box) now dot the correctional landscape. These organizations contract with probation and parole agencies to provide services to clients in the community.

Second, increased emphasis on accountability has reduced individual discretion. Professionals currently work within boundaries, often defined as guidelines, that specify policy options in different case types. For instance, a staff member may be told that each offender must be seen twice a month in the office and once a month in the community and that in each contact a urine sample must be taken. Such rules constrain discretion and provide a basis for holding staff accountable for their handling of offenders.

Third, the relationship between the professional and the client has become less important than the principles of criminal justice that underlie that relationship. Instead of training in psychology and counseling, for instance, the new corrections professional receives training in law and criminal justice decision making. Thus the sources of job satisfaction have shifted from helping offenders with their problems toward simply shepherding offenders through the system.

Thus, the new corrections professional is more accountable for decision making and is more oriented toward the system in carrying out agency policy. This has significant implications for motivation and training of staff, but it also means that in the traditional three-way balance between offender, staff, and bureaucracy, the latter has grown in importance.

Community Corrections Legislation

Corrections in the United States has always had a local focus. Corrections systems located only a few miles apart can vary dramatically in philosophy and practice because of differences in community values and interests. For instance, a person who crosses the border from Utah to Nevada goes from a state with one of the lowest incarceration rates in the United States to a state with one of the highest, even though the crime rates of the two states are nearly identical. Likewise, traveling from New Mexico to Arizona or from Kansas to Oklahoma or from Massachusetts to New York represents a journey between different corrections systems and philosophies. Figure 9.2 shows the differences in incarceration rates and crime rates in these pairs of adjoining states.

The differences in style and philosophy of correctional programs in different localities reflect a basic truth about law and order: Beliefs about right and wrong, and values

Most halfway houses are operated under government contract by nonprofit organizations. Good News Regeneration House, Brooklyn, New York, is a place for offenders to live while they work in the community and receive drug counseling.

A Nonprofit Corrections Agency: Connecticut Halfway Houses, Inc.

In 1962 Connecticut Halfway Houses, Inc. (CHHI), a private, nonprofit, community-based corrections agency, was founded by a group of concerned citizens with a grant from the Watkinson Foundation. Since 1966 CHHI has been delivering supervision, treatment, and comprehensive individualized services to sentenced offenders and those determined to be at risk of involvement with the criminal justice system, who have been referred under contract by agencies such as the Federal Bureau of Prisons, Federal Probation, the Connecticut Department of Corrections, and the Connecticut Office of Adult Probation. Alternatives to incarceration as well as residential and aftercare services are provided to over 2,200 offenders annually in fifteen programs and residential facilities located throughout the state. CHHI operates with an annual budget of over $3.5 million and a staff of 150.

Specialized services encompass case management, individual and group counseling, education, substance abuse services, AIDS education, relapse prevention, anger management, employment readiness training, literacy, life skills training, money management, and community service. A principal goal of the agency is to enhance the opportunities available to these people to become productive, contributing members of their families and communities.

Five residential programs serving a total of 126 men, adult females, and youthful offenders are operated by CHHI. Residential work release programs provide services to offenders who are either on pretrial status, on probation, approaching their sentence discharge date, or presently on supervised home release. Aftercare programs are offered as part of the discharge planning process and incorporate training in the use of community support services. Each residential facility provides professional services and counseling to enhance ex-offenders' rehabilitation and reintegration into the community.

Substance abuse counseling programs are offered to offenders who have been incarcerated or placed on probation because of behaviors influenced by their drug use (committing crimes to support a habit, possession or distribution of drugs). Services include in-depth assessment and evaluation of their drug/alcohol status and history, supervision, urine screening, and case management.

As part of Connecticut's commitment to intermediate sanctions, alternative incarceration centers have been established. The programs accept predominantly court-referred clients as part of a pretrial diversion program, as well as probation and supervised home prerelease violators. Clients are required to have daily contact with the centers, including providing an itinerary of their daily activities. Preapproved destinations, including places of employment, are spot-checked by telephone and with random site visits on an ongoing basis. Clients are required to submit to regular drug testing, participate in substance abuse counseling, and receive support services designed to meet their individual needs. Participation in community service work projects, designed to benefit the communities located near the centers, is viewed as an important program component and helps in developing community support. Supervised work crews provide labor to cities, towns, and charitable organizations. These projects have proved both a beneficial and cost-effective source of productive labor; more importantly, they offer offenders a way to give something back to their communities.

In 1991 President George Bush awarded Connecticut Halfway Houses, Inc., a certificate of merit for its community service projects. With the statewide growth in intermediate sanctions programs, the size of the annual budget and staff has tripled during the past three years. CHHI is currently investigating the development of new programs to serve the future needs of the criminal justice system.

about how to deal with wrongdoers, differ from one locality to the next. Over the years the concept of community corrections has revolved around many themes, but the core idea is that local governments know best how to deal with their own crime problems.

At its broadest level, the concept of community corrections is best understood as a goal: to reduce reliance on traditional maximum-security prisons in punishing offenders. In pursuit of this goal, community corrections embraces a wide spectrum of alternatives to incarceration among which judges and other criminal justice system officials may choose.

In the late 1960s and early 1970s, several states considered legislation to establish financial and programmatic incentives for community corrections. For example, in 1965 California passed the Probation Subsidy Act, which sought to reimburse counties for

Figure 9.2 Incarceration and Crime Rates in Selected Contiguous States, 1998

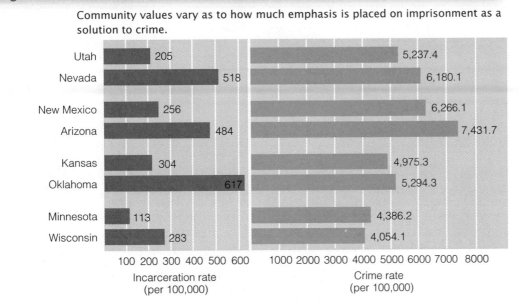

Community values vary as to how much emphasis is placed on imprisonment as a solution to crime.

State	Incarceration rate (per 100,000)	Crime rate (per 100,000)
Utah	205	5,237.4
Nevada	518	6,180.1
New Mexico	256	6,266.1
Arizona	484	7,431.7
Kansas	304	4,975.3
Oklahoma	617	5,294.3
Minnesota	113	4,386.2
Wisconsin	283	4,054.1

Incarceration rate (per 100,000)   Crime rate (per 100,000)

SOURCE: U.S. Department of Justice, Bureau of Justice Statistics, *Bulletin*, August 1998; Federal Bureau of Investigation, *Crime in the United States, 1994* (Washington, DC: U.S. Government Printing Office, 1995).

keeping offenders in the local corrections system instead of sending them to state facilities. The assumption was that up to 25 percent of all correctional commitments represented offenders who could be kept at the local level. Therefore the strategy undertaken was to develop a formula to determine the number of offenders who ordinarily would be sent to state institutions and to pay the counties a specified sum for each offender *not* sent to prison. The counties could then use the money to strengthen probation and other local correctional services so they could handle the additional offenders.

In 1973 Minnesota passed the first Comprehensive Community Corrections Act, which provided for funding of local corrections systems with money saved by state corrections when individuals were not sentenced to state facilities. Colorado in 1976 and Oregon in 1978 passed legislation patterned after Minnesota's. The experience of these pioneering states in community corrections was so well regarded that by 1995, more than half of the states had passed community corrections legislation, as shown in Figure 9.3. Some of these more recent legislative acts let local governments contract with private, nonprofit agencies to manage offenders. In these states halfway houses, drug treatment programs, and other correctional strategies can be established by private individuals who contract with local governments to deal with selected offenders.

Community corrections legislation is based on the idea that local justice systems have little incentive to keep their own offenders in local corrections. State-administered institutions are funded by state tax revenues, and it costs communities little to send large numbers of offenders to state-administered institutions. In contrast, it costs local citizens much more to keep offenders in jail or on local probation because they must supply the tax revenues to pay for those services.

Yet a year's incarceration in a state prison costs much more than local incarceration or probation (see Table 9.2). Therefore, in the long run, centralized, state-administered punishments seem more expensive than local corrections. If we also acknowledge that many offenders are sentenced to state prison when this extreme punishment is not necessary, we can easily see that the financial incentives that favor imprisonment run contrary to good correctional policy.

The payback system must establish some formula for determining what baseline prison commitment rates would be without the financial incentive provided by the legislation,

Figure 9.3 States with Community Corrections Acts

Many states provide financial incentives for local governments to keep offenders in local corrections agencies instead of sending them to state prisons.

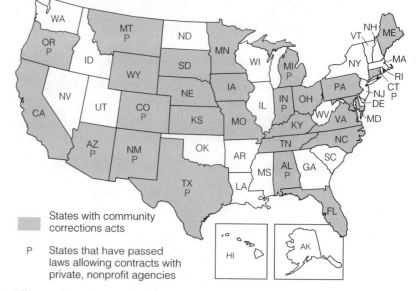

States with community corrections acts

P States that have passed laws allowing contracts with private, nonprofit agencies

SOURCE: M. Kay Harris, "Key Differences Among Community Corrections Acts in the United States: An Overview," *The Prison Journal*, June 1996.

and the same formula must apply to all the state's jurisdictions. This idea has problems, of course. Local corrections systems do not contribute equally to overincarceration of offenders; for example, urban and rural areas contribute differently. The funding formula, then, is likely to result in some serious inequities. For instance, California's formula did not adjust for counties that traditionally restricted incarceration; hence subsidies given to so-called progressive counties were unlikely to equal those given to more "conservative" counties. Further, California's original payback rate ($4,000 per offender) was not adjusted for inflation, and by 1975 this amount was worth less than $2,500 per offender. In contrast, Minnesota's formula factored inflation in and permitted adjustments for a locality's crime rate and the capacity of its corrections system. Yet the formula was criticized for providing lesser financial incentives to cities, which had more offenders and a correspondingly larger corrections system.

Ultimately, community corrections legislation has three aims:

Table 9.2 Costs of Incarceration and Intermediate Sanctions in Four States

In a study of Colorado, North Carolina, Ohio, and Virginia, intermediate sanctions proved far less expensive than imprisonment

Correctional Method	Cost per Year per Offender
Prison	$ 17,794
Jail	12,494
Probation	869
Intensive supervision	2,292
Community service	2,759
Day reporting	2,781
House arrest	402
Electronic monitoring	2,011
Halfway house	12,494
Boot camp	23,707

SOURCE: *Seeking Justice: Crime and Punishment in America* (New York: Edna McConnell-Clark Foundation, 1997), p. 34.

1. To reduce the rate and number of people sentenced to state correctional facilities
2. To reduce tax revenues spent on corrections by transferring both the costs and the funding to less expensive local correctional facilities
3. To reduce prison populations

Have these aims been achieved? The answer is complicated. Several evaluations have been made of California's Probation Subsidy Act.[31] All agree on one point: that availability of probation subsidies resulted in several local policy shifts and local compensatory decisions. Adult and juvenile commitments to state facilities decreased immediately after the enactment of the probation subsidy. These early findings led supporters of the subsidy to conclude it was extremely effective at reducing commitments.

Closer inspection raised questions as to whether the reduction in commitments also reduced the overall control of offenders. In the local justice systems the general intrusiveness of corrections increased for both adults and juveniles. More offenders were given jail terms, and more offenders received tighter control through commitment to local drug treatment and mental health facilities. Thus overall the subsidy primarily transferred incarceration of offenders from state-funded prisons to state-subsidized local corrections—hardly a resounding victory for community corrections.

The community corrections movement has had limited impact on prison populations in most states that have enacted such legislation. Generally their prisons remain extremely crowded. Parole decisions appear to have become more conservative in California and Minnesota, thus counterbalancing the modest reduction in commitments achieved by community corrections legislation. This has led some critics of community corrections to argue that the movement toward community corrections is only a surface shift in policies that emphasize incarceration, and talking about community corrections reform lets corrections continue its costly practices while creating an image of fiscal responsibility.[32]

So has community corrections legislation failed? All studies of community corrections have found that some offenders were shifted to local corrections, and this is encouraging. The problem is to control local correctional programs to ensure that the prison commitments are actually reduced under the new policies, as the legislation intended. As noted earlier, some community corrections acts let local governments contract with private, nonprofit businesses that provide services to offenders. Supporters claim these contracts create private jobs while reducing commitments to prison, and this aspect of community corrections acts may benefit everyone.

The Future of Intermediate Sanctions and Community Corrections

What does the future hold for intermediate sanctions and community corrections? Certainly three recurrent problems must be addressed.

First, some way must be found to overcome the tendency of the criminal justice system to resist placing offenders in less restrictive correctional contexts and instead to keep increasing the level of corrections. Even the most successful nonprison alternatives enroll only a few offenders who would otherwise have been incarcerated. The usual pattern is to first place offenders in prison and then release them to the community. New alternative programs fill up with people who formerly would have been placed on regular probation. Nonprison programs, whether intermediate sanctions or community corrections programs, must better recommend themselves to judges who are sentencing offenders for which such programs are intended.

Second, community support for these programs must increase. Citizens fear the offenders in their midst. Active measures must be taken to allay those fears, to help citizens become comfortable with a correctional mission that recognizes a wide array of programs other than incarceration-based punishments.

Third, the purposes of these sanctions must be clarified. No program can operate successfully for long if its goals are not clearly defined. The goals espoused by most programs today are competing generalizations: reduction of overcrowding, rehabilitation, protection of the community, reintegration, cost effectiveness, and so on. No legitimate government operation can reject any of these considerations, but some ordering of priorities and clarification of objectives must occur before these new forms of correctional functions can take their rightful place as core operations in the overall system.

Summary

Intermediate sanctions is a new movement that seeks to establish correctional programs falling between standard probation and prison. Although a basic justification for intermediate sanctions is that prisons are overcrowded, many jurisdictions have tried to develop a continuum of sanctions as a way of responding to the need for greater sentencing options.

Some intermediate sanctions programs are operated by the courts, and others by probation or correctional agencies. The main forms of intermediate sanctions are fines, community service, restitution, intensive supervision, home confinement, electronic monitoring, shock incarceration, and boot camp. These innovations have not been widely studied, and little can be said definitively about how well they work.

The goal of community corrections may be seen as diverting offenders from state prisons to locally administered correctional programs. Some states have enacted legislation to promote community corrections. The California Probation Subsidy Act was passed to encourage counties to maintain offenders in the community rather than send them to state correctional facilities. Colorado, Minnesota, and Oregon, among others, have passed similar legislation.

Some advocates of intermediate sanctions and community corrections have argued that they are cheaper than incarceration. This consideration has proved a powerful incentive to adopt this orientation. Community support for these programs is imperative if they are going to succeed. ■

For Discussion

1. Do intermediate sanctions work better as a way of improving on probation or of avoiding the negatives of imprisonment? Explain.
2. Should intermediate sanctions be run by traditional probation and prison systems or by new agencies seeking to serve as alternatives to them?
3. What does the experience of the California probation subsidy program tell us about the interdependence of various elements of corrections?
4. Why do states with similar crime rates sometimes have different incarceration rates?
5. Do you think that intermediate sanctions are acceptable to the general public in the current political climate? Why or why not?

For Further Reading

American Corrections Association. *Community Corrections.* Lanham, MD: ACA, 1996. A series of 21 papers on various aspects of intermediate sanctions, discussed from the viewpoint of the program administrator.
Anderson, David. *Sensible Justice: Alternatives to Prison.* New York: The New Press, 1998. Specially written for an informed lay audience, the book provides a comprehensive review of the argument for alternatives to incarceration, and develops a politically feasible case for expanded use of alternatives.
Byrne, James M., Lurigio, Arthur J., and Petersilia, Joan. *Smart Sentencing: The Emergence of Intermediate Sanctions.* Newbury Park, CA: Sage, 1992. Explores various issues in the design and implementation of intermediate sanctions programs.
Mair, George. *Evaluating the Effectiveness of Community Penalties.* London: Avebury Press, 1995. Evaluates electronic monitoring, intensive supervision, and community service, among other types of probation programs.

McGarry, Peggy and Madeline M. Carter, eds. *The Intermediate Sanctions Handbook: Experiences and Tools for Practitioners.* Washington, DC: National Institute of Corrections, 1993. Provides exercises and "how-to" advice for the successful design and implementation of intermediate sanctions programs.

Morris, Norval, and Tonry, Michael. *Between Prison and Probation: Intermediate Punishments in a Rational Sentencing System.* New York: Oxford University Press, 1990. Urges development of a range of intermediate punishments that can be used to sanction offenders more severely than nominal probation but less severely than incarceration.

Whitfield, Dick, and Scott, David, eds. *Paying Back: Twenty Years of Community Service.* Winchester, England: Waterside Press, 1993. Describes the problems and effectiveness of the community service experiment in England.

Notes

1. Norval Morris and Michael Tonry, *Between Prison and Probation: Intermediate Punishments in a Rational Sentencing System* (New York: Oxford University Press, 1990), p. 3.
2. Sally T. Hillsman, "Fines and Day Fines," in Michael Tonry and Norval Morris, eds. *Crime and Justice: A Review of Research,* vol. 12 (Chicago: University of Chicago Press, 1990), pp. 49–98.
3. Ken Pease, "Community Service Orders," in Michael Tonry and Norval Morris, eds., *Crime and Justice: A Review of Research,* vol. 6 (Chicago: University of Chicago Press, 1990), pp. 36–80.
4. "Nation's Probation and Parole Population Reached New High Last Year," Bureau of Justice Statistics, U.S. Department of Justice, News Release, August 16, 1998, p. 6.
5. Michael G. Turner, Francis T. Cullen, Jody L. Sunt, and Brandon K. Applegate, "Public Tolerance for Community-Based Sanctions," *The Prison Journal,* 77(1), March 1997, pp. 6–26.
6. Karla R. Spaulding, "Hit Them Where It Hurts': RICO Criminal Forfeitures and White-Collar Crime," *Journal of Criminal Law and Criminology,* 80, 1989, pp. 197–198.
7. *Austin v. United States,* 509 U.S. 602 (1993).
8. Michael Tonry and Michael Lynch, "Intermediate Sanctions," in Norval Morris and Michael Tonry, eds., *Crime and Justice: An Annual Review,* vol. 20 (Chicago: University of Chicago Press, 1995), pp. 99–144.
9. Frederick Allen and Harvey Treger, "Fines and Restitution Orders: Probationers' Perceptions," *Federal Probation,* 58(2), June 1994, pp. 34–38.
10. George Mair, *Part Time Punishment: The Origins and Development of Senior Attendance Centres* (London: Her Majesty's Stationery Office, 1991).
11. David W. Diggs and Stephen L. Peiper, "Using Day Reporting Centers as an Alternative to Jail," *Federal Probation,* 58(1), March 1994, pp. 9–13.
12. Peter Jones and Alan Harland, *Edgecombe: A Preliminary Analysis,* paper presented to the American Probation and Parole Association, (St. Louis Missouri, September 1, 1992).
13. Arthur J. Lurigio, David E. Olson, and James A. Swartz, "Chicago Day-reporting Center Reduces Pretrial Detention, Drug Use, and Absconding," *Overcrowded Times,* 9(3), June 1998, p. 4.
14. National Institute of Justice, Day Reporting Centers, Issues and Practices (Washington, DC: U.S. Department of Justice, 1995).
15. Joan Petersilia and Susan Turner, *Intensive Supervision for High-Risk Offenders: Findings from Three California Experiments* (Santa Monica, CA: Rand, 1990).
16. Michael P. Brown and Preston Elrod, "Electronic House Arrest: An Examination of Citizen Attitudes," *Crime and Delinquency,* 41(3), July 1995, pp. 332–346. See also Jen Kiko Begasse, "Oregonians Support Alternatives for Non-Violent Offenders, *Overcrowded Times,* 6(4), August 1995, p. 11.
17. Marc Renzema, "Home Confinement Programs, Development, Implementation, and Impact," in James M. Byrne, Arthur J. Lurigio, and Joan Petersilia, eds., *Smart Sentencing: The Emergence of Intermediate Sanctions* (Newbury Park, CA: Sage, 1992), p. 47.
18. Joseph B. Vaughn, "1994 Electronic Monitoring Survey," *Journal of Offender Monitoring,* 7(4), 1994, pp. 1–8.
19. Linda G. Smith and Ronald Akers, "A Comparison of Recidivism of Florida's Community Control and Prison: A Five Year Survival Analysis," *Journal of Research on Crime and Delinquency,* 30(3), August 1993, pp. 267–292.
20. Robert Lilly, Richard A. Ball, G. David Curry, and John McMullen, "Electronic Monitoring of the Drunk Driver: A Seven-Year Study of the Home Confinement Alternative," *Crime and Delinquency,* 39(4), October 1993, pp. 462–484.
21. Marc Renzema, "Satellite Monitoring of Offenders: A Report from the Field," *The Journal of Offender Monitoring,* 11(2), Spring 1998, pp. 7–11.
22. Doris L. MacKenzie, "Boot Camp Prisons and Recidivism in Eight States," *Criminology,* 33(3), 1995, pp. 327–358.
23. *San Francisco Examiner,* July 27, 1997.
24. Doris Layton MacKenzie and Alex Piquero, "The Impact of Shock Incarceration Programs on Prison Crowding," *Crime and Delinquency,* 40(2), April 1994, pp. 222–249.
25. Todd R. Clear and Anthony Braga, "Community Corrections," in James Q. Wilson and Joan Petersilia, eds., *Crime* (San Francisco: ICS Press, 1995), pp. 421–444.

26. Joan Petersilia and Susan Turner, "An Evaluation of Intensive Probation in California," *Journal of Criminal Law and Criminology*, 82(3), (1991, pp. 610–658.

27. William Spelmanq, "The Severity of Intermediate Sanctions," *Journal of Research in Crime and Delinquency*, 32(2), May 1995, pp. 107–135.

28. Ben M. Crouch, "Is Incarceration Really Worse? Analysis of Offenders' Preferences for Prison over Probation," *Justice Quarterly*, 10(1), March 1993, pp. 67–88.

29. Joan Petersilia, "Diverting Non-violent Prisoners to Intermediate Sanctions," *Corrections Management Quarterly*, 1(1), Winter 1997, pp. 1–15.

30. *Annual Report of the Oregon Sentencing Commission* (Salem: Oregon Sentencing Commission, 1992), p. 23.

31. Paul Lerman, *Community Treatment and Social Control* (Chicago: University of Chicago Press, 1975).

32. Rebecca D. Petersen and Dennis L. J. Palumbo, "The Social Construction of Intermediate Punishments, *The Prison Journal*, 77(1), March 1997, pp. 77–91.

CHAPTER TEN
Incarceration

tainless-steel handcuffs snugly fastened around subdued wrists. Waiting at an outer gatehouse. Watching the uniformed reception officer dispassionately size me up. Then escorted past double fences, inner fences, through steel doors, electronic steel grilles into the inner sanctum of concrete and steel.

Fear. The kind that chews at the stomach and makes the fingers tremble. Fear of known and unknown hidden dangers.

The atmosphere is tense and strange. Still wearing street-side clothes, I am a curiosity. After a number of rights and lefts and double-locked stairways, we come to Admitting and Processing.

Catalogued, tagged, photographed, and deloused. Issued, not issued, acceptable, not acceptable, and then ordered into a cell slightly bigger than a walk-in closet. When that door slams shut, an ache of mental and emotional pain seizes the senses brutally and completely.

This description, written for this text by Wayne B. Alexander, now serving a life term for murder and other crimes, shows how depersonalizing, jarring, and terrifying entrance into prison can be. Incarceration is something no person would want to endure (see the Focus box).

It should come as no surprise to criminal justice students that of the approximately 5.7 million adults under correctional supervision in the United States, only about 1.7 million are in jails and prisons. Yet when the subject of the criminal sanction arises, the general public thinks first of incarceration. And it is prison that legislators and politicians have in mind when they consider changes in the penal code or annual appropriations for corrections.

Since the early 1800s, when the penitentiary was invented, use of imprisonment has increased in the American criminal justice system. In many ways it remains the core sanction of corrections, though some recent trends have made its function ambiguous. For example, although scholars dispute the efficacy of imprisonment, penal code reforms have increased its use to add to the number of incarcerated adults. But we must recognize that the cost of maintaining offenders in institutions normally runs eight to ten times that required for probation and parole.

In this chapter and three of the four that follow, we focus primarily on the incarceration of adult males, who make up almost 95 percent of the prison population. The discussion links the modern prison with the history of American corrections so that we can understand its antecedents. In this chapter we will examine the following Questions for Inquiry.

Questions FOR INQUIRY

1. How are today's prisons linked to the past?
2. What are the goals of incarceration?
3. How is incarceration organized?
4. What major factors influence the design and classification of prisons?
5. Who is in prison?

Links to the Past

Reformers are frustrated by the sheer durability of prisons. For example, the oldest prison in America, New Jersey's Trenton State Prison, opened in 1798 and rebuilt in 1836, still houses offenders. Structures of stone and concrete are not easily redesigned when correctional goals change. Thus elements of all the major reform movements of the past can be found within these walls. In line with the Quakers' belief that offenders could be redeemed only if they were removed from the distractions of the city, most correctional facilities are still found in rural areas — Stateville (Illinois), Attica

F✺CUS Realization

Hearing the cell door slam shut the first time, there is a gripping realization, almost spiritual for some, that the consequences of crime are terribly real. Every memory, all of the past, good and bad, returns to haunt. Every single indelible moment is etched upon the mind's eye at some point, and painful memories invade conscious thought. The act, the arrest, pretrial and trial, conviction and sentencing, and most of all the last three hours flood involuntarily into mind and heart.

I look around at the cool, unforgiving gray concrete walls and feel the hopelessness. The helplessness of my predicament. The accommodations are welded and brazed and anchored into the concrete to last for years of use.

The gnawing fear that has been building steadily since hearing the door slam shut prompts me to jump up and test the door to see if it's really locked. It is.

Coming to terms with this reality begins one of the many emotional storms raging inside me. The raw fear penetrates and subsides, and the fight to control myself from crying out or pleading like a small child is a constant struggle.

This sensation of being torn apart from within by conflicting emotions vying for control is the most frightening human experience known. Nothing compares to the realization that I am being confined and controlled so totally. "Oh, God, no," I cry to myself. "Please don't let this be!"

After two hours the door slides back and a shout—"Chow!"—is heard. Steel doors slam, keys clang, and there is the shuffling of hundreds of feet. The strange, listless, angry, and embittered faces of the others offer painful insight into this subculture.

Lock in! 8:30 P.M. Until the morning meal, that door will be locked. Can I make it? The struggle rages again as I feel tears well up behind fatigued eyes. After two hours a uniformed arm pokes a flashlight into the cell for a moment and withdraws. Counted, and counted and counted again, I am among the best-monitored individuals outside an intensive care unit in the country. More than a half-dozen times a day I am counted to ensure that I still suffer. In addition, clothes, underwear, property, and every file about me bears the assigned number that was issued during the processing.

I didn't know until this day that it was possible to tag, count, and store human beings like merchandise in a warehouse. Yet in this modern maximum security "correctional institution," the insidiously antiseptic ritual of accepting an individual and transforming him into a number is as normal as sending youngsters on their way to school every morning on a yellow bus.

The consequences, again, become sparklingly clear and real. By committing a crime, I have plunged headlong into this nightmare of living death. I am condemned and I am so sorry; God, I'm sorry. I look around and realize there is no one to tell it to. In that moment I come to the realization that I have been forsaken. I have been cast out of a free society and branded with a number, never to achieve a position of trust or a level of responsibility that I might be capable of. I have come to the place of punishment and proved that the criminal justice system is alive and well in America.

I, the convicted, the incarcerated, come face to face with all these truths, only to sit mute upon my bunk, isolated by a society I so desperately want to apologize to.

SOURCE: Written especially for this text. Since 1974 Wayne B. Alexander has spent only a year and a half outside prison. Convicted of murder and other crimes, he is now serving a life term. Reprinted by permission.

(New York), Walla Walla (Washington)—far from most of the inmates' families, friends, and communities. Although many modern prisons feature "campuslike" settings, the stronghold remains the primary architectural style. Life on the "inside" varies with the type and locale of the institution and the characteristics of the inmates. Yet a prison is still a prison, whatever it's called and however it's constructed.

The image of the "big house," popularized in countless movies and television shows, is still imprinted on the minds of most Americans, although it has long ceased to be a realistic portrayal—if indeed it ever was. Moreover, much social science literature about prison society is based on studies conducted in big houses during the 1950s. Yet American correctional institutions have always been more varied than movies or novels portray them. Fictional depictions of prison life are typically set in a fortress, the "big house"—the maximum-security prisons where the inmates are tough and the guards are just as tough or tougher.

Prisons are built to last. Eastern Penitentiary opened in 1829 and was finally closed 150 years later in 1971. Today it stands as a historical relic as architects consider its restoration and reuse.

Although big houses predominated in much of the country during the first half of the twentieth century, many prisons, especially in the South, did not conform to this model. Racial segregation was maintained, prisoners were used as farm labor, and the massive walled structures were not so common.

The typical big house of the 1940s and 1950s was a walled prison with large, tiered cell blocks, a yard, shops, and industries. The prisoners, averaging about 2,500 per institution, came from both urban and rural areas, were usually poor, and, outside the South, were mostly white. The prison society was essentially isolated; access to visitors, mail, and other communication was restricted. Prisoners' days were very structured, and guards enforced the rules. There was a basic division between inmates and staff; rank was observed and discipline maintained. In the big house, few treatment programs existed; custody was the primary goal.

During the 1960s and early 1970s, when the rehabilitation model was dominant, many states built new prisons and converted others into "correctional institutions." Treatment programs administered by counselors and teachers became a major part of prison life, although the institutions actually continued to place their greatest emphasis on the custody goals of security, discipline, and order.

The civil rights movement of the early 1960s profoundly affected prisoners in general and minority prisoners in particular. Prisoners demanded their constitutional rights as citizens and greater sensitivity to their needs. As discussed in Chapter 5, the courts began to take notice of the legal rights of prisoners. Legal services were extended to corrections, and the traditional judicial hands-off policy evaporated. Suddenly administrators had to respond to the directives of the judiciary and run the institutions according to constitutional mandates.

During the past thirty years, as the population of the United States changed, so has the prison population, showing a major increase in the number of African-American and Hispanic inmates. There are more inmates from urban areas and more have been convicted of drug-related and violent offenses. Former street gangs, often organized along racial lines, today regroup inside prisons and have raised the levels of violence in many institutions. Finally, with the rise of public employee unions, correctional officers have used collective bargaining to influence working conditions, safety procedures, and training.

Now the focus of corrections has shifted to crime control, which emphasizes the importance of incarceration. Not only has the number of persons in prison greatly increased, but many states have removed educational and recreational amenities from institutions. Apparently some politicians believe that offenders have had it too "cushy" and that prisons should return to the strict regimes found early in this century. Some states have even reinstituted the chain gang as a way of "getting tough" on inmates (see the Focus box).

The last two decades have doubled the number of people held in prisons, building tensions within overcrowded institutions. Although today's correctional administrators seek to provide humane incarceration, they must struggle with limited resources and cell space. Thus, the modern prison faces all the problems that devil other parts of the criminal justice system: racial conflicts, legal issues, limited resources, and increasing populations. Can prisons still achieve their objectives? The answer depends, in part, on how we define the goals of incarceration.

FOCUS

The New Chain Gangs

*A*fter the Civil War the southern states achieved notoriety for brutal treatment of prisoners, many of whom were former slaves. Shackled together by iron chains, inmate work crews were forced to toil on the roads of the South. The viciousness of the chain gang bosses, captured in the movie Cool Hand Luke, was so famous that prisoners often crippled themselves to avoid the degrading and brutal work. As many as 45 percent died while in chains. This institutionalized cruelty so disturbed people that, beginning in the 1930s, the public outcry gradually shamed even the most backward states into abolishing the gangs.

Most penologists of today thus thought that chain gangs were a thing of the past, but in 1995 three states—Alabama, Arizona, and Florida—reinstituted them. The image of strings of prisoners clad in prison garb, lock-stepping in awkward rhythm, disturbs most penologists and many citizens, but many politicians and other citizens find the idea appealing. They agree with Alabama Governor Fob James that chain gangs will make prisons so much more unpleasant that they will help deter crime.

The reemergence of chain gangs raises fundamental questions about the benefits of brutal treatment: Does cruelty overpower offenders and intimidate them into being law abiding? Or does ruthlessness in penal practice unleash the same alienation and rage that led to crime?

One Alabama chain gang laborer said the experience "makes you start hating. It would make a person kill somebody to get away." Of course, proponents say this is precisely what they want—anyone this upset by the experience may think twice about committing another crime. However, even proponents ought to be troubled by a program that provokes murderous rage. And what are the consequences to society if the program does not deter crime?

There are other problems. In none of the three states will the program be extensive enough to involve more than 2 percent of the total inmate population, leading to conjecture that even if the chain gangs "work," they won't affect many prisoners. Also, the cumbersomeness of the chains interferes with the road crews' effectiveness. Of course, this is hardly a problem in Alabama, where the gangs break big rocks into smaller stones, which are then discarded, because using them to pave roads is not cost effective.

Conditions on today's chain gangs are presumably not as severe as those of yesteryear. Inmates spend twelve-hour workdays in the blistering sun, but authorities promise to curtail the gratuitous violence of the past. Of course, as Alabama corrections commissioner Ron Jones points out: "If they try to escape, our officers are going to shoot them." In any case, it is too early to say whether the new chain gangs will make our streets safer or merely make prisoners angrier. One thing is for sure—the "get tough" movement just got tougher.

SOURCE: Based on Adam Cohen, "Back on the Chain Gang," *Time* Magazine, May 15, 1995, p. 26; Brent Staples, "The Chain Gang Show," *New York Times Sunday Magazine*, September 17, 1995, pp. 62–63; Mireya Navarro, "Chain Gangs, with Limits, Return to Florida," *The New York Times*, November 21, 1995, p. A10.

The Goals of Incarceration

Security is what most people consider the dominant purpose of a prison, given the nature of the inmates and the need to protect the staff and the community. High walls, barbed-wire fences, searches, checkpoints, and regular counts of inmates serve the security function: few inmates escape. More important, the features set the tone for the daily operations. Prisons are expected to be impersonal, quasi-military places where strict discipline, minimal amenities, and restrictions on freedom carry out the punishment of criminals.

Three models of incarceration have been prominent since the early 1940s: custodial, rehabilitation, and reintegration. Each is associated with one style of institutional organization.

1. The **custodial model** is based on the assumption that prisoners have been incarcerated for the purpose of incapacitation, deterrence, or retribution. It emphasizes security, discipline, and order, subordinating the prisoner to the authority of the warden. Discipline is strict, and most aspects of behavior are regulated. This model was prevalent in corrections before World War II, and it dominates most maximum security institutions today.

custodial model

A model of a correctional institution that emphasizes security, discipline, and order.

rehabilitation model

A model of a correctional institution that emphasizes the provision of treatment programs designed to reform the offender.

reintegration model

A model of a correctional institution that emphasizes maintenance of the offender's ties to family and the community as a method of reform, in recognition of the fact that the offender will be returning to the community.

2. The **rehabilitation model,** developed during the 1950s, emphasizes treatment programs designed to reform the offender. According to this model, security and housekeeping activities are viewed primarily as preconditions for rehabilitative efforts. As all aspects of the organization should be directed toward rehabilitation, professional treatment specialists have a higher status than other employees. Since the rethinking of the rehabilitation goal in the 1970s, treatment programs still exist in most institutions, but very few prisons conform to this model today.

3. The **reintegration model** is linked to the structures and goals of community corrections. This model emphasizes maintaining offenders' ties to family and community as a method of reform, recognizing that they will be returning to society. Prisons that have adopted the reintegration model gradually give inmates greater freedom and responsibility during their confinement, moving them to halfway houses or work release programs before giving them community supervision.

Correctional institutions that conform to each of these models can be found, but most prisons are mainly custodial. Nevertheless, treatment programs do exist, and because almost all inmates return to society at some point, even the most custodial institutions must prepare them for reintegration.

We ask a lot of our prisons. As criminologist Charles Logan notes, "We ask them to correct the incorrigible, rehabilitate the wretched, deter the determined, restrain the dangerous, and punish the wicked."[1] Prisons are expected to pursue many different and often incompatible goals; so as institutions they are almost doomed to fail. Logan believes the mission of prisons is confinement. He argues that the basic purpose of imprisonment is to punish offenders fairly and justly through lengths of confinement proportionate to the seriousness of their crimes. If the goal of incarceration is to do justice through confinement, then he summarizes the mission of the prison as "to keep prisoners — to keep them in, keep them safe, keep them in line, keep them healthy, and keep them busy — and to do it with fairness, without undue suffering, and as efficiently as possible."[2] If the purpose of prisons is punishment through confinement under fair and just conditions, what are the implications for correctional managers? What measures should be used to evaluate prisons in line with these criteria? As you read the Comparative Perspective, consider prison conditions in our own country.

Organization for Incarceration

Prisons are operated by all fifty states and by the federal government. Offenders are held in 1,500 confinement facilities, 94 percent of which are operated by the states, and the remainder by the federal government. Among these prisons 80 percent are for men only, 10 percent are for women only, and 10 percent house both sexes.[3] For the most part prisons, as distinguished from jails, house convicted felons and those misdemeanants who have been sentenced to terms of more than one year. Note, however, that various state governments and the federal government differ in terms of bureaucratic organization for incarceration, number and types of institutions, staffing, and size of the offender populations. We will look at the federal and state systems in turn.

Federal Bureau of Prisons

The Federal Bureau of Prisons was created by Congress in 1930 within the Department of Justice. The bureau was assigned the responsibility for "the safekeeping, care, protection, instruction, and discipline of all persons charged or convicted of offenses against the United States." Before 1930 administrators of the seven federal prisons then in operation functioned relatively free from control by Washington. Today the bureau is highly

COMPARATIVE
PERSPECTIVE

World Report: Prison Conditions Around the Globe—Human Rights Watch

Prison massacres, dramatic protests, and violent guard abuse earned occasional news headlines in 1997, but the deplorable daily living conditions that were the plight of the great majority of the world's prisoners passed largely unnoticed. With scant public attention to the topic in most countries, correspondingly little progress was made in rectifying the abuses routinely inflicted in prisons and other places of detention. Many countries, moreover, fostered public ignorance of prison inadequacies by denying human rights groups, journalists, and other outside observers nearly all access to their penal facilities.

Unchecked outbursts of prison violence continued to violate prisoners' right to life. The killings of at least twenty-nine prisoners in a remote jungle facility in Venezuela led the country's Justice Ministry to promise reforms, and its Public Ministry to conduct an extensive investigation of the incident's causes. The Tajikistan government chose to cover up an even bloodier prison massacre. Although information about the events was scarce, reports indicated that the Tajik security forces stormed a prison in the northern city of Khujand, killing over a hundred prisoners. Earlier that week, inmates had rioted and taken several guards hostage to protest life-threatening detention conditions. The Tajik government apparently took no action to punish those responsible for the deaths.

In Morocco's Oukacha prison, twenty-two prisoners were burned alive; they had been crammed together in a cell reportedly built to hold eight. The cause of the fire was not announced, but the country's Justice Ministry did acknowledge that overcrowding might have played a role in the deaths. The most common cause of death in prison was disease, often the predictable results of severe overcrowding, malnutrition, unhygienic conditions, and lack of medical care. A special commission of inquiry, appointed after the death of a prominent businessman in India's high-security Tihar Central Jail, reported that the 10,000 inmates held in that institution endured serious health hazards, including overcrowding, "appalling" sanitary facilities, and a shortage of medical staff. Similar conditions prevailed in the prisons of the former Soviet Union, where tuberculosis continued its comeback. Russia's prosecutor general announced that about 2,000 inmates had died of tuberculosis in the previous year. In Kazakhstan, the disease, including drug-resistant strains, reached epidemic proportions. AIDS also plagued many prison populations.

Inadequate supervision by guards, easy access to weapons, lack of separation of different categories of prisoners, and fierce competition for basic necessities encouraged inmate-on-inmate abuse in many penal facilities. In extreme cases—as in certain Venezuelan prisons with one guard for every 150 prisoners, and an underground trade in knives, guns, even grenades—prisoners killed other prisoners with impunity. Rape, extortion, and involuntary servitude were other frequent abuses suffered by inmates at the bottom of the prison hierarchy.

In contrast, powerful inmates in some facilities in Colombia, India, and Mexico, among others, enjoyed cellular phones, rich diets, and comfortable lodging. With guard corruption rampant in so many prisons around the world, the adage "You get what you pay for" was only too appropriate.

Shielded from public view, and populated largely by the poor, uneducated, and politically powerless, prisons tended to remain hidden sites of human rights abuse. By struggling against this natural tendency towards secrecy and silence, the efforts of numerous local human rights groups around the world—who fought to obtain access to prisons, monitored prison conditions, and publicized the abuses they found—were critical. In some countries, moreover, government human rights ombudspersons, parliamentary commissions, and other monitors helped call attention to abuses. ∎

Source: "World Report, 1997: Prison Conditions Around the Globe," *Human Rights Watch Prison Project Report*, August 31, 1998, p. 1.

centralized, with a director appointed by the president, six regional directors, and a staff of over 30,000, who care for about 100,000 prisoners.[4]

To carry out its tasks, the Federal Bureau of Prisons has a network of facilities ranging from penitentiaries to correctional institutions, detention centers, prison camps, and halfway houses. This array of correctional services, shown in Figure 10.1, is much broader than can be found in any single state.

The jurisdiction of federal criminal law, unlike that of the states, is restricted to crimes involving interstate commerce, certain serious felonies such as bank robbery, violations of other federal laws, and crimes committed on federal property. Historically the federal prison has housed bank robbers, extortionists, people who have committed mail fraud, and arsonists. Yet since the "war on drugs" was instituted in the 1980s, the proportion of drug offenders in federal prisons has steadily increased and is now about 60 percent of the population. Interestingly, 30,000 — about 30 percent — of federal prisoners are citizens of other countries.[5] Federal prisoners are often a more sophisticated breed of criminal, from a higher socioeconomic class, than the typical state prisoner. Figure 10.2 compares some key characteristics of federal and state prisoners.

In recent years, however, the characteristics of federal prisoners have changed. Not only is the total number of offenders greater, but with the introduction of federal sentencing guidelines in 1987, the probability of imprisonment has increased substantially.

Figure 10.1 Institutions of the Federal Bureau of Prisons

Prisons run by the bureau are spread throughout the country and comprise a range of correctional institutions, detention centers, medical centers, prison camps, metropolitan correctional centers, and penitentiaries. Each is organized according to five security levels: minimum, low, medium, high, and administrative. Offenders are classified and assigned to an institution based on such factors as severity of the offense, length of incarceration, type of prior commitments, and history of violence.

SOURCE: U.S. Department of Justice, Federal Bureau of Prisons, *State of the Bureau* (Washington, DC: Federal Bureau of Prisons, 1998).

Figure 10.2 Comparison of Federal and State Prison Inmates

Compared to state prisoners, federal inmates tend to be older, to have more education and a higher prearrest income, to be married, and were employed prior to their arrest.

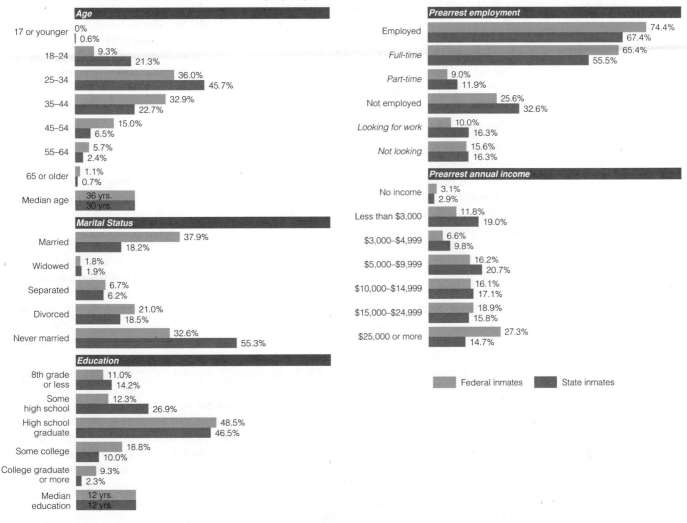

SOURCE: U.S. Department of Justice, Bureau of Justice Statistics, *Comparing Federal and State Prison Inmates, 1991* (Washington, DC: U.S. Government Printing Office, 1994), pp. 2–3.

Compared to the preguideline era, today's prisoners are incarcerated for longer periods, with a median expected time to be served of five and a half years.[6]

The federal government does not have enough pretrial detention space to house most people accused of violating the federal criminal law, so about two-thirds of pretrial detainees are housed in state or local facilities on a contractual basis. The U.S. Marshals Service has responsibility for placing these prisoners. Although all fifty states have laws requiring their correctional facilities to accept federal pretrial detainees, the marshals typically enter into intergovernmental service agreements with receptive jails. Because of crowding, however, the government recently has had increased difficulty finding state and local institutions that have room for federal prisoners. Local officials also fear that sophisticated federal prisoners will bring lawsuits challenging the conditions of their confinement and believe that federal officials expect the higher federal standards to be maintained at local expense.

The Bureau of Prisons currently operates ninety-three confinement facilities. Federal offenders are also housed in approximately 600 community corrections and detention contract facilities nationwide. Federal confinement facilities are classified in a security system ranging from level 1 (the least secure, camp-type settings) through level 4 (high-security institutions, U.S. Penitentiaries). Level 5 is the designation for administrative facilities with special missions such as the "Super Max" at Florence, Colorado. The bureau is organized so that the wardens report to one of the regional offices. In addition to the facilities administered by the bureau, fifty-one small federal detention centers and confinement facilities are operated by various branches of the military.[7]

Historically the federal system has been an innovator in the field of corrections, and for many years the operations of the Federal Bureau of Prisons were the most advanced in the country, rivaled only by California's vast system.

State Prison Systems

Although states vary considerably in how they organize corrections, the administration of prisons is a function of the executive branch of state government. This point is important because probation is often part of the judiciary, parole may be separate from corrections, and in most states jails are run by county governments. Only Alaska, Connecticut, Delaware, Hawaii, Rhode Island, and Vermont operate combined jail/prison systems.

Commissioners of corrections normally are appointed by state governors and are responsible for the operation of prisons. As discussed in Chapter 13, each institution is administered by a warden (often called a *superintendent*), who reports directly to the commissioner or a deputy commissioner for institutions. The number of correctional employees in state prisons has risen dramatically during the past decade, and upwards of 325,000 people — administrators, officers, and program specialists — now work in state institutions. In most jurisdictions these prison employees constitute three-quarters or more of all state correctional personnel.[8]

To a great extent the total capacity of a state's prisons reflects the size of the state's population. Yet, as discussed in Chapter 18, the number of offenders in a state's institutions reflects something more than crime rates or social factors. Sentencing practices, legislative appropriations for corrections, and politics also affect the incarceration rate.

In addition to organization, states vary considerably in the number, size, type, and location of correctional facilities. Michigan's state prison at Jackson, for example, has a capacity of 3,500, whereas specialized institutions house fewer than a hundred inmates. Some states (such as New Hampshire) have centralized incarceration in a few institutions, and other states (such as California, New York, and Texas) have a wide mix of sizes and styles — secure institutions, diagnostic units, work camps, forestry centers, and prerelease centers. For example, Alabama has thirteen correctional institutions (prisons), a disciplinary rehabilitation unit, an honor farm, a boot camp, a state cattle ranch, a prison for women, and a youth center for male felons under age 25, in addition to eleven community-based facilities.[9] (See Figure 10.3.)

The Design and Classification of Prisons

Since the era of John Howard in England and the Quakers in Philadelphia, penologists have pondered the optimal design of prisons. In all eras attempts have been made to design correctional institutions that would advance the current purpose of the criminal sanction. In this section we discuss some of the changes and concepts in prison design.

A cardinal principle of architecture is that form follows function: The design of a structure should serve the structure's purpose. Thus, during the penitentiary era, efforts were directed toward building institutions that would promote penance. When prison industry became the focus, a different design sought to enhance the efficiency of the workshops. When punishment through custody held sway, the emphasis was on the fortresslike edifice that ensures security. And during the rehabilitation era of the 1950s

Figure 10.3 The Alabama Prison System

The number and variety of institutions for felons in Alabama is typical of most medium-sized states. What factors might influence the location of penal institutions?

1. Bullock Correctional Facility, Union Springs
2. Draper Correctional Center, Elmore
   Elmore Correctional Center, Elmore
   Thomas F. Staton Correctional Center, Elmore
3. Easterling Correctional Facility, Clio
4. J. O. Davis Correctional Center, Atmore
   G. K. Fountain Correctional Center, Atmore
   Holman Prison, Atmore
5. Hamilton A & I, Hamilton
6. Limestone Correctional Center, Capshaw
7. Red Eagle Honor Farm, Montgomery
8. Kilby Corrections Facility, Mt. Meigs
   Disciplinary Rehabilitation Unit (Kilby CC), Mt. Meigs
9. St. Clair Correctional Facility, Springville
10. Frank Lee Youth Center, Deatsville
11. State Cattle Ranch, Greensboro
12. Julia Tutwiler Prison for Women, Wetumpka
13. Ventress Correctional Facility, Clayton
14. Donaldson Correctional Facility, Bessemer
15. Childersburg Boot Camp, Childersburg
16. Frank Lee Youth Center, Deatsville

SOURCE: American Correctional Association, *Juvenile and Adult Correctional Facilities Directory* (College Park, MD: ACA, 1997), pp. 4–6.

and 1960s, new prisons were built in styles thought to promote the treatment goal. At all times, however, the plans of the architects had to be "realistic" with regard to cost.

During the early 1800s, some of the greatest English and American architects specialized in designing penitentiaries whose spaces would serve the purposes of contemplation, industry, and isolation, thought to be the necessary conditions for reform. At that time people believed that improving inmate morals depended somewhat on the type of prison constructed.[10]

As discussed in Chapter 3, Eastern Penitentiary in Philadelphia, designed by English emigré John Haviland, is probably the best example of a structure shaped by commitment to moral uplift. The cell areas radiated from a central point like the spokes of a wheel from the hub. Each cell had its own exercise yard, with walls so arranged that other prisoners could not be seen. In many ways the European and American prisons of the nineteenth century were designed, like the great cathedrals of an earlier era, to overwhelm the people within them and impress on them the need to mend their ways.

The design and operational characteristics of today's prisons vary considerably from state to state. Some states and the federal government have created

The megaprison, often holding up to 3,500 offenders, may be cost-effective yet difficult to manage. Smaller institutions located closer to urban areas have been advocated by reformers.

Two mirror-glass watchtowers stand guard at the new Administrative Maximum Facility in Florence, Colorado. Designed to house 400 of the most "predatory" convicts in the federal system, it is often referred to as the "Alcatraz of the Rockies."

radial design

An architectural plan by which a prison is constructed in the form of a wheel, with "spokes" radiating from a central core.

telephone-pole design

An architectural plan for a prison calling for a long central corridor crossed at regular intervals by structures containing the prison's functional areas.

smaller facilities, but most institutions are old and large. The antiquated megaprisons found in many states have all the maintenance and operational problems of old, intensively used buildings. More than half of the nation's inmates are in prisons with average daily populations of more than a thousand, and about 35 percent are in prisons built more than fifty years ago. More than 12 percent of inmates are held in facilities built before 1888.[11]

Today's Designs

The buildings constructed to suit the purposes of one era often cannot be adapted to suit those of succeeding eras or changes in the sizes and characteristics of prison populations. At the same time, prisons are built to last, which means form may not continue to serve function. In any case four basic models can be found among America's prisons.

The Radial Design Prisons of the early nineteenth century tended to follow the **radial design** of Eastern Penitentiary (see Figure 10.4a). A control center at the hub makes it possible to monitor movement. From this central core one or more "spokes" can be isolated from the rest of the institution during periods of trouble. Even though Auburn Prison was administered to contrast with the separation and silence practiced at Eastern, it, too, was of the radial design. At other present-day locations, such as Leavenworth (Kansas) and Rahway and Trenton (New Jersey), the old design persists, but few newer prisons have been built to such specifications.[12]

The Telephone-Pole Design In a prison based on the **telephone-pole design,** a long central corridor (the pole) serves as the means for prisoners to go from one part of the institution to another (see Figure 10.4b). Jutting out from the corridor are cross-arms, each containing the prison's functional areas: housing, shops, school, recreation area, and so on. Continuous surveillance is possible from the central pole, and access to each functional area may be controlled independently.

The telephone pole is undoubtedly the design most commonly used for maximum-security prisons in the United States. For example, Graterford (Pennsylvania), Marion (Illinois), Somers (Connecticut), and Jackson (Georgia) are designed in this fashion. Built for custody, these prisons can house inmates according to classification levels, with certain housing areas designated for inmates with special needs, for those whose conduct merits extra privileges, and so on.

However, the telephone-pole prison can lead to overdetermination, a situation in which everything—

decisions, space, movement, and responsibility—is clearly and narrowly defined. All activities are scheduled. Social contacts are predetermined. The physical setting is limited and monotonous. . . . It is a condition in which groups can be easily supervised, where authority can be maintained and one in which accountability for personal action lies beyond the individual.[13]

Nagel argues that this design cuts off inmates from the world and that daily and seasonal variations are lost. For these reasons he believes confinement here "prepares [the inmate] only for confinement," not for reentry to the community.[14]

The Courtyard Style Some of the newer correctional facilities, including some maximum-security prisons, are built in **courtyard style** (see Figure 10.4c). Thus movement along the endless corridors of the telephone-pole design from one part of the prison to another is replaced by movement across the courtyard to the housing units and other functional areas. In some facilities of this type, such functional units as the dining hall, gym, and school are located in the entry yard area.

The Campus Style A design long used for correctional facilities for juveniles and women, the **campus style** also appears among some of the newer institutions for men (see Figure 10.4d). Relatively small housing units are scattered among the shops, school, dining hall, and other units of the facility. This style is thought to be an important development not only because of the humane features of the design but also because individual buildings can be used more flexibly. As in prisons of the courtyard style, inmates and staff must go outdoors to get from one part of the facility to another. Although the campus style might appear to provide less security than more conventional facilities, modern prison fences seem to keep escapes to a minimum. It must be emphasized, however, that most facilities of this type serve medium- and minimum-security populations.

The Location of Prisons

Most prisons for adults are located in rural areas. Originally the rationale was that inmates would more readily repent if isolated from urban distractions and family contacts. When more prisons were built later in the nineteenth century, the country setting was retained because the institutions were expected to maintain farms that would contribute to their self-sufficiency. Now, even though most prison inmates come from cities and reintegration is a prime correctional goal, new institutions are still being built in the countryside.

Part of the reason for this is related to land costs, but political factors also figure in the decision. Many citizens believe that serious offenders should be incarcerated, but not in their community. This attitude is often referred to as the NIMBY syndrome (Not In My Back Yard!). Research has disputed the contention that the building of a correctional institution lowers property values, but these concerns and such others as community safety have the political impact of preventing criminal justice planners from locating facilities in certain areas.

Some economically depressed localities have opened their doors to prison construction. They believe prisons will bring jobs and revitalize the local economy. An example is Fremont County, Colorado, where 18 percent of the population's 40,000 residents are "involuntary guests" at the four federal and nine state prisons. Already a home for state prisons,

courtyard style
An architectural design by which the functional units of a prison are housed in separate buildings constructed on four sides of an open square.

campus style
An architectural design by which the functional units of a prison are individually housed in a complex of buildings surrounded by a fence.

Figure 10.4 Prison Designs Used in the United States

These four basic designs are used throughout the country for most prisons housing adult felons. Each style has certain features related to the goals of "keeping and serving" the prisoners. How does architecture influence the management of these institutions?

a. Radial design   **b.** Telephone-pole design   **c.** Courtyard style   **d.** Campus style

Fremont residents bought 600 acres and donated the site to the U.S. government to lure the federal prisons. The thirteen prisons employ 3,100 workers, with an average salary of about $30,000. "Today, Main Street is bustling and unemployment is 4 percent."[15]

The Classification of Prisons

Prisons for men usually are classified according to the level of security deemed necessary: maximum, medium, and minimum. Thirty-eight states and the federal government have created prisons that are of even higher security than maximum. About 100,000 men, 8 to 10 percent of those behind bars, are currently kept in these prisons.[16] These institutions, often referred to as "maxi-max" or "super-max" prisons, are designed to hold the most disruptive, violent, and incorrigible prisoners. The federal Administrative Maximum Facility (ADX) at Florence, Colorado; California's Pelican Bay institution; and Connecticut's Northern Correctional Institute in Somers are examples of prisons designed to hold the "toughest of the tough" (see the Focus box).

FOCUS Maximum Takes on a New Meaning at This Prison

The state will soon begin transferring its most dangerous and disruptive inmates to the 300-cell, fortress-like Northern Correctional Institution in Somers, Connecticut's first "super maximum" security prison.

The inmates at Northern will be confined to individual 7-foot-by-12-foot concrete-encased cells 23 hours a day. When they are allowed out for a shower or fresh air, they will be handcuffed and in leg irons.

The cells are unpainted. No pictures will be allowed on the walls. Each has a small steel sink and toilet in one corner and a small steel desk with circular steel pull-out stool at the other end. The mattress on the metal bed frame has been X-rayed for possible contraband. "The word has already gotten out on this place through the inmate network," said David May, the warden, "and the word is that it's a place where you don't want to be." . . .

The new prison is for those men among the state's 15,000 inmates who present "chronic management problems," said Mr. May. . . . "Something like this within the prison system is a major deterrent." . . .

The concrete, bunker-style building is further reinforced by three fences: a 12-foot outer chain link fence topped with razor wire, a middle electrified fence that sets off lights and alarms if touched, and a 14-foot steel fence that curves inward, making it virtually impossible for someone to scale it.

Inside, newly arrived inmates will be admitted to Phase One, the most restricted and claustrophobic of the cell areas, where sensory deprivation is the main tool in instigating behavioral changes. No radio or television is allowed. There is minimal contact with others. One visit is allowed each week, but it is conducted with the inmate behind thick glass; the only communication is by speaker telephone. All meals are eaten in the cell. "The opportunities for socializing are extremely limited," Mr. May said.

Compliant inmates can progress to Phase Two, where they will be allowed out of their cells for classes and therapeutic programs and may win use of a radio and restricted television viewing. "We will have classes on anger management, communication skills, problem solving, decision making, things these inmates don't know how to do," Mr. May said. "They don't know how to assert themselves without laying a hand on someone."

In Phase Three inmates would be allowed communal dining with a handful of other inmates and limited time playing basketball in a prison gymnasium. The ultimate goal would be to transfer inmates back to a less confined facility, although some may stay indefinitely if their behavior continues to be a problem, Mr. May said. . . .

Leo Arone, regional director of the Department of Correction, said the "super max" prisons have had mixed success across the country, especially where recalcitrant inmates are transferred as a last resort and where they are forced to finish out their full sentences, even if the sentence is life without parole.

Perhaps most notorious is Pelican Bay, in northern California, which . . . was ordered by a Federal judge . . . to stop abuses. The judge, Thelton E. Henderson, noting near-total isolation and use of excessive force in the prison, said conditions there "may well hover on the edge of what is humanly tolerable."

Warning of the limitations of such prisons, Mr. Arone said, "If you lock a dog in a pen and throw food inside three times a day and never talk to him, after a year when you open the pen you're going to have a killer."

SOURCE: Jacqueline Weaver, "Maximum Takes on a New Meaning at This New Prison," *The New York Times,* February 19, 1995, p. 1. Copyright © 1995 by The New York Times Company. Reprinted by permission.

With changes in the number of prisoners and their characteristics, the distinction between maximum and medium security has disappeared in some systems. Crowding has forced administrators to house inmates requiring maximum security in medium-security facilities. Yet some penologists believe that many inmates now in maximum-security facilities could be housed at lower levels. However, others argue that the higher security level is necessary given the characteristics of today's inmates. They also argue that prison space is so expensive that it must be used cost effectively.

Most states have so few female prisoners that they are all housed in one institution; those who require higher levels of security are segregated. In contrast, male inmates are assigned to a specific type of facility, depending on such factors as the seriousness of the offense, the possibility of an attempt to escape, and the potential for violent behavior. Many states do not have an institution designed for each level of security, so a facility is often divided into sections for different categories of prisoners. There are no national design or classification standards, so a maximum-security facility in one state may be run as a medium-security facility in another. Yet some generalizations can be made.

The Maximum-Security Prison   Usually an awesome edifice surrounded by high stone walls studded with guard towers, the **maximum-security prison** (sometimes called a *closed custody prison*) is designed to prevent escapes and to deter prisoners from harming one another. Such facilities house 35.5 percent of all prisoners. Inmates live in cells, each with its own sanitary facilities. The barred doors may be operated electronically so that an officer can confine all prisoners to their cells with the flick of a switch. The purpose of the maximum-security facility is custody and discipline; there is a military-style approach to order. Prisoners follow a strict routine. Head counts are frequent, and surveillance of behavior—often through closed-circuit television—eliminates privacy.

California's Folsom Prison is a maximum-security institution. Although these inmates seem to be free to roam the facility, discipline is strict and security is tight.

maximum-security prison

A prison designed and organized to minimize the possibility of escapes and violence; to that end it imposes strict limitations on the freedom of inmates and visitors.

medium-security prison

A prison designed and organized to prevent escapes and violence, but in which restrictions on inmates and visitors are less rigid than in maximum-security facilities.

Because these structures are built to last, many that were built at the turn of the century, when custody was the dominant model of incarceration, are still in use, even though their design makes it difficult to adapt many of them to the more recent rehabilitation and reintegration models of corrections. The old prisons are not alone in their bad repute; a newer prison, Walpole State Prison in Massachusetts, built in the 1950s, has been described as the "concrete horror," one of the most dehumanizing facilities in the United States. Some of the most well-known prisons, such as Stateville, Attica, Yuma, and Sing Sing, are maximum-security facilities.

The Medium-Security Prison   The **medium-security prison** (holding 47 percent of inmates) externally resembles the maximum-security prison, but it is organized on a somewhat different basis and its atmosphere is less rigid. In some states a medium-security prison seems much closer to maximum than to minimum security. Prisoners have more privileges and contact with the outside world through visitors, mail, and access to radio and television. The medium-security prisons usually place greater emphasis on work and rehabilitative programs. Although the inmates may have committed serious crimes, they are not perceived as intractable, hardened criminals. Some of the newer facilities of this classification are constructed in the campus or courtyard style, though the barbed-wire fences, guard towers, and other security devices remain.

minimum-security prison

A prison designed and organized to permit inmates and visitors as much freedom as is consistent with the concept of incarceration.

The Minimum-Security Prison The **minimum-security prison** (with 17.5 percent of inmates) houses the least violent offenders, long-term felons with clean disciplinary records, and inmates who have nearly completed their term. The minimum-security prison lacks the guard towers and walls usually associated with correctional institutions. Often chain-link fencing surrounds the buildings. Prisoners usually live in dormitories or even in small private rooms rather than in barred cells. There is more personal freedom: inmates may have television sets, choose their own clothes, and move about casually within and among the buildings. The system relies on rehabilitation programs and offers opportunities for education and work release. Some states and the Federal Bureau of Prisons operate minimum-security prison camps where inmates work on forest conservation and fight wild fires. To the outsider it may seem that little punishment is associated with a minimum-security prison, but the inmates are segregated from society and their freedoms are restricted. It is still a prison.

Private Prisons

Corrections is a multibillion-dollar, government-funded enterprise that purchases supplies, materials, and services from the private sector. Many jurisdictions have long contracted with private vendors to provide specific institutional services and to operate aftercare facilities and program. Businesses furnish food and medical services, education and vocational training, maintenance, security, and industrial programs. Health care and food services are two of the fastest-growing sectors of the correctional enterprise. All of this has been referred to as "the corrections-commercial complex."[17]

Private enterprise has always played a role in American corrections. But with the rise of community corrections in the 1960s, there has been a great increase in the number and type of services purchased from nonprofit organizations operating halfway houses, group homes, juvenile care facilities, and work release programs. Now, with prisons and jails overcrowded and staff costs rising, private entrepreneurs have begun to build and run correctional facilities for adult offenders. They argue that they can operate such facilities as effectively, safely, and humanely as any level of government can, at a profit and at a lower cost to taxpayers.

The first privately operated secure correctional institution was the Intensive Treatment Unit, a twenty-bed, high-security, dormitory-style training school for delinquents opened in 1975 by RCA Corporation in Weaversville, Pennsylvania. In 1986 Kentucky's Marion Adjustment Center became the first privately owned and operated (by U.S. Corrections Corporation) facility for the incarceration of adult felons classified to at least a level of minimum security. By the end of 1997, 126 private prisons holding 77,010 adults were in operation in twenty-four states and the District of Columbia. The $1 billion-a-year private prison business is dominated by Corrections Corporation of America and Wackenhut Corrections Corporation, which together hold more than three-quarters of the market share of the private prison business.[18]

The private prison business was launched in the 1980s during a period of massive state expansion of prison capacity to deal with the skyrocketing incarceration rate. Many states contracted with private firms who promised that they could construct new facilities quickly. New prison construction has now leveled off, and some states now have excess capacity. Will there still be a demand for the private companies?

The experience of Cornell Corrections illustrates this problem. Cornell built a 300-bed facility in Rhode Island only to find that the federal prisoners slated to be housed there at $83 a day did not materialize. Rhode Island's political leaders pressed the U.S. Justice Department to fill the facility but to no avail. Facing angry bondholders and investors, Cornell hired an attorney to scout the country for states seeking beds for their prisoners. Only after North Carolina agreed to send 232 prisoners (including 18 murderers) to Rhode Island was Cornell's fiscal crisis, at least temporarily, relieved.[19]

Douglas McDonald has conceptualized four basic forms of public and private involvement in corrections, as shown in Figure 10.5. In his model he distinguishes between own-

Figure 10.5 Four Basic Forms of Public and Private Involvement in Correctional Administration

Ownership and operating authority are the key variables that help us differentiate forms of correctional administration.

<small>**SOURCE:** Douglas McDonald, "Private Penal Institutions," in Michael Tonry, ed., *Crime and Justice: A Review of Research,* vol. 16 (Chicago: University of Chicago Press, 1992), p. 365.</small>

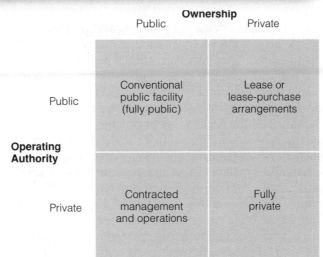

	Ownership	
Operating Authority	Public	Private
Public	Conventional public facility (fully public)	Lease or lease-purchase arrangements
Private	Contracted management and operations	Fully private

ership and operating authority. Thus some institutions are both fully owned and operated by either government or a private enterprise. Others, however, may be owned by government and operated under contract by a private entity, or owned by a private entity and operated by government on a lease or lease-purchase agreement. A number of prisons in Texas, Tennessee, and New Mexico are privately operated but state owned. [20]

The major advantages cited by advocates of privately operated prisons are that they provide the same level of care as the states but more cheaply and flexibly. Logan's study points to the difficulties of measuring the costs and quality of private prisons.[21] One issue is that many of the "true costs" (fringe benefits, contracting supervision, federal grants) are not taken into consideration. The quoted daily rates per prisoner in existing private facilities vary widely. In Texas the state pays the private companies about $30 a day on average for each prisoner, compared to $39.50 per day in state-run facilities. However, the $39.50 figure includes expensive maximum-security prisons which the private companies do not run. The private prison rate in Texas, is equivalent to $10,950 per year, much less than the costs per inmate held in most states.[22] A report by the U.S. General Accounting Office found that in a study of similar prisons in Tennessee—one private and two government—the per diem rates were almost the same.[23]

Provision of correctional services by private companies may result in lower costs, but public agencies must constantly monitor contracts to ensure compliance. The profit incentive may result in poor services, as evidenced by a 1995 detainee uprising at an Elizabeth, New Jersey, jail run by the Esmore Correctional Services Corporation for the Immigration and Naturalization Service. Undercutting a bid by the Wackenhut Corporation by $20 million, Esmore received a $55-million contract to run the facility in 1993. An investigation reported that Esmore demonstrated a "continuing cycle of contract violations" as indicated by understaffing, abuse of detainees, inadequate physical conditions, and health hazards.[24]

In 1997 the U.S. Supreme Court examined the question of the liability of guards in private prisons. You will remember that Section 1983 allows prisoners to sue public officials for constitutional violations. Because private companies are acting "under the color of state law" it has been assumed that they could be sued under Section 1983. But are guards employed by a private prison company provided with the "qualified immunity" of government employees who perform similar correctional work? Qualified immunity shields state employees from liability as long as their conduct does not violate "clearly established" rights. The Court said that private prison guards did not have this legal protection but are fully liable for their actions when they violate a protected right.[25]

Political, fiscal, ethical, and administrative issues must be examined before corrections becomes too heavily committed to the private ownership and operation of prisons. The political issues, including ethical questions of the propriety of delegating social control functions to people other than state employees, may be the most difficult to overcome. Some people believe the administration of justice is a basic government function that should not be delegated. They fear correctional policy would be skewed because contractors would use political influence to continue programs not in the public interest—for instance, they would press to maintain high occupancy, and would be interested only in skimming off the best inmates, leaving the troublesome to the public correctional system. We cannot yet demonstrate the fiscal value of private corrections: However, labor unions have opposed such ventures, pointing out that salaries, benefits, and pensions of workers in other spheres such as private security are lower than in their public counterparts. Finally, questions are raised about quality of services, accountability of service providers to correctional officials, and problems of contract supervision. Opponents cite many private services in group homes, day care centers, hospitals, and schools have been terminated because of reports of corruption, brutality, or substandard services.

The idea of privately run correctional facilities has stimulated much interest among the general public and within the criminal justice community. Privatization of criminal justice services may expand, or may be initiated at times of prison crowding, fiscal constraints on governments, and revival of free-enterprise ideology. The controversy about privatization has, however, forced corrections to rethink some strongly held beliefs. In this regard the possibility of competition from the private sector may have a positive impact.

Who Is in Prison?

The composition of the inmate population in terms of age, education, and criminal history helps determine how correctional institutions function. What are the characteristics of inmates in our nation's prisons? Do most inmates have long records of serious offenses, or are many of them first-time offenders who have committed minor crimes? Do all prisoners "need" incarceration? These questions are crucial to understanding the work of wardens and correctional officers.

Data on the characteristics of prisoners are limited. However, in a national survey of state prisons, the Bureau of Justice Statistics found (see Figure 10.6) that most prisoners are men in their late twenties to early thirties, have less than a high school education, and are disproportionately members of minority groups.

Recent studies indicate that recidivists who are convicted of violent crimes make up an overwhelming portion of the prison population. More than 60 percent of inmates have been either incarcerated or on probation at least twice; 45 percent, three or more times; and nearly 20 percent, six or more times. Two-thirds of the inmates were serving a sentence for a violent crime or had previously been convicted of a violent crime. These are major shifts from the prison populations of earlier decades, when only about 40 percent of all inmates had committed such offenses.[26] Today's prisoner has a history of persistent criminality. Beyond these shifts in the prison population, three additional factors affect correctional operations: the increased number of elderly prisoners, the many prisoners with HIV/AIDS, and the increase in prisoners sentenced to long incarceration.

Elderly Prisoners

Correctional officials have recently become aware of the increasing number of inmates over age 55. That number is now more than 30,000, with about 1,000 over 75 years old.[27] About half of these inmates are serving long sentences; the other half committed crimes late in life. Although older prisoners are still a small proportion of the total inmate population, their numbers are doubling every four years. If "three strikes" and "truth in sentencing" laws are fully implemented, the number of elderly prisoners will become a major problem for corrections within the next decade.

Elderly prisoners have security and medical needs that differ from those of the average inmate. In a number of states, special sections of the institution have been designated for this older population so that they will not have to mix with the younger, tougher inmates. Elderly prisoners are also more likely to develop chronic illnesses such as heart disease, stroke, and cancer.[28] In California the average yearly maintenance and medical costs for inmates over 55 is $46,800, double that of the norm.[29] One paradox is that while in prison the elderly inmate's life expectancy will be prolonged and his medical care will be much better than if he is discharged.[30]

Studies have shown that age is the most reliable predictor of recidivism. As people get older, they become less dangerous, statistically. Jonathan Turley has said that people undergo a "criminal menopause" as they age.[31] Only 1 percent of serious crime is committed by people over 60. With this knowledge, should the elderly be kept in prison until they die? California and some other states are considering community alternatives for low-security elderly prisoners. The Project for Older Prisoners (POPS) has been organized to cull low-risk geriatrics from overcrowded prisons.[32] The alternative to releasing elderly prisoners seems to be an ever larger population of them living in prison geriatric wards.

Prisoners with HIV/AIDS

In the coming years, AIDS is expected to be the leading cause of death among males aged 35 and younger. With 68 percent of the adult inmate population under 35, correctional officials must cope with the problem of HIV — the human immunodeficiency virus that causes AIDS — as well as AIDS itself and related health issues. As discussed in Chapter 6, in 1995 there were more than 27,000 HIV-positive inmates (2.3 percent of the prison population) and over 5,000 verified offenders (0.5 percent of the prison population) with AIDS. The rate of confirmed AIDS cases in state and federal prisons is six times higher than in the total U.S. population. Over 1,000 inmates died of AIDS while incarcerated that year, the second leading cause of death.[33] Because many inmates who are HIV-infected are undiagnosed, these numbers underestimate the scope of the problem.

The high incidence of HIV/AIDS among prisoners can be traced to increased incarceration for drug offenses. Many of these inmates engaged in intravenous drug use, shared needles, and/or traded sex for drugs or money. Male homosexual activity is

Figure 10.6 Sociodemographic and Offense Characteristics of State Prison Inmates

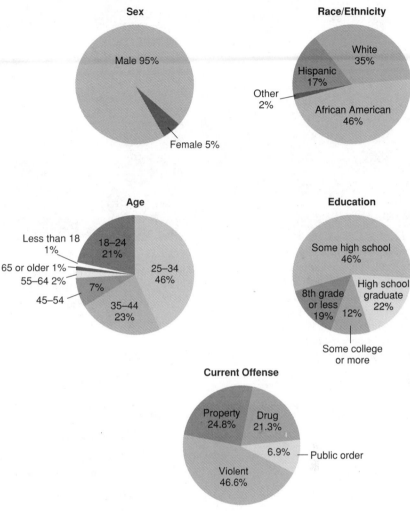

These data reflect the types of people found in state prisons. What do they indicate about the belief that many offenders do not "need" to be incarcerated?

SOURCE: U.S. Department of Justice, Bureau of Justice Statistics, *Survey of State Prison Inmates* (Washington, DC: U.S. Government Printing Office, 1993), p. 3.

These HIV-positive inmates at Mid-Orange Correctional Facility are attending a workshop designed to help them deal with the disease. Nationally, HIV/AIDS infects almost 3 percent of the prison population.

also a major way that HIV is transmitted. Although such behavior is forbidden in prison, "it has been estimated that 30 to 45 percent of prison inmates engage in such behaviors at one time or another." [34] Prisons and jails are ripe environments for transmission of sexual diseases. Some argue that the state has a compelling interest to education prisoners about the risk of unprotected sex or drug use in prison and even beyond the walls.[35]

To deal with offenders who have AIDS symptoms or who test positive for the virus, prison officials can develop policies on methods to prevent transmission of the disease, housing of those infected, and medical care for inmates with the full range of symptoms. Administrators are confronting a host of legal, political, medical, budgetary, and attitudinal factors as they decide what actions the institution should take. Policies concerning testing and segregated housing have been especially controversial, as reflected in Do the Right Thing.

DO THE Right THING

The Policy directive was precise:

> *All inmates will be tested for HIV. All inmates found to be positive will be placed in Wing A, regardless of their physical condition, conviction offense, or time remaining in their sentence.*

Testing for the deadly virus began at Elmwood State Prison soon after Warden True's directive was posted. All 753 inmates were tested over a three-week period, and every new prisoner entering the institution first had blood drawn at the medical unit for testing.

Six weeks after the directive was posted, the results were known. Most of the inmates breathed a sigh of relief in learning they were not positive. For a few, however, the call to report to the doctor was a prelude to a medical death sentence. The news that they had tested positive was traumatic. Most cursed, others burst into tears, still others sat in stunned silence.

The new policy was leaked to the press. The state chapter of the American Civil Liberties Union and the Howard Association for Prisoners' Rights called for a meeting with Warden True. In a press conference they protested the "state's invasion of privacy" and the "discriminatory segregation of gay and drug users, most of the latter being African-American and Hispanic." They emphasized that because it would be years before most of the infected would develop a "full" case of AIDS; corrections should respond with compassion, not stigmatization.

Warden True told reporters that he was responsible for the health of all inmates and that the policy had been developed to prevent transmission of the disease. He said that although the HIV inmates would be segregated, they would have access to all facilities available to the general inmate population but at separate times. He denied that he intended to stigmatize the twenty prisoners who had thus far tested positive.

What do you suppose Warden True considered in developing this policy? Is his policy likely to cause harm or good? Is it ethical to segregate a segment of the prison population? ∎

Long-Term Inmates

More prisoners serve long sentences in the United States than in any other Western nation. As discussed in Chapter 6, an increasing portion of the prison population consists of people who will serve more than seven years inside. About 9 percent are serving life sentences, and another 24 percent are serving sentences of over twenty-five years. These long-term prisoners are often the same people who will become elderly offenders, with all the attendant problems just discussed. [36]

Studies show substantial differences in the way the long-termer responds to incarceration. Some but not others experience severe stress, depression, and other health problems.[37] When severe emotional stress occurs, it tends to take place earlier, rather than later in the sentence.

Long-term prisoners generally are not control problems—they are charged with disciplinary infractions about half as often as short-term inmates. However, they do present a management problem for administrators, who must find ways of making long-term prison life livable. According to Timothy Flanagan, a leading authority on long-term inmates, administrators follow three main principles: (1) maximize opportunities for the inmate to exercise choice in living circumstances, (2) create opportunities for meaningful living, and (3) help the inmate maintain contact with the outside world.[38] Most long-term inmates will eventually be released after spending their prime years incarcerated. Will offenders be able to support themselves when they return to the community at age 50, 60, or even 70?

Summary

Prisons today are very unlike the prisons of the 1950s. The population is larger, the convicts are different, and the goals more ambitious. Most facilities were constructed when other goals were dominant and the population was different.

Three models of incarceration have been prominent during the past two decades: custody, rehabilitation, and reintegration. Each is linked closely to one goal of punishment, and implementation requires a particular organizational and administrative emphasis.

The architectural design of prisons has concerned administrators since the construction of Eastern Penitentiary. Of the various plans used, the telephone-pole design is most commonly found in maximum-security prisons. The campus, courtyard, and radial designs also are found in some states.

Correctional institutions are classified as either maximum, medium, or minimum security. This classification encompasses not only the physical aspects of the prison but also the internal organization of staff and the rules governing the prisoners. The higher the security level, the tighter the rules for prisoners and the more restricted their movements.

Because prison populations have more than doubled over the past ten years, the number of facilities and the staff to administer them have increased tremendously. Inmate characteristics and the problems they bring to institutions also have changed. In particular, the problems of long-term, HIV-infected, and elderly inmates are presenting correctional officials with new challenges. ■

For Discussion

1. Although the custodial model is the most popular for organizing a prison today, would any other model be appropriate?
2. What are the positive and negative aspects of the various prison designs? Do certain designs seem to correlate with certain goals of incarceration?
3. What ethical questions are raised by the emergence of prisons run by private, for-profit organizations?

4. Which characteristics of the prison population may present major problems for the managers of institutions?

5. If you were a warden, what would be your policy with respect to prisoners with AIDS?

For Further Reading

Johnson, Robert. *Hard Time: Understanding and Reforming the Prison.* Belmont, CA: Wadsworth, 1996. Makes a significant contribution to understanding the prison experience and the problems of adjustment.

Keve, Paul W. *Prisons and the American Conscience.* Carbondale: Southern Illinois University Press, 1991. Recounts the history of U.S. federal corrections from 1776.

Shichor, David. *Punishment for Profit: Private Prisons/Public Concerns.* Thousand Oaks, CA: Sage, 1995. Surveys the history and current debate over private prisons.

Wright, Richard A. *In Defense of Prisons.* Westport, CT: Greenwood Press, 1994. Critiques the critics of incarceration and analyzes deterrence and incapacitation in support of the prison.

Notes

1. U.S. Department of Justice, Bureau of Justice Statistics, Charles H. Logan, "Criminal Justice Performance Measures in Prisons," in John J. DiIulio, Jr., ed., *Performance Measures for the Criminal Justice System* (Washington, DC: U.S. Government Printing Office, 1993), p. 5.
2. Ibid.
3. U.S. Department of Justice, Bureau of Justice Statistics, *Correctional Populations in the United States, 1995* (Washington, DC: U.S. Government Printing Office, 1997), pp. 51, 54.
4. U.S. Department of Justice, Federal Bureau of Prisons, *State of the Bureau: Accomplishments and Goals* (Washington, DC: U.S. Government Printing Office, 1998), p. 51.
5. Ibid., pp. 48–50.
6. Ibid.
7. Ibid., pp. 43–47.
8. U.S. Department of Justice, Bureau of Justice Statistics, *Sourcebook of Criminal Justice Statistics, 1996* (Washington, DC: U.S. Government Printing Office, 1997), p. 87.
9. American Correctional Association, *Juvenile and Adult Correctional Facilities Directory* (College Park, MD: ACA, 1996), p. 4.
10. David B. Rothman, *Discovery of the Asylum* (Boston: Little, Brown, 1971), p. 83.
11. Camille G. Camp and George M. Camp, *The Correctional Yearbook 1995: Adult Corrections* (South Salem, NY: Criminal Justice Institute, 1995), p. 22.
12. William G. Nagel, *The New Red Barn: A Critical Look at the Modern American Prison* (New York: Walker, 1973), p. 36.
13. Ibid., p. 40.
14. Ibid., p. 41.
15. *The New York Times,* November 2, 1997, p. 14.
16. *The New York Times Magazine,* November 8, 1998, p. 54.
17. J. Robert Lilly, "The Corrections-Commercial Complex," *Crime and Delinquency,* 39, April 1993, p. 150.
18. Charles W. Thomas and Dianne Bolinger, *Private Adult Correctional Facilities Census,* 11th ed. (Gainesville: Center for Studies in Criminology and Law, University of Florida, 1998).
19. *The New York Times,* November 24, 1995, p. 1.
20. Douglas McDonald, "Private Penal Institutions," in Michael Tonry, ed., *Crime and Justice: A Review of Research,* vol. 16 (Chicago: University of Chicago Press, 1992).
21. Charles H. Logan, *Looking at Hidden Costs: Public and Private Corrections* (Washington, DC: National Institute of Justice, 1989).
22. *The New York Times,* June 24, 1997, p. A19.
23. *The New York Times,* July 13, 1997, p. D5.
24. *The New York Times,* July 23, 1995, p. 1.
25. *Richardson v. McKnight,* 000 U.S. 96-318 (1997).
26. U.S. Department of Justice, Bureau of Justice Statistics, *Survey of State Prison Inmates* (Washington, DC: U.S. Government Printing Office, 1993), p. 3.
27. U.S. Department of Justice, Bureau of Justice Statistics, *Sourcebook of Criminal Justice Statistics, 1996* (Washington, DC: U.S. Government Printing Office, 1997), p. 527; *The New York Times,* November 1, 1995, p. A1.
28. Philip G. Zimbardo, *Transforming California's Prisons into Expensive Old Age Homes for Felons: Enormous Hidden Costs and Consequences* (San Francisco: Center for Juvenile and Criminal Justice, 1994).
29. *The Hartford Courant,* February 18, 1997, p. A6.

30. Norval Morris and David J. Rothman, eds., *The Oxford History of Prisons* (New York: Oxford University Press, 1995), p. 253.
31. Ibid.
32. George F. Will, A Jailbreak for Geriatrics," *Newsweek*, July 20, 1998, p. 70.
33. U.S. Department of Justice, Bureau of Justice Statistics, *Bulletin*, August 1997.
34. Dorothy E. Merianos, James W. Marquart, and Kelly Damphousse, "Examining HIV-Related Knowledge Among Adults and Its Consequences for Institutionalized Populations," *Corrections Management Quarterly*, 1, Fall 1997, pp. 84–87.
35. Ibid.
36. Timothy J. Flanagan, ed., *Long-Term Imprisonment* (Thousand Oaks, CA: Sage, 1995), p. 10.
37. James Bonta and Paul Gendreau, "Reexamining the Cruel and Unusual Punishment of Prison Life," in Timothy J. Flanagan, ed., *Long-Term Imprisonment* (Thousand Oaks, CA: Sage, 1995), pp. 75–94.

CHAPTER ELEVEN
The Prison Experience

The gray bus with heavy wire mesh over the windows wends its way through the countryside. Inside, twelve passengers, the driver, and two uniformed guards sit quietly, each looking forward. The miles roll by. The riders do not seem to notice the stares of the curious in passing cars. There is tension in the air.

The twelve passengers are chained, one to another. More than anything else, the chain differentiates this bus and its passengers from a Greyhound bus. These are captives, being moved from the jail to the reception center of the state prison. The chain is there for security reasons, to prevent the captives from taking over the bus or escaping. But the links also symbolize to the bound people that they are powerless and that the state will determine most aspects of the experience awaiting them in prison. The symbolism of the chain is so great that in the language of the captives, the bus in which they are riding is called "The Chain" (see the Focus box).

Even the most hardened criminal must be tense and nervous on entering (or reentering) prison. For the "fish," the newcomer, the first few hours and days are a time of tremendous worry and anxiety. "What will it be like? Is it as bad as the stories told in the jail? How should I act? Will I be able to protect myself?" The new prisoner is apprehensive, like an immigrant starting out in a country where the language is incomprehensible, the customs are strange, and the rules are unfamiliar. But unlike the immigrant the prisoner has no freedom to choose where and with whom to live.

What does being incarcerated mean to inmates, guards, and administrators? How do prisons function? Are the officers really in charge, or do the prisoners "rule the joint"?

For the "fish," entering prison amidst the taunting of the inmates is a frightening experience. The new prisoner is apprehensive, like an immigrant starting out in a new country where the customs are strange and the rules unfamiliar.

As we examine the social and personal dimensions of prison life, imagine you are visiting a foreign land and trying to learn about its culture and daily activities. The prison may be located in the United States, but the traditions, language, and relationships are unlike anything you are used to.

In this chapter we explore the prison experience so that as citizens you can better understand this part of the criminal justice system and as potential correctional administrators you can learn more about the society of a maximum-security institution. We will look at prison society by addressing the following Questions for Inquiry.

Questions FOR INQUIRY

1. What is it like to be in prison, and how do prisoners adapt to "life in the joint"?
2. How extensive is the prison economy, and how does it work?
3. What is the nature of violence in prisons?
4. What can be done about prison violence?
5. What changes are taking place in prisons today?

Prison Society

The 1934 publication of Joseph Fishman's *Sex in Prison* marked the beginning of the scientific study of inmate subcultures in maximum-security institutions.[1] Since that time social scientists have been fascinated by the prison as a functioning community with its own values, roles, language, and customs. These studies have recognized that the inmates of a maximum-security prison do not serve their time in isolation. Rather, prisoners form a society with traditions, norms, and a leadership

F⊙CUS   Going In: The Chain

Michael Santos

Have you ever had a time in your life when you just wanted to die, when you thought death would be easier than facing the problems that you know are waiting for you? That was the feeling I had when I was 23 years old, just after a federal judge in Seattle sentenced me to serve forty-five years in prison for a nonviolent drug crime.

I remember my thoughts and experiences clearly as I was beginning that term. I had already been detained for about a year — awaiting my trial — before the judge sentenced me. A few weeks after conviction and the imposition of sentence, I knew I'd soon be on my way to prison. It would be a new experience, and one I wasn't looking forward to beginning.

My journey began when one of the guards from the jail came by my cell door early on a Saturday morning to wake me. "Roll up!" he hollered. "Roll up" is jail vernacular ordering a prisoner to pack all belongings and prepare for movement. The moment he said it, I felt it. His words were hanging in the air, like a threat, letting me know I was on my way to a place from where some don't return. "Okay, let's go," I said to myself as I tried to pump up my heart.

I didn't have much, as the jail really limits the amount of personal property a prisoner can keep. The guard marched me to a smoke-filled room where my ankles were shackled together and my wrists were cuffed to a chain wrapped around my waist. There were several other prisoners in the room. We were all chained together, because we were to ride the bus that would deliver us to prison.

I didn't know where I was going, not for several hours anyway. Then I found out. I was off to the U.S. Penitentiary in Atlanta. "Damn," I thought, "why would they be sending me to Atlanta? I'm from Seattle."

It didn't much matter what I thought. I was beginning to realize my thoughts didn't matter to anyone but me. When I was arrested, I pretty much lost my identity and became chattel, property of the U.S. government. Prison guards regulated everything in my life: the clothes I wore, the food I ate, the time I slept, the mail I sent or received. Lawyers even spoke for me. All I did was go through the motions of being human; someone else was always directing me. That is what it means to lose freedom.

What I did begin to think about was my own mortality. What was I going to be after release? I was a young man then, but I wouldn't walk the streets again until I was well over 50 years old. I'd been an adult for only a few years before I got locked up, now prison was going to be my life. Who would I be after release? An old man with nothing: no home, no automobile, no assets. A couple of friends might buy me a doughnut and a cup of coffee, but I'd have nowhere to go. I'd have to start life from nothing — at over 50 — and that was a chilling feeling.

The month-long bus ride was hell. We left Seattle, but rather than going directly to Atlanta, we worked our way across the West picking up and dropping off prisoners. I was restrained during the whole time, and the people sitting around me were, for the most part, guys who seemed like they'd been doing time forever. Most were covered with tattoos. I guess the tattoos were supposed to be frightening or something, like they were going to make the prisoner scarier and somehow meaner; they worked. I was learning everyone had their own way of dealing with time. Yet I had enough experience after my year in the county jail to know that I'd do my time alone.

structure.[2] Some may choose to associate with only a few close friends; others form cliques along racial or "professional" lines.[3] Still others may be the politicians of the convict society; they attempt to represent convict interests and distribute valued goods in return for support. Just as there is a social culture in the free world, there is a prisoner subculture on the "inside." Membership in a group provides mutual protection from theft and physical assault, the basis of wheeling and dealing activities, and a source of cultural identity.[4]

The concept of the prisoner subculture is useful as we try to understand inmate society. Like members of other groups who interact primarily among themselves and are physically separated from the larger world (such as soldiers, medical patients, or monks), inmates develop their own myths, slang, customs, rewards, and sanctions. But in recent times prisons have become less isolated from the larger society, and the concept of the prisoner subculture as isolated, separate, and opposed to the dominant culture may be incorrect. Although prisons do create special conditions that compel in-

When the bus finally approached the huge penitentiary in Atlanta, I was awestruck by the enormous wall that enveloped the entire prison. It stood 40 feet high, clearly separating the prisoners inside from the community. And the heavily armed guards standing outside the bus made clear there was nothing nice behind that wall.

I was scared, but I was determined to do whatever it took to make it through. I told myself repeatedly I was ready, but now, in retrospect, I realize I could never be ready. There was no room for fear, but fear was everywhere. I could smell it on the bus, on the men. We all waited, looking outside the windows in silence. I knew the only way I was going to make it was to stand up and face it, to go through it; it was with this absolute resolve that I was determined to return to the world.

Finally, the guards began calling us off by last name and prison number. It is not easy walking with a 12-inch chain connected to each ankle, and wrists bound to a chain that runs around the waist, but when my name was called, I managed to wobble through the bus's aisle, hopped down the steps, then began the long march up the stairs leading to the fortress. As I was moving to the prison's doors, I remember glancing over my shoulder, knowing it would be the last time I'd see the world from the outside of prison walls for a long time.

Once I was inside, the plain concrete walls reminded me my time was not going to be easy. As I was getting settled inside the walls, walking through the crowded halls, staring at the desperate faces, I felt the pressure. It was like I was on the road with a million drunk drivers all at once! They were angry with no apparent reason, as if they woke up in the morning and didn't even know themselves why they were mad.

Standing in line to eat breakfast is like going through a busy intersection when the traffic lights don't work; it's easy to crash, to get into a wreck without warning. Bam! That was how fast things happen in the penitentiary. I learned that killers stand 5 feet 6 to 5 feet 8. People who appear harmless are frequently the most dangerous men in the penitentiary. And there is no such thing as a fair fight in prison. You see guys over 6 feet tall, 220 pounds, hitting 5 feet 8, 150-pound guys with a piece of pipe when the smaller guy isn't looking. Fighters get respect from the other prisoners for this kind of thing, that is, recognition for doing "the right thing." I've seen people stabbed and piped in the showers, chow hall, the yard, the theater. People wore phone books taped to their bodies to protect themselves as they walked to the yard. Shanks were planted everywhere. Prison is really a gladiator school; a battle zone full of desperate men—a place where no one wants to be.

I remember reading somewhere that there are no atheists in foxholes, as every soldier placed in that situation is praying to God. Similarly, there really are no pacifists in prison, as even the most docile-seeming prisoner is capable of extreme violence, and often for no apparent reason. All prisoners feel the tension no matter where a man walks behind the walls, the threat of death is ever present. Seasoned prisoners want newcomers to either run with them or run away from them. They want to mold the way a prisoner behaves, who his friends are, and what he does. I refused to let the others dictate the kind of person I would be, so I pursued my own goals and decided to keep to myself while inside.

Serving a prison term is a consuming experience. Since I didn't want to be consumed, and didn't want to become like many of the people around me, I committed myself to building a better life and focusing on the future, on life outside of prison walls. I knew my road in prison would be long. I was certain the prisoners around me could make the road longer, and none of them could make it shorter. And that's why I've always structured my time to help me avoid them.

SOURCE: Written especially for this text. Michael Santos is serving his time in a minimum-security prison; 1998 marked his tenth year behind bars. Reprinted by permission.

mates to adapt to their environment, most inmates are now incarcerated for less than three years, and the culture of the outside world penetrates prison walls through television, magazines, newspapers, and contact with visitors and family (see the Workperspective). In short, the prison is very much a product of institutional and political relationships between the prison and the larger society.

Norms and Values

As in any society, the convict world has certain distinctive norms and values. Often described as the **inmate code,** these norms and values develop within the prison social system and help to define the inmate's image of the model prisoner. As Robert Johnson notes, "The public culture of the prison has norms that dictate behavior 'on the yard' and in other public areas of the prison such as mess halls, gyms, and the larger program and work sites."[5] He suggests that the culture emphasizes the use of hostility and manipulation in

inmate code

A set of rules of conduct that reflect the values and norms of the prison social system and help define for inmates the image of the model prisoner.

My Husband Is in Prison

WORK PERSPECTIVE

Tricia Hedin

Over the years, I've become quite resourceful in offering half-truths to those who ask about my marriage. "It is a commuter marriage," I say. Or "My husband is an artist, working on a government grant." Sometimes, particularly when I'm tired, I try to change the subject. When my spirits and energy are high, though, I say the simple truth: "He is in prison."

The truth requires stamina, as any prison wife will explain. There are pitying smiles, silent reproaches, numerous questions, and shocked responses. I believe that few marriages come under such close scrutiny as those of inmates and their spouses. There are many reasons for the questions, usually founded on a lifetime of media images. But as with other marriages, there are no generalizations that hold true for all prison marriages. There are, however, experiences all prison wives share.

During the four years I have visited my husband in prison—he is serving a twenty-year sentence with a ten-year mandatory minimum for bank robbery—I have discovered an incredible support system among inmate wives. Some of the women have jobs; others receive public assistance. Many of them are single-handedly raising their children. Often it is the first time they have been on their own. One fifty-year-old woman waiting to visit her husband described to me the first time she changed a light bulb in her oven and completed her income-tax form. Another talked about taking the family cow to be slaughtered. Yet there is a camaraderie among us. We come from different ethnic backgrounds and economic classes, but we understand each other. We understand that we have had to become strong.

Wives of prisoners must adjust to arbitrary treatment by prison guards and administrators who treat us as if we were criminals like our husbands. We are subjected to reprimands, searches, and a multitude of bureaucratic requirements designed to discourage continued contact. . . . Prison officials tend to discourage any type of networking among prisoners or their families. At the state penitentiary in Oregon, there is a rule against "cross-visiting": One inmate's visitor can't visit with another inmate. When we ask if the rule can be changed in order to promote a positive "community" atmosphere, we are told that there is no community among prison families nor does the prison wish to facilitate one.

Yet over and over again, women who are total strangers assist each other with advice about transportation and child care—and the techniques to fight bureaucratic battles. Our desire to keep our marriages and families intact is a taxing one. Coping with the incarceration of a loved one is difficult and can often result in financial burdens, health problems, and social ostracism. Divorce is common; not all prisoners react positively when their wives begin to take control of their own lives. Some marriages break down when the prisoner is released and both parties have difficulty adjusting to the changes they have undergone.

There are only seven states that allow conjugal visits between prisoners and their wives. Therefore, prison wives must struggle with decisions about their sexual lives. Some base their decisions on individual moral and religious beliefs and remain celibate. Some work out detailed agreements with their husbands that may allow

(continued)

one's relations with fellow inmates and staff. It makes caring and friendly behavior, especially with respect to the staff, look servile and silly.

Charles Terry, with twelve years of personal experience on the "inside" says that male prisoners must project an image of "fearlessness in they way they walk, talk, and socially interact."[6]

Thus inmates must suppress expressions of one's true feelings, because showing emotion about pain is seen as weakness. Terry believes that humor is one of the ways some inmates cope. It is used to bridge the gap between a normal and a convict identity—the world outside prison and the world within.

WORKPERSPECTIVE

My Husband Is in Prison *continued*

extramarital liaisons. Others base such decisions on the amount of time their husbands will be incarcerated. It is not sex with their husbands that most wives miss most of all; it is the intimacy and privacy. They long to be touched and held.

Organizations of prison wives are forming across the country, resulting in pressure for family-support groups, improved visitation conditions—including special play-rooms where fathers can see their children—and better transition programs for released inmates. Studies show that inmates who maintain close family ties are less likely to commit crimes again.

But becoming involved in prison reform can be especially difficult for us. We must plan our actions carefully because we are always aware that our husbands are under the control of prison officials. Many small injustices must be ignored because prison guards have the power to harass and punish. Still, I believe that change is possible. Some prison officials have begun to recognize that family members are often forgotten victims in the criminal justice sys-

tem and that we can assist in an inmate's rehabilitation. We know that prison is a destructive experience for those we care about, and we want to help lessen the negative impact. We also want to make sure they never return to prison.

I know the importance of love and trust in my relationship with my husband, of living in optimistic hope of a better future. I savor the time I spend in conversation with him, and I learn new ways of expressing intimacy in a crowded public area. I only hope that other prison wives will become proud of their special stamina. I hope that they, too, will cultivate connections with community leaders so they don't become isolated and that they will join to form the bridge from inside the prison walls to the outside world. For only we can help others understand that we are not crazy to love those who have made past mistakes. And we, who are strong enough to care, can really help keep our mates from going back to jail.

SOURCE: *Newsweek*, 15 December 1986, p. 14. Tricia Hedin is a freelance writer who resides in Eugene, Oregon. Reprinted by permission of the author.

The code also emphasizes the solidarity of all inmates against the staff. The two primary rules of the inmate code are "do your own time" and "don't inform on another convict." Based on his New Jersey study, Sykes refined the rules embodied in the code as follows:

1. *Don't interfere with inmate interests:* Never rat on a con, don't be nosy, don't have a loose lip, don't put a guy on the spot.
2. *Don't quarrel with fellow inmates:* Play it cool, don't lose your head, do your own time.
3. *Don't exploit inmates:* Don't break your word, don't steal from cons, don't sell favors, don't welsh on bets.
4. *Maintain yourself:* Don't weaken, don't whine, don't cop out, be tough, be a man.
5. *Don't trust the guards or the things they stand for:* Don't be a sucker, guards are hacks and screws, the officials are wrong and the prisoners are right.[7]

How does the "fish," the newcomer, learn the norms and values of the prison society? In jail awaiting transfer to the prison, the fish hears exaggerated descriptions of what lies ahead from fellow inmates. The ride on "The Chain" and the passage through the prison reception center further initiate the novice. The actions of the reception center staff, folktales passed on by experienced cons, and the derisive shouts of the inmates on the inside all serve as elements of a degradation ceremony that shocks the new prisoner into readiness to begin the **prisonization** process. But not all prisoners complete this process. Clemmer suggests that such factors as a short sentence, continuation of contacts with the outside, a stable personality, and refusal to become part of the group may weaken prisonization.[8]

The prisoner subculture designates inmates according to the roles they play in the society and the extent to which they conform to the code. Among the roles most frequently

prisonization

The process by which a new inmate absorbs the customs of prison society and learns to adapt to the environment.

Contemporary prison society is divided along racial, ethnic, and gang subgroups. There is no longer an inmate code to which all prisoners subscribe.

described in the literature are "right guy" or "real man" (an upholder of prisoner values and interests), "square John" (an inmate with a noncriminal self-concept), "punk" (a passive homosexual), and "rat" (an inmate who squeals or sells out to the authorities).

A single, overriding inmate code may not exist in present-day institutions. Instead, convict society has divided itself along racial and ethnic lines.[9] Reflecting tensions in American society, many prisons now are marked by racially motivated violence, organizations based on race, and voluntary segregation by inmates by race whenever possible — for example, in recreation areas and dining halls.

Do prisoners reject the views of conventional society? Research by Lucia Benaquisto and Peter Freed found that a vast majority of inmates held views on law and justice similar to those held by the general public. But as individuals they also view themselves as exceptions; it is the "other inmates" whose norms are contrary to those of society. The researchers suggest that while incarcerated the inmate must live and survive in an environment "where his movements and options are constrained, his person is insecure, and personal control is highly limited." Thus many inmates conform to the subculture even though their own values are contrary to the inmate code.[10]

Interviews with ex-convicts in California painted a picture of prison society in a greater degree of turmoil than in the past. This turmoil was created by the presence of gangs, changes in the type of person now incarcerated, and changes in prison policy. As the researchers found, "All these elements coalesced to create an increasingly unpredictable world in which prior loyalties, allegiances, and friendships were disrupted.[11]

In a changing society without a single code of behavior accepted by the entire population, the tasks of administrators become much more difficult. They must be aware of the different groups, recognize the norms and rules that members hold, and deal with the leaders of many cliques rather than with a few inmates who have risen to top positions in the inmate society.

Prison Subculture: Deprivation or Imported?

Where do the values of the prison subculture come from? How do they become integrated into a code? Sykes argues that the subculture arises within the prison in response to the pains and deprivations of incarceration.[12] These pains include the loss of liberty, autonomy, security, goods and services, and heterosexual relationships. They are an inescapable part of incarceration, and only through full integration into prison society are inmates able to adapt to and compensate for them. From this perspective the subculture develops within the institution as inmates try to adapt to the pains of incarceration.

An alternative theory holds that the values of the inmate community are also brought into prison from the outside world. John Irwin and Donald Cressey suggest that the prisoner subculture really combines three subcultures: convict, thief, and "straight."[13] They believe the system of values, roles, and norms that exists in the adult prison results from the convergence of the convict and the thief subcultures. The convict subculture is found particularly among state-raised youths who have been in and out of foster homes, detention centers, reform schools, and correctional institutions since puberty. They are used to living in a single-sex society, know the ways of institutional life, and in a sense make a home of prison. People who belong to the thief sub-culture look on crime as a career and are always preparing for the "big score." Irwin notes that thieves must exude a sense of "rightness" or "solidness" to be considered a "right guy" by their peers. Finally, the "square Johns" bring the culture of conventional society with them to the prison. They have been convicted for one-time offenses and identify more with the staff than with the other inmates. They want to avoid trouble and get through their terms as quietly as possible. In sum, the convict subculture results from the deprivations; the thief and straight subcultures are imported.

Unconvinced by these perspectives, Edward Zamble and Frank Proporino believe that inmate behavior results from how they cope, how they adapt to the prison environment.[14] They note that inmates come to prison with their own set of preincarceration experiences and values. However, even for the seasoned criminal, let alone the "fish," entering the institution is stressful. Each offender will adapt the best he or she knows how. Suppose two individuals are facing long terms. Both experience the same environment, restrictions, and deprivations of prison. Events in prison are often beyond their control. However, as a result of his background and attributes, one inmate "will interpret the lack of control as the result of his own inadequacy. In contrast, the second individual interprets the situation as one where others have used and abused him and are continuing to do so."[15] In dealing with their long sentences, the first "will likely immerse himself in the inmate social network and take on the behavior and values of other prisoners. . . . The second inmate will probably . . . have weaker ties to the inmate subculture. These behaviors will in turn affect the ways the two men are seen by both staff and other prisoners, and their subsequent treatment will differ."[16]

Thus whether the inmate subculture develops because of the deprivations of incarceration, or is imported with the offender, each prisoner adapts to the institution in his or her own way.

Adaptive Roles

On entering prison, a newcomer ("fish") is confronted by the question, "How am I going to do my time?" Some decide to withdraw into their own world and isolate themselves from their fellow prisoners. Others decide to become full participants in the convict social system. The choice is influenced by prisoners' values and experiences, and, in turn, helps determine strategies for survival and success.

Most male inmates use one of four basic role orientations to adapt to prison: "doing time," "gleaning," "jailing," and functioning as a "disorganized criminal." Irwin believes the great majority of imprisoned felons may be classified according to these orientations.[17]

Offenders do their time in a variety of ways. Some take advantage of prison programs while others do as little as possible. How would you do your time?

Doing Time Men "doing time" view their prison term as a brief, inevitable break in the criminal careers, a cost of doing business. They try to serve their terms with the least amount of suffering and the greatest amount of comfort. They avoid trouble by living by the inmate code, find activities to fill their days, form friendships with a few other convicts, and generally do what they think is necessary to survive and get out as soon as possible.

Gleaning Inmates who are "gleaning" try to take advantage of prison programs to better themselves and improve their prospects for success after release. They use the resources at hand: libraries, correspondence courses, vocational training, schools. Some make a radical conversion away from a life of crime.

Jailing "Jailing" is the choice of those who cut themselves off from the outside and try to construct a life within the prison. These are often "state-raised" youths who have spent much of their lives in institutional settings and who identify little with the values of free society. These inmates seek positions of power and influence in the prison society, often becoming key figures in the politics and economy of the joint.

Disorganized Criminal A fourth role orientation—the "disorganized criminal"—describes inmates who are unable to develop any of the other three role orientations. They may be of low intelligence or afflicted with psychological or physical disabilities and have difficulty functioning within prison society. They are "human putty" to be manipulated by others. These are also the inmates who cannot adjust to prison life, who develop emotional disorders, attempt suicide, and violate prison rules.[18]

As the number of these roles suggest, prisoners are not members of an undifferentiated mass. Individual convicts choose to play specific roles in the prison society. The roles they choose reflect the physical and social environment and contribute to their relationships and interactions in prison. How do most prisoners serve their time? Although the media generally portrays prisons as violent, chaotic places, research shows that most inmates want to get through their sentences without trouble. As journalist Pete Early found in his study of Leavenworth, roughly 80 percent of inmates try to avoid trouble and do their own time as easily as possible.[19]

The Prison Economy

In prison, as outside, people want goods and services. Although the state feeds, clothes, and houses all prisoners, amenities are scarce. A life of extreme simplicity is part of the punishment, and correctional administrators believe that to maintain discipline and security, rules must be enforced and all prisoners must be treated alike so none can gain higher position, status, or comfort levels because of wealth or access to goods. Prisoners are deprived of everything but bare necessities. Their diet and routine are monotonous and their recreational opportunities are scarce. They experience a loss of identity (due to uniformity of treatment) and a lack of responsibility. In short, the prison is relatively unique in having been deliberately designed as "an island of poverty in the midst of a society of relative abundance."[20]

In recent years the number of items that a prisoner may purchase or receive through legitimate channels has increased. In some state institutions, for example, inmates may now own television sets, civilian clothing, and hot plates. However, these few luxuries are not enjoyed by all prisoners, nor do they satisfy lingering desires for a variety of other goods. Some state legislatures have decreed that amenities will be prohibited and that prisoners should return to a Spartan environment.

Recognizing that prisoners do have some needs that are not met, prisons have a commissary or "store" from which inmates may, on a scheduled basis, purchase a limited number of items—toilet articles, tobacco, snacks, and other food items—in exchange for credits drawn on their "bank accounts." The size of a bank account depends on the amount of money deposited on the inmate's entrance, gifts sent by relatives, and amounts earned in the low-paying prison industries.

However, the peanut butter, soap, and cigarettes of the typical prison store in no way satisfy the consumer needs and desires of most prisoners. Consequently an informal, underground economy is a major element in prison society. Many items taken for granted on the outside are inordinately valued on the inside. For example, talcum powder and deodorant take on added importance because of the limited bathing facilities. Goods and services not consumed at all outside prison can have exaggerated importance inside prison. Unable to get alcohol, offenders may seek a similar effect by sniffing glue. Or, to distinguish themselves from others, offenders may pay laundry workers to iron a shirt in a particular way, a modest version of conspicuous consumption.

Mark Fleisher found an inmate running a "store" in most every cell block in the U.S. Penitentiary at Lompoc. Food stolen (from the kitchen) for late-night snacks, homemade wine, and drugs (marijuana) were available in these "stores."[21]

David Kalinich has documented the prison economy at the State Prison of Southern Michigan in Jackson.[22] He learned that a market economy provides the goods (contraband) and services not available or allowed by prison authorities. Through interviews Kalinich established the prices being charged. For example, a pint of liquor smuggled in from the outside costs $15 or six cartons of cigarettes. "Spud juice," an alcoholic drink made on the grounds by the inmates, sold for $5 a quart or fifteen packs of cigarettes. Kalinich found that the prison economy, like a market on the outside, responded to the forces of supply and demand and that risk of discovery replaced some of the risk associated with business in the free world. (See Michael Knoll's description of the prison economy in the Focus section.)

As a principal feature of the prison culture, this informal economy reinforces the norms and roles of the social system and influences the nature of interpersonal relationships. The extent of the economy and its ability to produce desired goods and services—food, drugs, alcohol, sex, preferred living conditions—vary according to the extent of official surveillance, the demands of the consumers, and the opportunities for entrepreneurship. Inmates' success as "hustlers" will determine the luxuries and power they can enjoy.

The standard currency in the prison economy is cigarettes. Because real money is prohibited and a barter system is somewhat restrictive, "cigarette money" is a useful substitute. Cigarettes are not contraband, are easily transferable, have a stable and well-known standard of value, and come in denominations of singles, packs, and cartons. Furthermore, they are in demand by smokers. Even those who do not smoke keep cigarettes for prison currency.

Certain positions in the prison society enhance opportunities for entrepreneurs. For example, inmates assigned to work in the kitchen, warehouse, and administrative office steal food, clothing, building materials, and even information to sell or trade to other prisoners. The goods may then become part of other market transactions. Thus, exchanging a dozen eggs for two packs of cigarettes may result in reselling the eggs as egg sandwiches, made on a hot plate, for five cigarettes each. Meanwhile, the kitchen worker who stole the eggs may use the income to get a laundry worker to starch his shirts or a hospital orderly to provide drugs or to pay a "punk" for sexual favors. "Sales" in the economy are one to one and are also interrelated with other underground market transactions.

Economic transactions may lead to violence when goods are stolen, debts not paid, or agreements violated. Disruptions of the economy may occur when officials conduct periodic "lockdowns" and inspections. Confiscation of contraband may result in temporary shortages and price readjustments, but gradually business returns. The prison economy, like that of the outside world, allocates goods and services, rewards and sanctions, and is closely linked to the society it serves.

Violence in Prison

Prisons are a perfect recipe for violence. They confine in cramped quarters a thousand men, some with histories of violent behavior. While incarcerated they are not allowed contact with women and live under highly restrictive conditions. Sometimes these conditions spark collective violence, as in the riots at Attica, New York (1971), Santa Fe,

(Text continues on p. 258)

Doing Business Behind the Walls or Bartering in the Joint

There's something going on — a deal, I think — on the tier in front of my house, cell number A-15, maximum unit, Arizona State Prison.

Outside on the tier — a narrow iron sidewalk enclosed in layers of green wire mesh — two prisoners stand arguing. In the grainy hall light, their bodies are just shadows, their words punctuated with tense, emotional hand gestures. One of the men begins removing cigarettes from the lining of a slightly modified blue denim jacket. His movements are precise, fluid, lightning fast, emptying two packs at a time into the hands of the man standing beside him. Ten packages. Twenty. Thirty. . . . As the cigarettes are being exchanged, the prisoners continue arguing, their words a jumble of language falling just short of where I'm standing.

Now the first man's coat is empty and both prisoners are silent. Forty packs of Camels have settled into the second man's denims. He arranges them to fit the contours of his body, while extracting from one pocket a small yellow plastic package. A balloon? He holds it briefly up to the light, runs one finger over its surface, then slips it into his mouth. The transaction complete, both traders hurry off.

Such exchanges are the basis for the prison economy. Had I followed the con with the cigarettes, I might have seen them traded for any of a dozen or so commodities necessary to a civilized existence. ("Civilized" — in a world that has been designed to be uncivilized — means not having to live on the bare essentials, the prison chow and the anonymous denim clothes, the institutional tobacco, and the harsh state soap dispensed to inmates.) Each of the goods or services acquired in the initial transaction would be consumed, or more likely, traded again according to the tastes of the owner. None of those transactions involve paper money. No green stuff and no Master Charge. No paper and no plastic. Yet the exchanges would be performed efficiently and to the satisfaction of both parties, each of whom might think they received the best end of the deal.

There's a lot of reasons why cigarettes are the favored unit of exchange: The demand is constant and their small size makes them readily concealable in a setting where bartering is illegal (although deals must often occur under the noses of the guards). Camel Regulars, the smallest available cigarette, are the most sought after, the most negotiable, and the most stable currency. They can be bartered for almost anything, from sex, drugs, and miscellaneous contraband, to televisions, jewelry, and a variety of services, including legal work performed by jailhouse lawyers.

Prices vary widely. A well-written appeal brief — suitable for submission to federal district courts — might bring anywhere from ten to twenty cartons of cigarettes depending on the competency of the prisoner lawyer, the amount of time and research involved, and the nature of the man's crime. Demand for legal services, which sometimes result in a retrial or reduction of sentence, remains very high. Sex is slightly cheaper, though the demand keeps abreast of the supply. A five-minute assignation with a prison drag queen might leave the john one carton poorer. The price could go higher though, according to how much he resembles a she. If he has recently received a hormone injection (occasionally available through the barter system), it could jack the price up by another carton. Add another few packs if he arrives wearing panties, mesh stockings, perfume, eye shadow, or lipstick. It cost him to score these things, so he's going to hustle you for whatever he can. If you've been locked up for a few years, chances are you'll put up with it.

A steak sandwich, on the other hand, might retail for from four to six packs, while the purchase of a watch, always a good hedge against inflation, would run a little higher. Figure three to four cartons for the watch, more if it's a name brand. Drug prices fluctuate more erratically. When available, a matchbox of the killer weed might cost from two to ten cartons of smokes, the price varying according to the drug's purity and place of origin, and the method used to bring it inside. When there's no dope around, other things get substituted. Catnip. Oregano. Parsley. To someone who hasn't had the real thing in a while, and doesn't have much chance of getting any, a little oregano can knock him out. Be careful about ripping people off here, though. There's only so far you can run. . . .

Despite official restrictions, bartering flourishes. Most guards prefer simply to look the other way — and avoid the confrontation associated with a bust. A few employees become actively involved: Manipulative prisoners con them into bringing contraband in, taking money out. With the aid of a guard, one fast-talking con was able to export the profits of his bartering operation outside the institution. Using the goods as security, he had his lawyer post an appeal bond and secure his release. . . .

Under the barter system one of the great joys — and great frustrations — is the flexibility of prices. In any transaction the final price is never predetermined but evolves according to both the buyer's and seller's ability to negotiate. That ability is both a necessity as well as an acquired art, one requiring patience, tenacity, and imagination. In deals not involving cigarettes, the beauty of these virtues becomes more apparent. . . .

I'm standing under the fifth tier, on a stairway crowded with prisoners, just after the evening meal. A little guy in a dirty blue cap — a convict renowned for his dealing skills — stands next to me holding a lamp. I have no idea where he got it. It's a large floor lamp with a shiny (and expensive-looking) brass stand, a bright yellow shade dotted with blue flowers. The thing seems totally incongruous here, where a small group of prisoners have congregated out of boredom or curiosity. It's the little guy in the cap that's doing all the talking:

"Ya see this, don't ya? Only lamp like it in the joint. How many of ya' ever seen a lamp like this 'round here? Right. None of ya'. And ya' know what? I made this. I put this together with my own hands, hustled the parts from the Industrial Block. You believe that? It's like something ya'd see inna living room, onna television, someplace out in the real world. Now, what-a-you scumbags gimme for this fine lamp?"

A voice in back, muffled by the crowd of denim bodies, yells back. "I'll give ya' two cases of Pepsi. A half dozen watermelon."

A louder voice—this is a black guy—all but drowns him out. "I ain't goin' to give you nothin'. Somebody stole that lamp. It's hot-er-n a firecracker."

The guy in the cap looks past the black dude, pretending not to hear him. "What am I goin' to do with some damn watermelons? You crazy? Keep them, gimme the Pepsi and four cartons of smokes."

Black prisoner: "I saw that lamp out in front of the counselor's office. You bastard—you're trying to get somebody busted!"

Man in back: "I'll give ya' the Pepsi, two bags of instant coffee, and a dozen watermelon."

Guy in the cap: "I said no watermelons. Got that? I want cigarettes. Three, four cartons. Them, or some weed. Got any weed?"

Man in back, stepping forward now: "I don't have any weed for a hot lamp. Best I can do is the Pepsi, the instant coffee, and my old *Playboy* magazines. I got about a dozen of them."

"How old are the magazines?"

"Couple years. No pictures torn out and no pages stuck together. I got the Bo Derek issue, and one with Brooke Shields."

"Still can't do business with ya." Hold it—you got Brooke Shields? Is that the real young broad? Sweet little teenager? Throw in Brooke Shields and your inflatable rubber party doll—You still got that? The one I traded you? One with the soft vinyl boobs? Throw the doll in and the lamp is yours."

When doing business in this manner, it's helpful to maintain a running stock of high-demand items: jewelry, postage stamps, electric razors and calculators, stereo tapes and headphones as well as food products from the inmate store.

Entry into this economic system is not as difficult as it might seem, or as it might be under another system. Inside, those willing to work and acquire capital will share in the wealth. All others have a rough time. The motivated prisoner knows that almost any object, service, skill, or talent has potential value as a unit of trade.

"Fish inmates"—new arrivals at the prison—enter the economy by bartering their labor, muscle, or time. They run errands and perform services, including laundry and housekeeping, for prisoners who pay them in property.

Possibly the most positive result of this trade system has been its effect on the prison arts. Convicts with no money, no meaningful job or activity—but with an excess of time, emotion, and imagination—discover talents. They teach themselves to write, to paint, and to fashion jewelry, leather goods, wood carvings, macramé, and pottery. Their first art is at times passionately original, expressive—and human. Fashioning it provides an outlet for energies normally denied within the prison environment.

The Arizona Department of Corrections, which for years remained indifferent toward the arts, has now become an art patron. Under director Ellis MacDougall, art materials and tools have been made legitimately available to prisoners through the mail as well as the visiting rooms. Facilities for hobby and craft work have been set up at several of the state's penal institutions.

The items made in these facilities command top prices, at least within the walls. One convict may contract another to have a portrait or leather belt done. Staff members sometimes purchase inmate art work for their homes, placing the money on the prisoner's bunks.

Purchases by staff members, as well as the general public, are sanctioned by the MacDougall administration. Prison art of all kinds is currently on display at the Department of Corrections central office in Phoenix. Additional display areas will soon be opened in Tucson, and at the women's prison in Phoenix.

D.O.C. spokesperson Judy Burris, who oversees prison art programs, says all prices are determined by the Department after an appraisal by experts. Profits go directly to the prisoners and prices are nonarguable.

Should you desire to negotiate regarding price or method of payment, you'll have to commit a felony and hope there's a cell available at Florence. If you decide to do that, leave your Master Charge and Visa cards outside. Throw away your bank cards, traveler's checks, and passbooks. On this side of the walls, those things won't do you any good.

SOURCE: "Doing Business Behind the Walls or Bartering in the Joint," *New Times Weekly*, April 1, 1982, pp. 11–12. Reprinted by permission.

The public thinks of riots, such as this one in New Jersey, when it thinks of prison violence. However, each year there are about 25,000 assaults by other inmates.

New Mexico (1980), Atlanta, Georgia, (1987), and Lucasville, Ohio (1993).

Although such events are widely reported in the news media, few people are aware of the level of everyday interpersonal violence in U.S. prisons. For example, each year about 150 prisoners commit suicide, about 90 perish in deaths "caused by another," and 400 die of unknown causes that were apparently not natural, self-inflicted, accidental, or homicide.[23] Annually there are about 25,000 assaults by other inmates.[24] Great numbers of prisoners live in a state of constant uneasiness, always looking out for people who might demand sex, steal their few possessions, or otherwise make their lives more painful. Yet some researchers have suggested that the level of violence varies by offender age, institutional security designation, and administrative effectiveness.[25]

Violence and Inmate Characteristics

For the person entering prison for the first time, the anxiety level and fear of violence is especially high. As one fish asked, "Will I end up fighting for my life ?"[26] Gary, an inmate at Leavenworth, told journalist Pete Early, "Every convict has three choices, but only three. He can fight (kill someone), he can hit the fence (escape), or he can fuck (submit)." [27]

Sexual assault is feared most by the "fish." The number is not known but Stephen Donaldson of Stop Prison Rape believes that more than 290,000 males behind bars are sexually assaulted each year. Victims tend to be young, physically small, first-timers, and convicted of less serious crimes. Not only are such attacks traumatic but the victim also becomes a target for further exploitation.[28] Incidents occasionally come to public attention when the victim goes to the press. For example, Michael Blucker sued Illinois prison officials for ignoring his requests for protection after he was gang raped in his cell. Blucker is now HIV-positive. The officials dispute Blucker's claims saying he prostituted himself to get drugs.[29]

Even if a prisoner is not assaulted, the potential for violence permeates the environment of many prisons, adding to the stress and pains of incarceration. Assaults in our correctional institutions raise serious questions for administrators, criminal justice specialists, and the general public. What causes prison violence, and what can be done about it? We consider these questions when we examine the three main categories of prison violence: prisoner–prisoner, prisoner–officer, and officer–prisoner.

To begin to understand that violence, we must first know more about the inmates, because violent behavior in prisons is related in part to the types of people who are incarcerated and the characteristics they bring with them. Innes and Verdeyen suggest that violent offenders can be divided into those who (1) have learned to be violent, (2) cannot regulate their violence because of mental disabilities, and (3) are violent and have severe personality disorders.[30] Three characteristics underlie these behavioral factors: age, attitudes, and race.

Age Studies have shown that young men between 16 and 24, both inside and outside prison, are more prone to violence than their elders.[31] Not surprisingly, 96 percent of adult prisoners are men, with an average age of 27 at admission.

The young not only have greater physical strength, but also lack those commitments to career and family that may restrict antisocial behavior. In addition, many young men have difficulty defining their position in society. Thus they interpret many interactions as challenges to their status.

"Machismo," the concept of male honor and the sacredness of one's reputation as a man, requires physical retaliation against those who insult one's honor. Observers have argued that many homosexual rapes are nonsexual; rather, they are political—attempts to impress on the victim the male power of the aggressor and to define the target as passive or "feminine."[32] Some inmates adopt a preventive strategy, trying to impress others with their bravado, which may result in counterchallenges and violence. Young inmates may seek to establish a reputation by retaliating for slurs on their honor, sexual prowess, and manliness. The potential for violence among such prisoners is obvious.

Attitudes One sociological theory of crime suggests that a subculture of violence exists among certain socioeconomic, racial, and ethnic groups. This subculture is found in the lower class, and in its value system violence is "tolerable, expected, or required."[33] Arguments are settled and decisions are made by the fist rather than by verbal persuasion. Many inmates bring these attitudes into prison with them.

Race Race has become a major divisive factor in today's prisons, reflecting tensions in the larger society. Racist attitudes seem acceptable in most institutions and have become part of the convict code. Forced association, having to live with people with whom one would not be likely to associate on the outside, exaggerates and amplifies racial conflict. Violence against members of another race may be how some inmates deal with the frustrations of their lives, both inside and outside prison. In addition, the presence of gangs organized along racial lines contributes to violence in prison.

Prisoner–Prisoner Violence

Although prison folklore may attribute violence to brutal guards, most prison violence is inmate to inmate. A study by Lee Bowker of four Virginia institutions registered a prisoner–prisoner assault rate of 9.96 attacks per 100 inmates per year. Matthew Silberman reported a rate at "Central" of 32.64 attacks per 1,000 inmates; and Ben Crouch and James Marquart found a similar rate in eight Texas prisons.[34] These levels of violence are not necessarily related to the size of the prisoner population in a particular facility. Uncounted inmates are injured by assaults. As Hans Toch has observed, the climate of violence in prisons has no free-world counterpart. "Inmates are terrorized by other inmates, and spend years in fear of harm. Some inmates request segregation, others lock themselves in, and some are hermits by choice."[35] It might be argued that most prisoners come from violent neighborhoods. But are they safer in prison than they would be on the outside?

Prison Gangs Racial or ethnic gangs are now linked to acts of violence in many prison systems. These gangs make certain prisons more dangerous than any American neighborhoods, as they continue street gang wars inside prison.[36]

These inmates show the signs of gang membership. Gangs organized along racial, ethnic, and geographic lines have become a major factor in many prisons.

Gangs are organized primarily to control an institution's drug, gambling, loan sharking, prostitution, extortion, and debt collection rackets. In addition, gangs protect their members from other gangs and instill a sense of macho camaraderie.[37]

Contributing to prison violence is the usual "blood in, blood out" basis for gang membership: A would-be member must stab a gang's enemy to be admitted, and once in cannot drop out without endangering his own life. Given the racial and ethnic foundation of the gangs, violence between them can easily spill into the general prison population. Many administrators try to separate rival gangs by housing them in separate units of the prison or moving members to other facilities.

Prison gangs exist in the institutions of forty states and also in the federal system, according to a national survey conducted by the American Correctional Association (see Figure 11.1). The survey identified thirty-nine major individual gangs nationwide; overall membership totaled about 6 percent of the U.S. prison population.[38]

Although the gangs are small, they are tightly organized and have even arranged the killing of opposition gang leaders housed in other institutions. Administrators say that prison gangs, like organized crime groups, tend to pursue their "business" interests, yet they are also a major source of inmate–inmate violence as they discipline members, enforce orders, and retaliate against other gangs.[39] The racial composition of prison gangs in Texas is shown in Table 11.1.

The racial and ethnic basis of gang membership has been well documented in California. Beginning in the late 1960s, a Chicano gang—the Mexican Mafia, whose members had known one another in Los Angeles—took over the rackets in San Quentin. In reaction, other gangs were formed, including a rival Mexican gang, La Nuestra Familia; CRIPS (Common Revolution in Progress); the Texas Syndicate; the Black Guerrilla Family; and the Aryan Brotherhood. Gang conflict in California prisons became so serious in the 1970s that attempts were made to break up the gangs by dividing members among a number of institutions. However, the ACA survey revealed a further proliferation of these gangs and increases in their membership.[40] Recent immigration patterns are reflected in new Chinese, Southeast Asia, and Central American gangs entering U.S. prisons.[41]

Figure 11.1 States with Prison Gangs

Racial and ethnic gangs are major causes of prison violence. What factors may account for the role of gangs in American prisons?

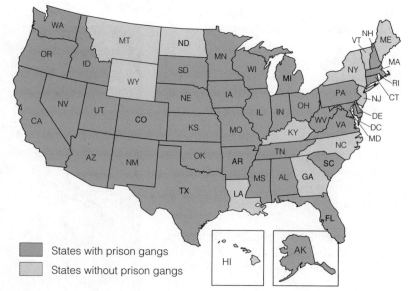

Source: American Correctional Association, *Gangs in Correctional Institutions: A National Assessment* (Laurel, MD: ACA, 1993), pp. 8–9.

Table 11.1 Prison Gangs in Texas

Texas has a major problem with prison gangs. As the data show they are racially and ethnically organized. How would you respond to gang membership if you were incarcerated?

Name of Gang	Racial Composition	Size of Membership	Year Formed
Texas Syndicate	Predominately Hispanic	296	1975
Texas Mafia	Predominately white	110	1982
Aryan Brotherhood	All white	287	1983
Mexican Mafia	All Hispanic	351	1984
Nuestro Carneles	All Hispanic	47	1984
Mandingo Warriors	All African American	66	1985
Self-Defense Family	Predominately African American	107	1985
Hermanos de Pistolero	All Hispanic	21	1985
Others	—	115	1985

SOURCE: Robert S. Fong, "The Organizational Structure of Prison Gangs: A Texas Case Study," *Federal Probation*, March 1990, p. 36.

The amount of prison violence attributable to gangs cannot be measured accurately. Although deaths certainly have resulted from gang violence, intimidation and assaults are undoubtedly much more prevalent. Administrators use a variety of strategies to weaken gang influence and to reduce violence.[42] These strategies include identifying members, segregating housing and work assignments, restricting possession or display of gang symbols, strip searches, mail and telephone monitoring, and no-contact visits.[43] Administrators have also set up intelligence units to gather information on gangs, particularly about illegal acts both in and outside of prison.[44] But in some prisons these new policies created a power vacuum within the convict society that was soon filled by newer groups with new codes of behavior.[45]

Protective Custody For many victims of prison violence, the only way to escape further abuse is to enter protective custody. Most prison systems have such a unit, along with units for disciplinary and administrative segregation. Inmates who seek protective custody may have been physically abused, have received sexual threats, have reputations as snitches, or fear assault by someone they crossed on the outside who is now a fellow inmate. Referred to as the "special management inmates," they pose special problems for prison administrators, who must provide them with programs and services.[46]

Life is not pleasant for these inmates. Often their physical conditions, programs, and recreational opportunities are little better than for inmates who are in administrative segregation because of misbehavior. Usually they are let out of their cells only briefly to exercise and shower. Their only stimulation is from books, radio, and television. Inmates who ask to "lock up" have little chance of returning to the general prison population without being viewed as a weakling—a snitch or a punk—to be preyed on. Even when administrators transfer such inmates to another institution, their reputations follow them through the grapevine.

Prisoner–Officer Violence

The mass media have focused on riots in which guards are taken hostage, injured, and killed. However, violence against officers typically occurs in specific situations and against certain individuals. In 1995 more than 14,000 prison staff members were injured by inmate assaults.[47] Correctional officers do not carry weapons within the institution because a prisoner may seize them. However, prisoners do manage to get lethal weapons and can use the element of surprise to injure an officer. In the course of a workday an officer may encounter situations that require the use of physical force against an inmate—for instance, breaking up a fight or moving a prisoner to segregation. Officers know that such situations are especially dangerous and may enlist others to help minimize the risk of violence. The officer's greatest fear is unexpected attacks. These may take the form of a missile thrown from an upper tier, verbal threats and taunts, or an officer's "accidental" fall down a flight of stairs. The need to be constantly watchful against personal attacks adds stress and keeps many officers at a distance from the inmates.

An injury to an officer may not be the only damage incurred. The authority of an officer assaulted by a prisoner is greatly reduced, especially if the officer's response is less than forceful. After such an incident, administrators often have no alternative but to transfer the officer to tower duty.[48]

Officer–Prisoner Violence

A fact of life in many institutions is unauthorized physical violence by officers against inmates. Stories abound of guards giving individual prisoners "the treatment" when supervisors are not looking. Many guards view physical force as an everyday, legitimate procedure. In some institutions, authorized "goon squads" comprised of physically powerful officers use their muscle to maintain order and the status quo.

From time to time, descriptions of incidents appear in the media about the excessive and illegal use of force by prison officials. Such an incident occurred July 10, 1996, in the Hays State Prison in northwestern Georgia when a top aide to the state prison commissioner touched off a bloody attack on prisoners when he grabbed an unresisting inmate by the hair and dragged him across the floor. The Commissioner watched "while inmates, some handcuffed and lying on the floor, were punched, kicked and stomped until blood streaked the walls."[49] The incidents led to a lawsuit and depositions in federal court by seven prison employees who witnessed the attacks.

How do we tell when prison officers are using force legitimately and when they are using physical violence to punish individual prisoners? Correctional officers are expected to follow departmental rules in their dealings with prisoners, yet supervisors generally can't directly observe staff–prisoner confrontations. Further, prisoner complaints about officer brutality are often not believed until an individual officer involved gains a reputation for harshness. Still, wardens may feel they must support their officers to retain, in turn, their officers' support. Levels of violence by officers against inmates are undoubtedly lower today than earlier. Nevertheless, officers are expected to enforce prison rules and may use force to uphold discipline and prevent escapes. However, definitions of appropriate force for the handling of particular situations typically are vague. We further discuss correctional officer use of force in Chapter 13.

Decreasing Prison Violence

Five factors contribute to prison violence, as listed by Lee Bowker: (1) inadequate supervision by staff members, (2) architectural design that promotes rather than inhibits victimization, (3) the easy availability of deadly weapons, (4) the housing of violence-prone prisoners near relatively defenseless people, and (5) a general high level of tension produced by close quarters.[50] The physical size and condition of the prison and the relations between inmates and staff also have a bearing on violence.

The Effect of Architecture and Size The fortresslike prison certainly does not create an atmosphere for normal interpersonal relationships, and size of the larger institutions can have management problems. The massive scale of the megaprison, which may hold up to 3,000 inmates, provides opportunities for aggressive inmates to hide weapons, dispense private "justice," and engage more or less freely in other illicit activities. Size may also result in some inmates "falling through the cracks," being misclassified and forced to live among more violent offenders.

The relationship between prison crowding and violence is unclear.[51] Some studies have shown that as personal space is reduced, the number of violent incidents rises.

Prisons housing offenders in a design capacity of 60 square feet per inmate are likely to have high assault rates. However, crowding can be measured in several ways (for example, number of people per area, amount of space per person, amount of unshared space per person, amount of time to oneself), and inmate perceptions of crowding seem to depend on a number of relative factors such as prior prison experience. Clearly, increased size of an institution's population strains such support facilities and services as dining halls, athletic areas, education and treatment programs, and medical care. These strains must be offset by increased resources so that quality of life can be maintained. In some institutions, the population has more than doubled without increases in violence. Good management seems to be a major factor in keeping conditions from deteriorating.

The Role of Management The degree to which inmate leaders are allowed to take matters into their own hands can affect the level of violence among inmates. When administrators run a tight ship, security measures prevent sexual attacks in dark corners, the making of "shivs" and "shanks" (knives) in the metal shop, and open conflict among inmate groups. A prison must afford each inmate defensible space, and an administrative goal should be the assurance that every inmate is secure from physical attack.

Effective prison management may decrease the level of assaultive behavior by limiting opportunities for attacks. Wardens and correctional officers must therefore recognize the types of people with whom they are dealing, the role of prison gangs, and the structure of institutions. John DiIulio argues that no group of inmates is "unmanageable [and] no combination of political, social, budgetary, architectural, or other factors makes good management impossible."[52] He points to such varied institutions as the California Men's Colony, New York City's Tombs and Rikers Island, the Federal Bureau of Prisons, and the Texas Department of Corrections under the leadership of George Beto. At these institutions, good management practices resulted in prisons and jails where inmates can "do time" without fearing for their personal safety. Wardens who exert leadership and effectively manage their prisons maintain an environment of governance so that problems do not fester and erupt into violent confrontations.

Measures suggested to reduce violence are not always clear-cut or applicable to all situations. The following steps have been proposed:

1. Improve classification so that violence-prone inmates are separated from the general population.
2. For inmates fearful of being victimized, create opportunities to seek assistance from staff.
3. Increase the size, racial diversity, and training of the custody force.
4. Redesign facilities so that all areas can be put under surveillance; there should be no "blind spots." Use smaller institutions.
5. Install grievance mechanisms or an ombudsman to help resolve interpersonal or institutional problems.
6. Augment the reward system to reduce the pains of imprisonment.

One administrative strategy that has helped bring order to violence-marked institutions is **unit management**.[53] This approach divides a prison into a number of small, self-contained "institutions" operating in semiautonomous fashion within the confines of a larger facility. Each of the units houses between fifty and a hundred inmates, who remain together as long as release dates allow and who are supervised by a team of correctional officers, counselors, and treatment specialists. The assumption is that by keeping the units small, staff will get to know the inmates better and recognize problems early on, and that group cohesion will emerge. Further, because the unit manager has both authority and accountability, policies presumably will be enforced consistently and fairly. The unit management approach to violence reduction has proved successful in a number of state and federal institutions.[54]

In sum, prisons must be made safe places. Because the state puts offenders there, it has a responsibility to prevent violence and maintain order. If violence is to be excluded

unit management

Tactic for reducing prison violence by dividing facilities into a number of small, self-contained, semiautonomous "institutions."

from prisons, limitations may have to be placed on movement within the institution, contacts with the outside, and the right to choose their associates. Yet these measures may run counter to the goal of producing men and women who will be responsible citizens when they return to society.

Summary

As in other situations in which people live together for extended periods, a system of norms and values develop in prison. Some criminologists argue the values of the prison society reflect the ways in which the prisoners adapt to the pain of imprisonment; others say the values are brought into the institution from the outside.

One way in which prisoners adapt to their environment is by creating a barter economy of desired services and goods. Prisons have canteens or stores in which some goods may be purchased, but their stocks are too limited to meet the inmates' needs. The resulting underground economy is a way of life for some inmates and a source of worry for administrators.

Violence is a major problem in correctional institutions. Violent behavior is related to the types of people who are incarcerated and the characteristics they bring with them, but institutional structure and administration also play a role. Many victims of prison violence escape further abuse only by entering protective custody, but this is a drastic step because they can never return to the general prison population.

Maintaining order in a prison can be a burdensome administrative task, given crowded conditions, violence, the character of some inmates, and the limited rewards and punishments available. Yet even in the most violent and fragmented institutions, a degree of order is still maintained. ■

For Discussion

1. Imagine you are a new prisoner. What are your immediate concerns? How will you handle them? What problems do you expect to face?
2. Are the values of today's prison culture a result of the deprivations of the prison, or do prisoners bring them from the outside? What about thirty years ago?
3. Which adaptive role might you choose if you were incarcerated? Which role might someone with fewer advantages choose?
4. What factors may account for the fact that the culture of the contemporary institution is at odds with the traditional view of prison society as united against the guards?
5. If you were the superintendent of a maximum-security prison, what policies would you adopt to end violence in the institution?

For Further Reading

Carroll, Leo. *Lawful Order: A Case Study of Correctional Crisis and Reform.* New York: Garland, 1998. History of Rhode Island's adult correctional institutions over the past forty years. Examines the transformation in response to changes in the external environment.

Earley, Pete. *The Hot House: Life Inside Leavenworth Prison.* New York: Bantam Books, 1992. An eyewitness account of day-to-day life inside the U.S. Penitentiary in Leavenworth, Kansas; written by the first journalist ever granted unlimited access to a maximum-security institution of the Federal Bureau of Prisons.

Fishman, Laura T. *Women at the Wall: A Study of Prisoners' Wives Doing Time on the Outside.* Albany: State University of New York Press, 1990. A study of how women cope while their husbands are in prison. A fascinating view of the world of prisoners' wives.

Johnson, Robert. *Hard Time: Understanding and Reforming the Prison,* 2nd ed. (Belmont, CA: Wadsworth, 1996). A significant contribution to understanding prison society.

Rideau, Wilbert, and Wikberg, Ron. *Life Sentences: Rage and Survival Behind Bars.* New York: Times Books, 1992. Describes life inside the Louisiana State Penitentiary; written by two former editors of *The Angolite,* the prison newspaper.

Sheehan, Susan. *A Prison and a Prisoner.* Boston: Houghton Mifflin, 1978. Gives a fascinating description of life in Green Haven Prison and the way one prisoner "makes it" through "swagging," "hustling," and "doing time"; contains an excellent discussion of the inmate economy.

Timilty, Joseph. *Prison Journal.* Boston: Northeastern University Press, 1997. The experiences of a Boston politician, sentenced to federal prison following his trial on a white-collar conspiracy charge.

Useem, Bert, and Kimball, Peter. *States of Siege: U.S. Prison Riots, 1971–1986.* New York: Oxford University Press, 1989. Surveys prison riots with case studies of the upheavals at Attica, Joliet, Santa Fe, Jackson, and Moundsville, and considers the nature and causes of prison riots.

Notes

1. Joseph Fulling Fishmen, *Sex in Prison* (New York: National Liberty Press, 1934).
2. Gresham M. Sykes, *The Society of Captives: A Study of a Maximum Security Prison* (Princeton, NJ: Princeton University Press, 1958), p. 107.
3. Leo Carroll, *Hacks, Blacks, and Cons: Race Relations in a Maximum Security Prison* (Lexington, MA: Lexington Books, 1974).
4. John Irwin, *Prisons in Turmoil* (Boston: Little, Brown, 1980). There has been surprisingly little scholarship on prison society since the early 1980s.
5. Robert Johnson, *Hard Time,* 2nd ed. (Belmont, CA: Wadsworth, 1996), p. 113.
6. Charles M. Terry, "The Function of Humor for Prison Inmates," *Journal of Contemporary Criminal Justice,* 13, February 1997, p. 26.
7. Sykes, pp. 63–108.
8. Donald Clemmer, *The Prison Community* (New York: Holt, Rinehart & Winston, 1940), pp. 299–304.
9. Carroll; Irwin.
10. Lucia Benaquisto and Peter J. Freed, "The Myth of Inmate Lawlessness: The Perceived Contradiction between Self and Other in Inmates' Support for Criminal Justice Sanctioning Norms," *Law and Society Review,* 30, 1996, pp. 481–511.
11. Geoffrey Hunt, Stephanie Riegal, Tomas Morales, and Dan Waldorf, "Changes in Prison Culture: Prison Gangs and the Case of the Pepsi Generation," in George F. Cole and Marc G. Gertz, eds., *Criminal Justice: Politics and Policies,* 7th ed. (Belmont, CA: Wadsworth, 1998), pp. 435-447.
12. Sykes, p. 107.
13. John Irwin and Donald R. Cressey, "Thieves, Convicts, and the Inmate Culture," *Social Problems,* 10, 1962, pp. 142–155.
14. Edward Zamble and Frank J. Porporino, *Coping, Behavior, and Adaptation in Prison Inmates* (New York: Springer-Verlag, 1988).
15. Ibid., p. 13.
16. Ibid.
17. Irwin, p. 67.
18. Kenneth Adams, "Adjusting to Prison Life," in Michael Tonry, ed., *Crime and Justice: A Review of Research,* vol. 16 (Chicago: University of Chicago Press, 1992), pp. 275–359.
19. Pete Earley, *The Hot House: Life Inside Leavenworth* (New York: Bantam Books, 1992), p. 44.
20. Virgil L. Williams and Mary Fish, *Convicts, Codes, and Contraband* (Cambridge, MA: Ballinger, 1974), p. 40.
21. Mark S. Fleisher, *Warehousing Violence* (Newbury Park, CA: Sage, 1989), pp. 151–152.
22. David B. Kalinich, *Power, Stability, and Contraband* (Prospect Heights, IL: Waveland Press, 1980).
23. U.S. Department of Justice, Bureau of Justice Statistics, *Correctional Populations in the United States, 1995* (Washington, DC: U.S. Government Printing Office, 1997), p. 105.
24. *USA Today,* August 8, 1997, p. 1.
25. Angela S. Maitland and Richard D. Sluder, "Victimization and Youthful Prison Inmates: An Empirical Analysis," *The Prison Journal,* 78, March 1998, p. 55.
26. Thomas J. Schmid and Richard S. Jones, "Suspended Identity: Identity Transformation in a Maximum Security Prison," *Symbolic Interaction,* 14, 1991, pp. 415–432.
27. Pete Earley, *The Hot House: Life Inside Leavenworth* (New York: Bantam Books, 1992), pp. 55–56.
28. *The New York Times,* December 29, 1993.
29. *The New York Times,* October 19, 1997, p. 7.
30. Christopher A. Innes and Vicki D. Verdeyen, "Conceptualizing the Management of Violent Inmates," *Corrections Management Quarterly,* 1, Fall 1997, pp. 1–9.
31. Leonore M. J. Simon, "Prison Behavior and the Victim–Offender Relationships Among Violent Offenders," *Justice Quarterly,* 10, September 1993, p. 263.
32. Wilbert Rideau and Ron Wikberg, *Life Sentences: Rage and Survival in Prison* (New York: Times Books, 1992), pp. 79–80.
33. Marvin E. Wolfgang and Franco Ferracuti, *The Subculture of Violence* (London: Tavistock, 1967), p. 263.

34. Data on prison violence are poorly reported. For these examples, see Lee H. Bowker, *Prison Victimization* (New York: Elsevier, 1980), p. 25; Matthew Silberman, *A World of Violence* (Belmont, CA: Wadsworth, 1995), p. 9; Ben M. Crouch and James W. Marquart, *An Appeal to Justice: Litigated Reforms of Texas Prisons* (Austin: University of Texas Press, 1989), p. 201.

35. Hans Toch, *Peacekeeping: Police, Prisons, and Violence* (Lexington, MA: Lexington Books, 1976), pp. 47–48.

36. C. Trout, "Taking a New Look at an Old Problem," *Corrections Today*, July 1992, pp. 62–67.

37. Geoffrey Hunt, Stephanie Riegal, Tomas Morales, and Dan Waldorf, "Changes in Prison Culture: Prison Gangs and the Case of the Pepsi Generation," *Social Problems*, 40, pp. 398–409.

38. American Correctional Association, *Gangs in Correctional Facilities: A National Assessment* (Laurel, MD: ACA, 1993). Because of definitional problems, the survey defined a prison gang as a "security threat group—two or more inmates acting together, who pose a threat to the security or safety of staff/inmates and/or disruptive to programs and/or to the orderly management of the facility/system."

39. S. Buentello, "Combating Gangs in Texas," *Corrections Today*, 54, July 1992, pp. 58–60.

40. American Correctional Association.

41. C. Ronald Huff and Matthew Meyer, "Managing Prison Gangs and Other Security Threat Groups," *Corrections Management Quarterly*, 1, Fall 1997, p. 11.

42. Huff and Meyer, pp. 10–18.

43. Salvador Buentello, "Texas Turnaround: New Strategies Combat State's Prison Gangs," *Corrections Today*, 54, May 1992, p. 59.

44. U.S. Department of Justice, National Institute of Corrections, *Management Strategies in Disturbances and with Gangs/Disruptive Groups* (Washington, DC: U.S. Government Printing Office, 1991).

45. Hunt et al.

46. Richard A. McGee, George Warner, and Nora Harlow, "The Special Management Inmate," in Timothy J. Flanagan, James W. Marquart, and Kenneth G. Adams, eds., *Incarcerating Criminals* (New York: Oxford University Press, 1998), pp. 99–106.

47. *USA Today*, August 8, 1997, p. 1.

48. Stephen C. Light, "Assaults on Prison Officers: Interactional Themes," *Justice Quarterly*, 8, June 1991, pp. 343–361.

49. *The New York Times*, July 1, 1997.

50. Lee H. Bowker, "Victimizers and Victims in American Correctional Institutions," in Robert Johnson and Hans Toch, eds., *Pains of Imprisonment* (Beverly Hills, CA: Sage, 1982), p. 64.

51. Gerald G. Gaes, "The Effects of Overcrowding in Prison," in Michael Tonry and Norval Morris, eds., *Crime and Justice: An Annual Review of Research*, vol. 6 (Chicago: University of Chicago Press, 1985). See also U.S. Department of Justice, Federal Bureau of Prisons, Gerald G. Gaes, "Prison Crowding Reexamined" (unpublished, 1990); Jeff Bleich, "The Politics of Prison Crowding," *California Law Review*, 77, October 1989, pp. 1125–1180.

52. John J. DiIulio, Jr., *No Escape: The Future of American Prisons* (New York: Basic Books, 1990), p. 12.

53. Innes and Verdeyen, p. 9.

54. J. Forbes Farmer, "A Case Study in Regaining Control of a Violent State Prison," *Federal Probation*, 55, 1988, pp. 41–47.

CHAPTER TWELVE
Incarceration of Women

As you approach New York's Bedford Hills Correctional Facility, you have no doubt it is a prison. You see guard towers, sliding gates of steel bars, and television security cameras. However, once inside you see things that seem out of place in a prison: a nursery, a playroom, colorful wall murals, a baby crying. In the middle stands Sister Elaine Roulet, an energetic nun who believes that mothers must maintain close ties with their offspring, even in the impersonal world of the prison.

In Bedford Hills, as in other prisons for women, nearly 80 percent of the inmates have children. Sister Elaine has pushed the New York Department of Correctional Services to develop a system of transportation, communication, and education to promote maternal bonding. Children born in the prison are cared for in the nursery for up to a year, and older children are brought to Bedford Hills for visits. In the summer the facility runs a camp for longer stays. As Sister Elaine says, "We have women in here who might not have been good citizens, but they were wonderful mothers. The kids have done nothing wrong to cause this painful separation. We need to do all we can to strengthen these bonds so the kids don't come back to prison later in a different way." She continues, sounding resigned, "Prisons are here to stay. You don't change systems. You change people."[1] Clearly Sister Elaine has set her sights on changing people.

Most states do not provide the level of services to female prisoners found in Bedford Hills. Because women make up such a small proportion of the prison population, a far larger portion of correctional budgets go to institutions for males. Yet female offenders usually have greater health, program, and security needs than do their male counterparts. In this chapter we review the history of women's incarceration and examine their life behind bars. We will seek answers to the following Questions for Inquiry.

Questions FOR INQUIRY

1. Why are women called the forgotten offenders?
2. What is the history of the incarceration of women?
3. What is it like to be incarcerated in a prison for women?
4. What are some major policy issues regarding the incarceration of women?
5. What problems do women face when they are released to the community?

Women: Forgotten Offenders

Often referred to as "the forgotten offenders," women traditionally have received discriminatory treatment from judges, few program resources from penal administrators, and little attention from criminal justice scholars. Various reasons have been given for this neglect of female criminals, including the facts that they make up such a small proportion of the correctional population, their criminality is generally not serious, and their place in the criminal justice system merely reflects the common societal attitude that puts all women in a subservient position.

Compared to prisons for men, those for women are fewer, smaller, and different. Criminologist Joanne Belknap argues that this has resulted in a three-pronged form of institutionalized sexism:

1. Women's prisons generally are located farther from friends and families, making visits from children, other family members, and friends more difficult, particularly for the poor.
2. The relatively small number of women in prison and jail is used to "justify" the lack of diverse educational, vocational, and other programs available to incarcerated women.
3. The relatively small number of women in prison and jail is used to "justify" low levels of specialization in treatment and failure to segregate the more serious and mentally ill offenders from the less serious offenders (as is done in male prisons and jails).[2]

The women's movement has focused attention on the condition of female offenders. Scholars have more actively sought to understand women's criminality, the nature of the subculture of women's institutions, and the special problems of this offender population. In a period when equal opportunity has become public policy, paternalistic and discriminatory decisions by judges, probation officers, wardens, and parole boards concerning female offenders have been both criticized and litigated in court. Although women prisoners have brought fewer legal cases contesting the conditions of confinement than have men, the right to equal protection under law has prompted state and federal judges to intervene in a number of disputes.[3]

Sister Elaine Roulet, the moving spirit behind the prison nursery at Bedford Hills Correctional Facility, shares a warm moment with inmate Evangelina Vasquez and her baby. As Sister Elaine has said, "This is my life, my passion."

Female offenders are incarcerated in 141 institutions for women, 162 coed facilities, and approximately 3,500 local and county jails.[4] Overall women make up only 6.4 percent of the U.S. prison population and only 11 percent of the jail population. However, the growth rate in number of incarcerated women has exceeded that of men since 1981. In fact, from 1985 to 1998 the male population in state and federal prisons increased 211 percent, whereas that of women increased by 311 percent. This growth has been particularly acute in the federal system which, because of the "War on Drugs" has had to absorb an additional 6,000 female inmates in the past ten years.[5] During the past ten years the number of women in state prisons for drug offenses has increased almost 450 percent.[6] The number of women now incarcerated in prisons and jails is more than 133,000.[7] Barbara Owen and Barbara Bloom argue that the increased number of women in prison has significantly affected the delivery of programs, housing conditions, medical care, staffing, and security.[8]

Some researchers have postulated that as women advance toward a position of equality with men in society, their behavior will become increasingly similar to men's, and so criminality among women also may increase. As a *New York Times* reporter noted, "Women wearing judges' robes or corporate pinstripes have become everyday images of society's changing gender roles. But what about women attired in Day-Glo prison jumpsuits?"[9] Others argue that differences in socializing women and men make it unlikely that the criminality of women will ever approach that of men, especially for violent crimes.

Females account for 24 percent of all arrests for the serious crimes tabulated by the Uniform Crime Reports (see Figure 12.1) but about 61 percent of people arrested for prostitution and commercialized vice, 41 percent of those arrested for fraud, and 36 percent of those arrested for forgery.[10] Women are more likely than men to be serving sentences for drug offenses and other nonviolent property crimes.[11] Given that there are far fewer female offenders and their crimes generally are far less serious than men's, many observers argue that it is rational for correctional public policy to focus on men.

Still, like the incarceration rate, the arrest rate for women has increased more than that for men over the past decade, particularly for drug and certain Index offenses — larceny-theft, robbery, aggravated assault, motor vehicle theft, and forcible rape. Although it is impossible to show direct links between women's status and their criminality, as they have moved into jobs from which they were formerly excluded, they may have gained the opportunities and skills to commit criminal acts. As Freda Adler remarked many years ago, "When we did not permit women to swim at the beaches, the female drowning rate was quite low. When women were not permitted to work as bank tellers or presidents, the female embezzlement rate was low."[12] Others challenge this view, pointing out that most property offenses committed by women consist of petty fraud and shoplifting, crimes that are not occupation-related. Owen and Bloom found that the

Figure 12.1 Percentage of Males and Females Arrested for Index Crimes

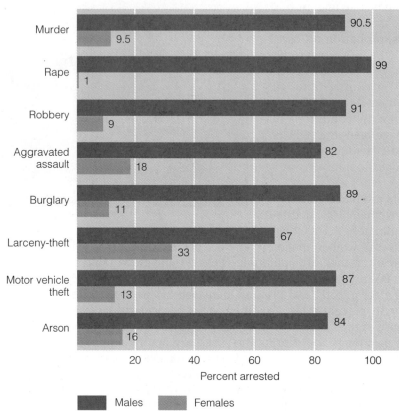

Although many more males are arrested, the proportion of arrests of females is highest for larceny, or theft. What might account for these data?

Crime	Males	Females
Murder	90.5	9.5
Rape	99	1
Robbery	91	9
Aggravated assault	82	18
Burglary	89	11
Larceny-theft	67	33
Motor vehicle theft	87	13
Arson	84	16

Percent arrested

■ Males   ■ Females

SOURCE: U.S. Department of Justice, Bureau of Justice Statistics, *Sourcebook of Criminal Justice Statistics* (Washington, DC: U.S. Government Printing Office, 1997), p. 380.

increased incarceration of women is a product of the "War on Drugs."[13] However, as Nichole Rafter suggests, the feminization of poverty over the past twenty years has meant that women and children now comprise 80 percent of the poor in the United States. She and other scholars believe that the poverty of young, female, single heads of households, and the way society treats them, has contributed to the increase in women's crime, particularly of property offenses.[14]

Women convicts traditionally have received lighter sentences than men for similar offenses. Judges have stated that when they sentence women, they feel compelled to treat them differently from men, and not only because children often are involved. Analysts believe this differential treatment arises from the fact that most jurists are men and hold typically male attitudes: Women are weak, are not to be taken seriously, and require gentle treatment. However, some scholars believe women are now being sentenced harshly whether they are first-time drug offenders or have been convicted of assaults against their husbands or boyfriends.

Historical Perspective

Not until the beginning of the 1800s did reformers start to press for separate correctional facilities and programs for female offenders. Prior to that time, all prisoners—men, women, children—in Europe and in the United States were housed together in jails and prisons. Historical records seem to indicate that women were punished the same as men: lashed, transported, imprisoned, and hanged. After John Howard's exposé of prison conditions in England in 1777 and the development of the penitentiary in Philadelphia, the issue of corrections for women was addressed. The sexes were then segregated, but the conditions under which women prisoners lived were atrocious.

Elizabeth Gurney Fry (1780–1845), a middle-class Quaker, was the first person to press for changes in the treatment of sentenced women and children. When Fry and several fellow Quakers visited London's Newgate Prison in 1813, they were shocked by the conditions in which the female prisoners and their children lived. Describing that first visit, Fry wrote, "The railing was crowded with half-naked women, struggling for the front situations with the most boisterous violence, and begging with the utmost vociferation." Fry felt she was venturing into a den of wild beasts, "shuddering when the door was closed upon her and she was locked in with such a herd of novel and desperate companions."[15] She agitated for separate facilities for women, with a domestic atmosphere, to be staffed by women. As a result, a parliamentary committee in 1818 heard evidence about conditions in the prisons, and reforms were ordered. Her 1827 book, *Observations in Visiting, Superintendence and Government of Female Prisons*, was influential in the movement to reform American prisons for women.

In the 1860s at Wethersfield Prison for Women, the inmates were trained for ironing, laundry work, and cooking; yet time was also spent learning such "ladylike" games as croquet.

The Incarceration of Women in the United States

News of Fry's efforts quickly reached the United States via the Quaker network.[16] Although reformers were excited about the development of the penitentiary, the issue of corrections for women had not yet been broached. In 1844 the Women's Prison Association was formed in New York by Sarah Doremus and Abby Hopper Gibbons with the goal of improving the treatment of female prisoners and separating them from male prisoners. Elizabeth Farnham, head matron of the women's wing at Sing Sing from 1844 to 1848, sought to implement Fry's ideas but was thwarted by the male overseers and legislators and was forced to resign.

Few women were incarcerated in the United States in the nineteenth century. Unlike their European counterparts, American judges were unwilling to pronounce women guilty of crime unless they were habitual offenders.[17] Thus the women convicted were, as inspectors at Sing Sing noted in 1844, "the most abandoned representatives of their sex." At this time, notes W. Davis Lewis, in the United States prison was "the end of the road for women too far lost to virtue to offer much hope for redemption." Because only men were believed to have the ability to reason (women were motivated solely by emotions), women who committed crimes posed a much more serious threat to order: As they had gone against their "nature" and were not amenable to reason, how could they be reformed? "It seems to have been regarded as a sufficient performance of the object of punishment, to turn them loose within the pen of the prison and there leave them to feed upon and destroy each other."[18]

Until 1870 most women inmates were housed in the same prisons and treated essentially the same as men.[19] Gradually separate quarters were established for female convicts in prisons intended primarily for men. Most incarcerated women were convicted for crimes against public order, especially prostitution, alcoholism, and vagrancy. The few women sentenced for more serious offenses were in out-of-the-way quarters without exercise yards, visitors' rooms, or even fresh air and sunlight. At Auburn in 1820, for example, "together, unattended, in a one-room attic, the windows sealed to prevent communication with men, the female prisoners were overcrowded, immobilized, and neglected."[20] Conditions of women imprisoned in other eastern and midwestern states before the Civil War have been similarly documented. All such reports indicate that the offenders were disregarded, sexually exploited, forced to do chores to maintain the prison, and kept in unsanitary facilities.

The Reformatory Movement

As we noted in Chapter 3, the 1870 meeting of the National Prison Association in Cincinnati marked a turning point in American corrections. Although the Declaration of Principles did not address the problems of female offenders in any detail, it endorsed separate, treatment-oriented prisons. Right after the Civil War, the House of Shelter, a reformatory for women, opened in Detroit. Run by Zebulon Brockway, it became the model for reformatory treatment. The first independent female-run prison was established in Indiana in 1873, followed by the Massachusetts Reformatory-Prison for Women in 1877, and the Western House of Refuge at Albion (Michigan) in 1893.[21]

The Quakers continued to be active in prison reform. In 1869 Sarah Smith and Rhoda M. Coffin were appointed to inspect correctional facilities for women. They found "the state of morals in our southern prisons in such a deplorable condition that they felt constrained to seek some relief for the unfortunate women confined there."[22] Women volunteers in corrections, following the example of Elizabeth Fry, became very active in serving their fellow human beings, acting out their religious convictions. This zeal was expressed by Maud Booth, a leader of the Salvation Army: "We must work for regeneration, the cleansing of the evil mind, the quickening of the dead heart, the building up of fine ideals. In short, we must bring the poor sin-stained soul to feel the touch of the Divine hand."[23]

Three principles guided female prison reform during this period: (1) separation of women prisoners from men, (2) provision of differential care, and (3) management of women's prisons by female staff. Nichole Rafter summarizes these principles: "Operated by and for women, female reformatories were decidedly 'feminine' institutions, different from both custodial institutions for women and state prisons and reformatories for men."[24]

Like the penitentiary movement, advocates of women's reformatories favored rural correctional institutions in areas, away from the unwholesome conditions of the city. However, the reformatory for women was not to emulate the fortresslike penitentiary, but rather of cottages around an administration building. Many states adopted this plan expecting that housing accommodating twenty to fifty women together would create a homelike atmosphere. For example, at the Massachusetts Reformatory Prison for Women in Framingham, which opened in 1877, the inmates lived in private rooms rather than cells, had iron bedsteads and bed linen, and, if they behaved well, "could decorate their quarters, enjoy unbarred windows, and have wood slats instead of grating on their doors."[25] Opportunities were provided for inmates to learn domestic skills suitable to their "true" female nature. The expectation was that upon release they would apply these skills in domestic service or in their own homes and families.

The women in these reformatories were primarily convicted of petty larceny, prostitution, or "being in danger of falling into vice." They tended to be viewed as errant or misguided women who needed help and protection within a female environment rather than as dangerous criminals who had to be isolated to safeguard society. The upper-middle-class Protestant women active in prison reform may have removed from the offenders the stigma of "fallen women," but they developed programs that treated the offenders as children. As Rafter points out, the women who lobbied state administrations for reformatories believed they were being helpful, "but in the course of doing good . . . [they] perpetuated the double standard that required women to conform to more difficult moral rules than men and punished them if they failed to do so."[26]

The reformatory movement was strongest in the East and Midwest; it gradually spread to parts of the South and West, but these regions were less influenced by the trend. In the South corrections was tied to the lease system of farm labor. When African-American women and children began to appear in large numbers before the criminal courts after the Civil War, officials had difficulty persuading farm leaseholders to accept these "dead hands," so the states created separate asylum farms for them.[27]

As time passed, the original ideals of the reformers faltered, as such reform impulses so often do, overcome by societal change, administrative orthodoxy, and legislative objections. In 1927 the first federal prison for women was opened in Alderson, West Virginia, with Mary Belle Harris as warden. She believed that much criminality among women resulted from dependency on men. She wanted her inmates to acquire skills to break this bondage and give them self-respect. These aims were incorporated into the programs at Alderson, which soon became a national model.

By the 1930s as the country moved away from rural and domestic values, increases in the offender population and greater emphasis on custodial care made reformatories seem out of touch with reality. Thus, by 1935 the women's reformatory movement had "run its course, having largely achieved its objective (establishment of separate prisons run by women) in those regions of the country most involved with Progressive reforms in general."[28]

The Post–World War II Years

No distinctive correctional model has arisen since the 1940s, perhaps because recent theories about the causes and treatment of criminal behavior do not discriminate between the sexes.

As women increasingly have been arrested for more serious crimes, and more drug law violators incarcerated, custody has become a more important goal than reformation. Rehabilitative programs, many based on psychological or sociological premises, were implemented in women's institutions in the 1940s and 1950s, as they had been in men's facilities. However, some scholars have argued that attention and resources were devoted mainly to men's institutions and that the less serious offenders found in women's prisons were accorded lower priority. Further, educational and vocational programs for women have been geared toward traditionally "feminine" occupations—hairdressing, food preparation, secretarial skills—that perpetuate gender stereotypes. With the deemphasis of rehabilitation and the rise in prison populations during the 1970s and 1980s, corrections for women was forced to defer to the rising concern about male offenders. The Comparative Perspective

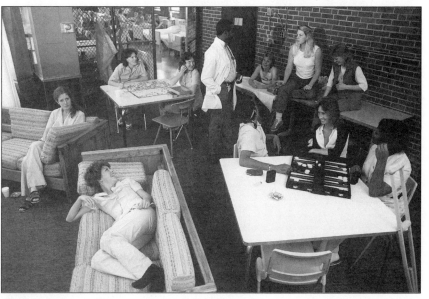

Although many institutions for women are small and built according to the campus design, they are often located far from the homes of the inmates' families.

COMPARATIVE PERSPECTIVE

A Canadian Prison Where the Great Spirit of Healing Dwells

Four years ago, Bridget Bruyere, 24, a Saulteaux Indian from Fort Alexander, Manitoba, was a prostitute in Winnipeg. She picked up a customer, accompanied him to his apartment and knifed him to death.

Convicted of second-degree murder, she spent time in two other correctional institutions—"where you open your windows and all you see is bars"—before her transfer to an unusual facility nestled in wooded hills near Maple Creek, a town of 2,500 in the cattle country of southwest Saskatchewan. Now she talks of her joy at being able to see trees and sky from her windows and go on walks amid the sage and prairie grass.

But the Okimaw Ohci Healing Lodge is more than a prison without bars and walls. It is the first Canadian penal institution specifically designed for Indian offenders.

The designers of the program hope that by embracing native customs like sun dances, sweat lodges and ceremonies involving smudge from the smoke and ash of sweet grass, up to 30 inmates will regain a sense of self-worth while learning skills needed to return to the world.

Ms. Bruyere, who quit school at grade nine but is now taking courses that will give her high-school equivalency and a knowledge of computers, said, "I can honestly say if drugs were offered me now, I'd be able to say no."

Denise Morning Cloud, 34, convicted on two counts of manslaughter, was having a coffee with Ms. Bruyere in the common room where guards, warden and deputy warden, prisoners and elders take meals together. "It helps quite a lot to know you're trusted, that people believe in you," she said.

Indians make up about 3 percent of Canada's overall population of 30 million, but are a far greater proportion of the prison population. The discrepancy is especially acute in Saskatchewan, where Indians are 10 percent of the population, but nearly three-quarters of the inmates.

"The over-representation of aboriginal people in federal, provincial and territorial court systems and prisons casts a long shadow over Canada's claim to be a just society," said a Canadian Royal Commission of Aboriginal Peoples.

Still, Canada has begun to develop culturally based corrections programs.

Sweat-lodge ceremonies now take place routinely at many prisons in the prairie provinces. "There is no question in my mind that these serve as a powerful agent for change for many who are searching for their identity," Allan MacLean, assistant warden of correctional programs at the Stony Mountain Penitentiary just north of Winnipeg, said in a recent interview.

The Okimaw Ohci Lodge—the name is Cree for Thunder Hills—is the most radical of all the government reforms. Prisoners are called residents and live in their own individual townhouse units, which can be adapted for live-in children. A nursery is ready, but final approval has not yet come to allow children. Practically all the staff are Indians.

Warden Norma Green, a Sioux who has worked for years in Indian social programs, calls the lodge a long-term investment. "If we do it properly," she said, "we will be on the road to healing." ■

SOURCE: *The New York Times*, July 17, 1996.

describes a program in Canada to help native women deal with their problems of identity and criminality.

Today there are increased demands that women be treated the same as men, yet as Nichole Rafter has pointed out, "equal treatment usually means less adequate treatment."[29] She argues that inferior care is the rule today and that gender differences are not taken into account.

Women in Prison

Life in women's prisons both resembles and differs from that in institutions for men. Women's facilities are smaller, security looser, inmate–staff relationships are less structured; physical violence is less common; the underground economy is not so well developed; and female prisoners seem less committed to the inmate code. Women also serve shorter sentences than men, so their prison society is more fluid as new members join and others leave.

Most women's prisons have the outward appearance of a college campus, often seen as a group of "cottages" around a central administration/dining/program building. Generally those facilities lack the high walls, guard towers, and cyclone fences found at most prisons for men. In recent years, however, the trend has been to upgrade security for women's prisons by adding barbed wire, higher fences, and other devices to prevent escapes.

The Okimaw Ohci Healing Lodge was designed so that Canada's female Indian offenders could participate in culturally based ceremonies and rituals, thus regaining a sense of their self-worth.

These characteristics of correctional facilities for women are offset by geographic remoteness and inmate heterogeneity. Few states operate more than one institution for women, so inmates generally are far from children, families, friends, and attorneys (see the Focus box). In addition, there is less pressure to design programs for individual offenders' security and treatment needs. Classifications are so broad that dangerous or mentally ill inmates are mixed with women who have committed minor offenses and have no psychological problems. The small numbers also limit the variety of vocational and educational opportunities available.

Joanne Belknap points out that the regime of women's prisons has been described as "discipline, infantilize, feminize, medicalize, and domesticize."[30] The tendency to treat women like children and the emphasis on "domesticating" them has been well documented. However, Belknap also notes that discipline for incarcerated women is generally overly harsh compared to that for men. For example, Dorothy McClellan found that in Texas female prisoners are far more likely to be cited for rule infractions, especially minor ones, and to receive more severe punishments.[31] Drugs were extensively used to "calm" inmates, and vaginal searches were frequently used to discover contraband. Coramae Mann notes, "What is ironic about this procedure is that these vagina examinations are frequent, yet the preventive Pap test for cervical cancer is not often given."[32]

Characteristics of Women in Prison

In most respects, incarcerated women, like male prisoners, may be viewed as disadvantaged losers in this complex and competitive society. Figure 12.2 summarizes some characteristics of female prisoners. A national survey of the backgrounds of women imprisoned found that about 62 percent had not finished high school, about half had been unemployed or had held unskilled jobs, and about 60 percent were Hispanic or African American.[33] What most distinguished incarcerated women from men were the nature of offenses, sentence lengths, patterns of drug use, and correctional history.

276

FOCUS Excerpts from a Prison Journal

"The Rose"

This is an interview with myself. I've decided to write a book on things happening to me . . . maybe someone else will read it and learn. I'm sitting in jail.

"Jail?" you say.

Sure. Haven't you ever seen one? That's the place you always believed, and were told, the bad people go. It's not true. They send good people there too. Look at me. I'm in a 12-by-20-foot cell with two other "criminally oriented" females. They're OK. One is here for not returning a car to the dealer she borrowed it from—known by some as grand theft auto. The other is in here for writing too many checks on an account with no money.

The bunks are always too high, the mattresses are flimsy, and the pillows are falling apart. The window's got no glass in it; the cold north breeze blows in and freezes your ass off. So, if you ever plan on going to jail, hope it's in the summer.

The wind blows in, sending shivering chills up your spine. Oh! what you'd give to stand outside, with the sunshine beaming down, the birds singing, a tree to touch, a decent glass to drink out of, a proper plate to have your food on, a fork to eat with, a room without names all over the walls. . . . Hanging your towels over the heater to dry so you'll have a dry towel the next time you take a shower. The heater is a little portable thing that looks like someone took their frustration out on it. And you have to put everything up so it doesn't get wet,

because the shower leaks and splatters all over everywhere. . . . Days of dripping shower, which is the worst sound in the world.

It's a sixty-eight-year-old building with steam heaters that whistle, jailers walking around with keys jingling, the elevator up and down all the time. They never come to get you. The phone rings from sunup to sundown. No calls for you. Calls only yours to be made when it's your turn. Knowing down inside no call will help you out of this mess.

The guys still flirt, no matter where—even through a little window in the door. . . . One of the girls is sitting under the sink having an obscene pipe conversation with Gary next door. He says it'll make him feel good, going down in history as an obscene pipe caller.

You'll never believe this. They're not trying to break out, just "escape to rape"—each other. I can hear the spoons digging now. Maybe they'll make it—by next year! The "escape to rape" fell through. We all knew it would, but it gave us something to do last night. We must've laughed for four hours straight. We got to do something. You can't just sit around and cry and find someone else to blame things on. A year is a long time when you live it in a box.

I made the news. Not like most of the people I went to school with. I'm going to write what it says so I'll never forget what Clovis, New Mexico, is really like.

Figure 12.2 Characteristics of Female Prisoners

Like their male counterparts, female prisoners typically are young, have little education, are members of minority groups, and are incarcerated for a serious offense.

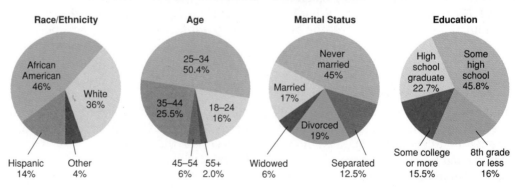

SOURCE: U.S. Department of Justice, Bureau of Justice Statistics, *Special Report* (Washington, DC: U.S. Government Printing Office, March 1994).

[They spelled my name right!], convicted of issuing a worthless check and distribution of a controlled substance, is charged with being an habitual offender. District Judge gave Ms. a two-year state penitentiary sentence with one year suspended and to be served on parole probation.

Ms. was originally given a suspended one-year sentence for issuing a worthless check. She was also previously given a five-year deferred penitentiary sentence for distribution of a controlled substance and was placed on probation.

Maybe someday I'll understand all this.

The worst feeling in the world was walking away and hearing my son scream for his mom. Knowing that I had to come back upstairs and be locked up. That's the hell in this hole—knowing people are close at hand and you can't touch or feel them.

I think what makes this so hard is that it's Christmastime. I'm almost crazy thinking I'm going to miss Santa Claus, Christmas carols, and my boys' smiling faces Christmas morning.

It's getting close to the time of my departure from a town I grew up in, learned to love. I feel a great loss as I'm going away knowing that returning may be a long ways away. Every passing moment brings thoughts I never conceived of having. I've never felt so alone. I've never felt so lost. I've never had so much taken from me in such a short time.

The strain of waiting for tomorrow has made me nervous, nauseous, and nuts. The three *N*'s. Sounds like a

bad disease. I go to a fate that I have no concept of, praying and hoping that I can handle it.

(Later, from the State Penitentiary)

I came through the gate knowing very well that it will be many months before I will be able to leave. The Annex (for women) is a building separate from the Big House (for men). I've only been here thirty minutes and I'm already talking like a convict. They gave me a number and issued me two blankets, dark green; two sheets, white; two towels, white; soap; toothbrush and toothpaste. They gave me some books, paper, pen, and envelopes, brought me to this square box half the size of the county jail cell. It has one of the hardest beds I've ever seen, a toilet, a sink, a footlocker, two small bookcases, and a window. You can look out and see desert.

So far the women and matrons here seem very adaptable and willing to help. I've already had cookies, two glasses of milk, and two cups of hot chocolate brought to me before I sleep in my new box, sweet box. Don't get me wrong. I'll take all my days of working, bill collectors, children crying—and headaches, worries, and woes. I'll take my problems just not to hear that steel door slam shut and the key turn in the lock, a matron walk down the hall leaving me with an empty feeling, and a sound of clanking, jangling keys falling off in the distance.

SOURCE: The 24-year-old author of this journal chose the pen name "The Rose." Her identity has been disguised to protect her and her family, including two sons, ages 2 and 6. These excerpts were written during the first five days following her conviction, while she was awaiting transfer from county jail to state prison. She served nine months in both maximum- and minimum-security facilities. Edited by Sue Mahan, from her interview notes. Reprinted by permission.

Offense Although the public commonly believes most female prison inmates are incarcerated for such minor offenses as prostitution, sentences for such crimes are normally served in jails; prisons hold the more serious offenders, both male and female. The survey found that 32.2 percent of the women prisoners were serving sentences for violent offenses (compared with 47.4 percent of male prisoners), 28.7 percent for property offenses (versus 24.6 percent of men), 32.8 percent for drug-related offenses (versus 20.7 percent of men), and 5.7 percent for public order offenses (versus 7.0 percent of men).[34] The most significant difference between the sexes is in violent offenses, and to a lesser extent in drug offenses. It is striking that in a similar survey conducted in 1986, only 12 percent of the women and 8.4 percent of the men were incarcerated for drug offenses.

Sentence Overall, women prisoners received shorter maximum sentences than did men. Half of the women had a maximum sentence of five years or less, whereas half of the men had a sentence of ten years or less. Like their male counterparts, however, increasing numbers of women are being sentenced to long terms (more than ten years) of incarceration. In the past most long-termers were murderers, but now more offenders are being given long, harsh sentences mandated by Congress and state legislatures as part of the War on Drugs.

In their study of a group of long-term female offenders in Louisiana, Doris MacKenzie and her colleagues found that the severity of offenders' needs and problems was much higher for women serving long terms. Because of the small number of women's prisons, opportunities for transfer to prisons closer to families are limited, as are jobs, educational opportunities, and social interactions. The researchers suggest that these difficulties accumulate and further burden the long-term female offender.[35]

Drug Use The national survey found that 32.8 percent of women in prison were serving time for drug-related offenses, but that habitual drug use before incarceration was much greater among females than this figure indicates. The researchers caution that few responded to the drug questions, but over half (54 percent) said that they had used drugs in the month before their current offense.[36] Thirty-seven percent said they had participated in at least one drug abuse treatment program other than any they were in at the time of the current offense. The extent of drug use has policy implications, because it indicates that a large percentage of female offenders need medical assistance while going through withdrawal in jails, and they need treatment programs while incarcerated.

Correctional History Almost 72 percent of the female prisoners had been on probation or incarcerated in a correctional facility before their current sentence.[37] Differences between men and women on this variable seem related primarily to experiences as juveniles: More men reported having been on probation and incarcerated as youths. Among recidivists, men and women were similarly rated on type of prior offense; crimes against property ranked highest for both sexes.

Drug offenses seem to account for the great increase of women in prison. National survey data on women offenders collected by the National Council on Crime and Delinquency found that drug dependence was the major factor women cited for committing their crime.[38] The upsurge in drug offenders and gang members has changed the character of the inmate society in many prisons for women. Delia Robinson, a veteran Connecticut inmate, told Andi Rierden that she especially disdains the young troublemakers who

> come in off the streets looking like zombies, bone thin and strung out on crack cocaine. "You can tell them by the abscesses on their bodies from shooting liquid dope cut with meat tenderizer. Before long these inmates fatten up on the prison's starchy food and the junk they order from commissary, smuggle in their drugs, and sleep around with women, even though they likely have a boyfriend or husband on the outside. Once released, they'll return to the streets, get arrested and then return to the Farm (prison). Once settled in they'll unite with old flames and "just chill."[39]

The Subculture of Women's Prisons

Studies of the subculture of women's prisons have been less extensive than those reported in Chapter 11 on male convict society. Just as there have been few ethnographic studies of men's prisons during the past two decades, there have been very few of women's prisons.

Much early investigation of separate women's prisons focused on types of social relationships among female offenders. As in all types of penal institutions, same-sex relationships were found, but unlike in male prisons, such relationships among women appeared more voluntary than coerced. Perhaps more importantly, scholars reported that female inmates tended to form pseudofamilies in which they adopted various roles—father, mother, daughter, sister—and interacted as a unit, rather than identifying with the larger prisoner subculture. Esther Heffernan views these "play" families as a "direct, conscious substitution for the family relationships broken by imprisonment, or . . . the development of roles that perhaps were not fulfilled in the actual home environment." She also notes the economic aspect of the play families and the extent to which they are formed to provide for their members.[40] Such cooperative relationships help relieve the tensions of prison life, assist the socialization of new inmates, and permit individuals to act according to clearly defined roles and rules.

When David Ward and Gene Kassebaum studied sexual and family bonding at the California Institute for Women in Frontera, they found homosexual roles but not familial roles. As have other studies of prisoner subcultures, Ward and Kassebaum examined adaptation to imprisonment through the development of roles expected of women in the larger society. The women in Frontera seemed to adapt less well to prison, and they did not develop the solidarity with one another that Donald Clemmer and Gresham Sykes found in male institutions. Yet societal expectations for gender and social roles of women were important in the prisoner subculture.[41]

Compared with the convict society in prisons for males, many female prisoners, such as these in Alabama's Julia Tutwiler Prison, form pseudofamilies, developing strong bonds with family members.

Researchers do not seem to have consensus on the extent and nature of same-sex relationships in women's prisons. Imogene Moyer, for example, points out that the evidence must be analyzed within a framework that recognizes factors in each institutional setting. Thus policies designed to keep prisoners separate, average length of time served, distance from relatives, and level of regimentation must be assessed before generalizations about social relationships can be made with any confidence.[42] Yet Robert Leger found the lesbians he surveyed had longer sentences, were arrested younger, were more likely to have been previously confined, and had served more time than had the heterosexual women with whom they were imprisoned.[43]

A more explicit attempt to compare the subculture of women's prisons with that of men's was made by Rose Giallombardo at the Federal Reformatory for Women in Alderson, West Virginia. Like Irwin and Cressey, Giallombardo hypothesized that many subculture features of the institution are imported from the larger society.[44] For example, she found that imprisoned women mitigate incarceration by developing marriage and kinship links with other inmates.

All societies have different expectations in regard to masculine and feminine roles. In the United States the woman has traditionally been wife and mother; the man has been expected to play an occupational role, and his status depends on the status of his work. Thus, notes Giallombardo, "The family group in the female prison is singularly suited to meet the internalized cultural expectations of the female role. It serves the social, psychological, and physiological needs of the female inmates."[45] Through prison homosexual marriage and kinship, Giallombardo believes, female inmates express and fulfill social needs. The cultural orientation of men, in contrast, precludes such groupings; prison "punks" and "fags" are scorned, and the dominant males' homosexual behavior is explained as a temporary adjustment to sexual deprivation.

Giallombardo suggests that in most respects the prison subcultures of men and women are similar, with one major exception: The informal social structure of the female prison helps inmates "resist the destructive effects of imprisonment by creating a substitute universe—a world in which the inmates may preserve an identity that is relevant to life outside the prison." The female inmates are somewhat collectivist, with warmth and mutual aid extended to family and kinship members; male prisoners adapt by self-sufficiency, a convict code, and solidarity with other inmates.[46]

The dispute over whether the subculture of prisoners is due to deprivation or is imported led to some interesting findings in women's institutions. When Esther Heffernan began her study of the District of Columbia Women's Reformatory in Occoquan, Virginia, she expected to find a unitary inmate social structure arising from within the institution, as Clemmer and Sykes had. But Heffernan found no "clear-cut pattern of acceptance or rejection of the inmate system, nor any relatively uniform perception of deprivations." Unlike the male maximum-security institution, Occoquan—like most other prisons for women—has a heterogeneous population with the whole spectrum of offenses. Heffernan demonstrates what Irwin and Cressey only suggest: Prisoners with similar orientations had developed "distinctive norms and values, a pattern of interrelationships and certain roles that served their own prison needs."[47] The typical offender types bring these orientations with them to the prison.

Heffernan discovered three adaptive roles: "square," "the life," and "cool," corresponding to noncriminal, habitual, and professional offenders in the institution. The term "square" in prison, as in the larger community, describes a person who adheres to conventional norms and values. A square is a situational offender, such as a woman who killed her spouse in a moment of rage. She attempts to maintain a conventional life in prison, to gain the respect of officers and fellow inmates, and to be a "good Christian woman." About 50 percent of the prison population are "in the life," and they, too, act in prison as they did on the outside: They are antisocial. These persistent offenders have been involved in prostitution, drugs, numbers rackets, and shoplifting. They have been in prison before and find community with others who have similar experiences. Their role requires them to stand firm against authority. "Cool," a term of general approval in jazz and among street gangs, is applied in the female prison to people who make a "controlled, pleasurable, manipulative response to a situation." They are professionals who "keep busy, play around, stay out of trouble, and get out." They manipulate others and do "easy time" by joining with like-minded inmates to gain as many amenities as they can without risking a short prison stay.[48]

These three role adaptations to incarceration correspond to criminal identities brought in from the outside. Prisoners who assume the various roles join together; thus three subsystems, each with its own perspective, exist within the prison society. Although divided, the inmates at Occoquan try to mitigate the deprivations of imprisonment through their informal social system.

In one of the few recent studies of prison culture, Barbara Owen found that the inmates at the Central California Women's Facility, holding over 4,500 women, developed various styles of doing time. These styles are based on the in-prison experience and are related to the day-to-day business of developing a program of activities and settling in to a routine. She found that one's style of doing time is influenced by the commitment to a deviant identity and the stage of one's criminal and prison career. These facts influence the extent to which an inmate is committed to the "convict code" and participating in "the mix."

The vast majority of inmates Owen observed and interviewed wanted to avoid "the mix"—"behavior that can bring trouble and conflict with staff and other prisoners."[49] A primary feature of "the mix" is anything for which one can lose of good time or can result in being sent to administrative segregation. Being in "the mix" was related to "'homo-secting,' involvement in drugs, fights, and 'being messy,' that is, being involved in conflict and trouble."[50] Owen found most women wanted to do their time and go home, but some "are more at home in prison and do not seem to care if they 'lose time.'" The culture of being "in the mix" is not imported from the outside but is internal to the prison, as some inmates prefer the pursuit of drugs, girlfriends, and fighting.

Male versus Female Subcultures

Research on the subcultures of male and female prisons reveals great similarities but also major differences. Comparisons are complicated by the nature of the research, because most studies have been conducted in single-sex institutions, and theories and concepts first developed in male prisons that have then been applied to female institutions. However, the following facts may help us understand subculture differences:

- Nearly half of male inmates, but only a third of female inmates are serving time for violent offenses.
- There is less violence in prisons for women than in prisons for men.
- Women show greater responsiveness to prison programs.
- Men's prison populations are divided by security levels; most women serve time in facilities where the entire population is mixed.
- Men tend to segregate themselves by race; this is less true with women.
- Men rarely become intimate with their keepers; many women share their lives with officers.

Some critics say that despite these differences "the treatment of imprisoned women is based on a correctional model that is based on muddy assumptions about violent men."[51]

A major difference between the two gender-specific societies relates to interpersonal relationships. In male prisons individuals act for themselves and are evaluated by others according to how they adhere to subculture norms. As James Fox noted in his comparative study of one women's and four men's prisons, men believe they must demonstrate physical strength and consciously avoid any mannerisms that may imply homosexuality. To gain recognition and status within the convict community, the male prisoner must strictly adhere to these values. Men, too, form cliques, but not the family networks found in prisons for women. Male norms emphasize autonomy, self-sufficiency, and the ability to cope with one's own problems, and men are expected to "do their own time." Fox found little sharing in the men's prisons.[52]

Women placed less emphasis on achieving status or recognition within the prisoner community. Fox writes, "They were less likely to impose severe restrictions on the sexual (or emotional) conduct of other members."[53] As noted previously, in prisons for women, close ties seem to exist among small groups akin to extended families. These family groups provide emotional support and share resources. As one female inmate told an interviewer:

> The families sort of try to look out for their own. Like, I have a family here. _____, she's kind of old and she has high blood pressure, and a lot of other things wrong with her, so she's my mother. And if she thinks that I'm getting something that she doesn't like, then we talk about it. I also have a brother, I have a sister, and we all sit and talk. But all the families aren't the same. Ours is sort of calm. _____ believes that we shouldn't get charge sheets, and if one of us gets a charge sheet, it's really something because we normally don't have any. So we try to stay on the cool side. When any of us gets a visit, we all cook together. When we go to the commissary, we put our sheets together and we buy food.[54]

The characteristics of male and female prisoner subcultures have been ascribed to the nurturing, maternal qualities of women. Some critics charge that such an analysis stereotypes female behavior and imputes a biological basis to personality where none exists. Of importance as well is the issue of inmate–inmate violence in male and female institutions. The few data that exist indicate that women are less likely to engage in violent acts against their fellow inmates than are men.[55] In any case, it will be interesting to see whether such gender-specific differences continue to be found among prisoners as the feminist perspective gains influence among researchers and as society comes to view women and men as equals.

Issues in the Incarceration of Women

As noted, the number of incarcerated women has hugely increased over the past ten years. Although departments of corrections have been playing "catch up" to meet the challenge of crowded facilities, demands for education and training, medical services, and methods for dealing with the problems of mothers and their children, persist. We next examine each of these issues and the policy implications they pose for the future.

Formal training in the skills needed to be a beautician is among the vocational programs found in many prisons. Critics charge that training programs in women's prisons are for jobs that are stereotypically "feminine."

Educational and Vocational Training Programs

A major criticism of women's prisons is that they lack the variety of vocational and educational programs usually available in male institutions and that existing programs tend to conform to stereotypes of "feminine" occupations — cosmetology, food service, housekeeping, sewing.[56] Such training does not correspond to the wider opportunities available to women in today's world. The programs also are less ambitious than those in men's prisons, which offer training for "real-world" jobs. Both men's and women's facilities usually offer educational programs so inmates can become literate and earn general equivalency diplomas (GEDs). However, unlike many facilities for men, few prisons for women offer college classes. The importance of vocational and educational opportunities during incarceration is underscored by the fact that on release most women must support themselves and many are financially responsible for children.

Research conducted in the 1970s by Ruth Glick and Virginia Neto[57] and by the editors of the *Yale Law Journal*[58] confirmed that fewer programs were offered in women's than in men's institutions and that the existing programs lacked variety. Merry Morash and her colleagues noted changes during the 1980s, but they too found gender stereotypes shaped vocational programs.[59] The American Correctional Association reported in 1990 that there are few work assignments for incarcerated women, but those that do exist teach marketable jobs skills.[60]

Better-paying employment opportunities in America are increasingly open only to people with the education necessary to meet the needs of a complex workplace. However, the educational level of most female offenders limits their access to these occupations. In some institutions less than half of the inmates have completed high school. Some corrections systems assign these women to classes so they can earn a GED, and other inmates can do college work through correspondence study or courses offered in the institution.

Critics of corrections have pointed out that although the female workforce in the broader community has greatly expanded since the 1970s and women now occupy positions formerly reserved for men, female prisoners are not being prepared for such jobs. Some correctional administrators say many inmates are not career-minded or interested in being self-supporting, but rather aspire to the traditional roles of wife and mother.

But the world the released offender will enter is unlikely to contain many men willing and able to support her and her children. Most women prisoners have no one to depend on but themselves. When they are released, they must find a job that will provide income and advancement. Without means of support, the released offender faces a life dependent on welfare or engaged in illegal activity to her and her children's needs. Programs to train offenders for postrelease vocations, as well as incentives to pursue new roles, are essential if offenders are to succeed in the community.

Medical Services

Women's prisons also lack proper medical services. Yet women usually have more serious health problems because of their socioeconomic status and limited access to preventive medical care. Compared to men, they have a higher incidence of asthma, drug abuse, diabetes, and heart disorders, and many women also have gynecological problems.[61] A higher proportion of women than men report receiving medical services in prison, yet women's institutions are less likely than men's to have a full-time medical staff or hospital facilities.[62]

HIV, tuberculosis, drug addiction, and mental illness affect women prisoners more than men. A national survey revealed that a higher percentage of female than male state prison inmates (4.0 percent versus 2.3 percent) tested positive for HIV. In addition, more than 11 percent of females had been confined overnight in a mental hospital before incarceration, and 54 percent had used drugs during the month before entering prison.[63]

Pregnant women also need special medical and nutritional resources. Surveys show that about 25 percent of incarcerated women were pregnant on admission to prison or had given birth during the previous year. However, a survey found that less than half received prenatal care, and only 15 percent received special diets and counseling.[64] There are no national data on the annual number of babies born in American jails and prisons, but a study in eight states found that 9 percent of female inmates had given birth behind bars.[65]

Pregnancies raise numerous issues for correctional policy, including special diets, abortion rights, access to delivery room and medical personnel, and length of time that newborns can remain with incarcerated mothers. Most pregnant inmates have characteristics (older than 35, history of drug abuse, prior multiple abortions, and sexually transmitted diseases) that indicate the potential for a high-risk pregnancy requiring special medical care.

Imprisonment can be very stressful for pregnant women as well. Not only do they have to cope with the physical aspects of incarceration, but they must also endure psychological stress over whether to have an abortion, who should care for the child after its birth, and separation from the child. Many prison systems are allowing nursing infants to stay with their mothers, creating in-prison nurseries, developing special living quarters for pregnant women and new mothers, instituting counseling programs, and improving standards of medical care.[66]

Saying that corrections must "defuse the time bomb," Leslie Acoca argues the failure to provide women inmates with basic preventive and medical treatments such as immunizations, breast cancer screenings, and management of chronic diseases "is resulting in the development of more serious health problems that are exponentially more expensive to treat." She says that poor medical care for the incarcerated merely shifts costs to overburdened community health care systems after release.[67]

Mothers and Their Children

Of greatest concern to incarcerated women is the fate of their children. Almost 80 percent of female inmates are mothers and on average have two dependent children. Thus on any given day, 167,000 American children—two-thirds under 10 years old—have mothers in jail or prison.[68] One study found that roughly half of these children do not see their mothers the entire time they are in prison.[69]

Because about 76 percent of incarcerated mothers were single caretakers of minor children before they entered prison, they do not have husbands or male partners able and willing to make a home for the children.[70] These children are placed with other relatives or in state-funded foster care while their mothers are in prison.[71] In a study of 133 inmates and their children, Phyllis Jo Baunach found that children are most often cared for by their maternal grandmothers. The knowledge that their children were with their grandmother gave these inmates peace of mind; they believed that

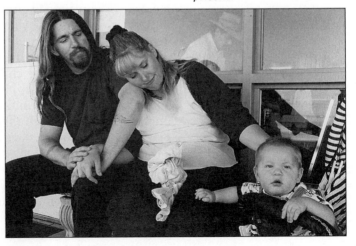

Shirley Carone and David Smith with David Jr. during visiting hours at Central California Women's Facility. That David not only takes care of their son but married Shirley and visits her regularly is most unusual in the world of women's prisons.

the youngsters were well cared for and that they would have no difficulty regaining custody when they were released. Baunach found that a higher proportion of the children of African-American inmates than of white inmates were cared for by relatives.[72] When inmates had no relatives or friends to assume the child care role, the children often were put up for adoption or placed in foster care. Having the fate of their children decided by welfare workers was traumatic for both mothers and children.

Anxiety about children bothers all imprisoned mothers, especially if strangers are caring for their children. In a survey of prison mothers, Acoca found that 13 percent had at least one child requiring special education, 10 percent said one or more of their children had been arrested as a juvenile and 15 percent said one or more had become a ward of the court.[73]

Enforced separation of children from their mothers can be devastating for both children and mothers. It is heart wrenching and stress inducing—and not fully shared by male inmates. Baunach found that regardless of race or age, women expressed guilt and shame that they had committed crimes that separated them from their children.[74] Those with drug problems may realize for the first time what their behavior has done to their children. Many are concerned about the eventual reunion, fearing that neither they nor the children will be able to readjust to each other after the long separation.

In most states babies born in prison must be placed with a family member or a social agency within three weeks of birth. However, critics have expressed great concern about such early termination of mother-infant bonding, thought to be so crucial for human development, and some innovative programs now let them stay together longer. For example, at the Women's Correctional Institution at Bedford Hills in New York, women move to the nursery for the last few months of pregnancy. They give birth at a nearby hospital and return to live in the nursery wing, caring for their infants for up to a year. Their primary responsibility is to care for their children and to learn parenting skills.[75] The story of Maria, who gave birth while incarcerated, is told in the Focus box.

Imprisoned mothers have difficulty maintaining contact with their children over the miles that separate them. Visits are short and infrequent, and phone calls are uncertain and irregular; and when the children do visit the prison, the surroundings are strange and intimidating. In some institutions children are even required to conform to the rules governing adult visitation: no physical contact and strict limits. Other correctional facilities, however, seek ways to help mothers maintain links to their children and nurture the relationships. For example, the Dwight Correctional Center in Illinois schedules weekend retreats similar to camping trips for women and their children. In their study of mothers in one institution, Susan Datesman and Gloria Cales found that 65 percent had visited with at least some of their children and that most kept in contact through phone calls and letters—70 percent at least once a week. The mothers emphasized the importance of visiting to maintain and strengthen relationships with children. One commented, "The main advantages of the visits are tightening up the relationships, watching your children grow, your children watching you grow, how you've changed, being able to love one another."[76]

Programs to address the needs of imprisoned mothers and their children are being designed. In some states children may meet with their mothers at almost any time, for extended periods, and in playrooms or nurseries where physical contact is possible. Some states transport children to visit their mothers; some institutions even let children stay overnight with their mothers. In both South Dakota and Nebraska, children may stay for up to five days a month. Four of the forty prisons that Virginia Neto and LaNelle Marie Bainer studied had family visiting programs that let the inmate, her legal husband, and her children be together, often in a mobile home or apartment, for up to seventy-two hours.[77]

The emphasis on community corrections as it developed in the 1970s gave rise to programs in which youngsters could live with their mothers in halfway houses. These programs have not expanded as much as expected, however, in part because children

FOCUS   Maria's Story

Maria is a soft-spoken woman in her mid-30s, of mixed African-American and Hispanic descent. Her slimness belies the fact that she delivered her second child less than three months ago in a nearby hospital.

Maria believes that she is extremely fortunate compared to most of the other pregnant and postpartum inmates who live in her housing unit. She is one of a handful of prison mothers participating in a small local program that provides foster mothers from the surrounding community to care for newborns. The foster mothers bring the children to the prison regularly for visits and help prepare both mother and child to live together successfully after the mother's release.

Without this program, Maria would have lost contact with her baby during the first months of his life because the child would have been sent immediately to a child welfare agency in Maria's county of commitment, hundreds of miles away from the prison. Maria describes the intense depression of the pregnant women she lives with who cannot participate in the program because of its limited size. She says that not knowing what will happen to their infants after delivery is the "worst things" for these women.

For Maria, the most difficult aspect of childbearing while incarcerated was returning from the hospital to the prison 10 hours after delivery without her baby and without medication to dry up her milk. She reports that in the days fol-

lowing the birth, her breasts became painfully engorged with milk and that she consequently developed an infection and high fever. She observes that other postpartum inmates in her unit have experienced the same problem.

Maria recalls that on the day of her last arrest she went to a local store to put some baby clothes on layaway because she had recently discovered that she was pregnant. She entered the store with her boyfriend who proceeded to steal a stack of Levi 501 jeans, which he hoped to sell for money to buy drugs. Maria claims that she had stopped using drugs due to her pregnancy and fear of HIV infection and that she had begged her boyfriend before they went shopping not to jeopardize their freedom by shoplifting. When the boyfriend was caught in the act of stealing, she was arrested also.

Because of her extensive history of past arrests and her status as a parolee and because she would not inform on her boyfriend, Maria was convicted for shoplifting and violation of parole and was sentenced to two years in state prison. Her boyfriend was not convicted and served no time for his offense. . . . Once she entered prison, her boyfriend [the father of her second child] severed all contact with her and has made no inquiries regarding their baby.

SOURCE: Leslie Acoca, "Hearts on the Ground: Violent Victimization and Other Themes in the Lives of Women Prisoners," *Corrections Management Quarterly*, 1, Spring 1997, p. 50.

upset prison routine. However, many states have furlough programs that let inmates visit relatives and children in their homes during holiday periods and some weekends.

Release to the Community

The limited data indicate that women on parole are just as successful as men. However, on release from prison women seem to have a greater variety of problems than men, are less confident in their ability to cope with those problems—and are less hesitant about admitting they need help. Because many are heads of households, they need extensive social services to help manage finances, work-related problems, child care, and household management; it is not enough for correctional workers to help them find employment and housing, as for men. In fact, parole officers have complained that female offenders in the community make many more demands on them than do male offenders.

Women need more postrelease training and support than men—not only employment help but also, perhaps, counseling for drug and alcohol abuse and help reestablishing family relationships. Some women have the support of relatives, but many are on their own and must care for young children. Even more burdensome is society's reaction to such women as criminals, a stigma very hard to shake.

Summary

The criminal justice system treats the female offender quite unlike her male counterpart. The differences may be traced to the level and type of female criminality, society's perceptions of the role of women, the relatively small number of women in the offender population, special needs of women with children, and limits on women's economic opportunities. At a time when the women's movement has focused national attention on the inequities to which women are subjected, the plight of the female offender has finally aroused the concern of correctional officials, legislators, and support groups. That only about 7 percent of the prison population is female has long been used to justify the limited allocation of resources to these offenders.

Early nineteenth-century reformers were appalled to find that women were not separated from men in penal institutions. With the establishment of separate institutions for women administered by women, the goal shifted to creating reformatories that would inculcate "feminine" habits by training in domestic skills. Reformers now push for vocational and other services for female inmates on a par with services offered to men.

Research on male prisoner subcultures has been replicated for women. Female inmates often confine interpersonal relationships to a close group of friends, or pseudo-families. About 80 percent of incarcerated women are mothers, and constantly concerned about separation from their children. Some institutions help women maintain contact with their children, but many prisons still make no such effort.

Gains made by women in the United States since the early 1970s might lead one to expect that differences between prisons for men and women have diminished. Some new resources have been provided, but these gains have often been offset by the increase in the prison population and by budgetary constraints. Female offenders may not be quite so overlooked as a generation ago, but they still receive far fewer services and less attention than their male counterparts. ■

For Discussion

1. How has fragmentation of corrections among federal, state, and local governments affected the quality of services for female offenders?

2. How might the unequal treatment of male and female offenders be rationalized? Should female offenders be given the same types of sentences as are given to men for similar crimes?

3. Imagine you are the administrator of a women's correctional center. What problems would you expect to encounter that are characteristic of the incarceration of women? How would you handle these problems?

4. What parental rights should prisoners have? Should children be allowed to live in correctional facilities with their mothers? What problems would this practice create?

5. How do the social structures of male and female correctional institutions differ? Why do you think they differ thus?

For Further Reading

Baunach, Phyllis Jo. *Mothers in Prison.* New Brunswick, NJ: Transaction, 1985. Represents one of the few studies to examine the relationship between female inmates and their children.

Belknap, Joanne. *The Invisible Woman: Gender, Crime and Justice.* Belmont, CA: Wadsworth, 1996. Gives an overview of the treatment of women by the criminal justice system.

Freedman, Estelle B. *Their Sisters' Keepers.* Ann Arbor: University of Michigan Press, 1981. Traces the history of the development of prisons for women in the United States.

Rafter, Nichole Hahn. *Partial Justice: Women, Prisons and Social Control,* 2nd ed. New Brunswick, NJ: Transaction, 1990. Recounts the history of prisons for women in the United States, with two new chapters on the "parity movement" and responses to sex discrimination against the incarcerated.

Rierden, Andi. *The Farm: Life Inside a Women's Prison.* Amherst, MA: University of Massachusetts Press, 1997. A case study of changes in the inmate population and administration during the late 1980s to early 1990s at Connecticut's Niantic Correctional Institution.

Notes

1. *The New York Times,* September 13, 1991, p. B2.

2. Joanne Belknap, *The Invisible Woman: Gender, Crime, and Justice* (Belmont, CA: Wadsworth, 1996), p. 97.

3. Nichole Hahn Rafter, "Gender and Justice: The Equal Protection Issue," in Lynne Goodstein and Doris MacKenzie, eds., *The American Prison* (New York: Plenum Press, 1989), p. 89.

4. Department of Justice, Bureau of Justice Statistics, *Correctional Populations in the United States, 1995* (Washington, DC: U.S. Government Printing Office, 1997), p. 54.

5. Mark S. Fleisher, Richard H. Rison, and David W. Helman, "Female Inmates: A Growing Constituency in the Federal Bureau of Prisons," *Corrections Management Quarterly,* 1, Fall 1997, pp. 28–35.

6. *The New York Times Magazine,* June 2, 1996, p.35.

7. Department of Justice, Bureau of Justice Statistics, *Bulletin,* January, 1998.

8. Barbara Owen and Barbara Bloom, "Profiling Women Prisoners: Findings from National Surveys and a California Sample," *The Prison Journal,* 75, June 1995, p. 166.

9. Clifford Krauss, "Women Doing Crime, Women Doing Time," *The New York Times,* July 3, 1994, p. 3.

10. Department of Justice, Bureau of Justice Statistics, *Sourcebook of Criminal Justice Statistics* (Washington, DC: U.S. Government Printing Office, 1997), p. 380.

11. Owen and Bloom, p. 167.

12. Freda Adler, "Crime, an Equal Opportunity Employer," *Trial Magazine,* January 1977, p. 31.

13. Owen and Bloom, p. 182.

14. Nichole Rafter, *Partial Justice: Women, Prisons and Social Control* (New Brunswick, NJ: Transaction, 1990), p. 178. See also Krauss.

15. R. Pitman, *Elizabeth Fry* (New York: Greenwood, [1884] 1969), p. 55.

16. Lucia Zedner, "Wayward Sisters: The Prison for Women," in Norval Morris and David J. Rothman, eds., *Oxford History of the Prison,* (New York: Oxford University Press, 1995), p. 333.

17. Feeley and Little point out that for much of the 1700s almost half of those indicted for felony offenses in London were women. The proportion dropped in the 1800s as the roles of women changed in the economy, the family, and society. See Malcolm M. Feeley and Deborah L. Little, "The Vanishing Female: The Decline of Women in the Criminal Process, 1687–1912," *Law and Society Review,* 25, 1991, pp. 720–757.

18. Davis Lewis, *From Newgate to Dannemora: The Rise of the Penitentiary in New York, 1796–1888* (Ithaca, NY: Cornell University Press, 1965), pp. 158–159.

19. Nichole Hahn Rafter, "Equality or Difference?" *Federal Prisons Journal,* 3, Spring, 1992, p. 17.

20. Estelle B. Freedman, *Their Sisters' Keepers* (Ann Arbor: University of Michigan Press, 1981), p. 15.

21. Zedner, p. 353.

22. Sara F. Keely, "The Organization and Discipline of the Indiana Women's Prison" (proceedings of the 58th Annual Congress of the National Prison Association, 1898), p. 275, quoted in Rose Giallombardo, *Society of Women* (New York: Wiley, 1966), p. 7.

23. Maud Ballington Booth, "The Shadow of Prison," proceedings of the 58th Annual Congress of the National Prison Association, 1898, p. 275, quoted in Giallombardo, p. 46.

24. Nichole Hahn Rafter, "Prisons for Women, 1790–1980, " in Michael Tonry and Norval Morris, eds., *Crime and Justice,* vol. 5 (Chicago: University of Chicago Press, 1983), p. 147.

25. Freedman, *Their Sisters' Keepers,* p. 69.

26. Rafter, "Prisons for Women," p. 165.

27. Lewis, p. 213.

28. Rafter, "Prisons for Women," p. 165.

29. Rafter, "Equality or Difference?" p. 19.

30. Belknap, p. 98.

31. Dorothy S. McClellan, "Disparity and Discipline of Male and Female Inmates in Texas Prisons," *Women and Criminal Justice,* 5, 1994, pp. 71–97.

32. Coramae Richey Mann, *Female Crime and Delinquency* (Tuscaloosa: University of Alabama Press, 1984).

33. Department of Justice, Bureau of Justice Statistics, *Special Report,* March 1994.

34. Ibid.

35. Doris Lawton MacKenzie, Jaems W. Robinson, and Carol S. Campbell, "Long-Term Incarceration of Female Offenders: Prison Adjustment and Coping," in Timothy J. Flanagan, ed., *Long-Term Imprisonment* (Thousand Oaks, CA: Sage, 1995), pp. 128–137.

36. Ibid., p. 7.

37. Ibid.

38. Leslie Acoca, "Hearts on the Ground: Violent Victimization and Other Themes in the Lives of Women Prisoners," *Correctional Management Quarterly,* 1, Spring 1997, pp. 44–55.

39. Andi Rierden, *The Farm: Life Inside a Women's Prison* (Amherst, MA: University of Massachusetts Press, 1997), p. 18.

40. Esther Heffernan, *Making It in Prison* (New York: Wiley, 1972), p. 88; MacKenzie, Robinson, and Campbell, p. 129.

41. David Ward and Gene G. Kassebaum, *Women's Prisons: Sex and Social Structure* (Hawthorne, NY: Aldine, 1965), p. 140.

42. Imogene L. Moyer, "Differential Social Structures and Homosexuality Among Women in Prisons," *Virginia Social Science Journal,* April 1978, pp. 13–14, 17–19.

43. Robert G. Leger, "Lesbianism Among Women Prisoners: Participants and Nonparticipants," *Criminal Justice and Behavior,* 14, December 1987, p. 463.

44. Rose Giallombardo, *Society of Women: A Study of a Women's Prison* (New York: Wiley, 1966), p. 6; John Irwin and Donald Cressey, "Thieves, Convicts, and the Inmate Culture," *Social Problems,* 10, Fall 1962, p. 145.

45. Giallombardo, p. 185.

46. Ibid., pp. 102, 103.

47. Heffernan, pp. 16, 17.

48. Ibid., pp. 41–42.

49. Barbara Owen, *"In The Mix": Struggle and Survival in a Women's Prison* (Albany, NY: State University of New York Press, 1998), p.179.

50. Owen, *"In the Mix,"* p. 179.

51. *The New York Times Magazine,* June 2, 1996, p. 35.

52. James G. Fox, *Organizational and Racial Conflict in Maximum-Security Prisons* (Lexington, MA: Lexington Books, 1982), pp. 100–102.

53. Ibid., p. 100.

54. Ibid. pp. 100–101.

55. Candace Kruttschnitt and Sharon Krmpotich, "Aggressive Behavior Among Female Inmates: An Exploratory Study," *Justice Quarterly,* 7, June 1990, p. 371.

56. Clarice Feinman, "An Historical Overview of the Treatment of Incarcerated Women: Myths and Realities of Rehabilitation," *The Prison Journal,* Autumn–Winter, 1983, pp. 12–24.

57. Ruth M. Glick and Virginia V. Neto, *National Study of Women's Programs* (Washington, DC: National Institute of Law Enforcement and Criminal Justice, 1977).

58. Ralph R. Arditi, Frederick Goldbert, Jr., M. Martin Hartle, John H. Peters, and William Phelps, "The Sexual Segregation of American Prisons," *Yale Law Journal,* 82, 1973, p. 1229.

59. Merry Morash, Robin N. Haarr, and Lila Rucker, "A Comparison of Programming for Women and Men in U.S. Prisons in the 1980s," *Crime and Delinquency,* 40, April 1994, pp. 197–221.

60. American Correctional Association, *The Female Offender: What Does the Future Hold?* (Alexandria, VA: Kirby Lithographic Company, 1990).

61. Lawrence Bershad, "Discriminatory Treatment of the Female Offender in the Criminal Justice System," *Boston College Law Review,* 26, 1985, pp. 389–438; S. Steven Yang, "The Unique Treatment Needs of Female Substance Abusers: The Obligation of the Criminal Justice System to Provide Parity Services," *Medicine and Law,* 9, 1990, pp. 1018–1027.

62. Bershad; Yang.

63. Department of Justice, Bureau of Justice Statistics, *Bulletin,* August 1995; *Sourcebook of Criminal Justice Statistics* (Washington, DC: U.S. Government Printing Office, 1997), p. 553.

64. John D. Wooldredge and Kimberly Masters, "Confronting Problems Faced by Pregnant Inmates in State Prisons," *Crime and Delinquency,* 39, Apri, 1993, p. 195.

65. *The New York Times,* November 30, 1992, p. A10.

66. Wooldredge and Masters, "Confronting Problems," p. 197.

67. Leslie Acoca, "Defusing the Time Bomb: Understanding and Meeting the Growing Health Care Needs of Incarcerated Women in America," *Crime and Delinquency,* 44, January 1998, pp. 49–69.

68. Department of Justice, Bureau of Justice Statistics, *Special Report,* March 1994, p. 6.

69. *The New York Times,* December 27, 1992, p. D3.

70. Leslie Acoca, "Hearts on the Ground: Violent Victimization and Other Themes in the Lives of Women Prisoners," *Corrections Management Quarterly,* 1, Spring 1997, pp. 44–55.

71. Denise Johnston, "Child Custody Issues of Women Prisoners: A Preliminary Report from the CHICAS Project," *The Prison Journal,* 75, June 1995, pp. 222–239.

72. Phyllis J. Baunach, "You Can't Be a Mother and Be in Prison . . . Can You?" in Barbara Raffel Price and Natolie J. Sokoloff, eds., *The Criminal Justice system and Women* (New York: Clark Boardman, 1982), pp. 155–169.

73. Acoca, p. 44.

74. Phyllis Jo Baunach, *Mothers in Prison* (New Brunswick, NJ: Transaction, 1985), p. 75.

75. Ibid.

76. Susan K. Datesman and Gloria L. Cales, "'I'm Still the Same Mommy': Maintaining the Mother–Child Relationship in Prison," *The Prison Journal,* 63, Autumn–Winter 1983, p. 147.

77. Virginia Neto and LaNelle Marie Bainer, "Mother and Wife Locked Up: A Day with the Family," *The Prison Journal,* 3, Autumn–Winter, 1983, p. 124.

CHAPTER THIRTEEN
Institutional Management

As Philip Carvalho and three of his fellow officers in the Massachusetts maximum-security prison at Walpole eat lunch together, their conversation is devoted almost entirely to shop talk. It is the small talk of infantry GIs dissecting the foibles of the higher echelons back at division headquarters.

"If the people out front who make up the rules had to come in here and enforce them, they'd never make them up. . . .

Correctional officers must face the problem of keeping order and preventing escapes. But they must also rely on a group of captives to do most of the work in the daily operation of the institution. This is a tall order!

"Yeah, they ought to have an officer out there with 'em when they make up those damn things. . . .

"Yeah, yeah, yeah, but then they'd pick some guy who never worked in the population . . . you want to bet on it . . . that's what they'd do. . . . "

"If you run this institution by the book they give you, you'd have a riot. You can't do it. It's impossible. Hey, they tell you a guy can't go to another tier to see another guy even if that guy's his brother."[1]

The prison differs from almost every other institution or organization in modern society. Not only are its physical features different, but also it is a place where a group of people devotes itself to managing a group of captives. Prisoners are required to live according to the rules of their keepers, and their movements are sharply restricted. Unlike managers of other governmental agencies, prison managers

- Cannot select their clients
- Have little or no control over the release of their clients
- Must deal with clients who are there against their will
- Must rely on clients to do most of the work in the daily operation of the institution and to do so by coercion and without fair compensation for their work
- Must depend on the maintenance of satisfactory relationships between clients and staff

With these unique characteristics, how should a prison be run? What rules should guide administrators?

Remember that a wide range of institutions fall under the heading of "prison." Some are treatment centers serving a relatively small number of clients; others are sprawling agricultural complexes; still others are ranches or forest camps. But most prisons have comparable management structures and offender populations.

In this chapter we look at the ways in which institutional resources are organized to achieve certain goals. At a minimum, prisoners must be clothed, fed, kept healthy, provided with recreation, protected from one another, and maintained in custody. In addition, administrators may be charged with offering rehabilitative programs and using inmate labor in agriculture or industry. To accomplish all this in a community of free individuals would be taxing. To do so when the population consists of some of the most antisocial people in the society is surely a Herculean undertaking. To understand how administrators approach these problems we will address the following Questions for Inquiry.

Questions FOR INQUIRY

1. What are the characteristics of the formal organization of a prison?

2. How are prisons governed?

3. What roles do correctional officers play?

4. What limits officers' use of power?

Formal Organization

The University of Texas, the General Motors Corporation, and the California State Prison at Folsom are very different organizations, each created to achieve certain goals. Differing organizational structures let managers coordinate the various parts of the university, auto manufacturer, and prison in the interests of scholarship, production, and corrections.

A **formal organization** is deliberately established for particular ends. If accomplishing an objective requires collective effort, people set up an organization to help coordinate activities and to provide incentives for others to join. Thus in a university, a business, and a correctional institution, the goals, rules, and roles that define the relations between the organization members (the organization chart) have been formally established.

Leadership is the crucial element of governance. Wardens find that "management by walking around" is an effective way of learning what concerns inmates and staff.

Amitai Etzioni, a theorist of administration, developed the concept of compliance as the basis for comparing types of organizations. **Compliance** is the way someone behaves in accordance with an order or directive given by another person. In compliance relationships, the order is backed up by one's ability to induce or influence another person to carry out one's directives.[2] This concept helps us recognize that people do what others ask because those others have the means — remunerative, normative, or coercive — to get the subjects to comply. **Remunerative power** is based on material resources, such as wages, fringe benefits, or goods, that people exchange for compliance. **Normative power** rests on symbolic rewards that leaders manipulate through ritual, allocation of honors, and social esteem. **Coercive power** depends on applying or threatening physical force to inflict pain, restrict movement, or control other aspects of a person's life.

Etzioni argues that all formal organizations employ all three types of power, but the degree to which they rely on any one of them varies with the desired goal. Thus, although the University of Texas probably relies mainly on normative power in its relationships with students and the public, it relies on remunerative power in relationships with faculty and staff. Although General Motors is organized primarily for manufacturing purposes, it may appeal to "team spirit" or "safety employee of the month" campaigns to meet its goals. And although the warden at Folsom may rely on remunerative power to manage staff and on normative power to encourage organization members to make it the best correctional facility in the United States, in working with prisoners he relies primarily on coercive power. The presence in high-custody institutions of "highly alienated lower participants" (prisoners), Etzioni says, makes the application or threat of force necessary to ensure compliance.[3]

Coercive power undergirds all prison relationships, but correctional institutions also vary in the extent to which physical force is used and in the degree to which the inmates are alienated. Correctional institutions may be placed on a continuum of custody or treatment goals. At one extreme is the highly authoritarian prison, where the movement of inmates is greatly restricted, staff–inmate relationships are formally structured, and the prime emphasis is on custody. In such an institution treatment goals take a back seat. At the other end of the continuum is the institution whose dominant goal is treatment, where the therapeutic aspect of the physical and social environment is stressed. Here the staff collaborates with inmates to overcome the inmates' problems. Between these ideal types lie the great majority of correctional institutions.

---

formal organization

A structure established for influencing behavior to achieve particular ends.

---

compliance

Obedience to an order or request.

---

remunerative power

The ability to obtain compliance in exchange for material resources.

---

normative power

The ability to obtain compliance by manipulating symbolic rewards.

---

coercive power

The ability to obtain compliance by the application or threat of physical force.

However, this custody–treatment continuum may neglect other aspects of imprisonment. As noted in Chapter 10, Charles Logan notes that we expect a lot of prisons: "to correct the incorrigible, rehabilitate the wretched, deter the determined, restrain the dangerous, and punish the wicked." He has proposed that we analyze prisons according to the goals of the "confinement model." In this model the purpose of imprisonment is to "punish offenders—fairly and justly—through lengths of confinement proportionate to the gravity of the offense."[4] Thus the mission with respect to prisoners has five features:

1. *Keep them in:* The facility must be secure, such that inmates cannot escape and contraband cannot be smuggled in.
2. *Keep them safe:* Inmates and staff need to be kept safe, not only from each other but from various environmental hazards as well.
3. *Keep them in line:* Prisons run on rules, and the ability of prison administrators to enforce compliance is central to the quality of confinement.
4. *Keep them healthy:* Inmates are entitled to have care for their medical needs.
5. *Keep them busy:* Constructive activity through work, recreation, education, and treatment programs are antidotes to idleness.[5]

All these dimensions of prison work must be carried out as fairly and as efficiently as possible, without causing undue suffering. The state may run correctional institutions with other goals as well, but these are the main models.

The Organizational Structure

For any organization to be effective, its leaders and staff must know the rules and procedures, the lines of authority, and the channels of communication. Organizations vary in their organizational hierarchy, in their allocation of discretion, in the effort expended on administrative problems, and in the nature of the top leadership.

Concepts of Organization The formal administrative structure of a prison is a hierarchy of staff positions, each with its own duties and responsibilities, each linked to the others in a logical chain of command. As Figure 13.1 shows, the warden is ultimately responsible for the operation of the institution. Deputy wardens oversee the functional divisions of the prison: management, custody, programs, industry and agriculture. Under each deputy are middle managers and line staff who operate the departments. Functions are subdivided according to prison size and population. For a description of the warden's job, see the Workperspective.

Figure 13.1 Formal Organization for a Prison for Adult Felons

The formal organization of an institution may say little about the political and informal relationships among staff members that really govern how the prison operates.

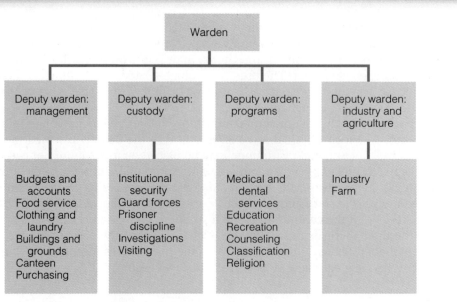

WORK PERSPECTIVE

Pamela K. Withrow

Warden, Michigan Reformatory

Becoming a warden was not my career aspiration. While in community college I was interested in criminal justice, but at that time it was a nontraditional career for women, and my counselors encouraged me to go to law school instead. So I entered a prelaw program at Michigan State University, earning a multidisciplinary social science bachelor's degree with emphases in psychology, sociology, and philosophy. Afterward I attended the University of Michigan School of Law for one semester, but financial circumstances dictated that I find a job. I looked for one in the field of criminal justice. The motivation for that choice was simple: my undergraduate education had been financed by the federal government's "LEAP" program, the education component of the Law Enforcement Assistance Administration (LEAA). Under LEAP at that time, not only could law enforcement workers attend college at no cost, those not yet in the field had their books and tuition subsidized, with all loans forgiven if the student subsequently worked in the criminal justice field for at least four years. A free college education was a powerful motivator for my choice of jobs!

My initial position was as a prison counselor for the Michigan Department of Corrections (DOC). As a welfare mother, I was hired under another federal program, WIC, which paid my salary for the first six months as an incentive for the agency to hire welfare recipients. My job was in the Corrections Camp Program, screening prisoner files for eligibility for community programs. This was excellent for training a new employee; I often noticed minor details in a prisoner's file that could have public safety implications. For example, occasionally I discovered that someone already at a minimum-security campus should be transferred to a secure prison.

I later worked for a year as an analyst in the planning section of the DOC central office, then as the supervisor of Camp Brighton, then as the warden's administrative assistant at the State Prison of Southern Michigan (commonly called Jackson Prison), and then as assistant deputy for housing at the same prison. In 1983 I was appointed warden at the Dunes Correctional Facility near Holland. This was the first time a woman had headed a state prison housing adult males in Michigan. In 1986 I moved on to the Michigan Reformatory, where I continue to serve as warden. Michigan Reformatory, the oldest prison in the state, has a capacity of approximately 1,200 prisoners. It is a close-security institution for young male offenders under age 26 who have unusually long sentences, are considered escape risks, or were unmanageable in other institutions.

The warden's job is much like that of a small-town mayor. Although you're not voted into office, staff or prisoner discontent can certainly result in your ouster! This is certainly true in that most prisons are organized by departments, with a hierarchical and often military-style chain of command ultimately reporting to the warden. But I like the mayoral analogy because prisons must provide almost all the goods and services a small town must make available to those who live and work there. These include the basics like the structure itself and heat, water, light, food, and clothing. Also, given the population living there, a large "police force"—corrections officers and their supervisors—is needed.

Although discussions of prison operations tend to focus on the prisoners, the most difficult decisions I make have to do with staff. The selection and promotion of qualified and ethical staff is critical, of course, but we usually have an employment record to assist with those decisions. The much more difficult task is dealing with staff members who are dishonest, who willfully violate the rules, or who simply prove to be unqualified. I've been a warden fifteen years as I write this, so I can speak with hard experience. Staff members have resigned in lieu of the discipline I would otherwise have had to impose. I have fired a few others for overfamiliarity with prisoners, excessive use of force, or involvement with drugs or alcohol. Prison staff function as a close-knit family, so it is very painful to remove personnel. You are not only letting that person go, but you're affecting the lives of co-workers and the employee's family. Worst of all, the offenders for whom we're supposed to be role models always discover the details of the dismissal and use that information to support their flawed belief that "everyone is dishonest; we just got caught." Nevertheless the integrity of the system requires that we discharge major violators to demonstrate to staff and prisoners that irresponsible behavior has serious consequences. So it must be done, but doing it is a more difficult part of the job than the very long hours I seem to have to put in to stay on top of things. The hours matter little when the work is as interesting and exciting as that provided by this career.

Three concepts explain the functioning of hierarchically structured organizations: unity of command, chain of command, and span of control. **Unity of command** is the idea that it is most efficient for a subordinate to report to only one superior. If a worker must respond to orders from two or more superiors, chaos ensues. Unity of command is tied to the second concept, **chain of command.** The person at the top of the organization cannot oversee everything, he or she must rely on lower-ranking staff to pass directives down. For example, the warden asks the deputy warden to have custody conduct a shakedown; the deputy warden passes the directive to the captain of the guard, who then has the lieutenant in charge of a particular shift carry out the search. The term **span of control** refers to the extent of supervision by one person. If, for example, there are many educational and treatment programs in a correctional institution, the deputy warden for programs may not be able to oversee them all effectively. This deputy warden's span of control is stretched so far that a reorganization and further division of responsibilities may be required.

Two other concepts clarify the organization of correctional institutions: line and staff. **Line personnel** are directly concerned with furthering the institution's goals. They have direct contact with the prisoners—the custody force, industry and agricultural supervisors, counselors, and medical technicians. **Staff personnel** support line personnel. They usually work under the deputy warden for management, handling accounting, training, purchasing, and so on.

The custodial employees, who make up over 60 percent of the personnel, normally are organized in a military-style hierarchy, from deputy warden to captain down to correctional officer. The professional personnel for the management, program, and industry functions (about 25 percent of the personnel), such as clinicians, teachers, and industry supervisors, are not part of the regular custodial organizational structure and have little in common with the custodial employees. All employees answer to the warden, but the treatment personnel and the civilian supervisors of the workshops have their own titles and salary scales. Their responsibilities do not extend to providing special services to the custodial employees. The top medical and educational personnel may formally report to the warden but in fact look to the central office of the department of corrections for leadership.

The multiple goals and separate employee lines of command often are a source of contention and ambiguity. In the larger prisons a sub-bureaucracy develops for each functional division, and the various divisions compete with one another to obtain resources, schedule inmates' activities, and use their labor.

The Warden The attitude a warden brings to the job has a huge effect on the organization. In the not-too-distant past the prison warden was an autocrat who ran the institution without direction from departments of corrections or intrusion of courts, labor unions, or prisoner support groups.[6]

Today's warden is the institution's main contact with the outside world. Responsible for operating the prison, he or she normally reports to the deputy commissioner for institutions in the central office of the department of corrections. When the warden's attention and energy are directed outward (to the central office, parole board, or legislature), daily operation of the prison is delegated to a deputy, usually the person in charge of custody. In recent years wardens in most states have lost much of their autonomy to managers in the central office who handle such matters as budgets, research and program development, public information, and legislative relations. The warden's job security, however, still rests on his or her ability to run the institution efficiently. At the first sign of trouble the warden may be looking for a new job, and in some states the top management of corrections seems constantly to be in flux. As former warden and correctional official George Bronson explains, today's prison warden must function effectively despite decreased autonomy and increased accountability.

Management Bureaucracies tend to increase personnel and resources used to maintain and manage the organization. This tendency can be especially strong in public bureaucracies, which strongly emphasize financial accountability and reporting to higher government agencies. Correctional institutions are no exception. Bureaucratic functions often fall to a deputy warden for management, who is responsible for house-keeping tasks: buying supplies, keeping up buildings and grounds, providing food, maintaining financial records, and the like. Some states, however, centralize many of these tasks in the office of the commissioner, to promote accountability and coordination among constituent institutions. For example, buying supplies from one warehouse that serves all state agencies has decreased the discretion of prison management to contract locally for provisions.

Most personnel assigned to manage services for correctional institutions have very little contact with the prisoners; in some facilities they work in buildings separate from the main plant. Only personnel directly providing services, such as the head of food services, have direct contact with the prisoners.

Custodial Personnel Later in this chapter we examine in detail the role of the correctional officer. Here it is important to note that in most institutions the custodial force has graded ranks (captain, lieutenant, officer), with pay differentials and job titles following the chain of command, as in the military.

Unlike the factory or the military, which has separate groups of supervisors and workers or officers and enlisted personnel, the prison requires its lowest status employee, the correctional officer, to be both a supervisor (of inmates) and a worker (for the warden). This is a major cause of role conflict and makes officers vulnerable to corruption by the inmates. Officers know the warden is judging their performance by the way they manage the prisoners, and they can seldom manage without at least some cooperation by the prisoners. Officers ease up on some rules so prisoners will more willingly comply with other rules and requests.

Program Personnel The modern correctional institution is concerned not only with punishing but also with encouraging prisoners' participation in educational, vocational, and treatment programs that will improve their chances of living crime-free after release. Such programs have been a part of corrections since the late 1800s, but the enthusiasm for rehabilitation that swept corrections after World War II created a wider variety of programs, as discussed in Chapter 14. Here we need only mention that rehabilitative and educational personnel have difficulty achieving their goals in institutions whose primary mission is custody.

Industry and Agriculture Personnel Since the invention of the penitentiary, inmate labor has been used for industry and agriculture. As we will show in Chapter 14, the importance of these functions has varied over time and among regions. In some southern prisons most of the inmates' time is spent tending crops. In the Northeast, prison farms have disappeared because they are uneconomical and ill matched to the urban backgrounds of most inmates.

From an organizational standpoint, industrial and agricultural production, like other programs, is usually administered outside of the strict custodial hierarchy. But unlike educational or treatment programs, work in a factory or farm requires supervisors. Administrators must often mediate disputes over the competing needs for officers in guard towers or housing units, for example, and in fields or factories.

The Impact of the Structure

The organizational structure of correctional institutions has changed over time. The traditional custodial prison was run as an autocracy, with the warden dominating the guard force and often disciplining employees as strictly as inmates. When rehabilitation became a goal and treatment and educational programs were incorporated, a separate structure for programs, often headed by a deputy warden, was added. Its employees were professionals in social and behavioral sciences, who frequently clashed with wardens over who dominated custody.

As some institutions increasingly focused on rehabilitation, correctional planners and scholars frequently contrasted the traditional prison organization with a collaborative model. Most of the 1967 President's Commission on Law Enforcement and Administration of Justice report, for example, referred optimistically to the future correctional institution in which a dedicated and professionally trained staff would work with other administrators and with prisoners to identify inmates' problems and to strive for rehabilitation.[7] Such an institution would require structural changes to de-emphasize the traditionally rigid control function, enlarge the decision-making role of treatment personnel, and allow input from the prisoners about the operation of the facility. However, by the 1980s it was hard to find either prisons being run this way or correctional leaders advocating that they be so run. Some observers say that the collaborative organizational style was never really followed in more than a few institutions.

Correctional institutions today are more humanely administered than in the past. This change is in part a response to the presence of rehabilitative personnel and programs, the increased training and professionalism of correctional personnel, the intrusion of the courts, and the growth of citizen observer groups that monitor operations. Society will no longer tolerate the harsh conditions once prevalent. For example, the deplorable situation at the Cummins Farm Unit at Arkansas State Prison described in Chapter 5 probably could not now exist for long without exposure in the media.

A formal organization chart does not convey the whole story of a prison's organization; no chart can show how the people who occupy the positions actually perform. As theorists explain, an informal network of behaviors exists alongside the formal structure with its rules and procedures, chain of command, and channels of communication. Every organization has individuals who ignore directives, bypass the chain of command in communicating to the top, and negotiate with others who perform parallel or associated functions.

How, then, do prisons function? How do prisoners and staff try to meet their own goals? Although the U.S. prison may not conform to the ideal goals of corrections and the formal organization may little resemble the ongoing reality of the informal relations, order is kept and a routine is followed.

Governing Prisons

Surprisingly little has been written about prison management.[8] Most relevant scholarly inquiry is by sociologists, who have looked at prisons as social systems rather than institutions to be governed. As political scientist John DiIulio points out, sociologists have written about the effects on inmates of life in prison, racial and ethnic cleavages, inmate argot and roles, and the informal distribution of authority in prisons. He notes that this research helps us understand prison society but does not offer policy recommendations to help correctional officials manage inmates and staff. In fact, most sociological research implies that administrators can do little to govern prisons because — despite formal rules and regulations (see the Focus box for one set of rules of conduct) — institutions are run mainly through the informal social networks of the keepers and the kept. DiIulio finds shocking the extent to which correctional officials seem to have accepted sociological explanations for institutional conditions, rather than correcting faulty management practices.[9]

What distinguishes a well-run prison from a substandard prison? DiIulio argues that the crucial variable is not the ethnic or racial distribution of the population, the criminal records of the inmates, the size of the institution, the degree of crowding, or the level of funding. What is important is *governance:* the sound and firm management of inmates and staff.

FOCUS

Rules of General Conduct, Michigan Department of Corrections

1. All residents are expected to obey directions and instructions of members of the staff. If a resident feels he/she has been dealt with unfairly, or that he/she has received improper instructions, he/she should first comply with the order and then follow the established grievance procedures outlined later in this booklet.

2. Any behavior considered a felony or a misdemeanor in this state also is a violation of institutional rules. Such acts may result in disciplinary action and/or loss of earned good time in addition to possible criminal prosecution.

3. Any escape, attempt to escape, walk away, or failure to return from a furlough may result in loss of good time and/or a new sentence through prosecution under the escape statute. At one time or another, most persons in medium or minimum custody have felt restless and uneasy. When this happens, we urge you to see your counselor or the official in charge for guidance and advice. Occasionally, the department has asked that those who have walked away impulsively not be prosecuted when they have turned themselves in immediately after the act, realizing their mistake.

4. Any resident may, if they feel they have no further recourse in the institution, appeal to the Director of Corrections, Deputy Director, the Attorney General, state and federal courts, Michigan Civil Rights Commission or the Governor in the form of sealed and uncensored mail.

5. Reasonable courtesy, orderly conduct, and good personal hygiene are expected of all residents. Standards for haircuts, beards, and general appearance are listed later in this rule book.

6. Residents cannot hold any group meetings in the yard. Meetings for all legitimate purposes require staff approval; facilities, if available, will be scheduled for this purpose and necessary supervision provided.

7. While residents are permitted to play cards and other games, gambling is not allowed. In card-playing areas there shall be no more than four persons at a table. Visible tokens or other items of value will be sufficient evidence of gambling. Games are prohibited during working hours on institutional assignments.

8. All typewriters, calculators, radios, TVs, electric razors, and other appliances, including musical instruments, must be registered with the institutional officials by make, model, and serial number.

9. Items under Paragraph 8 cannot be traded, sold, or given away without written approval of the Deputy Warden or Superintendent.

10. Residents cannot operate concessions, sell services, rent goods, or act as loan sharks or pawnbrokers.

11. All items of contraband are subject to confiscation.

12. When a resident desires to go from one place to another for a specific and legitimate reason, he/she should obtain a pass from the official to whom they are responsible, such as the housing unit supervisor, work foreman, teacher, etc.

13. No resident is allowed to go into another resident's cell or room unless specifically authorized.

SOURCE: Michigan Department of Corrections, *Resident Guide Book* (Lansing: Michigan Department of Corrections, n.d.).

What quality of life should be maintained in a prison? DiIulio states that a good prison "provides as much order, amenity, and service as possible given the human and financial resources."[10] *Order* is here defined as the absence of individual or group misconduct that threatens the safety of others — for example, assaults, rapes, and other forms of violence or insult. A basic assumption should be that, because the state sends offenders to prison, it is responsible for ensuring their safety there. *Amenity* is anything that enhances the comfort of the inmates, such as good food, clean cells, recreational opportunities, and the like. This does not mean that prisons are to function as hotels, but contemporary standards stipulate that correctional facilities should not be deleterious to inmates' mental and physical health. Finally, *service* includes programs designed to improve the life prospects of inmates: vocational training, remedial education, and work opportunities. Here, too, we expect inmates to be engaged in activities during incarceration that will make them better persons and enhance their ability to lead crime-free lives on release.

Running a prison in an authoritarian manner, backed up by force of arms, is neither effective nor efficient. Using a tactical team for a drug and weapons sweep, such as this one at Big Muddy Correctional Center, Illinois, is not usual.

If we accept the premise that well-run prisons are important for inmates, staff, and society, what are some of the problems that correctional administrators must address? The correctional literature points to four factors that make governing prisons different from administering other public institutions: (1) the defects of total power, (2) the limited rewards and punishments, (3) the co-optation of correctional officers, and (4) the strength of inmate leadership. After we review each of these research findings, we will then ask what kind of administrative systems and leadership styles can ensure that prisons are safe and humane and serve inmates' needs.

The Defects of Total Power

In his path-breaking investigation of the New Jersey State Prison, Gresham Sykes emphasized that although in formal terms correctional officials have formal power to extract compliance from the prisoners, in fact that power is limited and in many ways they depend on inmate cooperation.[11] Most citizens assume prisoners live according to an authoritarian regime: Officers give orders; inmates follow orders. Rules specify prisoner behavior, and are strictly enforced. The officers have a monopoly on the legal means of coercion and can be backed up by state police and National Guard. Staff members grant rewards and inflict punishment. In theory, any inmate who does not fall into line should end up in solitary confinement. Why, then, should questions arise about how the prisons are run?

Certainly we can imagine a prison society made up of hostile and uncooperative inmates ruled by force. Prisoners can be legally isolated from one another, physically abused until they cooperate, and put under continuous surveillance. Although all these things are possible, such practices would probably not be countenanced for long because the public expects correctional institutions to be run humanely.

Also, prisoners, unlike members of other authoritarian organizations such as the military, do not recognize the legitimacy of their keepers and therefore are not *moved* to cooperate. No sense of duty propels prisoners to compliance. This is an important distinction, because duty is the backbone of most social organizations. With it, rules are followed—and need not be explained first.[12]

The notion that correctional officers have total power over inmates has a number of other flaws. As John Hepburn points out, "The ability of the officials to physically coerce their captives into the paths of compliance is something of an illusion as far as the day-to-day activities of the prison are concerned and may be of doubtful value in moments of crisis."[13] Forcing people to follow commands is an inefficient way to make them carry out complex tasks; efficiency is further diminished by the ratio of inmates to officers (typically 40 to 1) and by the potential danger.

Of course, physical coercion *is* used to control prisoners. Such tactics may violate criminal statutes and administrative procedures, but they have long occurred in prisons throughout the United States—and cannot be considered idiosyncratic or sporadic. A study of a Texas prison, for example, found that a small but significant percentage of the officers used physical punishment. Force both controlled the prison population and induced cohesion among officers, maintaining a status differential between officers and inmates and helping officers win promotions.[14]

Rewards and Punishments

Correctional officers often rely on rewards and punishments to induce cooperation. To maintain security and order among a large population in a confined space, they impose extensive rules of conduct. Rather than use force to ensure obedience, however, they reward compliance and punish rule violations by granting and denying privileges.

Several policies may be followed to promote control. One is to offer cooperative prisoners rewards such as choice job assignments, residence in the honor unit, and favorable parole reports. "Good time" is given to inmates who do not break rules. Informers may also be rewarded, and administrators may ignore conflict among inmates on the assumption that it keeps prisoners from uniting against authorities.

The system of rewards and punishments has some deficiencies. One is that the punishments for rule breaking do not represent a great departure from the prisoners' usual circumstances. Because inmates are already deprived of many freedoms and valued goods — heterosexual relations, money, choice of clothing, and so on — not being allowed to attend, say, a recreational period does not carry much weight. In addition, according to the inmate code in a particular prison, the defiant convict may gain standing among the other prisoners. Finally, authorized privileges are given to the inmate at the start of the sentence and are taken away only if rules are broken, but few further rewards are authorized for progress or exceptional behavior. However, as an inmate approaches reintegration, opportunities for furloughs, work release, or transfer to a halfway house can serve as incentives to obey rules.

Co-optation of Correctional Officers

One way that correctional officers obtain inmate cooperation is by tolerating minor rule infractions in exchange for compliance with major aspects of the custodial regime. The correctional officer plays the key role in the interpersonal relationships among the prisoners and serves as the link to the custodial bureaucracy. The correctional officer

> must supervise and control the inmate population in concrete and detailed terms . . . must see to the translation of the custodial regime from blueprint to reality and engage in the specific battles for conformity. Counting prisoners, periodically reporting to the center of communications, signing passes, checking groups of inmates as they come and go, searching for contraband or signs of attempts to escape — these make up the minutiae of [the officer's] eight-hour shift.[15]

Officers and prisoners are in close association both day and night — in the cell block, workshop, dining hall, recreation area, and so on. The formal rules stipulate that a social distance be maintained between the two groups and that they speak and act toward one another accordingly, but both groups also recognize a certain interdependence. The officers need the cooperation of the prisoners so they will look good to their superiors, and the inmates count on the officers to relax the rules or occasionally look the other way. For instance, officers in a midwestern prison told researcher Stan Stojkovic that flexibility in rule enforcement was especially important as it related to the coping ability of prisoners. As one officer said, "Phone calls are really important for guys in this place . . . you cut off their calls and they get pissed. So what I do is give them a little extra and they are good to me." Yet the officers also told Stojkovic that they would be crazy to intervene to stop illicit sex or drug use.[16]

Even though officers are backed by the state and have the formal authority to punish any prisoner who does not follow orders, they often discover the best course of action is to make "deals" or "trades" with the inmates. As a result, officers buy compliance or obedience in some areas by tolerating rule breaking elsewhere.

Officers are expected to maintain "surface order." They must ensure that the inmates are conforming voluntarily to the most important rules, things are running smoothly, and there is no visible trouble and no cause for alarm. Because officers' job performance is judged on their ability to maintain surface order, both officers and prisoners have a tacit understanding and bargain accordingly. Stojkovic summarizes the assumptions underlying the accommodative relationships between officers and inmates as follows:

1. Negotiations are central to prisoner control because correctional officers cannot have total control over the inmates.
2. Once an officer defines a set of informal rules with prisoners, the rules must be respected by all parties.
3. Some rule violations are "normal" and consequently do not merit officers' attention or sanctioning.[17]

Correctional officers must be careful not to pay too high a price for cooperation. Officers who establish underground relationships can be manipulated by prisoners into smuggling contraband or committing other illegal acts. Officers are under pressure to work effectively with prisoners and may be blackmailed into doing illegitimate favors in return for cooperation. When leadership is thus abdicated, authority passes to the inmates.

Inmate Leadership

In the traditional prison of the big-house era, administrators enlisted the inmate leaders to help maintain order. As Richard Korn and Lloyd W. McCorkle wrote in 1954,

> *Far from systematically attempting to undermine the inmate hierarchy, the institution generally gives it covert support and recognition by assigning better jobs and quarters to its high-status members provided they are "good inmates." In this and other ways the institution buys peace with the system by avoiding battle with it.*[18]

Descriptions of the contemporary maximum-security prison raise questions about administrators' ability to run institutions in this way. When the racial, offense, and political characteristics of inmate populations of many prisons began to change in the mid-1960s, the centralized convict leadership structure was replaced by multiple centers of power. As official authority broke down, some institutions became violent, dangerous places.

Prisons now seem to function more effectively than in the recent past. Although they are more crowded than ever, riots and reports of violence have declined. In many prisons the inmate social system may have reorganized, so that correctional officers again can work through prisoners respected by fellow inmates. Yet some observers contend that when wardens maintain order in this way, they enhance the positions of some prisoners at the expense of others. The leaders profit by receiving illicit privileges and favors, and increase their influence among inmates by distributing benefits.

Disciplining Prisoners

Maintaining order can be burdensome to prison administrators, given the factors just discussed. In an earlier era prisoners were kept in line with corporal punishment. Today withholding privileges, erasing good-time credits, and placing inmates in "the hole" (the adjustment center, or segregation) constitute the range of punishments available to discipline the unruly, and the Supreme Court has curbed administrators' discretion in applying even these punishments. Procedural fairness must be included in the process by which inmates are sent to solitary confinement and in the method by which good-time credit may be lost because of misconduct.

On entering the prison, the newcomer is given a manual, often running up to a hundred pages, specifying the rules that govern almost all of prison life, from permitted clothing to dining room conduct and standards of personal hygiene. Prominently listed are types of behavior that can result in disciplinary action: rioting, gambling, sexual activity, possession of currency, failure to obey an order, and so on. Prisoners are warned that some rule infractions are also violations of the state's criminal law and may be handled by the criminal justice system;[19] most infractions, however, are dealt with by an institutional committee. This disciplinary committee may commit an inmate to punitive segregation for the number of days speci-fied for each class of offense or hand down other sanctions. The manuals vary from state to state; some merely list vio-lations and give disciplinary committees broad discretion as to the punishment.

A national survey of state prison in-mates found that over half (53 percent) had been charged with violating prison rules at least once in their current sen-tence.[20] Younger inmates and those with more extensive criminal careers or drug histories were the most likely to have vio-lated prison rules. Also, inmates in larger prisons or maximum-security prisons had more rule violations than prisoners in other types of facilities. Further, whites and African Americans commit-ted infractions at the same rate — ap-proximately 1.5 violations per inmate per year. And more than 90 percent of the inmates charged with violating prison rules were found guilty in prison administrative proceedings.

The Disciplinary Process Custodial offi-cers act like cops with regard to most prison rules. Minor violations may warrant merely a verbal reprimand or warning, but

Correctional officers are the linchpins of management because they are in constant contact with inmates. They must enforce the rules yet gain the cooperation of the prisoners. A difficult job!

more serious violations may earn the prisoner a "ticket": a report forwarded to higher au-thority for action. Some correctional systems distinguish between major and minor viola-tions. Major tickets go to the disciplinary committee; lesser tickets receive summary judgment by a hearing officer, whose decision may be appealed to a supervising captain, whose decision may, in turn, be appealed to the committee. In some systems all discipli-nary reports go to a hearing officer, who investigates the charges, conducts the hearing, and determines the punishment. The decisions of the hearing officer may be reviewed by the commissioner of corrections, who can reduce the punishment but not increase it.

Such procedures are relatively new. Less than thirty years ago, formal codes of insti-tutional conduct either did not exist or were ignored; punishment was at the full discre-tion of the warden, and inmates had no opportunity to challenge the charges. Beginning in 1970, in a series of decisions, the U.S. Supreme Court granted inmates certain (lim-ited) procedural rights: to receive notice of a complaint, to have a fair hearing, to con-front witnesses, to have help in preparing for the hearing, to be given a written statement of the decision.[21] However, the Court also has emphasized the need to bal-ance prisoner rights with state interests. Thus, two years after it guaranteed prisoners fundamental due process rights, the Court ruled that counsel was not included.[22]

As a result, most prisons developed rules that specify some elements of due process in disciplinary proceedings. In many institutions a disciplinary committee receives charges, conducts hearings, and determines guilt and punishment. Normally discipli-nary committees are composed of three to five members of the correctional staff, includ-ing representatives of custody, treatment, and classification, with a senior officer acting as chairperson. Sometimes the committees also include inmates or outside citizens.

As part of the procedure, the inmate is read the charge, is allowed to present his or her version of the incident, and may present witnesses. In some institutions an inmate advocate may help the prisoner. If the inmate is found guilty, a sanction is imposed. The inmate may usually appeal the decision to the warden and ultimately to the commissioner. Yet even with these protections, prisoners are still powerless and may fear further punishment if they challenge the disciplinary decisions of the warden too strenuously.

Sanctions   Punitive segregation and loss of privileges and good time are the sanctions most often imposed for violating institution rules. The privileges lost may include visits, mail, access to the commissary, and recreation periods.

The most severe sanction by a disciplinary committee is confinement in punitive segregation. Most institutions limit the amount of time that an inmate can spend in segregation and regulate conditions with respect to food, medical attention, and personal safety. Twenty days of continuous punitive segregation is the maximum in many prisons, but inmates may be returned to "the hole" after a token period outside.

Maintaining order among offenders who live in close proximity in conditions of deprivation is a major task. Officers recognize they must walk a very narrow line between overrestrictiveness and overpermissiveness. They must recognize, too, that their objective is to encourage cooperation and conformity to the rules. But they must also understand that rewards and punishments are limited and that courts now insist that due process be observed in disciplining and proceeding against violators. This all adds up to a tall order, but with good management practices the objective can be reached. One index of a poorly run institution is a large number of disciplinary violations, showing that staff and prisoners can't prevent disruptive behavior or function with mutual tolerance, if not respect.

Leadership: The Crucial Element of Governance

Amazingly, most of the time prisons work: Order is maintained and activities are carried out. As Edwin Sutherland and Donald Cressey observed, any prison is made up of

> *synchronized actions of hundreds of people, some of whom hate and distrust each other, love each other, fight each other physically and psychologically, think of each other as stupid or mentally disturbed, "manage" and "control" each other, and vie with each other for favors, prestige, power and money.*[23]

Still, most prisons do not fall into disarray, although at times certain institutions have approached chaos. Examples include Soledad in California, during a period of racial and political unrest in the 1960s; Walla Walla in Washington in the 1970s, when an experiment with inmate self-government was attempted; and the Eastham Unit and some other Texas prisons prior to court-ordered reforms in the 1980s. But these are exceptions, and many correctional facilities are well governed. What elements affect the quality of life in U.S. prisons? What is the role of management?

Organizational structures in prisons are bureaucratic, yet management styles vary. Studying the management of selected prisons in California, Michigan, and Texas, John DiIulio found differences in leadership philosophy, political environment, and wardens' administrative style. DiIulio maintains that quality of prison life as measured by levels of order, amenity, and service is mainly a function of management quality. Prisons can be governed, violence can be minimized, and services can be provided to the inmates if correctional executives and wardens exhibit leadership. He comments,

> *Prison managers must effect a government strong enough to control a community of persons who are most decidedly not angels. At the same time, however, prison managers must be subject to a vigorous system of internal and external controls on their behavior, including judicial and legislative oversight, media scrutiny, occupational norms and standards.*[24]

The Focus box describes the unique management practices of Warden Dennis Luther.

Prison systems perform well if leaders can cope with the political and other pressures that contribute to administrative uncertainty and instability. In particular, management is successful when prison directors

1. Are in office long enough to learn the job, make plans, and implement them.
2. Project an appealing image to a wide range of people, both inside and outside of the organization.
3. Are dedicated and loyal to the department, seeing themselves as engaged in a noble and challenging profession.
4. Are highly hands-on and proactive, paying close attention to details and not waiting for problems to arise. They must know what is going on inside, yet also recognize the need for outside support. In short, they are strangers neither in the cell blocks nor in the aisles of the state legislature.[25]

From this perspective, making prisons work is a function of administrative leadership and the application of sound management principles. Governing prisons is an extraordinary challenge, but it is a task that can be and has been accomplished. DiIulio's

FOCUS   A Model Prison

Set in the woods outside of Bradford, Pennsylvania, is the Federal Correctional Institution, McKean. Opened in 1989 as a medium-security facility, it houses more than 1,000 male inmates. Until he retired in July 1995, McKean's warden was Dennis Luther, an administrator who during his sixteen years in prison work gained a reputation for unorthodox policies.

At a time when politicians were railing against "country club" prisons and the need to "make 'em bust rocks," Luther ran an institution that earned a 99.3 accreditation rating from the American Correctional Association, the highest in the Bureau of Prisons. Badly overcrowded and with an increasing number of violent offenders, McKean cost taxpayers $15,370 a year for each inmate, well below the federal average of $21,350. Amazingly, in six years there were no escapes, no murders, no suicides, and only three serious assaults against staff and six recorded against inmates.

How did Luther do it? According to Luther each prison has its own culture, which is often violent and abusive, based on gangs. The staff in such institutions feel they are unable to change it. At McKean, Luther set out to build a different type of culture, based on unconditional respect for the inmates as people. As he says, "If you want people to behave responsibly, and treat you with respect then you treat other people that way." This credo has been translated into twenty-eight beliefs, the product of Luther's years of experience. These "Beliefs About the Treatment of Inmates" are posted all over the institution to remind both staff and inmates alike of their responsibilities. They include

1. Inmates are sent to prison *as* punishment and not *for* punishment.
2. Correctional workers have a *responsibility* to ensure that inmates are returned to the community no more angry or hostile than when they were committed.
3. Inmates are *entitled* to a safe and humane environment while in prison.
4. You must believe in man's *capacity* to change his behavior. . . .
10. Be *responsive* to inmate requests for action or information. Respond in a timely manner and respond the first time an inmate makes a request. . . .
12. It is important for staff to *model* the kind of behavior they expect to see duplicated by inmates. . . .
14. There is an *inherent value* in self-improvement programs such as education, whether or not these programs are related to recidivism. . . .
18. Staff *cannot,* because of their own insecurities, lack of self-esteem or concerns about their masculinity, condescend or degrade inmates. . . .
26. Inmate discipline must be *consistent* and *fair.*

Merely posting the "Beliefs" in prominent places will not create a superior prison culture. The credo must be put into practice. Here are some examples:

1. *Front-line staff.* If you want to get front-line staffers to treat inmates with respect, top managers must treat staffers with respect. Luther has said, "Line-level people have good ideas, not only about how to do their job, but about how to do *your* job better." With this in mind he created the Line Staff Advisory Board, a rotating group of front-line workers who meet with him to talk through complaints, suggestions, and rumors.

2. *"Management by walking around."* Through contact with staff and inmates in the dining hall, on the yard, and in the cell blocks, a warden becomes a visible presence who can hear suggestions and complaints. Often he or she is able to nip problems before they fester and explode. This presence sets an example of the extent to which the warden is concerned about the problems of inmates and staff.

(continued)

3. *Inmate involvement.* Regular "town hall" meetings with inmates provide opportunities for two-way communications. Proposed changes in regulations or procedures are first brought to the inmates for comment (for example, items to be offered in the commissary).

4. *Inmate Benefit Fund.* The Inmate Benefit Fund (IBF) was created to generate money inmates could use to purchase items for which taxpayer dollars were not available. Using their own funds, inmates could order items from Bradford stores and restaurants that would ease their stay in McKean. Orders were placed with the IBF and delivered to the institution for a modest handling charge. With 2,000 inmates substantial sums were generated by these surcharges. The inmates could use these funds to purchase additional educational and recreational programs for the population. Besides helping inmates gain access to these programs, the IBF spending contributed to the local economy.

5. *Education.* McKean has a higher percentage of inmates enrolled in classes than almost any other federal prison. Luther believes prison time should be spent preparing offenders for their return to the community. Courses are taught by staff members of the prison's education department, professors from neighboring colleges, and inmates. The latter teach adult continuing education courses and act as mentors and tutors.

Luther expects inmates to be responsible, and he holds them to a higher standard than found in most prisons. After a few minor incidents, the warden ordered "closed movement" during evening hours. This restricted inmate activity and was meant to be permanent. A group of inmates asked if he would restore "open movement" if the prison was incident-free for ninety days. Luther agreed, and the prison has remained "open."

Inmates who meet the standards are rewarded. Weekly inspections are held in each cell block and inmates who score high are given additional privileges. Those whose disciplinary record is clean and excel in the programs can earn their way to the "honor unit." And those who show consistently good behavior are allowed to attend supervised picnics on Family Day.

Dennis Luther is convinced his methods will work in any prison, even those plagued by violence, overcrowding, and gangs. Many staff members feel the same way. They believe McKean is a shining example of the difference good management can make.

SOURCE: Adapted from Robert Worth, "A Model Prison," *Atlantic Monthly*, November 1995, pp. 38–44; Tom Peters, *Liberation Management* (New York: Knopf, 1992), pp. 247–255.

research challenges the common assumption of many correctional administrators that "the cons run the joint." Rather, as the success of such legendary administrators as George Beto of Texas, William Fauver of New Jersey, Anna Kross of New York's Rikers Island, and William Leeke of North Carolina demonstrate, prisons can be managed so that inmates can serve their time in a safe, healthy, and productive environment.[26]

Correctional Officers: The Linchpin of Management

Over the past twenty-five years, the correctional officer role has changed greatly. The officer is no longer responsible merely for "guarding." Now the correctional officer is the crucial professional, has the closest contact with the prisoners, and is expected to perform a variety of tasks. As correctional officer Philip Carvalho points out in the Focus box, officers are expected to counsel, supervise, protect, and process the inmates under their care. In many jurisdictions hours are long, pay low, entry requirements minimal, and turnover high. Given these conditions, why would someone want to enter this field?

Who Becomes a Correctional Officer?

The early criminal justice literature either ignored the prison officer or painted a picture of an individual with a "lock psychosis" resulting from the routine of numbering, counting, checking, and locking. Some prison studies give the impression that officers were incompetent and psychologically inferior, performing the only job to which they could gain access. They were viewed as the primary opponents of rehabilitation, at loggerheads with both inmates and administrators. Some observers have referred to guards in

FOCUS A Day on the Job—In Prison

The buzzer of the white clock radio drones through the bedroom. The hands of the luminous dial point to 5:20 A.M.

For Philip Martin Carvalho, the jarring sound is the same prelude to the morning ritual that millions of Americans call "going to work." But unlike most other job-bound early risers, his workplace is different: It's behind eight steel, barred doors within the walls of the Massachusetts maximum-security prison at Walpole.

Phil Carvalho holds the rank of senior correctional officer. He has covered virtually every custody assignment in the eight years he has been in a prison that has been jarred by inmate riots and strikes by its personnel. Since last January, his post has been Ten Block, the segregation unit where Massachusetts houses up to sixty of its toughest and most incorrigible inmates. . . .

Phil Carvalho punches the time clock, moves through the first of the electronically controlled steel doors, opens his lunch bag for inspection by another officer, empties his pockets of keys and small change, and removes his buckled belt before stepping through the archway of the metal detector. The unseen electronic eye doesn't flicker any alarm. . . .

Ten Block is a steel, barred island within the walled continent of the prison . . . insulated and isolated for those who live there and those who work there. It is an island cut off from the institutional mainland by more than the click, bang of steel. Because it confines or segregates those who have assaulted guards and inmates, it is often territory that is ostracized by other guards and inmates.

Ten Block also is an island marked by the paraphernalia of violence. Handcuffs dangling from a pegboard . . . a trio of fire extinguishers within easy reach on the floor . . . a convex Plexiglas riot shield resting in the corner. Its sixty cells are divided between two floors, fifteen to a corridor. Some of the cells on the first floor have solid steel doors in front of the bars, which are clanged shut when an inmate does punitive isolation time.

When Carvalho arrives, nine young officers already are beginning to fill cardboard trays with muffins, cereal, and paper cups of coffee from the kitchen wagon. Like Carvalho, all are volunteers for Ten Block.

"Yeah, you gotta be crazy to work here," one of them says, "but it's got good days off." Most of the officers have been spit at by some of their charges. Some have been hit by urine and excrement.

Before Carvalho has a chance to move through the door of the cubicle that serves as an office, one of the three phones inside rings.

"Ten. Carvalho."

The phone is sandwiched between the cheek and the shoulder of the 220-pound, six-foot two-inch Carvalho. For the next eight hours, it will ring incessantly, with rare moments of silence. For Carvalho, the telephone is something more than an electronic instrument.

He growls at it, purrs into it, persuades, cajoles, allowing the cadence of his voice to vary with the purpose of his message. "Yeah, right. Hey, sweetheart, do me a favor. . . ."

The conversations are always on a first-name basis, sometimes flecked by touches of jailhouse humor that softens the harshness of where they take place. There is a subconscious line between Carvalho and the inmates that marks the perimeter between levity and insolence, between what is permitted and what is not. Since he arrived in Ten Block, Phil Carvalho never has been spit at or assaulted by anything more than a barrage of four-letter words.

In the office, the phones are ringing again.

"Ten. Carvalho."

"Yeah, O.K. Sullivan's visit canceled. O.K. Thanks."

"Ten. Carvalho."

"No. I can't do it. I don't have a place to put him. Look, sweetheart, he can have a legal aid visit. Yeah, but not today. I got visits at 11, at 11:30, at 1:30, and a disciplinary board. Yeah, try tomorrow. Sorry. You're doing a great job . . . a great job." . . .

An officer comes into the cubicle with a handful of small brown envelopes. Carvalho counts them, records the total and the time in the dog-eared logbook in front of him.

"Medication," he says. "O.K., give 'em out."

Ten Block distributes medication more frequently than meals. Four times a day, inmates may receive prescriptions that include sedatives, tranquilizers, and sleeping pills. During the morning distribution, fourteen of twenty-eight inmates on the first floor receive pills. Five milligrams of Valium four times a day plus a sleeping pill at night is not unusual.

"I can't understand it," says Carvalho. "These guys when they're on the street can't be gettin' that medication. Impossible. Some of 'em need it for their nerves. Being in this situation they need something to calm them down. But the pain pills they put out, the depressants . . . it's unbelievable. . . ."

"Yeah, Charlie?"

"Listen, Phil, you gotta get that son-of-a-bitch out of here. . . ." The voice in the dimly lighted cell details a complaint against an officer on the three-to-eleven shift.

Other inmates shout their own litany of complaints. Hands holding mirrors protrude from the other fourteen cells in the section, giving their owners a glass-reflected picture of the officer and the visitor.

"The only thing I can tell you," Carvalho responds, "is that I've got to get McLaughlin down here."

Thomas McLaughlin is deputy superintendent at Walpole. He is one of the key reasons why Phil Carvalho

(continued)

volunteered for Ten Block. "He backs you up. And he's there when you need him. All these guys," Carvalho says, pointing to the young officers, "they're there when you need 'em. . . ."

When McLaughlin arrives, Carvalho takes him through the corridor where the inmates are complaining about the officer. They move from cell to cell like army medics making rounds in a crowded hospital. The deputy superintendent is a listener. Occasionally, he asks a question, sometimes he nods, but his face shows neither a flicker of sympathetic agreement nor cynical disbelief. Later, he tells Carvalho there will be a meeting with the night officer at the end of the shift.

"Hey, Phil . . .Phil . . ." Another voice from the cell in the corridor. Carvalho again moves into the narrow hallway.

"Hey, Phil, I need a legal visit. My case comes up on the fourteenth."

"O.K. I'll take care of it."

From a hall phone, Carvalho dials an extension, "Yeah, Phil Carvalho. I need a legal visit for . . ."

The demands made on Carvalho are not phrased in convoluted euphemisms. They are direct. They deal with basic wants in the limited, cramped world of the segregation unit . . . an appointment for a visitor, a phone call to a relative . . . some writing paper. Sometimes the demands attempt to stretch the narrow boundaries of Ten Block. Either way, the answers are equally direct. Carvalho's booming voice, intoning, "I'll try," or "Yes," or "No," leaves little room for doubt.

The noon food wagon arrives, and the officers dish out the meal into the paper trays. After the inmates are served, the officers grab a tray and bring it into the office, a few at a time. Some have brought their lunch and eat it piecemeal between running upstairs or into the cell corridors. Elsewhere in the prison, most corrections officers eat in the staff mess hall. In Ten Block, there is no formal sit-down dining.

Carvalho, between bites, dials the phone again. "Yeah, Russ. He's back in Block Three. Yeah, he's back. My count is fifty-eight." The count of inmates is reported to control at the beginning of the shift, at noon, or whenever any inmate leaves or returns to Ten Block. . . .

A young officer comes in and hands Carvalho another packet of brown envelopes. Medication. Second distribution. Carvalho registers them in the log.

The logbook is something of a barometer for the shift. It records the traffic like a counter at a busy intersection. And it offers some distinctions between the shifts.

The preceding three-to-eleven P.M. shift had seven entries for its entire eight-hour segment. The eleven-to-seven A.M. shift showed three entries. By noon, Carvalho had written twenty-one separate items into his log.

The clock on the office wall ticks the shift slowly to an end.

Fifty minutes and twenty-seven traffic-congested miles later, Carvalho is back in his private world on the outer fringes of suburbia. He is greeted by his wife and his 14-year-old daughter, Cheryl. . . . Supper is on the table a half hour later.

The small talk is about an afternoon shopping trip in search of parochial school uniforms for Cheryl. There is no small talk about Ten Block.

"He doesn't talk about the job," his wife, Shirley, says. "He tells his father about the job and his father tells his mother and she tells me some things. That's how I get information about the prison. If he comes home and he's in a good mood, I'll know he had a fine day. If he comes home a little bit aggravated, then I know he had a bad day and I'll just go about my business."

When Shirley is out of earshot, Carvalho acknowledges her worrying. "I know it affects my wife. I'll tell her, 'I'm not going in today,' and she'll say, 'Oh, good. Call in sick.' And then I tell her I'm only kidding. And I trudge in there. But I must like it because I keep goin' back."

"It has its good days and its bad. Today was a good day," he says.

The Plexiglas protective shield remained unused. No inmate had refused to return to his cell. None of the young officers had urine or excrement thrown at them. The fire extinguishers remained in their places.

Shirley nods in agreement. Today Phil Carvalho came home in a good mood.

SOURCE: Edgar May, "A Day on the Job — In Prison," *Corrections Magazine,* December 1976, pp. 6–11. Reprinted by permission of the Edna McConnell Clark Foundation.

general as "frightened, hostile people,"[27] and the report of the commission that investigated the 1971 Attica riots labeled the guards there as racists. Who are the correctional officers? Have they been accurately depicted? What kind of person accepts a job that offers low pay and little hope of advancement?

Studies have shown that a primary incentive for becoming a correctional officer is the security of a civil service job. In addition, because most correctional facilities are located in rural areas, prison work often is better than other available employment, and the salary often can be supplemented by overtime or part-time work. Until the push of the last twenty years for greater professionalism among corrections workers, many guards joined the ranks because they had few employment opportunities.

Today, because they need more well-qualified correctional officers, most states have given priority to recruiting quality personnel. Salaries have been raised so that the yearly average entry-level pay runs between $16,000 in some southern and rural states to over $30,000 in states such as Massachusetts and New Jersey.[28] In addition to their salaries, most officers can earn overtime pay, supplementing base pay by up to 30 percent. The annual turnover rate among officers seems inversely proportional to compensation level, with some low-paying states losing 25 percent of their force annually.[29]

Over the past quarter century, federal courts, the 1964 Civil Rights Act, and affirmative action programs, have dramatically changed the racial and gender composition of the correctional officer force. Today approximately 32 percent of correctional officers are members of minority groups and 19 percent are women.

How do these increases in the number of minority and female officers shape the work environment among correctional officers? Dana Britton found in her study that black male and female officers are less satisfied with their jobs than their male counterparts. She also found that black and Hispanic male officers felt they were more effective working with inmates than did their white counterparts. And female correctional officers were also found to be more contented with their work than male officers.[30] Figure 13.2 shows the racial/ethnic composition of correctional officers and inmates in adult systems.

Women officers are no longer limited to work with female prisoners. For example, in Alabama, where almost 25 percent of correctional officers are women, fully 97 percent work in male institutions. In Mississippi 43 percent of correctional officers are women, and 92 percent of them work in male institutions. However, in the Federal Bureau of Prisons, only 10.2 percent of the staff are women, and only 8 percent of them work among male inmates.[31]

An increasing number of women officers work in male institutions. As has been true in other formerly all-male domains, female officers reported initial difficulties in being accepted by their male counterparts.

Just as female police officers often have found themselves excluded from certain assignments and from full integration into the social group that constitutes the force, women in corrections feel discriminated against.[32] In a study of women officers in two prisons for men, Lynn Zimmer found that their male counterparts were opposed to sexual integration of the guard force.[33] Male officers argued that women could not handle the violence and confrontations with inmates that occur in prisons. But a study by Denise Jenne and Robert Kersting found that women officers tended to respond to violent situations as aggressively as their male coworkers, and sometimes more aggressively.[34] Women officers also seem to have less trouble with the inmates than did their male counterparts, although they were harassed when they first appeared on the job. In some states male prisoners raised the issue of privacy when female officers

Figure 13.2 Racial/Ethnic Composition of Correctional Officers and Inmates, Adult Systems Nationwide

Although the racial/ethnic composition of correctional officers does not equal the racial/ethnic composition of the inmate population, great strides have been made during the past quarter century.

<small>Source: U.S. Department of Justice, Bureau of Justice Statistics, *Sourcebook of Criminal Justice Statistics* (Washington, DC: U.S. Government Printing Office, 1997), p. 88; *Bulletin*, January 1998, p. 6.</small>

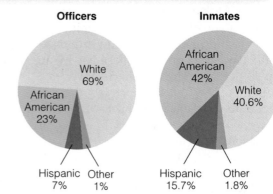

Officers: White 69%, African American 23%, Hispanic 7%, Other 1%

Inmates: African American 42%, White 40.6%, Hispanic 15.7%, Other 1.8%

were assigned to cell block duty; courts have upheld inmate objections with regard to women supervising shower and toilet facilities.[35]

Most states now have training programs for correctional officers, modeled on police training programs, that give recruits at least a rudimentary knowledge of job requirements and corrections rules. The classroom work, however, often bears little resemblance to problems confronted in the cell block or on the yard. Therefore, on completing the course, the new officer is placed under the supervision of an experienced officer. On the job, the new officer experiences real-life situations and learns the necessary techniques and procedures. Through encounters with inmates and fellow officers, the recruit becomes socialized to life behind the walls and gradually becomes part of that subculture.[36]

For most correctional workers, custodial officer is a dead-end job. Although officers who perform well may be promoted to higher ranks such as correctional counselor, very few ever move into administration. However, in some states and in the Federal Bureau of Prisons, people with college degrees can move up the career ladder to management positions without having to advance through the ranks of the custodial force.

Role Characteristics

Correctional officers are street-level bureaucrats who are expected to engage in "people work" within an organizational setting. Today, officers are expected to help inmates deal with their personal problems, yet because they work in a bureaucracy are also expected to treat clients impersonally and to follow formally prescribed procedures. Fulfilling these contradictory role expectations is difficult in itself, and the difficulty is heightened by the long-term physical proximity of officers and inmates.

Although most prison work is thought to be routine, guarding is not an undifferentiated occupation. Officers supervise the cell blocks, dining areas, and shops; transport prisoners to hospitals and courts; take turns serving on the disciplinary board; perch with rifles in guard towers; and protect the prison gates. Unscheduled activities range from offering informal counseling to breaking up fights to escorting prisoners on family visits in the community.

In most states the custodial staff is organized along paramilitary lines, with ranks of officer, sergeant, lieutenant, and captain. The sergeant supervises a complement of officers in one area of the prison—housing unit, hospital, and so on. The lieutenants are the main disciplinarians of the institution, conducting shakedowns, breaking up fights, and supervising the removal of inmates to segregation. The few captains on a staff have primarily administrative responsibilities and serve as the link between custodial personnel and the warden and other top management officials.

The military nomenclature and organization extend to the relationships among staff members. Officers are subject to inspections; in some institutions they may be given "tickets" (disciplinary reports) by their superiors; and when they are housed in quarters attached to the facility, rules govern their off-duty behavior. To guard against officers smuggling contraband into the institution, the staff is kept under rigorous discipline. That the rules for and organization of the officers parallel those that govern the inmates is not lost on the correctional staff. "We're all doing time here," they say, "except that we're doing it in eight-hour shifts."

Job Assignments

Officers may be assigned to one of seven job assignments. These vary as to their location within the institution, the duties required, and the nature of the contact with the inmate population. Assignments include (1) block officer, (2) work detail supervisor, (3) industrial shop and school officer, (4) yard officer, (5) administration building assignment, (6) wall post, and (7) relief officer.[37]

Block Officers Of all the correctional staff, officers in the cell blocks have the closest contact with prisoners and the greatest potential for inducing behavior change in them. Work in the housing units of some prisons is dangerous because the officers lack weapons, are greatly outnumbered, and can be easily overwhelmed by the prisoners.

In units housing 300–400 inmates, the five to eight block officers are responsible for moving their charges to the dining hall, work sites, infirmaries, and the like. They must oversee unit maintenance, watch for potential breaches of security, handle inmates' personal problems and answer their questions, enforce rules, ensure inmate safety, and carry out the warden's orders. So the cell block officer must have management and leadership skills.

Work Detail Supervisors Inmates provide labor for feeding, cleaning, and maintaining the institution. A portion of the custodial staff must supervise various work details connected with these tasks. The work area is a more relaxed place than the cell block. The work groups are small, the officer and prisoners may engage in conversation, and esprit may develop as they work. This is especially true when people work a particular job and shift over an extended period of time. In the kitchen, laundry, welding shop, or hospital, for example, the inmate–officer relationship is analogous to worker and foreman in a factory. Yet the correctional officer has no counterpart in business or industry.

Studying field operations at a plantation-style southern prison, Ben M. Crouch found officers focused on two goals: "completing the agriculture task at hand and returning to the building the same number of inmates 'turned out' at the beginning of the day."[38] Officers showed little interest in the rules of dress and demeanor that so concerned building personnel. Although most fights between inmates were stopped immediately, on some occasions the two antagonists were allowed to "duke it out" — unheard-of in a cell block. Crouch found that officers in the field adopted a paternalistic style that evoked the unequal relationship of parent to child. Social distance between inmate and supervisor in the field was not as great as inside, so informality arose between them.

Industrial Shop and School Officers In industrial shops and in the prison school, officers primarily have maintenance and security responsibilities. They work alongside civilians, such as shop supervisors, teachers, and counselors. Here the correctional officers act principally to ensure that the inmates who are supposed to be in the shops or school are there at the appointed time. The officers keep attendance, ascertain the whereabouts of absentees, attempt to prevent pilfering, and handle inmate problems and complaints.

Yard Officers As Lombardo observes, "In the blocks inmates are at home; in the school, shops, and on work details they are at work; but in the yard inmates are 'on the street.'" The yard is probably the most unstructured environment in the prison. Officers maintain a presence in the area, but they have no specific duties other than "supervising" the inmates. They are expected to preserve order and to be concerned about security. According to one guard, "In the yard it's mainly the observation of key individuals — the supposed troublemakers. You keep an eye on them so they're not causing any trouble that the prison doesn't need."[39]

Administration Building Assignments Officers in the administration building are generally removed from contact with the inmates and interact mainly with administrators, officials from the commissioner's office, and civilians. They provide security at the gates, supervise the visitors' room, and escort outsiders to offices. Because the appearance and behavior of these officers may color the general public's impression of the institution, they are selected carefully for these assignments.

Wall Posts Officers assigned to the towers or along the walls have almost no contact with inmates. Alone with telephone and weapon, the tower guard is solitary and bored. Traditionally these assignments have been reserved for new recruits and partially incapacitated veterans or for officers who don't get along with inmates. In recent years, with increases in prison violence, some correctional officers have sought to flee frustration and trouble by transferring from the cell blocks, dormitories, and yard to the safety of the towers.

Relief Officers Relief officers are assigned to a variety of tasks, depending on vacancies in the staff due to vacations and sick days. Because they work for only short periods in any particular area of the institution, they do not develop close contacts with the inmates. Relief officers are experienced workers who can step into any assignment as needed.

Problems with the Officer's Role

As with many correctional occupations, prison officers are expected to serve conflicting custodial and treatment goals. They are held responsible for preventing escapes, maintaining order, and ensuring the smooth functioning of the institution; yet they are also expected to counsel inmates and demonstrate an understanding attitude. Beyond the incompatibility of those roles lies the impossible rehabilitative ideal of treating each inmate as an individual in a large people-processing institution. Officers must use discretion yet somehow behave both custodially and therapeutically. Thus if they enforce the rules, they may be considered too rigid, yet if their failure to enforce rules threatens security, orderliness or maintenance, they are not doing their job.

Officers complain that the rules are constantly changing, so neither they nor the inmates know where they stand. Many look back nostalgically to the days when they were clear in purpose, unchallenged in authority, and respected by inmates. Whether such days ever existed seems not to be asked.

The correctional officer unquestionably is the key figure in the penal equation, the one on whom the whole system depends. And given the current emphasis on humane custody, the officer must be able to have a positive influence on inmates. As seen in Do the Right Thing, officers also confront ethical dilemmas on the job. In sum, correctional officers are asked to carry out an almost impossible mandate.

DO THE Right THING

After three years of daily contact, correctional officer Bill MacLeod and inmate Jack Douglas, who was serving a three- to five-year sentence, knew each other very well. They were both devoted to the Red Sox and Celtics. Throughout the year they would chat about the fortunes of their teams and the outlook ahead. MacLeod got to know and like Douglas. They were about the same age and had come from similar backgrounds. Why they were now on opposite sides of the cell bars was something MacLeod could not figure out.

One day Douglas called to MacLeod and said that he needed money because he had lost a bet to a guy, gambling on the Red Sox. Douglas said his wife would send him the money but that it couldn't come through the prison mail to him, because a check or money order would show on his commissary account.

"The guy wants cash. If he doesn't get it, I'm dead." Douglas took a breath. "Could you bring it in for me? She'll mail the money to you at your home. You could just drop the envelope on my bed."

"You know the rules. No gambling and no money," said MacLeod.

"But I'm scared shitless. It'll be no big deal for you and it will make all the difference for me. Come on, we've gotten along well all these years. I think of you as being different from those other officers."

What should MacLeod do? Is it likely to be a one-time occurrence with Douglas?" What if MacLeod's sergeant finds out? What if other inmates learn about it? ■

Use of Force

In Chapter 5 we described the case of Keith Hudson, an inmate at the state penitentiary at Angola, Louisiana, who was handcuffed and beaten by two correctional officers. Hudson had refused to stop washing his clothes in his cell toilet during the early morning hours. The U.S. Supreme Court ruled that the officers had "maliciously and sadistically used force to cause harm," thus violating Hudson's rights under the Eighth Amendment.[40]

Although corporal punishment and the excessive use of force is not permitted, correctional officers may use force in many situations. They often confront inmates who challenge their authority or are attacking fellow inmates. Officers are unarmed and outnumbered, yet are expected to maintain order and uphold institutional rules. Under these conditions corrections officers feel justified in using force.

When and how much force may be used? All correctional agencies now have formal policies and procedures with regard to the legitimate use of force. In general these policies allow only levels of force necessary to achieve legitimate goals. Officers violating these policies may be subject to an inmate lawsuit and dismissal. Christopher Smith lists five situations in which it is legally acceptable for officers to use force.[41]

1. *Self-defense:* If officers are threatened with physical attack, they may use a level of force that is reasonable to protect themselves from harm.
2. *Defense of third persons:* As in self-defense, an officer may use force to protect an inmate or another officer. Again, only reasonably necessary force may be used.
3. *Upholding Prison Rules:* If prisoners refuse to obey prison rules, it may be necessary for officers to use force to maintain safety and security. For example, if an inmate refuses to return to his or her cell it may be necessary to use handcuffs and forcefully transfer the prisoner.
4. *Prevention of a Crime:* Force may be used to stop a crime from being committed. For example, theft or destruction of property.
5. *Prevention of Escapes:* Officers may use force to prevent escapes because they threaten the well-being of society and order within correctional institutions. Although escape from a prison is a felony, officials may not shoot the fleeing inmate at will as

in the past. Today, agencies differ as to their policies toward escapees, some limit the use of deadly force to prisoners thought to be dangerous, others require warning shots. However, officers in Nebraska and Texas may face disciplinary action if they fail to use deadly force. Although the U.S. Supreme Court has limited the ability of police officers to shoot fleeing felons, the rule has not been applied to correctional officers.

Correctional officers face challenges to self-control and professional decision making. Inmates often "push" officers in subtle ways such as moving slowly, or use verbal abuse to provoke officers. Correctional officers are expected to run a "tight ship" and maintain order, often in threatening situations where they are outnumbered and dealing with troubled people who are difficult to control. In confrontation situations they must defuse hostility, yet uphold the rules—a difficult task at best.

Unionization

Collective bargaining for prison workers is a fairly recent phenomenon. The first unions for prison employees with collective bargaining rights were established in 1956 in Washington, DC, and New York City. However, the movement did not register major gains until the 1970s, when many states passed laws permitting unionization by public employees. By 1981 correctional employees were unionized in twenty-nine of fifty-two jurisdictions (state, federal, and District of Columbia).[42] The unions that represent correctional officers include two national public employee associations, the American Federation of State, County, and Municipal Employees (AFSCME), a part of the AFL-CIO, and the Service Employees International Union (SEIU); the International Brotherhood of Teamsters, and locally based state employee organizations. Custodial and program staff may belong to separate unions, resulting in conflict in some states; in others, different perspectives on correctional goals cause conflict among union groups.

Like other labor organizations, unions representing prison employees seek to improve wages and working conditions. Because the members are public employees, most are prohibited by law from striking, but some work stoppages and "sickouts" have occurred, and several commissioners have lost their jobs under union pressure. For example, in 1979 the 7,000 officers of the New York State system went on strike for seventeen days, and the governor was forced to call up more than 12,000 National Guard troops to maintain order.[43] In Connecticut 800 officers went on strike for three days, and 100 officers called in sick at the New Jersey State Prison. Although all these work stoppages were settled within a short time, they had an impact beyond the specific issues in dispute.

In addition to bargaining with management over wages and working conditions, unions representing correctional workers are active in politics. Like other public employee organizations, they seek to persuade legislators to pass laws and budgets to benefit their members. Their lobbying has often benefited corrections as a whole, because improvements in the system usually enhance conditions in which officers work. This fact has not been lost on commissioners and other correctional administrators, who often solicit the help of organized labor at budget time. Unlike other recipients of government services, prisoners are not interested in promoting the aims of their department. Given the absence of supportive clients, commissioners may depend on correctional employees and their unions to help advance legislative goals.

The great expansion of the incarcerated population over the past decade has increased the number of correctional officers from 223,078 in 1989 to 323,353 in 1994. In some states this growth has greatly increased union power. In California, for instance, where the number of officers has increased 500 percent since 1980, their union has become a potent political force lobbying not only for better wages and working conditions but also for expansion of prison facilities. This union has become a major contributor to political campaigns, helped pass the "three strikes" legislation, has lobbied against private prisons, supported victims' rights, and pushed for hiring more correctional officers.[44]

With the rise of prison employee unions, relationships between employees and administration are now more formalized: The rights and obligations of each side are stipulated by a labor contract, and wardens can no longer dictate working conditions. Thus unionization has brought officers not only better pay and job security but also greater control over their work. Seniority now determines work assignments, and officers have an increased role in setting institutional policies. Nonetheless, many people fear that unions and pro-inmate groups may form alliances on certain issues to oppose the administration.

Summary

Managing a correctional institution is exacting and complex. The formal structure of a coercive organization does not begin to describe the actual management of the prison. Although the warden, administrators, clinicians, and officers have formal state authority, their power is far from total. The relationship between managers and prisoners is much more dynamic than the organizational chart in the front office indicates.

Successful management depends on the leadership abilities of the top administrators. Effective styles of leadership change over time with shifts in the inmate community, decisions from the correctional commissioner's office, and political pressures from outside.

As the largest employee group in correctional institutions, custodial officers play a crucial role: They are the line personnel in constant contact with the prisoners. The officer is both a manager and a worker—a manager to the inmates, a low-status worker to the supervisors. Placed in an environment where most interactions are with prisoners, the officer is nevertheless expected to maintain a formal distance from them. ■

For Discussion

1. How have American prisons changed since the "big house" era? What do these changes mean for management?
2. As the superintendent of a prison, what sort of management problems must you face? What people can help you solve them?
3. In what way is the idea of total power in the institutional setting defective?
4. As a correctional officer assigned to manage a forty-man housing unit in a maximum-security prison, what problems might you face? How would you handle them?
5. Would you like to be a correctional officer? What aspects of the job make it attractive? What aspects make it unattractive?

For Further Reading

Crouch, Ben M., ed. *The Keepers: Prison Guards and Contemporary Corrections.* Springfield, IL: Thomas, 1980. Provides an excellent collection of articles about the role of correctional officers and the changes in that work that have taken place over time.

DiIulio, John J., Jr. *Governing Prisons.* New York: Free Press, 1987. Represents a major critique of the sociological view of prisons, and argues that governance by correctional officials is the key to maintaining good prisons and jails.

Irwin, John. *Prisons in Turmoil.* Boston: Little, Brown, 1980. Gives a sociological perspective on the changes that took place in American prisons during the 1970s and their implications for the lives of inmates and officers.

Jacobs, James B. *Stateville.* Chicago: University of Chicago Press, 1977. A classic study of a maximum-security prison. Analyzes changes over a half century.

Lombardo, Lucien X. *Guards Imprisoned.* New York: Elsevier, 1981. Takes an in-depth look at the working life of correctional officers as they perceive and experience it.

Phillips, Richard L., and Charles R. McConnell, *The Effective Corrections Manager.* Gaithersburg, MD: Aspen, 1996. An in-depth guide for prison managers. Covers all the major issues of correctional management.

Wright, Kevin N. *Effective Prison Leadership.* Binghamton, NY: William Neil Publishing, 1994. A guide for prison executives in developing an effective leadership style.

Zimmer, Lynn. *Women Guarding Men.* Chicago: University of Chicago Press, 1986. Explores the innovative policy of employing women as correctional officers in prisons for men.

Notes

1. Edgar May, "A Day on the Job—In Prison," *Corrections Magazine,* December 1976, p. 6.
2. Amatai Etzioni, *A Comparative Analysis of Complex Organizations* (New York: Free Press, 1961), p. 3.
3. Ibid., pp. 5–7, 27.
4. Charles Logan, "Criminal Justice Performance Measures for Prisons," *Performance Measures for the Criminal Justice System* (Washington, DC: U.S. Government Printing Office, 1993), pp. 19–57.
5. Ibid., ch. 5.
6. James B. Jacobs, *Stateville* (Chicago: University of Chicago Press, 1977).
7. President's Commission on Law Enforcement and Administration of Justice, *Task Force Report: Corrections* (Washington, DC: U.S. Government Printing Office, 1967), pp. 19–57.
8. Kevin N. Wright, *Effective Prison Leadership* (Binghamton, NY: William Neil Publishing, 1994), p. 2.
9. John J. DiIulio, Jr., *Governing Prisons* (New York: Free Press, 1987), p. 13.
10. Ibid., p. 12.
11. Gresham Sykes, *The Society of Captives* (Princeton, NJ: Princeton University Press, 1958), p. 41.
12. Jon R. Helpburn, "The Exercise of Power in Coercive Organizations: A Study of Prison Guards," *Criminology,* 23, 1985, pp. 145–164.
13. Ibid., p. 49.
14. James Marquart, "Prison Guards and the Use of Physical Coercion as a Mechanism of Prisoner Control," paper presented at the Annual Meeting of the American Sociological Association, San Antonio, Texas, August 1984.
15. Sykes, p. 53.
16. Stan Stojkovic, "Accounts of Prison Work: Corrections Officers' Portrayals of Their Work Worlds," *Perspectives on Social Problems,* 2, 1990, pp. 211–230.
17. Ibid., p. 223.
18. Richard Korn and Lloyd W. McCorkle, "Resocialization Within Walls," *Annals,* 293, 1954, p. 191.
19. Research in New York prisons revealed that although an estimated 6,000 crimes may be committed by inmates, few are referred for prosecution. David R. Eichenthal and Laurel Blatchford, "Prison Crime in New York State," *The Prison Journal,* 77, December 1997, pp. 456–466.
20. Department of Justice, Bureau of Justice Statistics, *Special Report* (Washington, DC: U.S. Government Printing Office, 1989), p. 1.
21. *Wolff v. McDonnell,* 94 S.Ct. 2963 (1974).
22. *Baxter v. Palmigiano,* 425 U.S. 308 (1976).
23. Edwin H. Sutherland and Donald R. Cressey, *Criminology* (Philadelphia: Lippincott, 1970), p. 536.
24. DiIulio, Governing Prisons, p. 235.
25. Ibid., p. 242.
26. John J. DiIulio, Jr., *No Escape: The Future of American Corrections* (New York: Basic Books, 1991), ch. 1.
27. James B. Jacobs and Norma Crotty, *Guard Unions and the Future of Prisons* (Ithaca: New York State School of Industrial and Labor Relations, 1978), p. 2.
28. Department of Justice, Bureau of Justice Statistics, *Sourcebook of Criminal Justice Statistics* (Washington, DC: U.S. Government Printing Office, 1995), p. 98.
29. Department of Justice, Bureau of Justice Statistics, *Sourcebook of Criminal Justice Statistics* (Washington, DC: U.S. Government Printing Office, 1997), p. 89.
30. Dana M. Britton, "Perceptions of the Work Environment Among Correctional Officers: Do Race and Sex Matter?" *Criminology,* 35, February 1997, pp. 85–105. See also: Kevin N. Wright and William G. Saylor, "Male and Female Employees' Perceptions of Prison Work: Is There a Difference?" *Justice Quarterly,* 8, December 1991, pp. 505–524.
31. Department of Justice, Bureau of Justice Statistics, *Sourcebook of Criminal Justice Statistics,* 1995, p. 98.
32. Nancy C. Jurik, "Organizational Barriers to Women Working as Corrections Officers in Men's Prisons," in Timothy J. Flanagan, Jams W. Marquart, and Kenneth G. Adams, eds., *Incarcerating Criminals* (New York: Oxford University Press, 1998), pp. 136–148.
33. Lynn E. Zimmer, *Women Guarding Men* (Chicago: University of Chicago Press, 1986).
34. Denise L. Jenne and Robert C. Kersting, "Aggression and Women Correctional Officers in Male Prisons," *The Prison Journal,* 76, December 1996, pp. 442–460.
35. Mark R. Pogrebin and Eric D. Poole, "The Sexualized Work Environment: A Look at Women Jail Officers," *The Prison Journal,* 77, March 1997, pp. 41–57.
36. Ben M. Crouch and James W. Marquart, "On Becoming a Prison Guard," in Stan Stojkovic, John Klofas, and David Kalinich, eds., *The Administration and Management of Criminal Justice Organizations,* 2nd ed. (Prospect Heights, IL: Waveland Press, 1994), p. 301.
37. Lombardo, p. 3.

38. Ben M. Crouch, "The Book vs. the Boot: Two Styles of Guarding a Southern Prison," in Ben M. Crouch, ed., *The Keepers* (Springfield, IL: Thomas, 1980), pp. 207–224.

39. Lombardo, p. 42.

40. *Hudson v. MacMillan,* 503 U.S. 1 (1992)

41. Christopher R. Smith, *Law and Contemporary Corrections* (Belmont, CA: Wadsworth, 1999), ch. 6.

42. David Duffee, "Careers in Criminal Justice: Corrections," in Sanford H. Kadish, ed., *Encyclopedia of Crime and Justice* (New York: Free Press, 1983), p. 1232.

43. Jacobs and Crossy, p. 3.

44. *The New York Times,* November 7, 1995, p. 1.

CHAPTER FOURTEEN
Institutional Programs

The median time served in U.S. prisons is twenty-nine months.[1] Imagine where you were two and one-half years ago and what you were doing. Now imagine you had spent every day, every hour since then living behind bars. Think of what you would have missed. Think, too, of how long the prison term would have seemed to have lasted—decades, an eternity. The theme in prison, the one thread that links all prisoners, is time: "time in the joint," "doing time," "good time," "time left," "straight time." "How much time did you get?" "When do you come up for parole?" "What's your maximum release date?" Calendars are prominent in the cells, and some inmates carefully mark the passing of each day.

Institutional programs mitigate the oppressiveness of time in prison. They also provide opportunities for prisoners to improve their lives, whether the programs involve counseling, education, or merely recreation. When rehabilitation is a dominant correctional goal, the parole board sees participation in a treatment program as an indication of readiness for supervision in the community. But perhaps the major merit of programs is the fact that they keep prison time from becoming dead time. When minutes crawl, the soul grows bitter.

In this chapter we examine the wide variety of prison programs in today's prisons. We investigate the role these programs play in prison life, and we evaluate their effectiveness from the viewpoint of both inmates and management. We will seek answers to the following Questions for Inquiry:

Questions FOR INQUIRY

1. Why is managing time important for prison administrators and inmates?
2. What is the classification process, and how is it used?
3. What types of rehabilitative programs are available in most prisons?
4. Why are prison industries important, and how do they operate?
5. Why do administrators believe recreation programs are important?

Managing Time

Prison administrators use institutional programs to help manage time. Work assignments occupy the middle hours of the day; treatment and recreational periods are held before and after work assignments; and special programs (Junior Chamber of Commerce meetings, Bible study, Alcoholics Anonymous sessions) take up the remaining hours. Experienced administrators know that the more programs they offer, the less likely inmates' boredom is to translate into hostility toward the staff. The less cell time, the fewer tensions. "It is absolutely the most important ingredient in managing a safe and secure institution, to keep the inmates productively occupied, in either work or education or

As the old saying goes, "Idle hands are the Devil's playground." Experienced administrators know that the more programs offered, the less likely inmates' boredom will translate into "mischief-making."

prison program

Any formal, structured activity that takes prisoners out of their cells and sets them to instrumental tasks.

drug treatment or structured recreation," says J. Michael Quinlan, a former director of the Federal Bureau of Prisons.[2]

Administrators use prison programs as incentives for good behavior. Inmates know that when they break the rules, they will be denied access to programs, and this will make time go slower.

We use the broadest possible definition of **prison program** in this chapter. A program is any formal, structured activity that takes prisoners out of their cells and lets them do something. Programs range from group therapy sessions to chair-making factories, from baseball teams to reading groups. Some programs are designed to rehabilitate, others use inmate labor to reduce costs of running the facility. But all prison programs serve the fundamental need to manage time.

There are four types of programs. The most controversial are rehabilitative ones. Many such programs attempt to improve job skills or education; others seek to alter the propensity for criminal behavior by psychological, behavioral, or social treatment. A second type of program is industrial. Here prisoners make various products. The third type involves daily maintenance—janitorial and kitchen tasks, laundry, and the like. Maintenance programs are all but universal because every prison needs them. The fourth type are recreational programs designed to keep inmates physically fit and involved in positive activities.

Constraints of Security

No matter how beneficial a program is, it must not conflict with security. As criminologist Donald J. Newman once remarked, even if a thousand evaluations showed that pole-vaulting was a valuable skill, it still would never be taught in prison.

Security requirements impinge on programs in a variety of ways. Whenever a program requires sharp tools or materials that could be fashioned into tools, heavy security prevails. This is a particular problem for maintenance, but it also affects many industrial programs. Plumbing and electrical operations use knives, pipes, hammers, and wrenches—weapons. Common prison industries as woodworking, welding, and auto repair likewise use potentially lethal objects.

Security requires repeated tool counts, searches, and detailed accounting of materials. Inmates are often searched twice a shift, and inventories taken three or more times a day. The heavy emphasis on security has two important consequences. First, unceasing surveillance further demoralizes the inmates and sharpens their sense of captivity. Prisoners are lined up and checked out so often that their consciousness of themselves as security risks is constantly reinforced. The most rudimentary tasks call for a level of control that exacerbates an already dehumanizing environment.

Second, security requirements make maintenance and industrial programs inefficient. Each time a tool is used, it must be signed out and signed in; each time material is obtained, paperwork must be done. Even coffee breaks are circumscribed by security measures. Captives are seldom the most industrious workers, and prison security measures don't improve efficiency.

Despite the negative effects, most authorities strenuously support tight control of potentially dangerous items. Even one handcrafted knife or bludgeon is a serious physical risk to inmates and staff. Stabbings and other mayhem occur far too often. Yet cynics question the utility of intrusive security; even in the most closely monitored prisons shakedowns uncover hundreds of contrived weapons and other contraband. Prisoners are ingenious at creating weapons; even such items as spoons and ballpoint pens can be turned into weapons. The only remedy—and a weak one—is unremitting vigilance. And some programs are simply impractical, because the equipment and materials are too easily misused.

Institutional security affects rehabilitative programs in a different way. In classwork or counseling, inmates know their interactions with other prisoners are observed closely for security violations. Even in therapy a prisoner knows any remark made to a staff member touching on a possible violation may well have unpleasant consequences. Here, too, security makes it difficult to bridge the gap between the keepers and the kept.

The effect of that gap on rehabilitative programs can be very serious. The relationship between the therapist and the client is of central importance to treatment success. Many writers have analyzed this matter in some detail; a vivid description by Thomas Harris appears in his popular book *I'm OK, You're OK.*[3] Harris points out that patients in therapy find it difficult to solve their problems as long as they feel what he calls "not OK": dependent, untrustworthy, incompetent. Yet these are precisely the feelings security practices arouse in prisoners. Prison therapists thus must fight the environment in which they work: It's not easy to make a prisoner feel OK.

In sum, although the objectives of a program—to improve the prisoners' sense of themselves or to make them more vocationally competitive—may be laudable, achieving such objectives in a prison is difficult. The need for tight security dilutes the effectiveness of prison programs, except as a means to fill time.

The Principle of Least Eligibility

Institutional programs also are affected by society's expectation that prisoners will not receive free any extra services for which law-abiding citizens must pay. According to this **principle of least eligibility,** prisoners, having been convicted of wrongful behavior, should be the least eligible of all citizens for social benefits beyond the bare minimum required by law. Taken to its extreme, the principle would prohibit many institutional benefits for offenders, such as education courses and cosmetic surgery.

In 1994 Senator Kay Bailey Hutchison, a Texas Republican, led the fight in Congress against Pell Grants for prisoners, arguing that paying tuition for college courses for inmates used $2 million and displaced 100,000 law-abiding students. In fact any student who meets Pell eligibility requirements, in prison or in the community is funded and of the 4 million grants awarded each year only 23,000 went to prisoners. And research shows that inmates who take educational programs while incarcerated are the least likely to return.[4]

Administrators find it difficult to justify the practice of offering services to prisoners that may exceed in quality those available to law-abiding citizens. The general public often is quite hostile to creative programming for inmates, and this sentiment affects virtually all programs. The story is told of a miniature golf course, built on the grounds of a Connecticut prison by inmates in their off-hours and with their own funds, that was left unused after a newspaper reporter exposed it in a series of stories on the "country-club prison."

The principle of least eligibility reflects a strong public ambivalence about correctional programming. Brandon Applegate, Francis Cullen, and Bonnie Fisher found that citizens surveyed support rehabilitation as part of correctional policy.[5] Yet the public does not want programs that seem to reward criminal conduct. Therefore prison programs frequently represent only weak versions of free-society programs. If the prison offers job training programs, they do not prepare inmates for positions in the most prestigious or high-paying occupations. If the prison offers psychological services, they frequently take the form of group or individual counseling sessions rather than intensive therapy. Educational classes tend to be very basic and barely remedial.

Consider the public reaction to a recent suit brought by an Oregon prisoner, who forced the state to pay $17,000 for a sex-change operation. The surgery is considered a

principle of least eligibility

The doctrine that prisoners ought to receive no goods or services in excess of those available to people who have lived within the law.

legitimate (if unusual) procedure in free society, but its free provision to a member of the least eligible class was interpreted by many observers as unwarranted exploitation of the public by the offender. Yet such an operation is often justified in terms of the psychological or social well-being of the prisoner and its positive effects on future behavior.

Classification

classification

A process by which prisoners are assigned to types of custody and treatment.

Inmates who wish to participate in programs face still another constraint: the procedures used to classify them with respect to security and programs. At Elmira Reformatory in the 1800s, Zebulon Brockway initiated a process of **classification** so that inmates could be grouped according to custody requirements and program needs. During the rehabilitation era classification was important because treatment was based on a clinical assessment of the inmate's needs. Although rehabilitation is less emphasized today, ongoing classification is still important for prison management. Instead, classification now focuses on the offender's potential for escape, violence, or victimization by other inmates.

During incarceration, prisoners may be reclassified as they encounter problems or finish treatment programs. Classification also changes if inmates transfer to another institution and if they are approaching release to the community.

The Classification Process

In most corrections systems, all prison-bound offenders pass through a reception and orientation center where, for a period typically lasting three to six weeks, they are evaluated and classified. In some states the center is a separate facility, but generally each institution has its own reception center. Social scientists have likened reception and classification to a process of mortification. Much as the army recruit is socialized to military life by basic training, the college student to a fraternity by pledge week, and the monastic brother to a religious order through the novitiate, the sentenced felon is introduced to the new status of prison inmate by the reception process. This is a deliberately exaggerated degradation ceremony that seeks to depersonalize the inductee. Newcomers are stripped of personal effects and given a uniform, rule book, medical examination, and shower—in part to underscore that they no longer are free citizens.

In some systems classification consists merely of sorting prisoners on the basis of age, severity of offense, record of prior incarceration, and institutional conduct. Such approaches serve mainly as a management tool to ensure that inmates are assigned to housing units appropriate to their custody level (low, medium, high, segregation), separated from those who are likely to victimize them (for example, separating the young, slight, and timid from the "gorillas"), and grouped with members of their work assignment (for example, kitchen duty).

At rehabilitative institutions, batteries of tests, psychiatric evaluations, and counseling are administered so that each prisoner can be assessed for treatment as well as custody. Treatment resources are limited in most prisons, so they must be allocated to benefit the inmates who most need them. The diagnostic process serves this purpose.

The classification decision often is made by a committee consisting of the deputy warden and the heads of departments for custody, treatment, education, industry, and the like. In some systems a classification committee makes decisions about an inmate's program and custody status. At the hearing caseworkers or counselors present information from presentence reports, police records, and the reception process. The inmate appears before the committee, personal needs and assignments are discussed, and decisions are made. However, because it is difficult to assemble so many top administrators for classification hearings, some institutions delegate the task to two or three staff members on the reception team. They make assignments according to procedures prescribed by the department of corrections and the institution's needs. The Workperspective describes the role of a classification officer.

WORK PERSPECTIVE

Karl G. Lewis

**Classification Counselor,
Connecticut Department of Correction**

I was hired by the Department of Correction soon after completing my B.A. in English literature. I attended the Academy and was assigned to the high-security unit at the Connecticut Correctional Institution–Cheshire as a classification officer. Here I began my criminal justice education, working with a wide variety of offenders in the general population, punitive housing, and protective custody. After a year as a trainee, I was promoted to Correctional Rehabilitation Service Officer–I, a line classification officer with responsibility for decisions on housing, programs, and work.

At the urging of the deputy warden, I enrolled in the Master of Public Affairs Program at the University of Connecticut. My graduate work, completed part-time, allowed me to study criminal justice agencies in the web of government. After a stint at a minimum-security prerelease facility, I was promoted to Classification Officer–Senior Grade. I then transferred to the Connecticut Board of Parole as a Case Analyst, working with board members in the hearing process. During an administrative reorganization, I was reassigned to the high-security unit at Cheshire with expanded responsibilities.

Senior classification officers are part of a unit management team, often acting as a treatment or custody supervisor in the absence of the unit manager. The decisions I had to make as a custody supervisor had to be the most difficult, and the most important, of my career.

When working with general-population, high-security inmates, custody supervisors commonly receive requests for transfer to the segregated housing unit known as Protective Custody (P.C.). One day in the summer of 1996, while monitoring a recreation period, an inmate asked to speak to me in private. He told me he wanted to "check in" to P.C. He said he owed a debt to certain gang members over cigarettes. The inmate, who looked much

younger than his 24 years, was unwilling to identify the parties who were threatening him, other than general details, for example, "the tall Spanish guy from the upper tier." If he identified the perpetrators he risked being labeled a "snitch," which could lead to serious, even mortal consequences.

Although the inmate was agitated, I could not justify even temporary segregation given the dearth of detail. However, if I sent him back to his own housing unit he might be a danger to himself, staff, other inmates, or the orderly operation of the institution. As a precaution, I transferred the inmate to a different part of the facility where he would have no contact with his tormentors. This would give me time to investigate.

It turned out that the inmate's story was a fabrication. In fact, he was in considerably more difficulty than he was willing to admit. Reviewing his criminal history, I saw he had been convicted of sexually assaulting a child in an adjoining state in the late 1980s. He had had adjustment problems in other facilities, having twice requested, unsuccessfully, to be transferred to P.C. A department intelligence officer learned that the child was the son of a high-ranking prison gang leader in the other state. It was therefore only a matter of time before an inmate at Cheshire found out and the young sexual offender became a target.

With this information, I was able to justify reclassification to protective custody.

Cheshire's 200-bed P.C. unit serves the entire correctional system and houses snitches, sexual offenders, and former Latin Kings and Aryan Brotherhood gang members. Divided into two units, inmates eat, recreate, and participate in programs only in Protective Custody—they have no contact with the general population. The inmate I placed in P.C. had eighteen to thirty-six months to go on a four-year definite sentence for a drug-related burglary. It is unlikely that he will leave P.C. until he is released.

In practice, classification committees often revert to stereotypes rather than diagnostic criteria in assigning inmates. Common stereotypes include members of racial or ethnic gangs, predators who demand everything from sex to cigarettes, weak victim types, and informers seeking protection, and those who do not fit into any one category. Inmates often contribute to stereotyping by their behavior with staff. By fitting each inmate to a stereotype, the staff routinize classification, serving the staff and organizational needs.

Classification decisions are often made on the basis of the institution's needs rather than those of the inmate. Enrollment in certain treatment and training programs is limited, and demand is great. Thus inmates may find that the few places in, for example, the electrician course are filled and there is a long waiting list. Because the institution's housekeeping must be done by inmates, large numbers of inmates must be assigned to these tasks. This issue is posed in Do the Right Thing.

DO THE Right THING

Members of the classification committee examined the case folders of the inmates who would appear before them. This morning ten newly admitted prisoners were to be classified as to housing and program. Each folder contained basic information about the inmate's education, prior employment, offense, sentence, and counselor's evaluation.

In the small talk before the first inmate arrived, Ralph MacKinnon, chief of the classification unit, warned the other members that the computer program was filled and the waiting list was long. However, there was a great need for workers making mattresses for state institutions.

"But Ralph, some of the guys trying to learn computer programming just can't hack it," said counselor Michael Harris. "I've got a man coming before us who was a math major in college and has already had some computer experience. He would greatly benefit from the extra training."

"That's fine, Mike, but we can't let someone jump ahead, especially when the mattress factory needs workers. I promised Jim Fox we would get him some help."

"But shouldn't we put people into programs that would help them when they get out?" responded Mike.

If you were on the classification committee what would you do? ■

Classification is the process of evaluating an offender's needs and developing custody and treatment programs.

Objective Classification Systems

As prison space becomes scarcer and more valuable, administrators feel pressured to ensure that it is used as efficiently as possible and that levels of custody are appropriate. The courts require systems of classification to "be clearly understandable, consistently applied and conceptually complete. Methods of validation must be implemented and means of redress for irregularity must be provided."[6]

New predictive and equity-based systems seek to classify inmates more objectively. Predictive models are designed to distinguish inmates with respect to risk of escape, potential misconduct in the institution, and future criminal behavior. Clinical, socioeconomic, and criminal factors (such as previous prison escapes) are given point values, and the total point score determines security level. Equity-based models of classification use only a few explicitly defined legal variables reflecting current and previous criminal characteristics. Such variables as race, employment, and education are not used because it is seen as unfair to manage inmates on the basis of these characteristics. However, in reality the two models frequently use similar variables to classify inmates, the main difference being that predictive models use statistical techniques.

Objective systems are more efficient and cheaper because line staff can be trained to administer and score the instrument without help from clinicians and senior administrators. A staff member can determine appropriate custody level by entering relevant data, adding up total points for factor scores, and applying numerical criteria to indicate classification. Inmates who score 25 or above, for example, might be sent to maximum security, those who score 15 or below to minimum security, and the remainder to medium security. Classification serves the program and custody goals of the institution, but the process also places a label on each prisoner. The inmate may take from the classification process a new identity and a knowledge of the official evaluation. When prisoners become aware of the labels given them by evaluators, they interpret those labels as the viewpoint of the officials who have almost unlimited power over their lives.

Most states overclassify inmates, placing them in higher custody levels than appears necessary simply because more high-security space is available. As a result, treatment assignments for which prisoners in maximum security are not eligible (such as work release) are simply unavailable to the vast majority of inmates.

This classification policy can have negative consequences for prisoners, because many privileges are linked to classification level. For example, in Colorado early release from prison is restricted to inmates classified as minimum security. In many states the amount of good time that can be earned is tied to security classification. Further, release on parole often depends on a record of successful participation in treatment or educational programs. Prisoners often have difficulty explaining to the parole board that they really did want to learn a skill but were given no opportunity to do so.

Rehabilitative Programs

Rehabilitative programs aim to reform the offenders' behavior. Some people argue that imprisonment is so painful that it is itself reformative: Offenders change their ways to avoid repeating the experience. The reformative power of prison itself often is called its "special deterrence effect."

But many scholars contend that imprisonment by itself is not reformative enough, that the inmate's prison activities must also be reformative. There is much dispute about what rehabilitative programs should be offered and emphasized: psychological, behavioral, social, vocational, substance abuse, and religious.

Psychological Programs

Psychological help in its various forms—psychotherapy, counseling, and so on—is routinely sought by millions of Americans to help them weather various crises. In prison, psychological programs seek to treat the underlying emotional or mental problems that led to criminality. Of course, this assumes that such problems are indeed the primary cause of most offenders' criminality—or even that the concept of mental illness makes sense. These assumptions underlie the medical model, discussed in Chapter 3. However, critics have challenged this model repeatedly and vigorously.

In his famous critique, psychiatrist Thomas S. Szasz questioned the applicability of the medical model used for physical ailments to the human "problems in living" commonly called mental illness.[7] The notions of diagnosis, prognosis, and treatment are irrelevant to these problems and also mislead people who try to deal with them.

Other critics of mental health treatment in prisons take a much less radical stance: They say mental illness is an inadequate explanation of criminal behavior. Many additional factors enter an offender's decision to behave criminally: opportunity, rational motivation, skill, acquaintances, anger. No one can demonstrate convincingly that some mental problem underlies all or even most of such decisions. Indeed, studies of correctional populations find that only about 8 percent of prisoners, 7 percent of jail inmates, and 6 percent of probationers suffer from serious mental illnesses.[8] These rates are much higher than the general population, but still represent only a small minority of the correctional population.

The lack of consensus on diagnoses of mental illness indicates some of the drawbacks in the general concept that mental illness underlies much criminal behavior. Trained psychiatrists, for example, disagree on the diagnosis of patients' mental problems as often as half the time. If the experts cannot agree on the nature of an "illness," then perhaps the idea of the "illness" itself has no merit.

psychotherapy

In generic terms, all forms of "treatment of the mind"; in the prison setting, coercive in nature.

Psychotherapeutic Approaches The unreliability of mental illness diagnosis may be one reason why treatments have been so ineffective. Robert Martinson's ground-breaking review of over two hundred evaluations of treatment programs, discussed in Chapter 3, provides perhaps the most stark conclusion: With few exceptions, rehabilitative efforts had no appreciable effect on recidivism.[9] Martinson was referring to a wide variety of programs, but his conclusion was particularly applicable to programs designed to improve offenders' emotional or psychological functioning.

That these programs do little for offenders should not be surprising. Most experts would agree that psychotherapy, the generic term used to refer to all forms of "treatment of the mind," has narrow prospects for success even with motivated, voluntary, free patients. There, the most common arrangement for psychotherapy is entrepreneurial. The individual enters a voluntary, financial contract with the therapist for help; either party is free to terminate the agreement at any time. Because the client is the purchaser, it is easy to see why the therapist keeps the client's interest foremost during the treatment process.

The psychotherapy approach is problematic in prison. It is not the offender but society that purchases the therapist's services. The interests of the purchaser—society—assume more importance to the therapist than do those of the offender. This turns the accepted practices of most therapy upside down. The centerpiece is not the offender; instead, it is society's desire that the offender develop a crime-free lifestyle. This is why so many complain that prison psychotherapy probes into aspects of their lives with which they do not need help.

coercive therapy

Treatment in which the therapist determines the need for and the goals of treatment processes, whether or not the client agrees.

When a third party (such as society) establishes both the need for and the goals of therapy, it is called **coercive therapy.** With coercive therapy the patient finds it hard to resist the imperative of getting help, even though treatment may be inappropriate. Indeed, coercive therapy has a Catch-22 aspect: Any reluctance on the offender's part to admit help is needed is interpreted as "resistance," a sure sign that the prisoner does indeed need the therapy.

Because of the many problems with prison psychotherapy, programs that address inmates' emotional health have become less common in recent years. Most experts agree that mental abnormalities play an insignificant role in the criminality of most offenders. Today most prison counselors do not practice psychotherapy with inmates. Instead, they tend to focus their work on concrete problems that prisoners may face in adjusting to the prison environment or in dealing with family crises that occur during incarceration.

Group Treatment Approaches Unlike traditional psychotherapy, prison programs that address prisoners' emotions and thoughts tend to use group therapy, in which offenders come together to discuss mutual problems. Group treatment is considered important because humans are social animals. Most of our behavior occurs in groups, and we learn to define ourselves and to interpret our experiences in groups. This fact is particularly appropriate to criminology, because a large proportion of crime is committed by groups or in groups, and much criminal behavior is reinforced by group norms, by manipulation, and by elaborate rationalizations. Therefore prison treatment groups are often highly confrontational. Group members are asked to "call" the manipulations and rationalizations others are using to justify their deviant behavior, and they are encouraged to participate wholeheartedly in the process. Theoretically inmates can then come to understand their own versions of those manipulations and rationalizations.

Most groups in prison use structured approaches in which the group undertakes a series of patterned discussion topics or activities that are targeted not at the offender's emotions, but at thought processes. Four of the most common group approaches are reality therapy, confrontation therapy, transactional analysis, and cognitive skill building.

Reality therapy has a very simple core tenet: People's problems decline when they behave more responsibly. Things get difficult when people fail to behave in ways consistent with life's realities. The therapist's role is to return the client consistently and firmly to the real consequences of his or her behavior, with particular attention to the troubles that follow inappropriate behavior. Reality therapy is popular in corrections for three reasons. First, it assumes that the rules society sets for its members are inescapable. Second, its techniques are easy for staff to learn. Third, the method is short-term and thus highly adaptable to prison.

In **confrontation therapy** a professional group leader encourages group members to confront each other's rationalizations and manipulations, which are common to criminal thoughts and actions. These sessions can become quite vocal, and inmates trying to defend themselves can get very angry in reaction to aggressive accusations by peers. The intent of the therapy is to pressure inmates into giving up their manipulative rationalizations, and especially to accept responsibility for the harms their crimes have caused. Confrontive techniques are often used with offenders whose criminal styles include heavy reliance on denial, especially sex offenders. Studies show these methods can backfire, leading some offenders to deepen involvement in secretive criminal ways,[10] and the techniques can be so aggressive that some experts question whether they are ethical and whether they model the very exploitive behavior they seek to prevent.[11]

Transactional analysis focuses on the roles (ego states) that people play with others. Three general ego states are involved: The Parent is judging and controlling; the Adult is mature, realistic, and ethical; the Child is playful, dependent, and sometimes naughty. The aim of transactional analysis is to lead people to a realization that their problems commonly result from approaching the world as an angry Parent or weak Child rather than as a responsible Adult. The life stance of many prisoners has been that of naughty Child: "Try to catch me." The therapist's role is largely that of teacher; he or she spends much time explaining the concepts of transactional analysis and showing the client how to use them in analyzing his or her own life. Like reality therapy, transactional analysis is considered well suited to corrections because it is simple, straightforward, and short term. Moreover, a formal therapy "contract" between the client and the therapist helps to eliminate some of the insidious aspects of coercive therapy.

Cognitive skill building focuses on changing the thought patterns that accompany criminal behavior. Advocates argue that offenders develop antisocial patterns of reasoning that make them believe criminal behavior makes sense. To replace these thought patterns, offenders need to learn new skills and techniques for day-to-day living. The group leader uses a variety of procedures to teach these new skills, including role-playing and "psychodramas" — that re-create emotionally stressful past occurrences. Sometimes called *cognitive restructuring*, the aim of the cognitive approach is to teach offenders new ways to think about themselves and their actions.

Recent evaluations of reasoning-based group programs in prison settings find that offenders who complete these programs perform better after release from prison than do others who have not been in the program.[12] However, proponents of these methods stress that not all inmates are suitable for group methods and that the programs must be operated by skilled staff. Too often offenders have little motivation to attend group sessions, prison security undermines the integrity of the process (members are asked to

---

reality therapy

Treatment that emphasizes personal responsibility for actions and their consequences.

confrontation therapy

A treatment technique, usually done in a group, that vividly brings the offender fact to face with the consequences of the crimes for the victim and society.

transactional analysis

Treatment that focuses on how a person interacts with others, especially on patterns of interaction that indicate personal problems.

cognitive skill building

A form of behavior therapy that focuses on changing the thinking and reasoning patterns that accompany criminal behavior.

report statements made by others in the group), or group leaders lack professional competence. Under such conditions, groups will fail.

Behavior Therapy

behavior therapy

Treatment that induces new behaviors through reinforcements (rewards and punishments), role modeling, and other active forms of teaching.

Much recent work in psychotherapy has focused on treating behavior rather than the mind. Correctional **behavior therapy** postulates that the differences between people labeled *deviant* and *nondeviant* lie not within the individual but in that person's responses to problems in the environment. According to this idea, what needs reformation is not the offender's mind or emotions but his or her behavior. The method seeks to change behavior directly by identifying and altering the environmental conditions that promote problem behavior. The assumption is that behavior is learned and has some positive payoff. It can be unlearned if that payoff is eliminated and a more rewarding payoff is found for different behavior.

The target of the behavior change effort is not criminality per se but the variety of problem behaviors that surround a criminal lifestyle: verbal manipulation and rationalization; deficiency in social skills, such as conversation; inability to control anger and frustration; and so on. Obviously such behavior can make it difficult to keep jobs, avoid conflict, and handle disappointment. The underlying belief is that criminal behavior typically is related to such crucial personal experiences.

token economy

A type of behavior therapy that uses payments (such as tokens) to reinforce desirable behaviors in an institutional environment.

The **token economy** is a systematic behavior therapy in which any benefits the offender wants—television or recreation time, library privileges, and so forth—must be purchased with tokens. The tokens can be earned only by completing certain approved tasks, such a work assignment or good grades. Thus the inmate gradually develops behavior patterns that mirror the values held in the larger society: People must earn what they get; one must save up for desired things; postponing gratification is often the best way to obtain greater gratification.

Experience with token economies suggests that they can often be powerful techniques for managing the prisoner's time in prison. In some token economies virtually everything has a price—choice of menu, furloughs for family visits, availability of night reading—and prisoners quickly learn that if they want to do reasonably comfortable time, they had better earn the currency to buy it.

Unfortunately follow-up studies of token economies do not show that what is learned in prison is transferable to life outside. It is questionable whether responsible behavior on the street always pays off in the direct manner of the token economy. In fact, the departing prisoner may rejoin friends and acquaintances who promote a very different idea: The way to the good life is to take it. Very often strong peer pressure moves the former offender back into a criminal lifestyle in which the law-abiding reinforcement patterns of the token economy count for little.

Critics of behavior therapy in general raise two points. First, the technique is often successful with the target behaviors but fails to alter criminality. Second, the methods of therapy often lead to serious abuses of coercive power in corrections: To force alterations in behavior, the therapist takes advantage of the inmate's powerlessness. To many observers such manipulation is a frightening misuse of government power.

Social Therapy

social therapy

Treatment that attempts to make the institutional environment supportive of prosocial attitudes and behaviors.

The idea of social treatment was introduced by Maxwell Jones in 1956 under the label therapeutic community. Since then the limitations of behavior and psychological programs have led authorities to develop other therapy systems that attempt to create healthy social support patterns among offenders. The broad term **social therapy** is applied to these programs (often referred to as milieu therapy or positive peer culture) because they seek to develop a prosocial environment within the prison to help the offender develop noncriminal ways of coping outside. They are based on the idea that people learn lawbreaking values and behaviors in social settings from peers to whom they attach importance. To permanently alter these values and behaviors, the peer relationships and interaction patterns must be changed.

The primary aim of this model is to change the institution into a more democratic operation in which all inmates have a say in what goes on. In its most developed form the therapeutic community is governed by three principles:

1. *Emphasis on productive work and rapid return to the community.* Every form of activity within the institution is used to help the inmate get ready for early release as a responsible citizen.
2. *Reorientation of inmates through educational techniques.* Group dynamics and group pressures are used liberally for constructive purposes. Group treatment is often regarded as more effective than individual treatment.
3. *Widely diffused authority among staff and inmates.* The authority that in custodial prisons rests on rank or position is supplemented by authority based on treatment competence, thus including inmates. The system is strongly democratic rather than authoritarian.[13]

The approach assumes that true change occurs when offenders begin to take responsibility for the social climate within which they must live. All actions are directed toward developing an inmate culture that promotes a law-abiding lifestyle with appropriate social attitudes. Such a program requires significant shifts in institutional policy to support a prosocial institutional climate. Thus (1) institutional practices must be democratic rather than bureaucratic, (2) programs must focus on treatment rather than custody, (3) humanitarian concerns have priority over institutional routines, and (4) flexibility is valued over rigidity.

It is exceedingly difficult to turn a prison into a therapeutic community. Three strategies are used to do so. First, efforts are made to recruit staff and inmates whose personal orientations toward the work are consistent with the therapeutic community ideal. All correctional staff, including guards and professionals, are trained in the techniques of social treatment. Inmates must have normal intelligence and willingness to verbalize their feelings.

Second, the prison architecture is made to fit the therapeutic aims. Thus the facility must be "open," with few locked doors, cells, and bars; it must be suitable for dormitory-style living and must have freely available space.

Third and most significant, small inmate groups are convened daily to discuss prison management, staff–offender interaction, and offender behavior. The functioning of a group is both democratic, in that many of the policy decisions are discussed fully before they are adopted, and therapeutic, in that each member of a group (whether staff or inmate) agrees to take responsibility for the emotional well-being of all other members. Sometimes a group will confront individual members about negative behavior; other times the group will help an individual to work out a particular problem. Through this regularly scheduled social interaction, the aims of the therapeutic community are most fully realized.

The therapeutic community has been criticized as both impractical and ineffective in reducing crime. The impracticality of the idea is apparent from a description of its intent. How can a prison, intentionally established as a degrading, painful, intrusive setting be transformed into a caring, supportive environment? How can the keepers, trained to control the kept but vulnerable to their threats, ever give up meaningful institutional authority to groups of inmates without risking their own security and that of the institution?

The programs that have lasted long enough to be evaluated have yielded ambiguous results. Most reviews found that parolees from therapeutic milieus did no better or worse than parolees from traditional prisons. Interestingly, early evaluations of social treatment settings for juveniles showed positive results, but more recent reanalyses cast doubt on those findings.

Belief in the potential of these programs to rehabilitate offenders, especially drug-dependent offenders, has recently undergone something of a renaissance. For carefully selected groups of offenders, certain social treatment programs, properly run, have been shown to be effective.[14]

Vocational Rehabilitation

One of the oldest ideas in prison programming is to teach prisoners a skill that can help them get a job on release. **Vocational rehabilitation** has much to recommend it, because offenders constitute one of the most undereducated and underemployed groups in the U.S. population, and the unemployment rate of former offenders is more than three times that of nonoffenders. Certainly, then, offenders have limited capability to succeed as wage earners. Many people believe that criminal behavior stems from this kind of economic incapacity, and they urge the wide use of educational and vocational programs to counter it.

Educational Programs It has been estimated that over 200,000 state and federal inmates participate in an educational program while incarcerated, making education one of the most popular prison programs in the corrections system.[15] Even so, prison education programs face difficult practical and fiscal problems (see the Focus box).

Many prisoners' ability to learn is hampered by a lack of basic reading and computational skills. Moreover, research has increasingly shown a link between learning disabilities and delinquency; many offenders have experienced disciplinary as well as academic failure in school. Thus prison education must cope with inmates who have neither academic skills nor attitudes conducive to learning.

The problems of prison education are exacerbated by other factors. Inmates normally are well beyond the age associated with their current educational attainment. For example, it is not unusual for a 29-year-old prisoner to be performing at a sixth-grade level. Very few available texts are appropriate for such adults. Imagine a 32-year-old two-time robber with self-inflicted tattoos struggling through a passage in a second-grade reader about Johnnie and Susie learning how to bake cookies. The sheer inappropriateness of the material to the age and interests of inmates drives many of them away from remedial schooling.

Similarly, the needs of adults differ from those of youthful students. Their attention span is longer, their life experience much broader, and their sophistication greater. Adult learning curricula are unlike typical school curricula, but prison budgets seldom permit purchase of specialized educational aids, so the education programs often have to make do with inappropriate, inadequate, outdated materials.

The typical correctional education program is directed toward the General Equivalency Diploma (GED). Applicants for the GED take a written exam that assesses general comprehension and ability in basic academic areas — reading, writing, science, and mathematics. The GED is considered equivalent to a high school diploma, and many prisoners seek it because it can satisfy the minimum educational requirement of most nonprofessional jobs in the United States.

How successful is prison education as a rehabilitative program? Not many studies have been done on the subject. Early studies tended to find disappointing results, but more recent research shows that prisoners who complete educational courses while incarcerated do better on release than other prisoners — with some studies even showing arrest rates one-seventh that of the general parolee population.[16] Critics point out that this higher success rate may be due to the fact that it is the better-risk prisoners who take the courses.

This success has not meant that educational programs are being expanded. Given the cost of building and operating new prisons, budgets for education have come under attack. And as noted, some citizens ask why prisoners should have access to services not available to ordinary citizens.

A survey conducted in 1994 found that thirty-one states and the federal prison system allowed inmates to take college courses — and even obtain a bachelor's degree — while locked up. Many offenders paid for college using Pell Grants, a federal program

F CUS Educational Programs in Federal Prisons

Michael Santos

Educational programs are among the few activities individuals in federal prisons can pursue in order to bring meaning and hope to their lives. Such opportunities enable prisoners to escape the monotony of institutional life and to work on their personal goals and plans for their futures. Whether an individual spends time in formal classes or studies independently by using available library services, education departments are areas in the prison where the walls seem more permeable.

Prison libraries vary in size. Some of the older and larger ones hold upward of 20,000 books; those in newer institutions usually contain only a few thousand. All federal prisons participate in the interlibrary loan system, which enables an inmate to order nearly any title he or she needs from a nearby library. So although gates, walls, and gun towers isolate federal prisoners from the wider community, they still are able to learn languages and travel the world learning about different cultures through their access to literature and other educational materials.

Unfortunately, many of the men and women in prison have poor reading skills; some cannot read at all. This has always been a problem, yet the situation became even more severe after Congress passed the 1994 Comprehensive Crime Control Bill, as it tied federal prisoners' eligibility to earn good time with verification of high school equivalency. In other words, inmates who cannot pass the high school equivalency examination are ineligible to receive time off their sentences for good behavior. Furthermore, individuals who do not have a high school diploma or certificate verifying high school equivalency are limited to the amount of money they can earn from prison jobs.

Prisoners who need help developing their reading skills or preparing for the high school equivalency exam, can find it in the education department of each prison. Every facility conducts Adult Basic Education (ABE) classes and General Equivalency Diploma (GED) classes. In fact, Congress mandates all prisoners who lack high school equivalency to participate in GED classes for at least 120 days. Staff members usually teach these classes, though many institutions use inmate tutors to work with some inmates on an individual basis.

Inmates who complete the GED, or those who already have high school diplomas can advance to the vocational technology (VT) programs. These give prisoners opportunities to learn trades that might translate into jobs on their release from prison. Each prison offers its own selection of VT courses, many of which culminate with actual state licenses that let successful participants ply their trades in communities outside of prison walls once their sentences are completed. Some of the more popular VT programs in federal prisons include barbering, building trades, culinary arts, horticulture, and the operation of basic computer programs.

Besides the ABE, GED, and VT classes, people in prison can also pursue collegiate studies. In fact, until the 1994 Crime Bill passed, most federal prisons had agreements with local colleges and universities. Those agreements let nearby institutions send professors into the prison to teach classes. Many citizens complained about this practice and the 1994 Crime Bill eliminated funding for the prison college program. Still, a small minority of federal prisoners continue to prepare themselves for release by studying independently through correspondence courses at cooperating universities. Financial assistance for tuition through Pell Grants, however, is no longer available for prisoners.

Inmates in some institutions work together in order to create their own communities of learning. For example, at Federal Correctional Institution McKean, in Bradford, Pennsylvania, inmates asked the administration to designate one of the housing units as an education unit. Individuals in serious pursuit of self-improvement programs apply through the supervisor of education for assignment to that unit. Those who live in the education unit work to strengthen it in various ways. They correspond with libraries in an effort to solicit donations of books and other learning materials; they offer classes in some of the common living areas; and they work as tutors to help each other grasp concepts that might be more difficult to understand independently.

Educational programs help prisoners prepare for release. Besides that, they help prisoners move through their sentences. For the prisoner who allows his or her mind to lie dormant, time creeps at a snail's pace. Those who keep focused and work to enhance their skills in prison can document their accomplishments as time passes; in other words, educational programs empower people in prison by letting them make use of their time instead of letting the time use them.

SOURCE: Written especially for this text.

that provides assistance to low-income college students. However, prisoners are no longer eligible for federal education loans to help finance their studies and many colleges have ceased to offer courses inside prisons. Political and fiscal pressure has also cut basic education budgets in over half the states.[17]

Vocational Programs

Vocational programs attempt to teach offenders a marketable job skill. However, these programs also suffer from the principle of least eligibility: Training is often directed toward less desirable jobs in industries that already have large labor pools — barbering, printing, welding, and the like. Other problems also plague prison vocational programs. For one thing, participants often are trained on obsolete or inadequate equipment, because prisons generally lack the resources to upgrade. A story is told about a very popular print shop apprenticeship program at one large state reformatory in which inmates were trained on presses donated by the local newspaper. On parole the inmates discovered that their acquired skill was unmarketable because the machinery they had learned to operate was so inefficient that the newspaper had junked it (which was why it had been donated). Vocational programs rarely teach up-to-date skills.

Offenders also often lack the attitudes necessary to obtain and keep a job — punctuality, accountability, deference to supervisors, cordiality to co-workers. Further, they may lack the ability to locate a job opening and survive an interview. Therefore a skill is not the only thing prisoners need to be taught; most prisoners also need help with the entire vocational lifestyle. But the prison regimen, which tells prisoners what to do and where to be each moment from morning to night, can do little to develop attitudes needed outside the walls.

civil disabilities

Legal restrictions that prevent released felons from voting and holding elective office, engaging in certain professions and occupations, and associating with known offenders.

Yet another problem is perhaps the most resistant of all. The **civil disabilities** that attach to the former offender, discussed in more detail in Chapter 16, severely limit job mobility and flexibility. Occupational restrictions force offenders into low-paying, menial jobs, which may lead them back to crime. In one state or another, barred occupations include nurse, beautician, barber, real estate salesperson, chauffeur, worker where alcoholic beverages are sold, cashier, stenographer, and insurance salesperson. Nearly six thousand occupations are licensed in one or more states, and ex-convicts may find the stigma of being a convicted offender either difficult or impossible to overcome. The fact that some prison vocational programs promoted for rehabilitative purposes lead to restricted occupations seems to have been ignored.

Despite their detractors, prison vocational programs receive considerable support from many experts because poor job skills seem so closely tied to the problems inmates face on release into the community. The additional income and taxes produced by vocationally trained inmates may actually offset the cost of their training programs and may also reduce recidivism among participants.

Substance Abuse Programs

The link between crime and substance abuse is strong. Studies of offenders at the time of arrest estimate that 50–80 percent test positive for drugs and that 50–75 percent of these arrestees need some form of drug treatment.[18] To serve this large clientele, substance abuse treatment programs have grown rapidly in all parts of the criminal justice system. In 1993, the last year for which data are available, 1.1 million offenders were enrolled in drug or alcohol treatment units — double the number in 1980.[19]

For years people have questioned the effectiveness of drug treatment programs for habituated offenders. Follow-up studies routinely found high rates of rearrest for those leaving these programs, and most offenders had instances of relapse as well. The failure of these programs to eradicate drug use among participants led many to believe that drug treatment did not work. Yet more recent research has demonstrated that even though failure rates are high, drug treatment can be a valuable, cost-effective crime reduction strategy. For example, one study of drug-involved offenders used a "continuum" approach, in which the principles taught in a prison-based treatment program were reinforced in specialized work release centers and supported by special aftercare parole supervision. After 18 months, 76 percent of the offenders in this program were drug-free, and 71 percent were arrest-free, compared to only 19 percent drug-free and 30 percent arrest-free in the nontreatment comparison group.[20]

One reason for this reinterpretation of drug treatment programs is that different researchers frame the question differently. Instead of asking simply whether the offender relapses to drug use, some researchers ask a more complex evaluation question: Do program participants return to drugs and crime at lower rates than similar offenders who were not in the program? The usual answer is yes.

This more complex question stems from a recognition of how difficult it is to overcome drug addiction. Even a small rate of abstinence among program participants may represent a big difference in drug use and crime compared to nonparticipants. And participants who eventually fail often spend more time drug-free on the streets before relapse, and their new crimes are less serious. These effects can result in significant savings in criminal justice costs and losses of victims — as much as $7 saved for every $1 spent on treatment.[21]

Recent research suggests that the most effective substance abuse treatment programs share several components:

1. The program occurs in phases, with a residential treatment phase lasting between six and twelve months.
2. During residential treatment participants gradually earn more privileges in a therapeutic treatment setting.
3. Multiple treatment modalities are used, including individual psychotherapy, group therapy, and vocational rehabilitation.
4. Residential staff and community officials closely coordinate plans for release.
5. Treatment continues after release in the form of therapy groups augmented by drug testing.[22]

Religious Programs

Religious programs do not easily fit any programming categories discussed thus far. Nevertheless, they do fit our definition of prison programs in that inmates become involved in religious programs to ease the burden of prison time. Because the First Amendment guarantees the right to belief and practice, religious programs are available to all prisoners.

The two main religions in prison are Christianity and Islam, but U.S. prisons host the same array of faiths as exist in free society. For instance, in the West and Southwest, Native Americans may fast and sit in "sweat lodges," where the devotee may spend up to a day in quiet contemplation. In the Northeast and Southwest, daily Catholic masses are common. In prisons in the southern "Bible Belt," religious programs tend to be heavily evangelical Christian.

Few studies have been conducted of religion in prison. A recent national study found that religious activity helps inmates adjust to prison, and can reduce rule infractions.[23] Interviews with religious inmates indicated a number of reasons why religion is helpful in prison. For example, involvement in religion often provides both a psychological and even a physical "safe haven" from harsh realities, and enables inmates to maintain ties with their families and with religious volunteers from the outside. Many administrators believe that strong religious inmate groups — even nontraditional religions such as

Speaking to prisoners in Illinois, the Rev. Jesse Jackson urged the inmates to replace guns and drugs with prayer and job training. He said the cost of locking them up shows that skimping on education is a mistake.

Islam—make a prison easier to run, because these inmates help stabilize the prison culture.

But there is also the problem of "jailhouse religion"—inmates who pretend to "get religion" to look good for correctional authorities, particularly parole boards. This may not really be a significant problem, however, because research has shown that parole boards generally do not consider this in their release decisions.

The key issue here is whether religious participation helps offenders stay out of trouble after release. Evidence on this question is spotty, but a recent evaluation of the Prison Fellowship (PF) gives some basis for speculation. This multifaceted religion program was developed by Watergate conspirator Charles Colson after completing a prison sentence during which he was converted to Christianity. The program works with prisoners in intensive sessions during incarceration but also provides follow-up support after release. The study found that PF graduates did slightly better after release than a comparison group of non-PF inmates; the differences were most pronounced for low-risk offenders.[24] Whether these differences are due to the self-selection of better risks for the PF program, and why the results do not hold for high-risk offenders, remain open questions.

The Rediscovery of Correctional Rehabilitation

After Martinson's 1975 study indicated that prison rehabilitation programs were ineffective, the number of treatment programs began to decrease. According to the new vision, prison was a place that should provide safe and secure custody while punishing offenders. Yet even though some correctional officials willingly abandoned the rehabilitation ideal, many others believed eradicating rehabilitation from prisons was unwise. In recent years these penologists have become a strong minority voice calling for a renewed emphasis on rehabilitative programs in corrections. In a book titled *Reaffirming Rehabilitation,* Francis Cullen and Karen Gilbert argue that correctional treatment is more humane than mere custody and punishment and that these programs can be effective when appropriately designed and implemented.[25]

Following their lead, a team of Canadian researchers analyzed a large number of recent evaluations of correctional treatment and identified six conditions under which treatment programs will be effective:

1. The programs are directed toward high-risk clients.
2. The programs respond to offenders' problems that caused the criminal behavior.
3. The treatments take into account offenders' psychological maturity.
4. The treatment providers are allowed professional discretion on how to manage offenders' progress in treatment.
5. The programs are fully implemented as intended.
6. Offenders receive follow-up support after completing the treatment programs.[26]

Such studies have sparked a new interest in rehabilitation among influential penologists. The National Institute of Corrections has funded a series of demonstration programs designed to show how treatment programs can be effectively implemented in corrections. Whether this emphasis on treatment will again become as popular among policymakers as before remains to be seen. Although research supporting rehabilitation is growing, some scholars argue that the new studies are misleading and overstate results.[27]

Prison Industry

American prisoners have always worked, and making them work has been seen as a way to accomplish many correctional objectives. Hard labor was historically seen as a central part of punishment. In recent years this idea has gained new popularity with the re-emergence of chain gangs in a few southern states. It was even a popular belief at one time that prisoners' labor was legally forfeited as a result of their criminality and that the state could expect to profit from their incarceration.

Labor was also a way to manage the restlessness and idleness of prison time. Meaningful and productive work came to be seen as one of the best ways to make the long days of prison go faster, and paying inmates for their labor was a way to help them make their hard lives less harsh through buying daily amenities and goods for their cells. Most important, labor also has been viewed as part of the reformative process. As seen in the Comparative Perspective, Sweden has developed prison industries directly aimed at reintegrating inmates.

Some scholars recently have declared that historians have focused too heavily on the humanitarian and reformist basis for the rise of the penitentiary and reformatory. They argue that this view does not adequately reflect economic motives for the emergence of the prison. In fact, prisons provide a captive labor pool, and restriction on inmate wages make possible the production of goods at very low cost.

The theme of labor for profit is accompanied by a concern about idleness. Much of the history of prison industry revolves around the search for suitable ways to occupy inmates' time while also serving the financial interests of forces outside the walls. Four approaches have resulted: (1) the contract labor, piece price, and lease systems; (2) the public account system; (3) the state use system; and (4) the public works and ways system.

The Contract Labor, Piece Price, and Lease Systems

From the first days of U.S. prisons, inmates' labor was sold to private employers, who provided the machinery and raw materials for the work they would do. The products made by this **contract labor system** were then sold on the open market. Alternatively, in the **piece price system,** the contractor established a purchase price for goods that inmates produced with raw materials provided by the contractor. These arrangements were extremely exploitive. Inmates worked in sweatshops, and the fees for their labor were paid to the prisons; "free" during the day, they returned to the prison at night. In the **lease system,** a variation of the piece price system, the contractor maintained the prisoners, working them for twelve to sixteen hours at a stretch. These systems enabled many prisons in the later 1800s—even the vaunted Auburn—to operate in the black. The low wages increased the contractors' profit margins. The prisoners, of course, worked for nothing and gained nothing.

Not surprisingly, these arrangements led to extreme corruption as well as exploitation. With sizable contracts at stake, kickbacks and bribes became common business practices. And wardens took advantage of easy opportunities to line their pockets—and caused predictable public scandals when they were caught.

It was not long before organized labor began to attack the prison labor arrangements. In fact, late in the nineteenth century a coalition of humanitarian reformers and labor leaders lobbied successfully for laws prohibiting contract inmate labor. States then began to experiment with alternative forms of free-market inmate labor.

The Public Account System

When contract labor was outlawed, Oklahoma led the way in instituting the **public account system.** Instead of selling inmate labor to private entrepreneurs, the state prison itself in 1909 began to make twine, buying raw materials and using inmate labor. Similar twine-making factories existed in Minnesota and Wisconsin prisons. At first the reform was enormously successful, reducing costs of twine to Oklahoma farmers and generating profits that defrayed two-thirds of the costs of prison operations, but ultimately the experiment failed. The financial pressure that wardens had felt earlier did not die with the contract labor system, and they often succumbed to it by

contract labor system

A system under which inmates' labor was sold on a contractual basis to private employers, who provided the machinery and raw materials with which they made salable products in the institution.

piece price system

A labor system under which a contractor provided raw materials and agreed to purchase goods made by prison inmates at a set price.

lease system

A variation on the piece price system in which the contractor provided prisoners with food and clothing as well as raw materials. In some southern states prisoners were leased to agricultural producers to perform field labor.

public account system

A labor system under which a prison bought machinery and raw materials with which inmates manufactured a salable product.

COMPARATIVE PERSPECTIVE

Prison Industries in Sweden

The *Kriminalvardsstyrelsen*—literally the "criminal care administration"—is the agency that runs the Swedish corrections system. Rehabilitation and reintegration of offenders is the overriding goal of the Swedish correctional system. This can be seen in the extent to which Sweden has developed educational, vocational, and work programs in their prisons.

On a given day, the *Kriminalvardsstyrelsen* is responsible for about four thousand inmates serving sentences and about seven hundred awaiting trial. In most countries, a half dozen institutions would be considered more than enough to hold the small number of inmates. But in Sweden the treatment focus emphasizes small institutions, hence there are 19 national prisons, designed for people sentenced to more than one year; 56 local institutions, used primarily to house people with terms of less than one year, and 24 remand prisons holding people awaiting trial. The maximum capacity of these institutions ranges from 10 to 300, most hold between 20 to 40, more akin to halfway houses in the United States. The prisons have a total capacity for 1,700 inmates housed in "open" institutions—without walls or fences and 2,400 in closed facilities.

The time served in Sweden by serious offenders is indeed shorter than in the United States. The penal code authorizes incarceration at either a fixed term of 14 days to 10 years, or a life sentence. The latter is rare and is usually commuted to a determinate sentence of between 15 and 20 years.

Sixty-five percent of Swedish prisoners serve sentences of three months or less, 13 percent three to six months, 9.5 percent six to twelve months, 8 percent twelve to twenty-four months, and only 4 percent more than two years. Included are drunk drivers (30 percent of all offenders sent to prison) and 75 percent of those convicted of a traffic offense who receive the maximum sentence of one month. In Sweden there is no distinction between felons and misdemeanants: All enter the same correctional system.

The Act on Correctional Treatment in Institutions passed in 1974 puts great emphasis on reintegration of prisoners into the community. It states that the "natural" form of correctional care is noninstitutional and that every effort should be made to keep offenders out of prison and to maximize contacts with the outside world for those who are incarcerated. To accomplish this goal, judges are instructed to make greater use of probation; inmates in local institutions are given the right to leave the facility during the day to work, study, and participate in recreation; furloughs for short or long terms are authorized; and long-term prisoners not viewed as security risks are given short-term periods of release to study, secure treatment, or for other reasons that would facilitate the prisoner's adjustment to society.

The factory program at the national prison Tillberga is an example of the reintegrative focus of Swedish penology. About 80 inmates are at this facility, and of these, about 40 are employed in constructing prefabricated houses sold on the open market. All inmate-workers are members of the national construction union and are paid free-market wages negotiated by that union. The union agreed to this idea on three conditions: that the inmates would be paid the same wages as other building trade members; the houses would be sold at the same price as private companies; and the housing market remained strong.

However, the inmates do not pay national income taxes (normally 30 percent of a wage), so their pay envelope actually contains 70 percent of that received by their outside counterparts. Many prisoners are not attracted to the Tillberga scheme, because they are only given 25 percent of their wages to spend. The remainder is placed in a savings account that the inmate receives on release.

Sweden has a reputation of taking social welfare policies further than any developed nation. The Swedish political ideology emphasizes similarities among citizens rather than differences and encourages a sense of collective responsibility that seeks to protect the rights and needs of its weakest members. Governmental policies have been developed to assist these citizens, even those who have broken the law. ■

SOURCE: Adapted from Michael S. Serrill, "Profile/Sweden," *Corrections Magazine*, 3, June 1977, p. 11; Richard J. Terrill, *World Criminal Justice Systems*, 2nd ed. (Cincinnati, OH: Anderson, 1992), pp. 196–205.

padding budgets and altering records. In any case, it was impossible to sustain full employment of inmates by an industry that had such a narrow market. And when prisons began to turn a profit on goods that the private sector also produced, private industry and labor stopped cooperating.

The State Use System

In response to the problems associated with using inmate labor to produce goods for the competitive market, many states turned to a **state use system,** in which prisoners are employed to produce goods and services used only in state institutions and agencies. Many experts consider this arrangement reasonable and beneficial, and many states mandate that their agencies must purchase goods produced by inmate labor when they are available. This requirement creates something of a state monopoly on certain products. Today the state use system is the most common form of prison industry.

> **state use system**
>
> *A labor system under which goods produced by prison industries are purchased by state institutions and agencies exclusively and never enter the free market.*

The state use system has several advantages. Prison labor, which by many accounts is cheaper than free labor, is not allowed to compete with other labor pools in the open market. At the same time, the state can purchase some goods more cheaply. Under this system state agencies often buy a great variety of prison-made items — school chairs and desks, soap and paper towels, milk and eggs, and so on.

The state use system also has drawbacks. Even when prison products are used only by government, the system preempts the free labor market. Moreover, many of the goods produced within the system — license plates, for example — have no close equivalents outside, so skills the inmates acquire in prison often are not transferable to outside industries. Even when an analogous outside industry exists, prison industry is so inefficient and its methods so outmoded that prisoners often must shed what they learned there before they can succeed in private industry. Farming, for example, is a common prison industry, yet the enterprise typically teaches few advanced agricultural methods; prisoners usually do manual chores, although farmhand positions are drying up across the country. The prison farm may be good economics, but it is poor schooling.

The Public Works and Ways System

In a version of the state use system called the **public works and ways system,** inmates work on public construction and maintenance projects, filling potholes, constructing or repairing buildings and bridges, and so on. This approach was introduced in the 1920s, when the automobile was gaining popularity and surfaced roads were needed.

> **public works and ways system**
>
> *A labor system under which prison inmates work on public construction and maintenance projects.*

Advocates praise the tremendous economic benefits of this system and point out that prisoners learn new skills while producing goods and services useful to society. However, prisoners do the more arduous jobs on a project, and then outside craftworkers are hired for the skilled work. Some detractors say it is exploitation; the state receives a benefit but does not fairly compensate prisoners.

Prison Industry Today

Until very recently, the trend has been away from free-market use of prison labor and toward state monopolies. From 1885 to 1940 the private use of inmate labor, once the most popular form of prison industry, vanished. One reason was that the public had become increasingly aware of the exploitive character of prison industry. Southern prison systems expanded dramatically after the Civil War, and former slaves accounted for much of the growth. The labor of most of these prisoners was contracted out in one way or another, leading some critics to argue that industrial capitalists had replaced plantation owners as exploiters of the former slaves.

The Prison Blues line of sportswear produced by inmates at Oregon's maximum security prison has shown that correctional industries can compete successfully in the marketplace.

With the rise of the labor movement, state legislatures passed laws restricting the sale of prisoner-made goods so as not to compete with free workers. As early as 1819, New York had required boots and shoes produced at Auburn to be labeled "State Prison." In another application of the principle of least eligibility, whenever unemployment began to soar, political pressures mounted to prevent prisons from engaging in enterprises that might otherwise be conducted by private business and free labor.

In 1900 the U.S. Industrial Commission endorsed the state use plan, and in 1929 Congress passed the Hawes-Cooper Act, followed by additional legislation in 1935 and 1940, which banned prison-made goods from interstate commerce. In an excess of zeal, by 1940 every state had passed laws banning imports of prison-made goods from other states. These restrictions crippled production and ended the open-market system of employing prisoners. With the outbreak of World War II, however, President Franklin Roosevelt ordered the government to procure goods for the military effort from state and federal prisons. Later, under pressure from organized labor, President Harry Truman revoked the wartime order, and prisoners returned to idleness. By 1973, then President Nixon's National Advisory Commission on Criminal Justice Standards and Goals found very few inmates throughout the corrections system had productive work.

The past decade has seen a renewed interest in channeling prison labor into revived industrial programs that would relieve idleness, allow inmates to earn wages that they could save until release, and reduce the costs of incarceration to the state. In 1979 Congress lifted restrictions on interstate sale of products made in state prisons and urged correctional administrators to explore private-sector ways to improve prison industry (see the Focus box). In the same year the Free Venture program of the Law Enforcement Assistance Administration made funds available to seven states to develop industries. These programs would operate according to six principles: (1) a full workweek for inmate employees, (2) wages based on productivity, (3) private-sector productivity standards, (4) responsibility for hiring or firing inmate workers vested in industry staff, (5) self-sufficient or profitable shop operations, and (6) a postrelease job placement mechanism. Once again inmate labor would compete with free labor. By 1994 sixteen states were engaged in Free Venture prison industry, and five states—Nevada, New Hampshire, South Carolina, Tennessee, and Washington—allowed inmates to earn wages approaching federal minimum wage. Figures 14.1 and 14.2 show some of the employment and payment practices for prison industries.

The change in attitude toward prison industries may be related to the fact that many large U.S. firms, in search of cheap labor, have moved operations to Third World countries. Because of increased shipping costs and problems of administering plants overseas, some manufacturers may view prison labor as an attractive alternative. Union opposition may weaken if it can be shown prisoners are not taking jobs away from taxpaying free workers. Indeed, some studies estimate that even if every prisoner were employed in a prison job, the total productivity of prisoners would be less than one-tenth of 1 percent of the gross domestic product—indicating that prisoners would take very few "free-world" jobs.[28] In the federal prison system, which employs inmates to supply the prison with goods and services, prison-made goods are less than two-tenths of 1 percent of all federal prison expenditures.[29]

Early indications are that the supposed efficiencies of private industry in corrections are less dramatic than expected. Inmate labor is cheaper than free labor, but recent reforms include higher wages for prisoners than those formerly paid by private contractors, and security requirements drive up the costs of prison industry. However, even if a renewed prison industry is neither efficient nor damaging to free-market labor, indica-

FOCUS   Prison Blues

The toll-free number for one of Oregon's fastest booming new businesses is 1-800-597-7472. If you call to place an order, you will be buying from a government-run business operating out of Oregon's maximum security prison, Eastern Oregon Correctional Institution, employing inmates who manufacture stylish denim jeans, shirts and jackets.

You will also be participating in one of the most innovative semiprivate sector programs in prison industry today: Unigroup Correctional Industries of Oregon. Made possible by [Oregon] Senate Bill 780 in 1984, Unigroup was established in 1989 to market prison-made products ranging from jeans and shirts to bedroom furniture, priced at market value. The inmates who make the products are paid minimum wage plus incentives. Eighty-five percent of the wage goes to victim restitution, prison maintenance, family support, and taxes. The rest they get to use personally—most of it going into a savings account available to them upon release.

The idea for Prison Blues grew out of administrator Fred Nichol's conviction that prisons need to teach inmates self-reliance and work skills, and there's no better way to do that than employment in competitive, free market industry. So he created Unigroup to create a prison-based manufacturing group.

According to the group's marketing manager, Brad Haga: "The concept was simple enough: select a consumer product that had universal appeal, build a state-of-the-art factory inside a corrections facility, hire seasoned private sector supervisors to train and manage inmate workers, market the product across the United States."

And they did. For one thing, the curiosity factor attracted a lot of free media coverage. After all, the Prison Blues owned a corner on a fascinating market concept: "made on the inside to be worn on the outside." A private advertising consulting firm helped Prison Blues get on the *ABC News* with Peter Jennings, the *Phil Donahue Show*, *The Paul Harvey Radio News Show*, and a one-page splash in *The New York Times Sunday Magazine*—a total of $2.5 million in free publicity in 1993 alone! The popularity of the distinctive product grew so quickly that Unigroup's goal for the year 2000 appears easily attainable: 450 inmates in the production line and $26 million in sales.

Prison Blues is certainly a winner from a business standpoint. But is it good correctional practice?

No comprehensive studies have been done of the recidivism rate of former workers—the idea is still too new for that. Inmates who work for Unigroup proclaim that the effort has given them a new interest in "real world" skills and has changed their attitudes toward work. Whether this will translate into greater success after release remains to be seen, and critics wonder if the experience in Unigroup gives some inmates false hope for a better life after prison.

Former Oregon Corrections Director Frank Hall, under whom the program was developed, says that in the long run the issue is not about jeans, but about reforming prisoners and reinventing prisons. It is too early to know for sure, but if the program helps inmates become self-responsible and increases public confidence in prisons, he may be right. Perhaps the story is summed up by a message tagged to every item sold by Prison Blues: "In the end, inmates are giving you high-quality, great-fitting jeans, and you are giving them a second chance."

Source: Brad Haga, "Prison Blues: Jeans Change Public Perceptions, Offer Innovative Solutions," *Corrections Compendium*, 19, October 1994, pp. 1–4.

tions are that it makes sense to have inmates work. A Federal Bureau of Prisons study shows that employed inmates have fewer disciplinary infractions in prison, get better jobs when released, and stay out of trouble with the law longer than do unemployed prisoners.[30]

Prison Maintenance Programs

Running a prison is like running a town. The typical prison must provide every major service available in a community and more: fire department, electrical and plumbing services, janitorial maintenance, mail delivery, restaurant, drugstore, administrative recordkeeping, and so on. These operations must be coordinated. If only to keep the costs of these services manageable, prisoners do the bulk of the work. The one thing abundant in a prison is human resources, and perhaps the most frequent types of jobs in any given prison have to do with its day-to-day maintenance.

In most prisons, maintenance jobs constitute an elaborate pecking order of assignments and reveal something about prestige and influence within the facility. The choice jobs involve access to power. For example, a clerical job

Figure 14.1 Percentage of Eligible Inmates Working in Prison Industries

Participation of inmates in prison industry varies greatly by state.

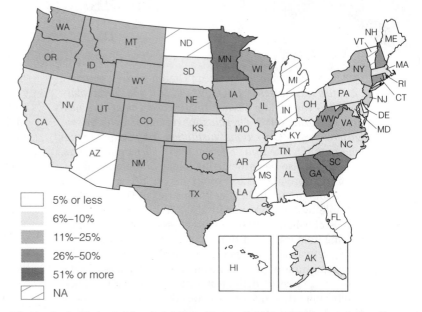

SOURCE: Amanda Wunder, "Working for the Weekend: Prison Industries and Inmate Employees," *Corrections Compendium*, October 1994, pp. 9–21.

in the records room (which contains inmates' files) gives the inmate a corner on one of the most sought-after commodities in prison: information. The records room inmate can learn who is doing time for what, who is eligible for privileges (such as reclassification, reassignment, and parole), and what decisions are being made about whom. The contents of inmates' files are confidential, but it is hard to prevent the

Figure 14.2 Hourly Payments to Prisoners Engaged in Industry

Some states employ large percentages of their inmates in prison industries, whereas others do not. But no states pay sizable wages to prisoners, and some pay only a few pennies per hour.

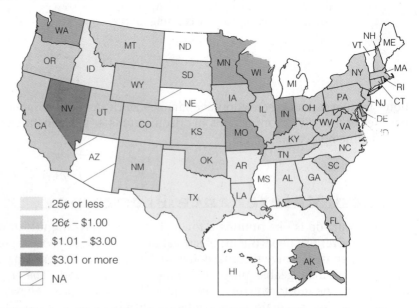

SOURCE: Amanda Wunder, "Working for the Weekend: Prison Industries and Inmate Employees," *Corrections Compendium*, October 1994, pp. 9–21.

records room clerk from sneaking a look—or from trading the information for goods or favors.

Clerical support jobs are similarly prestigious. Desk assignments permit access to authority figures (and very likely to such favors as flexibility in scheduling, better food, and sometimes information) and make inmates who get them the first contributors to the institutional rumor mill. Often inmates must qualify as trusties before they are given clerical assignments.

Among the most desirable jobs are those that allow access to goods or services that can be sold within the prison economy. For example, an inmate who works in the laundry can charge two packs of cigarettes as insurance that another inmate's clothing will be returned neatly folded and without rips or tears.

Also desirable are jobs that provide access to contraband goods. For example, inmates on kitchen detail can filch extra food to trade or sell. Library assignments let prisoners make liberal use of law books and other popular reading material. Assignments to the dispensary, even with very tight security on drugs and other medical items, and to the stockroom can pay off in various ways.

Different benefits can be derived from other assignments. The electrician's aide and the message runner, for instance, usually have flexible schedules and relatively varied tasks that make the time go faster.

The least desirable jobs are the most plentiful: janitorial services. Mop details are frequently initial job assignments in which new inmates must prove themselves for later reassignment; they are also given as disciplinary measures. Mopping halls and cleaning latrines is not particularly interesting work; repeated three or more times a day in the same areas, the tasks become painfully monotonous.

Prison maintenance jobs are essential to managing the prison in two ways. First, they lower the cost of operations by eliminating the need to hire outside labor. Second, the job hierarchy provides rewards and punishments to enforce prison discipline. Prisoners who cooperate receive choice assignments; others get the dirty work.

Prison Recreation Programs

When prisoners are not at work, in treatment, or in their cells, they are probably engaging in recreation. Organized recreation is a favorite pastime—and often central to the prison experience. Most men's prisons have sports teams—baseball, basketball, even football—and many regularly compete with outside teams. Many prisons also provide such activities as table tennis, weight training, music, drama, and journalism clubs.

Many politicians have urged elimination of weight lifting and other recreational programs. What arguments could an administrator use in support of these programs?

Recreation programs have two primary functions in addition to filling time. First, they are integral to prison social life. Prisoners vary in intellect and physical capacities; variety in programs enables inmates to form positive social contacts with others who share their interests and abilities. Second, prison recreation and leisure pursuits can be rehabilitative in several ways. They can teach such social skills as cooperation and teamwork; they provide a means for prisoners to grow in experience and enhance their self-image; and they serve as a productive counterpoint to the general alienation of prison.

Recreation programs also present security risks. Whenever prisoners congregate, they can plan disruptions. Especially in recreation, where prisoners compete, tempers may flare. Although prisons without leisure activities would be torture, recreation requires careful management.

Recently the public has reacted against recreational programming, feeling that free-time programs make prison too easy and even enjoyable. Politicians have thus pressed to shut down recreational programs, especially weight lifting. Administrators point out that inmates in these programs are often the best behaved; they also argue that trying to run a prison without such activities will cause prisoner unrest.[31] Still, the popular sentiment that prison should be unbearable tends to eradicate any programming not directly related to rehabilitation.

Prison Programming Reconsidered

Our discussion of prison programs has focused on types of activities used to occupy prisoners. Underlying this discussion is the question, Is this prison time useful? The answer is equivocal.

Offenders are often sent to prison in the expectation that treatment and rehabilitative programs will prepare them to adjust to society when they are released. This ideal is at best ephemeral, because most rehabilitative programs have serious shortcomings and limited effectiveness. The degree to which a prison can focus on rehabilitation is in question. Surprisingly, a large number of inmates are not considered to need education, vocational training, or drug/alcohol rehabilitation. Of those who need help in these areas, often less than half actually participate in available programs.

Nonrehabilitative programs—prison industry and maintenance—pose their own problems for administrators. And the need for security severely constrains prison practices.

Yet a programless prison is unthinkable. Time is burden enough for prisoners to manage; to provide no opportunity to fill the time with positive pursuits is out of the question. Structured activities must be available. Moreover, it is not realistic to suppose that outside workers would perform daily chores to keep a prison operating—for low wages and at some personal risk.

Some experts have said prison programs ought to be voluntary. Their philosophical arguments in favor of free choice and against coercion and exploitation certainly sound reasonable. But given the realities of prison life—the need to run the prison, occupy time, and give both staff and prisoners hope that life will be better for inmates after they leave—it is unlikely prison programs will change in any dramatic way.

Summary

Managing inmates' time is a major problem of prison managers. There are not enough activities to keep inmates busy. Idle time allows inmates to behave in ways that frustrate the rehabilitative, industrial, and maintenance goals and functions of the institution. However, security needs make certain activities unsuitable, and the principle of least eligibility makes many controversial.

Classification is the process in which prisoners are grouped by such considerations as security level, program and housing needs, and reassessment schedule. Classification originated as a diagnostic tool for identifying behavioral problems that caused criminality and as a means of determining how best to help the offender. Unfortunately, organizational needs too often preempt individuals' needs in classification decisions.

Rehabilitative programs are designed to help offenders and to act as special deterrents so that the offenders will not return to crime. These programs are psychological, behavioral, vocational, social, and religious in orientation; they address substance abuse problems as well.

Prison industries have always been a part of American corrections; however, organized labor and legislation restricting sale of prisoner-made products have seriously blocked their success. Federal efforts have given new life to prison industries in some states and in the federal system.

Maintenance programs provide the institution with labor and reduce idleness. As in other program areas, most institutions find they have more labor than uses for it. The exception is recreation programs, which usually have plenty of takers.

The role of programs in prisons changes with the nature of the population, management goals, and outside influences. As rehabilitation has declined as a goal of corrections, emphasis on programs — with the exception of prison industries — has also declined. ◼

For Discussion

1. How strictly should the principle of least eligibility be applied? Support your viewpoint.
2. What factors limit the possibility of running prison industries as profit-making ventures? What could be done to improve the profitability of prison industries?
3. How much value do the various rehabilitative programs have? Are some programs more effective than others? Why or why not?
4. Should prisoners be forced to participate in programs? As a correctional officer, what would you do if an inmate did not want to leave his or her cell?
5. Is a programless prison a possibility?

For Further Reading

Andrews, Don A., and Bonta, James. *The Psychology of Criminal Conduct.* Cincinnati: Anderson, 1994. Discusses the theory and practice of offender rehabilitation.

Glaser, Daniel. *Profitable Penalties: How to Cut Both Crime Rates and Costs.* Thousand Oaks, CA: Pine Forge Press, 1997. Summarizes effective correctional practices, and how those practices can be used to prevent crime at lower correctional costs.

Johnson, Robert. *Hard Time: Understanding and Reforming the Prison,* 2nd ed. Belmont, CA: Wadsworth, 1996. Examines strategies for making prisons safer and more humane places.

McGuire, James, ed. *What Works: Reducing Reoffending.* New York: Wiley, 1995. Offers a collection of essays on and studies of successful rehabilitation programs.

Palmer, Ted. *A Profile of Correctional Effectiveness and New Directions for Research.* Albany: State University of New York Press, 1994. Describes and analyzes the most effective strategies for offender treatment.

Notes

1. Patrick A. Langan and Jodi M. Brown, "Felony Sentences in the United States, 1994," *Bureau of Justice Statistics Bulletin* (Washington, DC: U.S. Department of Justice, July 1997, p. 9.
2. *The New York Times,* July 16, 1995, p. 3.
3. Thomas Harris, *I'm OK, You're OK* (New York: Harper & Row, 1960).
4. James S. Kunen, "Teaching Prisoners a Lesson," *The New Yorker,* July 10, 1995, p. 37.
5. Brandon K. Applegate, Francis T. Cullen, and Bonnie S. Fisher, "Public Support for Correctional Treatment: The Continuing Appeal of the Rehabilitative Ideal," *The Prison Journal,* 77, September 1997, pp. 237–258.
6. *Ramos v. Lamm,* 458 F.Supp. 128 (1979).
7. Thomas S. Szasz, *The Myth of Mental Illness* (New York: Harper & Row, 1969), p. 30.
8. See H. J. Steadman, S. Fabisiak, J. Dvoskin, and E. J. Holohean, "A Survey of Mental Disability Among State Prison Inmates," *Hospital and Community Psychiatry,* 38, 1987, pp. 1086–1090; National Alliance for the Mentally Ill, *Criminalizing the Mentally Ill* (Alexandria, VA: NAMI, 1992); Betsy Fulton, "Offenders with Mental Illnesses on Probation and Parole: The Importance of Information," in *Responding to the Mental and Substance Abuse Health Care Needs of Persons on Community Corrections* (Seattle: National Coalition for Mental and Substance Abuse Health Care in the Criminal Justice System, 1995).
9. Robert Martinson, "What Works? Questions and Answers About Prison Reform," *Public Interest,* Spring 1974, p. 25.

10. Jon Kear-Colwell and Phillip Pollock, "Motivation or Confrontation — Which Approach to the Child Sex Offender?" *Criminal Justice and Behavior,* 24(1), March 1997, pp. 30–33.
11. William D. Pithers, "Maintaining Treatment Integrity with Sexual Abusers," *Criminal Justice and Behavior,* 24(1), March 1997, pp. 34–51.
12. Kris R. Henning and B. Christopher Frueh, "Cognitive-Behavioral Treatment of Incarcerated Offenders," *Criminal Justice and Behavior,* 23(4), December 1996, pp. 523–542.
13. Hassim Solomon, *Community Corrections* (Boston: Holbrook, 1976), p. 51.
14. Ted Palmer, *The Re-emergence of Correctional Intervention* (Newbury Park, CA: Sage, 1992).
15. "Education in U.S. Prisons: Survey Summary," *Corrections Compendium,* March 1994, pp. 5–6.
16. Don Andrews and James Bonta, *The Psychology of Criminal Conduct* (Cincinnati: Anderson, 1994); *The New York Times,* July 16, 1995, p. 3.
17. Jamie Ellis, "Prison Programs Reduced," *Corrections Compendium,* 19(3), March 1994, pp. 1–4.
18. Gregory P. Falkin, Michael Prendergast, and M. Douglas Anglin, "Drug Treatment in the Criminal Justice System," *Federal Probation,* 58(3), September 1994, pp. 31–40.
19. Department of Health and Human Services, Substance Abuse and Mental Health Services Administration, *Overview of the FY94 National Drug and Alcoholism Treatment Unit Survey (NDATUS): Data from 1993 and 1980–1993* (Rockville, MD: U.S. Department of Health and Human Services, May 1995), p. 4A.
20. James A. Inciardi, "A Corrections-Based Continuum of Effective Drug Abuse Treatment," *National Institute of Justice Research Preview* (Washington, DC: U.S. Department of Justice, June 1966).
21. Elizabeth Mauser, Kit R. Van Stelle, and D. Paul Moberg, "The Economic Impact of Diverting Substance-Abusing Offenders into Treatment," *Crime and Delinquency,* 40(4), October 1994, pp. 568–588.
22. James A. Inciardi, Dorothy Lockwood, and Robert M. Hooper, "Delaware Treatment Program Presents Promising Results," *Corrections Today,* February 1994, pp. 34–40.
23. Todd R. Clear, Bruce D. Stout, Harry S. Dammer, Linda L. Kelly, Patricia L. Hardyman, and Carol A. Shapiro, *Prisoners, Prisons, and Religion,* unpublished report, Rutgers University, Newark, New Jersey, November 1992.
24. Tom O'Connor, "The Impact of Religious Programming on Recidivism, the Community and Prisons," *The IARCA Journal on Community Corrections,* 6(16), June 1995, pp. 13–19.
25. Francis Cullen and Karen Gilbert, *Reaffirming Rehabilitation* (Cincinnati: Anderson, 1982).
26. Don A. Andrews, Ivan Zinger, Robert D. Hoge, James Bonta, Paul Gendreau, and Francis Cullen, "Does Correctional Treatment Work? A Clinically Relevant and Psychologically Informed Meta-Analysis," *Criminology,* 28(3), 1990, pp. 369–429.
27. John T. Whitehead and Steven Lab, "A Meta-Analysis of Juvenile Correctional Treatment," *Journal of Research on Crime and Delinquency,* 26, 1989, pp. 276–295.
28. Timothy Flanagan and Kathleen Maguire, "A Full Employment Policy for Prisons in the United States: Some Arguments, Estimates and Implications," *Journal of Criminal Justice,* 21, 1993, pp. 117–130.
29. Robert C. Greiser, "Do Correctional Industries Adversely Affect the Private Sector?" *Federal Probation,* 53(1), 1989, pp. 18–24.
30. William G. Saylor and Gerald G. Gaes, *PREP Study Links UNICOR Work Experience with Successful Post-Release Outcome* (Washington, DC: U.S. Bureau of Prisons, Office of Research and Evaluation, n.d.).
31. Wesley Johnson, Katherine Bennet, and Timothy J. Flanagan, "Getting Tough on Prisoners: Results from the National Corrections Survey, 1995," *Crime and Delinquency,* 43(1), January 1997, pp. 24–41.

Release from Incarceration

An African-American minister active in party politics, a retired corporate executive, a man who owns a small business, and a woman interested in civic affairs sit as a parole board to consider the lengths of the sentences of Maurice Williams and nineteen other inmates. Convicted of first-degree robbery, Williams is serving his first major sentence, five to ten years. As he enters the hearing room at the maximum-security prison, he seems relaxed and confident, more sure of himself than most inmates at parole hearings. His time in prison has been productive: he has earned a high

At a Tennessee parole hearing, Pauline Edwards opposes the release of Robert Corliss, convicted of killing her son. In most states victims may comment in writing about a release decision, but they are not permitted to appear before the board.

school general equivalency diploma, he has received a good report from the director of the drug treatment program and a supporting report from the prison psychiatrist; and his brother has written that he will give him a job in his grocery store in the old neighborhood. Still, he is a bit nervous. He has never been before the parole board previously, and he wonders about the people he is facing. Who are they? What do they know about him? How will they react to his file?

The minister asks Williams about his plans for the future. He answers that he will live with his brother and work in the store. The woman wants to know if he will be hanging out with his old buddies. Williams tries to assure her that although many still live nearby, he will avoid them. "I've learned my lesson. I'm gonna keep away from those guys." After a few more minutes during which the members shuffle through the papers in his file, Williams is told that he can return to his cell and that he will learn the board's decision by evening.

In the discussion that follows Williams's departure, several panel members express skepticism about his prison performance and wonder if he is merely a con artist who will do anything to earn early release. The businessman predicts that Williams will fall back into trouble soon after he hits the streets: "I know that neighborhood. It will be impossible for him to stay away from those influences." Eventually they compromise and decide to grant Williams an extended parole—that is, he will be paroled, but not on the date he first becomes eligible. One member has already started to study another of the files stacked before him. It is 9:20 A.M. One case down on a typical hearing day and nineteen to go.

Much of the public fails to recognize that more than 95 percent of individuals sent to prison will return to live in the community. Maurice Williams's parole hearing was typical of the release procedures used across the country when rehabilitation was the dominant goal of the criminal sanction. The parole board used its discretion to fix the release date.

Today scenes similar to this one still occur, but fewer states maintain parole boards or allow boards the wide discretion they had in the past. In this chapter we examine the mechanisms for prison release. Supervision of ex-inmates on parole and their adjustment to the community is discussed in Chapter 17. Here we will examine the following Questions for Inquiry:

Questions
FOR INQUIRY

1. What is parole, and how does it operate today?

2. What is the origin of parole?

3. How is the release decision made?

4. How are releasing authorities organized?

5. What steps are taken to ease the offender's reentry into the community?

Release from One Part of the System to Another

Parole is the conditional release of an offender from incarceration but not from the legal custody of the state. Thus offenders who comply with parole conditions and do not further conflict with the law receive an absolute discharge from supervision at the end of their sentences. If a parolee breaks a rule, parole may be revoked and the person returned to a correctional facility. Parole, then, rests on three concepts:

1. *Grace or privilege:* The prisoner could be kept incarcerated, but the government extends the privilege of release.
2. *Contract of consent:* The government enters into an agreement with the prisoner whereby the prisoner promises to abide by certain conditions in exchange for being released.
3. *Custody:* Even though the offender is released from prison, he or she is still a responsibility of the government. Parole is an extension of correctional programs into the community.

Only felons are released on parole; adult misdemeanants are usually released directly from local institutions on expiration of their sentences. With the incarcerated population more than doubling during the past twenty years, it is not surprising that the number of parolees has also grown, as shown in Figure 15.1.

Every year almost 370,000 felons are conditionally released from prison and allowed to live under parole supervision in the community. Today 685,000 persons are under parole supervision, a rate of 346 for every 100,000 adult residents.[1]

During most of the twentieth century, the term *parole* referred to both a release mechanism and a method of community supervision. It is still used in this general sense, but since the spread of the deserved punishment model of the criminal sanction (see Chapter 4), the dual usage is no longer appropriate in many states. Now we must

parole

The conditional release of an inmate from incarceration under supervision after part of the prison sentence has been served.

Figure 15.1 Numbers of Adults Under Parole Supervision, 1980–1997

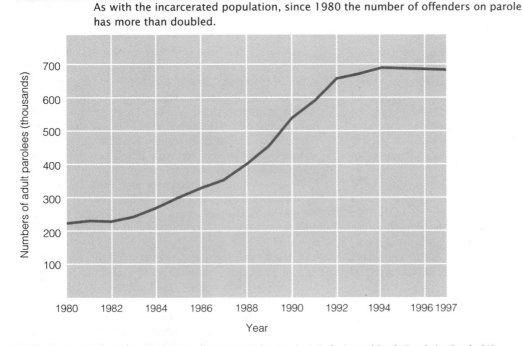

As with the incarcerated population, since 1980 the number of offenders on parole has more than doubled.

SOURCE: U.S. Department of Justice, Bureau of Justice Statistics, "Nation's Probation and Parole Population Reached New High Last Year," Press Release, August 16, 1998.

distinguish between a releasing mechanism and supervision. Although releasing mechanisms have changed, most former prisoners must still serve a period of time under parole supervision.

A variety of organizational structures have been developed to effect the release of prisoners, but parole is an activity solely of state and federal (not local) governments. In many states the parole board is part of the department of corrections; in others it is an autonomous body whose members are appointed by the governor.

As you read this chapter, keep in mind that, like so many other correctional activities, the decision to release is made in the context of complex and competing goals. Traditionally parole has been justified in terms of rehabilitation. In theory parole board members evaluate the offender's progress toward rehabilitation and readiness to abide by laws. In practice they consider other factors as well. Even where determinate sentencing or parole guidelines are in effect, correctional officials can influence release; the decision is not as cut-and-dried as proponents have claimed.

Many questions bear on the release decision no matter what procedures are followed. How will the public react? Who will be blamed if the offender commits another crime? Is the prison so crowded that an early release is necessary to open up space? How will the offender's release affect judges and prosecutors? The Focus box considers the U.S. Supreme Court decision that a state can deny release to an offender who has completed his sentence.

Origins of Parole

Parole in the United States evolved during the 1800s following the English, Australian, and Irish practices of conditional pardon, apprenticeship by indenture, transportation of

FOCUS   *Kansas v. Hendricks*

Over a thirty-year period, Leroy Hendricks was convicted of six sexual offenses against children and spent much of his adult life in prison. Every time he finished serving a prison sentence or gained parole release, he eventually victimized more children and returned to prison. After serving nearly ten years in prison for his most recent crime—molesting two teenage boys— he was scheduled to move to a halfway house in the community as the first step toward release in 1994.

As Hendricks neared the end of his latest prison sentence, the Kansas legislature passed a new law permitting the state to hold sex offenders in mental hospitals *after* they served their prison sentences. As a result of Kansas's new Sexually Violent Predator Act, Hendricks was transferred from a prison to a mental hospital at the end of his sentence. Hendricks had served the prison sentence imposed for his crime. Yet after serving his full sentence, he did not gain his freedom. The new law permitted Kansas to keep him locked up forever.

Is it fair to serve a full prison sentence for a crime and still remain behind bars? Hendricks believed the Kansas law was unfair. He took his case to court claiming the law was

punishing him a second time for his crime. If that was true, the Kansas law could be violating the constitutional right not to be placed in "double jeopardy"—to be tried or punished twice for the same offense. Hendricks also argued that the law improperly imposed a new punishment on him *after* he committed his crime and served his sentence. Thus he claimed that the Sexually Violent Predator Act was an "*ex post facto* law," prohibited by the U.S. Constitution because it applies new rules and punishments that did not exist at the time an offender violated previously existing laws.

Should Hendricks be entitled to release? Is it fair to create new rules that keep people locked up after they serve their full prison sentences? Was Hendricks being punished twice for his crimes?

In 1997, the Supreme Court tackled the issues raised by Hendricks. Hendricks remained locked up. Four of the nine justices believed Kansas had unfairly created new rules after the fact when it kept Hendricks in custody. The majority of the Supreme Court — only five justices — decided that this was not a second or after-the-fact punishment, because Kansas sought to use the law to provide "treatment" rather than to impose "punishment."

criminals from one country to another, and the issuance of "tickets of leave." These were all methods of moving criminals out of prison. Such practices generally did not develop as part of any coherent theory of punishment or to promote any particular goal of the criminal sanction. Instead, they were responses to problems of overcrowding, labor shortages, and the cost of incarceration.

As noted in Chapter 2, England relied on transportation as one of the major sanctions until the mid-1800s. When America gained independence, Australia and other Pacific colonies became outlets for England's overcrowded prisons; offenders were given conditional pardons known as "tickets of leave" and sent to those outposts of the empire.

A key figure in developing parole in the 1800s was Captain Alexander Maconochie (1787–1860), who administered British penal colonies in Tasmania and elsewhere in the South Pacific and later in England. Maconochie criticized definite prison terms and devised a system of rewards for good conduct, labor, and study. He developed a classification by which prisoners could pass through the stages of increasing responsibility and freedom: (1) strict imprisonment, (2) labor on chain gangs, (3) freedom within an area, (4) a ticket-of-leave or parole with conditional pardon, and (5) full liberty. This procedure assumed that prisoners should be prepared gradually for release. In the transition from imprisonment to conditional release to full freedom, we can see the roots of the U.S. system of parole.

In Ireland, Sir Walter Crofton (1815–1897) built on Maconochie's idea of requiring prisoners to earn their early release. After a period of strict imprisonment, offenders transferred to an intermediate prison where they could earn marks based on work, behavior, and education. Prisoners who graduated through Crofton's three successive levels were released on parole, with conditions. Most importantly, parolees had to submit monthly reports to the police. In Dublin, a special civilian inspector helped releasees find jobs, visited them, and supervised their activities. Crofton contributed the concepts of the intermediate prison, assistance, and supervision to the modern system of parole.

The English and Irish developments soon traveled across the Atlantic. Conditional pardons and term reductions for good time had been a part of American corrections since the early 1800s, but such offenders were released without supervision. Gaylord Hubbell, warden of Sing Sing, and Franklin Sanborn, secretary of the State Board of Charities for Massachusetts, also championed the Irish system. In 1870 the National Prison Association incorporated references to the Irish system into the Declaration of Principles, along with such other reforms as the indeterminate sentence and classification based on a mark system.[2]

With New York's passage of an indeterminate sentence law in 1876, Zebulon Brockway, superintendent of Elmira Reformatory, began to release prisoners on parole when he believed they were ready to return to society. Initially the New York system did not require police supervision, as in Ireland, because parolees were placed in the care of private reform groups. As the number of parolees increased, however, the state replaced the volunteer supervisors with correctional employees.

In the United States, as states adopted indeterminate sentencing, parole followed. By 1900 twenty states had parole systems and by 1925 forty-six states did; Mississippi and Virginia finally followed suit in 1942.[3] Beginning in 1910, each federal prison had its own parole board made up of the warden, the medical officer, and the superintendent of prisons of the Department of Justice. The boards made release suggestions to the attorney general. In 1930 Congress created the U.S. Board of Parole, which replaced the separate boards.[4]

Although used in the United States for over a century, parole remains controversial. When an offender who has committed a particularly heinous crime, such as Charles Manson, becomes eligible for parole or when someone on parole has again raped, robbed, or murdered, the public is outraged. During the 1970s debate on rehabilitation, both parole and the indeterminate sentence were criticized on the grounds that release was tied to treatment success, that parole boards were abusing their discretion, and that inmates were being held in "suspended animation"—one more pain of imprisonment.

In states with determinate sentences, the decision to release becomes a matter of calculating the amount of time served plus good time, and subtracting it from the sentence.

Remember, however, that although parole may be justified in terms of rehabilitation, deterrence, or protection of society, it has other effects as well. Insofar as it reduces time spent in prison, it affects plea bargaining, the size of prison populations, and the level of discipline in correctional facilities.

Release Mechanisms

Except for the small number who die in prison, all inmates will eventually be released to live in the community. Until the mid-1970s all states and the federal government had systems that allowed parole boards to determine the exact date for an inmate to leave prison. Since the critique of rehabilitation in the 1970s and the move to determinate sentencing and parole guidelines, fifteen states have abolished their parole boards. However, three of these states, Colorado, Connecticut, and Florida, re-established the equivalent of parole boards after finding that abolition did not increase actual time served because prison crowding became so great that inmates had to be released early.[5]

There are now three basic mechanisms for persons to be released from prison: (1) discretionary release, (2) mandatory release, (3) unconditional release. Figure 15.2 shows the percentage of felons released by the various mechanisms.

Discretionary Release

discretionary release

The release of an inmate from prison to conditional supervision at the discretion of the parole board within the boundaries set by the sentence and the penal law.

States retaining indeterminate sentences allow **discretionary release** by the parole board within the boundaries set by the sentence and the penal law. This is a conditional release to parole supervision. This approach (illustrated by the case of Maurice Williams) lets the parole board assess the prisoner's readiness for release within the minimum and maximum terms of the sentence. In reviewing the prisoner's file and asking questions about the prisoner, the parole board focuses on the nature of the offense, the inmate's behavior, and participation in rehabilitative programs. This process places great faith in the ability of parole board members to accurately predict the future behavior of offenders.

Mandatory Release

Figure 15.2 Methods of Release from State Prison

Felons are released from prison to the community, usually under parole supervision through various means depending upon the law.

Source: U.S. Department of Justice, Bureau of Justice Statistics, *Correctional Populations in the United States, 1996* (Washington, DC: U.S. Government Printing Office, 1998), p. 36.

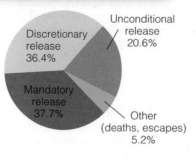

Discretionary release 36.4%

Unconditional release 20.6%

Mandatory release 37.7%

Other (deaths, escapes) 5.2%

Mandatory release is so named because it occurs after an inmate has served time equal to the total sentence minus good time, if any, or to a certain percentage of the total sentence as specified by law. Mandatory release is used by federal jurisdictions and states with determinate sentences and parole guidelines (see Chapter 4). Without a parole board to make discretionary decisions, mandatory release is a matter of bookkeeping to check the correct amount of good time and other credits and make sure the sentence has been accurately interpreted. The prisoner is released conditionally to parole supervision for the rest of the sentence minus good time. Yet because of the growth of prison populations many states have devised ways to get around the rigidity of mandatory release by placing inmates in the community through furlough, home supervision, halfway houses, emergency release, and other programs.[6]

Unconditional Release

An increasing percentage of prisoners are given **unconditional release.** These are inmates who are released from any further correctional supervision and cannot be returned to prison for any remaining portion of the sentence for a current offense. Such offenders have been incarcerated until the end of their sentence, had their sentence commuted, or been pardoned.

The Organization of Releasing Authorities

The structuring of a releasing authority raises certain questions. For example, should it be autonomous or consolidated with the corrections authority? How should field services be administered? Should the parole board sit full or part time? And how should board members be appointed? Over the past decade states have tended to create strong links between the paroling authority and the department of corrections, emphasizing parole board professionalism. The organization of parole in Japan is described in the Comparative Perspective.

Consolidated versus Autonomous

Parole boards tend to be organized either inside a department of corrections (consolidated) or as an independent agency of government (autonomous). Some argue that a parole board must be independent to insulate members from the activities and influence of corrections staff. An independent parole board may be less influenced by staff considerations such as reducing the prison population and punishing inmates who do not follow rules. Critics counter that an independent parole board can become unresponsive to corrections needs and programs and is too far removed from prison activities to understand individual cases.

Whether a parole board is independent or a part of the corrections department, it cannot exist in a vacuum. Board members cannot ignore the public's attitudes and fears about crime. If a parolee commits a crime and public indignation is aroused, the board members make decisions more cautiously, to avoid public condemnation.

Parole boards may also be influenced by departments of corrections and must maintain good relations with them. For example, if an autonomous board conflicts with the department, the department may not provide the board with information it needs. Information about particular offenders may become "unavailable," or the state may provide biased information about particular offenders that officials wish to see punished. By contrast, a board closely tied to corrections officials may get information and cooperation. However, such a board runs the risk of being viewed by prisoners and the general public as merely the rubber stamp of the department.

Field Services

Questions similar to those concerning the organization of the releasing authority surround the organization of field services. Should community supervision be administered by the paroling authority or by the department of corrections? When the parole board administers field services, proponents say, consistent policies can be developed. During the past decade, however, there has been a movement to make the transition from prison to the community more gradual, and most departments have instituted such preparole programs as work release and educational release. Therefore, it is argued, the institutional staff and the parole board must be coordinated—more easily done if they are in the same department.

---

mandatory release

The required release of an inmate from incarceration to community supervision on the expiration of a certain time period, as stipulated by a determinate sentencing law or parole guidelines.

unconditional release

The release of an inmate from incarceration without any further correctional supervision; the inmate cannot be returned to prison for any remaining portion of the sentence for the current offense.

COMPARATIVE PERSPECTIVE

Parole Release in Japan

Japan is probably the safest country in the developed world. To understand why Japan's crime rate is so low it might help to talk to a short, squat man with rumpled clothes, a gentle smile and big, leathery hands who once crushed his neighbor's head with a hammer.

This 62-year-old man, who killed his neighbor after robbing him of money, is on parole after 15 years in prison. No one in his family ever visited him. His wife and son have told him never to return to their village. His three daughters have even refused to see him. "I have four grandchildren—I think," he said. He has never even seen their pictures.

More than any other developed country, Japan has resolved to "just say no" to crime. Japanese society ostracizes offenders and demands that they not just be caught but that they also confess and show remorse.

But as in the United States, few Japanese offenders die in prison; almost all are released on parole to live under supervision in the community.

Aftercare programs have been available for Japanese offenders since the 1880s. But not until the 1950s were all elements of community treatment for ex-offenders—probation, parole, and aftercare—brought together on a national basis.

Today, decisions to release offenders from prison and place them under supervision in the community are made by eight regional parole boards (RPBs). Sitting in panels of three, the members review applications for parole from prisons and training schools. They also have the authority to revoke an individual's parole on the recommendation of a local office.

The service units of the RPBs coordinate parole. One-third of the sentence must be served. The warden, not the inmate, files the application; he thus clearly uses parole to manage prisoners. The prison directly helps select parolees by sending information to the RPB for parole.

A parole officer visits the home specified in the inmate's job/living plan. The officer checks the situation over, and recommends changes, if necessary. The report goes to the prison and the RPB. Sometimes the inmate has to revise and submit another plan.

Then the regional parole board looks at the inmate's character, behavior, and other circumstances. A board member interviews the person. Parole conditions are set partly by law and partly by administrative actions. For example, Parker writes (pp. 53–54) that parolees must "(1) maintain a fixed residence and pursue a lawful occupation; (2) refrain from associating with persons having criminal or delinquent tendencies; (3) maintain good behavior; (4) obtain advance permission from a parole supervisor before changing a place of residence or traveling for an extended period; and (5) comply with any special conditions imposed by the parole board at the time of release."

Japanese probation, parole, and aftercare focus on community. Unpaid volunteers do the supervision; private organizations administer aftercare, paid only partly by governmental subsidies.

The Japanese public largely believes that people can correct themselves. Repentant offenders tend to get out; others end up in prison. "Rehabilitation" is a way to earn the right to be reincluded in society. ∎

Source: Adapted from Nicholas D. Kristof, "Japanese Say No to Crime: Tough Methods at a Price," *The New York Times*, May 14, 1995, p. 1; L. Craig Parker, Jr., *Parole and the Community Based Treatment of Offenders in Japan and The United States* (New Haven, CT: University of New Haven Press, 1986), pp. 53–54; Elmer H. Johnson, *Japanese Corrections: Managing Convicted Offenders in an Orderly Society* (Carbondale: Southern Illinois University Press, 1996), pp. 266–267, 294.

Full Time versus Part Time

A third set of questions concerns full-time versus part-time boards. Because of the increased complexity of corrections, many people, in both discretionary and mandatory release states, hold that administration of parole should be a full-time enterprise. The type of person who is able to serve full time on a parole board differs considerably from one who serves part time. Membership on a board that meets full time attracts criminal justice professionals, who usually are well paid. However, members of part-time boards, paid by the day, are thought to better represent the community because they have other careers and are independent of the criminal justice system.

Appointment

Members of the paroling authority may be appointed by the governor or by the head of the corrections department. Some people believe gubernatorial selection insulates the members from the department, provides "better" members, and permits greater responsiveness to public concerns. Others believe the parole mechanism should be apolitical and should be operated by people who really know something about corrections.

Selection of members for parole boards is often based on the assumption that people with training in behavioral sciences can tell which candidates have been rehabilitated and are ready to return to society. The statutory qualifications for parole board membership in five states are listed in Table 15.1. However, in many states political considerations dictate that members should include representatives of specific racial groups or geographical areas. For example, the Mississippi board recently consisted of a contractor, a businessman, a farmer, and a clerk; the Florida board included a newspaperman, an attorney, and a man with experience in both business and probation; the Washington State board had people with training and experience in sociology, government and law, the ministry, and juvenile rehabilitation.

The Decision to Release

An inmate's eligibility for release to community supervision on parole depends on requirements set by law and the sentence imposed by the court. As noted, in states with determinate sentences or parole guidelines, release is mandatory once the offender has served the required amount of time. In nearly half the states, however, the release

Table 15.1 Statutory Qualifications for Parole Board Membership in Selected States

Although many states require that board members meet certain educational criteria, political considerations are important in other states.

Jurisdiction	Statutory Qualifications for Membership
Montana	Academic training that qualifies board member for professional practice in a field such as criminology, education, psychiatry, psychology, law, social work, sociology, or guidance counseling. Related work experience in these areas listed may be substituted for these educational requirements. One board member must have particular knowledge of Indian culture and problems.
New York	Each member of the board shall have graduated from an accredited four-year college or university with a degree in the field of criminology, administration of criminal justice, law enforcement, sociology, law, social work, corrections, psychology, psychiatry, or medicine, and shall have had at least five years of experience in one or more of such fields.
Ohio	No person shall be appointed a member of the board who is not qualified by education or experience in correctional work, including law enforcement, probation, parole, in law, in social work, or in a combination of the three categories.
Pennsylvania	An individual shall have at least six years of professional experience in parole, including one year in a supervisory or administrative capacity, and a bachelor's degree. Any equivalent combination of experience and training shall be acceptable.
West Virginia	Each member of the board shall have had experience in the field of social science or administration of penal institutions and shall be familiar with the principles, practices, and problems thereof and shall be otherwise competent to perform the duties of his office.

SOURCE: Edward E. Rhine, William R. Smith, and Ronald W. Jackson, *Paroling Authorities: Recent History and Current Practice* (Laurel, MD: American Correctional Association, 1991), p. 36.

decision is discretionary, and the parole board has authority to establish a release date. The date is based on the sufficiency of rehabilitation and the individual's characteristics as an inmate.

Discretionary Release

Based on the assumptions of indeterminate sentences and rehabilitative programs, discretionary release is designed to allow the parole board to release inmates to conditional supervision in the community when they are deemed "ready" to live as law-abiding citizens.[7]

Procedure Eligibility for a release hearing in discretionary states varies greatly. In prison films and novels, one regularly hears inmates say that they are going to "apply" for parole. In fact, one does not apply. Appearance before the parole board is a function of the individual sentence, statutory criteria, and the inmate's conduct before incarceration. Often the offender is eligible for release at the end of the minimum term of the sentence minus good time. In other states eligibility is at the discretion of the parole board or is calculated at one-third or one-half of the maximum sentence. However, many states provide a variety of mechanisms for release, as shown in Table 15.2.

Table 15.2 Ten Release Mechanisms in South Carolina

Until a task force on overcrowding consolidated some of the provisions, South Carolina recognized more than ten ways to leave a prison (besides escape or death). All the following types of release have been specified in the state statutes or administrative procedures.

Type of Release	Eligibility	Calculation
Discretionary parole	All felons	"Life," eligible at 20 years Less than 10 years, eligible at 1/4 of sentence 10 years or more, eligible at 1/3 of sentence
Good time	All felons	Lifers earn 15 days off maximum term for every 30 days in prison; others can earn 20 days for every 30 days in prison
Earned work credits	All felons on special work assignments	1 day off maximum term for every 2 days in work assignment up to 180 days per year
Extended work release	All felons with no more than 1 prior conviction	Placed on work release status 2 months before parole eligibility
Supervised furlough I	All felons with: clean disciplinary record less than 5-year sentence less than 2 prior convictions	Released 6 months before parole eligibility
Supervised furlough II	All felons with 6 months' clean record	Released 6 months before parole elibibility
First-day-of-month rule	All felons	Released on first day of month in which eligibility is reached (after other reductions)
Emergency release provision	Felons within 90 days of eligibility for parole	When prison reaches state of crisis because of crowding, governor may roll back sentences to reduce numbers
Provisional parole	All felons	Released 90 days before eligibility at discretion of parole board
Christmas parole	All felons	If parole eligibility is reached between 18 December and 30 January, released on 18 December at discretion of parole board

As an example of the computation of parole eligibility, look again at the case of Maurice Williams (see Figure 15.3). At the time of sentencing Williams had been held in jail for six months awaiting trial and disposition of his case. He was given a sentence of a minimum of five years and a maximum of ten years for robbery with violence. Williams did well at the maximum-security prison to which he was sent. He did not get into trouble and was thus able to amass good-time credit at the rate of one day for every four that he spent on good behavior. In addition, he was given meritorious credit of thirty days when he completed his high school diploma equivalency test after attending the prison school for two years. After serving three years, three months, and four days of his sentence, he appeared before the board of parole and was granted release into the community.

Release Criteria What criteria guides the parole board decision? Parole boards give inmates a formal statement of the criteria for making the decision. These standards normally include at least eight factors concerning the inmate:

1. Nature and circumstances of offense and current attitude toward it
2. Prior criminal record
3. Attitudes toward family members, victim, and authority in general
4. Institutional adjustment, and participation and progress in programs for self-improvement
5. History of community adjustment
6. Physical, mental, and emotional health
7. Insight into causes of past criminal conduct
8. Adequacy of parole plan

Although the published criteria may help familiarize inmates with the board's expectations, the actual decision is discretionary and is typically based on various other kinds of information as well as fundamental moral judgments about the severity of the crime, the prisoner's culpability, and the adequacy of the term served as punishment for the crime. It is frequently said that parole boards release only good risks, but as one parole board member has said, "There are no good-risk men in prison. Parole is really a decision of when to release bad-risk persons." In the Workperspective, Joel Barfoot, formerly a member of the Alabama Board of Pardons and Paroles describes some characteristics of offenders who are the best risks for parole.

Other considerations weigh heavily on the parole board members. If parole is not regularly awarded to most prisoners who gain eligibility, morale among all inmates may suffer as they fear that they will not gain release when anticipated. The seeming arbitrariness of parole boards was one of the major causes of prison riots during the 1970s.

Figure 15.3 **Computing Parole Eligibility for Maurice Williams**

Various good-time reductions to the minimum sentence are allowed in most correctional systems to determine eligibility for parole. Note how a five- to ten-year sentence can be reduced to a stay of three years, four months.

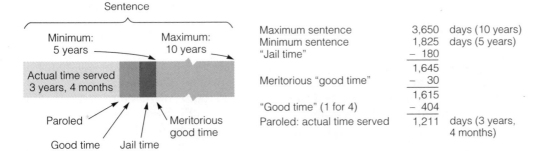

	days
Maximum sentence	3,650 days (10 years)
Minimum sentence	1,825 days (5 years)
"Jail time"	− 180
	1,645
Meritorious "good time"	− 30
	1,615
"Good time" (1 for 4)	− 404
Paroled: actual time served	1,211 days (3 years, 4 months)

Sentence

Minimum: 5 years — Maximum: 10 years

Actual time served 3 years, 4 months

Paroled — Good time — Jail time — Meritorious good time

WORKPERSPECTIVE Joel Barfoot

Alabama Board of Pardons and Paroles (chairman until 1994)

With my background as a sheriff and my conservative political viewpoint, you might presume that I would be the most conservative board member, but that distinction belongs to an African-American minister and civil rights activist. My "lock 'em up and throw away the key" mentality began to shift when I saw people being locked up who could just as well have been handled through alternative means. This only makes victims out of every tax-paying citizen.

As parole board members, we focus on three areas: (1) public protection, (2) rehabilitation, and (3) punishment. Public protection is our key concern—we must be reasonably sure that the release of an inmate won't endanger the public.

We review files approximately sixty days before the parole hearing to determine suitability for parole. We look at the crime itself, time served, disciplinary record while in prison, program participation in prison, prior record, protest letters, letters in favor of the inmate, warden reports, institutional parole officer's reports, and any other miscellaneous information. At the parole hearing itself we review the file and listen to anyone who wishes to speak in behalf of or against the inmate. At this time we can either grant or deny parole.

One factor that causes prison overcrowding and puts pressure on the parole board in Alabama is the Habitual Offender Act. Another problem is disparity in sentencing. Because of these problems, someone who walks away from the work release program or steals a small amount of property, for example, can receive a life sentence, while someone who sets his or her child on fire may get only ten years. In such cases the board makes an effort to adjust and equalize the sentences so that offenders serve approximately the same time for the same offense.

Which offenders make the best candidates for parole? Let's examine a few types.

- *Murderers.* Surprisingly, convicted murderers generally make the best parolees. Predatory and multiple murderers should be kept in prison, but people who murder in the heat of the moment can usually be rehabilitated.

- *Sex offenders.* Because recidivism rates for these offenders are high, they are poor candidates for parole. If sex offenders are paroled, it is usually after they have completed an intensive treatment program, and they are placed under strict supervision with a strong aftercare program.

- *Drug offenders.* Although these offenders have a high parole revocation rate, we try to get them into treatment programs to work out their problems rather than simply return them to prison. And if we do revoke parole, we do so for only a few months to get the parolee some help inside.

- *Property offenders.* Most of these offenders are also substance abusers and if they can get this problem under control, they usually succeed on parole. An exception is some female offenders, who don't consider the consequences of these crimes or are kleptomaniacs.

- *Assaulters.* After participating in mental health workshops and intensive programs in anger management and anger-induced acting-out, these offenders become better candidates for parole. Ongoing counseling on being paroled is important, however.

Because we are really playing God with inmates' lives as well as the general public, we take our responsibilities seriously—a bad decision can have a catastrophic effect on so many people.

The prospect of gaining parole is a major incentive for many prisoners to follow rules and cooperate with corrections officials.

Parole board members are also concerned about the public and the adequacy of the parole plan. They don't want public criticism for making controversial decisions. Thus, notorious offenders, such as Sirhan Sirhan, the man convicted of assassinating presidential candidate Robert Kennedy in 1968, and multiple murderer Charles Manson, are unlikely ever to gain parole release even if they behave well in prison.

The Prisoners' Perspective: How to Win Parole "If you want to get paroled, you've got to be in a program." This statement reflects one of the most controversial aspects of discretionary release: its link to treatment. Although corrections authorities emphasize the voluntary nature of most treatment services and clinicians argue that coercive therapy cannot succeed, inmates still believe they must "play the game." Most parole boards cite an inmate's progress in self-improvement programs as one criterion for release. A Connecticut inmate noted, "The last time I went before the board they wanted to know why I hadn't take advantage of the programs. Now I go to AA and group therapy. I hope they will be satisfied."

Although prisoners' participation in programs is technically voluntary, the link between participation and release poses many legal and ethical problems as illustrated by the case of Jim Allen in Do the Right Thing.

In some states, inmates convicted of drug or sex offenses may be expected to participate in treatment programs. However, the correctional system may not have enough places in these programs to serve all of them. Offenders may wait long periods before gaining admission, or they may be in an institution that does not have the treatment they need. Because they cannot force the prison system to transfer them to the appropriate institution, inmates may become frustrated hearing about other people gaining parole while they are not given an opportunity to prove themselves to the board. Moreover, some kinds of treatment programs, especially for sex offenders, may involve intrusive counseling therapies or medications that have lingering physical effects and a limited likelihood of success. Yet, threatened with denial of parole if they refuse to participate, prisoners may not feel able to decline such treatments.

DO THE Right THING

The five members of the parole board questioned Jim Allen, an offender with a long history of sex offenses involving teenage boys. Now approaching 45 and having met the eligibility requirement for a hearing, Allen respectfully answered the board members.

Toward the end of the hearing, Richard Edwards, a dentist who had recently been appointed to the board, spoke up: "Your institutional record is good, you have a parole plan, a job has been promised, and your sister says she will help you. All of that looks good, but I just can't vote for your parole. You haven't attended the behavior modification program for sex offenders. I think you're going to repeat your crime. I have a 13-year-old son, and I don't want him or other boys to run the risk of meeting your kind."

Allen looked shocked. The other members had seemed ready to grant his release.

"But I'm ready for parole. I won't do that stuff again. I didn't go to that program because electroshock to my private area is not going to help me. I've been here five years of the seven-year max and have stayed out of trouble. The judge didn't say I was to be further punished in prison by therapy."

After Jim Allen left the room, the board discussed his case. "You know, Rich, he has a point. He has been a model prisoner and has served a good portion of his sentence," said Brian Lynch, a long-term board member. "Besides we don't know if Dr. Hankin's program works."

"I know, but can we really let someone like that out on the streets?"

Are the results of the behavior modification program for sex offenders relevant to the parole board's decision? Is the purpose of the sentence to punish Allen for what he did or for what he might do in the future? Would you vote for his release on parole? Would your vote be the same if his case had received media attention? ∎

Consequences of Discretionary Parole During a riot at New Jersey's Rahway Prison, inmates held aloft a banner that boldly proclaimed, "Abolish parole!" Why? Although inmates criticize the somewhat capricious actions of some parole boards, they also point out that indeterminate sentences and discretionary release leave them constantly in limbo. The uncertainty is demoralizing.

When release is discretionary, the parole board's power is much like that of the sentencing judge. Detractors emphasize that unlike the judge, the board makes its decisions outside the spotlight of public attention. In addition, they contend that, whereas sentencing is done with due process of law, there are few such rights at a parole hearing.

Supporters of discretionary release maintain that parole boards can make their decisions without community pressure and can rectify sentencing errors. Arguably, legislatures often respond to public pressure by prescribing unreasonably harsh maximum sentences—thirty, fifty, even a hundred years. But most penal codes also prescribe minimum sentences that are closer to the actual times served; thus the parole board is able to grant release after a "reasonable" period of incarceration.

Structuring Parole Decisions

In response to the criticism that the release decisions of parole boards are somewhat arbitrary, many states have adopted parole guidelines to help their members. Release is usually granted to prisoners who have served the amount of time stipulated by the guidelines and who meet the following three criteria:

1. They have substantially observed the rules of the institution in which they have been confined.
2. Their release will not depreciate the seriousness of the offense or promote disrespect for the law.
3. Their release will not jeopardize the public welfare.

As with sentencing guidelines, a "severity scale" ranks crimes according to their seriousness and a "salient factor" score measures the offender's criminal history (drug arrests, prior record, age at first conviction, and so on) and risk factors regarded as relevant to successful completion of parole (see Tables 15.3 and 15.4).

By placing the offender's salient factor score next to his or her particular offense on the severity scale, the board, the inmate, and correctional officials may calculate the **presumptive parole date** soon after the offender enters prison. This is the date by which the inmate can expect to be released if there are no disciplinary or other problems during incarceration. The presumptive parole date may be modified on a scheduled basis. The date of release may be advanced because of good conduct and superior achievement, or may be postponed if there are disciplinary infractions or a suitable community supervision plan is not developed.

presumptive parole date

The presumed release date stipulated by parole guidelines if the offender serves time without disciplinary or other incidents.

The Impact of Release Mechanisms

Parole release mechanisms do more than simply determine the date at which a particular prisoner will be sent back into the community. Parole release also has an enormous impact on other parts of the system, including sentencing, plea bargaining, and the size of prison populations.[8]

One important effect of discretionary release is that an administrative body—the parole board—can shorten a sentence imposed by a judge. Even in states that have mandatory release, various potential reductions built into the sentence mean the full sentence is rarely served. "Good time," for example, can reduce punishment even if there is no parole eligibility.

To understand the impact of release mechanisms on criminal punishment, we need to compare the amount of time actually served in prison with the sentence specified by the judge. In some jurisdictions up to 80 percent of felons sentenced to prison are released to the community after their first appearance before a parole board. Eligibility for discretionary release is ordinarily determined by the minimum term of the sentence

Table 15.3 Criminal History/Risk Assessment under the Oregon Guidelines for Adult Offenders

The amount of time to be served is related to the severity of the offense and to the criminal history/risk assessment of the inmate. The criminal history score is determined by adding the points assigned each factor in this table.

	Factor	Points	Score
A.	No prior felony convictions as an adult or juvenile:	3	
	One prior felony conviction:	2	
	Two or three prior felony convictions:	1	
	Four or more prior felony convictions:	0	____
B.	No prior felony or misdemeanor incarcerations (that is, executed sentences of ninety days or more) as an adult or juvenile:	2	
	One or two prior incarcerations:	1	
	Three or more prior incarcerations:	0	____
C.	Verified period of three years conviction-free in the community prior to the present commitment:	1	
	Otherwise:	0	____
D.	Age at commencement of behavior leading to this incarceration was ____; D.O.B. was _____.		
	Twenty-six or older and at least one point received in Items A, B, or C:	2	
	Twenty-six or older and no points received in A, B, or C:	1	
	Twenty-one to under twenty-six and at least one point received in A, B, or C:	1	
	Twenty-one to under twenty-six and no points received in A, B, or C:	0	
	Under twenty-one:	0	____
E.	Present commitment does not include parole, probation, failure to appear, release agreement, escape, or custody violation:	2	
	Present commitment involves probation, release agreement, or failure to appear violation:	1	
	Present commitment involves parole, escape, or custody violation:	0	____
F.	Has no admitted or documented substance abuse problem within a three-year period in the community immediately preceding the commission of the crime conviction:	1	
	Otherwise:	0	
	Total History/Risk Assessment Score:		____

SOURCE: Adapted from State of Oregon, Board of Parole, *ORS* Chapter 144, Rule 255-35-015.

minus good time and jail time. As noted, good time allows the minimum sentence to be reduced for good behavior during incarceration or for exceptional performance of assigned tasks or personal achievement. Jail time—credit given for time spent in jail while an offender awaits trial and sentencing—also shortens the period that must be served before an inmate's first appearance before the parole board.

Although states vary considerably, on a national basis felony inmates serve an average of a little over two years before release. Offenders who receive long sentences actually serve a smaller proportion of such sentences than do offenders given shorter sentences. For example, a robbery offender may be given a term of 12–60 months and serve 69 percent of the term before being released after 23 months. By contrast, an offender sentenced to a term of 181–240 months will actually serve 38 percent of the term, 83 months. Figure 15.4 shows the average time served for selected offenses.

Table 15.4 Number of Months to Be Served Before Release Under the Oregon Guidelines

The presumptive release date is determined by finding the intersection of the criminal history score (Table 15.3) and the category of the offense. Thus an offender with an assessment score between 6 and 8, convicted of a category 3 offense, could expect to serve between 10 and 14 months.

	Criminal History/ Risk Assessment Score			
Offense Severity	**11–9** **Excellent**	**8–6** **Good**	**5–3** **Fair**	**2–0** **Poor**
Category 1: bigamy, criminal mischief I, dogfighting, incest, possession of stolen vehicle	6	6	6–10	12–18
Category 2: abandonment of a child, bribing a witness, criminal homicide, perjury, possession of controlled substance	6	6–10	10–14	16–24
Category 3: assault III, forgery I, sexual abuse, trafficking in stolen vehicles	6–10	10–14	14–20	22–32
Category 4: aggravated theft, assault II, coercion, criminally negligent homicide, robbery II	10–16	16–22	22–30	32–44
Category 5: burglary I, escape I, manslaughter II, racketeering, rape I	16–24	24–36	40–52	56–72
Category 6: arson I, kidnapping I, rape II, sodomy I	30–40	44–56	60–80	90–130
Category 7: aggravated murder, treason	96–120	120–156	156–192	192–240
Category 8: aggravated murder (stranger-stranger, cruelty to victim, prior muder conviction)	120–168	168–228	228–288	288–life

SOURCE: Adapted from State of Oregon, Board of Parole, *ORS* Chapter 144, Rule 255-75-026 and Rule 255-75-035.

The probability of release well before the end of the formal sentence encourages plea bargaining by both prosecutors and defendants. Prosecutors can reap the benefits of quick, cooperative plea bargains that look tough in the eyes of the public. Meanwhile, the defendant agrees to plead guilty and accept the sentence because of the high likelihood of early release through parole.

Beyond the benefits of parole to prosecutors, supporters of discretion for the paroling authority argue that it has invaluable benefits for the overall system. Discretionary release mitigates the harshness of the penal code. If the legislature must establish exceptionally strict punishments as a means of conveying a "tough-on-crime" image to frustrated and angry voters, parole can effectively permit sentence adjustments that make the punishment fit the crime. Everyone convicted of larceny may not have done equivalent harm, yet some legislatively mandated sentencing schemes may impose equally strict sentences. Early release on parole can be granted to an offender who is less deserving of strict punishment, such as someone who voluntarily makes restitution, cooperates with the police, or shows genuine regret.

A major criticism of parole is that it has shifted responsibility for many primary criminal justice decisions from a judge, who holds legal procedures uppermost, to an administrative board, where discretion rules. Having legal education, judges are knowledgeable about constitutional rights and basic legal protections. In contrast, parole

Figure 15.4 Estimated Time to Be Served by Adults Convicted of Selected Offenses

The data indicate that the average felony offender spends about two years in prison. What would be the public's reaction to this fact?

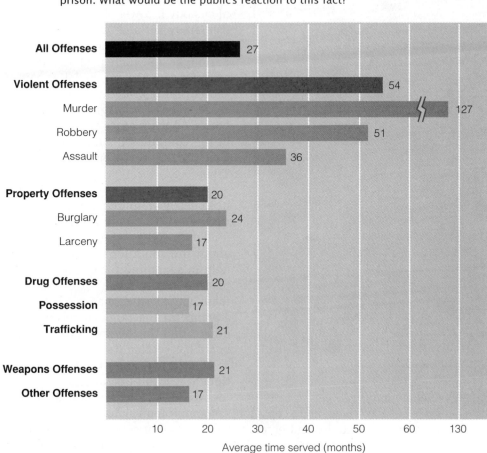

Source: U.S. Department of Justice, Bureau of Justice Statistics, *Bulletin*, January 1997, p. 4.

board members may not have such knowledge. In most states with discretionary release, parole hearings are secret, with only board members, the inmate, and correctional officers present. Often no published criteria guide decisions, and prisoners are given no reason for denial or granting of parole. Should society place such power in the hands of parole boards? Because there is so little oversight over their decision making and so few constraints on their decisions, some parole board members will make arbitrary or discriminatory decisions inconsistent with the constitutional system and civil rights. Generally, the U.S. legal system seeks to avoid determining people's fate through such methods.

Release to the Community

The development of community corrections has had a tremendous impact on most aspects of the system. Some of the most striking effects have been on the nature of incarceration and on decisions concerning release.

Out of the philosophy of community corrections came the reintegration model of prison life. Here the goal is to prepare offenders for reentry into society through the gradual allocation of freedoms and responsibilities during incarceration. Where this

Upon completion of her sentence, a mother greets her daughter. When an offender is released, family and community relations have to be reforged.

model has been adopted, prisoners are placed at a high level of custody when they enter the institution and are periodically evaluated. As they progress, the level of custody is lowered so they can reestablish family ties and begin to heal the damage done by their crime and incarceration. Furloughs and increased visitation often are arranged. Toward the latter part of the sentence, the offender may be placed on work release, transferred to a halfway house, or given other opportunities to live in the community. Characteristics of selected prerelease programs are shown in Table 15.5.

In most states prison programs have been designed to prepare the offender for release to community supervision. The offender receives prerelease counseling about the conditions of supervision and help in searching for employment and a place to live. In some corrections systems these activities begin as much as a year in advance of the targeted release date; in others they begin only after the parole board has set that date.

California, for example, provides a three-week, full-time training program for inmates who are within fifteen to forty-five days of release. Inmates are given training in the attitudes needed to get and keep a job, communication skills, family roles, money management, and community and parole resources. The prisoners and their needs are evaluated. Each prisoner is then given a list of five objectives to achieve within thirty days of being paroled, as well as the names and addresses of five public or private agencies that can be contacted for assistance. During the training program, each prisoner participates in at least one mock job interview and acquires a California driver's license.

A similar program in North Carolina includes transfer of the participating inmates to a housing unit reserved for prereleases. One week of the four-week period is devoted to family readjustment training. With the emphasis on reintegration and community supervision, offenders are no longer confined to one cell in one institution for the duration of their terms. Instead, they move about a great deal from one security level to another and from one institution to another as they prepare for release.

Summary

During most of the 1900s, parole boards decided when most prisoners would be released to the community. With the advent of determinate sentencing and parole guidelines, releasing power has essentially been taken from the board in many states. It is now necessary to distinguish between discretionary release and mandatory release.

Parole in the United States evolved in the 1800s from practices in England, Ireland, and Australia. Alexander Maconochie and Walter Crofton made significant contributions to the development of parole.

Discretionary release is influenced by the rehabilitation model. Parole boards consider such factors as participation in treatment programs, readiness for the community,

Table 15.5 Characteristics of Prerelease Programs in Selected States

Corrections systems have developed programs to help ease inmates' transition to the community. Note the variety of organizations prepared to assist the offender on release.

State	Eligibility	Role of Outside Agencies and/or Volunteers
Arkansas	Inmate must have a projected release date of not more than 120 days at a time of transfer; must not have pending felony detainers; has not been convicted of a sex offense or exhibited a history of abnormal sexual behavior while incarcerated; does not have a pending prior disciplinary charge; and does not require special medical consideration which cannot be handled by the unit/center.	The Arkansas Employment Security Division (outside agency) assists in obtaining employment for prerelease inmates and assists with transportation for them to and from job interviews. Outside community volunteers provide religious activities and some counseling.
Florida	Before release from community correctional centers, immediately prior to participation in community work release.	Citizen volunteers are utilized as well as other community, private, and state agencies.
Maryland	Twelve months from next parole hearing or expiration date; maintain as infraction-free adjustment for a minimum of six months; first- and second-degree sex offenses are precluded along with those convicted of three serious offenses with at least one prior commitment.	Provide various services, including employment readiness, drug and alcohol therapy, vocational training, and some psychological services.
Oregon	Inmate must be within six months of an established release date and must be minimum custody.	Utilize practicums and volunteers for counseling inmate club activities, and religious services. Also present a release services seminar twice a month which relies almost solely on volunteer instruction.
South Carolina	No detainers; participation is during final 30 days of incarceration, prior to good-time release. Parole board may specify participation prior to effecting parole.	Approximately 75 percent of all prerelease programming is conducted by other agencies and volunteers. They are the primary providers of all such services.

Source: Adapted from *Corrections Compendium*, March 8, 1984, pp. 5–8. Copyright © 1984 Contact Center, Inc. Reprinted by permission.

seriousness of the offense, and availability of suitable employment. Mandatory release is determined on the basis of a determinate sentence or parole guidelines. These mechanisms limit the discretion of correctional officials.

The release decision affects the size of the prison population, the plea bargaining process, and the lengths of sentences. One criticism of discretionary release is that it shifts responsibility from the judge to the parole board.

Releasing authorities are organized in a variety of ways. Parole boards may be autonomous or consolidated, may meet full time or part time, and may administer field services.

Increased reliance on the reintegration model of institutional operation has affected the way prisons are run. Where this model has been implemented, inmates are placed in housing units of decreasing security levels as their release dates approach. Furloughs, work and educational release, halfway houses, and prerelease training are elements of the reintegration model. ■

For Discussion

1. What are the implications of mandatory release for the corrections system? How will corrections adjust to this harnessing of the discretion of parole boards and judges?

2. What factors should a parole board consider when it evaluates a prisoner for release?

3. Suppose, as a parole board member, you are confronted by a man who has served six years of a ten- to twenty-year sentence for murder. He has a good institutional record, and you do not believe him to be a threat to community safety. Would you release him to parole supervision at this time? Why or why not?

4. Suppose you have been asked to decide whether the department of corrections or an independent agency should have authority over release decisions. Where would you place that authority? Why?

5. Given the current public attitude toward criminals, what do you see as the likely future of parole release?

For Further Reading

Glaser, Daniel. *The Effectiveness of a Prison and Parole System.* New York: Bobbs-Merrill, 1964. Represents a classic study of the links between incarceration and parole.

Rhine, Edward E., Smith, William R., and Jackson, Ronald W. *Paroling Authorities: Recent History and Current Practice.* Laurel, MD: American Correctional Association, 1991. Reports the results of a national survey conducted by the ACA Task Force on Parole.

Stanley, David T. *Prisoners Among Us.* Washington, DC: Brookings Institution, 1976. Represents the only major published account of parole release decision making, with an emphasis on parole board discretion.

Von Hirsch, Andrew, and Hanrahan, Kathleen J. *The Question of Parole.* Cambridge, MA: Ballinger, 1979. Examines parole from the "just deserts" perspective and urges its reform.

Notes

1. Department of Justice, Bureau of Justice Statistics, *Bulletin,* August 1998, p. 5.
2. Harry Elmer Barnes and Nedgley K. Teeters, *New Horizons in Criminology* (Englewood Cliffs, NJ: Prentice-Hall, 1944), pp. 550,553.
3. Lawrence M. Friedman, *Crime and Punishment in American History* (New York: Basic Books, 1993), p. 304.
4. Peter B. Hoffman, "History of the Federal Parole System: Part I (1910-1972)," *Federal Probation,* 61, September 1997, p. 23.
5. Fox Butterfield, "Eliminating Parole Boards Isn't a Cure-All, Experts Say," *The New York Times,* January 10, 1999, p. 12.
6. Pamela L. Griset, "The Politics and Economics of Increased Correctional Discretion Over Time Served: A New York Case Study," *Justice Quarterly,* 12, June 1995, p. 307.
7. Susette Talarico, "The Dilemmas of Parole Decision Making," in George F. Cole, ed., *Criminal Justice: Law and Politics,* 5th ed. (Pacific Grove, CA: Brooks/Cole, 1988), pp. 442–451.
8. Samuel Walker, *Taming the System: The Control of Discretion in Criminal Justice, 1950–1990* (New York: Oxford University Press, 1993), p. 141.

CHAPTER SIXTEEN

Making It: Supervision in the Community

Returning to the streets after years behind bars is a shock; the most normal, unremarkable events seem to take on overwhelming significance. Max, who spent six years in prison, recently described his postrelease experience to a team of researchers:

"The first few days out were a flash. That's all I can say, man. There's cars and dogs and trees and people, you know, and you walk

With a bus ticket and $50 "gate money," Barry Pizzo returns to the free world. What will be the problems that he must immediately face?

down the street and there's mailboxes and there's houses and screen doors. And it all comes back to you. Things that you'd wanted to do, places that you'd wanted to go, things you wanted to see. It's all there, and you try to get them all at once. That's one reason why a lot of people are going back, man, because they're trying to do everything at once. I'm still flashing. Sometimes I think I'm back in the joint, man. I say, "Wow, where am I? I'm free. I'm here. I'm doing fine."[1]

The popular notion is that once offenders have completed their prison sentences, they have paid their "debt" and are ready to start life anew. The reality is that the vast majority of offenders released from prison remain subject to correctional authority for some time. For many offenders this authority is represented by the parole officer; for others it is the staff of a halfway house or work release center. The "freedom" of release is constrained: The whereabouts of offenders are monitored, and their associations and daily activities are checked.

The freedom of offenders who are released outright — either because they have completed their maximum term (the maximum sentence minus good time) or, as in the state of Maine, because there is no parole supervision — is also less complete than may seem. The former inmate still has many serious obstacles to overcome: long absence from family and friends, legal and practical limitations on employment possibilities, the suspicion and uneasiness of the community, even the strangeness of everyday living. The outside world can seem alien and unpredictable after even a short time in the artificial environment of prison.

No truly "clean start" is possible. The status of former convict is nearly as stigmatizing as the old status of convict, and in many ways more frustrating. Most people look at the parolee askance, and the experience can be embittering.

In this chapter we focus on "making it" — the struggles of former inmates to not return to prison. Many fail; about half of all released offenders return to prison within six years. The number who succeed is impressive. Most are under the scrutiny of agents of the state; all face significant legal, familial, and social strains. How many of us would not be vulnerable to misconduct under such pressures? Released offenders are playing against a stacked deck, and the fact that so many succeed is testimony to their perseverance. The following Questions for Inquiry are addressed in this chapter.

Questions FOR INQUIRY

1. What are the major characteristics of the postrelease function of the corrections system?
2. How is community supervision structured?
3. What are residential programs, and how do they help parolees?
4. What are some problems parolees confront?
5. What are the relationships among parolees, officers, and the bureaucracy?
6. Why are some parolees viewed as dangerous, and how is society handling this problem?
7. How effective is postrelease supervision?

Overview of the Postrelease Function

Parolees are released from prison on condition that they abide by laws and follow rules designed both to aid their readjustment to society and control their movement. The parolee may be required to abstain from alcohol, keep away from undesirable associates, maintain good work habits, and not leave the community without permission. These requirements, called **conditions of release,** regulate conduct that is not criminal but that is thought to be linked to the possibility of future criminality. Specific conditions of release are set forth in Figure 16.1, a parole contract that New Jersey parolees are required to sign.

Community Supervision

Restrictions on parolees are rationalized on the grounds that people who have been incarcerated must readjust to the community gradually so they will not simply fall back into preconviction habits and associations. Some people hold that trying to impose on parolees standards of conduct not imposed on others is both wrong and likely to fail. Moreover, new parolees find themselves in such daunting circumstances that they may have great difficulty living according to the rules.

When releasees first come out of prison, their personal and material problems are staggering. In most states they are given only clothes, a token amount of money, a copy of the rules governing their release, and the name and address of the parole officer to whom they must report within twenty-four hours. Although a promised job is often a

conditions of release

Restrictions on parolees' conduct that must be obeyed as a legally binding requirement of being released.

Figure 16.1 Conditions of Release, New Jersey

Newly released offenders must comply with specific conditions in order to remain in good standing on parole.

condition of release, an actual job may be another matter. Most former convicts are un-skilled or semiskilled, and parole stipulations may prevent them from moving to areas where they could find work. If they are African American and under age 30, they join the largest group of unemployed in the country, with the added handicap of former convict status.

Reentry problems help explain why most parole failures occur rela-tively soon after release — nearly one-quarter during the first six months. With little preparation offend-ers move from the highly structured, authoritarian prison life into the complex, tempta-tion-filled free world. They are expected to summon up extraordinary coping abilities, but not surprisingly, the social, psychological, and material overload sends many parolees back. Figure 16.2 summarizes some key characteristics of parole violators.

Revocation

When people fail on parole, their parole is revoked and they are returned to prison to continue serving their sentences. Parole can be revoked for two reasons: (1) committing a new crime or (2) violating conditions of parole (a "technical violation"). Technical vi-olations are controversial because they involve noncriminal conduct, such as failure to report an address change to the parole officer.

Critics of parole argue that it is improper to reimprison a parolee for minor infrac-tions. In practice, revocations seldom result from a single rules violation — prisons are far too crowded. To be returned to prison on a technical violation, a parolee usually must show persistent noncompliance or else give the parole officer reason to believe he or she has returned to crime. Observers believe most revocations occur only when the parolee is arrested on a serious charge or cannot be located by the officer.

Perspectives on the parolee's status in the community have changed over the years. Early reformers saw parole decisions as grace dispensed by the correctional authority. Such parole could be revoked at any time and for any reason. Later reformers began to view parole as a privilege, earned by good behavior in prison and retained by adherence to parole conditions. More recently some commentators have begun to describe parole as a right of prisoners who have served enough time in prison, and they urge that tech-nical violations be eliminated as a basis for return to prison. The "rights" view does not now prevail officially in any parole system, although the state of Washington strictly limits the penalties that may be imposed on technical violators.

If parole is a privilege, then its revocation is not subject to due process or rules of evidence. In some states liberal policies of granting parole have been justified on the grounds that parole can be swiftly revoked whenever the offender violates the parole rules. Under the New York statute, for example, if a parole officer has reason to be-lieve a parolee has lapsed or is about to lapse into criminal conduct or into the com-pany of criminals, or has violated any important condition of parole, the officer may rearrest the parolee. The officer's power to recommend revocation because the parolee is "slipping" hangs over the parolee like the proverbial sword of Damocles, suspended by a hair.

When the parole officer alleges a technical violation of parole, the U.S. Supreme Court requires a two-stage revocation proceeding. Although the Court exempted revoca-tion proceedings from the normal requirements of a criminal trial, many due process rights must be accorded the parolee.[2] In the first stage the parole board determines whether there is probable cause that a violation has occurred. (Probable cause is the criterion for deciding whether evidence is strong enough to uphold an arrest or to sug-gest issuing an arrest or warrant; also, the facts upholding the belief that a crime has been committed and that the accused committed the offense.) The parolee then has the right to be notified of charges, be informed of evidence, be heard, present witnesses, and confront the parole board's witnesses (providing no witness would be endangered by such a confrontation). In the second stage the parole board decides if the violation is severe enough to warrant return to prison.

Figure 16.2 Personal Characteristics of Failed Parolees

Parole violators tend to be unmarried, African-American men in their late twenties and early thirties.

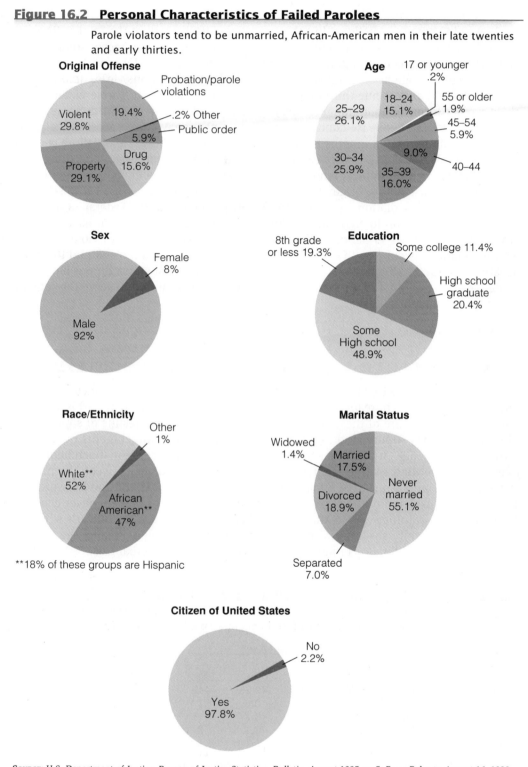

Original Offense

Probation/parole violations 19.4%
.2% Other
Public order 5.9%
Violent 29.8%
Property 29.1%
Drug 15.6%

Age

17 or younger .2%
18–24 15.1%
55 or older 1.9%
45–54 5.9%
40–44 9.0%
35–39 16.0%
30–34 25.9%
25–29 26.1%

Sex

Female 8%
Male 92%

Education

8th grade or less 19.3%
Some college 11.4%
High school graduate 20.4%
Some High school 48.9%

Race/Ethnicity

Other 1%
White** 52%
African American** 47%

**18% of these groups are Hispanic

Marital Status

Widowed 1.4%
Married 17.5%
Divorced 18.9%
Never married 55.1%
Separated 7.0%

Citizen of United States

No 2.2%
Yes 97.8%

Source: U.S. Department of Justice, Bureau of Justice Statistics, *Bulletin*, August 1995, p. 5; Press Release, August 16, 1998.

Data on the number of parole revocations is difficult to determine. A combined revocation and recommitment rate of approximately 25 percent within three years of release has been reported for years; these data, however, do not distinguish between people returned to prison for technical violations and those returned for new criminal offenses. Recent studies using standard definitions of revocation rates have put this figure higher in some jurisdictions, but they also have disclosed that the total failure rate varies dramatically, from 25 percent to over 50 percent. In addition, recent studies show that successful completion of parole shifts from time to time (see Table 16.1).

The degree to which these rates reflect technical rules violations varies among states as well. Overall, almost one-third of all new prison admissions are parole violators (including other forms of conditional release); of this group, nearly two-thirds are returned to prison for violating release conditions, without a new conviction.[3] Most of these violations occur in the initial months following release—the highest rate of failure is in the first year of release—but parolees can fail even after years of successful adjustment.

Information on the typical length of reconfinement for a technical parole violation indicates that those whose original charges are the most serious can expect to serve the most time for their violation (see Table 16.2). The guidelines of the Federal Parole Commission recommend up to eight months for revoked parolees who do not have a history of violations and a longer period (eight to sixteen months) for persistent violators, those whose violations occur less than eight months after release, and those found to have a negative employment/school record during supervision. Most states do not have such guidelines. The offender whose parole is revoked may be required to serve the remainder of the unexpired sentence.

The Structure of Community Supervision

Three forces influence the newly released offender's adjustment to free society: the parole officer, the parole bureaucracy, and the experiences of the offender. Carl B. Klockars notes that the structure of these relationships can determine the results of supervision. Klockars describes supervision as a series of stages in which attachments develop, as shown in Figure 16.3. In the initial stages of supervision, the strongest attachment is between the officer and the bureaucracy, with a minor attachment between the parolee and the officer and a negative attachment between the parolee and the bureaucracy. The parolee's suspicion of the bureaucracy's rules and fear of its policies never changes. As the parolee and officer get to know each other better, however, the officer's strongest attachment gradually shifts from the bureaucracy to the parolee. Finally, the two develop rapport, the ability to communicate positively and with mutual trust.[4]

Table 16.1 Trends in State Parole Discharges, 1988–1997

The percentage of parolees who successfully complete their term and are discharged from supervision varies from time to time. What factors might account for these shifts?

Method of Parole Discharge	All Discharges			
	1988	1991	1992	1997
Successful completions	35.1%	40.6%	49.2%	44%
Absconded	0.5	0.7	0.8	1
Returned to jail/prison[a]	61.8	57.0	48.2	41
Transferred	0.2	0.1	0.1	2
Death	1.0	1.1	1.1	1
Other	1.4	0.5	0.6	11
Number of parole discharges	114,528	176,361	206,623	410,839

[a]Includes those returned to prison with a new sentence, technical parole violations, and those returned pending parole revocation on new charges.:

SOURCES: U.S. Department of Justice, Bureau of Justice Statistics, *National Corrections Reporting Program*, 1992 (Washington, DC: U.S. Department of Justice, 1995); *News Release*, August 16, 1998.

Table 16.2 Expected Time to Be Served by Parole Violators Returned to Prison

The typical parole violator serves a little over two years for the violation, but serious offenders serve at least four times that amount.

Most Serious Current Offense	Time Expected to Serve in Prison	
	Mean	**Median**
Total	63 months	28 months
Violent offenses	124	83
Homicide[a]	217	173
Sexual assault[b]	119	90
Robbery	105	75
Assault	102	59
Other[c]	187	105
Property offenses	46	24
Burglary	55	31
Larceny	31	17
Other property[d]	41	22
Drug offenses	37	23
Possession	28	19
Trafficking	44	26
Other	18	11
Public order offenses	34	20
Other offenses	85	81
Probation/parole violation	27	12
Number of inmates	135,611	135,611

[a]includes murder, nonnegligent manslaughter, and negligent manslaughter.
[b]includes rape.
[c]includes kidnapping.
[d]includes motor vehicle theft, fraud, stolen property, and arson.

SOURCE: U.S. Department of Justice, Bureau of Justice Statistics, *Bulletin*, August 1995.

This model explains why parolees' rule violations are often overlooked: The parole officer identifies more closely with the offender than with the bureaucracy. But the process does not always follow that pattern. Often rapport never develops, and the attachment between the parolee and the officer sours. When strain develops between the parolee and the other forces, it is very difficult for the offender to succeed.

Figure 16.3 Positive and Negative Attachments at Three Stages of the Supervision Process

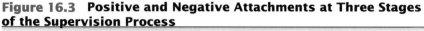

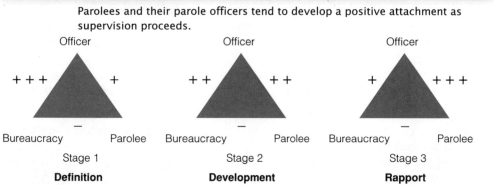

SOURCE: *The Effectiveness of a Prison and Parole System* by Daniel Glaser © 1964. Adapted by permission of Prentice-Hall, Inc., Upper Saddle River, NJ.

Parole officers are responsible for both supervising the activities of ex-offenders and helping them find the resources they need to successfully establish their lives outside of prison.

What determines the outcome of the supervision process? The answer lies in a complex web of attitudes, situations, policies, and random events. First consider in detail two major forces: the parole officer and the bureaucracy.

Agents of Community Supervision

Parole officers are usually asked to play two roles: cop and social worker. As cops they can restrict many aspects of the parolee's life, enforce conditions of release, and initiate revocation for violations. In states that subscribe to the concept of parole as grace, officers may search the parolee's living quarters without warning, arrest him or her for suspected violations without bail, and suspend parole pending a hearing. One common practice when parolees misbehave is to "hold" them in jail for a day or two to warn them not to challenge the officer's authority. Like other street-level bureaucrats in the criminal justice system, officers have extensive discretionary power. The officer's relationship with the offender thus has an authoritative component that can hinder the development of rapport and mutual trust.

Parole officers are responsible for assisting parolees' adjustment to the community as well as for policing their actions. They must act as social workers by helping parolees find jobs and restore family ties. They must be prepared to mediate between parolees and organizations and to channel parolees to such human service agencies as psychiatric clinics. As caseworkers, officers must develop a relationship that fosters trust and confidence; which is not likely to develop if parolees are made constantly aware of the officers' ability to send them back to prison.

How can parole officers reconcile these conflicting role demands? One suggestion is that the responsibilities be divided, so that the officer carries out the supervision and other people perform casework functions. Alternatively, the officer can be charged solely with casework, and local police can check for violations. Georgia has experimented with having a team of two supervisors handle a caseload jointly. One person (often a former police officer) was the surveillance officer, and the other was the probation officer, providing assistance. However, an evaluation of the system found that the distinction often became vague: Parolees often looked to surveillance officers for help and saw probation officers as enforcing the conditions of supervision.[5] Despite the conflict, the job seems to require that any person having supervisory contact with the offender perform both roles. Criteria for those providing parole services have been summarized as follows:

1. *Be known.* Parolees must know where to go, or where to find out where to go.
2. *Be open for business.* Parolees may encounter problems at any time, so guidance or temporary remedies must be available around the clock.
3. *Be reachable.* Parolees must have easy access to parole services or be given transportation.
4. *Be comprehensive.* Parolees must have access to remedial services, whatever the difficulty—money, drugs or alcohol, family problems.
5. *Be trusted.* Parolees must feel they will not be punished or threatened when they reveal a problem.
6. *Be voluntary.* Parolees are unlikely to respond to coercion or to forced treatment. In the free community they must make their own choices, and compelling participation will delay their rehabilitation.[6]

Daniel Glaser has analyzed the various ways in which parole officers adapt their personal styles and orientations.[7] Officer role orientations may be divided along the dimensions of assistance and control, yielding four conceptions of parole work, as shown in Figure 16.4.

Paternal officers protect both the offender and the community by assistance, lectures, praise, and blame. They have ambivalent emotional involvement with offenders

Figure 16.4 Differing Role Orientations of Parole Officer

Daniel Glaser has identified four different types of parole officers based on their attitudes toward the job.

SOURCE: Adapted from Daniel Glaser, *The Effectiveness of a Prison and Parole System,* abridged ed. Copyright © 1969 by Macmillan Publishing Company. Reprinted by permission.

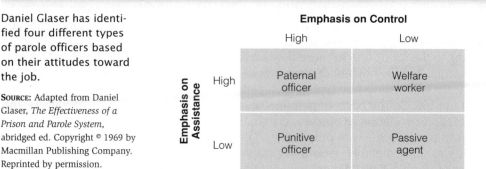

and with others in the community, taking first one side and then the other. Paternal officers tend to have little formal training but much dedication and experience.

Punitive officers are guardians of middle-class morality and try to make the offender conform by threats and punishment. They stress control and protection of the public against offenders, and are suspicious of the people they supervise.

Welfare workers seek the greater good for their clients, and toward that end they aid each client's individual adjustment. They believe the community's protection lies in that personal adjustment. Emotionally neutral, their diagnostic and treatment skills take into account the situation, needs, and capacities of their parolees.

Passive agents see their jobs as sinecures and expend only minimal energy on them. Often political appointees, they have little interest in the parolees but like the pay, independence, and opportunities to pursue their own interests.

There is some dispute about the ways officers balance concern for assistance and concern for control. Some people believe that the roles are incompatible and that effectiveness requires choosing to emphasize one. Others argue that the effective officer must be able to shift from role to role. A recent study of role adoption in supervision approaches suggests that an officer's emphasis on control is largely a product of personal preferences but that the degree of emphasis on assistance depends on the overall philosophy of the organization.[8]

The parole officer's style has been referred to as a "hidden condition" of supervision. This hidden condition embodies certain expectations about how clients will behave and therefore how to treat them. Glaser's paternal officers take a parental approach; welfare workers approach the job as professional caseworkers; punitive officers see themselves as community protection agents; passive agents are bureaucrats. Each approach leads to a style of interaction with parolees—gruff, distant, or friendly—that is an informal determinant of the supervision process. In fact, style can overwhelm other aspects of the work. For instance, Elliot Studt's famous study of parole officers in California revealed that their individual styles were so varied that each could be thought of as almost a separate agency.[9]

The second hidden condition of supervision is the supervision plan. In most agencies each officer and parolee develop a supervision (or treatment) plan that states what the parolee is going to do about the problems (unemployment, drug abuse, marital conflict, and so on) that hinder adjustment to the community. The officer has a great deal of discretion in developing this plan and may put a lot of energy into it or very little. This latitude may explain why officers who are oriented toward providing assistance tend to write significantly more supervision objectives for their clients and to get involved in more areas of parolees' lives.

As street-level bureaucrats, officers are also affected by organizational demands unrelated to either assistance or control. Richard McCleary's study of parole officers in Cook County (Chicago) disclosed that decisions about individual parolees are influenced by the organization's definition of the situation, the officer's own perception of the parolee, and the officer's professional reputation. Members of the parole bureaucracy strive to maintain desirable professional conditions: a good working atmosphere, independence from supervisory oversight, and the use of discretion. Certain parolees are viewed as threatening to the status quo because they make trouble for their officers and for the officers' superiors, and they therefore elicit special responses from their officers.

McCleary believes that by typing each parolee from the start, the officer neutralizes potential trouble. On the basis of parolees' files, initial interviews, and home visits, the officer categorizes clients as sincere, criminally inclined, or dangerous. "Dangerous" refers not to parolees who are potentially violent, but rather to those few who may act irrationally or unpredictably, who don't respond to warnings, and who go out of their way to make trouble. The "dangerous" parolees are the most worrisome, for an officer has more difficulty maintaining control over them. McCleary found that, surprisingly, one way is to bargain with them:

> All right, Johnny, this is how it is. I've got you on paper for the next seven years, but I'll make a deal with you. You give me two years of good behavior and I'll recommend you for early discharge. When I say "good behavior," though, I mean cooperation. When I tell you to do something, you do it. You don't argue with me about whether I'm right or wrong or whether it's fair or not, or even whether I have the right to tell you to do it. You just do it. If you give me two years of cooperation like that, I'll give you an early discharge.[10]

Thus parole officers represent one set of forces that affect a parolee's chance of making it. Officers may support parolees or may hinder their adjustment. Parole officers "read" parolees and then decide how they will treat them. They have the formal power to revoke parole on the basis of violations, but they have even greater informal power — to make life for parolees difficult or easy, depending on the way they approach their jobs.

The Community Supervision Bureaucracy

Parole officers do not work in a vacuum. Although the job often attracts people who like flexible schedules and substantial latitude, every officer works in an organizational context, usually in close contact with other officers. Parole officers therefore face limits in their approaches to cases. The limits derive from both the specific need to manage a heavier workload than is feasible in the available time and the general need to respond to organizational philosophies and policies.

Workload   In his award-winning essay on human services, Michael Lipsky pointed out that the difficulties faced by many clients of human services are so complex that "the job . . . is in a sense impossible to do in ideal terms."[11] One tool that parole organizations find useful in the face of this reality is a classification system that structures the relationship between the officer and the parolee. The system lets the parole bureaucracy prescribe rules for allocating officers' time, with priority given to the parolees most in need because there is not enough time for ideal supervision. The system in New York is typical (see Table 16.3). In general, officers spend more time with the new releasees than with those who have been out for some time. The level of supervision is later adjusted to "active" or "reduced" surveillance, depending on how the releasee functions in the community. As the officer gains confidence in the parolee, only periodic check-ins may be required. Finally, at the end of the maximum length of the sentence or at the time specified by the parole board, the former convict is discharged from supervision.

Reformers have long held that parole caseloads be no more than thirty-six per officer. In reality, caseloads vary dramatically but average about eighty parolees per officer. This is smaller than the average probation caseload, but the services required by parolees are greater.

The caseload influences the number of contacts made with parolees and the amount of assistance that can be given to each. Some states structure low, specialized caseloads

Table 16.3 An Example of the Varying Levels of Supervision Provided to Releasees

Most parole systems vary the amount of supervision they provide based on the risk posed by the offender, the length of time on parole, and the response to the supervision.

Type of Contact	Supervision Level		
	Intensive	Active	Reduced
Reporting to parole office	Weekly or semimonthly	Monthly or up to but not exceeding every two months	Quarterly or less frequently up to and including annually
Employment check	Monthly	Every two months	Same as reporting
Employment visit	Every three months	Every three months	At least as frequently as reporting
Home visit	Every three months	Monthly	Not mentioned
Other and collateral visits	More frequently than active or reduced	Not mentioned	Not mentioned

SOURCE: David T. Stanley, *Prisoners Among Us* (Washington, DC: Brookings Institution, 1976), p. 96.

for officers who supervise certain types of parolees, but even with specialized caseloads, time available for parolees can be minimal, often less than an hour a month. One reason for the small contact time with parolees is that officers have organizational responsibilities. Part of the day may be spent in the field helping parolees deal with other service agencies—medical, employment, educational—but much is spent in the office meeting bureaucratic paperwork and administrative requirements. Parole officers spend as much as 80 percent of their time at nonsupervisory work.

Philosophy and Policy   Originally parole officers worked directly for parole boards, and some boards still favor this arrangement. In recent decades, however, parole field staffs increasingly had become part of departments of corrections. With the growing emphasis on parole's links to other aspects of community corrections and on the use of prerelease programs, halfway houses, and other community-based services, the rationale is that institutional and field activities need to be coordinated months before an inmate's release on parole.

Many states combine probation and parole staffs because they perform similar functions. As pointed out, however, probation officers have ties to judges, whereas parole is seen as part of corrections. Parole has a greater law enforcement orientation: Parole agents in some states carry guns, and all are sworn officers. Agents with social work orientations thus seem more likely to gravitate toward probation.

Field service operations can be classified with the help of a grid based on two key policy issues. The first is the degree to which the system emphasizes offender control (surveillance and monitoring of offenders' actions) over offender change (providing assistance to clients). This distinction is similar to that made by individual parole officers, but here it operates at the organizational level and represents organizational philosophy. The second is the degree to which staff members are assigned either general workloads (a cross-section of clients) or specialized workloads (subgroups of clients sharing a similar characteristic, such as drug abuse). This structural dimension is related to both organizational resources and policy. As Figure 16.5 shows, these dimensions suggest four stereotypical case management models in field services: traditional, program, advocacy, and broker.[12]

Figure 16.5 Various Approaches to Case Management in Correctional Field Services

The approach depends on the agency's goals and service delivery structure.

SOURCE: Adapted from Todd R. Clear and P. Kevin Benoit, "Case Management in Probation and Parole Supervision," in John O. Smykla, ed., *Probation and Parole* (New York: Macmillan, 1984), p. 234.

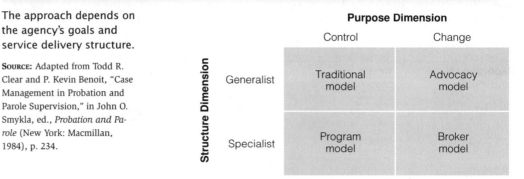

The traditional and program models stress offender control and rely primarily on the skills and abilities of their own staffs. Referring parolees to other agencies (such as public welfare) for help is ordinarily considered tangential to parole supervision and direct contact with the offender. In contrast, advocacy and broker models stress offender change and make more referrals to external agencies. The officer's main function is seen as helping offenders become involved with social service agencies whose programs they need. Of course, all parole agencies must support both control and change functions, but agencies differ in the priorities they set.

In traditional model agencies, clients are distributed more or less randomly to parole officers to keep caseloads at equal size. In such agencies, which are the most common across the United States, officers are fairly well isolated from their peers and supervisors. An officer's work ordinarily draws little attention unless a client creates a problem (perhaps by a new arrest), so the officer monitors cases closely to avoid unpleasant surprises. Officers have much latitude, and it is understood that they will be left alone until a client's behavior draws a superior's attention. They are often just told, "Cover your bases."

Program model agencies assign specialized caseloads so parole officers can concentrate on particular problems. Thus one officer may handle drug users, another may supervise unemployed offenders, and so on. The argument for specialization is that homogeneous workloads make better use of staff expertise, and officers are better able to understand and respond to similar clients. Yet this strategy breeds discontent among officers because the specialties often conflict. For one thing, it is difficult to equalize workloads. Who can tell, for instance, whether it takes more or less effort to supervise thirty drug addicts than to supervise forty sex offenders? Moreover, because officers want to think of their jobs as important, they often clash over whose work (and special clientele) is the most central to the agency's mission. Staff members devote much effort to showing how they are trying to prevent new offenses, because recidivism is the common denominator across all specialties. The underlying value of offender control thus emerges, because workers with special assignments are normally judged on how well they manage the potential criminality of their clients.

The broker model agency, by contrast, emphasizes offender change: helping offenders cope with factors that may lead to criminality by referring them to helpful agencies. The officer's main role is to determine the client's most serious problems, locate agencies that handle such problems, and help the client make use of the agencies' services. Only in unusual cases does the officer provide direct counseling or delivery of services. Staff members specialize in different service areas—for instance, one person may specialize in employment agencies, another in substance abuse agencies. Once a client's needs are diagnosed, he or she meets with staff members whose specialties cover those needs and who can provide referrals to other agencies. Although many people are impressed by the way the broker approach involves offenders with the community, some believe that the small amount of direct contact between officers and offenders leads to a lack of accountability and control over offenders.

Accountability is increased in the advocacy model, in which community service agencies work more closely with offenders and parole agencies. Rather than simply referring offenders to other agencies, advocacy model parole staff accompany offenders to the agencies and provide support throughout treatment. To facilitate community work, caseloads are usually organized by geographical region. The advocacy approach provides the most intensive level of assistance and control and also requires the most staff resources. It is not realistic to expect most correctional field service units to follow this approach because their resources are too limited. Moreover, some people think it is inappropriate for workers to be so heavily involved in the lives of offenders.

Constraints on Officers' Authority   Parole officers often are portrayed as having absolute authority over their clients, as being able to manage offenders in any way they see fit. It is more accurate to say that in using discretion, officers balance many constraints.

The bureaucratic context pressures parole officers to "go along with the system," just as police officers are pressured to cover for their partners. In this respect parole resembles other correctional functions: Line workers are isolated from administration and depend on one another for support. They feel constrained to behave supportively and to let well enough alone. As one parole supervisor said,

> I won't stand for one of my parole officers (POs) second-guessing another. If I tolerated that, I'd have grudges going on here. Pretty soon I'd have an office full of snitches. A few years ago, I had a PO who couldn't keep his nose out of the other caseloads. I spoke to him about it but that didn't do any good. He thought he was the conscience of the Department of Corrections. I finally got fed up with his meddling and I gave him a taste of his own medicine. I went over to his files and found unfinished work for him to do.[13]

Parole officers perform their jobs in ways that maintain office norms without threatening their co-workers. The knowledge of office norms reduces their discretion, however, because often they are forced to take certain actions in regard to problems that in the absence of organizational pressures they would have handled another way. In recent times, for example, jails and prisons have become so overcrowded that officers have felt informal (but very clear) pressures not to crowd the institutions further with revocations for "nonserious" violations. Officers learn that they would be wise to act only on the most serious misbehaviors of their clients and ignore the rest.

The bureaucracy of parole, then, is a force in the offender's postrelease experience in several ways. First, it structures the activities of parole officers according to traditional philosophical orientations. Second, it provides rules and policies for managing workloads that would otherwise be unbearable. Finally, it provides a context of unwritten and informal norms that define appropriate and inappropriate officer conduct.

Finding and holding a job is one of the major problems faced by those released from prison. San Francisco's Delancey Street Foundation for many years has been a leader in training ex-offenders in such skills as floristry, baking, and carpentry.

Residential Programs

Residential programs serve offenders when they are first released from prison. Most house a limited number of offenders at any one time (usually between ten and twenty-five) in medium- or minimum-security facilities. Treatment staff help offenders work out plans to address their problems, placing heavy emphasis on involving the offenders in regular community functions.

community correctional center

A small group-living facility for offenders, especially those who recently have been released from prison.

Residential programs are often referred to as **community correctional centers.** Most require that offenders live on the premises while working in the community. They usually provide counseling and drug treatment, and impose strict curfews on residents when they are not working. Many of these facilities are renovated private homes or small hotels, permitting a less institutional atmosphere. Individual rooms, along with group dining and recreation areas, help these facilities achieve a homelike character. By obeying the rules and maintaining good behavior in the facility, residents gradually earn a reduction in restrictions—for instance, the ability to spend some free time in the community. The idea is to provide treatment support to the offender while promoting the step-by-step adjustment to community life.

Residential centers face problems, however. With very high staff–resident ratios, they are relatively expensive to operate; they represent a real savings in costs only when they enable a jurisdiction to avoid construction of a new prison. Studies also show that some centers have high failure rates—one-third or more of the residents may be rearrested in a year. But the main problems with these centers are political. Misbehavior by residents makes them unpopular with the local community. Just one serious offense can result in a strong public backlash. Citizens typically do not want groups of ex-convicts living in their midst (as noted earlier, NIMBY stands for "Not In My Back Yard."

The most common type of community correctional center is the halfway house, or **work release center.** This idea originated in Wisconsin in 1913 with the passage of the Huber law, which let prisoners work in gainful occupations outside the prison as long as they returned to their cells at night.

work release center

A facility that allows offenders to work in the community during the day while residing in the center during nonwork hours.

Two kinds of work release programs are available today. In the more secure of the two, prisoners work during the day (often in groups) and then return at night to a group housing unit. In the other version, sometimes called *work furlough,* offenders work and live at home during the week and return to the prison for the weekend.

The idea underlying the halfway house is straightforward: Return to the community after institutionalization requires an adjustment, and a relatively controlled environment improves adjustment. Because studies indicate that the highest failure rates of parolees occur in the early months of parole, this idea seems plausible. Recently halfway houses have become more than mere stopping points for prisoners released from custody; they now employ direct treatment methods (such as therapeutic community techniques) to help offenders confront the problems they face when they return to the community. By these standards, how have the release programs fared?

The earliest studies of residential release programs tended to find that these offenders performed slightly worse on parole than those given regular parole supervision and had higher rates of return to prison. Later studies have uncovered more positive results. A large study of work release in the state of Washington found that although those on work release do no better than others released from prison, arrest rates for work release inmates were quite low, and work release played a role in the successful adjustment of one-fourth of those released for the state's prisons.[14] Although there is still incontestable scientific evidence that these centers "work," the research certainly indicates that remaining in prison is not preferable to work release.

One basic problem is the schizophrenic environment within which the programs operate. The pressures of institutional crowding establish a premium for these programs; without them many corrections systems would be unable to manage their ballooning populations. Yet relying on release programs makes leaders of corrections systems vulnerable to highly publicized failures, especially when a parolee commits another heinous crime.

Certainly release programs do not inevitably lead to reintegration of offenders. Perhaps this approach is faulty: Prisoners do not necessarily benefit from more supportive assistance at the release stage. Or, more likely, contemporary release programs have a more fundamental problem: The negative impact of the prison experience on offenders is not easily eradicated by the simple mechanism of graduated release. In any case, the only thing we know for sure is that the effectiveness of programs designed to handle offenders who are being released from incarceration has been disappointing.

The Offender's Experience of Postrelease Life

The new releasee faces three harsh realities: the strangeness of reentry, unmet personal needs, and barriers to success. Each must be dealt with separately; each poses a challenge to the newly released offender (see the Focus box).

The Strangeness of Reentry

Although release from prison can be euphoric, it can also be a letdown, particularly for parolees who return after two, three, or more years away. The images in their minds of friends and loved ones represent snapshots frozen in time, but in reality everyone has changed (as has the parolee): moved away, taken a new job, grown up, or, perhaps most disturbing, become almost a stranger. Initial attempts to restore old ties thus can be threatening and deeply disappointing. How many relationships—with spouses, children, and old friends—can survive the strain of long separation unscarred?

Moreover, freedom is now an unfamiliar environment. In the prison every decision about daily life is made by others, so routine decision-making skills atrophy.

There are plenty of sad-funny stories about parolees looking at a menu for the first time in years and panicking at the prospect of choosing a meal and ordering it. Compare this simple task to the more important tasks of getting a job, finding housing, and so on.

The Problem of Unmet Personal Needs

Parolees are aware they must meet critical needs to make it on the streets. One parolee said,

> The first few days I was out were about the roughest days of this entire period . . . no money, no transportation, no job, and no place to live. Now these things have a way of working themselves out in time, but you have to contact the right people, and sometimes it's hard to find the right people. I was lucky enough to make a contact with a fellow at the Service Center and he gave me enough money to tide me over out of a fund that they had. I'd say the first week was rough.[15]

When asked to name their needs, parolees have very practical concerns: Education, money, and a job tend to top the list. Yet they are not always realistic in their thinking about how to meet their needs. Many parolees are unable to identify the specific things to avoid doing in order to stay out of trouble.

Barriers to Success

Soon after release, offenders learn that they have achieved an in-between status: They are back in society but not totally free. They face restrictions on opportunities beyond the close monitoring of the parole officer. Many restrictions are statutory, stemming from a common law tradition that people who are incarcerated are "civilly dead" and have lost all civil rights. Compounding their adjustment problems are a myriad of impediments to employment.

Civil Disabilities The right to vote and to hold public office are two civil rights that are generally limited on conviction of a felony. Three-fourths of the states return the right to vote after some period of time; fifteen do so after offenders have served their full sentence and ten disenfranchise for life anyone convicted of a felony. Only through a pardon is full citizenship restored. Twenty-one states return the right to hold public office to felony offenders following discharge from probation, parole, or prison; nineteen states permanently restrict that right except for pardoned felons. Many states deny felons other civil rights, such as serving on juries, holding public office, and holding positions of public trust (which include most government jobs).

FOCUS   Coming Out—The Man Who Fell to Earth

In the gray light of the prerelease unit, I stand with a group of twelve convicts. Each of us is uncomfortable with the idea of freedom, as nervous as if we were about to pull a robbery. I've been waiting for this day for five years, a few of the others have been waiting longer. In those years, I've become accustomed to waiting—it's the nature of doing time. Brief conversation flares up around me, dies, flares up again, returning each time to the topic of freedom: life in the mythic "free world" to which we're returning.

One man, incarcerated four years, mentions lobster, his voice bright with anticipation. "I'm gonna eat lobster in a restaurant. I'm gonna be waited on. A four-course meal. After I've finished with the food, I'm going home with the waitress."

"I think that the woman should come before the meal," argues a twentyish B&E artist. "The woman, then the food. It's not like we haven't eaten here inside the walls."

A dealer down five years for heroin sales has another point of view. He says that drugs should take precedence. "Junk is the best thing on the streets. And I hear it's cheaper these days. Better quality than a few years ago."

"The dope'll send you back here, though," counters another man. "Stick with women, money, cars. Pick an easy hustle. Or, what the hell, you could even go to college."

Listening, I juxtapose the fantasy and the grim visible landscape. What lies beyond the coils of barbed wire has become wholly abstract and vague, an imagined place only a little more tangible than the surface of Mars. "Freedom, man," one voice says, and the others repeat it. "Freedom." The word sounds so good. Sounds glorious. Sounds so damned easy.

The "free world" address to which we're delivered later is the Department of Corrections halfway house in Tucson. For us, this is the last stop of a release process that began with a parole board or work furlough hearing. This phase involves a final fingerprinting, a fast series of mug shots, and the filling out of various forms. We do the paperwork quickly, then listen as a parole officer rattles off the rules: "No illegal drugs or alcohol. No association with ex-felons. . . . You will be gainfully employed at all times and report all income to the Parole Department."

As the litany continues, I tell myself I can do it, that I'll do anything to avoid coming back.

I lived for the first week at the home of a friend, Jay, an instructor who taught a writing class in the institution. Jay and his wife greeted me casually at the front door, but at that point, free just two hours, I was almost too uptight to speak.

Their initial questions concerned the nature of my experience inside, and they seemed hopelessly difficult to answer. I tried, though, describing for them the banalities of the prison routine, the extortion activities of gangs, and a dining room incident in which I'd been forced to watch as a friend's throat was slashed. They listened and nodded politely. I talked to them another twenty minutes before I gave up, asking tentatively if I might go outside. Jay reminded me I didn't need a movement pass out here, and I realized abruptly where I was.

I spent an hour that night walking the streets of Tucson, checking things out and exploring the world I'd stumbled into. I felt a euphoria that faded as I realized I knew no one out here, I had no place to go and nothing to do. I felt like a guest—an uninvited guest—from some other world. Something like the protagonist in *Brother from Another Planet* or *The Man Who Fell to Earth*. When I arrived finally at the strangest place of all, a McDonald's, I ordered a cheeseburger. "This is better than lobster," I told another customer. He stared back at me in silence as if I really had arrived from another planet.

The biggest problem was where to get a job and some income. My fifty dollars in gate money, the check I'd received from the state on the day of my release, I'd donated to Jay as a down payment on my room and board. Securing a job with a prison record is not easy, and my years of college were of substantially less interest to prospective employers than my FBI rap sheet.

Most interviews went like this: I'd arrive early at the interview, wearing a meticulously laundered prison-industries shirt. I'd inform the receptionist that I was interested in applying for a job. She'd stare at me, examine my clothes and inside-the-walls haircut, and then shove an application in my face. That application, at first glance, seemed simple. I'd sail through the "Education History," stumble only a little on the "Employment History"—where had I worked for the last five years?—but then stop dead at the box asking "Have you ever been convicted of a felony?"

My parole officer had warned me I must be totally honest about my criminal history. So I wrote in the threatening box, "I will explain in person." But I wasn't able to explain away five years of incarceration.

The job for which I was hired a week later was with an apartment painting crew, working for fifty cents less than the minimum wage. The employer justified the low wage by saying that no money would be deducted for taxes, that I'd be paid "under the table." I told him that was fine. I got along pretty well with my co-workers, Hispanics from Central America, most of them in the country illegally. In my ragged Spanish I told them I felt somewhat as they must have felt: like an alien, someone who'd jumped a border and now lived precariously in a foreign country.

I kept the painting job two weeks before I was accepted as a senior at the University of Arizona in its program in creative writing. In preparing for school, I decided I needed some clothes. My subsequent trip to a shopping mall was one of my strangest postrelease experiences.

In prison I'd lived in a cell with just one other occupant, isolated, when the doors closed, from the rest of the population. On the yard I'd kept a safe distance from other cons, allowing no one to come very close and never letting anyone get behind me. To allow another con to get behind you in maximum was to risk a shank in the back or a possible assault. At the Tucson mall there were suddenly hundreds of people on all sides, front and back, shoving, crowding. Intellectually I understood that I was in no danger, but the old alarms went off anyway, the joint-induced paranoia. I ran out of the mall without buying anything, too nervous even to notice the girls, swarms of them, dressed up and perfumed. I thought of them later in my apartment. Afterward I went shopping only in smaller stores. Never again in a mall.

My experience at the university had the same paranoia, alienation, and sense of confusion. I was certain, even in my free-world clothes, that every student I passed could identify me as an ex-felon, not a real student but a kind of impostor. I wore student clothes and used student language, picking up the slang of the university just as I'd picked up prison slang my first days in the joint.

I never felt as though I totally belonged. The few people I talked to regularly were students or teachers in the writing program, and I never told them everything—about how it really felt to walk down a university hall four weeks out of prison, for instance, in a mixture of terror and dread. I never talked at all about my distrust of people, which prison had reinforced so well. Outside it was different. Outside it was just as deadly not to trust, to remain apart. Because I didn't understand that, I stayed apart from other students and after a while I felt as if I were doing fine. I was free, but I acted like I was doing time.

Other habits were equally difficult to change. Before my incarceration as an addict, I'd shoplifted regularly to finance my habit. I didn't use drugs my first months free, but I occasionally boosted small things from stores, not big things and not things I needed. Once in the university bookstore I slipped a copy of War and Peace inside my shirt. I was sure no one had seen me, that I'd been fast enough. On my way out I found myself blocked by a security cop, his badge flashing notice of my pending arrest.

I thought that incident—petty larceny, a misdemeanor—would send me back to prison, but the bookstore didn't press charges. My parole officer only told me that the next time I'd go back to the walls so fast my head would swim. When I told him there wouldn't be another slip, I meant it, yet I wondered to myself if I could ever live out here. My life was becoming a kind of treadmill, and I could feel myself tiring.

At that time I'd been out of prison seven months. I still felt only a little more at home in the free world than I had my first days out of the joint. When I formed relationships, they tended to be superficial and brief. I still couldn't talk about feelings, how it felt to awaken and make simple decisions, like what to have for breakfast, what clothes to put on, how to structure my day. In prison all of these choices had been made by someone else, a guard or administrator. Then I could move through my days and make no decisions at all. Any freedom I had was mental, and it was nothing like what confronted me outside: total freedom to administer my own life. The weight of that responsibility became a source of fear and anxiety, something I needed to talk about and didn't, something that eventually helped lead me back to drugs.

When I returned to drugs, I did so cautiously, still hoping to complete my degree and to enter graduate school the following year. The only drugs I let myself use were prescription narcotics, substances provided by a doctor. To compensate for using them—the guilt I felt in getting high—I began to work harder in school, adding more courses and taking a part-time job as a tutor. I wanted to finish my B.A. as quickly as possible and my grades had to be high enough for a graduate scholarship. That scholarship had already been dangled in front of me. I just needed another point or two on my average.

Before the academic year ended, my drug use had become an addiction, something I wasn't able to control. Because my relationships were all so tenuous, I told no one what was happening. I considered informing my parole officer and requesting placement in a drug treatment program, but I realized that doing so would be admitting to a violation of parole: no use of illegal drugs or narcotics.

When I was eventually arrested, I'd been out of prison a year and was only a few months from graduation. The new charges, two of them—obtaining narcotics by fraud—came after I accepted prescriptions for Percodan under a false name. I left my apartment, which was littered with textbooks, term papers, and my student clothes, on the arms of two detectives. On the way to the county jail I took a long look at the city I was leaving, a world I never really got to know, and wondered what it might have been like actually to live there.

The transport bus that carried me back was a duplicate of the bus that had carried me to freedom a year before. The other passengers, about a dozen returning convicts, seemed almost identical to the group that had left prison with me. The talk was flat, resigned, bitter. When a man asked why I was going back, I didn't say anything and just stared at him in silence, my mind glazed with anger and despair.

SOURCE: While incarcerated the author was able to furhter his education, gaining a college degree. Upon release on parole he earned a master's degree. He is now a teacher. Reprinted by permission of the author.

A 1998 report by Human Rights Watch and the Sentencing Project points out that 1.4 million African-American men—13 percent of black men—cannot vote because of their criminal records. Thus in Alabama and Florida one-third of black men are permanently disenfranchised, and in Iowa, Mississippi, New Mexico, Virginia, Washington, and Wyoming, the ratio is 1 to 4.[16]

Employment   Barriers to employment are both formal and informal. Employers hesitate to hire parolees because they view a conviction as evidence of untrustworthiness. Thus to the cumulative effect of statutory and informal discrimination must be added many offenders' unrealistic expectations for employment. One parolee explains,

> *Contrary to my prison expectations, finding employment was not an easy task. In fact, it took me over six weeks to find my first job, even though, at least for the first month, I made a conscientious and continuing effort to find employment. I quickly found that I had no marketable skills. My three years' experience working for a railroad before I was imprisoned provided me with no work skills transferable to other forms of employment. Nor did my prison assignments in the tag shop (making license plates and street signs), in the soap shop (making soap), or as a cellhouse worker prove to be of any assistance. The only job openings available to me were nonskilled factory work and employment in service-oriented businesses. Finally, after six weeks, I found employment mixing chemicals in vats for placement later in spray cans. After two weeks the personnel manager told me that he had to discharge me because I had lied about my criminal history (I had). Even though my foreman spoke up for me, supposedly company policy had to be followed.[17]*

The legal barriers to employment are perhaps the most frustrating because they constitute an insurmountable wall between the offender and job opportunities. In many states a number of occupations require licenses that are denied to any ex-convict. The courts have upheld these bans when the work has a connection to the criminal conduct of the offender.[18] For example, it is constitutional for a state to restrict employment of convicted child molesters in day care centers. Other statutes bar from specified jobs any person who "gave evidence of moral turpitude or a lack of good moral character"—characteristics that many people attribute to convicts. A study of changes in legal restrictions on ex-offenders' employment over the last ten years showed that some prohibitions had been eliminated, but others had been imposed. Some of the changes are dramatic, so that in many states ex-offenders have now penetrated professions closed to them for centuries; yet public reaction to specific cases has resulted in new prohibitions in some locations.[19]

Making matters worse, such statutes bar employment in some job areas that are most important to former offenders. All states, for instance, restrict former offenders from employment as barbers (even though many prisons provide training programs in barbering), beauticians, and nurses. Further, well-paying jobs tend to be reserved for people with no criminal record. Indeed, newly released offenders may find themselves legally barred from jobs they held before they were incarcerated. In most states civil service regulations or special statutes bar or restrict the employment of former offenders. Even a prior arrest for a felony without a conviction can lead to rejection. Cities and counties have more restrictions than state governments. Even a prior arrest as a juvenile is an absolute bar to employment in a criminal justice occupation in many states, despite the fact that criminal justice agencies that have hired former convicts rate their job performance equal to or better than that of the average employee.

The options for most offenders, however, remain severely limited. The quandary is real: Should offenders tell prospective employers about their criminal records and risk being denied a chance to prove themselves? Or should they lie and risk being fired if their criminal records come to light? These questions are highlighted by studies finding that employers are reluctant to hire ex-convicts, especially when their crimes involved violence.[20]

A 9-year follow-up study of employment and earnings of 1,176 men released from Georgia prisons in the 1970s confirmed the difficult prospects faced by ex-offenders.

Both employment and earning levels were quite low for this group, and incomes were worst for African Americans and those without high school degrees. Unemployment rates of the oldest ex-offenders were particularly high, regardless of the amount of time in prison.[21]

The only real solution for offenders is **expungement** of their criminal records. In theory, expungement means the removal of a conviction from state records. In practice, although offenders whose records have been expunged may legally say they have never been convicted, the records are kept and can be made available on inquiry. Moreover, expungement legal procedures generally are both cumbersome and inadequate. Expungement provides little true relief.

The same is true of **pardons,** executive acts of clemency that effectively excuse the offender from suffering all the consequences of conviction for a criminal act. Contemporary pardons serve three main purposes: (1) to remedy a miscarriage of justice, (2) to remove the stigma of a conviction, and (3) to mitigate a penalty. Full pardons for miscarriages of justice are rare, but do occur. For example, you may have read of individuals released from prison and pardoned after the discovery that the crime had been committed by someone else. Pardons are most commonly given to expunge the criminal records of first-time offenders, but overall they are given only infrequently.

Thus offenders must have certain misgivings about reentry: adjustment to a strange environment; the unavoidable need for job training, employment, money, and support; and limitations on opportunities. The stigma of conviction stays with the former felon. And the general social condemnation of ex-convicts adds to the pressures of continuing correctional authority, personified by the parole officer or work release counselor. If offenders believe that the cards are stacked against them, they have reason for thinking so.

expungement

A legal process that results in the removal of a conviction from official records.

pardon

An action of the executive branch of the state or federal government excusing an offense and absolving the offender from the consequences of the crime.

Making It as a Game

One way to think about the postrelease situation is as a game with three players: the parolee, the parole officer, and the parole bureaucracy. The game consists of a series of moves and countermoves, with each participant having certain objectives and certain strategies for attaining them.

The parole bureaucracy seeks stability. Parole always has been subject to attack because its failures are highly visible (in the form of new crimes, sometimes sensationalized in the media) and its critics perceive it as institutionalized leniency. Thus most parole agencies avoid controversy and negative public attention. They base their policies on accountability and crime prevention in order to avoid or minimize appearances of failure.

The parole officer is looking for satisfying work in an organizational context in which even a well-intended action can have unintended consequences. Officers learn to cover all the bases, but the need to do so often conflicts with a very real desire to help offenders. Job satisfaction comes largely from seeing offenders make it, and so parole officers experience role ambivalence. On the one hand, they

Former boxing heavyweight champion Mike Tyson, under community supervision after his release from an Indiana prison, was sent to prison in Maryland for assaulting two men in a minor car accident.

are painfully aware of the agency's vulnerability to public reaction and the leadership's concern that proper procedures be followed. On the other hand, they witness daily the limitations of and impediments before their parolees. They cannot speak with certainty about everyone in their caseloads, nor can they realistically enforce all the rules. So they balance these pressures, sometimes choosing to go to bat for parolees and other times coming down hard on them to protect the bureaucracy.

For all but the truly deviant offenders, the primary goal on parole is to avoid returning to prison. But parolees seek to advance a wide variety of individual aims as well. Some want to live a mainstream life, with a well-paying job and a fulfilling family life; others seek money, thrills, fast times. Whatever the goal, newly released offenders frequently butt up against the weight of the bureaucracy and the orientation of the parole officer. And the offenders are at a distinct disadvantage in the game because they have little formal power and stand to lose the most.

The parole supervision "game," then, is the series of moves and countermoves of the three players as they try to achieve their main goals and offset their primary liabilities. Offenders do what they can to live their lives well while avoiding return to prison. Officers look for opportunities to work creatively and effectively without running afoul of official policy and procedure. The bureaucracy strives to present an image of rationality and effectiveness to an outside world that is often looking for validation of its doubts about the legitimacy of parole as an institution.

Parole officers and the bureaucracy have substantial interests at stake in the game and face significant limitations as well. In some respects the officers are in the most vulnerable position. The bureaucracy expects caseloads to be managed effectively, yet caseloads are usually far too large to permit supervision without cutting corners. Meanwhile offenders see officers as potential adversaries who may snatch away their freedom. Parole workers thus must balance their interests. Without information and (at least surface) cooperation from parolees, the officers' job is nearly impossible. In efforts to avoid problems with the agency, officers informally depend on offenders' conduct, so they select strategies designed to elicit cooperation. The last thing they want is to be forced to revoke a client's parole, and they do so only in the most extreme and well-documented cases.

Parole officers function with serious technical uncertainty. They can never be sure what supervision approach will work best or how the parolee will respond. Officers choose strategies knowing they may not work. Thus officers are aware that (1) they do not have enough time to do all that should be done for clients, (2) their course of action may not turn out satisfactorily, and (3) a case action will be reviewed only if it fails. In short, for the officers the situation has a constant potential for negative feedback.

The bureaucracy, for its part, operates in a volatile sociopolitical environment. Parole failures are serious events and can lead to public disenchantment. On such occasions the bureaucracy needs to show that its actions were reasonable; it needs records that demonstrate the extent of supervision and justify its handling of the case.

A key element in the parole game is paperwork—records kept on cases. Paperwork performs two vital functions for the bureaucracy. First, it forces all parole officers to consider a uniform set of criteria in making decisions about classification and supervision. Thus the use of forms promotes the regularity in procedure and policy that is a fundamental need of a bureaucracy operating under conditions of uncertainty. Second, paperwork ultimately forms the foundation on which the agency builds its defense against potentially damaging outside scrutiny. When courts review a parole officer's decisions or when the media express an interest in a case, the best response is that "proper procedures were followed." Paperwork alerts the officers to procedures and to policy.

Because of the volume of paperwork and the frequency of minor violations, parole officers realistically cannot write up every incident that occurs. Therefore they often use informal means (such as increased parolee reporting or heavier surveillance) to respond to misbehaviors, rather than taking the formal route of issuing warrants for violations. Said one officer: "If the cops catch one of my men shooting up, I go through the motions of requesting a warrant. But if I catch the man myself, I handle it my own way. My way accomplishes the same thing and only takes one tenth of the time. If I went by the book, they'd have me down here six days a week writing reports."[22]

From the parole officers' point of view, the game involves picking and choosing among actions that may be taken on the wide variety of incidents. Sometimes a promise not to write down an incident may persuade a parolee to cooperate; at other times filing a form may more effectively persuade a parolee to "come around." To move the relationship toward rapport, the officer is using informal discretion to decide which information to record. The officer's primary need is for the offender to play the game by the rules—to report as directed, communicate productively, and stay clean.

The parolee influences what gets put down on paper by following the parole officer's lead. If the officer wants a client to play it straight, the parolee must make a convincing show of doing so. If the officer wants minimal interaction, the parolee must accede. Most parolees have an inflated view of the officer's power, recognizing that the officer regularly decides whether or not to record information. So the parolee must convince the officer that the information does not portend larger subsequent problems.

The parole bureaucracy is the playing field where they come together. Pressures to revoke (or to ignore minor violations), a history of recriminations against officers whose parolees have had major problems, a tradition of close supervision of officers' actions— such organizational characteristics are the backdrop of the officer–parolee interaction. When the bureaucracy's need to protect itself against criticism conflicts with an officer's desire to handle misbehavior informally, the strength of the bureaucratic norms is likely to determine whether the officer will follow the book or take a chance.

The game ends when supervision is terminated, and the manner of termination determines who won. It is possible for all three parties to win: Offenders can be terminated in a "positive adjustment status"—a success. But in many ways one or more parties can lose. Offenders lose if they return to prison. Officers also lose a great deal in such situations. Apart from knowing that their approach did not work, officers always may need to be second-guessed. Supervisors may review files and ask why some action was or was not taken. When supervision has clearly failed, it is difficult to defend subjective decisions to a third party who was not involved.

So when a parolee loses, the officer also loses—unless that bulky file of paperwork can justify the actions taken. When an officer reports a technical violation, the decision-making authority may refuse to revoke parole, and then the officer is forced to try to supervise the victor-parolee—not the best situation. Finally, a high return rate leads the public to question the agency's effectiveness. So revocation is a last resort, invoked only for the more dangerous offenders. This fact is known to experienced parolees, and it gives them some leeway to maneuver as they play the supervision game.

The Parolee as "Dangerous"

Few images are more disturbing than that of a recent parolee arrested for committing a new violent or sexual crime, especially when that crime is against a stranger.[23] The most heinous of these incidents make national news and captivate the nation's attention. Recent examples include the arrest and conviction of a California parolee for the brutal murder of 12-year-old Polly Klaas, which spurred a national movement toward life sentences for third-time felons,[24] and the rape and murder of 7-year-old Megan Kanka in New Jersey by a paroled sex offender, which led to a series of "sex-offender notification" laws, called "Megan's Law" after the victim.[25] By 1997, 32 states and the federal government had passed sex offender notification laws and many other states were considering such laws.[26] Figure 16.6 shows an example of a sex offender notification bulletin from Washington State, and Table 16.4 shows some differences among seven states' notification statutes.

Figure 16.6   Sex-Offender Notification Bulletin, State of Washington.

Is it fair to tell a person's neighbors that he has been in prison for a sex offense? How should it be done?

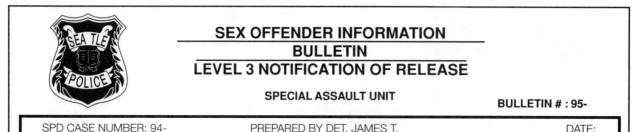

SEX OFFENDER INFORMATION
BULLETIN
LEVEL 3 NOTIFICATION OF RELEASE

SPECIAL ASSAULT UNIT

BULLETIN # : 95-

SPD CASE NUMBER: 94-   PREPARED BY DET. JAMES T.   DATE:

The Seattle Police Department is releasing the following information pursuant to RCW 4.24.550 and the Washington State Supreme Court decision in <u>State v. Ward</u>, which authorizes law enforcement agencies to inform the public of a sex offender's release when, at the discretion of the agency, the release of information will enhance public safety and protection.

The individual who appears on this notification has been convicted of a sex offense that requires registration with the sheriff's office in the county of their residence. Further, their previous criminal history places them in a classification level which reflects the <u>potential</u> to reoffend.

This sex offender <u>has served</u> the sentence imposed on him by the courts and has advised the King County Department of Public Safety that he will be living in the location below. <u>HE IS NOT WANTED BY THE POLICE AT THIS TIME.</u> THIS NOTIFICATION IS NOT INTENDED TO INCREASE FEAR; RATHER, IT IS OUR BELIEF THAT AN INFORMED PUBLIC IS A SAFER PUBLIC.

The Seattle Police Department has no legal authority to direct where a sex offender may or may not live. Unless court ordered restrictions exist, this offender is constitutionally free to live wherever he chooses.

Sex offenders have always lived in our communities; but it wasn't until passage of the Community Protection Act of 1990 (which mandates sex offender registration) that law enforcement even knew where they were living. In many cases, law enforcement is now able to share that information with you. Citizen abuse of this information to threaten, intimidate or harass registered sex offenders will not be tolerated. Further, such abuse could potentially end law enforcement's ability to do community notifications. We believe the only person who wins if community notification ends is the sex offender, since sex offenders derive their power through secrecy.

The Seattle Police Department Crime Prevention Division is available to help you set up block watches and to provide you with useful information on personal safety. Crime Prevention may be reached at 684-7555. If you have information regarding current criminal activity of this or any other offender, please call 9-1-1.

Ogden, Willard W M   3/30/68
Age 27

5'7" 155 lbs., Brown hair, Blue eyes,

Scars on right hand and right forearm.

Willard Ogden was released from the Washington State Penitentiary at Walla Walla after serving 5 years and 8 months for a conviction of Statutory Rape in the first degree and Indecent Liberties. These crimes were committed in Richmond, Washington during June and July of 1988. The victim was a 3-year-old female who resided in the same apartment complex as Ogden. The crimes were accomplished by leading the child into some woods near the apartment complex and behind a nearby school gymnasium. Ogden was often seen at the complex only in the company of small children. He sometimes offered them cookies. Ogden is an untreated sex offender who has refused deviancy treatment. He is at a high risk to reoffend. Odgen is on Post Release Supervision with the Department of Corrections. He has registered as a sex offender as required by law and has recently moved to the 800 block of Casparus St. in downtown Seattle.

Additional sex offender information:
As of the date of this bulletin, there are 8,703 sex offenders who have registered as required (since 2/28/90) and are living in Washington State. 1,900 of these are registered to King County addresses. 863 are registered to addresses within the city limits of Seattle. State-wide there are an additional 2,132 sex offenders who are required to register and have not and are actively

NOTE: "Willard Ogden" is a pseudonym, and this is not a picture of the actual offender.

SOURCE: Carl Poole and Roxanne Leib, *Community Notification in Washington State: Decision-Making and Costs* (Olympia: Washington State Institute for Public Policy, July 1995), p. 24.

The fact of repeat violence fuels a public perception that parolees represent an ongoing threat to the public welfare. It also contributes to a belief that the criminal justice system is too lenient, with the result that communities are made unsafe. For many parole officers, notification laws or the lack of such a law, presents an ethical dilemma (see Do the Right Thing). But how accurate are the public perceptions, and how necessary are the laws?

DO THE Right THING

The state had not adopted its own version of Megan's Law requiring police and neighborhood notification of the presence of a sex-offender parolee in the community. As parole officer Todd Whetzel sat in his office looking over the record of his newest client, John Paterson, the word *pedophile* leaped from the paper.

Paterson had been convicted of molesting an 11-year-old boy and had served seven years of a ten-year term before his release on parole. The 37-year-old Paterson was to live with his mother in Mansfield, the community of 50,000 where he grew up. Examining the record, Whetzel noted that the molestation had occurred in the capital city, some two hundred miles from Mansfield. He didn't remember a news story in the *Mansfield Chronicle* about the crime or the sentence imposed. For all he knew, only Paterson, his mother, and he knew of the conviction.

Whetzel thought about the alternatives. On the one hand, the law did not *require* notification and to release the information would violate Paterson's privacy. Certainly it would be almost impossible to help Paterson find a job if his secret was known. On the other hand, what if Paterson should molest a child in Mansfield? ■

Certainly ex-offenders represent a greater risk to community safety than do other citizens. But such isolated tragedies can exaggerate the actual danger to the public, especially considering that parolees are such a tiny proportion of the citizens on the streets. A recent study in Louisiana found that slightly over one-third of parolees were rearrested for a violent crime, but this represented less than 2 percent of all the arrests for violence statewide.[27] Even though the arrest rates of parolees may seem high, keeping these offenders incarcerated would have prevented only a small fraction of all violent crime in Louisiana.

The California response to Polly Klaas's death was to pass a law mandating very long prison terms, up to life without parole, for all third-time felons. The law is so broad it even applies to a man who recently strong-armed a pizza from a vendor along a boardwalk. Implementing the law will cost the state an estimated $3.7 billion by 2003 — nearly every available dollar of California state revenues.[28]

Some people worry that the public preoccupation with potential parolee criminality makes it harder for parolees to succeed. Certainly new laws such as sex offender notification open up the possibility that some citizens will want to harass parolees and refuse to let them live in their

Determined to keep a child molester from moving into his mother's home, these Dilley, Oregon, neighbors banded together to buy the property.

Table 16.4 Major Provisions of Sex Offender Notification Laws

Important differences in sex offender notification laws make it harder on sex offenders in some states than in others.

State	Year Statute Went Into Effect	How Long Offenders Remain Subject to Notification	Notification Mandatory or Discretionary	Notification Proactive or Only in Response to Request	Sex Offenses Covered by Statute
Alaska	1994	*for life:* 2 or more convictions *15 years:* 1 conviction	mandatory by administrative regulation	upon request	all offenses
Connecticut	1996	10 years after end of probation or parole	discretionary	proactive	selected offenses
Louisiana	1992	10 years after release	mandatory	proactive	all offenses
New Jersey	1994	indefinitely, but may petition for relief 15 years after release	mandatory	proactive	selected offenses
Oregon	1993, 1995	for life; may petition for waiver after 10 years	varies[1]	proactive and upon request	selected offenses
Tennessee	1995	10 years minimum; then may petition for relief	discretionary	proactive	all offenses
Washington	1990	for life, 15 years, or 10 years depending on seriousness of offense	discretionary	proactive and upon request	all offenses

[1]Mandatory if under supervision; discretionary if not.

SOURCE: U.S. Department of Justice, National Institute of Justice, Peter Finn, "Sex Offender Community Notification," *Research in Action*, February 1997, p. 4.

neighborhoods. Most of the laws expressly forbid such harassment by private citizens, and a New Jersey man was arrested after he fired five bullets into the home of a paroled rapist who had lived quietly in the neighborhood for sixteen years.[29] (The Focus box describes the problems faced by a paroled child molester.)

Postrelease Supervision

We've seen that postrelease supervision can be viewed as a game. But how effective is that game? How do we determine that effectiveness? What might the game be like in the future? Will its rules change?

How Effective Is It?

The effectiveness of corrections is usually measured by rates of recidivism, the percentage of former offenders who return to criminal behavior after release. One problem with

Implementing Agency	Immunity Explicitly Provided to Implementers	Who May Be Notified	Retroactivity	Information That May Be Disseminated
State Dept. of Public Safety	provided	anyone	retroactive	limited by statute
probation	not provided	anyone	not retroactive	unrestricted
offenders— supervised by probation	provided	limited by statute	retroactive to June 1992	limited by statute
prosecutor and police	provided	people likely to encounter the offender	retroactive	not specified
probation and police	not provided	anyone	retroactive	unrestricted
Tennessee Bureau of Investigation	provided	not specified	retroactive	"relevant" information
police	provided	not specified	retroactive	not specified

statistics on recidivism is that the concept means different things to different people. The rates reported vary from 5 to 50 percent, depending on how one counts three things: (1) the event (arrest, conviction, parole revocation), (2) the duration of the period in which the measurement is made, and (3) the seriousness of the behavior. Typically an analysis of recidivism is based on rearrest or reimprisonment for either another felony conviction or a parole violation for up to three years after release.

Recent figures show that only about half of parolees nationwide successfully complete their parole terms, although this figure appears to be improving. Of the 391,298 parolees who terminated supervision in 1995, 60 percent were not returned to prison.[30] But it is hard to know how much of this success results from parole work and how much reflects the sheer determination of the parolee. When Howard Sacks and Charles Logan compared a group of court-ordered releasees with a similar group under parole supervision, they found that those discharged without supervision recidivated — had a new conviction for any crime — faster, especially during the first year. By the third year, 77 percent of the parole group had relapsed, compared with 85 percent of those discharged directly to the street.[31]

388

FOCUS

No "Perverts" Allowed

Carolyn Holt remembers the Tuesday evening when the town watch committee came around to tell her a child molester was moving in down the street. "I was terrified," says Holt, whose three young grandsons often visit her house in Riverside, N.J. "After that we used to tell the kids going down the street to school, 'There's a pervert in that house, don't go in.'" Local TV swarmed over the story, and outraged citizens demanded that the offender, Richard Marter, get out of town.

Such stories have become increasingly common in New Jersey since Megan's Law took effect. The statute requires police to notify neighbors when a sex offender like Marter moves into the area. By the weekend, Marter, who served 16 years after enticing a 7-year-old boy into his car and then fondling him, had been "ridden out of town on a rail," remembers Holt; parole officials moved Marter to the neighboring town of Beverly. "It was fear," says Mark Minton, building manager of Marter's rooming house in Riverside. "He was afraid someone might kill him."

Within another week, neighbors had hounded him out of Beverly, too. "He basically got chased up the Delaware River," says Mark Waligore, managing editor of *The Trentonian*, a tabloid that covered the story closely. According to his elderly aunt, Marter now sells newspapers in Trenton and lives anonymously in a single room. "He calls me from time to time to say he's O.K.," says the aunt, Harriet Chew. "He's been through enough."

Critics contend that Megan's Law is not only unconstitutional but also encourages vigilantism. Indeed, two men recently broke into an apartment in Phillipsburg, N.J., where they thought child molester Michael Groff was staying. They attacked the wrong man. Groff, like Marter, is now on the move again. " I don't feel sorry for the criminal at all, " says Carolyn Holt. "I don't care how much time they serve, it'll never be enough."

SOURCE: *Newsweek*, February 6, 1995, p. 25. © 1995 Newsweek, Inc. All rights reserved. Reprinted by permission.

The effectiveness of traditional parole work has been questioned based on studies of small parole caseloads. These studies find that the assumptions underlying attempts to reduce caseload size are incorrect. When parole caseloads are reduced to between thirty and thirty-five clients per officer, the officers do not spend more total time with clients (instead, they improve on the quality of paperwork), nor do the offenders become more likely to succeed.

On the other hand, growing evidence suggests that supervision can be effective if structured to achieve certain aims. For example, behavioral treatment combined with close surveillance and sporadic urine testing for drug addicts on parole can significantly reduce rates of new addiction, new crime, and drug-related death.[32]

A very important strategy for improving supervision effectiveness is case management. One element of case management is to impose on the supervision effort a structure of established approaches that are likely to be successful, rather than leaving the supervision style to the officer's discretion. A Texas parole study compared discretionary supervision methods to a structured strategy including a standardized intake interview, carefully monitored classification and case planning, and systematic officer performance appraisal. Under the new, more structured approach, parolees fared better in terms of criminal behavior and social adjustment (as measured by such factors as employment).[33] Similarly, an *"in vivo* treatment" system of supervision for drug-involved parolees provided the second element of successful case management: tangible services such as job training and money for transportation to work, with close monitoring of progress. An evaluation of this aspect of case management found that case management sets the stage for full recovery from addiction and crime-free adjustment to the community.[34]

The effectiveness of parole supervision has earned mixed reviews. Yet because parolees who remain crime free for two years often succeed thereafter, correctional administrators continue to revise parole practices in ways that will help offenders make it.

COMPARATIVE PERSPECTIVE

Parole Supervision in Japan

When Japan organized correctional services after World War II, some argued that probation and parole supervision should combine professional and volunteer workers. A shortage of funds precluded expanded professional service, and volunteers had historically contributed to the rehabilitation of offenders. Japan also has a tradition of voluntary social welfare systems firmly rooted in the community. The Offender's Rehabilitation Law called on all people to "render help, in accordance with their position and ability, in order to achieve the goals (of rehabilitation of offenders, etc.)." With passage of the Volunteer Probation Officer Law in 1950, people were nominated to serve in this capacity. They were charged with helping offenders to rehabilitate themselves in society and with fostering a constructive public attitude that would help to promote crime prevention.

Today, almost 50,000 volunteers work individually with the one to ten cases assigned to them, supervised by 800 professional officers. Appointed for two-year terms, volunteers are assigned according to their place of residence to one of 764 "rehabilitation areas." The volunteers in each area form an association of officers that is nationally linked to provide for volunteer solidarity, to coordinate training, and to gain resources.

Volunteer officers tend to be older (more than half are over 50) and are from a variety of backgrounds. The largest group (23 percent) comes from such primary industries as agriculture, fishing, and forestry. The second largest category (18 percent) consists of people officially classified as unemployed but mainly homemakers and retired. Religious professionals comprise the next largest category. Only 5 percent of the officers are lawyers, doctors, and other professionals, somewhat in contrast to the community activities of this group in Western countries. Although there is a diversity of backgrounds, most volunteers are middle class.

The volunteer regularly meets a client at home and also visits the client's family. The volunteer continues to observe the offender in these contacts and tries to advise, assist and support him or her. Assistance is also given to the offender's family, with due respect to the dignity and freedom of the individual. Sometimes the volunteer has to visit the client's place of employment. The greatest concern is how to maintain client contact while at the same time keeping the offender's criminal background from the knowledge of neighbors and employers. Contact is generally twice a month, but in special cases it occurs almost every day. Volunteers feel they should be readily available to clients and their families, even during weekends or late at night in case of emergency, particularly in remote areas where professional services are few.

The volunteer probation and parole service in Japan is believed to have unique merits lacked by the professional officer. It is believed that through this nonofficial relationship the offender can regain self-respect and identify with the law-abiding culture. Also, as members of the community where their clients live, volunteers know the particular setting and local customs. Yet some professional officers believe they could do a better job than the volunteers.

The nature of probation and parole in Japan draws heavily on that country's unique sense of community. By sharing a common culture and social experience, the Japanese are closely bound to one another in a consensual society. For offenders, rehabilitation requires earning one's way back into community membership.

The Japanese approach to probation and parole is quite different from the United States. Perhaps it would only be successful in a country where there is not great cultural diversity and where community pressures are a major aspect of social control.

SOURCES: Drawn from Yasuyoshi Shiono, "Use of Volunteers in the Non-Institutional Treatment of Offenders in Japan," *International Review of Crime Policy*, 27, 1969, pp. 25–31; Kenichi Nakayama, "Japan," in George F. Cole, Stanislaw Frankowski, and Marc G. Gertz, eds., *Major Criminal Justice Systems*, 2nd ed. (Newbury Park, CA: Sage, 1987), p. 168; L. Craig Parker, Jr., *Parole and the Community Based Treatment of Offenders in Japan and the United States* (New Haven, CT: University of New Haven Press, 1986); Elmer H. Johnson, *Japanese Corrections* (Carbondale: Southern Illinois University Press, 1996).

What Are Its Prospects?

Many changes have been made in the way offenders are released from prison, as noted in Chapter 15, but these changes are not reflected in supervision practices. Even states that have altered release laws or policies seem to recognize that offenders need some help or control in the months after release, and research suggests that parole does help them stay crime free, at least during the early months on the outside. Therefore postrelease supervision, whether in the form of parole, work release, or some other program, probably will continue to be part of the experience of most incarcerated offenders. Yet as the Comparative Perspective shows, supervision of parolees in Japan is based on very different principles from in the United States.

The nature of supervision, however, is likely to change significantly over the next few years. Increasing evidence suggests that it is not appropriate for all offenders but should be oriented toward those who are most likely to fail and who require close supervision. The broad discretionary power of the parole officer is disappearing. In its place a much more restrictive effort is becoming popular, one in which limited special conditions are imposed and stringently enforced. The helping role of the officer — as counselor, referral agent, and so forth — is being freed from the coercive role, and the help offered is increasingly seen as an opportunity that offenders may choose not to take. Postrelease supervision is likely to be streamlined in years to come as the courts continue to review officers' decisions and their agencies' policies.

What is not likely to change is the situation of the released offender. Poor training and poor education lead to poor job prospects; public distrust of offenders leads to discrimination. These conditions will continue to be the realities of the postrelease experience. Offenders will need to hone their strategies if they are to succeed in the community.

Summary

The postrelease function has three main participants: the offender, the community supervision agent, and the bureaucracy. The goals of postrelease supervision — assistance and control — do not mix well, and both clients and officers must struggle with the resulting inconsistencies. A parole officer is expected to develop a relationship with a client, and the two come to depend on each other as they work toward a successful outcome to their joint endeavor. Technical uncertainty permeates the entire system, and actions taken by officers and clients always contain risks. The operation is carried out in a bureaucratic context that limits both participants' ability to choose among courses of action.

As a result, postrelease supervision is much like a game. Offenders seek ways to convince parole officers that they are adjusting well to the community in order to avoid reimprisonment; officers seek ways to avoid accusations that their decisions have been inappropriate; the bureaucracy seeks to maintain an image of effectiveness with the general public. Each participant has substantial ability to influence the others' capacity to get what they desire out of the postrelease relationship. They are in a classic pattern of exchange: They try to support one another's needs as long as their own needs are being met.

Research has shown that postrelease supervision is of limited effectiveness unless it is structured to deal individually with particular offenders and their particular problems. It is by this means that the parole officer can do the most to help the offender make it.

For Discussion

1. Imagine that you have just been released from prison after a five-year term. What are the first things you will do? What problems can you expect to face?

2. Why is it said that probation officers tend to take a social work approach and parole officers tend to take a law enforcement approach? How might these differences in approach be explained?

3. Why are some parole officers reluctant to ask that a client's parole be revoked for technical violations? What organizational pressures may be involved?

4. Why are so many occupations closed to convicted felons?

5. Do you think neighborhood notification laws for released sex offenders increase public safety? Or do these laws make it harder for sex offenders to succeed? Why?

For Further Reading

McCleary, Richard. *Dangerous Men: The Sociology of Parole,* 2nd ed. Albany, NY: Harrow & Heston, 1992. Studies the bureaucracy of parole supervision.

O'Leary, Vincent, and Clear, Todd R. *Community Corrections into the 21st Century.* Washington, DC: National Institute of Corrections, 1995. Reviews methods for managing offender risk in the community.

Paylor, Ian. *The Housing Needs of Ex-Offenders.* London: Avebury Press, 1995. Describes the problems encountered by ex-offenders in establishing suitable living arrangements after leaving prison.

Sacks, Howard R., and Logan, Charles H. *Does Parole Make a (Lasting) Difference?* West Hartford: University of Connecticut School of Law Press, 1979. Examines the impact of parole supervision on parole success.

Simon, Jonathan. *Poor Discipline: Parole and the Social Control of the Underclass.* Chicago: University of Chicago Press, 1993. Explores the use of parole to control poor and disadvantaged members of society.

Studt, Elliot. *Surveillance and Service in Parole Supervision.* Washington, DC: U.S. Government Printing Office, 1973. Represents a classic study of parole officers and parolees.

Notes

1. Taken from Rosemary J. Erickson, Wayman J. Crow, Louis A. Zurcher, and Archie V. Connett, *Paroled but Not Free* (New York: Human Sciences Press, 1973), p. 15.

2. *Morrissey v. Brewer,* 408 U.S. 471 (1972).

3. Calculated from Jodi M. Brown and Patrick A. Langan, *State Court Sentencing of Convicted Felons, 1994* (Washington, DC: Bureau of Justice Statistics, U.S. Department of Justice, March 1998), pp. 4, 5; and *Correctional Populations in the United States, 1995,* (Washington, DC: Bureau of Justice Statistics, U.S. Department of Justice, 1997), p. 11.

4. Carl B. Klockars, "A Theory of Probation Supervision," *Journal of Criminal Law, Criminology, and Police Science,* 63, 1972, pp. 550–557.

5. Billie S. Erwin, *Evaluation of Intensive Probation Supervision in Georgia* (Atlanta: Georgia Department of Offender Rehabilitation, February 1985), p. 16.

6. David T. Stanley, *Prisoners Among Us* (Washington, DC: Brookings Institution, 1986), p. 170.

7. Daniel Glaser, *The Effectiveness of a Prison and Parole System* (New York: Bobbs-Merrill, 1969), pp. 292–293.

8. Todd R. Clear and Edward E. Latessa, "Surveillance vs. Control: Probation Officers' Roles in Intensive Supervision," *Justice Quarterly,* 10(3), 1993, pp. 441–462.

9. Elliott Studt, *Surveillance and Service in Parole* (Washington, DC: U.S. Government Printing Office, 1973).

10. Richard McCleary, *Dangerous Men: The Sociology of Parole,* 2nd ed. (Albany, NY: Harrow & Heston), 1992, p. 113.

11. Michael Lipsky, *Street-Level Bureaucracy* (New York: Russell Sage Foundation, 1980), p. 82.

12. Todd R. Clear and P. Kevin Benoit, "Case Management in Probation and Parole Supervision," in John O. Smykla, ed., *Probation and Parole* (New York: Macmillan, 1984), p. 234.

13. McCleary, p. 63.

14. Susan Turner and Joan Petersilia, "Work Release in Washington: Effects on Recidivism and Correctional Costs," *The Prison Journal,* 76(2), June 1996.

15. Gordon Waldo and Ted G. Chiricos, "Work Release and Recidivism: An Empirical Evaluation of Social Policy," *Evaluation Quarterly,* 1, 1986, pp. 87–108.

16. *The New York Times,* October 23, 1998, p. A12.

17. Robert M. Grooms, "Recidivist," *Crime and Delinquency,* 28, October 1982, pp. 542–543.

18. Clair A. Cripe, *Legal Aspects of Corrections Management* (Gaithersburg, MD: Aspen, 1997), p. 402.

19. Kathlen M. Olivares, Velmer S. Burton, Jr., and Francis T. Cullen, "The Collateral Consequences of a Felony Conviction: A National Study of State Legal Codes Ten Years Later," *Federal Probation,* 60(1), July 1996, pp. 10-18.

20. Shelly Albright and Furjen Denq, "Employer Attitudes Toward Hiring Ex-Offenders," *The Prison Journal,* 76(2), June 1996, pp. 118–137.

21. Karen E. Needels, "Go Directly to Jail and Do Not Collect? A Long-term Study of Recidivism, Employment, and Earnings Patterns Among Prison Releasees," *Journal of Research in Crime and Delinquency,* 33(4), November 1996, pp. 471–496.

22. McCleary, p. 133.

23. Roxanne Lieb, Vernon Quinsey, and Lucy Berliner, "Sexual Predators and Social Policy," in Michael Tonry, ed., *Crime and Justice: A Review of Research*, vol. 23 (Chicago: University of Chicago Press, 1998), pp. 43–114.

24. Peter Benekos and Alidaa M. Verlo, pp. 3–7.

25. "Megan's Law Passes New Jersey Legislature," *The New York Times*, September 19, 1994, p. A1.

26. Peter Finn, *Sex Offender Community Notification* (Washington, DC: National Institute of Justice Research in Action, U.S. Department of Justice, February 1997).

27. Michael R. Geerken and Hennessey D. Hayes, "Probation and Parole: Public Risks and the Future of Incarceration Alternatives," *Criminology*, 31(4), November 1993, pp. 549–564.

28. Franklin Zimring, "The Voodoo Economics of California Crime," *Overcrowded Times*, 5(5), October 1994, p. 3.

29. *The New York Times*, July 1, 1998, p. A23; November 14, 1998, p. A19.

30. Department of Justice, Bureau of Justice Statistics, *Correctional Populations in the United States, 1995*, (Washington, DC: U.S. Government Printing Office, 1997), p. 130.

31. Howard R. Sacks and Charles H. Logan, "Does Parole Make a (Lasting) Difference?" in George F. Cole, ed., *Criminal Justice: Law and Politics*, 4th ed. (Pacific Grove, CA: Brooks/Cole, 1984), pp. 362–378.

32. Douglas Anglin, "What Works with Substance Abusing Offenders," paper presented to the IARCA Conference on What Works, Seattle, November 3, 1994.

33. Greg Markley and Michael Eisenberg, *Follow-Up Study of Texas Parole Case Management Project* (Austin: Texas Board of Pardons and Paroles, 1987).

34. Steven S. Martin and James A. Inciardi, "Case Management for Drug Involved Offenders," *The Prison Journal*, 77(2), June 1997, pp. 168–183.

CHAPTER SEVENTEEN
Corrections for Juvenile Offenders

Between February 1997 and April 1999, nine highly publicized incidents occurred in the United States in which teenagers shot and killed their teachers and fellow students. The events in Alaska, Arkansas, California, Colorado, Kentucky, Mississippi, Oregon, Pennsylvania, and Tennessee were lead stories in the news for weeks. The horrific conduct, and the way it forced itself onto the public agenda, led to calls for fundamental reform of juvenile justice. Predictable calls came for "getting tough" with serious offenders, as well as demands for actions to strengthen families and reduce youth alienation.

In this chapter, we explore the juvenile correctional system. Although separate from adult corrections, the juvenile system is linked to adult correctional activity at many points. What sets the juvenile correctional system apart are differences in philosophy, procedures, and programmatic emphasis. The philosophy of juvenile corrections places a higher premium on rehabilitation and prevention, compared to punishment, than does its adult counterpart. The procedures of juvenile corrections are less dominated by firm due process rules, and instead attempt to build in a degree of informality and discretionary decision making. This informality is in part intended to enable program administrators to develop innovative strategies for correctional programming that promise to keep juvenile offenders from returning to crime as adults. The following Questions for Inquiry will guide our examination of juvenile corrections.

Questions FOR INQUIRY

1. What is the extent of youth crime today?
2. How did juvenile corrections in the United States develop?
3. What is the rationale for dealing differently with juvenile offenders and adult offenders?
4. What is serious juvenile delinquency?
5. In what ways are juvenile offenders sanctioned?
6. What special problem is posed by youth gangs?
7. How does the future of juvenile corrections look?

The Problem of Youth Crime

It disturbs us to think of a child as "dangerous" or "sinister," but we are forced by daily news to consider the unpleasant truth that some young people commit serious crimes. Each year about 100 children under the age of 13 are arrested for homicide, 600 for forcible rape, and a troubling 7,600 for aggravated assault.[1] Many of these cases become local or national news stories. The incidents remind us that some juveniles are capable of deeply distressing behavior. Because these cases alarm and frighten us, the need for greater confidence in the juvenile justice system has become a major issue for correctional professionals and policymakers.

The juvenile crime incidents just described are quite rare. In a nation with 78.5 million people 19 years of age or younger, there were 2.8 million arrests of juveniles in 1996, only 135,000 of which (about 5 percent) were for violent crimes.[2] Compare this with the 13 million arrests of adults, 650,000 for violent crimes, in that same year. When it comes to serious crime, juveniles are a much smaller problem than adults are.

Yet we are particularly unsettled by juvenile crime for reasons beyond the numbers. Young people represent our future. We expect them to be busy growing up, learning how to become productive citizens and developing skills for a satisfying life. We do not expect them to be committing crimes that damage the quality of community life. And because they are starting criminal behavior so young age, we worry about the future—how long before a young person's criminal career fades? How much damage will be left in its wake?

History of Juvenile Corrections

Throughout history children who get in trouble have faced dire circumstances. During the Middle Ages children were seen as property of the male head of the household, and the patriarch could deal with his possessions however he wished. Brutality was not uncommon. When a parent lacked resources, their children went without food. When parents ran afoul of the law, children lost their protectors and were left to fend for themselves. When children themselves broke the law, they faced the same kinds of punishments faced by adults. The plight of children was a factor in the reform of laws dealing with children in England during the 1600s and 1700s.

Wounded student Ryan Attleberry is led to an ambulance in Springfield, Oregon, after fellow student Kipland Kinkel sprayed the crowded Thurston High School cafeteria with gunfire, killing two and wounding nineteen. Earlier Kinkel had killed his parents.

Juvenile Corrections: The English Antecedents

During the early 1600s in England, governments began to consider the plight of the child. In much the same way as the crown claimed property rights throughout the realm, children were seen as being under the protection of the king or queen. Under the doctrine of **parens patriae**—literally, "parent of the nation"—the crown could act as guardian of any child, especially one with rights to inherited property.

The Elizabethan Poor Laws (1601) established the basis for officials to take charge of vagrant and delinquent children, placing them under the authority of church wardens and other overseers. Most ended up in poorhouses or workhouses, working under oppressive, slavery-like conditions. The same fate befell the children of widows, when their mother lacked means of support. And when children broke the law, they were processed by the same authorities who handled adult criminals, and were exposed to adult punishments.

In the 1800s, reformers such as John Howard visited the gaols and poorhouses in England and were appalled by the decrepit conditions and the treatment of women and children in these dark, disease-filled facilities. As we saw in Chapter 2, reformers called for a new, reformative approach to imprisonment. The plight of children in the system helped galvanize public sentiment for change.

___
parens patriae
___

The "parent of the country"; the role of the state as guardian and protector of all people (particularly juveniles) who are unable to protect themselves.

Juvenile Corrections in the United States

The English procedures were maintained in the American colonies and continued into the 1800s. The earliest attempt by a colony to deal with problem children was passage of the Massachusetts Stubborn Child Law, in 1646. With this law, the Puritans of the Massachusetts Bay Colony conveyed their view that the child was evil and emphasized the need of the family to discipline and raise youths. Those who would not obey their parents were to be dealt with by the law.

Table 17.1 outlines the shifts in how the United States has dealt with the problems of youth. Five periods of American juvenile justice history can be defined. Each period was characterized by changes in juvenile justice that reflected the social, intellectual, and political currents of the time. During the past two hundred years, population shifts from rural to urban areas, immigration, developments in the social sciences, political reform movements, and the continuing problem of youth crime have all influenced how Americans have treated juveniles. We have touched on the Puritan period; next we examine the refuge period.

Table 17.1   Juvenile Justice Developments in the United States

Period	Major Developments	Causes and Influences	Juvenile Justice System
Puritan 1646–1824	Massachusetts Stubborn Child Law (1646)	A Puritan view of child as evil B Economically marginal agrarian society	Law provides: A Symbolic standard of maturity B Support for family as economic unit
Refuge 1824–1899	Institutionalization of deviants, House of Refuge in New York established (1825) for delinquent and dependent children	A Enlightenment B Immigration and industrialization	Child seen as helpless, in need of state intervention.
Juvenile Court 1899–1960	Establishment of separate legal system for juveniles; Illinois Juvenile Court Act (1899)	A Reformism and rehabilitative ideology B Increased immigration, urbanization, large-scale industrialization	Juvenile court institutionalized legal irresponsibility of child.
Juvenile Rights 1960–1980	Increased "legalization" of juvenile law; *Gault* decision (1967); Juvenile Justice and Delinquency Prevention Act (1974) calls for deinstitutionalization of status offenders	A Criticism of juvenile justice system on humane grounds B Civil rights movement by disadvantaged groups	Movement to define and protect rights as well as to provide services to children.
Crime Control 1980–present	Concern for victims, punishment for serious offenders, transfer to adult court of serious offenders, protection of children from physical and sexual abuse	A More conservative public attitudes and policies B Focus on serious crimes by repeat offenders	System more formal, restrictive, punitive; increased percentage of police referrals to court; incarcerated youths stay longer periods.

NOTE: A status offender is a juvenile who has committed an act that is considered unacceptable for a child, such as truancy or running away from home, that would not be a crime if committed by an adult.

SOURCES: Adapted from U.S. Department of Justice, *A Preliminary National Assessment of Status Offender and the Juvenile Justice System* (Washington, DC: U.S. Government Printing Office, 1980), p. 29; Barry Krisberg, Ira M. Schwartz, Paul Litsky, and James Austin, "The Watershed of Juvenile Justice Reform," *Crime and Delinquency*, 32, January 1986, pp. 5–38.

The Refuge Period (1824–1899)   During the early 1800s reformers urged creation of institutions where delinquent, abused, and neglected children could learn good work and study habits, live in a disciplined and healthy environment, and develop "character." The first such institution was the House of Refuge of New York, which opened in 1825. By 1850 almost every large city had such an institution operated by private charities. According to the reformers, residents were to be trained in job skills, provided with religious instruction, and held accountable with strict, but sympathetic, discipline.

In practice, these ideals were difficult to attain. Most refuge houses came to resemble the adult prisons of the day, with cruelty by staff, hostilities among the inmates, and an overriding sense of harshness and alienation in daily life. Although reformers felt they were bringing a kind of "social love" into the lives of wayward youth, what in fact occurred was at best an indifferent institutionalization, and at worst a kind of social oppression. Historians have pointed out that the rhetoric of the reformers was well meaning, and their intentions sincere, but the actual impact of these reforms was quite different than intended.

Some have described the refuge house movement as an aspect of the conflict between the native-born upper classes and the burgeoning inner-city immigrant poor, commonly referred to in those days as "the dangerous classes." The teeming cities alarmed the elites as cauldrons of social problems that threatened the core of contemporary civic life.

In the mid-1800s, when frontier settlements were crying out for labor, delinquent and neglected urban children, removed from their homes, were often "placed out" to these faraway places to work on farms or in small businesses. These arrangements were not unlike those made for the indentured servants of the previous century.

Eventually, critics began to complain about the growing abuses of the refuge house strategy. It had become apparent that the adult court system was not a satisfactory approach for dealing with juveniles. These courts often treated juveniles more harshly than adults who had committed the same crimes. It had also become obvious that the problems of urban youth had not been solved.

During the Progressive Era at the end of the 1800s, reformers called "the child savers"[3] called for new ways to deal with children in trouble. A reform group in Chicago ushered in the modern juvenile justice system.

The Juvenile Court Period (1899–1960)   The first juvenile court was established by legislative act in Cook County (Chicago) Illinois, in 1899. The impetus for the reforms came from the Chicago Women's Club, which had asked the Chicago Bar Association to conduct a study of the problems of handling juvenile offenders and to recommend a model code for a new system. The thrust of the resulting legislation was to give judges broad discretion in handling juvenile cases.

Based on the revitalized idea of *parens patriae,* the new juvenile court was to take the role of guardian, the substitute parent to the child. Decisions about a juvenile's fate was linked less to guilt or innocence, and more directly to "the best interests" of the child. The main tenets of the juvenile court can be summarized as informality, individualization, and intervention.

Informality was intended to move away from the formality and due process requirements of the adult courtroom. Instead of rules of evidence and cross-examination, judges would run the sessions as conversations in which interested people such as parents, teachers, and social workers could comment on the case. The court was encouraged to establish a relaxed, informal atmosphere so that the needs of the child could be understood. Formal rules were thought to hinder the exploratory conversation and unnecessarily limit the potential solutions.

Individualization was based on the idea that each child ought to be treated as a unique person with unique circumstances. It was considered mistaken to handle a case solely on the basis of misbehavior type. Two children, each of whom had broken into a home, might have different needs that led each to the misconduct. Criminality was thus seen as a "symptom" of trouble, only one of the problems facing the child. By treating each child as different, more fitting solutions to children's' problems could be crafted.

Intervention was the method of the juvenile court. The final aim of all juvenile processing was "adjustment"—to help the child develop a law-abiding lifestyle. Thus, the court was not to punish children, but to identify and solve the problems that led them astray and to provide treatment that would avert a life of crime.

To implement this approach, the juvenile court developed its own language, procedures, and rules. In place of standard adult processing practices, the juvenile justice system established a version revised to achieve its new aims. Table 17.2 compares the terminology of the adult and juvenile systems.

There was widespread enthusiasm for the new juvenile court model. Following the Chicago example, every state had revised its penal code and established a separate juvenile court within a few years. The age of jurisdiction often varied—some states took

In the nineteenth century some states adopted a parental role and placed young people who were deemed "out of control" into institutions such as reform schools to shape their behavior and "character" into socially acceptable modes.

Table 17.2   Comparison of Terminology in the Adult and Juvenile Justice Systems

Function	Adult System Term	Juvenile System Term
Taking into custody	Arrested	Detained (police contact)
Legal basis for holding	Charged	Referred to court
Formal charges	Indicted	Held on petition
Person charged	Defendant	Respondent
Determination of guilt	Trial	Hearing
Outcome of court case	Verdict	Finding
Term for "guilty"	Convicted	Adjudicated (as responsible)
Sanction	Sentence	Disposition
Custodial sentence	Incarcerated	Placed or committed
Incarceration facility	Prison	Training school
Release supervision	Parole	Aftercare

delinquent

A child who has committed an act that if committed by an adult would be criminal.

neglected

A child who is not receiving proper care because of some action or inaction of his or her parents.

dependent

A child who has no parent or guardian or whose parents are unable to give proper care.

juveniles as old as 18 or 19, whereas others allowed anyone over the age of 16 to be handled as an adult. The courts were given jurisdiction over delinquent, neglected, and dependent children. A **delinquent** child is one who has committed an act that if committed by an adult would be criminal. A **neglected** child is one who is not receiving proper care, because of some action or inaction of his or her parents. This may include not being sent to school, not receiving medical care, being abandoned, or not receiving some other care necessary for the child's well-being. A **dependent** child either is without a parent or guardian, or is not receiving proper care because of the physical or mental disability of a parent/guardian.

Despite the enthusiasm, problems arose with the informal approach. Sometimes judges and attorneys ran roughshod over rights, imposing the law in ways that seemed opposed to the youngsters' true interests. Judges were allowed to tailor dispositions, but many suspected that lower-class children and ethnic minorities received harsher, less sympathetic treatment. And the failure of intervention to stem recidivism led the community to distrust the effectiveness of juvenile court.

The Juvenile Rights Period (1960–1980)   By the 1960s liberal reform groups, such as the American Civil Liberties Union, rallied to protect the rights of juveniles. In a series of decisions (see Table 17.3), the U.S. Supreme Court extended to juveniles many of the due process rights accorded adults.

The Crime Control Period (1980–Present)   During the past twenty years conservative critics have argued that young people are treated far too leniently by the juvenile authorities. Stories are told about crimes that would have landed an adult in jail, but for which a juvenile received nothing more than probation. Alarm over serious and violent juvenile offenses has resulted in a broad public movement for increased use of waiver to adult court. This pressure to treat juveniles as adults and meting out stern punishment for serious crimes has eroded some enthusiasm for the juvenile court reforms of a century ago.

Even though the reforms of the last forty years have changed the procedures and to a lesser extent the practices of the juvenile justice system, in many respects the underlying philosophy of the juvenile court remains very much as these original reformers intended. Juveniles receive a different version of treatment by their justice system, one that places less emphasis on punishment and more emphasis on individualized treatment. The rationale for this difference is that juveniles differ in important ways from adults, ways that ought to be considered in the way the law works. How do other societies handle this problem? For a view of juvenile justice in Norway, see the Comparative Perspective.

Table 17.3 Major Decisions by the U.S. Supreme Court Regarding the Rights of Juveniles

Since the mid-1960s, the Supreme Court has gradually expanded the rights of juveniles, but has continued to recognize that the logic of a separate system for juvenile offenders justifies differences from some adult rights.

Kent v. United States (1966)	Requires "essentials of due process" for juvenile offenders.
In Re Gault (1967)	Specifies the "essentials" of due process required by *Kent*—notice, hearing, counsel, cross-examination.
In Re Winship (1970)	Requires a standard of "beyond a reasonable doubt" for delinquency matters.
McKeiver v. Pennsylvania (1971)	Holds that jury trials are not required for juvenile court hearings.
Breed v. Jones (1975)	Waiver to adult court following adjudication in juvenile court violates the constitutional guarantee against double-jeopardy.
Smith v. Daily Mail Publishing Co. (1979)	The press may report certain aspects of juvenile court cases and matters.
Eddings v. Oklahoma (1982)	The age of a defendant must be considered as a mitigating factor in capital crimes.
Schall v. Martin (1984)	Preventive pretrial detention is allowed for juvenile defendants who are found "dangerous."
Stanford v. Kentucky (1989)	Set minimum age for capital punishment at 16.

Why Treat Juveniles and Adults Differently?

Differences between juveniles and adults are used to justify separate justice systems. Even though each offender is different, on average juveniles represent a different set of challenges to correctional professionals. Five such differences are identified as follows.

Juveniles Are Young and May Easily Change   Most correctional professionals believe juveniles are more susceptible to the influence of treatment programs. Younger offenders are not as entrenched in negative peer associations, nor do they penetrate as deeply into criminal activity as more experienced, older offenders. The habits of the young are less well formed and may be more easily altered.

But the youthfulness of juveniles is a double-edged sword. Age is a predictor of recidivism: the younger the juvenile offender — and the more serious the misconduct — the more likely that offender will be arrested again. As a consequence, the general experience of correctional workers is that younger offenders are more malleable, but this is countered by the fact that so many of the very young will find it hard to stay out of trouble.

Juveniles Have a High Rate of "Desistence"   All else being equal, age is the best predictor of recidivism: the younger the offender, the more likely that offender will fail under community supervision. But that statistic can be misleading, because juvenile offenders, as a group, have lower failure rates than adults. This is true because it is not uncommon for youth to get arrested. Yet most juveniles who get in trouble with the law once never get arrested again. For all youths, the failure rate increases as age of first involvement in juvenile crime decreases. Despite the high success rate of juveniles, even the very young, a look at those who fail will turn up large numbers whose criminality began at a very early age.

COMPARATIVE
PERSPECTIVE

The Hidden Juvenile Justice System in Norway

There is no punishment for crimes in Norway for children under age 15. Thus, there are no special courts to try criminal cases against juvenile offenders. Older teenagers may be tried in ordinary courts and sentenced to prison. However, most sentences consist only of a suspended sentence or probation or several months in an open prison.

In practice, the prosecutor transfers the juvenile case directly to a division of the "social office," the *barnevern*—literally, child protection. After a trial the judge may also refer the child to this office. Police evidence is turned over to the social workers, not for prosecution, but for "treatment."

The usual first step in treatment is that the *barnevern* takes emergency custody of the child and places the child in a youth home. If the parents or guardians do not give consent, the child welfare committee will consider arguments against the placement. Here, the question is the appropriate treatment for the child.

The *barnevern* is most often associated in the public mind with handling of cases of child abuse and neglect. In such a case, the board will turn over custody of the child to the social workers for placement in a foster home or youth home. Once the custody is removed from the parents, the burden of proof is on the parents to retain custody. Social

workers are well aware of numerous cases of recovering alcoholics who, even after recovery, have been unable to retain custody of their children.

In contrast to the U.S. juvenile court, the Norwegian model is wholly dominated by the social worker. The function of the judge is to preside over the hearing and to maintain proper legal protocol, but the child welfare office presents the evidence and directs the case. The five laypeople who constitute the [social welfare committee] are advised by the child welfare office well before the hearing of the "facts" of the case. Before the hearing, the youth will have been placed in a youth home or mental institution "on an emergency basis"; the parents' rights will have already been terminated.

The hearing is thus a mere formality after the fact. There is overwhelming unanimity among members of the board and between the board and social worker administrators. The arguments of the clients and of their lawyers seem to "fall on deaf ears."

Proof of guilt brought before the committee will generally consist of a copy of the police report of the offenses admitted by the accused and a school report written by the principal after he or she has been informed of the law

Juveniles' Families Are an Important Part of Their Lives   For juvenile offenders, the role of family is critical to the success of correctional efforts. This is true because the juvenile is, by virtue of age, deeply connected to the immediate family (parents, siblings, and extended family) in ways that do not characterize adult relationships. Under the laws of most states, for example, the juvenile actually becomes a ward of the state and the court (usually through probation officers) accepts joint responsibility for the young offender. Under the law, then, the court system is a partner with the family in the supervision effort. It is thought reasonable to take this approach, because the child's delinquency is taken as evidence that the parents are not capable of effective supervision without support from the court.

Juveniles Are Easily Influenced by Their Peers   With isolated exceptions, juvenile crime is a group phenomenon. Young people gather to socialize and a common part of their behavior is testing boundaries and challenging each other to try new things. We often associate "gangs" with the criminal behavior of young people, but all studies find that group criminality can arise, even when gangs are not involved. Especially during the preadoles-

breaking. Reports by the *barnevern*-appointed psychologist and social worker are also included. The *barnevern,* in its statement, has summarized the reports from the point of view of its arguments (usually for placement). Otherwise, the reports are ignored.

The hearing itself is a far cry from standard courtroom procedure. The youth and his or her parents may address the board briefly. The attorney sums up the case for a return to the home. Expert witnesses may be called and questioned by the board concerning, for instance, their treatment recommendations.

Following the departure of the parties, the *barnevern* office presents what amounts to "the case for the prosecution." There is no opportunity to rebut the testimony and no opportunity for cross-examination.

Placement in an institution is typically for an indefinite period. No notice of the disposition of the matter is given to the press. This absence of public accountability may serve more to protect the social office than the child.

Children receive far harsher treatments than do adults for similar offenses. For instance, for a young adult first offender the typical penalty for thievery is a suspended sentence. A child, however, may languish in an institution for years for the same offense.

A *barnevern's* first work ought to be to create the best possible childhood. However, the *barnevern* also has a control function in relation to both the parents and the child, and the controller often feels a stronger duty to the community. The institutionalization of children with behavior problems clearly reflects this social control function. Approximately half of the children under care of the child welfare committee are placed outside the home and the other half placed under protective watch.

The system of justice for children is therefore often very harsh. This is in sharp contrast to the criminal justice system for adults, which is strikingly lenient. Where punishment is called *treatment,* however, the right of the state can almost become absolute. The fact that the state is represented by social work administrators creates a sharp ethical conflict for those whose first duty is to the client.

What we see in Norway is a process of juvenile justice that has not changed substantially since the 1950s. Due to flaws within the system, including the lack of external controls, the best intentions of social workers "have gone awry." Where care and protection were intended, power and secrecy have prevailed. Juvenile justice in Norway today is the justice of America yesterday. ■

SOURCE: Condensed from Katherine Van Wormer, "The Hidden Juvenile Justice System in Norway: A Journey Back in Time," *Federal Probation,* March 1990, pp. 57–61.

cence and teen years, peer relationships are the most important influences on most youths. It is not easy for youths to resist the pressure to engage in group delinquent acts.

Juveniles Have Little Responsibility for Others For an adult, successful adjustment to the community involves taking on productive adult roles: parent, worker, citizen. By contrast, juveniles are typically only responsible for their own individual behavior. Juvenile self-responsibility typically concerns other things such as school performance and behavior, compliance with a curfew, and developing interpersonal skills.

Differences Between Adults and Juveniles in Perspective

These differences underscore some of the reasons why a separate juvenile justice system makes sense to most correctional professionals: Young offenders differ from older offenders in sufficiently important ways to justify different strategies carried out by separate correctional authorities. Advocates for juvenile justice emphasize the need for strategies of juvenile offender management that take into account important facts:

- Juveniles are appropriate candidates for many rehabilitation programs that may not work for adults.
- Juveniles are a lower risk than adults.
- Juveniles' families and peers are important influences that correctional efforts may shape.
- Juveniles are responsible for preparing for adult lives, but not yet for succeeding in adult roles.

However, these differences do not always work out as juvenile correctional workers might intend. For example, family dynamics often contribute to delinquent behavior. Inadequate parental supervision may leave the child too free to get into trouble. Or conflicts between the child and adults may promote delinquency as the child's way of "getting back" or even unintentionally calling attention to the conflict. Abuse, alcoholism or drug addiction, or mental illness of the child's parents may contribute to problems that end in delinquency. It is not uncommon for such adults to resist taking a positive role in the supervision effort. They may be hostile to the efforts of the correctional worker, or may excuse the child's misbehavior or even condone it.

Peer groups can also cause problems. Minor delinquents can drift from the everyday rule-breaking of truancy, fighting, and drinking, into far more serious crime. This can especially happen when the group pressures for ever-greater risk taking. Although we might all remember instances of violating curfews, drinking alcohol, and other delinquent acts that seemed merely "fun," many of the most serious forms of delinquency begin with just this sort of misbehavior.

Finally, keeping a juvenile offender in the ordinary environment of most young people — schools and neighborhoods — may not be easy. When a child disrupts the school setting through aggressive or threatening behavior, the school authorities usually want that youngster removed. When neighbors are afraid of the open violence of a gang member, there will be strong pressure for the judge to send that person to a juvenile institution. When a juvenile fails in the school and on the streets, few options are available to keep that person from sinking deeper into the correctional system.

The Problem of Serious Delinquency

The juvenile justice system is predicated on what we might call "normal" delinquency. This term may seem a contradiction but emphasizes that delinquent behavior is common in teenage years; certainly for young males in difficult living situations, it is almost expected. There is no legal or textbook definition of what is "normal"; rather, there is a set of assumptions about kinds of misbehaviors associated with growing up. Because some level of delinquency is, in this sense, "normal," people may react to it with less alarm than to similar misbehavior by adults. People may believe juveniles require not a punitive correctional response, but a developmental one, because their behavior is a part of a common adolescent pattern.

It would be naive to think that the juvenile justice paradigm applies equally to every young person who breaks the law. As noted, for each difference between adults and juveniles, there are well-known cases where the distinction did not apply. Some juveniles are already hardened and are unlikely to change; some will continue criminal behavior well into adulthood; some lack meaningful families with whom to engage in supervision; some are loners, unaffected by peer influences; some are already in adult roles, with jobs, spouses, and children. What should we do when a youthful offender does not act as we would expect a juvenile to act?

One of the most important considerations appears to be the age of the juvenile, and whether the behavior is age appropriate. There are big differences in what people find "normal" between the ages of, say, 14 and 17. Even though this difference is less than three years, a 14-year-old might sometimes be angry and engage in hostile, irrational behavior and be thought only "troubled." However, the same behavior by a 17-year-old will be seen as immature. In the same way, when a very young juvenile—for example, a preteen—engages in an extremely violent act, we are alarmed by the antisocial behavior of a young person who should be learning to live by society's norms. Clearly, assumptions about the "normalcy" of delinquency depend on the degree to which the type and degree of misbehavior fits the juvenile's age and level of development.

Likewise, people expect misbehavior to take place in a social context. It does not surprise or unduly alarm us to learn that so much delinquency occurs in adolescent groups, where youngsters who are learning to be socially connected to one another occasionally resort to delinquency as a way of becoming a member of their group. Gangs are, of course, an extreme example, but even them people can understand, although most have trouble understanding impersonal gang violence and broad-scale gang criminality. The lone child who commits crime for personal pleasure rather than social acceptance is comparatively rare, and people do not perceive such behavior as "normal" in a young person's development.

The public also finds it hard to understand when a youngster engages in gratuitous violence. Some kids commit petty property offenses, stealing things they want or vandalizing places they resent. A few get into schoolyard fights. But children who kill each other or plot to hurt someone are deeply unsettling. The label "delinquent" seems far too weak for these acts.

Unusual juvenile criminality has been one reason why some question the wisdom of having a separate juvenile justice system. They say society ought to treat all criminal acts with the seriousness they deserve, regardless of age. To the extent that age contributed to the gravity of the act, it could be taken as an aggravating or mitigating factor in sentencing. And certainly, age would also be a consideration in designing and managing correctional programs. Offenders could be assigned to programs based partly on age and maturity. But critics of juvenile justice argue for ending the separate system of justice, because there are so many exceptions to the stereotypes on which the juvenile justice system is based.

Although there are many proposals to reform juvenile justice, so far no nationwide movement seeks to abolish juvenile court. Thus today's most common approaches are applied within the separate system of justice for juveniles, described in the next sections.

Sanctioning Juvenile Offenders

Originally, separating juvenile justice from adult justice was intended to enable justice workers to give the highest priority to preventing crime by rehabilitating delinquents. Juvenile corrections agencies provide a range of services from diversion to probation, detention, and aftercare. Rehabilitation does indeed figure prominently in their practices, but that ethic is very fragile in reality.

Overview of the Juvenile Justice System

Juvenile corrections suffers from the same type of fragmentation as its adult counterpart, with agencies sometimes operated under the courts, sometimes under the executive branch; sometimes housed together with the institutional function, sometimes separated from it; sometimes run by counties, sometimes run by the state. Such fragmentation makes it very difficult to generalize about juvenile corrections policies. Nearly any policy arrangement a person can imagine exists somewhere, and what is true of one locale may not be true in the next jurisdiction down the road.

In 1996, the most recent year for which we have data, 2.9 million juveniles were arrested, 19 percent of all arrests made by the police. Of all people arrested, 95 percent are between ages 10 and 49. As Figure 17.1 shows, juveniles were involved in a much smaller proportion of violent crime arrests than property crime arrests. Less than a third

Figure 17.1   Percentage of Arrests Involving Juveniles

Juveniles were involved in a much smaller proportion of violent crime arrests than property arrests.

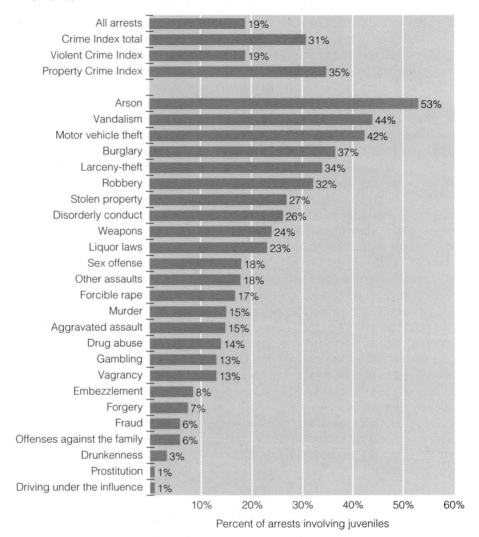

Category	Percent
All arrests	19%
Crime Index total	31%
Violent Crime Index	19%
Property Crime Index	35%
Arson	53%
Vandalism	44%
Motor vehicle theft	42%
Burglary	37%
Larceny-theft	34%
Robbery	32%
Stolen property	27%
Disorderly conduct	26%
Weapons	24%
Liquor laws	23%
Sex offense	18%
Other assaults	18%
Forcible rape	17%
Murder	15%
Aggravated assault	15%
Drug abuse	14%
Gambling	13%
Vagrancy	13%
Embezzlement	8%
Forgery	7%
Fraud	6%
Offenses against the family	6%
Drunkenness	3%
Prostitution	1%
Driving under the influence	1%

Percent of arrests involving juveniles

Source: U.S. Department of Justice, *Crime in the United States, 1996* (Washington, DC: U.S. Government Printing Office, 1997), table 38.

of juveniles were arrested for Index crimes—murder, sexual assault, aggravated assault, robbery, burglary, theft/fraud, auto theft. Of juvenile arrestees, 75 percent were male and 68 percent were 16 years of age or older. Juvenile arrests disproportionately involved minorities. People of color comprise 20 percent of the juvenile population, but were arrested out of proportion to their numbers. Especially troubling is the fact that of those arrested for murder, 61 percent were members of minorities; rape, 45 percent; robbery, 60 percent.

Such numbers are alarming: to think that 76,600 juveniles were arrested for aggravated assault, a serious and violent personal crime. And arrest rates are increasing for girls faster than for boys. Yet we must take these numbers in their proper context. In all, less than 0.5 percent of all Americans aged 10–17 were arrested for a violent offense in 1996. Violent crime among young people is alarming, but it is not common. Still, over one-third of the increase in violent crime between 1985 and 1994 was due to juveniles.[4]

In fact, serious juvenile offenders (those who commit felonies) are not all violent, nor are they chronic. Violent offenders commit felonies that threaten physical harm. Chronic juvenile offenders offend in repetitive patterns. Figure 17.2 shows the overlap of these types of offenders—some juveniles engage in all three patterns, but most are one type of offender only. And violent offenders are the least frequent.

These differences mean that the offense alone is not enough to predict whether or not the offender is someone of whom we should be afraid. Among juveniles, the rate of false positives (incorrect predictions of dangerousness) is very high. Studies show that instead of relying on the offense alone to identify the highest risk juvenile offenders, we should be concerned about other factors in the juvenile's history. Among them are

- Persistent behavior problems during elementary school years
- Onset of delinquency, aggression, or drug use between the ages of 6 and 11
- Antisocial parents
- Antisocial peers, poor school performance, impulsivity, and weak social ties between the ages of 12 and 14
- Membership in delinquent gangs
- Drug dealing[5]

Disposition of Juvenile Offenders

Annually about 1.7 million juvenile offenders are referred to juvenile court. The first decision made in a juvenile court is whether or not to file a petition of juvenile jurisdiction. If the petition is granted, there is a hearing on the merits of the charges, with the

Figure 17.2   The Overlap of Violent, Serious, and Chronic Juvenile Offenders

The offense types of juvenile offenders who most concern us differ in their patterns in important ways.

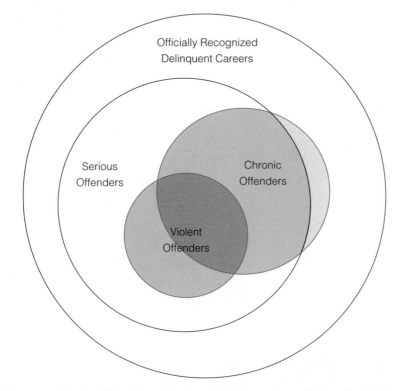

Source: U.S. Department of Justice, Office of Juvenile Justice and Delinquency Prevention, *Juvenile Offenders and Victims: 1997 Update on Violence* (Washington, DC: U.S. Government Printing Office, 1997), p. 25.

intention of making the juvenile a ward of the court, if the charges are sustained. Cases that are not petitioned involve informal dispositions in which the juvenile consents to whichever outcome is determined by the court.

As Figure 17.3 shows, nearly half of the referrals to juvenile court do not result in a petition. Of these cases, nearly half have their charges dismissed, and another one-third are assigned to an informal probation. On rare occasions, nonpetitioned juveniles receive placements, typically in mental health facilities, while more commonly some alternative sanction is agreed to.

When a petition is filed, the court must consider whether it will take jurisdiction in the case. In about 1 percent of cases, jurisdiction is waived to adult court. In the usual case, the juvenile must decide whether or not to contest the charges—if so, an adjudication hearing follows, in which the accuracy of the charges are considered. Almost half the time, the charges are sufficiently minor, the facts in so little dispute, or the likely disposition sufficiently acceptable, that the juvenile waives this hearing and the court proceeds directly to disposition of the charges. Without an adjudication hearing charges

Figure 17.3   Juvenile Court Processing of Delinquency Cases

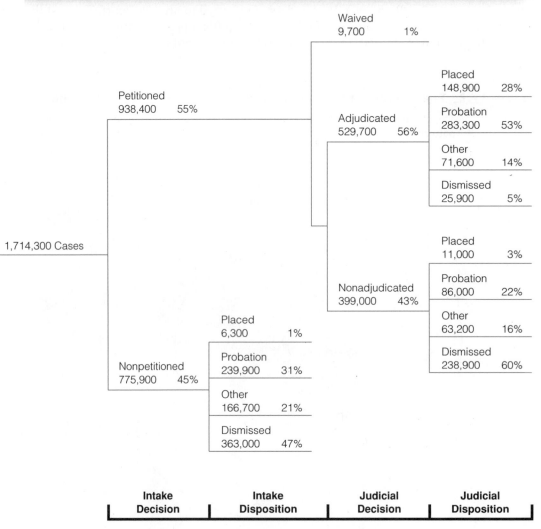

Source: Melissa Sickmund, Anne Stahl, Terrence A. Finnegan, Howard N. Snyder, Rowan S. Poole, and Jeffrey A. Butts, *Juvenile Court Statistics, 1995* (Washington, DC: Office of Juvenile Justice and Delinquency Prevention, 1998).

are usually dismissed. It is also common for the juvenile to accept a probation term or some other moderate penalty.

The juvenile usually contests the charges in the petition if they are serious or the disposition is potentially severe. Rarely (5 percent) is this strategy successful in getting the charges dismissed. And even though the usual disposition is a term of probation, almost one-third of adjudicated offenders get placed — in a reform school, training school, or some other institution for juveniles.

This review of the juvenile justice process shows some reasons why the process has had its critics in recent years. Among adult felons, for example, 82 percent of those convicted of violent crimes receive sentences involving terms of confinement, and 32 percent of those con-

Juveniles sent to reform or training schools live under a strict regime. Here delinquents are marched to school on the center's grounds.

victed of property offenses get incarcerated.[6] This compares to juvenile court dispositions that involve some form of confinement for only 31 percent of juveniles adjudicated for offenses against persons, and 28 percent for property offenses.[7] These differences in outcomes most trouble some observers of the juvenile justice system.

Waiver   Those who are uneasy with the juvenile justice system often favor an increased use of waiver to adult court. Waiver — also referred to as "transfer to adult court" — is an option available when the court believes the circumstances of the case — the seriousness of the charges or the poor prospects of rehabilitation — call for the young person to be handled under adult court procedures and laws. Waiver has been a controversial idea but a recent surge in state legislation to broaden the waiver statutes has increased the number of crime categories that are automatically waived to adult court — especially for serious crimes such as murder and sexual assault.[8]

Despite the public policy outcry about waiver, rates of waiver have stayed almost constant at about 1.4 percent of all petitions since 1985. The only change appears to have been a slight increase in the proportion of African Americans subjected to waiver.[9] There are also questions about the uses of waiver decisions, as most of those juveniles who are transferred to adult court are property offenders, not violent offenders.[10] Among juveniles transferred to adult court for violent crimes, only 59 percent are convicted of that offense, further suggesting that the waiver decision may not automatically be the toughest option for a serious juvenile offender. On the other hand, waiver supporters point out that of those convicted of violent offenses, 79 percent receive an incarceration, a percentage very similar to that for adults.[11] This may seem effective in the long run, but waiver opponents question the value of the results. At least one study suggests that these juveniles may end up serving less actual time in confinement than those not waived on the same type of offense.[12] Also, recent evidence shows that waiver of juveniles to adult court decreases their chances of avoiding crime in the future. One Florida study found that transferred cases were re-arrested more rapidly and more frequently than similar offenders handled in juvenile court, suggesting that adult punishments may actually exacerbate crimes rather than deterring them.[13]

Because the number of juveniles waived to adult court is so small, the number of juveniles serving time in adult facilities is also small. Recent data suggest that less than 8 percent of prisoners are 21 years old or younger, and only about 0.5 percent are 17 or younger. Barely over 100 adult prison inmates are 15 or younger, and only about

1 percent of all prison admissions are juveniles waived to adult court.[14] The young offender in adult facilities is a management problem because of special needs, not because of large numbers.

Diversion   The conceptual opposite of waiver is diversion. Although waiver attempts to avoid the lenient treatment of the juvenile justice system, diversion seeks to avoid burdensome consequences of formal processing. Diversion makes an informal adjustment to the case. It can occur at any stage of the juvenile justice process, but is most often chosen prior to filing formal charges in a petition to the court.

Diversion can take two major forms. The most direct form is simply to stop processing the case, in the expectation that the main objectives of the justice process have been achieved — the juvenile has realized the wrongness of the conduct and has shown a convincing willingness to refrain from it in the future. This form of diversion is seldom final — if the young person returns to court on a new referral, the old charges may be considered again with the new one.

Increasingly, juveniles are diverted to specific programs. This option may be selected when the court determines that the young person's delinquency is a result of certain problems in the child's life that may best be addressed by a program designed to help the juvenile, and the finding of delinquency would not be helpful. These diversion programs often deal with developmental issues such as the child's social skills or response to frustration in school performance. Diversion to mental health treatment for emotionally disturbed youth is also commonly preferred to formal processing.

The logic of diversion is based on the developmental pattern of delinquency. It is thought that most juveniles drift into delinquent behavior as a gradual part of growing up. As their misconduct becomes more serious, they "signal" a need for help to get out of the pathway to delinquency. The diversion strategy tries to provide that help as early as possible. For example, recent studies show that misbehaviors such as stubbornness, resistance to authority, and interpersonal aggressiveness, when they are exhibited at the early, preadolescent ages, are indicative of a risk of later delinquency.[15] Other studies find that truancy is a predictor of later delinquency.[16] That is why diversion programs to help disruptive children learn to cope and to retain children in school are considered important aspects of delinquency prevention, not requiring formal juvenile processing of every child referred to court.

Correctional Programs for Juvenile Offenders   The impact of correctional treatment programs differs from programs for adults in two ways. First, juvenile treatment programs show somewhat greater success than adult programs. And second, the payoff of juvenile treatment programs, when they are successful, is considerably more valuable than adult programs. That is not to say that adult programs lack cost-effectiveness, just that whatever the benefits of adult correctional programming, they appear to be surpassed by their juvenile counterparts.

The research on effectiveness of juvenile correctional programs identifies a handful of particularly promising strategies. Most of these programs are "early intervention" programs, designed to identify children at high risk of delinquency and provide a concentration of services to help them change their destinies. For youngsters aged 11–18, for example, limited basic social skills and poor school performance are two important predictors of delinquency. Programs that increase social interpersonal competence — usually through cognitively oriented skill development strategies — and decrease school failure have been shown to reduce delinquency. For girls, programs that improve family discipline and problem solving also prevent delinquency.[17] There seems to be a growing body of evidence that the systematic support of all aspects of family life for families in which at-risk youth are being raised have both long-term effects of reducing delinquency and antisocial behavior, and also save money.[18]

The money savings can be considerable. A study by Rand Corporation researchers reviewed the size of impact of successful early intervention programs. They found these programs prevented so much delinquency and other social problems that they saved enormous money. One program they studied, for example, was a "graduation incentives" program that established monetary and other incentives for participants who did not drop out of high school, and then provided tutoring and related assistance intensively to help them succeed. This program cost about $12,500 per participant, but statistically speaking, it prevented more than four crimes per participant, and each crime costs well more than the program. Using cost-per-crime estimates, these researchers found that expanding available and proven early intervention programs in California would reduce crime twice as much as expanded use of incarceration, at one-fifth the cost.[19]

Evidence for the value of early intervention for at-risk youth is very strong, yet political support remains weak. A public that is willing to invest billions in bricks and mortar for more prison cells seems to see intervention programs as "soft" social welfare. Until political energy develops for expanding intervention programs, the promised benefit will remain only promises.

Detention Approximately one out of five juvenile arrestees is detained—almost 400,000 per year.[20] Most juvenile detention is very brief, a day or two until there is an initial appearance before a juvenile court judge (or judicial referee, who represents the court in detention hearings). After a petition decision is made, most juveniles are released to their families. But some juveniles, found to endanger others or at risk of flight, are kept in detention for days or weeks until an adjudication hearing can be scheduled.

In all but the largest cities, juveniles are detained by the same authorities and in the same facilities. Federal law requires that juveniles housed in adult jails be segregated from adult prisoners and be taken before a magistrate for an initial appearance within 24 hours of arrival in the facility. As minors under special protection of the court, these juveniles also have legal rights to education and basic services, yet most juveniles receive little special programming.

Nevertheless, such programming clearly should be a priority. Many juveniles in detention have special needs that make treatment appropriate. Juvenile delinquents disproportionately suffer from learning disabilities that make them lag in school performance—time in detention only makes matters worse after release. Still other juveniles are members of gangs, which places them at risk of assault by other members detained in the same facilities. In general, detention centers for juveniles are places where great strides could be made in preventing delinquency by dealing with youth in crisis, but far too little is being done today.[21]

Juvenile Probation The differences between adult and juvenile probation are subtle, and stem from the differences between adult and juvenile offenders, described in the first section of this chapter. Juvenile probation officers often try to develop personal relationships with their clients, something discouraged for adult probation officers. To achieve this bond, juvenile probation officers often engage in recreation with their clients, or accompany them to social activities. Through this bond officers seek the youngster's trust, which they hope will form the basis for long-lasting behavior change. Sometimes officers will mix the child on probation with other young people who are not under court supervision, to further reintegration into more socially acceptable peer relationships. Often adult mentors are used to give children effective role models; mentoring programs reduce antisocial activities and school misbehavior by as much as one-third.[22]

In carrying out supervision the probation officer must work closely with community social service agencies that are involved with the juvenile and the family. Probation officers spend time in the schools, talk to teachers and guidance counselors, and learn about programs for troubled youth. This especially includes recreational programs and youth counseling programs. Probation officers also establish close contact with family service agencies, welfare providers, and programs that support young mothers and provide substitutes for missing fathers. In some respects, the probation officer serves as linchpin for the array of community services that might be used to help a young person stay out of trouble. The Workperspective by Bill Stewart describes his career in juvenile probation.

Although the ideals of rehabilitation and reintegration are important in all community supervision, they receive special emphasis among juvenile probation workers. It is important to recognize, however, that juvenile probation is changing. A sense of unease about how juvenile probation handles serious offending among youth has led

WORKPERSPECTIVE Bill Stewart

Assistant Chief Probation Officer,
Dorchester District Court, Massachusetts

I was introduced to the criminal justice system when, as a teenager, I accompanied my father to two local state prisons where he taught inmates to officiate sports. I was captivated by the attention they paid him and by the faces of the inmates. They did not look different from us but we were going home. They were not.

Criminal justice was my primary interest as a history major in college. For my senior thesis, I arranged to spend a night as an inmate in the county jail. There I learned first-hand what incarceration sounded, smelled, and felt like.

On graduation, I applied for probation positions but was not initially hired, so I taught high school for the next four years. Finally I was hired as a probation officer. I thought that now I would have the chance to really work with "kids" that needed help.

I have worked almost exclusively with youth gangs during the past twelve years. Most of the cases involved assaults or drug sales. With a caseload of 150 to 200, most of my work was in the courthouse, what with all the paperwork and court appearances involved. I became part of "Fortress Probation," dealing with files and not the youths those files represented. Under our job contract, I was only required to do my work from 8:30 A.M.. to 4:30 P.M., the police were expected to supervise my clients.

On November 12, 1992, that role changed when my partner, two Boston police officers, and I took to the streets to enforce terms of probation at night. Five minutes into that first ride, an offender told me that probation and police riding together was not fair, the rules can't be changed. And on that statement "Operation Nite Lite," a police–probation partnership, was founded.

Promoted to assistant chief in 1993, I now co-supervise the Youthful Offender Field Service unit comprised of eight probation officers. These offenders range in age from 17 to 24, the group has the highest recidivism rate and most likely to shoot or be shot. They sign special terms of probation with curfew and area restrictions, and must provide weekly proof of school attendance or work search. The job of the probation officers entails direct supervision in the community through home, job, and school visits during the daytime. On a voluntary basis officers ride with police officers making area and curfew checks on high-risk clients at night. Initially this new community probation was frowned on by many officers as not being part of the job. But it is now a facet of probation that is readily accepted by all officers in the unit because they have seen things change. What was once a simple police–probation partnership has became a multiagency program called "Operation Ceasefire." On a monthly basis, some twenty different agencies, from the U.S. Attorney to police, probation, and community members, sit as equal members at the table exchanging ideas and working together to make our neighborhood safer. We've found we cannot solve all the community's problems, but we can stop the violence.

What this proactive role has taught those of us in probation is that, it is impossible to change an offender while sitting behind a desk. The offender did not get to be like he is yesterday. And he is not going to change his behavior just because we have told him to do so. You have to follow him into his world to really understand him, and to be there when he needs limits set or when he just needs someone to talk with so that he can make sense of the world around him.

to a new interest in the techniques and practices of adult supervision: surveillance and control.

Working in the Schools   Most juveniles spend a significant portion of their day in school—and up to the age of 16, juveniles are required by law to be in school. Juvenile justice agencies—in particular, probation—typically develop school-based programs to increase overall effectiveness with youth under supervision of the juvenile court. School-based programs typically have three objectives: keep potential truants in school, reduce school violence, and increase academic performance of at-risk youths.

Programs have been developed that are effective for each of these objectives. Successful school safety programs focus on reducing bullying behavior and eliminating weapons and drugs on school grounds.[23] School dropout programs create networks of services within the community, and the concentration of efforts seeks to increase the youth's academic self-confidence and personal commitment to staying in school.[24] With over 500,000 juveniles processed by the juvenile justice system returning to public schools, there is a need to find effective programs for these identified, at-risk youth.[25]

Unfortunately, school programs that appear to make sense do not always work as expected. Studies have found, for example, that juveniles who work while in school are more likely to engage in delinquency, and their likelihood of delinquency increases with the hours worked.[26] Thus, work programs that appear to offer youths transitions into adult wage-earner roles may also hasten delinquent involvement.

Intermediate Sanctions for Juveniles   The complaint that few sanctioning options exist between traditional probation and custodial dispositions is perhaps even more true in juvenile justice than in criminal justice. One reason for slowness in developing juvenile intermediate sanctions is that traditional juvenile corrections already resembles intermediate sanctions. Adult probation is interested in intensive supervision as an intermediate sanction, but adult ISP (intensive supervision probation) caseloads are often of about the same size as many traditional juvenile caseloads—in the twenties or thirties. The adult system develops electronic monitored home detention; the juvenile system has routinely used curfews restricting youth to home except during school hours. Community service and restitution have been standard juvenile court dispositions for many years.

Some juvenile probation agencies have begun to develop intensive supervision approaches that are far more intensive than adult ISPs. A juvenile ISP officer may carry 15 cases or fewer, and may well see each client almost on a daily basis—more than once a day if necessary. Police–probation partnerships have been used to strengthen juvenile intensive supervision, because the police can add a component of surveillance to the probation services. Juvenile corrections systems have also developed work-based community service, restitution centers where young people work to pay back the victim, and after-school assignments that minimize free time. Under intermediate sanctioning approaches, juveniles may be required to complete programs to increase awareness of the impact of crimes on victims, and they may be sent to summer camps that require community service labor cleaning parks and other public places.

One of the most widespread new intermediate sanctions for juvenile offenders is "boot camps," described in Chapter 9. As noted there, the results have not been promising. In fact, some studies show that boot camp graduates actually do worse than those placed in other alternatives.[27] This has led to the development of specialized aftercare caseloads of boot-camp graduates, to try to reduce their failure rate.[28]

Juvenile Community Corrections   Despite the lukewarm evaluations of juvenile community corrections (see Chapter 22), interest has continued in this approach, for two main reasons. First, most people realize that removing a young person from the community is an extreme solution, for extreme cases. Disrupting community and family relationships can interfere with long-term prospects for successful adjustment by damaging these already fragile supports. Second, and just as compelling, for most youth the institutional stay will be short — 6 months to a year in custody is very common. Eventually the youth returns to the community, and the real work of successfully adjusting to community life occurs there. Advocates of community corrections ask, "Why wait?"

There are some additional advantages to community corrections for juveniles. The cost of custody in a juvenile training school is usually at least double that for an adult in prison, which means there is more money to work with in creating incentives to keep offenders out of trouble and in designing and implementing effective alternatives in the community. Moreover, public opinion toward youthful offenders is not as harsh as that toward adult offenders, so it is easier to obtain public support for juvenile community corrections. Finally, because youth incarceration numbers are smaller than the adult numbers, it is easier to show success in saving money by diverting offenders to local programs.

A program in Ohio, gaining national acclaim, seeks to return funds to communities that retain juvenile offenders rather than send them to state-run schools. RECLAIM Ohio — Reasoned and Equitable Community and Local Alternatives — provides a significant payback to county leaders who can show that juveniles who might have been sent to training schools paid by state taxes are instead being kept in local, innovative programs designed especially for local needs. The program has proven popular because it appeals to conservative ideals of cost-effective public policy and local control, while appealing to liberal beliefs in rehabilitation of juvenile offenders.[29]

Juvenile Incarceration   A wide variety of facilities are designed for the secure placement of juveniles: foster homes, residential centers, reform schools, and training schools. These places vary in the degree of security and the amount of programming available. We will describe them in the order of the degree of close custody they provide.

Foster homes and residential centers typically take small numbers of delinquents. These locations are not considered punitive — judges use foster homes and residential centers when the juvenile's family cannot provide an adequate setting for the child's development. Foster homes are often run by a married couple, and children live in them, sometimes as cohabitants with the adults' biological children. The court pays the couple a per diem fee for each foster child, usually not enough to cover all the expenses involved, and the adults in the home provide supervision in cooperation with probation officers. Foster children attend the local school system and operate under whatever restrictions the foster parents and probation officer deem suitable — curfews, associations, leisure activities, and the like. Residential centers operate much like foster homes, with residents attending locals schools and living under limited numbers of restrictions. The main difference is that residential centers are run by professional staff, not adult volunteers. It may also be the case that a small amount of residential treatment programming occurs in residential centers, usually group counseling sessions.

Reform schools and training schools offer far less freedom to the child placed within them, do not hesitate to impose a strict regime, and see one of their functions as punishment. These twenty-four-hour facilities allow the residents very limited freedom. School is on campus, and the residents also do work to maintain the facilities. In almost every way, reform schools and training schools are the equivalent of adult prisons, developed for adolescents under custody. So they have some of the same problems that plague adult prisons and jails: violence, sexual assault, staff–resident conflict, and disciplinary problems of control. Because the residents are younger and somewhat more volatile than adults, behavioral control is often an everyday issue, fights and aggression are common. Poor management practices, such as those described in Do the Right Thing, can lead to difficult situations.

D O   T H E   Right   T H I N G

Residents of the Lovelock Home had been committed by the juvenile court because they were either delinquent or neglected. All twenty-five boys, aged 7 to 15, were streetwise, tough, and interested only in getting out. The institution had a staff of social services professionals who tried to deal with the educational and psychological needs of the residents. Because state funding was short, these services looked better in the annual report than to an observer visiting Lovelock. Most of the time the residents watched television, played basketball in the backyard, or just hung out in one another's rooms.

Joe Klegg, the night supervisor, was tired from the eight-hour shift that he had just completed on his "second job" as a daytime convenience-store manager. The boys were watching television when he arrived at seven. Everything seemed calm. It should have been, because Joe had placed a tough 15-year-old, Randy Marshall, in charge. Joe had told Randy to keep the younger boys in line. Randy used his muscle and physical presence to intimidate the other residents. He knew that if the home was quiet and there was no trouble, he would be rewarded with special privileges such as a "pass" to go see his girlfriend. Joe wanted no hassles and a quiet house so that he could doze off when the boys went to sleep.

Does the situation at Lovelock Home raise ethical questions, or does it merely raise questions of poor management practices? What are the potential consequences for the residents? For Joe Klegg? What is the state's responsibility? ■

Juvenile Aftercare   The term *aftercare* refers to services provided to juveniles after they have been *placed*—removed from their home and put under some form of custodial care. Aftercare operates in a way similar to adult parole. It receives juveniles who have been under some form of custody—typically the state's training school, but sometimes a foster home or residential placement—and provides supervision and support during the period of readjustment to community life. The importance of aftercare rests on the fact that youth face significant obstacles of adjustment after they have been away from their homes, and the chances of failure for such youth are quite high.

Aftercare workers know that youth who have been returned from confinement face significant adjustment problems and require substantial attention and support. First of all, a youth who has been placed in a custodial setting by the court has either engaged in some form of serious criminal behavior or has shown a pattern of persistent disobedience of less serious laws and of court-ordered rules of behavior. In either case, there is a potential for trouble. The serious offender has committed a frightening crime and faces a fearful community, a family that may not welcome the return, and a school system that doubts the juvenile's readiness to behave. The persistent delinquent has been a source of trouble to family, neighbors, school officials, and others, and will not be received with open arms. The aftercare worker negotiates the return to the community by helping the juvenile understand the community's apprehension, while showing the community evidence that the juvenile deserves a second chance.

The aftercare worker also must closely follow the adjustment, even while advocating for the juvenile. The risk of recidivism is high enough that the community feels a stake in the aftercare scrutiny. All involved in the aftercare system recognize that a careful balance is needed between support and control, because these juveniles include the most serious cases in the juvenile justice system. By the same token, much is to be gained. When an aftercare worker can successfully negotiate a juvenile through the first months of return to the community, a lifetime of crime can be avoided.

Antonio Fernandez, Latin King's gang leader and fellow member Dennis Capello, form the gang symbol of a crown outside of Federal court in New York City. Their deposed leader, Luis Felipe, is on trial on charges of orchestrating the murder of his rivals.

The Special Problem of Gangs

No discussion of juvenile justice would be complete without a comment on the special problem of gangs. It is estimated that America has over 840,000 gang members operating in over 31,000 gangs,[30] and that these young offenders are involved in over half a million serious crimes.[31] Studies show that gangs vary widely in makeup, and it is important to bear in mind that most gangs are not violent and many gang members engage in positive as well as negative social behaviors. An important distinction must also be made between traditional street gangs that provide the social connections that many adolescents need and that engage in varieties of criminal conduct, and drug gangs that are organized into cohesive business structures and often use violence as a method of business.

Gangs permeate the work of correctional officials. In custodial facilities, they offer a profound challenge to control the population and to manage the potential for intergang conflict. In community settings, gangs provide hostile competition to the prosocial programs developed by correctional leaders. For the community, gangs are a primary source of fear and peril. Especially where gang members are armed, the presence of the gang can be a central destabilizing force in neighborhood life.

Recent initiatives have shown some success with gangs. One of the most impressive has been the Boston Gun Project, described in the Focus box.[32] This project involved a coordinated effort of prosecutors, probation officers, street gang workers, and police, to target gun use by gang members. They focused on "getting the message out" that gun violence would not be tolerated, and they backed it up by prosecuting fully any gang member found involved in a gun crime. Homicides went down from weekly events to near zero, within the first year.

The Future of Juvenile Justice

High-profile gang criminality and the recent spate of school shootings has ended the anonymity of juvenile correctional work. Public policymakers are turning their attention to the juvenile justice system, and there is reason to think that the decades of reform in adult corrections since the 1970s will be replayed in the juvenile justice arena. What will this mean?

The public is today enamored of "get-tough" measures, and we are already beginning to see the influence of this thinking on juvenile justice. There is more pressure to increase waiver of serious juveniles to the adult court, where their sentences may be longer and their punishments harsher. Local political leaders call for tougher probation, and training schools populations are growing. These are all the familiar echoes of changes in the adult criminal justice system, and few are surprised to see them arising again in respect to juveniles, now that the public spotlight has landed there.

It is unlikely, however, that the reform process for juveniles will exactly reproduce the adult process. No matter how the extreme case is portrayed in the papers, the everyday juvenile offender remains unsophisticated and susceptible to change under appropriate programs. Most juvenile crime is still minor misbehavior, not at all like the highly charged cases of serious violence that dominate the news. To paint all

FOCUS

Operation Ceasefire and Operation Nite Lite

On November 12, 1992, Boston probation officers Bill Stewart and Rick Skinner accepted an offer from their friends, police officers Bob Merner and Bob Fratalia to spend Saturday evening in the back seat of a squad car touring the streets of Dorchester, a troubled inner-city area. Merner and Fratalia were members of the police department's gang unit who had been collaborating with probation officers in efforts to deal with a growing problem of gang violence in another troubled neighborhood, Roxbury.

A few hours into the evening, the cruising police car got an emergency call reporting a gunshot victim in a nearby street. Arriving at the scene, the four saw a crowd of about twenty-five residents — mostly young men — milling around a face-down body, dead from a bullet to the head. This was a familiar scene to the police, but the presence of the probation officers gave it a new twist. Stewart and Skinner recognized many of the bystanders as young men on probation and under curfew orders, who were out on the town. The victim also turned out to be one of Stewart's probationers. In all, perhaps a dozen curfew-violating probationers were at the scene. As Stewart recalls, "They were amazed to see me out there at night with the cops. They tried to cover their faces. They knew that, unlike the cops, I could recognize them." Officer Fratalia was also amazed. Bystanders at a crime scene normally claim to have seen nothing, but Stewart was able to elicit information from the young people who faced having their probation revoked for curfew breaking.

Out of this experience Operation Nite Lite, the simple idea of enforcing juvenile probation curfews, was born. Operation Nite Lite brings probation into the field and aims probation services at juvenile gang members with guns. Where gang violence is a serious problem, there can be no higher priority than reducing gang street violence.

Operation Nite Lite is a part of a broader effort in Boston known as Operation Ceasefire, a coordinated attempt to end gang gun violence. Ceasefire is based on the knowledge that a few offenders account for a substantial proportion of all crime and that these offenders are often concentrated in particular city neighborhoods.

Operation Ceasefire uses two strategies. First, interagency collaboration identifies individuals and gangs at risk for committing violence. A task force of federal, state, and municipal criminal justice and social service agencies regularly meet to share information, identify gang members to be targeted, discuss tactics to increase investigation effectiveness, and to develop a repertoire of interventions and strategies.

A second strategy is aimed at increasing deterrence through swift and certain sanctioning. When a violent act is committed, the various agencies can at their discretion not only arrest suspects, but also shut down drug markets, strictly enforce probation restrictions, make disorder arrests, deal more strictly with cases in adjudication, deploy federal enforcement power, and so on.

Operation Ceasefire develops in gang members a new set of expectations regarding violent behavior. When gang members seek rehabilitative services, the program assists them. But when they persist in violent activity, the coordinated agencies hit them with undesirable sanctions until the violence stops.

The Boston program has been going strong since late 1992, and has had unexpected success. Firearm homicides have dropped from 65 per year to 21. Firearm homicides by juveniles have dropped from 10 to an astounding 0 for two years running. National attention has been focused on Boston's success story.

Source: Todd R. Clear and David R. Karp, *Community Justice: Preventing Crime and Achieving Justice, Report to the National Institute of Justice* (Tallahassee: Florida State University, 1999).

juvenile offenders with a broad, adult criminal brush would not only be unwise, but also inaccurate.

So some middle ground will be found. The relative anonymity of the juvenile justice system is past. Juvenile justice policy and practice will be scrutinized, and pressured to conform to the stricter adult system. Few observers will note the irony that even as the pressure mounts to toughen juvenile justice, dissatisfaction remains high with the adult model toward which they are moving.

Summary

The history of juvenile justice in the United States can be divided into five periods: Puritan, House of Refuge, juvenile rights, and crime control. Creation of the juvenile court in 1899 established a separate juvenile justice system dealing with delinquency, neglected children, and dependent children. The philosophy of juvenile justice is based on the assumption that decisions should be in the best interest of the child. This requires that police officers, judges, and correctional workers be granted discretion so as to tailor decisions that best meet this goal. However, under some circumstances judges may waive jurisdiction and a juvenile may be dealt with in the adult criminal justice system.

The juvenile justice system operates its own agencies for institutional and community correctional functions. The differences between juveniles and adults are reflected in the practices of juvenile justice agencies, as the main objective is to move these errant children toward responsible adulthood. Programs in juvenile justice have not always been effective in achieving this goal. In this country, the juvenile justice system has been criticized both for being too lenient and for insufficiently protecting juveniles' rights. ■

For Discussion

1. How has the experience of growing up changed over the last few centuries? Why are these changes important for juvenile justice?
2. How do the differences between adults and juveniles affect policies in juvenile justice? How are adults and juveniles similar under the law?
3. Are the many differences in terminology between the adult and juvenile systems important? Why or why not?
4. In what ways do juvenile institutions differ from adult institutions? How does this affect institutional management? What does it mean for juveniles who are housed in adult facilities?
5. Should we have a separate juvenile justice system? Why or why not?

For Further Reading

Chesney-Lind, Meda, and Randall G. Sheldon. *Girls: Delinquency and Juvenile Justice.* Pacific Grove, CA: Brooks/Cole, 1992. Reviews the literature on girls who get into trouble with the law. Includes types and extent of delinquency with an overview of the special problems juvenile justice faces in responding to female delinquents.

Decker, Scott H., and Barick Van Winkle. *Life in the Gang: Families, Friends, and Violence.* New York: Cambridge University Press, 1996. Follows the life of a juvenile gang in St. Louis for a year, documenting their trouble with the law. Examines juvenile justice efforts to deal with family and community problems.

Glick, Barry, and William Sturgeon. *No Time to Play: Youthful Offenders in Adult Correctional Systems.* Lanham, MD: American Correctional Association, 1998. Analyzes programmatic, management, and policy issues involved with juvenile offenders housed in adult facilities.

McCall, Nathan. *Makes Me Wanna Holler: A Young Black Man in America.* New York: Random House, 1994. Describes the problems faced by young black males in contemporary society.

Puntz, Patricia, and Mary Ann Scali. *Beyond The Walls: Improving Conditions of Confinement for Youth in Custody.* Washington, DC: Office of Juvenile Justice and Delinquency Prevention, January 1998. Discusses attempts to develop innovative and effective treatment programs in juvenile institutions.

Notes

1. Jeffrey A. Butts and Howard Snyder, "The Youngest Delinquents: Offenders Under the Age of 15," *Juvenile Justice Bulletin* (Washington, DC: U.S. Department of Justice, 1997).
2. Howard S. Snyder, "Juvenile Arrests in 1996," *Juvenile Justice Bulletin* (Washington, DC: U.S. Department of Justice, November 1997).
3. Anthony Platt, *The Child Savers: The Invention of Delinquency* (Chicago: University of Chicago Press, 1970).
4. *Juvenile Offenders and Victims* (Washington, DC: Office of Juvenile Justice and Delinquency Prevention, February 1996), p. 20.
5. Snyder, *Serious and Violent Juvenile Offenders* (Pittsburgh, PA: National Center for Juvenile Justice, 1997).
6. Patrick Langan and Jodi Brown, *Felony Sentences in State Courts* (Washington, DC: Bureau of Justice Statistics, U.S. Department of Justice, January 1997), p. 4.

7. *Juvenile Court Statistics, 1995* (Washington, DC: Office of Juvenile Justice and Delinquency Prevention, May 1998), p. 10.

8. Jeffrey A. Butts and Adele V. Harrell, "Delinquents or Criminals: Policy Options for Young Offenders," *Crime Policy Report* (Washington, DC: Urban Institute, 1998), p. 8.

9. Carol J. DeFrances and Kevin J. Strom, *Juveniles Prosecuted in State Criminal Courts* (Washington, DC: Office of Juvenile Justice and Delinquency Prevention, U.S. Department of Justice, March 1997), p. 4.

10. James C. Howell, "Juvenile Transfers to Criminal Court," *Juvenile and Family Justice Today*, 6(1), Spring 1997, p. 14.

11. Kevin J. Strom, Steven K. Smith, and Howard N. Snyder, *Juvenile Felony Defendants in Criminal Courts* (Washington, DC: Bureau of Justice Statistics, U.S. Department of Justice, September 1998), p. 6.

12. Eric J. Fritsch, Tony J. Caetti, and Craig Hemmons, "Spare the Needle but Not the Punishment: The Incarceration of Waived Youth in Texas Prisons," *Crime and Delinquency*, 42(4), October 1996, pp. 593–609.

13. Lawrence Winner, Lonn Lanza-Kaduce, Donna M. Bishop, and Charles E. Frazier, "The Transfer of Juveniles to Criminal Court: Re-examining Recidivism over the Long Term," *Crime and Delinquency*, 43(4), October 1997, pp. 548–563.

14. Dale Parent, Terence Dunworth, Douglas McDonald, and William Rhodes, *Transferring Serious Juvenile Offenders to Adult Courts* (Washington, DC: National Institute of Justice, U.S. Department of Justice, January 1997), p. 5.

15. Barbara Tatem Kelley, Rolph Loeber, Kate Keenan, and Mary DeLamatre, *Developmental Pathways in Boy's Disruptive and Delinquent Behavior* (Washington, DC: Office of Juvenile Justice and Delinquency Prevention, U.S. Department of Justice, December 1997).

16. Eileen M. Gary, *Truancy: First Step to a Lifetime of Problems* (Washington DC: Office of Juvenile Justice and Delinquency Prevention, U.S. Department of Justice, October 1996).

17. Gottfredson, Denise C., M. D. Sealock, and C. S. Koper, "Delinquency," in R. J. DiClemente, W. B. Hansen, and L. E. Ponton, eds., *Handbook for Adolescent Youth Risk Behavior* (New York: Plenum, 1996).

18. Hirokazu Yoshikawa, "Long-Term Effects of Early Childhood Programs on Social Outcomes and Delinquency," *The Future of Children*, 5(3), Winter 1995, pp. 51–75.

19. Peter W. Greenwood, Karyn E. Model, C. Peter Rydell, and James Chiesa, *Diverting Children from a Life of Crime: Measuring Costs and Benefits* (Santa Monica: Rand, April 1996).

20. *Juvenile Court Statistics, 1995* (Washington, DC: Office of Juvenile Justice and Delinquency Prevention, U.S. Department of Justice, May 1998), p. 7.

21. Kenneth E. Kerle, "Juveniles," in *American Jails: Looking to the Future* (Boston: Butterworth-Heinmann, 1998).

22. Jean Baldwin Grossman and Eileen M. Garry, *Mentoring — A Proven Delinquency Prevention Strategy* (Washington, DC: Office of Juvenile Justice and Delinquency Prevention, U.S. Department of Justice, April 1997).

23. June L. Arnette and Marjorie C. Walsleben, *Combating Fear and Restoring Safety in the Schools* (Washington, DC: Office of Juvenile Justice and Delinquency Prevention, U.S. Department of Justice, April 1998).

24. Sharon Cantelon and Donni LeBoeuf, *Keeping Young People in School: Community Programs That Work* (Washington DC, Office of Juvenile Justice and Delinquency Prevention, U.S. Department of Justice, June 1997).

25. Sarah Ingersoll and Donni LeBeouf, *Reaching Out to Youth Out of the Education Mainstream* (Washington, DC: Office of Juvenile Justice and Delinquency Prevention, U.S. Department of Justice, February 1997).

26. John Paul Wright, Francis T. Cullen, and Nicholas Williams, "Working While in School and Delinquent Involvement: Implications for Social Policy," *Crime and Delinquency*, 43(2), April 1997, pp. 203–221.

27. Michael Peters, David Thomas, and Christopher Zamberlan, *Boot Camps for Juvenile Offenders* (Washington, DC: Office of Juvenile Justice and Delinquency Prevention, U.S. Department of Justice, September 1997).

28. Blair B. Bourque, Mei Han, and Sarah M. Hill, *A National Survey of Aftercare Provisions for Boot Camp Graduates* (Washington, DC: National Institute of Justice, U.S. Department of Justice, May 1966).

29. Melissa M. Moon, Brandon K. Applegate, and Edward J. Latessa, "RECLAIM Ohio: A Politically Viable Alternative to Treating Youthful Felony Offenders," *Crime and Delinquency*, October 1997, pp. 438–456.

30. James C. Howell, *Youth Gangs: An Overview* (Washington, DC: Office of Juvenile Justice and Delinquency Prevention, U.S. Department of Justice, August 1998).

31. David Curry, Richard A. Ball, and Scott H. Decker, *Estimating the National Scope of Gang Crime from Law Enforcement Data* (Washington, DC: National Institute of Justice, U.S. Department of Justice, August 1966).

32. David M. Kennedy, Anne M. Piehl, and Anthony A. Braga, "Youth Violence in Boston: Gun Markets, Serious Youth Offenders, and a Use-Reduction Strategy," *Law and Contemporary Problems*, 59(1), 1996, pp. 147–184.

PART THREE

Correctional Issues and Perspectives

As Americans begin the twenty-first century, corrections

is confronted by a number of issues concerning current

practices and future trends. In Part 3 we examine

several of these issues and look at new developments

as the corrections system faces the future.

CHAPTER EIGHTEEN
Incarceration Trends

Anyone who is at all attentive to public issues knows that the United States has a large and expanding prison population. Extensive media coverage of the increased number of Americans in prison makes the issue difficult to ignore. Incarceration rates in the United States are second only to Russia in the developed world. The United States has ten times the population of Canada but about thirty-five times the prison population.[1] Observers believe that since the middle of the 1970s the United States has been engaged in an experiment testing the proposition that crime can be reduced if a greater number of offenders are imprisoned.[2] Paradoxically, although crime in the United States has been declining for the past six years, the incarceration rate continues to climb. It has been suggested that the imprisonment boom of the past decade has developed a built-in dynamic that is independent of changes in the crime rate.[3]

Over the past decade the incarceration rate has more than doubled. Since 1990 the prison population has grown at an average of 7.7 percent each year, a trend that shows no sign of abating.[4] One response has been to build more institutions, resulting in a prison construction boom and increased employment of correctional officers. Correctional budgets have climbed an average of 8 percent annually since 1986, and many states have diverted money from education, welfare, and health programs to meet the soaring needs of corrections. Five states now have corrections budgets of more than $1 billion per year. California is the leader, spending $3.6 billion on operations and another $500 million on new prison construction.[5]

The increase in the prison population has led to calls for a moratorium on further construction and the development of intermediate punishments to remove from prisons those who "don't belong" there. However, supporters of current policies argue that the prison population is high because the level of violent crime in the United States is also high. Some researchers have even argued that the costs to society of incarcerating some types of criminals is less than the cost of their remaining on the streets.

In this chapter we explore explanations for the recent rise in incarceration. We also consider ways to deal with the crowding crisis and examine the impact of crowding on prison systems. Finally, we evaluate the argument that incarceration is cost effective for society.

Questions FOR INQUIRY

1. What explanations are given for the dramatic increase in the incarceration rate?
2. What can be done to deal with the prison population crisis?
3. What is the impact of prison crowding?
4. Does incarceration pay?

Explaining Prison Population Trends

For most of the past fifty years the numbers of persons incarcerated in the United States remained fairly stable.[6] During the 1940s and 1950s, the incarceration rate was maintained at about 110 per 100,000 population. For a brief period in the 1960s, when rehabilitation and community corrections was stressed, the incarceration rate actually decreased. However, since 1973, when the overall crime rate started to level off, the incarceration rate has almost quadrupled. As criminologist Alfred Blumstein asks, "With so dramatic an increase in the incarceration rate, why have we not seen a significant decline in the crime rates?"[7]

As noted by Allen Beck of the Bureau of Justice Statistics, this growth has brought about dramatic changes in the demographic and offense composition of the prison population. African Americans and Hispanics make up a larger percentage of inmates than

Figure 18.1 Incarceration Rate per 100,000 Population, 1940–1998

Between 1940 and 1973 the incarceration rate held steady. Only since 1975 has there been a continuing increase. The rate today is more than double what it was in 1985.

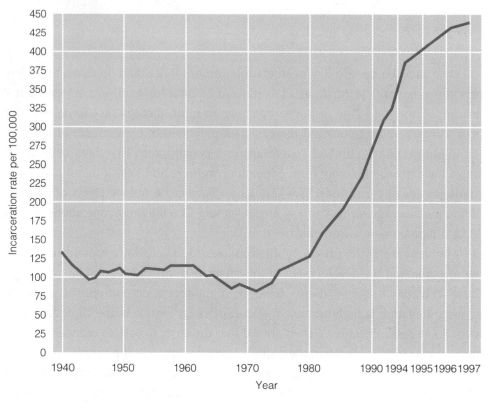

SOURCE: U.S. Department of Justice, Bureau of Justice Statistics, *Bulletin* (Washington, DC: U.S. Government Printing Office, August 1998).

ever. Prisoners are more likely to be middle-aged, and more women are being incarcerated. Since 1980 the percentage of inmates serving time for violent offenses has declined, and the number incarcerated for drug violations has increased.[8]

Every June and December the Bureau of Justice Statistics takes a census of the U.S. prison population. As Figure 18.1 shows, from a low of 98 per 100,000 population in 1972, the incarceration rate has steadily risen, and by the end of 1997 it was 445. The census found 1,244,554 men and women in state and federal *prisons.* An additional 567,079 were being held in local *jails.*[9]

But it is important to emphasize that the size and growth of the prison population is not evenly distributed across the country. As Figure 18.2 shows, seven of the ten states with the highest incarceration rates are in the South. In 1997 the South incarcerated 506 people for each 100,000 inhabitants, a ratio much higher than the national average of 445.[10] Because Arizona, California, and Nevada are included in the top ten, the South is not alone with high incarceration rates.

Many argue that southern attitudes toward crime and punishment account for that region's high prison population. The penal codes in many southern states provide for the longest sentences, and inmates there spend extended periods in institutions. It is also the region with the highest African-American population, which is incarcerated in numbers far greater than its proportion of the overall population. Research by Edmund McGarrell found that states with proportionately large African American populations have more punitive traditions, leading to greater use of incarceration as a response to crime.[11]

The skyrocketing prison population has created a correctional crisis of overcrowding. In many states new inmates have been crowded into already bulging institutions, some making do in corridors and basements. At year end 1997, 34,000 state prisoners were

Figure 18.2   Sentenced Prisoners in State Institutions per 100,000 Civilians, December 31, 1997

What can be said about the differences in incarceration rates among the states? There are not only regional differences but also differences among adjacent states that seem to have similar socioeconomic and crime characteristics.

WA 233
OR 232
MT 255
ND 112
MN 113
NH 184
VT 140
ME 129
ID 323
SD 303
WI 283
NY 386
MA 278
WY 326
NE 200
IA 243
MI 457
PA 291
RI 213
NJ 351
CT 397
NV 518
UT 205
CO 342
IL 342
IN 301
OH 429
DE 443
CA 475
KS 304
MO 442
WV 174
VA 407
MD 413
D.C. 1,682
AZ 484
NM 256
OK 617
AR 392
KY 372
TN 309
NC 370
SC 536
MS 531
AL 500
GA 472
TX 717
LA 672
AK 420
FL 437
HI 288

SOURCE: U.S. Department of Justice, Bureau of Justice Statistics, *Bulletin* (Washington, DC: U.S. Government Printing Office, August 1998), p. 3.

being held in county jails until prison space becomes available.[12] Judges in some states have demanded changes, because they believe the crowding violates the Constitution.

In most states prison construction has become a growth industry, with massive public expenditures for new facilities that are often filled as soon as they open. Today many states spend more on the incarceration of offenders than on higher education, and many have cut spending for poor children while increasing prison spending.[13]

Why this increase? As we have noted, there seems to be little relationship between the crime rate and the incarceration rate. If this is now the case, what factors explain the growth? Here we will explore five reasons often cited for the increase: (1) demographic change, (2) increased arrests and higher probability of incarceration, (3) tougher sentencing, (4) prison construction, (5) and the war on drugs. None of these reasons should be viewed as a single explanation. Rather, each contributes to the equation, with some having a greater impact than others.

Demographic Change

The size of the prison population is influenced by the number of people "at risk"—that is, those most likely to commit crimes and be sent to prison. Criminologists have long considered men between the ages of 16 and 24 to be "crime prone." Much of the rise in crime during the early years of the 1970s was attributed to the fact that the "baby boomers," the large cohort of people born in the years immediately after World War II, had reached their crime-prone years by 1968. Whereas arrest rates begin to peak around age 18, rates of imprisonment do not peak until age 25. Only after successive periods of probation or of incarceration in youth facilities or in jail does the average young offender graduate to state or federal prison.

Analysts in the late 1970s attributed the rise in incarceration to the fact that members of the baby boom cohort were now entering correctional institutions. At that time many criminal justice planners argued that the rise in prison populations during the early 1980s was only a temporary phenomenon reflecting the passage of baby boomers through their life cycle.[14] If states could weather this temporary increase, prison populations would re-

Not only has the number of arrests increased, but so has the likelihood of going to prison upon conviction.

turn to "normal" levels. However, more recent research by Patrick Langan has shown that demographic factors account for only about 20 percent of the prison population explosion of the 1980s.[15] The decrease in crime during the 1990s has been attributed by many to the small size of the young male ("crime prone") cohort, yet there has been no corresponding decline in incarceration.

Increased Arrests and More Likely Incarceration

Some analysts have argued that the billions spent by federal, state, and local governments on the crime problem may be paying off. When the crime rate began to rise dramatically in the mid-1960s, the incarceration rate was proportionally low. Crime rates for serious offenses have now declined, but arrest rates have gone up. Between 1980 and 1990 the adult arrest rate increased by 45 percent, yet for some offenses the growth was much greater. For example, drug violations up 114 percent, aggravated assault up 74 percent, and sexual assaults other than rape up 60 percent. In recent years arrest rates for most serious crimes have dropped.[16]

Compounding the impact of more adult arrests for serious offenses is the increased probability of being sent to prisons on conviction. Reacting to public opinion and legislative actions, judges have been more willing to sentence serious offenders to incarceration. As Figure 18.3 shows, between 1980 and 1994 (the latest available data) the likelihood of incarceration on arrest increased fivefold for drug violations, fourfold for weapons offenses, and twofold for larceny-theft, motor vehicle theft, and sexual assault other than rape. For only one crime—murder/nonnegligent manslaughter—did the likelihood of incarceration decrease.[17]

Not only is the probability of a prison sentence greater today than in the past, but also increased numbers of offenders are being sent to prison for probation and parole violations. In 1980 82.4 percent of those entering prison did so directly as a result of a court sentence. This percentage dropped to 64.5 percent in 1994, reflecting increase in number of inmates sent to prison for violating conditions of probation or parole. Beck's analysis shows that 42 percent of the growth in total admissions to state prisons from 1980 to 1994 can be attributed to this factor.[18]

Tougher Sentencing Practices

Some observers hold that a hardening public attitude toward criminals is reflected in longer sentences, in a smaller proportion of those convicted being granted probation, and in fewer inmates being released at the time of their first parole hearing.

As discussed in Chapter 4, in the past two decades the states and the federal government have passed laws that increase sentences for most crimes. In addition, new mandatory sentencing laws greatly limit the discretion of judges with regard to the length of sentences for certain offenders. The shift to determinate sentences, the new truth-in-sentencing laws, and a drop in the percentage of prisoners released on their first appearance before the parole board, has increased the amount of time served for most offenses.

The tougher sentences do not seem to be the major factor in keeping offenders incarcerated for longer periods. Since the 1980s the likelihood of being incarcerated has risen but the average maximum sentence has remained about constant at six years to state prison and six and a half to federal prison.[19] Even with the increasing use of mandatory

Figure 18.3 Commitments to State Prison Relative to Arrests for Selected Offenses, 1980 and 1994

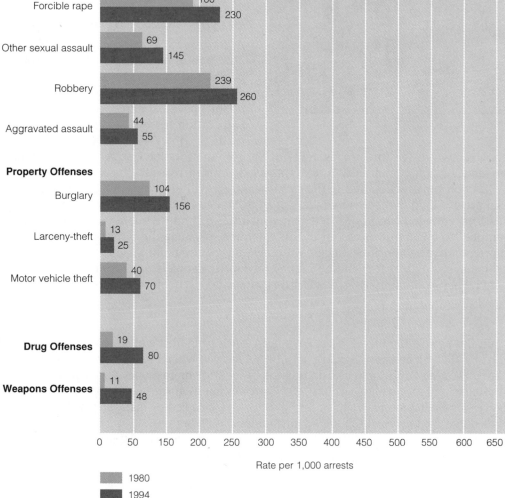

Not only have there been more arrests, but for most offenses a greater proportion of those arrested are sent to prison.

Rate per 1,000 arrests

1980
1994

Source: Allen J. Beck, "Growth, Change, and Stability in the U.S. Prison Population, 1980–1995," *Corrections Management Quarterly*, 1, Spring 1997, p. 11.

minimum sentences and sentencing enhancements during that period, the percentage of inmates who received a maximum sentence of ten years or longer declined.

What has changed is the increasing amount of time actually served.[20] Release from state prison is usually by parole board, whereas federal offenders sentenced under the Sentencing Reform Act of 1984 must serve at least 85 percent of the sentence. Today a smaller percentage of state inmates are being released on their first appearance before the parole board than in 1980. The number of releases relative to the number of inmates dropped from 37 per 100 state prisoners in 1990 to 31 per 100 in 1996.[21] The new federal sentencing law and the tighter state parole release policies partially explain the growth of the prison population.

The doubling of the incarceration rate has created a boom in the prison construction industry. Many people now wonder if it is possible for a state to build itself out of the crowding crisis.

Thus the combination of longer time served and fewer releases presents an anomalous situation. From 1990 to 1996 the number of inmates climbed 60 percent, however, the number of new admissions rose grew only 17 percent during those years.[22] Keeping people in prison longer seems to account for much of the growth of incarcerated population.

Prison Construction

According to organization theorists, available public resources such as hospitals, parks, and so on, are used to their fullest capacity. Prisons are no exception. When prison space is limited, judges reserve incarceration for only the most violent offenders. However, when new cells are constructed those same judges may not hesitate to sentence less serious offenders to prison. Creation of additional prison space may thus increase the incarceration rate.

Prison construction during the 1990s was a growth industry with 213 state and federal prisons built in the first five years at an estimated $30 billion.[23] For health and safety reasons, crowded conditions in existing facilities cannot be tolerated. Many states attempted to build their way out of this dilemma, because the public seemed to favor more punitive sentencing policies, which would require more prison space. Yet opinion polls have shown that spending money for more prisons is not a high priority for the general public. If the issue is new prisons versus new schools, education wins.[24]

The War on Drugs

Crusades against the use of drugs have been a recurring theme of American politics since the late 1800s. The latest manifestation began in 1982 when President Ronald Reagan declared "War on Drugs" and asked Congress to set aside more money for drug enforcement personnel and for prison space. In 1987 Congress imposed stiff mandatory minimum sentences for federal drug law violations, laws that were copied by many states. The war continued into the Bush and Clinton administrations, with both presidents urging Congress to appropriate billions for an all-out law enforcement campaign against drugs.

The War on Drugs has succeeded on one front by packing the nation's prisons with drug law offenders, but many scholars believe that's about all it has achieved.[25] With additional resources and pressures for enforcement, the number of people sentenced to prison for drug offenses has increased steadily. In 1980 only 19 per 1,000 of new court commitments to state prisons were for drug offenses; by 1994 this had risen to 80 per 1,000. Today, 23 percent of state prisoners are incarcerated for drug offenses and the percentage in federal prisons is even higher, at almost 60 percent.[26]

Public Policy Trends

It is difficult to point to one factor as the major cause of the doubling of the incarceration rate during the past decade. As we've seen, a number of plausible hypotheses exist. But as Connecticut's former commissioner of corrections, Larry Meachum, has noted, "Prison population is not driven by crime. It is driven by public policy."[27] Public policies are forged in the political arena. Politicians are aware that the public is concerned about crime, have little sympathy for offenders, and support increased punishments. In this political environment correctional policies have emerged in Congress and in state legislatures based on the assumption that crime can be controlled through greater use of incarceration. Alfred Blumstein has noted that in a democracy political leaders respond to public demands to deal with a problem such as crime. However, as he also notes, demands for increased punishments do not solve the problem, but merely alleviate the political pressure to "do something."[28]

To "do something" about crime, government leaders have enacted policies designed to incarcerate a greater number of offenders for longer periods of time. This objective has been implemented through increased law enforcement and prosecution spending, mandatory sentencing laws, truth in sentencing requirements, enhanced drug law enforcement, and tough parole policies. But it is not clear that these policies have been successful.[29] Proponents of the policies argue that the decline in crime can be attributed to the fact that large numbers of criminals are in prison. However, some critics argue that incarcerating vast numbers of offenders is extremely expensive and has harmed society, especially in poor, minority communities.

Given current public attitudes toward crime and punishment, fear of crime, continued (but decreasing) high crime rates, and the expansion of prison space, incarceration rates likely will remain high. Perhaps only when the costs of this form of punishment have a greater impact on the pockets of taxpayers will attitudes and policies shift, with a greater emphasis being placed on alternatives to incarceration. At present, however, correctional administrators and policy makers must deal with the problem of crowded prisons.

Dealing with the Prison Population Crisis

At year end 1997, thirty-six states and the federal prison system reported operating at 100 percent of capacity or more. The federal system was estimated to be operating at 19 percent, and overall the state systems were operating at 15 percent above capacity.[30] Crowded prisons may violate constitutional standards, increase violence, decrease access to programs and services, and create major administrative problems.

The increase in the prison population comes at a time when the public seems to be urging a more punitive approach to crime yet seems reluctant to provide the money to carry out such a policy. Further, given the lag time of up to seven years from authorization of a prison construction project until completion, the immediate demand for space cannot be satisfied. Thus states are adopting a variety of strategies to manage prison crowding, a problem that exists in all states and that has a definite impact on corrections nationally. A mixture of approaches may best suit the needs of a particular corrections system.

Alfred Blumstein suggests four possible approaches that states may take to address the crowding crisis.[31] Each approach has economic, social, and political costs, and each entails a different amount of time for implementation and impact. For example, the null strategy could be implemented immediately, whereas intermediate sanctions would require several years to develop the necessary organizational structures before they would begin to reduce prison crowding. New construction would take the longest, often seven or eight years.

The Null Strategy

Proponents of the **null strategy** say that nothing should be done, that prisons should be allowed to become increasingly congested. This, of course, may be the most politically acceptable approach in the short run; taxpayers need not pay for new construction. In the long run, however, the resulting crowding may turn prisons into powder kegs as staff members become demoralized and prisoners take control. And ultimately the courts may declare conditions in the facilities unconstitutional and take over their administration.

Opponents of incarceration on philosophical grounds may support this approach because they fear that other strategies will only result in greater numbers being imprisoned. They may reason as well that with the prisons filled, nonviolent offenders will be placed on probation or diverted from the system. This reasoning reflects the reality that society does, in effect, let off minor offenders when serious crime has become endemic. When serious crime is not viewed as a problem, however, society penalizes less serious

null strategy

The strategy of doing nothing to relieve crowding in prisons on the assumption that the problem is temporary and will disappear in time.

offenses. Thus, if murder is relatively uncommon, more criminal justice resources are devoted to shoplifters, drug users, or prostitutes.

The Construction Strategy

The approach that usually comes to mind when legislators or correctional officials confront prison crowding is to expand the size and number of facilities. But given contemporary state budgets and the recent unwillingness of voters in some states to authorize bond issues for new prisons, the **construction strategy** may not be as feasible as it seems.

Legislatures typically estimate new prison construction costs at approximately $75,000 per cell. For a hypothetical 500-bed medium-security facility, this would total around $31 million. However, the true cost of constructing and operating a comparable prison begins with a base construction cost of $61,015 per cell (approximately $30 million for the facility alone). Additional costs such as architects' fees, furnishings, and site preparation raise the figure to $82,246 per cell ($41 million for the facility). To this must be added operating costs, which, estimated conservatively at $19,000 per inmate per year, totals $9.5 million per year. The thirty-year bill to taxpayers for construction and operation thus totals about $250 million—for what legislators view shortsightedly as a $30-million commitment.[32]

As noted previously, opponents of new construction believe that, given the nature of bureaucratic organizations, prison cells will always be filled. This has been the experience of many states that have adopted the construction strategy (see the Focus box).

Intermediate Sanctions

Prisons are a costly and scarce resource. Rather than merely build more institutions, some observers have argued that prison space should be reserved for those violent offenders who have not been deterred by prior punishments. As discussed in Chapter 9,

construction strategy

A strategy of building new facilities to meet the demand for prison space.

FOCUS

Connecticut: Trying to Build Its Way Out

In the early 1980s Connecticut's prison system became overcrowded, driven by the public demand that the criminal justice system "get tough" on crime. A state long wedded to the concepts of rehabilitation and community corrections, Connecticut's incarceration rate in 1981 was 95 per 100,000 population, well below the national rate of 153. As political pressures increased, however, the legislature toughened sentencing laws, eliminated supervised home release, and mandated that an increasing portion of sentences be served. Immediately the incarceration rate began to rise.

In 1987 Connecticut launched a $1-billion construction effort to double capacity by adding thirteen new prisons and expanding nine others. Connecticut's prison-building program was rivaled in scope only by California's. The expansion was inaugurated at a time when the state's economy was booming and there was a budget surplus.

However, by the time the new facilities came on line in the early 1990s, a recession had set in and the state had a major budget deficit. Opening the new prisons became a problem as operating costs skyrocketed. Several stood vacant awaiting legislative appropriations to hire additional staff, yet the flow of newly sentenced offenders continued to increase.

From 1985 to 1997 the number of Connecticut inmates increased from 5,790 to 14,100, the correctional budget rose from $92.5 million to $417 million, and the incarceration rate swelled from 127 to 387 per 100,000 inhabitants (the highest in the Northeast). All this has occurred in a state in which the amount of reported crime has not changed appreciably, although the number of arrests, especially for drug offenses, increased dramatically. In 1994 Connecticut led all states by recording a one-year prisoner growth rate of 20 percent. By 1995 the new prisons were operational—and filled.

intermediate sanctions have been advocated as one way to punish in the community those individuals who require some kind of punishment and supervision short of incarceration. Intermediate sanctions include community service, restitution, fines, boot camp, home confinement, and intensive probation supervision. Judges can fashion sentences using combinations of these punishments to fit the needs of the offender and the severity of the offense.

Some critics contend that even if such alternatives were fully incorporated, they would affect only first-time, marginal offenders; they are not appropriate for serious criminals if crime control is a goal. They also assert that the availability of intermediate sanctions merely widens the net of social control, with the result that a greater number of citizens come under correctional supervision.

Prison Population Reduction

Corrections normally has little or no control over the intake of its raw material — offenders. Only in nine states have legislatures required that sentencing guideline framers consider prison capacity when stipulating incarceration lengths. For example, to reduce prison use North Carolina's new guidelines directs judges to use intermediate sanctions for nonviolent offenders.[33] Thomas Marvell found that in six of these states the incarceration rate declined.[34] For example, the Minnesota Sentencing Guideline Commission is under such a requirement. That state had the second lowest incarceration rate in the nation from 1985 to 1997 (113 per 100,000 population), and the growth rate continues to be low. From 1996–1997 the Minnesota inmate population grew 2.9 percent compared to the national rate of 5.1 percent. In 1990 Texas developed a county "shipping formula" based on such factors as that jurisdiction's prior admissions, crime rate, population, and unemployment level.[35] Under this model, the state prison fills beds according to the formula.

The main ways that correctional officials are able to reduce prison populations is through various "back door strategies," such as parole, work release, and good time, to get offenders out of prison before the end of their terms so as to free space for newcomers. In recent years, however, many legislatures have passed laws mandating that higher portions of sentences be served and have reduced good-time allocations.

Blumstein argues that certain offenders can be safely released early. He points to research on deterrence suggesting that certainty of punishment (the probability of going to prison) is more important than severity (the time served). With regard to the goal of incapacitation, he also argues that the longer the time served in prison, the more likely it is that the inmate would have terminated his criminal career. Research has shown that criminal careers are relatively short, with 10–20 percent of offenders "retiring" from crime annually, so that a long period of incarceration at the end of a criminal career is "wasted." About 10 percent of those in prison would have terminated their criminal career were they on the outside.[36] Proponents also point to studies claiming that incapacitation has its primary effect during the period immediately following conviction. From these perspectives, shorter sentences may be more effective than longer ones.

The Impact of Prison Crowding

Prison crowding directly affects the ability of correctional officials to do their work because it decreases the proportion of offenders in programs, increases the potential for violence, and greatly strains staff morale. The makeup of the inmate community in terms of age, race, and criminal record also affects how institutions are operated. Because prison space is an expensive resource, it can be expected — in the absence of expansion — that corrections will be working increasingly with the most serious offenders as first-time and less violent criminals are placed on probation for lack of cells.

In many states prison crowding has forced the creation of "temporary" housing units. What are some of the problems to be expected under these conditions?

As discussed both here and in Chapter 10, the overwhelming number of inmates are recidivists or have been convicted of a violent crime. A Bureau of Justice Statistics study showed that more than 60 percent of inmates have been either incarcerated or on probation at least twice; 45 percent of them, three or more times; and nearly 20 percent, six or more times. Two-thirds of the inmates were serving a sentence for a violent crime or had previously been convicted of a violent crime.[37] These are major shifts from the prison populations of earlier decades, when only about 40 percent of all inmates had committed such offenses. Corrections now faces a different type of inmate, one who is more prone to violence, in a prison society where racial tensions are great.

As a direct consequence of the higher incarceration rate, courts have cited a number of states for maintaining prisons so crowded that they violate the Eighth Amendment's prohibition against cruel and unusual punishments.[38] Courts have imposed population ceilings, specified the number of offenders per cell, the minimum floor space per person, and ordered the removal of prisoners from overcrowded prisons and jails.

Does crowding cause inmate ill health, misconduct, violent behavior, and postrelease recidivism? Crowding as an influence on behavior cannot be measured merely by the number of inmates housed in a prison designed for a certain capacity. The architecture of the building, whether living units are comprised of cells or dormitories, inmate characteristics, management practices, and the past experiences of prisoners with regard to social density all impinge on the problem. At the least, most researchers would agree on the following points. First, prisoners housed in large, open-bay dormitories are more likely to visit clinics and to have high blood pressure than are prisoners in other housing arrangements (single-bunked cells, double-bunked cells, small dormitories, large partitioned dormitories). Second, prisons that contain dormitories have somewhat higher assault rates than do other prisons. Finally, prisons housing significantly more inmates than a design capacity based on sixty square feet per inmate are likely to have high assault rates.[39]

In the current political climate support for continued high levels of incarceration remains firm, yet the great expense of building and operating new prisons may limit continued expansion. What is not discussed is the extent to which incarceration influences crime rates. Analysts have cast serious doubt on the common assumption that states build prisons in response to crime and that their reliance on imprisonment in turn reduces crime. Yet others argue that the stability of the crime rate since the mid-1970s is a result of increased incarceration.

Does Incarceration Pay?

Opponents of current penal policies note that the United States ranks second in the industrialized world for incarcerating citizens.[40] To be in the same category as Russia strikes many Americans as inconsistent with the freedom we so highly prize. Many of these critics argue that offenders whose crimes do not warrant the severe deprivation of prison nonetheless are being sent to prison. They also argue that the unintended consequences of imprisonment such as disrupted families and disintegrated communities are factors not considered in the policy debate.[41]

Supporters of incarceration believe that current policies have succeeded in lowering the crime rate. They say that most inmates have committed serious crimes, often with violence, and that they are repeat offenders. To not incarcerate repeat offenders, they claim, is costly to society.

Is incarceration misused in the United States? One explanation of why we incarcerate more people is simply that we have more crime than do other countries such as England, Germany, and Japan. For example, more than 150 countries, both developed and less developed, have lower murder rates than the United States. This point is buttressed by research comparing the likelihood of imprisonment for robbery, burglary, or theft in the United States, Canada, England, and the former West Germany.[42] As Figure 18.4 shows, there was little difference among the countries.

But the propensity to incarcerate is only one dimension of penal policy. As James Lynch notes, sentence length is a second important dimension. He compared the length of sentences in five industrialized democracies: Australia, Canada, England, the Federal Republic of Germany, and the United States.[43] He found that, except for homicide, the time served in confinement in the United States was generally longer than in Australia and England for similar offenses. For Canada and the United States the differences were minimal for violent offenses; however, longer sentences were handed down for crimes of violence in the former West Germany than in common law countries. And whereas U.S. prisoners are kept in custody for substantially longer periods of time than in Australia, Canada, and England, those in West Germany served longer periods than in the United States.

There is a long reform tradition critical of incarceration, and only recently have proponents of the current penal policies argued that prisons have value.[44] A major debate among researchers and policymakers concerns the cost-effectiveness of imprisonment, a debate sparked by a 1987 report by Edwin Zedlewski, an economist at the National Institute of Justice.[45] Zedlewski said that the annual per-prisoner cost of incarceration was $25,000. Using national crime data and the findings of victimization

Figure 18.4 Percentage of Adult Arrestees Incarcerated After Conviction, Selected Offenses

Comparison of the incarceration rates among these four countries shows little difference.

NOTE: West Germany includes burglary and auto theft in the theft category; therefore there is no separate figure for burglary.

SOURCE: U.S. Department of Justice, Bureau of Justice Statistics, *Special Report* (Washington, DC: U.S. Government Printing Office, February 1987), p. 2.

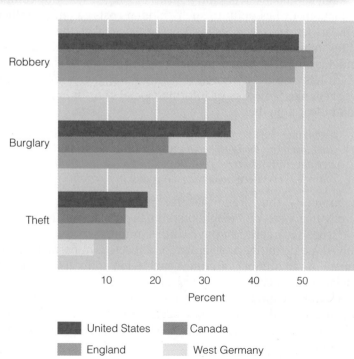

surveys, he estimated that the typical offender commits 187 crimes a year when on the street, at a "social cost" of $430,000. Thus, he argued, incarceration has a benefit–cost ratio of just over 17:1. In other words, putting a thousand felons behind bars costs $25 million a year. But allowing these same felons to remain at large costs society about $430 million a year in additional crimes.

Critics immediately retorted that Zedlewski's report overstated the number of crimes committed per offender and the social costs per crime.[46] These critics pointed out that if Zedlewski's statistics were accurate, the huge increase in the prison population since 1973 should have saved enough money to almost cancel out the national debt and should have reduced crime to a negative number by 1992.[47] Obviously, this didn't happen.

However, John DiIulio used a similar approach to estimate the cost effectiveness of imprisonment in Wisconsin. He concluded that imprisoning a typical felon costs Wisconsin $14,000 per year, but letting him roam the streets harming victims costs society $28,000 per year.[48] Still, crime in Wisconsin has increased despite the growth in its prison population. Also employing a cost–benefit analysis, Thomas Marvell concluded that locking up each additional state prisoner prevented about twenty-one crimes a year. Comparing national costs of incarceration to benefits of crimes prevented, he concluded that the current size of the prison population was about right from an economic viewpoint.[49]

In a 1997 review of the evidence Zedlewski says that "prisons are good investments in that the value of crimes averted has exceeded the confinement costs of averting them." Yet he also notes that there is a point at which continued expansion of prison capacity may be less cost effective as greater numbers of lower-level offenders are incarcerated.[50]

But is the incarceration of *all* prisoners cost effective? Recent studies by DiIulio, Anne Piehl, and Burt Useem in New Jersey, New York, Arizona, and New Mexico raise questions about the social costs of incarcerating "drug-only offenders." These are prisoners whose only adult crime have been drug crimes. Each of the states imprisons a substantial portion of drug-only offenders. Studies have shown that for each drug offender incarcerated, a replacement enters the market. DiIulio and coresearchers believe that the incarceration of large numbers of drug offenders is not an efficient use of valuable prison space. Some of the cells could be better reserved for high-rate property and violent offenders.[51]

But should incarceration policies be judged solely by comparing prison costs to crime reduction? Critics point to such "hidden costs" as those inflicted on offenders' families who are left without a wage earner and caretaker, the loss of young men to their communities, the redirection of governmental resources from societal needs such as health care and education, and the damage done to children by the absence of a parent.[52]

It has also been argued that removing young men from their families and friends weakens the networks of informal social control in their communities. Dina Rose and Todd Clear note that

> high-crime neighborhoods are also high-incarceration neighborhoods. In these places, children are more likely to experience family disruption, lack of parental supervision, property devoid of effective guardians, and all other manner of deteriorated informal social controls that otherwise deflect the young from criminal behavior.[53]

In summary, they argue that the "prison can never be a substitute for absent adults, family members, and neighbors in making places safe."[54]

Does incarceration pay? Until a number of crucial methodological problems are solved, no definitive answer can be expected. In particular, we need a more accurate estimate of the number of crimes each felon commits, a better method of calculating the social costs of crime and incarceration, and a way of determining costs that includes correctional capital, operating costs, and indirect costs. And even if we were to refine the method and obtain a more accurate view of the cost–benefit differential, certain political and moral issues would have to be addressed before a rational incarceration policy could be designed.

Summary

After decades of stability, the incarcerated population in the United States has more than doubled in the past decade. The states and the federal government have responded with a massive program of prison construction. Some of the reasons advanced for this growth include demographic changes, improved law enforcement and prosecution, tougher sentencing practices, prison construction, and the war on drugs. Methods of dealing with prison crowding include doing nothing, building more prisons, implementing more intermediate sanctions, and reducing prison populations.

Corrections is in the position of being unable to control the inputs to its portion of the criminal justice system and must rely on legislatures to appropriate the funds to finance construction and operations. After a period of expanding prison budgets, states now are facing the reality that incarceration is expensive. Some analysts, however, argue that incarcerating criminals is more cost effective than allowing them to live in the community. Critics say that incarceration imposes undue costs on offenders' families and communities. It also diverts resources from the health care and educational needs of society. The incarceration policies of the past decade are now under scrutiny. Have they served to decrease crime? Can they decrease crime in the future? Or are they simply a means of controlling that portion of the population that lacks the education and training to function in today's high-tech world? Currently no clear answers to these questions are available. ■

For Further Discussion

1. Which of the many hypotheses advanced to explain the doubling of the incarceration rate seem most plausible to you? What other reasons might be added?
2. Which of the strategies for dealing with crowded prisons seems most viable to you? Why did you choose that one?
3. Imagine that you are incarcerated in a double-celled prison that is over capacity. What are some of the factors that will influence the way you serve your time?
4. How would you respond to the argument that the American prison is becoming a place where the urban poor receive better housing, health care, education, and job training than they do on the outside?
5. The incarceration rate has become a political issue; how would you summarize the two sides?

For Further Reading

Irwin, John, and Austin, James. *It's About Time: America's Imprisonment Binge,* 2nd ed. Belmont, CA: Wadsworth, 1997. Argues that the "grand imprisonment experiment" that has dominated recent American crime reduction policy has failed miserably and should be abandoned.

Morris, Norval. *The Future of Imprisonment.* Chicago: University of Chicago Press, 1974. An early critique of imprisonment, with recommendations for future correctional policies.

Zimring, Franklin E., and Hawkins, Gordon. *The Scale of Imprisonment.* Chicago: University of Chicago Press, 1991. Questions the scale of society's prison enterprise compared to other criminal sanctions and to the general population, and calls for a political economy of imprisonment.

Notes

1. Marc Mauer, *Americans Behind Bars: U.S. and International Use of Incarceration, 1995* (Washington, DC: The Sentencing Project, 1997). *Halifax (Canada) Chronicle Herald,* August 3, 1998.
2. Todd R. Clear, *Harm in American Penology* (Albany: State University of New York Press, 1994), p. 38; John Irwin and James Austin, *It's About Time: America's Imprisonment Binge* (Belmont, CA: Wadsworth, 1997).
3. *The New York Times,* August 9, 1998, p. A18.
4. Department of Justice, Bureau of Justice Statistics, *Bulletin,* August 1998, p. 1.
5. Steven R. Donzinger, ed., *The Real War on Crime: The Report of the National Criminal Justice Commission* (New York: HarperCollins, 1996), p. 48.

6. Alfred Blumstein, "Stability of Punishment: What Happened and What Next," in Thomas G. Blomberg and Stanley Cohen, eds., *Punishment and Social Control* (New York: Aldine DeGruyter, 1995), pp. 259–274.

7. Alfred Blumstein, "U.S. Criminal Justice Conundrum: Rising Prison Populations and Stable Crime Rates," *Crime and Delinquency*, 44, January 1998, p. 129.

8. Allen J. Beck, "Growth, Change, and Stability in the U.S. Prison Population, 1980–1995," *Corrections Management Quarterly*, 1, Spring 1997, pp. 1–14.

9. Department of Justice, Bureau of Justice Statistics, *Bulletin*, August 1998, p. 1.

10. Ibid., p. 3.

11. Edward F. McGarrell, "Institutional Theory and the Stability of a Conflict Model of the Incarceration Rate," *Justice Quarterly*, 10, March 1993, p. 23.

12. Ibid.

13. *Overcrowded Times*, April 1995, p. 1.

14. Alfred Blumstein, Jacqueline Cohen, and Harold Miller, "Demographically Disaggregated Projections of Prison Populations," *Journal of Criminal Justice*, 8, January 1980, pp. 1–26.

15. Patrick A. Langan, "American's Soaring Prison Population," *Science*, 251, March 1991, p. 1572.

16. Beck, p. 9. See also Lawrence A. Greenfeld, Allen Beck, and Darrell Gilliard, "Prisons: Population Trends and Key Issues for Management," *Criminal Justice Review*, 21, Spring 1996, pp. 4–20.

17. Beck, p. 11.

18. Ibid. p. 10.

19. Department of Justice, Bureau of Justice Statistics, *Bulletin*, July 1997, p. 7.

20. Department of Justice, Bureau of Justice Statistics, *Truth-in-Sentencing in State Prisons*, Press Release, January 10, 1999.

21. Ibid.

22. Fox Butterfield, "Inmates Serving More Time, Justice Department Reports," *The New York Times*, January 11, 1999, p. A10.

23. *The New York Times*, August 8, 1997, p. A16.

24. *Newsweek*, May 18, 1992, p. 63.

25. *Newsweek*, June 14, 1993, p. 32.

26. Department of Justice, Bureau of Justice Statistics, *Bulletin*, August 1998, p. 12.

27. *Hartford Courant*, January 28, 1992, p. A6.

28. Alfred Blumstein, "Prisons," in James Q. Wilson and Joan Petersilia, eds., *Crime* (San Francisco: Institute for Contemporary Studies, 1995), p. 399.

29. Todd R. Clear, "Ten Unintended Consequences of the Growth in Imprisonment," *Corrections Management Quarterly*, 1, Spring 1997, pp. 25–31.

30. Department of Justice, Bureau of Justice Statistics, *Bulletin*, August 1998, p. 9.

31. Blumstein, "Prisons," p. 402.

32. Edna McConnell Clark Foundation, *Time to Build?* (New York: Edna McConnell Clark Foundation, 1984), pp. 18–19; Edna McConnell Clark Foundation, *Seeking Justice: Crime and Punishment in America* (New York: Edna McConnell Clark Foundation, 1997), p. 9.

33. Michael Tonry, "Intermediate Sanctions in Sentencing Guidelines," in Michael Tonry, ed., *Crime and Justice: A Review of Research*, vol. 23 (Chicago: University of Chicago Press, 1998), pp. 199–253.

34. Thomas B. Marvell, "Sentencing Guidelines and Prison Population Growth," *Journal of Criminal Law and Criminology* 85 (1995): pp. 696–709.

35. James w. Marquart, Steve Jay Cuvelier, Madju Bodapati, and Shihlung Huang, "Testing the Prison Allocation Formulation over Time," *Criminal Justice Research Bulletin*, 7(2), 1992, p. 4.

36. Blumstein, "Prisons," p. 409.

37. Department of Justice, Bureau of Justice Statistics, *Special Report* (Washington, DC: U.S. Government Printing Office, 1988), p. 2.

38. Richard B. Cole and Jack E. Call, "When Courts Find Jail and Prison Overcrowding Unconstitutional," *Federal Probation*, March 1992, pp. 29–39.

39. Gerald G. Gaes, "The Effects of Overcrowding in Prison," in Michael Tonry and Norval Morris, eds., *Crime and Justice: A Review of Research*, vol. 6 (Chicago: University of Chicago Press, 1985), p. 95.

40. Edna McConnell Clark Foundation, *Seeking Justice*, p. 4; Marc Mauer, *Americans Behind Bars: The International Use of Incarceration, 1995* (Washington, DC: The Sentencing Project, 1997).

41. Todd R. Clear, "Ten Unintended Consequences."

42. Department of Justice, Bureau of Justice Statistics, *Special Report: Imprisonment in Four Countries* (Washington, DC: U.S. Government Printing Office, 1987), p. 2. See also Warren Young and Mark Brown," Cross-National Comparisons of Imprisonment," in Michael Tonry, ed., *Crime and Justice: A Review of Research*, vol. 17 (Chicago: University of Chicago Press, 1993), pp. 1–50.

43. James P. Lynch, "A Cross-National Comparison of the Length of Custodial Sentences for Serious Crimes," *Justice Quarterly*, 10, December 1993, pp. 639–660.

44. See, for example, John J. DiIulio, Jr., "The Value of Prisons," *The Wall Street Journal*, May 13, 1992; Edwin W. Zedlewski, "Why Prisons Matter: A Utilitarian Review," *Corrections Management Quarterly*, 1, Spring 1997, pp. 15–24.

45. Department of Justice, National Institute of Justice, Edwin W. Zedlewski, "Making Confinement Decisions," in *Research in Brief* (Washington, DC: U.S. Government Printing Office, 1987).

46. Franklin E. Zimring and Gordon Hawkins, "The New Mathematics of Imprisonment," *Crime and Delinquency,* October 1988, pp. 425–436.

47. Zimring and Hawkins, "New Mathematics." See also Franklin E. Zimring and Gordon Hawkins, *Incapacitation: Penal Confinement and the Restraint of Crime* (New York: Oxford University Press, 1995), ch. 7.

48. John J. DiIulio, Jr., "Crime and Punishment in Wisconsin," *Wisconsin Policy Research Institute Report,* 3, December 1990, p. 53. See also John J. DiIulio, Jr., and Anne Morrison Piehl, "Does Prison Pay?" *The Brookings Review,* Fall 1991, pp. 28–35.

49. Thomas B. Marvell, "Is Future Prison Expansion Worth the Cost?" *Federal Probation,* 58, 1994, pp. 59–62.

50. Zedlewski, "Why Prisons Matter."

51. Anne Morrison Piehl and John J. DiIulio, Jr., "'Does Prison Pay?' Revisited," *The Brookings Review,* Winter 1995, pp. 21–25.; John J. DiIulio, Jr., Anne M. Piehl, and Burt Useem, "New Estimates of the Criminality of Inmates from New York, Arizona, and New Mexico," unpublished manuscript, Princeton University, 1998.

52. Edna McConnell Clark Foundation, *Seeking Justice,* pp. 9-10; Clear, Penal Harm; Clear, "Ten Unintended Consequences," pp. 25–31.

53. Dina R. Rose and Todd R. Clear, "Incarceration, Social Capital, and Crime: Implications for Social Disorganization Theory," *Criminology,* 36, August 1998, pp. 441–480.

54. Ibid.

CHAPTER NINETEEN
Race, Ethnicity, and Corrections

What do you think about the O. J. Simpson trial? Do you think he committed the murders? Do you think justice was served by the verdict of "not guilty"? According to surveys, if you are white you likely are outraged by the verdict, but if you are African American you can understand why the jury acquitted him.

The O. J. case is but one illustration of a somber fact of life in the United States: It is not possible to talk about crime and punishment without thinking about race. For one thing, people of color are far more likely than whites to be caught up in the criminal justice system. In 1997, for example, an astounding 3,098 per 100,000 African-American males, and 1,278 Hispanic males—compared to 370 per 100,000 white American males—were incarcerated in U.S. prisons and jails.[1] Today African Americans comprise about one-half of the prison population but only about 12 percent of all U.S. residents. African Americans are seven times more likely than whites to have been incarcerated at some time in a state or federal prison. If current rates continue, more than one in four African-American men in the United States will go to prison during their lifetimes.[2]

When all punishments—probation, intermediate sanctions, incarceration, parole—are taken into account, one in three African-American men in their twenties are currently under correctional supervision.[3] And in America's inner cities the figures are even more astounding. For example, a study of Baltimore found that about 56 percent of young African

Americans were under correctional super-vision.[4] In Washington, DC, half of all African-American men aged 18–35 were under some form of correctional control.[5]

These figures have alarming implica-tions. For many Americans — especially young men of color — the penal system is not an abstraction, but a reality of every-day life. Those who are not themselves reporting to correctional authorities prob-ably have a brother, uncle, or father who is. Under these circumstances the law represents a kind of continuum of state presence, from the police presence on the streets to the courthouse and jail down-town to the prison out in the countryside.

This pervasiveness of corrections in the lives of people of color has evolved gradually, made possible by the 1980s war on drugs and the enormous growth of our penal system. Since 1973 the cor-rectional population overall has increased by nearly 400 percent and has dispropor-tionately affected Americans of color and their families.[6]

Mumia Abu-Jamal, sentenced to death in Philadelphia for the killing of a police officer, charges that the criminal justice system is racist as evidenced by his prosecution, trial, and sentence.

But sheer numbers do not tell the full story. In the everyday thinking of many Amer-icans, crime — particularly violent street crime — is a racial phenomenon. When white Americans imagine burglars, robbers, or rapists, they often think of African-American men and they think of such men fearfully. This has crucial consequences for relations among the races in the United States.

As we shall see, there are differing viewpoints about where these images come from and how accurate they are. The fact that so many white Americans feel this way, how-ever, is itself an important social fact. It means that ordinary African American or His-panic males walking down the street, minding their own business, will frequently find themselves confronted with suspicious looks or fearful, even hostile glares from fellow citizens.[7] How many whites have ever crossed the street in order to avoid walking near a group of young men of color who seemed, somehow, menacing? Where did the notion to fear young men of color come from?

In this chapter we explore the complex implications of feelings about race and ethnicity for the corrections system. Strong feelings abound when it comes to matters of race, class, crime, and punishment, and often the debate is instructed more by heat than by light. We begin by discussing the concepts of race and ethnicity. We then focus on the indisputable fact that African Americans and Hispanics are subjected to the criminal justice system at considerably higher rates than other ethnic and racial groups. Two questions arise: What are the causes of this disparity? What are its main effects? The following Questions for Inquiry will guide our discussion.

Questions FOR INQUIRY

1. What are race and ethnicity?

2. How do varying visions of race and punishments influence our thinking on this issue?

3. What is the significance of race and punishment?

The Concepts of Race and Ethnicity

The United States is a multiracial, multiethnic society. From colonial times, through the period of the slave trade, and then through the mass migrations from all over the world, ours has been one of the most diverse societies ever to exist. By culture and by law we are all Americans, yet we recognize that we are not a melting pot, but rather a mosaic, with each new immigrant group seeking its place in the broader community. Where once immigrants felt great pressure to become assimilated to the dominant white European society and to sacrifice their own cultural identity, the trend since the end of World War II has been to honor the many cultures that comprise the nation.

Although we can point to countless immigrant groups that have successfully moved up the socioeconomic ladder and into the middle class, we know that many members of both old and new groups have not. Native Americans, who lived here long before the arrival of Europeans, were decimated by disease and war, finally to be herded to reservations, where most have lived a precarious existence. African Americans, most of whose ancestors were brought to this country as slaves, have been held back by racial discrimination and economic exploitation. Newer groups such as Hispanics and Asians also have faced discrimination, have had to work at low-wage jobs, and have been restricted in their efforts to achieve.

Race and ethnicity are complex concepts. **Race** is usually assumed to be a biological concept that divides humankind into categories related to skin color and other physical features. Social scientists, however, also look at the ways in which groups define themselves and are defined by others. Today the concept of race is controversial because so many Americans have interracial backgrounds that it is difficult to accept a purely biological approach. Race is also controversial to the extent that it has political and social implications. For example, many transfers of funds from the federal government to the states for social programs are calculated on race-based formulas.

Ethnicity is a concept that is used to divide people according to their cultural characteristics—language, religion, and group traditions. Ethnicity is usually reported by subjects themselves, as opposed to a visual identification.[8] Although we tend to think of ethnic groups as existing among white Americans—for example Irish, Italians, Poles—the concept can also be used to distinguish ethnic groups within the black, Asian, and Hispanic communities. Thus in the Northeast sizable black communities are made up of immigrants from Africa and the West Indies whose culture differs from that of the larger group of African Americans who migrated to the northern cities from the agricultural South. Asians have immigrated from many countries, and are multiethnic, multilingual,

race

Traditionally, a biological concept used to distinguish groups of people based on their skin color and other physical features.

ethnicity

Concept used to distinguish people according to their cultural characteristics—language, religion, and group traditions.

and multiracial. Hispanics are also multiethnic and multiracial. We use the category "Hispanic" to distinguish Spanish-speaking Americans, yet this group is made up of people, some of whom are black, from Mexico, Cuba, Puerto Rico, and other countries.

In this chapter we will focus primarily on correctional issues that relate to African Americans and Hispanic Americans. Members of these two groups are under correctional supervision out of proportion to their numbers in the general population, so issues of racial (and ethnic) disparities are most apparent with regard to these Americans.

Visions of Race and Punishment

African Americans and Hispanics are subjected to the criminal justice system at much higher rates than the white majority. A central question is whether these racial and ethnic disparities are the result of discrimination. A **disparity** is a difference between groups that can be explained by legitimate factors. For example, the fact that 18- to 24-year-old men are arrested out of proportion to their numbers in the general population is a disparity explained by the legal factor that they commit more crime. It is not thought to be the result of a public policy of singling out young males for arrest. **Discrimination** occurs when groups are differentially treated without regard to their behavior or qualifications, for example, if people of color are routinely sentenced to prison regardless of their criminal history.

Explanations for the cause of racial disparities in the criminal justice system can be roughly grouped according to three themes. Some observers argue that these disparities are due to the fact that the system operates as a giant sieve to differentiate offenders, and more men of color end up under correctional authority because they commit more crimes. Others claim that the sieve is racist and that men of color are treated more harshly by the system. And still others argue that the criminal justice system operates within the broader context of our society's racism and merely represents one vehicle for its expression. We consider each of these views in turn.

The View of Differential Criminality

Nobody denies that there is disparity in the involvement of people of color in the criminal justice system. There is, however, controversy over whether the disparity results from discrimination. In their recent book *The Color of Justice,* Samuel Walker, Cassia Spohn, and Miriam DeLone point out that the criminal justice system is supposed to take into account differences between serious offenders and petty offenders, and such considerations might result in disparity.[9] Logically then, more people of color will end up in corrections if they are more likely to commit more serious crimes and have more serious prior records than do whites.

A number of perspectives can be incorporated into this view. The most extreme versions contend that some people are, by nature, more predisposed to commit crimes.[10] This position implies the existence of something akin to a "criminal class" of people who constitute an ongoing danger to society. When this view incorporates a conclusion that one of the predisposing factors toward criminality is having dark skin, we can see why the view is vulnerable to charges of racism. Nonetheless, some people believe that sociobiological factors result in large numbers of Hispanics and African Americans being processed by the criminal justice system.

In fact, the evidence to support a view that people of color are inherently more likely to be involved in crime is paltry at best and nonexistent at worst. **Self-report studies,** in which individuals are asked to report on their own criminal behavior, have shown that nearly everyone admits to having committed a crime during his or her lifetime, although most people are never caught. Table 19.1 shows the results of the first self-report study, conducted on a cross-section of citizens in 1947, in which an astonishing 99 percent of respondents admitted to at least one criminal offense since turning 16.[11] A more recent

disparity

The inequality of treatment of one group by the criminal justice system, compared to the treatment accorded other groups.

discrimination

Differential treatment of groups without reference to an individual's behavior or qualifications.

self-report study

An investigation of behavior (such as criminal activity) based on subjects' responses to questions concerning activities in which they have engaged.

Table 19.1 Percentage of Men and Women Who Admitted Committing Offenses, by Type of Crime, 1947

Most adults have committed a serious offense in their lifetime.

Type of Crime	Men	Women
Petty theft	89%	83%
Disorderly conduct	85	76
Malicious mischief	84	81
Assault	49	5
Tax evasion	57	40
Robbery	11	1
Falsification and fraud	46	34
Criminal libel	36	29
Concealed weapons	35	3
Auto theft	26	8
Other grand theft	13	11
Burglary	17	4

SOURCE: Adapted from James Wallerstein and Clement J. Wyle, "Our Law-Abiding Law-Breakers," *Probation,* 35, April 1947, p. 112.

study of 4,000 students found that 49 percent of African-American youths and 44 percent of white youths reported having committed a delinquent act during the preceding year.[12] Studies of illicit drug use find that whites are slightly more likely than African Americans to admit to using illegal substances.[13] Even though self-report studies have been criticized on methodological grounds, the argument that African Americans are more criminal than whites by nature is not sustained by the evidence.[14]

Less stringent versions of this argument rest on the fact that criminality is related to socioeconomic disadvantage and that many people of color suffer from great disadvantage. Figure 19.1 shows the percentage of children of whites, African Americans and Hispanics who live in poverty; Figure 19.2 compares the incomes of white and African-American families. These figures show the vast racial disparity in wealth in the United States—and studies show that this disparity is increasing.[15]

Figure 19.1 Children in Poverty, by Race and Ethnicity

One of the most disturbing aspects of contemporary American society is the increasing proportion of children who live in poverty.

SOURCE: Samuel Walker, Cassia Spohn, and Miriam DeLone, *The Color of Justice: Race, Ethnicity, and Crime in America* (Belmont, CA: Wadsworth, 1996), p. 67.

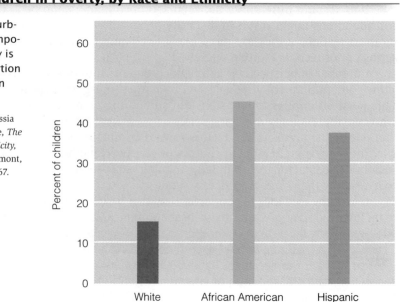

Figure 19.2 Median Family Income of White and African-American Families, 1970 and 1990

Disparity of income continues to be a basic characteristic of American society.

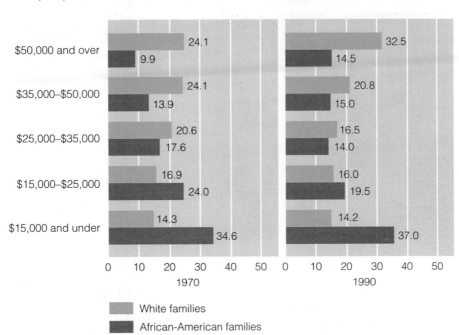

SOURCE: Samuel Walker, Cassia Spohn, and Miriam DeLone, *The Color of Justice: Race, Ethnicity, and Crime in America* (Belmont, CA: Wadsworth, 1996), p. 63.

Social problems such as poverty, single-parent families, and unemployment are well known to contribute to higher crime rates. It would be natural, according to this view, to expect Hispanic and African-American males to engage in more crimes. Not only do these higher criminality rates result from disadvantage, they also reproduce it—the victims of African-American offenders are most often other people of color who live in the communities where the crimes are committed. As John DiIulio points out, "No group of Americans suffers more when violent and repeat criminals are permitted to prey upon decent, struggling, law-abiding inner-city citizens and their children than . . . black America's silent majority."[16]

Proponents of this view point out that African-American and Hispanic males are arrested more frequently than white males and for more serious offenses.[17] Almost two decades ago, Alfred Blumstein showed that arrest rates of African Americans explained their higher imprisonment rates for serious offenses such as homicide and robbery, but not for other crimes, notably property and drug offenses.[18]

Those who see African Americans as more criminal due to social factors differ in their solution to the problem. Some, such as DiIulio, think we can do little other than impose long prison sentences, especially for repeat offenders, and "let 'em rot."[19] They say we need, instead, to focus our resources on today's youth in order to prevent them getting into serious crime in the first place. Others argue that we need new crime control policies that work to reduce the social problems contributing to the higher crime rates of African Americans and Hispanics. Still others contend that the social disadvantage under which these people have to live should be taken into account when they are sentenced.

The View of a Racist Criminal Justice System

Racial disparities become racial discrimination if people who are otherwise similar in their criminality are treated differently by the criminal justice system because of their

Some argue that the War on Drugs has targeted police resources on the urban poor. Who would be incarcerated if these same resources had been targeted against the suburban consumers of cocaine?

race. It is true that African Americans account for 30 percent of all arrests while comprising only 12 percent of the population, but just because people of color are arrested more often than whites does not mean they are more crime-prone than whites. For example, evidence suggests that even though African Americans are arrested for drug offenses more frequently than whites, they do not seem to use drugs more frequently.[20] The conviction and death sentence of Mumia Abu-Jamal discussed in the Focus box has given rise to charges that the Philadelphia criminal justice system is racist.

Drug sentences have been proven to contribute to high rates of incarceration of African Americans. A detailed study by Human Rights Watch of New York State's drug offender sentencing laws concluded that enhanced penalties for drug offenders resulted in disproportionately harsh sentences for African Americans and Hispanics.[21] A study conducted for the U.S. Sentencing Commission concluded, "the main reason that sentences were longer than whites . . . was that 83% of all Federal offenders convicted of trafficking in crack cocaine were black, and the average sentence imposed for crack trafficking was twice as long as that for trafficking in powdered cocaine."[22]

Such facts raise questions about bias in the criminal justice system. Do police, prosecutors, and judges treat whites and nonwhites equally? A great deal of research has been conducted on race and criminal justice processing, but no simple conclusions can be drawn. Some scholars argue that evidence of overt discrimination is weak, at best showing only small amounts of bias in decisions of police officers and judges.[23] In 1983 the National Research Council of the National Academy of Sciences (NAS) commissioned a major review of more than seventy reports on race and criminal justice. Overall, the NAS scholars asserted that "factors other than racial discrimination in sentencing account for most of the disproportionate representation of blacks in U.S. prisons."[24]

The disparity between crime rates and punishment patterns is a key factor in the claim by some scholars that the criminal justice system is biased against minority groups. The rate of incarceration of lower-class and minority citizens is indeed greater than even their higher rates of offending would justify. Figure 19.3 compares the race of offenders, as identified by victims, to the race of arrestees and shows that the odds of African-American offenders being arrested are higher than those of white offenders. One recent study in New York State found that differences in incarceration rates of African Americans and whites reflected "significant disparities that could not be attributed to arrest charges [or] prior criminal charges."[25] If these studies are correct, small, seemingly insignificant disparities at each stage of the criminal justice process may add up into significant overall disparities.

Criminal justice system officials need not act in overtly racist ways in order to produce this kind of gap between arrest rates and punishment rates. At each stage of the process, the criminal justice system operates according to principles that, although not overtly discriminatory to men of color, may tend to disadvantage them. For example, while African Americans constitute 13 percent of monthly drug users, they represent 35 percent of arrests for drug possession, 55 percent of convictions, and 74 percent of prison sentences.[26] The number of minority arrests may be greater because police patrols are more heavily concentrated in residential areas where nonwhites live, areas where drug use may be more open and more likely to be observed by police. Further, a study of 150,000 cases in Connecticut found that on average an African-American or

Mumia Abu-Jamal Faces Execution: Did He Receive a Fair Trial?

Mumia Abu-Jamal, a radio journalist in Philadelphia and member of the Black Panther Party, was convicted and sentenced to death for the killing of Police Officer David Faulkner. According to Mumia, he was driving a cab through a rundown district of Philadelphia the night of December 9, 1981, when he was shot and beaten by police and then charged with the murder of Officer Faulkner. Mumia's supporters believe the real killer of the officer is still at large.

In a full-page advertisement in *The New York Times*, Mumia's legal defense organization raised questions about the evidence presented at his trial. They also listed the following aspects of racial bias in the criminal justice system and asked, "Should procedures like this take away someone's life?"

The Judge had sentenced more people to death than any other sitting judge in the United States. Six former Philadelphia prosecutors have sworn in court documents that no accused could receive a fair trial in the court of Judge Albert Sabo.

The Jury was impaneled only after eleven qualified African Americans were removed by peremptory challenges from the prosecution, a practice that was recently revealed as having been taught to prosecutors in a special training video tape.

The Defense Attorney testified that he didn't interview a single witness in preparation for the 1982 trial and he informed the court in advance that he was not prepared. Jamal was also denied the right to act as his own attorney.

The Defense Investigator quit the case before the trial because the meager court-allocated funds were exhausted. Neither a ballistics expert not a pathologist were hired because of insufficient funds.

The Prosecutor used the fact that 12 years earlier Jamal had been a member of the Black Panther Party as an argument for imposing the death penalty, a practice condemned as unconstitutional by the U.S. Supreme Court in another case.

The Racial Bias of Philadelphia's courts now has 120 people on death row—all but thirteen of them non-white.

You be the judge and jury. Do these elements show racial bias in the Philadelphia criminal justice system? Should Mumia Abu-Jamal receive a new trial?

SOURCE: Mumia Abu-Jamal, *Live from Death Row* (Reading, MA: Addison Wesley, 1995); *The New York Times*, October 22, 1998, p. A11.

Figure 19.3 Comparison of Uniform Crime Report and National Crime Victimization Survey Data on Offender Race, 1992

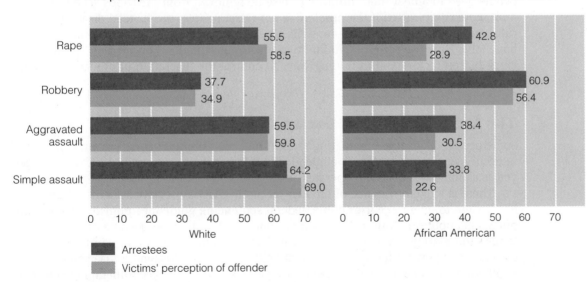

The perception of the race of the offender (arrestee) differs from the race of those arrested.

White:
- Rape: Arrestees 55.5, Victims' perception of offender 58.5
- Robbery: Arrestees 37.7, Victims' perception of offender 34.9
- Aggravated assault: Arrestees 59.5, Victims' perception of offender 59.8
- Simple assault: Arrestees 64.2, Victims' perception of offender 69.0

African American:
- Rape: Arrestees 42.8, Victims' perception of offender 28.9
- Robbery: Arrestees 60.9, Victims' perception of offender 56.4
- Aggravated assault: Arrestees 38.4, Victims' perception of offender 30.5
- Simple assault: Arrestees 33.8, Victims' perception of offender 22.6

Arrestees
Victims' perception of offender

SOURCE: Samuel Walker, Cassia Spohn, and Miriam DeLone, *The Color of Justice: Race, Ethnicity, and Crime in America* (Belmont, CA: Wadsworth, 1996), p. 45.

Hispanic-American man must pay *double* the bail that would be paid by a white man for the same offense.[27] Most pretrial release practices take into account factors such as employment status, living arrangements, and prior criminal record. Clearly the under-employed and unemployed tend to be unable to make bail and thus languish in jail awaiting trial. Prosecutors also may be less likely to dismiss charges against poor, un-employed, single men—many of whom are African American—especially if they have a prior record. And poor defendants are less likely to have a private attorney. Research has shown that all these factors are related to sentence severity.

These step-by-step decisions of the system mean that African Americans, the unem-ployed, and the poor often appear at sentencing hearings with more extensive prior records and fewer prospects for reform. Thus what appears discriminatory may simply represent the functioning of an impersonal bureaucratic system. After all, evidence of discrimination in sentencing is disputable and ambiguous. According to a National Acad-emy of Sciences report, "Some studies find statistical evidence of discrimination; others find none. While there is no evidence of a widespread systematic pattern of discrimina-tion in sentencing, some pockets of discrimination are found for particular judges, par-ticular crime types, and in particular settings."[28]

Perhaps criminal justice system officials, acting under the daily pressures and rou-tines of bureaucratic decision making, use filtering criteria to move cases along through the process. The criteria they use would be difficult to dispute: When a crime is not se-rious, when the suspect or defendant appears contrite and unlikely to repeat the of-fense, when the evidence is weak or contradictory, or when the accused has a respectable prior history, then the system chooses not to proceed with the case or to downgrade the punishments. Is this truly racism?

We may not so easily dismiss arguments that the system is racist. For one thing, the result of the system's decisions cannot be disputed—African American and Hispanic men end up in prison and jails in proportions that exceed their contribution to crime rates and arrest rates. According to a recent sophisticated review of thirty-eight studies published since 1975, over two-thirds of the studies uncovered system biases disadvan-tageous to African Americans, whereas less than one-tenth found biases in favor of African Americans. The authors concluded that "race is a consistent and frequently sig-nificant disadvantage when [imprisonment] decisions are considered . . . [but] race is much less of a disadvantage when it comes to sentence length."[29]

Some reformers have considered ways to eliminate racism from the criminal justice system. The solution depends on how the problem is defined. If racism exists because individuals within the system are themselves racist, then the solution is plain: These people need to adjust their attitudes or else be removed from their jobs. The problem is a bit more complicated if the problem is not racist people, but instead disadvantageous rules and practices, such as treating the unemployed with less leniency than those who have jobs. Here the solution would lie in revamping the decision-making criteria to ex-clude biased factors and in finding ways to control the discretion of officials to use the new criteria.

The View of a Racist Society

Some people claim that eliminating racism from the criminal justice system is not likely to occur because the system is embedded in a larger racist society. In fact, the strongest voices claim that the system operates as an instrument of such racism.

There is indeed evidence of broader racism in the way society asks the criminal jus-tice system to operate. For example, federal sentencing guidelines punish crack cocaine offenders about one hundred times more harshly than powder cocaine offenders, even though these drugs are virtually identical. The only difference is that whites tend to use cocaine in its powder form, whereas inner-city people of color tend to use crack cocaine. In addition, sentencing studies find a stronger association between unemployment rates and imprisonment rates than between crime rates and imprisonment rates, suggesting that prison is used as a place to confine people who cannot find jobs when the economy falters—and many of these unemployed are African-American males.[30] Finally, Michael Tonry comments that the recent War on Drugs was "foreordained to affect disadvantaged black youths disproportionately [and was based on] the willingness of the drug war's planners to sacrifice young black Americans"[31] (see the Focus box).

Many observers further believe that the relationship between racism and the criminal justice system is reciprocal. As Coramae Richey Mann argues, "At every level of contemporary human existence—education, housing, politics, health, law, welfare, economics, religion, and the family—racism and racial discrimination in American institutions have contributed to and continue to perpetuate . . . minority status [and] criminal activity."[32]

Thus, confronted with the reality of crime by people of color, the criminal justice system reacts in a way that reflects public horror and revulsion by removing large numbers of people of color from their communities. Racist institutions, it is argued, help produce the higher crime rate among minorities, and then racist fears of people of color help justify treating them more harshly when they are caught.

Admittedly the image of the "black criminal" has been useful to white people for various purposes. In the South, fear of African-American rapists of white women was an excuse to lynch some young males and keep the rest in perpetual fear of summary execution.[33] As recently as 1988, the image of Willie Horton, an African-American convicted felon released under Massachusetts Governor Michael Dukakis's administration, was used to fuel white fears of crime and help portray George Bush as "tough on crime." Bush eventually was elected president, with strong support from voters fearful of street crime. And when Susan Smith wanted to cover up her murder of her two young sons, she invented an African-American assailant, and the general public believed her without batting an eye.

If people of color are overrepresented in the justice system because the larger society is racist, the solution may seem a bit daunting. Nobody knows a way to rapidly rid our society of policies, practices, and, perhaps most importantly, attitudes of racism. Even an optimist would think that a generation or more of vigilance to eradicate racism may be necessary.

Police, Minorities, and the War on Drugs

The Los Angeles police called it "Operation Hammer." Mobilizing up to a thousand officers a night, they began conducting massive "sweep" arrests of suspected gang members. On one weekend alone in October 1989, they arrested over a thousand people, all of whom were African American or Hispanic. In addition to the massive violations of civil liberties (with people being arrested on little, if any, evidence), Operation Hammer did not reduce either gang membership or drug trafficking. Most of those arrested were quickly released, and few were ever prosecuted.

The nature of police drug enforcement strategies [such as Operation Hammer] explains much of the racial disparity in arrests. With conventional street crimes (robbery, rape, burglary), the police are reactive, responding to citizen calls for service. Drug possession and sale, on the other hand, are "victimless" crimes, with no one calling the police. Consequently, enforcement efforts are proactive: the police initiate investigations at their own discretion. The evidence suggests that police departments choose to target drug enforcement efforts at minority group neighborhoods and not areas where white professional and middle-class people engage in drug use.

In "Operation Pressure Point," a highly publicized drug crackdown in New York City, the police dramatically increased the arrest of street dealers, who were racial minorities, while harassing and scaring off potential drug buyers who drove in from the suburbs, virtually all of whom were white. This practice represented a differential and discriminatory treatment of people involved in drugs.

Source: Samuel Walker, Cassia Spohn, and Miriam DeLone, *The Color of Justice: Race, Ethnicity, and Crime in America* (Belmont, CA: Wadsworth, 1996), p. 100.

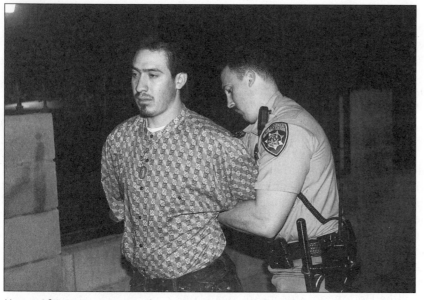

Young African-American and Hispanic males contend that they are always being hassled by the police. Is this racism, or effective police work?

Which Is It: Race or Racism?

We can illustrate how complicated this issue is with a hypothetical case.[34] Suppose that Wilson, who is white, and Edwards, who is African American, each was convicted of burglary. If Wilson received a sentence of probation with a $5,000 fine and 200 hours of community service while Edwards received a six-month jail sentence, would you think that the verdict was racist?

Would it change your opinion to learn that at sentencing, Wilson's attorney argued that a jail term would cost Wilson his job as a construction worker and would leave his unemployed wife and two children without a source of financial support? Or to learn that Edwards had no job and that his two children had already been living without his income as he sat in jail, awaiting trial? When the law tries to take into account these sorts of concerns, however reasonable they seem, it runs the risk of inadvertently penalizing those who have fewer resources.

The situation becomes even more complicated if we learn that this is Wilson's first offense but that Edwards has been before the court on a previous charge. The jail term makes a bit more sense for a repeat offender. But we have to keep in mind that young African-American men often experience arrests that result in charges being dropped, for whatever reason. To consider such arrests at sentencing may be unfair and indirectly biased.

What if the reason Wilson received a fine is that he had a job in the first place and could afford to pay? Edwards might claim that he went to jail because he was unemployed, but that if the system would help him get a job he could pay a fine.

All these scenarios raise the question of whether the system is reasonable, biased, or simply part of a larger set of social inequities. There is no obvious answer. That is one of the reasons recent studies of race and criminal justice find that "the criminal justice system is neither completely free of racial bias nor systematically racially biased."[35]

The Significance of Race and Punishment

In some respects it does not matter which of the competing views is most accurate. The real repercussions of racial disparities in the criminal justice system have already become a force to be reckoned with by criminal justice policymakers.

The fact that such a high percentage of young African-American men are behind bars must be understood in terms of what these young men cannot be doing. They cannot be earning a living, attending school, parenting their children, or supporting their partners; they cannot be voting or otherwise partaking of "free" society. We can only speculate about the implications of the fact that so many of this generation's young men of color have passed through the criminal justice system. But we must wonder whether this experience might not further alienate this group and prevent them from identifying with the society that sent them there. For the many children in some neighborhoods who grow up with fathers, uncles, and brothers absent from home due to the system, does it breed respect for the law, or revulsion and enmity? Does the prison stand as a fearful symbol of deterrence or as a contemptible symbol of the inevitable power of the state to disrupt a person's life? In the effort to establish and preserve order, does the disproportionate impact of corrections on people of color instead produce suspicion and even social disruption? In short, does the heavy-handed use of the criminal justice system in minority communities exacerbate the very problems of social disorder it is trying to restore?

Some of the importance of racial differences is symbolic. The year-long trial of O. J. Simpson for the alleged murders of his ex-wife Nicole Brown Simpson and Ronald Goldman amply demonstrates the way in which themes of race intertwine with justice processes in the United States. One of the main prosecution witnesses, Los Angeles police officer Mark Fuhrman, was exposed as a blatant racist who admitted to beating up and framing African-American suspects — and enjoying it. The defense argued that O. J. was the victim of a racist frame-up. The prosecution was forced to play catch-up, conceding the racism but claiming that the evidence proved the defendant's guilt anyway. Three-quarters of white Americans agreed, but three-quarters of African Americans thought O. J. was innocent, and perhaps framed by a racist system.

The Simpson trial serves as a microcosm of the fruits of our disparate correctional practices. Whether or not the criminal justice system has achieved the great disparities in punitive results due to its own or society's racism, the point is that many citizens believe such disparities exist. And at least as many do not. The result is a polarization of attitudes about race that discolors the capacity of our society to remember its traditional values of fairness, equity, and equal opportunity.

How do we interpret the problems of race that we see in our corrections system? And what can we do to overcome them?

Most people believe there are three solutions. First, we must open up the corrections system to greater participation by people who come from the groups historically disadvantaged by the disparate treatment. Special efforts to employ young men and women from minority groups will in the long run reduce the predominance of white policymakers in this area. Studies of African-American police officers, judges, and correctional officers find that their decisions about cases are remarkably similar to their white co-workers, but their greater presence in criminal justice roles of authority at least is beneficial to us all. The fact that there were African-American lawyers on both sides of the Simpson case helped deflect some of the more flagrant impressions of racism.

Second, we must ferret out and refuse to tolerate incidents of blatant racism in justice practices or policy. This is easier said than done, of course, because there is so much disagreement about what exactly is a racist policy. For example, should people who do not have jobs be as eligible for bail as those who have stakes in the community? Should police spend as much time aggressively combating white-collar crime as they do street crime? Ensuring that criminal justice policies are free of racial and ethnic bias is nonetheless a high priority for tomorrow's correctional leaders.

Finally, we must recognize that as long as racism is a force in the larger society, any attempts to eradicate it from the criminal justice system will have only marginal prospects for success. As long as some groups are unfairly excluded from society's opportunities, they will feel less stake in obeying its laws. And the corrections system will be their adversary.

Summary

People of color are vastly overrepresented in the criminal justice system, especially young African American and Hispanic males. The reasons for this are disputed. Some say that these groups commit more crimes and end up being punished more as a result. Others say that the criminal justice system and the larger society are racist and that this bias results in greater punishment for those groups.

Whatever the explanation, the greater involvement of minorities in the corrections system gives at least the appearance of unfairness and leaves many of these groups believing that the system is biased against them because of their ethnicity or race. The result is a decline in the overall credibility of the criminal justice system. ■

For Further Discussion

1. What are the five main reasons that people of color are overrepresented in the criminal justice system? Is this a problem? What, if anything, can be done to change the pattern?
2. What impact does a high incarceration rate have on minority communities? Does this impact have implications for the effectiveness of the criminal justice system? How?
3. How does the close relationship between politics and criminal justice policy reflect issues of race and punishment?
4. If you were writing a sentencing code, would you give people lighter sentences if they came from disadvantaged backgrounds? Why or why not?
5. What are the most important steps to take to reduce racial differences in punishments? Why?

For Further Reading

Abu-Jamal, Mumia. *Life from Death Row.* Reading, MA: Addison Wesley, 1995. An African-American journalist and political activist writes from inside death row. He points to racism in the criminal justice system and in American society.

Free, Marvin D., Jr. *African Americans and the Criminal Justice System.* New York: Garland, 1996. An overview of the role played by race in the criminal justice system.

Hawkins, Darnell, F., ed. *Ethnicity, Race, and Crime: Perspectives Across Time and Place.* Albany: State University of New York Press, 1995. Addresses issues regarding race and crime from historical, economic, and political perspectives.

Kennedy, Randall. *Race, Crime, and the Law.* New York: Pantheon, 1997. A controversial examination of attitudes of both the left and the right on the issues of race and criminal justice. Provides a historical overview of racial bias in the American system of criminal justice, but also attacks underenforcement of law in the African-American community.

Lopez, Antoinette Sedillo. *Criminal Justice and Latino Communities.* New York: Garland, 1995. An excellent collection of articles on crime and the criminal justice system as it impacts Latino communities.

Mann, Coramae Richey. *Unequal Justice—A Question of Color.* Bloomington: Indiana University Press, 1993. Argues that people of color are systematically disadvantaged by the design and operation of the criminal justice system.

Tonry, Michael. *Malign Neglect: Race, Crime, and Punishment in America.* New York: Oxford University Press, 1995. Provides a critical assessment of the impact of criminal justice policy on African-American males and suggests reforms of those policies.

Walker, Samuel, Cassia Spohn, and Miriam DeLone. *The Color of Justice: Race, Ethnicity, and Crime in America.* Belmont, CA: Wadsworth, 1996. Gives an up-to-date review of studies of race, crime, and justice at all stages of the criminal justice system, from arrest to punishment.

Notes

1. Darrell K. Galliard and Allen J. Beck, *Prisoners in 1997,* Bureau of Justice Statistics Bulletin (Washington, DC: U.S. Department of Justice, August 1998), p. 11.
2. Thomas P. Bonczar and Allen J. Beck, *Lifetime Likelihood of Going to State or Federal Prison,* Bureau of Justice Statistics Bulletin (Washington, DC: U.S. Department of Justice, March 1997).
3. Mark Mauer, *Young Black Americans and the Criminal Justice System: Five Years Later* (Washington, DC: The Sentencing Project, 1995).
4. Michael Tonry, *Malign Neglect: Race, Crime, and Punishment in America* (New York: Oxford University Press, 1995), p. 30.
5. Eric Lotke, "Hobbling a Generation: Young African American Men in Washington, DC's Criminal Justice System—Five Years Later," *Crime and Delinquency,* 44(3), July 1998, pp. 355–366.
6. Tonry, *Malign Neglect,* p. 59.
7. Cornel West, *Race Matters* (Boston: Beacon Press, 1993).
8. Robert J. Sampson and Janet L. Lauristen, "Racial and Ethnic Disparities in Crime and Criminal Justice in the United States," Michael Tonry, ed., *Crime and Justice: A Journal of Research,* vol. 21 (Chicago: University of Chicago Press, 1997), pp. 311–374.
9. Samuel Walker, Cassia Spohn, and Miriam DeLone, *The Color of Justice: Race, Ethnicity, and Crime in America* (Belmont, CA: Wadsworth, 1996), pp. 15–16.

10. James Q. Wilson and Richard J. Herrnstein, *Crime and Human Nature* (New York: Simon & Schuster, 1985). See also Richard J. Herrnstein and Charles Murray, *The Bell Curve: Intelligence and Class Structure in American Life* (New York: Free Press, 1994).

11. James F. Wallerstein and Clement J. Wyle, "Our Law-Abiding Law-Breakers," *Probation*, 35, April 1947, pp. 107–119.

12. Travis Hirschi, *Causes of Delinquency* (Berkeley: University of California Press, 1969).

13. Andrea J. Kopstein and Patricia T. Roth, *Drug Abuse Among Race/Ethnic Minorities* (Washington, DC: National Institute of Drug Abuse, 1990), p. 13.

14. For critiques of these studies, see Sampson and Lauristen, p. 329.

15. Walker, Spohn, and DeLone, ch. 3.

16. John J. DiIulio, Jr., "The Question of Black Crime," *The Public Interest*, Fall 1994, p. 3.

17. John DiIulio, "The Question of Black Crime," *The Public Interest*, Fall 1994.

18. Alfred Blumstein, "On the Racial Disproportionality of the United States' Prison Population," *Journal of Criminal Law and Criminology*, 73, 1982, pp. 1259–1281.

19. John DiIulio, "Let 'em Rot," *Wall Street Journal*, January 26, 1995, editorial page.

20. Alfred Blumstein, "Making Rationality Relevant: The American Society of Criminology 1992 Presidential Address," *Criminology*, 31(1), January 1993, p. 1.

21. "Cruel and Unusual: Disproportionate Sentences for New York Drug Offenders," *Human Rights Watch*, 9(2,B), March 1997.

22. Douglas C. McDonald and Kenneth E. Carlson, *Sentencing in Federal Courts: Does Race Matter?* (Washington, DC: U.S. Department of Justice, December 1993).

23. William Wilbanks, *The Myth of a Racist Criminal Justice System* (Monterey, CA: Brooks/Cole, 1987).

24. Alfred Blumstein, Jacqueline Cohen, Susan Martin, and Michael Tonry, eds., *Research on Sentencing: The Search for Reform*, vol. 1 (Washington, DC: National Academy Press, 1983).

25. New York State Office of Justice Systems Analysis, *The Incarceration of Minority Defendants: An Identification of Disparity in New York State, 1985–1986* (Albany: New York State Division of Criminal Justice Services, July 1991), p. i.

26. Fox Butterfield, "More Blacks in Their 20's Have Trouble with the Law," *The New York Times*, October 5, 1995, p. A18.

27. Steven R. Donziger, ed., *The Real War on Crime: The Report of the National Criminal Justice Commission* (New York: HarperCollins, 1996), p. 111.

28. Blumstein et al., p. 93.

29. Theodore G. Chiricos and Charles Crawford, "Race and Imprisonment: A Contextual Assessment of the Evidence," in Darnell F. Hawkins, ed., *Ethnicity, Race, and Crime: Perspectives Across Time and Place* (Albany: State University of New York Press, 1995).

30. Theodore G. Chiricos and William D. Bales, "Unemployment and Punishment: An Empirical Assessment," *Criminology*, 29(4), December 1991, pp. 701–724.

31. Tonry, *Malign Neglect*, p. 123.

32. Coramae Richey Mann, "The Contribution of Institutionalized Racism to Minority Crime," in Darnell F. Hawkins, ed., *Ethnicity, Race, and Crime: Perspectives Across Time and Place* (Albany: State University of New York Press, 1995), p. 259.

33. Stuart Tolnay and E. M. Beck, *A Festival of Violence: An Analysis of the Lynching of African-Americans in the American South, 1882–1930* (Urbana: University of Illinois Press, 1994).

34. For an excellent review of the literature on racial discrimination and the criminal justice system, see: Ronald Weitzer, "Racial Discrimination in the Criminal Justice System: Findings and Problems in the Literature," *Journal of Criminal Justice*, 24, 1996, pp. 309–322.

35. Walker, Spohn, and DeLone, p. 229.

CHAPTER TWENTY
The Death Penalty

Saying "I love you all very much" and smiling as she was given a lethal injection, Karla Faye Tucker was executed in February 1998, becoming the first woman put to death in Texas since the Civil War.[1]

Karla Faye's execution ended a case that attracted great attention around the world and reopened debate about capital punishment. The prospect of executing a woman exposed a raw nerve in society, but also prompted many death penalty supporters to insist that Tucker had gained undeserved sympathy as a soft-spoken, gentle-looking, born-again Christian who pleaded for mercy. Those calling for clemency were an eclectic coalition that included Pope John Paul II, Bianca Jagger, Amnesty International, the ACLU, one of the jurors in her case, and the brother of one of her two victims. Most surprising was the plea for clemency by televangelist Pat Robertson, a supporter of the death penalty. One Christian columnist, F. M. Richbourg, III, of Dallas, described Ms. Tucker as "this miraculously sweet-spirited little soldier in the war against criminal wickedness." Her case became a staple for radio and television talk shows in the weeks leading up to her execution.

On a summer night in June 1983, 23-year-old Karla Faye, her 37-year-old boyfriend, Daniel Garrett, decided to break into the apartment of Jerry Lynn Dean to steal motorcycle parts. Ms. Tucker killed Dean with a pickax and then hit Deborah Thornton, who was cowering under the bed sheets, with the ax. Because Tucker's arms were tired, Thornton did not die until she was polished off by Garrett. Just after the killings Karla Faye said she had experienced a surge of sexual pleasure every time she swung the pickax.

Karla Faye Tucker confessed to her crimes, expressed remorse, testified against Garrett at his trial, but received no leniency in return. In 1984 Tucker and Garrett were sentenced to death. During her long stay in prison Tucker became an active Christian who organized Bible study groups and married the prison chaplain. Her transformation from a drugged-out prostitute to a Bible-quoting missionary caused Robertson to describe Tucker "an extraordinary woman" whose "authentic spiritual conversion" cried out for mercy.

Condemned killer Karla Faye Tucker reads her Bible prior to becoming the first woman in 135 years to be executed in Texas. The fact that she was a woman and had become a "born-again" Christian drew support for clemency from around the world, including Pope John Paul II and televangelist Pat Robertson.

Despite the pleas for clemency, the Texas Board of Pardons and Paroles voted 16 to 0, with two abstentions, not to change the sentence. Governor George Bush refused to intervene. Karla Faye Tucker became the second woman to be executed since the Supreme Court reinstated capital punishment in 1976 and the third since 1962.

Tucker's death added fuel to the raging debate over capital punishment. Should her sentence have been converted to life imprisonment because she was a Christian woman who had expressed remorse? Why do the 43 women on death rows make up such a small fraction of the nearly 3,500 awaiting execution? Public opinion polls revealed that many supporters of the death penalty favored clemency for Karla Faye. In this chapter we discuss the many facets of the death penalty debate, focusing in particular on the moral, political, and legal aspects. In addition, we examine the death row population, which contains a disproportionate number of lower-class, undereducated minority men. We will frame our discussion by addressing these Questions for Inquiry.

The Debate over Capital Punishment

Among the goals of the criminal sanction, retribution, deterrence, and incapacitation are usually cited as the basis for the death penalty. Retribution reflects the belief that one who takes another's life deserves a punishment equal to the victim's fate; deterrence reflects the hope that the execution will deter others from crime; and incapacitation, making the offender no longer able to commit crimes.

Ernst van den Haag, a supporter of capital punishment, notes that arguments about the death penalty are either moral or utilitarian. As a moral argument supporting retribution, van den Haag says, "Anyone who takes another's life should not be encouraged to expect that he will outlive his victim at public expense. Murder must forfeit the murderer's life, if there is to be justice."[2] Opponents of the death penalty argue that God has a right to take a life, but instruments of society do not. Opponents also emphasize that mistakes can and have been made, resulting in innocent people being executed. Further, they claim that the death penalty is discriminatory in that poor people and racial minorities are disproportionately given this sentence. Van den Haag counters by claiming that abolitionists would continue to oppose capital punishment even if they could be certain that "none but the guilty are executed, and without discrimination or capriciousness."[3] Summarizing the philosophical basis for the death penalty, Marvin Wolfgang has said, "There is no rationale of punishment or disposition of a convicted offender that requires the death penalty."[4]

The utilitarian argument for capital punishment is based on the belief that executions of wrongdoers deter others from committing the crime. As noted in Chapter 4, the general deterrence position sounds reasonable to most people, yet there is no effective means to prove it scientifically. Some argue that it is impossible to show if someone was actually deterred from committing an act because they recognized the consequences.[5]

However, over 200 studies have looked closely at murder rates, comparing states with the death penalty with those without the sentence.[6] Most of these studies have found no deterrent effect of the penalty. For example, Ruth Peterson and William Bailey examined homicide rates in adjacent states over a twelve-year period. They found that the murder rate in states *with* the death penalty was higher than those that had abolished it.[7] In a 1983 study, Richard Lempert echoed the findings of most researchers by concluding, "The death penalty in general and executions in particular do not deter homicide." [8]

Challenging much of the deterrence research, economist Isaac Ehrlich argued in 1975 that each execution in the United States from 1933 to 1969 prevented seven or eight murders because of the deterrent effect.[9] His findings were greeted eagerly by death penalty supporters. However, almost immediately his methodology was questioned.[10] A panel of the National Academy of Sciences reanalyzed Ehrlich's data and found no deterrent effect.[11]

In 1991 a San Francisco public television station sued the state for permission to provide live coverage of California executions. The suit and the publicity it generated contributed to the ongoing debate over the death penalty in this country and highlighted the various arguments in support of and opposed to capital punishment.

According to supporters, the death penalty indeed deters criminals from committing violent acts—individuals will be less likely to kill if they know that they face execution for doing so. In addition, the death penalty serves justice by paying back killers for their horrible crimes. Society exacts an appropriate measure of revenge ("an eye for an eye"), and victims' families can be reassured that the murderer received a just punishment and will not kill others. By executing murderers, society emphasizes the high value placed on life. And the death penalty prevents murderers from doing further harm. Finally, the death penalty is less expensive than holding violent criminals in prison for decades or for life. By executing these serious offenders, the state can save up to $1 million in incarceration costs over the lifetime of each murderer.

According to opponents of capital punishment, there is no evidence that the death penalty deters violent crime. Many people who kill are under the influence of alcohol or drugs, psychologically disturbed, in an emotional rage, or otherwise unable to control themselves. Thus the threat of capital punishment never enters

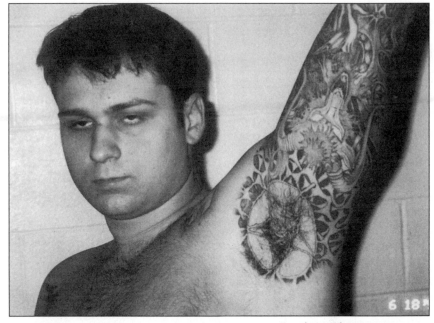

Death penalty opponents are severely tested by killers such as John William King, found guilty of the brutal death of James Byrd Jr., who was chained to a truck and dragged for two miles in Jasper, Texas. What should society do with people such as King?

their minds when they commit violent crimes. In addition, it is wrong for a government to participate in the intentional killing of its citizens. State-sponsored executions convey the harmful message that life is cheap and that violence is an appropriate response to violence. Further, the death penalty is applied in a discriminatory fashion. Historically members of racial/ethnic minority groups convicted of murder have been significantly more likely to receive the death penalty than members of the majority group. Also, poor defendants who cannot obtain pretrial release on bail and who are represented by public defenders are more likely to receive the death penalty than are other convicted murderers. Finally, innocent people have been executed.

The Death Penalty in America

The death penalty has been controversial ever since colonial times. As discussed in Chapter 2, until the middle of the 1700s, criminal punishment in Europe and the American colonies focused on the body of the offender. Along with mutilation, whipping, and dismemberment, death was a common punishment for a range of felonies—from premeditated murder, to striking one's mother or father (New York), to witchcraft and adultery (Massachusetts). Executions were carried out in public until the 1830s, when most were withdrawn behind prison walls.[12] In some regions, however, particularly in the West and South, public executions continued into the twentieth century. The last public execution in the United States took place on August 14, 1936, when an estimated 20,000 spectators converged on the small town of Owensboro, Kentucky.[13] The death penalty has strong historical roots in American culture.

Yet even though capital punishment was common, as far back as the 1600s critics argued that the death penalty was immoral, an ineffective deterrent, "a violation of the ideal of proportionality in sentencing, and a breach of the increasingly widespread belief that the criminal could be reformed."[14]

Death Row Population

Between 1930 and 1967, when the Supreme Court ordered a stay of executions pending a hearing on the issue, 3,859 men and women were executed by state and federal authorities (see Figure 20.1). In 1935, 199 people were put to death; after that the number

Figure 20.1 Persons Executed in the United States, 1930–1998

The steady decline in the number of executions after 1940 gave abolitionists the impression that, as in Europe, the death penalty would eventually be a thing of the past. That belief was shattered when states resumed executions in 1977.

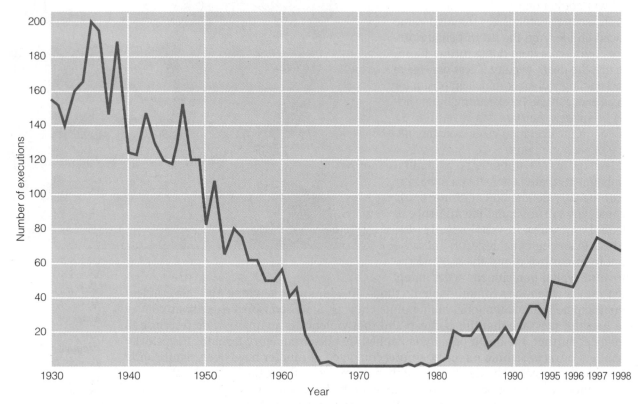

Sources: U.S. Department of Justice, Bureau of Justice Statistics, *Bulletin*, December 1997; NAACP Legal Defense and Educational Fund, *Death Row, USA* (New York: NAACP, Winter 1999); NAACP Death Penalty Information Center, *Year End Report, 1998, www.essential.org/dpic/* February 3, 1999.

of executions began to fall steadily. An average of 128 individuals per year were executed during the 1940s, 72 during the 1950s, and 19 during the 1960s. This decline led many observers to believe that the United States, like the countries of Europe, ultimately would cease applying the death penalty either by law or de facto through lack of use.[15] But this was not the case. After the Supreme Court reaffirmed the constitutionality of the death penalty in 1976, state legislatures quickly enacted new laws providing for the execution of convicted murderers under some circumstances, and executions resumed.

The numbers of people facing the death penalty has increased dramatically since 1976 (Figure 4.4). Almost 3,500 men and 50 women are awaiting execution. Two-thirds are in the South, with the greatest number in California, Texas, and Florida. In recent years executions have spread from its southern base to states around the country.

Public Opinion

In a democracy public opinion is viewed as having an important impact on public policy. Since 1936 the Gallup Organization has been asking the public, "Do you favor or oppose the death penalty for persons convicted of murder?" Responses to this question have shifted greatly over the past sixty years. Although the majority of Americans favored capital punishment until 1960, public support gradually declined, reaching a low of 40 percent in 1965. However, with the rise in crime in the late 1960s, opinion shifted to a tougher stance.[16] Legislators, always ready to respond to public concerns, began to press for changes in sentencing laws and urged that the death penalty be reinstituted. By 1993 there had been a major reversal of public opinion, with 72 percent of Americans supporting the death penalty. Yet a number of populous states, such as Michigan and Massachusetts, still reject capital punishment in favor of life sentences for murderers. Figure 20.2 traces these shifts in public support for the death penalty.

However, some analysts have argued that opinion on the death penalty is somewhat confusing. They say it is difficult to determine whether the public is supporting capital punishment in general, or whether people are merely supporting the right of the government to take a life under specific circumstances. Much depends on the wording of the question.[17]

Others point to the fact that support for capital punishment plunges when alternatives, such as life imprisonment without the possibility of parole (LWOP) are presented. Mark Costanzo says that the public is about evenly split when respondents are asked to choose between LWOP and death.[18] More than 20 percent of those who support capital punishment switch to LWOP when given the option. A survey of Tennessee prosecutors, public defenders, and state legislators found support for the death penalty decline when LWOP was an option.[19] Even in such strong death penalty states as Arkansas, Georgia, Indiana, and Oklahoma, the split is about even.[20] Costanzo believes that the possibilty that murderers will be released on parole is an important consideration for a large segment of the public. If they could be assured that the murderer would never be released they would be less supportive of capital punishment.[21]

However, in a survey of several hundred respondents in a large American city, Durham, Elrod, and Kindade found continued high support for the death penalty.[22] Given seventeen homicide scenarios and asked the appropriate sentence—death, LWOP, or a prison term—60.8 percent called for death. This may seem low compared to the Gallup Poll results, but very high when it is acknowledged that only about 2 percent of persons convicted of murder are sentenced to death.

Figure 20.2 Attitudes Toward the Death Penalty for Persons Convicted of Murder, 1965–1996

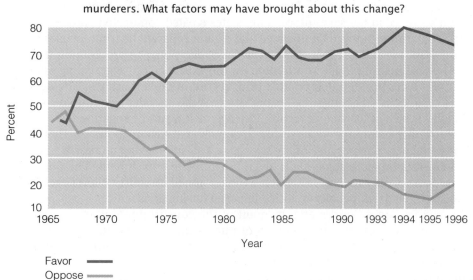

There has been a major reversal of public opinion on the death penalty since 1965. Currently about 72 percent of Americans support capital punishment for convicted murderers. What factors may have brought about this change?

Favor
Oppose

NOTE: Percentages do not add up to 100, because some respondents were undecided.

SOURCE: U.S. Department of Justice, Bureau of Justice Statistics, *Sourcebook of Criminal Justice Statistics* (Washington, DC: U.S. Government Printing Office, 1997), pp. 161, 164.

With thirty-eight states and the federal government now authorizing capital punishment, about 300 death sentences are pronounced each year, and the number of people on death row has risen to more than 3,500. However, as of this writing, the number of executions since 1976 has never exceeded seventy-four (1997) in any one year. Capital punishment remains a controversial issue, one that the courts, correctional professionals, scholars, and the public seem unable to resolve.

The Death Penalty and the Constitution

Death obviously differs from other punishments in that it is final and irreversible. As a result, the Supreme Court has examined the decision-making process in capital cases to ensure that the Constitution's requirements regarding due process, equal protection, and cruel and unusual punishment are fulfilled. Because life is in the balance, capital cases must be conducted according to higher standards of fairness and more careful procedures than other kinds of cases. Several important Supreme Court cases illustrate this fact.

Key U.S. Supreme Court Decisions

In *Furman v. Georgia* (1972), the Supreme Court ruled that the death penalty, as administered, constituted cruel and unusual punishment. The decision invalidated the death penalty laws of thirty-nine states and the District of Columbia.[23] Although a majority of justices objected to the way in which the death penalty was applied, they could not agree on reasons why it was unconstitutional. Two justices argued that the death penalty always violates the Eighth Amendment's prohibition on cruel and unusual punishment, but other members emphasized that the procedures used to impose death sentences were arbitrary and unfair.

Over the next several years, thirty-five states enacted new capital punishment statutes that provided for more careful decision making and more modern methods of execution, such as lethal injection (see Figure 20.3).

The new laws were tested before the Supreme Court in 1976 in the case of *Gregg v. Georgia*.[24] The Court upheld those laws that required the sentencing judge or jury to take into account specific aggravating and mitigating factors in deciding which convicted murderers should be sentenced to death. Instead of deciding the defendant's guilt and imposing the death sentence in the same proceeding, states created "bifurcated" proceedings in which a trial determines guilt or innocence and then a separate hearing focuses exclusively on the issues of punishment. Under the *Gregg* decision, the prosecution uses the punishment-phase hearing to focus attention on the existence of "aggravating factors," such as excessive cruelty or a defendant's prior record of violent crimes. The decision makers must also focus on "mitigating factors" such as the offender's youthfulness, mental retardation, or lack of a criminal record. The aggravating and mitigating factors must be weighed together before the judge or jury can make a decision about whether to impose a death sentence. The purpose of the two-stage decision-making process is to ensure thorough deliberation before someone is given the ultimate punishment. The Court also endorsed "proportionality review" in which a higher appellate court reviews each death sentence to see if the death penalty was also imposed in similar cases.[25]

Despite the Supreme Court's endorsement of the constitutionality of capital punishment, opponents of the death penalty continue to challenge it with new cases. Instead of making the broad claim that capital punishment is unconstitutional, these cases challenged aspects of it such as racial discrimination in capital sentencing and the execution of minors and the mentally retarded.

The U.S. Supreme Court may have dealt a fatal blow to the hopes of death penalty opponents in April 1987. In the case of *McCleskey v. Kemp* the Court rejected a constitutional challenge to Georgia death penalty law on the grounds of racial discrimination.[26]

Figure 20.3 Methods of Execution Authorized by States

An increasing number of states authorize the use of lethal injections. What reasons might be given for the acceptance of this method?

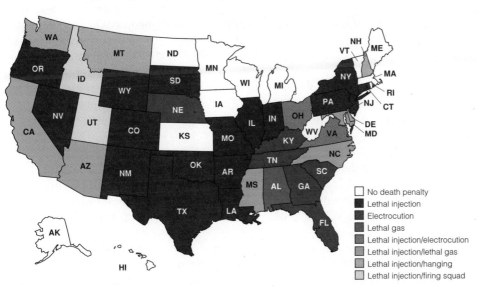

- ☐ No death penalty
- Lethal injection
- Electrocution
- Lethal gas
- Lethal injection/electrocution
- Lethal injection/lethal gas
- Lethal injection/hanging
- Lethal injection/firing squad

SOURCE: U.S. Department of Justice, Bureau of Justice Statistics, *Bulletin*, December 1997, p. 5.

Warren McCleskey, an African American, was sentenced to death for killing a white police officer during a furniture store robbery. Before the U.S. Supreme Court, McCleskey's attorney cited research showing a disparity in the imposition of the death penalty in Georgia based on the race of the victim and, to a lesser extent, the race of the defendant. Researchers had examined over two thousand Georgia murder cases and found that defendants charged with killing whites had received the death penalty eleven times more often than had those convicted of killing African Americans. Even after compensating for 230 factors, such as the viciousness of the crime or the quality of the evidence, the study showed that the death sentence was four times more likely to be imposed when the victim was white. Although 60 percent of Georgia homicide victims are African Americans, all seven people put to death in that state since 1976 had been convicted of killing white people and six of the seven murderers were African Americans.[27]

By a 5–4 vote the justices rejected McCleskey's assertion that Georgia's capital sentencing practices violated the equal protection clause of the Constitution by producing racial discrimination. The slim majority of justices declared that McCleskey would have to prove that the decision makers acted with a discriminatory purpose in deciding his case. The Court also concluded that statistical evidence showing discrimination throughout the Georgia courts did not provide adequate proof. McCleskey was executed in 1991.

Continuing Legal Issues

In recent years there has been a shift in the challenges to capital punishment. Although the case law since *Furman* would indicate that capital punishment is legal so long as it is imposed fairly, some opponents now argue that it is cruel and unusual per se to uniformly execute all individuals receiving the sentence of death. They claim, for example, that certain classes of death row inmates should not be executed because they are insane, were underage at the time they committed the crime, or are mentally retarded. According to this argument, it is morally wrong to execute a person who does not have the mental capacity of an adult. The effectiveness of defense counsel in capital cases is also an issue. Because most defendants in capital cases are poor, they are assigned counsel by the state. Critics charge that these attorneys are inadequate and do not have the fiscal resources to mount an effective defense. A fourth issue, the length of appeals, has been a major concern of Chief Justice William Rehnquist.[28]

Execution of the Insane Insanity is a recognized defense for commission of a crime because *mens rea* (criminal intent) is not present. But should people who become mentally disabled after they are sentenced to death be executed? The Supreme Court responded to this question in 1986 in *Ford v. Wainwright*.[29] In 1974 Ford was convicted of murder and sentenced to death. There was no suggestion at his trial or sentencing that he was mentally incompetent. Only after he was incarcerated did he begin to exhibit delusional behavior, claiming that the Ku Klux Klan was part of an elaborate conspiracy to force him to commit suicide and that his female relatives were being tortured and sexually abused somewhere in the prison.

With evidence of these delusions, Ford's counsel invoked the procedures of the Florida law governing the determination of competency of a condemned inmate. Three psychiatrists examined Ford for thirty minutes in the presence of witnesses, including counsel and correctional officials. Each psychiatrist filed a separate and conflicting report with the governor, who subsequently signed a death warrant. Ford then appealed to the Supreme Court.

Justice Thurgood Marshall, writing for the majority, concluded that the Eighth Amendment prohibited the state from executing the insane—the accused must comprehend both the fact that he had been sentenced to death and the reason for it. Marshall cited the common law precedent that questioned the retributive and deterrent value of executing a mentally disabled person. In addition, he argued, the idea is offensive to humanity. The justices also found the Florida procedures defective because they did not provide for a full and fair hearing on the competence of the offender.

Although one might think that the *Ford* decision would end questions about competency to be executed, the issue arose again in Arkansas in 1991.[30] Rickey Ray Rector killed two men, one of whom was a police officer. He then shot himself in the temple, lifting three inches off the front of his brain, leaving him with the mental capabilities of a small child. He was convicted at trial and given the death sentence. In prison he howled day and night, jumped around, exhibited other aspects of abnormal behavior, and seemed to have no idea that he was to be executed.

The U.S. Supreme Court rejected his appeal. The Arkansas Parole and Community Rehabilitation Board unanimously turned down a recommendation that Governor Bill Clinton commute the death sentence to life imprisonment without parole. Clinton declined to halt the execution, and Rector was given a lethal injection on January 24, 1991.

Although the Supreme Court has ruled that the insane should not be executed, the issue of how competence should be determined is still an issue. A second issue concerns the morality of treating an offender's mental illness so that they *can* be executed, a policy opposed by the American Medical Association. The Supreme Court has not directly addressed this issue with regard to death row inmates. However, in *Washington v. Harper* (1990) it did say that a state could require a prison inmate to take a drug to control his schizophrenia. But the court based the decision on the state's interest in reducing the danger such an inmate has to himself and to others.[31]

Execution of Juveniles The laws of eight states do not specify a minimum age for offenders receiving capital punishment. In some states the minimum age is the same as the age at which a juvenile may be transferred to criminal court and tried as an adult. Most (fifteen) states set age 18 as the minimum for which capital punishment is authorized.[32] Since 1642, when the Plymouth Colony in Massachusetts hanged a teenage boy for bestiality, about three hundred juveniles have been executed in the United States.[33] Death penalty opponents have argued that adolescents do not possess the same capacity as adults to understand the consequences of their actions.

The Supreme Court has been divided on the issue of the death penalty for juveniles. In *Thompson v. Oklahoma* (1988), the Court narrowly decided that William Wayne

Thompson, who was 15 when he committed murder, should not be executed.[34] A plurality of four justices held that executing juveniles did not comport with the "evolving standards of decency that mark the progress of a maturing society." The dissenters said that Thompson had been correctly sentenced under Oklahoma law. Within a year the Court again considered the issue in *Stanford v. Kentucky* (1989) and *Wilkins v. Missouri* (1989) and this time the justices upheld the death sentences imposed on offenders who were 16 and 17 years old, respectively, at the time of their crimes.[35] All the justices agreed that interpretation of the cruel and unusual punishment clause rests on the "evolving standards of decency that mark the progress of a maturing society." However, the justices disagreed as to the factors that should be used to make that determination. With the Supreme Court evidently sanctioning executions of juveniles under some circumstances, Louisiana put to death Dalton Prejean, a juvenile at the time of the offense, on May 18, 1990. There are currently seventy-three males on death rows who were under age 18 at the time of their offenses.[36] The schoolyard killings in Jonesboro, Arkansas and other homicides by juveniles have raised calls to lower the age that young people may be charged as an adult.

Unkempt, unwashed, and declared schizophrenic, triple killer Horace Edwards Kelly confronted the California courts with a dilemma. State law prohibits the execution of an inmate who has become insane while in prison—even if the inmate was found competent at the time of the crime and during trial. Should Kelly die? You decide.

Execution of the Retarded   An estimated 250 offenders on the nation's death rows are classified as retarded, and they account for 13 percent of executions.[37] It is argued that retarded people have difficulty defending themselves in court because they have problems remembering details, locating witnesses, and testifying credibly in their own behalf. It is also asserted that executing the retarded serves neither retributive nor deterrent purposes, because the general public may believe that it was the fact of the mental disability that caused the offender to commit the crime.[38]

In 1989 the Supreme Court decided that the Eighth Amendment does not prohibit execution of the mentally retarded. The case involved Johnny Paul Penry, a convicted killer with an IQ of about 70 and the mental capacity of a 7-year-old.[39] The court noted that only Georgia and Maryland prohibited execution of the mentally retarded. Now, years after the Supreme Court decision, Penry is still on death row in Texas, in part because of the lengthy appeals process.

In contrast, Alabama executed Horace Dunkins, Jr., who had an IQ of 69, on July 14, 1989. Adding to the injustice of executing a retarded person was the manner in which the execution was carried out. Because the first bolt of electricity left Dunkins still alive, a second flick of the switch was needed to kill him.[40]

Appeals   The long appeals process for death penalty cases is a source of ongoing controversy. The average length of time between sentencing by a trial court and the date that the sentence is carried out is between seven and eight years. During this time sentences are reviewed by the state courts and, through the writ of habeas corpus, by the federal courts.

The writ of habeas corpus is the only means by which the federal courts can hear challenges by state inmates to their convictions and sentences. A long time is required to exhaust state appeals before filing a habeas corpus petition in the federal courts. Intervening court decisions have frequently changed the law to help the offender's case. Yet in two 1990 decisions the Court limited the ability of death row inmates to base appeals on new favorable rulings issued after their convictions.[41]

In a major ruling affecting death penalty appeals, the Court sharply curtailed the ability of offenders to file multiple challenges to the constitutionality of their sentences. In *McCleskey v. Zant* (1991), the Court ruled that, except in exceptional circumstances, the lower federal courts must dismiss a prisoner's second and subsequent habeas corpus petitions. Observers believe that this ruling will result in states carrying out death sentences more quickly.[42]

Appeals to the federal courts were further restricted by the Supreme Court in 1993 when a majority of the justices said that an offender who presents belated evidence of innocence is not ordinarily entitled to a new hearing in a federal court before execution. This ruling centered on the case of Leonel Herrera, who was convicted in Texas and sentenced to death for the 1982 murder of two police officers. Ten years later Herrera's nephew asserted in an affidavit that before he died in 1984, his father, Raul Herrera, Sr., told him that it was he and not his brother, Leonel, who had shot the officers. Statements from three other people who previously had named Raul as the murderer were presented to the court. Texas law provides only thirty days for filing a motion for a new trial based on newly discovered evidence. The Supreme Court rejected Herrera's argument that his case should be reopened because of the new evidence. The Chief Justice, writing for the majority, observed that only in "truly persuasive" cases should a hearing be held.[43] Herrera was executed on May 12, 1993. His last words were, "I am innocent; I am innocent. God bless you all."

Chief Justice Rehnquist has actively sought to reduce the opportunities for capital punishment defendants to have their appeals heard by multiple courts.[44] In 1996 President Clinton signed the Anti-Terrorism and Effective Death Penalty Act that requires death row inmates to file habeas appeals within one year and requires that federal judges issue their decisions within strict time limits.[45]

Appellate review is a time-consuming and expensive process, but it also has an impact. From 1977—the year after the Supreme Court upheld the constitutionality of revised state capital punishment laws—to 1996, a total of 5,154 people entered prison under sentence of death. During those twenty years, 358 people were executed, and 1,957 were removed from under a death sentence by appellate court decisions and reviews, commutations, or death while awaiting execution.[46]

Radelet, Lofquist, and Bedau have examined the case of sixty-eight death row inmates later released because of doubts about their guilt.[47] These cases account for one of every five inmates executed during the period 1970–1996. Correction of the miscarriage of about one third of the defendants took four years or less, but it took nine years or longer for another third of the defendants. Had the expedited appeals process and limitations on habeas corpus been in effect, would these death sentences have been overturned?

Counsel   In 1984 the Supreme Court ruled in *Stickland v. Washington* that defendants in capital cases had the right to representation that meets an "objective standard of reasonableness."[48] As noted by Justice Sandra Day O'Connor, the appellant must show "that there is a reasonable probability that, but for counsel's unprofessional errors, the result of the proceeding would have been different."[49]

David Washington had been charged with three counts of capital murder, robbery, kidnapping, and other felonies, and an experienced criminal lawyer was appointed as defense counsel. Against his attorney's advice Washington confessed to two murders, waived a jury trial, pleaded guilty to all charges, and chose to be sentenced by the trial judge. Believing the situation was hopeless, his counsel did not adequately prepare for the sentencing hearing and sought neither character statements nor psychiatric examination. On being sentenced to death, Washington appealed. The Supreme Court rejected his claim that his attorney was ineffective since he did not call witnesses, seek a presentence investigation report, or cross-examine medical experts.

Most death penalty defendants are indigent and are provided counsel by the state. Critics argue that defense in capital cases is a highly specialized area of the law and that inexperienced attorneys should not be assigned to indigent cases. In most jurisdictions, especially in the South, counsel appointed to represent capital defendants receive very small fees, often limited by statute to $1,000 per case. For example, Alabama pays attorneys $20 per hour and Mississippi pays only $11.75.[50] Few attorneys are willing to put in the hundreds of hours required in a capital case for these amounts. Stephen Bright estimates that he was paid less than $2 per hour for representing a capital defendant in Mississippi.[51] The defense also has limited resources to investigate the case and to call expert witnesses. One Texas lawyer delivered a twenty-six-word statement at sentencing: "You are an extremely intelligent jury. You've got that man's life in your hands. You can take it or not. That's all I have to say." This client was executed in 1992.[52]

To address some of these concerns, the federal government has established fifteen death penalty resource centers supported by federal and state funds. The centers recruit, train, and assist lawyers who handle appeals from death row, but they do not provide for attorneys at the trial.[53]

Who Is on Death Row?

Of the 22,000 arrests each year for murder and nonnegligent manslaughter, only about 300 receive the death penalty. What factors contribute to some offenders being given incarceration while others are sentenced to death? The Supreme Court has ruled that juries must weigh aggravating and mitigating factors before recommending the sentence in capital cases. But what other factors might contribute to the selection of only a few for execution? Can it be *who* they are? Where the crime was committed? Who was the prosecutor? Was race a factor? In sum, is the process capricious, akin to a lottery as some scholars have said?[54]

Who Are They?

Death row inmates tend to be poorly educated men from low-income backgrounds. Further, the number of minority group members on death row is far out of proportion to their numbers in the general population (see Figure 20.4). The criminal history of these death row inmates shows that 66 percent have a prior felony conviction, 9 percent have a prior homicide conviction, and 34 percent were on probation or parole or in prison at the time of the capital offense.[55]

As noted early, only forty-seven women currently are on death row. Karla Faye Tucker and Judy Buenoano were the last women to be executed, in 1998, by Texas and Florida, respectively. Although one of seven arrestees for murder is a woman, judges and jurors seem reluctant to sentence them to death, as evidenced by the life in prison sentence given Susan Smith, convicted or murdering her two young sons. However, what some might view as a double standard may end as public attitudes toward women change.

Where Was the Crime Committed?

Of particular interest is the distribution of death row inmates among the states, as shown in Figure 20.5. About 56 percent of those under sentence of death are in the South, 22 percent in the West, and 15 percent in the Midwest. Less than 7 percent are in the northeastern death penalty states of Connecticut, New Hampshire, New Jersey, New York, and Pennsylvania. Also revealing is the fact that of the 434 executions from 1976 to January 1998, two thirds have been carried out in six states: Texas (144), Florida (39), Virginia (46), Missouri (29), Louisiana (24), and Georgia (22).[56]

Figure 20.4 Characteristics of Death Row Inmates

Like other prisoners, death row inmates tend to be younger, less educated males. Minority group members on death row also are disproportionately represented.

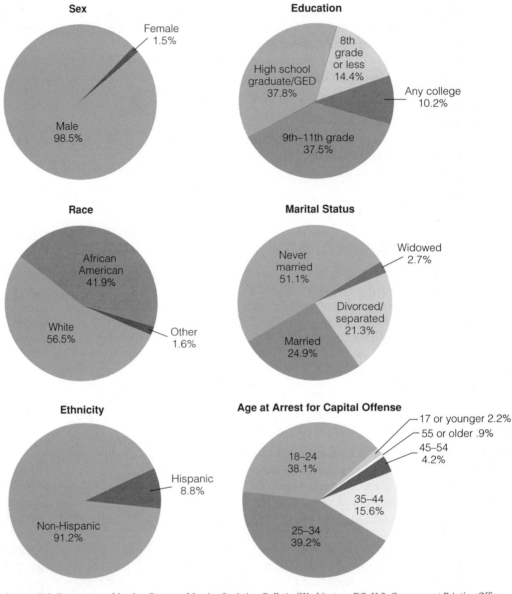

Sex

Female 1.5%

Male 98.5%

Education

8th grade or less 14.4%

High school graduate/GED 37.8%

Any college 10.2%

9th–11th grade 37.5%

Race

African American 41.9%

White 56.5%

Other 1.6%

Marital Status

Never married 51.1%

Widowed 2.7%

Divorced/separated 21.3%

Married 24.9%

Ethnicity

Hispanic 8.8%

Non-Hispanic 91.2%

Age at Arrest for Capital Offense

18–24 38.1%

17 or younger 2.2%

55 or older .9%

45–54 4.2%

35–44 15.6%

25–34 39.2%

Source: U.S. Department of Justice, Bureau of Justice Statistics, *Bulletin* (Washington, DC: U.S. Government Printing Office, December 1997), p. 8.

Who Was the Prosecutor?

But even within states, the probability that a prosecutor will ask for the death penalty differs. For example, of the ninety-two people executed in Texas from 1976 to 1995, thirty-seven were from the Houston area, where district attorney Johnny B. Holmes, Jr., is a vocal advocate of the death penalty. In contrast, Dallas area district attorney John Vance is more circumspect; only five people from that area have been executed, and the death row population is about a quarter that of Houston's.[57] The discretionary power of prosecutors and the local political environment explain much of these differences.[58] As James Liebman, an expert on the death penalty, says, "Lots of states have death belts. In southern Georgia, there are lots of death sentences; in northern Georgia, there aren't. In Tennessee, there are tons of death sentences in Memphis and East Knoxville, but not in Nashville."[59]

Figure 20.5 Prisoners Under Sentence of Death, by State

Why is there such variation among the states in applying the death penalty?

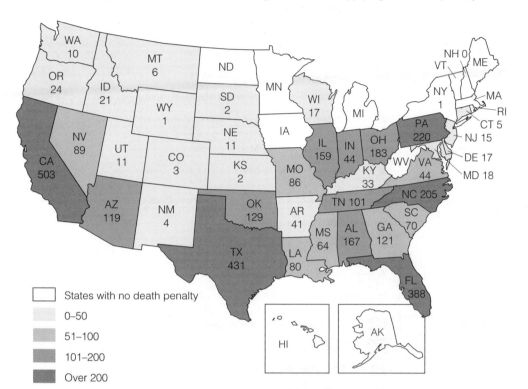

States with no death penalty

0–50

51–100

101–200

Over 200

SOURCE: NAACP Legal Defense and Education Fund, *Death Row USA* (New York: NAACP Defense and Education Fund, 1998).

Political factors may be at work in these states to the extent that prosecuting attorneys and judges expect to be reelected if they campaign on their death penalty record.[60]

Was Race a Factor?

Research by David Baldus and others found that imposition of the death penalty in Georgia was influenced by the race of the murder victim and, to a lesser extent, the race of the offender.[61] Of over two thousand Georgia murder cases, defendants charged with killing white people had received the death penalty eleven times more often than had those charged with killing African Americans. Even after compensating for 230 factors, the death sentence was four times more likely to be imposed when the victim was white. Although 60 percent of Georgia homicide victims are African American, all seven people put to death in that state since 1976 had been convicted of killing white people; six of the seven murderers were African American. The factors influencing imposition of the death penalty in Georgia are shown in Figure 20.6.

Is Georgia unique, or is the victim's race a determinative factor in other states? Samuel Gross and Robert Mauro examined the death penalty in eight states—Arkansas, Florida, Georgia, Illinois, Mississippi, North Carolina, Oklahoma, and Virginia. In each state they found that the death sentence was more likely to be imposed if the victim was white rather than African American. The ratios varied from 10:1 in Georgia and Mississippi to 5:1 in Virginia.[62]

Does the evidence from Georgia indicate racism, or are other factors at work? Robert Bohm examined racial disparity and discrimination in two Georgia judicial circuits and suggested that it is institutional racism, such as the few African-American prosecutors, defense attorneys, and judges in the system, that influences capital punishment decisions.

Figure 20.6 Imposing the Death Penalty in Georgia

Researchers have identified the various aspects of a murder that increase or decrease the chance of a death penalty.

Factors that reduce the chance of a death penalty	● Defendant was not the triggerman.
	● Defendant was under seventeen.
	● Circumstances involved family, lover, liquor, or barroom quarrel.
	● Defendant was retiree, student, juvenile, or housewife.
Neutral factors	● Defendant was African American.
	● Defendant was female.
Factors that increase the chance of the death penalty	● Victim was a police or correctional officer on duty.
	● Victim was a stranger.
	● Victim was weak or frail.
	● Armed robbery was involved.
	● One or more whites were victims.
Increase more	● Victim was twelve or younger.
	● Murder was for hire.
	● Defendant killed two or more people.
	● Mental torture was involved.
	● Rape was involved.
Increase greatly	● Defendant's motive was to collect insurance,.
	● Physical torture was involved.

SOURCES: *The New York Times,* February 24, 1995, p. B4. Figure based on David Baldus, George Woodworth, and Charles Pulaski, *Equal Justice and the Death Penalty: A Legal and Empirical Analysis* (Boston: Northeastern University Press, 1990).

He believes that one result of the Supreme Court's decision in *McCleskey v. Kemp* is that it will be almost impossible to show racism in individual cases. Bohm quotes Georgia state senator Gary Parker as saying, "The Supreme Court's decision in *McCleskey v. Kemp* has been interpreted by prosecutors and judges in the South as a clear message that they are not to be held accountable in the courts for racial discrimination that occurs in capital trials."[63]

A 1998 study on racial disparities in death penalty cases found that African-American defendants in Philadelphia are nearly four times more likely than other defendants to be sentenced to death, even when controlling for levels of crime severity and the defendant's criminal history. The researchers also found that unlike the South where the victim's race is a factor, in northern states more disparity in defendants' race is present, with blacks more likely to be charged.[64]

A Continuing Debate?

Although public opinion polls show high support for the death penalty and about 300 offenders per year are given this sentence, the number of executions remains low. Does this mean Americans are ambivalent about actually carrying out the punishment? What might it tell us about capital punishment as we enter the new century? Debate on this important public policy issue has gone on for more than two hundred years, yet there is still no consensus.

Opponents of the death penalty argue that poor people and members of minority groups receive a disproportionate number of death sentences. Yet some have challenged this view as not being supported by research.[65]

Opponents also cite the finality of death, in light of the number of acknowledged mistakes that have been made in the past, as sufficient reason to oppose capital punishment.[66] A recent study found 68 cases of defendants who were released between 1973 and 1995 because of doubts about their guilt. Researchers found that nationally as many as eight defendants have been released each year because of such factors as perjured testimony, withheld evidence, or mistakes of identification.[67]

Opponents further note that the cost to try, convict, and execute a murderer is much higher than trying that individual as a noncapital case and keeping him or her in prison for twenty years. A study of death penalty cases in North Carolina showed that the *extra* cost to the public of prosecuting a capital case rather than noncapital is more than

FOCUS Awaiting Execution

Stephen Gettinger

At 10 A.M. Wednesday, I found it too easy to visualize what Robert Austin Sullivan was going through as he awaited his execution at the Florida State Prison at Starke.

He had described his fears to me dozens of times, in letters and in prison: choking down his last meal, feeling the razor as it shaved his head and leg, feeling the leather belts cinch him into the big oak chair that inmates call "Old Sparky."

Several years ago, I sat in that same chair, for a few minutes, and tried to imagine what it would be like: gagged and bound, drinking in one last vision before they dropped the hood over my eyes. Would there be one caring face in that crowd of witnesses, or only eyes hardened against me?

Mr. Sullivan slept with that vision for ten years, longer than anyone else on death row. Doing research for a book, I first met him in June 1976. College-educated and middle-class, he was more like me than most of those who populate death rows across the country. Mr. Sullivan didn't blink at my questions: What do you imagine it will feel like? Do you dream about it? Will you fight the guards when they come to get you? His direct answers, delivered with a slight stutter, and his wide eyes told me he thought about these things all too often.

A week later, I was back on death row taking photographs. In response to questions from Mr. Sullivan, I told him gently that the Supreme Court had rejected his appeal the day before. He said his lawyer hadn't bothered to call him. Mr. Sullivan's photograph shows him behind bars of his cage, a portly young man standing in his underwear, looking wistful.

In May 1979, Mr. Sullivan peered across the prison yard at the dim movements in the death house as John Spenke-

link was executed. Later, he wrote a long reconstruction of the incident filled with disturbing detail: "A special lubricant solution was applied to his shaved head and leg to increase the conductivity and to reduce burning." . . .

News reports said that Mr. Sullivan was calm during the night before his execution but that he broke down and cried several times in the death chamber. His last words, according to one witness, were: "I hold malice to none. May God bless you all."

I have tried to blot out the scene with images of the murder of which Mr. Sullivan was convicted: Donald Schmidt, assistant manager of a restaurant, kidnapped from his office at midnight, driven out to a deserted spot in the woods, kneeling blindfolded while a shotgun blew his head open. But there is a nagging chance that Mr. Sullivan may not have done it: His evidence that he was not involved, while questionable, was never given a full examination in court. Aside from that, the firm belief grows that one nightmare does not cancel out another. The horror inflicted on thirty-six-year-old Robert Sullivan diminishes us all: executioners, observers, those who ignored it.

Albert Camus wrote: "The devastating, degrading fear that is imposed on the condemned for months or years is a punishment more terrible than death. For there to be equivalence, the death penalty would have to punish a criminal who had warned his victim of the date at which he would inflict a horrible death on him and who, from that moment onward, had confined him at his mercy for months. Such a monster is not encountered in private life."

Source: Adapted from S. Gettinger, "Awaiting Execution," *The New York Times,* December 5, 1983. Copyright © 1983 by The New York Times Company. Reprinted by permission.

A group photo is taken of twenty-eight of the seventy-five former death row inmates released because later evidence proved their innocence. The group assembled at a conference on Wrongful Convictions and the Death Penalty held at Northwestern University.

$216,000. And if the case ultimately results in an execution, the *extra* cost is more than $2.16 million.[68] A report adopted by the Judicial Conference of the United States found the cost of defending a person charged with a capital offense, for which the U.S. Attorney General did not authorize seeking the death penalty, to be $55,772. If the death penalty was sought, the defense costs were $218,112. Prosecution costs were $192,333 and $269,139 respectively.[69]

Data from other parts of the nation support this view. It has been estimated that California would save $90 million annually if the death penalty were abolished[70] and the New York Department of Correctional Services has estimated that reinstating the death penalty will cost the state $118 million each year.[71]

In a highly publicized *Wall Street Journal* article conservative scholar John J. DiIulio surprised many by writing that the death penalty should be abolished because "as it has been administered, is administered and will likely to continue to be administered [it] is arbitrary and capricious. . . . Since we can't apply it fairly, we ought to consider abolishing it."[72] He pointed to the disparity among the great number of murders committed each year, the smaller number of persons who receive the death penalty, and the infinitesimally small number who are executed. This results in a ratio of people murdered to people executed for murder, of about 1,000 to 1.

Proponents of the death penalty claim that it deters criminals from committing violent acts and that justice demands that retribution, regardless of cost, be accorded murderers. They further argue that, given the high levels of violent crimes in the United States, we must retain the severest penalties. To give someone a life sentence of incarceration for murder diminishes the worth of the victim, is costly to society, and does not lessen the possibility that the offender will do further harm either while incarcerated or on release on parole. In answer to the charge that the death penalty is administered in an arbitrary and capricious manner, scholars such as Walter Berns and Joseph Bessette say that in the post-*Furman* era, "the system now in place serves as a filter, reserving the death penalty for the worst offenders."[73]

Will the United States increase the pace of executions, allow the number of capital offenders in prison to grow, or provide some alternatives such as life imprisonment without parole for convicted murderers? These questions remain unanswered.

Summary

Capital punishment continues to be a highly controversial sanction. Issues of morality, utility, and equity dominate the debate, as they have in the United States for some two hundred years.

With the number of individuals on death row rising each year but the number of executions remaining low, questions have been raised about the future of this punishment. Since the 1976 Supreme Court decision in *Gregg v. Georgia,* thirty-eight states have rewritten their statutes so as to provide for the death penalty. In that same time the Court has addressed issues related to the death penalty, including the execution of the mentally ill, juveniles, and the retarded. Of late, Chief Justice Rehnquist has urged the judiciary to limit opportunities for appeals so as to ensure that the penalty is carried out.

The characteristics of those on death row show that, compared to the general population, they are more likely to be low-income, undereducated, minority men. The data also show that the southern states are most likely to impose the death penalty and that the race of the victim is an important factor.

Although public opinion seemingly supports the death penalty, some argue that this support is shallow. It is also argued that life imprisonment without parole might be an acceptable alternative. ■

For Discussion

1. What are the major arguments supporting and opposing capital punishment? Which seems to you the most important?

2. Should the death penalty be imposed on a person whose crime was committed as a juvenile? Do you believe the "evolving standards of decency" of our society support such an execution?

3. Why is there support for the death penalty in the United States when it has been abolished in Europe?

4. What alternatives to death might achieve the retributive, deterrent, and incapacitative goals of capital punishment?

5. What does the future hold for the death penalty?

For Further Reading

Acker, James R., Robert M. Bohm, and Charles S. Lanier, eds., *America's Experiment with Capital Punishment.* Durham, NC: Carolina Academic Press, 1998. An outstanding collection of essays on the death penalty.

Bedau, Hugo Adam. *Death Is Different.* Boston: Northeastern University Press, 1987. Argues that the death penalty differs from other punishments in its morality, its politics, and its symbolism; written by a major opponent of the death penalty.

Costanzo, Mark. *Just Revenge.* New York: St. Martin's Press, 1997. An excellent overview of capital punishment, exploring its symbolism, costs, expected benefits, politics, and consequences.

Johnson, Robert. *Death Work,* 2nd ed. Belmont, CA: Wadsworth Publishing, 1998. Studies the individuals on death row—both prisoners and correctional officers—and the impact of capital punishment on their lives.

Mello, Michael A. *Dead Wrong: A Death Row Lawyer Speaks Out against Capital Punishment.* Madison: University of Wisconsin Press, 1997. For seventeen years a death row lawyer in Florida, the author describes his motivation and experiences.

Prejean, Helen. *Dead Man Walking.* New York: Random House, 1993. Recounts the story of a Roman Catholic nun, spiritual adviser to two Louisiana death row inmates, who confronts both the viciousness of these murderers and the pain of the families of their victims; written by a death penalty opponent but also a victims' advocate.

Tucker, John C. *May God Have Mercy: A True Story of Crime and Punishment.* New York: W. W. Norton, 1997. Case study of the indictment, trial, and execution in 1992 of Roger Coleman, convicted of the murder of his sister-in-law. New evidence was not considered by the court, because Coleman's appointed attorney filed a document a day late.

Von Drehle, David. *Among the Lowest of the Dead.* New York: Times Books, 1995. A journalist's account of the culture of death row: the condemned, their attorneys, and the relatives of the victims.

Notes

1. Drawn from Beverly Lowry, "The Good Bad Girl," *The New Yorker,* February 9, 1998, pp. 60–69; *The New York Times,* January 1, 1998, p. A1, February 3, 1998, p. A4, February 4, 1998, p. A1.
2. Ernest van den Haag, "For the Death Penalty," *The New York Times,* October 17, 1983. See also Ernest van den Haag, "Justice, Deterrence and the Death Penalty," in James R. Acker, Robert M. Bohm, and Charles S. Lanier, eds., *America's Experiment with Capital Punishment* (Durham, NC: Carolina Academic Press, 1998), pp. 139–156.
3. Ibid.
4. Marvin E. Wolfgang, "We Do Not Deserve to Kill," *Crime and Delinquency,* 44, January 1998, p. 22.
5. Michael L. Radelet and Ronald L. Akers, "Deterrence and the Death Penalty: The Views of the Experts," *Journal of Criminal Law and Criminology,* 87, Fall 1996, pp. l–16. In a survey of "top criminologists," the authors found agreement that captial punishment fails to deter.
6. Mark Costanzo, *Just Revenge* (New York: St. Martin's Press, 1997), p. 96.
7. Ruth D. Peterson and William C. Bailey, "Murder and Capital Punishment in the Evolving Context of the Post–*Furman* Era," *Social Forces,* 66, 1988, pp. 774–807. See also Peterson and Bailey, "Is Capital Punishment an Effective Deterrent for Murder?" in James R. Acker, Robert M. Bohm, and Charles S. Lanier, eds., *America's Experiment with Capital Punishment* (Durham, NC: Carolina Academic Press, 1998), pp. 157–182.
8. Richard O. Lempert, "The Effect of Executions on Homicides: A New Look in an Old Light," *Crime and Delinquency,* 29, 1983, pp. 88–115.
9. Isaac Ehrlich, "The Deterrent Effect of Capital Punishment: A Question of Life and Death," *American Economic Review,* 65, 1975, pp. 397–417.
10. William J. Bowers and Glenn L. Pierce, "The Illusion of Deterrence in Isaac Ehrlich's Research on Capital Punishment," *Yale Law Journal,* 85, 1975, pp. 187–208.
11. Klein, B. E. Forst, and V. Filatov, "The Deterrent Effect of Capital Punishment: An Assessment of the Estimates," in A. Blumstein, J. Cohen, and D. Nagin, eds., *Deterrence and Incapacitation* (Washington, DC: National Academy of Sciences).
12. Louis P. Masur, *Rites of Execution: Capital Punishment and the Transformation of American Culture, 1776–1865* (New York: Oxford University Press, 1989).
13. Harry Elmer Barnes and Negley K. Teeters, *New Horizons in Criminology,* 3rd ed. (Englewood Cliffs, NJ: Prentice–Hall, 1959), p. 308.
14. Ibid., p. 4.
15. Franklin Zimring and Gordon Hawkins, *Capital Punishment and the American Agenda* (New York: Cambridge University Press, 1986).
16. Thomas J. Keil and Gennaro F. Vito, "Fear of Crime and Attitudes Toward Capital Punishment: A Structural Equations Model," *Justice Quarterly,* 8, December 1991, p. 447. The authors find a link between fear of crime in the neighborhood and a greater willingness to endorse the death penalty.
17. Frank P. Williams, III, Dennis R. Longmire, and David B. Gulick, "The Public and the Death Penalty: Opinion as an Artifact of Question Type," *Criminal Justice Research,* 3, 1988, p. 3.
18. Costanzo, *Just Revenge,* pp.123–128.
19. John T. Whitehead, "Good Ol' Boys" and the Chair: Death Penalty Attitudes of Policy Makers in Tennessee," *Crime and Delinquency,* 44, April 1998, pp. 245–256.
20. J. Bowers, M. Vandiver, and P. H. Dugan, "A New Look at Public Opinion on Capital Punishment: What Citizens and Legislators Prefer," *American Journal of Criminal Law,* 22, 1994, pp. 77–150.
21. Costanzo, p. 124.
22. Alexis M. Durham, H. Present Elrod, and Patrick T. Kinkade, "Public Support for the Death Penalty: Beyond Gallup," *Justice Quarterly,* 13, December 1996, pp. 705–730.
23. *Furman v. Georgia,* 408 U.S. 238 (1972).
24. *Gregg v. Georgia,* 428 U.S. 153 (1976).
25. Leigh B. Bienen, "The Proportionality Review of Capital Cases by State High Courts After *Gregg:* Only 'The Appearance of Justice?'" *Journal of Criminal Law and Criminology,* 87, Fall 1996, pp. 130–285.
26. *McCleskey v. Kemp,* 478 U.S. 1019 (1987).
27. David C. Baldus, George F. Woodworth, and Charles A. Pulaski, Jr., *Equal Justice and the Death Penalty: A Legal and Empirical Analysis* (Boston: Northeastern University Press, 1990).
28. Mark A. Small, "A Review of Death Penalty Caselaw: Future Directions for Program Evaluation," *Criminal Justice Policy Review,* 5, June 1991, p. 117; Candace McCoy, "The Death Penalty Continued," *Federal Probation,* March 1990, p. 77.
29. *Ford v. Wainwright,* 477 U.S. 399 (1985).
30. Marshall Frady, "Death in Arkansas," *The New York Times,* February 23, 1993, p. 105.
31. *Washington v. Harper,* 494 U.S. 210 (1990).
32. Department of Justice, Bureau of Justice Statistics, *Bulletin,* December 1997, p. 5.

33. Ron Rosenbaum, "Too Young to Die?" *New York Times Magazine,* March 12, 1989; NAACP Legal Defense and Education Fund, *Death Row, USA* (New York: NAACP Legal Defense and Education Fund, 1998.

34. *Thompson v. Oklahoma,* 108 S.Ct. 2687 (1985).

35. 492 U.S. 361 (1989)

36. NAACP Legal Defense and Educational Fund, *Death Row U.S.A.* (New York: NAACP Legal Defense and Education Fund, 1998).

37. Victor L. Streib, "Executing Women, Children and the Retarded: Second Class Citizens in Capital Punishment," in James R. Acker, Robert M. Bohm, and Charles S. Lanier, eds., *America's Experiment with Capital Punishment* (Durham, NC: Carolina Academic Press, 1998), p. 212.

38. Philip L. Fetzer, "Execution of the Mentally Retarded: A Punishment Without Justification," *South Carolina Law Review,* 40, 1989, p. 419.

39. *Penry v. Lynaugh,* 45 Cr.L.Rptr. 3188 (1989).

40. *The New York Times,* July 15, 1989, p. 6.

41. *The New York Times,* March 6, 1990, p. A20.

42. *McCleskey v. Zant,* 111 S.Ct. 1454 (1991).

43. *New York Times,* January 26, 1993, p. 1.

44. Robert D. Pursley, "The Federal Habeas Corpus Process: Unraveling the Issues," *Criminal Justice Policy Review,* 7, June 1995, p. 115.

45. *Newsweek,* May 6, 1996, p. 72.

46. Department of Justice, Bureau of Justice Statistics, *Bulletin,* December 1997, p. 9.

47. Michael L. Radelet, Williams S. Lofquist, Hugo Adam Bedau, "Prisoners Released from Death Rows Since 1970 Because of Doubts About Their Guilt," *Thomas M. Cooley Law Review,* 13, 1996, p. 907.

48. Welsh S. White, "Effective Assistance of Counsel in Capital Cases: The Evolving Standard of Care," *University of Illinois Law Review,* 1993, p. 323.

49. *Strickland v. Washington,* 466 U.S. 668 (1984).

50. Robert Scheer, "Equal Justice: $11.75 an Hour versus $1.5 Million," *Los Angeles Times,* February 19, 1995, p. M5.

51. Stephen B. Bright, "Race, Poverty and Disadvantage in the Infliction of the Death Penalty in the Death Belt," *The Machinery of Death* (Washington, DC: Amnesty International USA, 1995).

52. *Newsweek,* November 9, 1998, p. 64.

53. *Newsweek,* June 1, 1992, p. 39; Kevin Cullen, "The New Freedom Riders," *Boston Globe Magazine,* June 25, 1994, p. 16.

54. Richard A. Berk, Robert F. Weiss and Jack Boger, "Chance and the Death Penalty," Law and Society Review, 27, 1993, p. 80; Robert E. Weiss, Richard A. Berk and Cathrine Y. Lee, "Assessing the Capriciousness of Death Charging," *Law and Society Review,* 30, 1996, p. 607.

55. Department of Justice, Bureau of Justice Statistics, *Bulletin,* December 1997, p. 10.

56. *The New York Times,* January 25, 1998, p. WK1.

57. *The New York Times,* February 2, 1995, p. 1.

58. Tina Rosenberg, "The Deadliest D.A.," *The New York Times Magazine,* July 16, 1995, p. 21.

59. *The New York Times,* February 2, 1995, p. B6.

60. Kenneth Bresler, "Seeking Justice, Seeking Election, and Seeking the Death Penalty: The Ethics of Prosecutorial Candidates' Campaigning on Capital Convictions," *Georgetown Journal of Legal Ethics,* 7, 1994, p. 941.

61. David Baldus, Charles Pulaski, and George Woodworth, "Comparative Review of Death Sentences: An Empirical Study of the Georgia Experience," *Journal of Criminal Law and Criminology,* 74, 1983, pp. 661–685. Victim–based discrimination has been found in a number of southern states. See, for example, Alan Widmayer and James Marquart, " Capital Punishment and Structured Discretion: Arbitrariness and Discrimination After *Furman,*" in Clayton A. Hartjen and Edward E. Rhine, eds., *Correctional Theory and Practice* (Chicago: Nelson–Hall, 1992), pp. 178–196.

62. Samuel R. Gross and Robert Mauro, *Death and Discrimination: Racial Disparities in Capital Sentencing* (Boston: Northeastern University Press, 1990), pp. 109–110.

63. Robert M. Bohm, "Capital Punishment in Two Judicial Circuits in Georgia," *Law and Human Behavior,* 18, 1994, p. 335.

64. *The New York Times,* June 7, 1998, p. A22.

65. Stanley Rothman and Stephen Powers, "Execution by Quota?" *The Public Interest,* Summer 1994, pp. 3–17.

66. Hugo Adam Bedau, William S. Lofquist, and Michael L. Radelet, "Miscarriages of Justice in Potentially Capital Cases," *Stanford Law Review,* 40, November 1987, pp. 21–179.

67. Radelet, Lofquist, and Bedau, "Prisoners Released," pp. 907–966.

68. Philip J. Cook and Donna B. Slawson, with Lori A. Gries, *The Cost of Processing Murder Cases in North Carolina* (Durham, NC: Terry Sanford Institute of Public Policy, 1993).

69. Judicial Conference of the United States, *Federal Death Penalty Cases: Recommendations Concerning the Cost and Quality of Defense Representation* (Washington, DC: U.S. Government Printing Office, 1998), pp. 2–3.

70. *The Sacramento Bee,* March 28, 1988, p. 1.

71. *New York Newsday,* June 14, 1989, p. 60. See also Robert M. Bohm, "The Economic Costs of Capital Punishment," in James R. Acker, Robert M. Bohm, and Charles S. Lanier, eds., *America's Experiment with Capital Punishment* (Durham, NC: Carolina Academic Press, 1998), pp. 437–458.

72. John J. DiIulio, "Abolish the Death Penalty, Officially," The *Wall Street Journal,* December 15, 1997, p. A11; DiIulio, "Letter to the Editor," *Wall Street Journal,* January 16, 1998, p. A15.

73. Walter Berns and Joseph Bessette, "Why the Death Penalty Is Fair, *The Wall Street Journal,* January 1, 1998, p. A16.

CHAPTER TWENTY-ONE
Surveillance and Control in the Community

The Goals of Surveillance

The Techniques of Surveillance and Control
    Drug Controls
    Electronic Controls
    Human Surveillance
    Programmatic Controls

Control: A Double-Edged Sword
    Social Control and Personal Liberty
    The Politics of Surveillance and Community Protection

The Limits of Control
    Technology
    Human Responses
    Moral and Ethical Limits

Toward an Acceptable Community Control

Summary

Y ou awaken in the early morning to the sound of your phone ringing. The alarm clock next to your bed tells you it is 3:45 A.M. The loud phone startles you awake, but oddly it does not surprise you. This happens every third or fourth day, at irregular intervals in the nighttime. Putting the receiver to your ear, you mutter a slight obscenity.

The voice on the other end of the line is not a human voice; it is one of those robot-voiced machines. It says, "This is the Madison County Community Control Department. Please enter your offender code."

You type into the phone the first five digits of your social security number.

"Thank you," says the heartless voice. "Please verify your identity by placing your index finger on the Veri-Pad." Next to the phone is a heat-sensing pad. You put your right index finger on it and wait for three seconds while it registers the information it is receiving from your skin.

The voice intones: "Mr. Juan Agostino, have you committed any crimes since your last observation?"

You are not unnerved by the question — it is a part of the routine for these night-time calls. And you know the Veri-Pad is also a lie detector.

You answer, "No."

There is a slight pause. Then the voice continues: "Thank you, Mr. Agostino. You have tested negative for drugs, for alcohol, and for new crimes, and you are in residence as required. You are approved to remain in the community until the next contact." The voice clicks off.

You hang up the phone with a curious sense of annoyance but also relief. Nine months ago, you were convicted of burglary — your second conviction. If you can put up with the intrusion for another year, you will not have to go to prison.

You glance at the alarm clock, which reads, March 15, 2005 . . . 3:50 A.M. At 6:30 the alarm will go off, and you will have to get up and go to work. . . .

This scenario may sound farfetched, but it is not. The technologies it describes either exist now and are being used or are nearly perfected. They are the technologies of social control, and they are especially designed to be applied to offenders in the community.

Perhaps you do not find the scenario particularly dismaying; if so, it is a sign of how far our society has come in normalizing community surveillance. Thirty years ago the description would have provoked outrage from liberals and conservatives alike.

Today the techniques of community control surround us, and we are no longer amazed or alarmed by them.

In this chapter we explore one aspect of corrections that has grown more rapidly than perhaps any other in the past twenty years — community surveillance. That surveillance in the community has been increasingly responsible for sending or returning offenders to prison is reflected in the steady increase in the percentage of new prison admissions who are probation or parole violators (see Figure 21.1). In fact, more than one out of every six prison admissions is a probationer or parolee who was not convicted of a new crime, but instead was sent to prison for violating the rules of probation or parole.[1]

This chapter argues neither for nor against this trend, but it does begin with an assumption: Personal liberty is the precious ability to live freely with our families, in our homes and communities, without being subjected to inordinate controls over our autonomy. Any correctional trend that touches on this supposedly inviolate aspect of American life raises profound questions. We will use the following Questions for Inquiry to guide our examination of these important issues.

Questions FOR INQUIRY

1. What are the goals of surveillance?
2. What techniques of surveillance and control are now in use?
3. In what ways may "control" be a "double-edged" sword?
4. What are the limits of control?
5. How do we develop an acceptable system of community control?

Figure 21.1 Percentage of New Prison Admissions Who Are Probation or Parole Violators, 1926–1995

People who are placed under community supervision are finding it harder than ever to "make it." How much of this is due to increased surveillance?

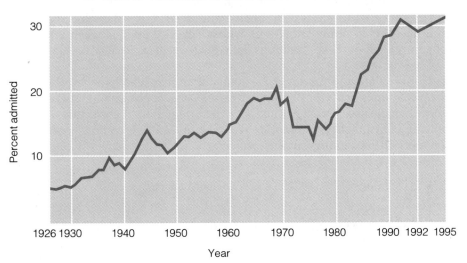

NOTE: Data for 1972-1973 not available; graph extrapolated.

SOURCE: U.S. Department of Justice, Bureau of Justice Statistics, *Bulletin,* August 1995, p. 4; *Correctional Populations in the United States, 1995* (Washington, DC: U.S. Government Printing Office, 1997).

The Goals of Surveillance

Community surveillance of offenders has multiple goals. The main goal might seem to be community protection: We keep offenders under surveillance to keep ourselves safe from them. Certainly the rationale for most surveillance programs and the way they are described to the public fit this goal. The rhetoric of "tough" supervision is designed to instill confidence in a doubting public that offenders living in the community pose no threat.

However, most offenders are not "dangerous" for two reasons. First, many offenders, once caught and processed by the system, will not become reinvolved in crime. Second, even when offenders continue their criminal behavior, most of their crimes represent petty acts that cause losses to their victims but do not really endanger them. Providing surveillance for such offenders suggests that "protection" is not necessarily the most important aim.

A more basic motivation for surveillance programs is the insidious political problem of institutional overcrowding. The electoral climate of the 1980s required politicians to promise zero tolerance for crime. Yet increasing prison capacity requires increases in public spending — and taxes — certainly a difficult political choice. Therefore, although most offenders must live in the community, the "get-tough" movement has severely limited tolerance for offenders in the community.

Policymakers have thus tried to build community surveillance, claiming that such programs are as "safe as prison." This claim is debatable. In any case, the key point is that the "tough surveillance" aspect of these new community programs allows corrections to retain many offenders in the community without having to address public fear of crime. Thus surveillance serves as a form of a program assurance — the public can have confidence in the corrections system keeping so many offenders on the streets because they are being watched so closely.

Surveillance has other goals as well. Treatment providers point out that without some degree of surveillance, it is not possible to know for sure if a given treatment is having an effect. They argue that some form of drug use surveillance, for instance, is essential to any drug treatment program. Deterrence-minded people argue that tough surveillance deters crime in two ways: (1) It makes offenders less willing to decide to commit a crime because they are being watched so closely, and (2) it catches active criminals earlier in their recidivism.[2]

The intermediate sanctions movement, discussed in Chapter 9, is an expression of this concern. It is based on the argument that for many offenders probation is not stringent enough but prisons are too expensive and destructive. This has led to the creation of a range of community sanctions whose severity falls between incarceration and probation. Each of these sanctions calls for some degree of surveillance and control.

Along with surveillance technologies, systems of control also have grown. These are technical ways to limit behavior, through either physical constraints or other means. The advent of technical surveillance has changed the orientation of corrections. Instead of merely applying punishment or promoting rehabilitation, the corrections system controls the offender's behavior to prevent misconduct.

The Techniques of Surveillance and Control

Technologies of correctional surveillance and control have multiplied in recent years. Corrections uses four general control strategies: drugs, electronics, human surveillance, and control programs. They may be used either separately or in combination.

Drug Controls

It is perhaps ironic that in a society so concerned about drug abuse, a main strategy for controlling human behavior uses chemicals. Yet a long tradition of prescribing drugs for this purpose exists in the United States. Here we describe only a few such drugs, but the extent of their use underscores the importance of chemical controls.

Antabuse is frequently given to alcohol abusers. Combined with alcohol, it makes a person become violently nauseated and therefore suppresses the desire for alcohol. But Antabuse also seriously reduces sexual response. The drug is controversial because it is seldom taken voluntarily and its side effects are so undesirable. For example, imagine the predicament of a prisoner who wants to visit his spouse on a furlough but is required to take Antabuse as a condition of the furlough.

The War on Drugs has brought forth new techniques of surveillance such as this drug-sniffing dog.

Sometimes called "chemical castration," the drug **Depo-Provera** constrains the male sexual response. It is used to reduce or eliminate the sex drive of men convicted of certain sex offenses. The drug is fairly effective in eliminating men's capacity to sustain an erection, but critics do not find this a good argument for its use. They argue that the aggression of sex offenses, as in assaulting children and women, is not inhibited by reduced sexual performance. Moreover, the causes of sexual deviance are not altered by the drug's use.

The drug **Thorazine** long has been prescribed for people suffering from certain psychiatric problems that lead to violent behavior. Thorazine is a very strong drug that creates a lethargic mood in its users and, by diminishing the capacity for excitement and expressive emotions, reduces the likelihood of violence. Precisely this lowering of the person's affect leads many to criticize its use.

For offenders who suffer from depression, the drug **Prozac** is often prescribed. Widely used among nonoffenders, this drug decreases the low, sad feelings that accompany depression. Although few offenders commit crimes as the direct result of depression, it can be a contributing factor to some criminality, in that people who are unmotivated to get a job or improve their life may be undeterred by the threat of punishment for crime.

Although certainly not an exhaustive list, these are some of the drugs more commonly used to control criminal behavior. These examples illustrate the range of problems addressed through drugs and the variety of physical, biological, and emotional responses these drugs produce. They also show the controversial nature of chemical controls—they often have adverse side effects, and they are never 100 percent effective.

Antabuse

A drug that, when combined with alcohol, causes violent nausea; it is used to control a person's drinking.

Depo-Provera

A "chemical castration" drug that eliminates sexual response among males.

Thorazine

A drug used to control violent or aggressive behavior caused by psychiatric problems.

Prozac

A drug used to decrease the negative emotions associated with depression.

Electronic Controls

Perhaps the dominant penal innovation of the 1980s was electronic monitoring. As noted in Chapter 9, electronic monitoring has much to recommend it: It represents "high-tech" corrections, and costs less than prison. Since initial application in the early 1980s, electronic monitoring has become a major industry, and thousands of offenders now are monitored each day.

The electronic age has made possible a quantum leap in surveillance technology. For example, the technology now exists for visual monitoring via telephone lines. Therefore video screens could be used to ensure that the offender is actually at home during the phone call. The probation officer could simply call the offender on the phone and then conduct a face-to-face interview without ever leaving the office.

Also possible is routine, random video surveillance without telephone hookup. Under this system the probation officer could activate a video camera in the offender's home at any time and obtain direct, unbiased information about the offender's behavior and compliance with the law.

As another level of surveillance, consider the technology of the "electric fence" that is used to confine some dogs. It establishes a perimeter (usually the yard) outside of which the dog may not venture without triggering an electric shock. Certainly this kind of technology might be easily adapted to keep certain offenders away from schools, bars, or other areas. In theory, at least, it could allow extensive freedom within the necessary restrictions. The Focus box describes efforts at electronic monitoring in England and the United States.

FOCUS Update on Electronic Monitoring: "The Bag" Beats "The Tag"

The English are not wild about "tagging offenders" — as they refer to electronic monitoring. But their prison population has risen so drastically, by 10,000 offenders in two years to a total of more than 62,000, that some are beginning to consider the idea.

By American standards, their alarm seems misplaced. We house almost twenty times as many offenders in our prison systems, and incarcerate our citizens at five times the rate they do. A host of electronic monitoring executives from this country have made it their business to visit England and with "aggressive marketing" convince the English it is time to get into the business of tagging offenders to deal with prison growth.

In 1989, the British Home Office conducted an experiment with tagging as a condition of bail. The results were widely seen as a "fiasco" — more than half the tagged offenders violated their conditions or were rearrested while under monitoring, and the program cost the equivalent of about $20,000 per offender. But that did not stop the government from undertaking a plan to use tagging on a field test basis with curfew orders on probationers — typically unemployed men in their twenties and thirties, convicted of a repeat drunkenness-related offense, such as brawling.

The Home Office evaluation of the new project is under way, and early results are only a bit more positive than the first round. Magistrates (English lower-court judges) are loath to assign the tag as a condition, and offenders are resistant to its use — only 83 offenders were sentenced to tagging in the first twelve months, and although the majority of cases did well, and the scheme cost less than $1,500 per person overall, the results are still meager. The Chief Probation Officers Association has written an official policy statement that tagging "does not add anything that cannot already be achieved through existing community penalties." Everyone acknowledges that tagging cannot work unless it is a part of a supportive, service-oriented probation approach.

Meanwhile, in the United States, the brave new world of electronic monitoring gets braver. Disenchanted with the limitations of telephone-based systems, some agencies are now experimenting with global positioning systems (GPSs). The weakness of the traditional system includes the fact that once the offender has left the property, his or her whereabouts are undetermined — all that is known is that the offender is not home. So the offender is monitored when under curfew, but at other times is free to be anywhere — even prohibited places.

The GPS system solves that. It requires the offender to carry a "bag" (some systems use a box) at all times. The device transmits a signal to the satellite system developed by the U.S. military for surveillance purposes, which routes the information back to central control. What is actually being tracked is the device in the bag, but the bag has the capacity to inform central control if the offender's bracelet (and presumably the offender) has ceased to be within a short distance — say, 20 feet — of the bag. Thus the central control officer can know at all times where the bag is and whether the offender is nearby: twenty-four-hour, worldwide electronic surveillance.

The companies who produce the technology charge $18 per day — about half the cost of jail. The marketers also indicate that their accuracy is far superior to the traditional systems, and with additional gadgetry the accuracy can be enhanced even more. The prospect of being able to monitor any offender all the time is no longer mere science fiction.

Sources: Prison Reform Trust, "Electronic Tagging: Monitoring in the U.K. and Europe," *Journal of Offender Monitoring*, 11, Winter 1998, pp. 13–19; Marc Renzema, "Satellite Monitoring of Offenders: A Report from the Field," *Journal of Offender Monitoring*, 11(2), Spring 1998, pp. 5–11.

Human Surveillance

The technological advances of electronics and drugs are more systematic than mere human interaction. However, unlike these other techniques, personal contact allows the correctional worker to process an array of subtle information — body language, attitudes, odors, and so forth. When it comes to surveillance, no approach can fully supplant the basic strategy of increasing the offender's contact with the experienced correctional worker.

Intensive supervision systems have been used to increase both the frequency and diversity of surveillance. The frequency is increased by reduced caseloads and minimum contact requirements for every offender under supervision. Typically these offenders are seen at least weekly and sometimes more often than that. What makes the surveillance effective is not just how much contact there is, but where and when it occurs. Offenders are seen at the office, in their homes, and at work; they are seen at regular intervals and in "surprise" visits without prior notification. The dominant effect is an aura of surveillance in which no aspect of the offender's life is totally free of potential observation.

In short, through routine, random contacts, the correctional officer is able to observe a wider range of the offender's behavior in a broader array of situations, which yields a deeper understanding of the offender's compliance with the law.

Programmatic Controls

The most widely used techniques of surveillance and control are established elements of treatment programs. Drug testing is a good example. In these programs urine samples are routinely taken to test for potential drug use. Normally the offender is required to submit a urine sample (with a correctional worker watching as it is "produced" to ensure that it is truly the offender's urine and not a substitute), which is then sent to a lab for testing.

Not only is this procedure awkward and invasive, it is untimely, involving substantial delay between the time of surveillance (the actual urine evaluation) and subsequent arrest and revocation if the urine proves "dirty." Recently, on-the-spot tests have been developed, usually involving a drug-sensitive strip of paper. Some are used with urine samples; others are performed on saliva samples. In addition, because some drugs leave no traces of their presence in the urine and saliva within hours of their use, some programs have adopted the expensive alternative of hair testing. Traces of some illegal drugs can be detected in human hair for a year or more after the drug's ingestion.

Programs also sometimes provide for systems of surveillance and control. The most famous example is Vermont's Relapse Prevention Program for sex offenders. This program trains the offender to recognize potential signs of deviant sexual behavior. These signals include sudden changes in mood, renewed drinking, loss of a job, depression, and so forth. What makes this program unusual, however, is that selected individuals living in the offender's community — family, friends, therapists, and co-workers — also are taught to look for the same signs. In effect, these people become additional eyes and ears for the correctional worker, who contacts them regularly to see if the offender is showing a behavior change that should concern the authorities. The community thus augments the system by providing additional surveillance.[3]

Control: A Double-Edged Sword

Many of us might initially regard the idea of tighter surveillance of offenders as a good thing. Even if the prime goal is to increase public confidence in corrections, arguably this is much needed. But the other aims of community protection — more effective treatment of offenders and improved deterrence of crime — are desirable as well.

The potential uses of surveillance technology for observing and tracking offenders in the community is only now being realized.

Social Control and Personal Liberty

Various forms of surveillance are common in modern society — and are not necessarily bad. Parents put listening devices in infants' rooms so they can hear when the baby wakes up; banks put video monitors in their ATMs to photograph people who withdraw money; airports x-ray all bags to check for weapons; businesses and stores check credit cards. With the advent of the information age, surveillance has become a more likely option for preventing problems than ever before.

Yet Americans also have a tradition of respect for individual privacy — and unquestionably surveillance invades privacy. We are especially suspicious of any invasion of the home, no matter what its benefits might be; thus the increase in community surveillance comes at a price. The main cost is civil liberty. Just as studies have shown that families suffer from a member's incarceration, they also show that house arrest, electronic monitoring, and intensive supervision place stress on the family. Sometimes these measures infringe directly on the privacy of innocent people. For instance, think about the scenario described at the beginning of the chapter. Can you imagine the annoyance of Juan Agostino's wife whenever the phone rings in the middle of the night? Or the sense of personal violation provoked by the surreptitious video monitoring?

Critics of the new community surveillance argue that historically, whenever government is allowed to intervene into citizens' lives without restraint, tyranny results. Unless we jealously protect our civil liberties from intrusion by the state, freedom will inevitably and continually erode. These critics point out that airport metal detectors were supposed to be a temporary measure when they were first developed and that the social security number was also supposed to have no official use other than keeping track of social security benefits.

Advocates of control concede these points. But they also note that airplane hijackings have decreased and that life is more convenient with social security numbers. Moreover, surveillance is almost always less restrictive than prison (suggesting that convicted criminals' rights to privacy are not strong); and the right to privacy might be deemed less important than the need to prevent crime.

Admittedly, however, when new technologies are developed for corrections, it is difficult to stop them from spreading, for they quickly become quite popular. Who can argue against electronic fences for criminals if it can be shown that they work? Already some city streets are blocked off to prevent drug sales. The image of a future society in which whole sections of town are cordoned off from certain people for legal reasons may not be farfetched.

Thus the new surveillance and control emphasis of corrections is a major change, not just for the field but also for the community at large. Technological surveillance and control change our communities, perhaps in some ways we would not choose. And the debate about freedom and control is a very old one, one that cannot be resolved in a few pages.

The Politics of Surveillance and Community Protection

Community surveillance and control are highly controversial issues in modern U.S. politics. To better understand this controversy, we can compare traditional conservative and

liberal views about the appropriate role of government in the community and then assess how the problem of crime influences those views.

Traditionally, conservatives have opposed governmental intrusion into personal affairs. They seek as much autonomy as possible for individual citizens and want the government to be conservative (reluctant) in taking action. The basic idea is that
interpersonal relations should be unencumbered by governmental oversight. Yet when it
comes to crime, this position is reversed: Conservatives call for broad and extensive
governmental action and control. Thus the existence of crime in the community serves
to refract the ordinary conservative idea of governmental restraint into a modern view
of government as protector of the individual and property rights. Ironically, the primary
conservative spokespeople advocate for all sorts of electronic, chemical, and human
control over fellow citizens.

At the other end of the spectrum, the traditional liberal view calls for the use of
governmental power to promote equal access of all citizens to the benefits of society.
Thus liberals seek programs that alleviate social inequalities, which often requires a
fairly extensive level of governmental involvement in communities, especially in the
form of ameliorative social programs. Yet when it comes to crime, liberals are suspicious
of governmental surveillance and control, and they seek firm limits on these approaches.
Instead of being concerned about the way crime reduces victims' access to social benefits, liberals often express their concern about potential overinvolvement by government
in offenders' lives.

Why this shift? Much of it has to do with the ways in which the traditional political
positions contrast the values of social order and personal liberty. Conservatives strongly
emphasize social order. They view crime as a serious threat to normal social relations,
throwing the ordinary processes of human commerce out of kilter. To prevent such
crime-fueled distortions of society, conservatives are willing to sacrifice offenders' interest in being free of undue governmental control. Although conservatives ordinarily want
individuals to look out for their own interests, where crime is concerned they want the
government to manage the interests of the private citizens.

In contrast, because they value liberty, liberals tend to be alarmed by the intrusion
of government into the lives of individuals — both offenders and nonoffenders. They
view any governmental control of citizens as inherently dangerous and believe that the
cost of extending governmental power into the home far outweighs any potential benefits in controlling crime. Liberals want government to guarantee equal access of all citizens to the social arena, but they feel that governmental action against crime reduces
rather than advances human liberty.

There is another, more practical, issue in the politics of community surveillance and
control: Which communities will be controlled? In the United States, street crime is
much more pervasive in the inner cities, where minorities and the poor are concentrated. It is these communities that are targeted for control, and the practical politics of
community crime control is expressed through the expanded intrusion of governmental
power into the lives of poor and minority citizens. This is probably another reason why
the traditional viewpoints of conservatives and liberals diverge on the problem of crime.
Liberals, more than conservatives, are troubled by the image of massive, government-
run surveillance programs applied to minority, inner-city residents.

The Limits of Control

A few years ago, when the first rumblings of the "get-tough" movement were felt, criminologist Nils Christie wrote an essay against punishment entitled *Limits of Pain*.[4] His
argument, which has become a classic criticism of penal reform, was that the focus of
liberals on reforming punishment might backfire and result in an expansion of the penal
system and the number of people under governmental control.

His predictions turned out to be correct—although as we'll see in the Epilogue, not everyone argues this has harmed society. Imprisonment has grown in scope and cost. Community correctional programs have become tougher, more oriented toward control and surveillance, and quicker to reincarcerate offenders who don't comply with strict requirements. We might well ask, What are the limits of this trend?

Technology

The most direct limit on this trend is technical. All technologies can fail, and determined offenders often can figure out a way to defeat even the most ingenious technical apparatus. The growing number of crimes committed by people who are being monitored electronically attests to this fact.

Technologies also are limited in terms of capacity. Even though marvelous things are done with computers these days, anyone who works with them will have experienced the "bugs" that can develop in these systems. Big companies like IBM or AT&T can afford to spend large sums of money to constantly upgrade information capability, but corrections systems need reliable computers that do not require extensive management. Thus the correctional version of an information system is usually not state-of-the-art. Advances in surveillance and control technologies require sophisticated technical support, which often is lacking for corrections.

Human Responses

A second limitation in control is human. Corrections workers often choose the field because they like working with people. They may resent the intrusion of technical surveillance into their work; others take exception to the shift in goals from helping to controlling. In either case they may undermine the change in policy through active or passive resistance. It is always possible to find some staff who enjoy surveillance, but in most agencies they are a minority.

Offenders also resent surveillance and control. Although there may be little they can do about it directly, they can resist in indirect ways. For instance, the unenthusiastic offender may come to the probation office late, sulk during interviews, act sullen when the officer visits the home, and generally let it be known that the tight control is unwanted.

In addition, like all of us, offenders are relatively unpredictable. Any system of control is based partly on prediction—how the offender will respond to the system and what the offender will and will not be able to do about it. By acknowledging that offenders are not completely predictable, we also are saying in yet another way that there is no foolproof way to control them.

Moral and Ethical Limits

Some of the scenarios about community control are downright distasteful, bringing to mind images of totalitarian regimes in which the powerful use mind control to squelch all dissent. There is, of course, a difference between dissent and crime. But the correctional population of the United States consists disproportionately of young, urban, African-American and Hispanic men, and we should be cautious in developing whole systems of control and surveillance to surround them. After a while, it begins to appear almost as though the homes, streets, schools, and families of an entire social subgroup are being subjected to official control and invaded by technologies of surveillance. The image is not an attractive one.

At some point the tradeoff between safety and freedom becomes a concern. In terms of street crime, some of the safest societies in history have been the totalitarian regimes of Nazi Germany and Stalinist Russia. There are worse things to live with than crime in the streets.

Toward an Acceptable Community Control

How do we resolve this dilemma? Stanley Cohen has written eloquently about this problem, arguing that there is nothing inherently wrong with "control."[5] The issue is who benefits from it. If the sole purpose of correctional control is to strengthen the capacity of government to rule citizens' lives and to reduce individual and community autonomy, then the control is a net negative and helps destroy communities. But if the surveillance and control are designed to maintain communities by allowing offenders to find ways to continue to live there despite their offense, then the approach is inclusive and helps to build communities.

The distinction is not an obvious one, and few of the modern correctional forms of surveillance and control can be easily classified as truly "inclusive" or ultimately anti-community. We can, however, begin to get an idea of the value of the various correctional methods by asking certain questions. For example, is the surveillance/control truly being used in lieu of imprisonment? That is, without this control would the offender actually be in jail or prison? Second, is the risk to the community such that without this control the offender would be highly likely to engage in crime? In other words, is the surveillance/control really necessary, or is it being used to mollify public sentiment that is basically erroneous? Third, could some other less intrusive method achieve the same basic result? That is, is the technology being used only because it is high-tech, not because it succeeds better than traditional alternatives? Fourth, are steps being taken to eliminate the indirect intrusions of the surveillance into the lives of innocent individuals who live or work with the offender? Finally, is the offender allowed opportunities to demonstrate self-control, so that surveillance/control can be gradually reduced?

To the degree that there are positive answers to these questions, we might think of the corrections system as being necessary, limited, and offender focused.

Summary

As more and more offenders live in the community, technologies of surveillance and control have grown. They include drug controls, electronic controls, program controls, and human actions, all designed to watch offenders more effectively and to exert more control over their actions.

This shift in community corrections has resulted from a change in the goals of corrections. It has also served the latent goal of increased public confidence in corrections. But the increase in surveillance and control comes at a cost in terms of civil liberties. Only if society carefully designs and implements these programs can the costs be minimized. ■

For Discussion

1. Would electronic fences be a good thing for some offenders? If so, which offenders? How would you use the fences?

2. In mandating that some offenders submit to control via drugs such as Antabuse or Depo-Provera, what tradeoffs between civil liberties and community safety might be necessary?

3. What might be the value of electronically monitored house arrest for pretrial detainees? In answering this question, refer to the questions posed in the chapter's final section.

4. Do offenders' family members have a right to have their privacy protected from correctional surveillance? Why or why not?

5. Should high school students be tested regularly for illegal drug use? Why or why not?

For Further Reading

Cohen, Fred. *Deprivation of Liberty.* Raleigh, NC: Carolina Academic Press, 1992. Analyzes the legal and historical issues involved in social control in community and institutional settings.

Cohen, Stanley. *Visions of Social Control.* Cambridge, MA: Polity, 1985. Assesses community-based correctional surveillance and control.

———. *Against Criminology.* New Brunswick, NJ: Transaction, 1988. Describes the recent history of thinking about crime control strategies, with a special emphasis on penology.

Sherman, Lawrence. *Ethics in Criminal Justice Education.* Hastings-on-Hudson, NY: Institute for Social Ethics, 1982. Reviews problems in criminal justice education and suggests standards.

Notes

1. Department of Justice, Bureau of Justice Statistics, *Correctional Population in the United States, 1995* (Washington, DC: U.S. Government Printing Office, 1997), p. 95.
2. Joan Petersilia and Susan Turner, *Intensive Supervision for High-Risk Probationers* (Santa Monica, CA: Rand Corporation, 1990).
3. Marlatt and J. R. Gordon, *Relapse Prevention* (New York: Guilford Press, 1985); see also L. Bays, R. Freeman-Congo, and D. D. Hiedebran, *How Can I Stop? Breaking My Deviant Cycle* (Orwell, VT: Safer Society Press, 1990).
4. Nils Christie. *Limits to Pain* (Oxford, England: Martin Robinson, 1981).
5. Stanley Cohen, *Against Criminology* (New Brunswick, NJ: Transaction, 1988), pp. 104–124.

CHAPTER TWENTY-TWO
Community Justice

Walter Harrison is a probation officer, on his way to work. But you wouldn't know it from the look of things: it is 7 P.M., and his destination is the local police precinct in Roxbury — a tough, inner-city neighborhood in Boston. There he will partner up with another probation officer and two police officers, members of the Gang Unit of the Boston Police Department assigned to police the gangs of Roxbury.

Their workday begins with a strategy session, in which the police-probation team reviews the files of twelve gang members they expect to see sometime throughout the evening. They know the names and faces well, but the review serves as a reminder. Each gang member has a

Frequent home visits are an important part of community justice. Here Officer Corey Burke drops by unannounced to visit an offender in his apartment. These visits serve to involve family members in restoring the offender.

criminal record—many include multiple arrests for violent crimes involving guns. And each gang member is on probation for a recent conviction, with an evening curfew as a condition of probation. The team's job is to make sure that the probationers are obeying the curfew. They also want to make sure that, whatever else, the young men they see are not carrying guns. This probation team wants the violence to stop.

The officers start their shift by setting priorities—who needs to be seen most; where might they expect to find problems; what new information has come to light about one of the probationers; what they have learned from recent forays into the field. After talking through their cases and setting objectives for the night's tour, they drive into the streets of Roxbury in an unmarked car. It is 8 P.M., the time by which every gang member on probation must be at home.

The first stop is a local park where youths congregate at night. They pull up near a small group of young people, and look for the familiar faces of the gang members on probation. Although they recognize many of the youths—and adolescents signal that they recognize the unmarked car—there are no probationers there. One youth approaches the car; for a brief time he and the officers engage in an almost friendly banter. The youth's older brother is on probation and is doing well, and Harrison asks about how things are with the family. After a few minutes, the team drives off. The interaction has been calm and even cordial—everybody seems to know what is going on.

The team pulls up to a three-story run-down apartment building, and makes the first curfew check. James Sampson, 16-year-old on probation for illegal possession of a gun, lives here. The police officers check the area for safety issues, noting the area surrounding the home and any exits to the house. The probation officers approach the front door. Sampson's mother meets them at the door, and seems almost glad to see them. What proceeds is a fairly typical home visit, with routine questions about Sampson's activities, especially his new job. The officers make an effort to keep things cordial and relaxed, because they want to show respect for the probationer and his family. The visit goes well. As they leave, Sampson's mother thanks them and says with emotion that curfew means she no longer has to wonder if "my Jamie" will die on the streets in the middle of the night. It is a sentiment the team has heard before, even from the former gang members. The team heads on to its next stop. They are engaged in a new kind of correctional work in the community.

Some observers see a trend in what is going on in Boston and a number of other cities and states. In Milwaukee, for example, probation and police work together to deal with a variety of problems facing high-crime neighborhoods; in Portland, Oregon, prosecutors have moved into the highest-crime neighborhoods to begin dealing with the problems of everyday citizens who live there; in Phoenix, probation staff have opened up neighborhood centers where they run literacy programs for residents; in Vermont, citizens are a part of sanctioning boards called Reparative Panels, and they impose sanctions on offenders sent to the boards from the courts. Each of these is an example of a change in the way justice works—a change toward "community justice."[1]

In this chapter we will examine the growing community justice movement with special attention to the role of corrections. We will address the following Questions for Inquiry.

Questions FOR INQUIRY

1. What is community justice? How does it differ from criminal justice?
2. What arguments have been given in favor of community justice?
3. What are some of the problems with community justice?
4. What are the future prospects of community justice?

What Is Community Justice, and How Does It Differ from Criminal Justice?

The concept of **community justice** is a new idea that has gathered considerable support among practitioners and policymakers across the country. Community justice initiatives of one sort or another have recently been undertaken in a large number of municipalities. The particulars of these initiatives vary, because the settings in which they have been developed vary. It stands to reason that different places will undertake differing strategies, when they seek to confront the particulars of their own crime problems. The rapid growth in new and innovative community justice projects is remarkable for two reasons. First, they have arisen as a result of local desires to develop more proactive responses to crime. Second, they are not funded by any large federal grants, but rather are drawn from local resources that are redirected from traditional approaches to community justice strategies.

What Is Community Justice?

Community justice is not a simple idea that can be explained in a single sentence. It can be thought of as at once a **philosophy** of justice, a *strategy* of justice, and a series of justice *programs*.

A Philosophy of Justice As a philosophy, community justice is based on the pursuit of a vision of justice that is more ambitious than the traditional three tasks of criminal justice—the apprehension, conviction, and punishment of offenders. In addition to these ordinary aspects of criminal justice, community justice recognizes that crime and the problems that result from crime are a central impediment to the quality of community life. Thus the community justice approach seeks not only to respond to criminal events, but also sets as a goal the improvement of quality of community life, especially for communities afflicted by high levels of crime.

A Strategy of Justice The strategy of the community justice approach combines three contemporary justice innovations: community policing, environmental crime prevention, and restorative justice. Each of these innovations has proven promising as a way of preventing crime and reviving community safety.

Community Policing The community policing approach to law enforcement employs problem-solving strategies to identify ways to prevent crimes by getting to root causes instead of relying on arrests as a way to respond to criminal events. Rather than reacting to 911 calls for service, community policing attempts to identify crime "hot spots" and change the dynamics of those places that seem to make crime possible. Rather than keeping citizens at arm's length, police officers actively seek to develop partnerships with residents and citizen groups in pursuit of safer streets. Rather than a hierarchical paramilitary structure, community policing seeks to decentralize decision making to officers at the local areas, and seeks to design area-specific strategies for overcoming the crime.

By the end of the 1990s, the community policing movement had become enormously successful. Over 80 percent of police departments said they practiced some form of community policing, and most observers credited the approach as partly responsible for the drop in crime in the latter half of the decade.

Environmental Crime Prevention   The environmental crime prevention approach begins with an analysis of why crime tends to concentrate in certain locations and certain times. "Hot spots" of crime exist and in some cities, 70 percent of crimes occur in 20 percent of the city's locations. By analyzing the reasons for that pattern, this approach looks for ways to revise the physical environment of crime—houses, streets, and other public space as a means of thwarting crime.

What about those places produces such high concentrations of crime? And what can be done about those places?

These are the questions that occupy the attention of environmental crime prevention specialists. These new professionals make it their business to change the places crimes tend to occur in ways that reduce crime. They bring light to darkened street corners that otherwise attract gangs as hangouts, establish procedures to keep elevators in repair so that people need not use isolated stairways to get to their apartments, change the traffic flow in streets that used to serve as drug markets, and restore open areas so that they serve as playgrounds rather than vacant lots.

Restorative Justice   The restorative justice approach to sanctioning offenders seeks to restore the victim, the offender, and the community, to a level of functioning that existed prior to the criminal event. The restorative justice approach calls for offenders to admit what they have done and take steps to make restitution. Victims and offenders are often brought together to identify the steps that offenders may take to help victims recover from the crime. Then the offender gets involved in programs designed to help reduce the chances of re-offending.

Programs   Programs of community justice include a varied package of methods. A brief listing of a few illustrates the range and innovative nature of community justice:

- Crime-mapping is used to identify where the problem of crime is most concentrated.
- Citizen advisory groups are used to help identify local crime problem priorities.
- Citizen partnerships between justice agencies and citizen groups are used to improve the legitimacy of justice programs and to help justice officials tailor their strategies to make them.
- Police, prosecutors, judges, and corrections officials are organized locally to enable them to develop local strategies of crime prevention.
- Citizens and victims are involved in sentencing decisions to increase their confidence in the wisdom of the sanctions.
- Offender community service is used to sanction offenders and restore victims and their communities.

Most of all, community justice is concerned with taking seriously the problems faced by people who live amid high levels of crime, some of whom are themselves involved in crime. When Walter Harrison, described at the beginning of this chapter, goes to work, he is practicing community justice in a way that is not any one of these particular programs, but reflects them all. He is not out to arrest kids, but to help keep them safe. He is not saying, "I am a probation officer, not a policeman"; rather, he is trying to practice probation in a way that is relevant to the particular needs of the offenders, their families, and their neighbors, each of whom is concerned about being safe.

How Is Community Justice Different?

Community justice is different from traditional criminal justice in three important ways: It is based on the neighborhood rather than on the legal jurisdiction; it is problem solving rather than adversarial; and it is restorative rather than retributive.

A Neighborhood Focus   Neighborhoods are typically quite different from legal jurisdictions. For most important crimes, it is the state or federal government that has legal jurisdiction with political boundaries. But crime problems vary greatly within those jurisdictions. We see this when we compare cities such as Miami to towns such as Lake City; both lie within Florida, but each has its own unique crime and justice problems. Even within a city, crime problems vary with the income levels, racial composition, and economic status of each neighborhood. The Miami neighborhoods of Liberty City and Coconut Grove contrast starkly in their socioeconomic and crime characteristics. Would we want standardized criminal justice policies to be applied in both neighborhoods? Research in Chicago was able to define 343 coherent neighborhoods. Each had a different social profile, crime problem, and justice concerns.[2] It follows that these local areas have different needs for justice services and priorities.

Traditional justice practices attempt to develop standardized approaches to crime problems that are applied uniformly across the entire legal jurisdiction. By contrast, community justice attempts to tailor strategies to fit important differences across neighborhoods within the same legal jurisdiction.

A Problem-Solving Focus   Problem solving in the context of community justice differs from adversarial justice in its fundamental aims. The adversarial process is thought to have succeeded when the innocent citizen is found not guilty and the guilty citizen fairly punished. In contrast, the problem-solving approach succeeds when the problem about which it is concerned is resolved. That is why the traditional criminal justice system is concerned almost exclusively with offenders, and ends this concern once the offender's punishment has been concluded. Community justice extends its sights and seeks to solve the underlying problems faced by offenders, victims, and others in the neighborhood.

A Focus on Restoration   Restoration is the solution sought under the problem-solving philosophy of community justice. This means that the losses suffered by the victim as a result of the crime are restored, the threat to local safety is removed, and eventually the offender is restored to being a fully participating member of the community. When the crime is so serious that full restoration is not possible, community justice seeks as much restoration as can be provided. The Vermont Reparative Sentencing Boards, described in the Focus box, is one way of implementing the goal of restoration.

These three differences: a focus on neighborhoods, problem solving, and restorative justice, show how the community justice approach strikes a different path from traditional criminal justice. It is not so much that community justice replaces the need for criminal justice, but that it augments by filling in where the justice system fails to meet community needs.

Table 22.1 compares some of the ways that community justice differs from traditional criminal justice. The latter operates as a centralized bureaucracy staffed by professional workers whose job is to process criminal cases. Community justice strives to be a localized, community presence of specialists who deal with the problems that result from crime by developing partnerships with various agencies and citizen groups. Of course, community justice is not the opposite of criminal justice. Agents involved in

FOCUS
Restorative Justice in Vermont

One night in Morrisville, Vermont, Newton Wells went looking for a good time and wound up in an experiment.

The 22-year-old college student was charged with assault last November after nearly driving into two police officers who were breaking up a party. Facing a felony conviction, Wells took a different way out. He pleaded guilty to a lower charge and volunteered to be sentenced by a county "reparative" board. Instead of a judge, a businessman, a counselor, a retired chemistry teacher, and a civil servant issued his punishment.

Flinty Vermonters have a long history with community sanctions. In colonial days, thieves were nailed by their ear lobes to the village hitching post, the better to contemplate their wrongs. Today, offenders are more likely to be sentenced to make public apologies, restitution, or chop wood for the elderly—to "repair" the community. . . .

Restorative justice programs are designed to compensate victims, rehabilitate offenders, and involve the community, in a new and a direct way, in the justice process. . . .

Vermont's sentencing boards, which have been meting out punishments statewide since late 1995, are not without controversy. Defense lawyers say sanctions can vary widely, raising the issue of fairness. Others question the constitutionality of private citizens acting as judges.

And then there is what might be called the "Crucible" factor: the unease even some Vermonters feel about letting fellow citizens sit in judgment upon them. . . .

The boards, typically four to six volunteers, handle misdemeanors and low-grade felonies such as drunken driving and writing bad checks. And while such crimes normally would not merit jail time, removing the cases from the traditional criminal justice system has the side benefit of freeing corrections department resources.

People accused of nonviolent crimes agree to be sent to the community sentencing program as part of a plea bargain that is approved by a judge.

Board members meet with offenders in hour-long sessions, hear explanations and apologies, and tailor the penalties. The idea is to make the punishment related to the crime, often in a novel way.

In Morrisville, college student Wells was ordered to work 30 hours with troubled youths, and to meet with the police he menaced so that they could vent their anger about his driving.

In Rutland, a man who drove 105 mph down a residential street was sentenced to work with brain-injured adults, some of them survivors of high-speed crashes.

In Hyde Park, a teenager who vandalized a home got 55 hours on a work crew. His job was repairing plaster on an aging opera house. . . .

Panel members get involved in ways they never could if they were serving as jurors. In Rutland, Jack Aicher tells shoplifters they've committed crimes against the "community." Everyone pays higher prices, he says, to cover the store's loss.

Victims are encouraged to sit in on hearings but to date few have. Board members say some may fear facing their antagonists, while others don't wish to be inconvenienced. Flor Tutiakoff of Barre says board members try to act as surrogates for the "victims and the entire community."

Proponents say board sanctions are typically tougher than conventional probation. But offenders opt for the citizen panels to get their sentences concluded quickly. In Vermont, probation can last more than a year and can include special sanctions such as drug tests and rehabilitation programs. Reparative board punishments are concluded within 90 days.

In the corrections department's view, the boards have worked out well. Citizens handled about 650 cases last year or one-third of Vermont's ordinary probation caseload. They will soon handle 100 percent if corrections officials get their way.

Meanwhile, the percentage of nonviolent offenders in the state's eight prisons has dropped from about 50 to 28 percent. The decline is ascribed, in part, to the effect of the boards. By handling low-level offenders, the community panels have freed state probation officers to deal with more serious cases. Those probation officers are then able to monitor criminals serving their sentences in work camps or on furlough rather than in jail as a way of relieving overcrowding.

SOURCE: *USA Today*, February 12, 1997, *http://www.usatoday.com.* © 1997 USA Today. Reprinted with permission.

community justice operate under the same penal code, use the same legal authority, and face the same constitutional constraints.

What is different is that community justice is not as concerned with the individual offender as much as it is with the general issue of community safety. Because of this variation community justice work tends to use the tools of justice, in different ways and sets different action priorities. For example, community policing officers make arrests, just as is done by traditional law enforcement officials. But criminal justice has often

Table 22.1 Community Justice and Criminal Justice—Some Comparisons

Community justice differs from criminal justice in the key strategies employed by each.

Community Justice	Criminal Justice
Based in a neighborhood	Based in a state or local jurisdiction
Focus on solving crime problems	Focus on processing cases
Uses partnerships with citizens and social service agencies	Uses professionals who operate isolated of citizens and other agencies
Goal is improved community safety	Goal is apprehension, conviction, and punishment of offenders

seen the arrest as "closing" a case, especially when it is followed by a conviction. Community justice workers see the arrest as a first part of the problem-solving process involving the impact of the crime and the future of the person who has been arrested. In cases where crimes do not result in arrest, community justice workers see just as much a need for problem solving and restoration of community safety as in those where an arrest identifies an offender. Community justice concerns itself with the life of the community, and the community includes victims, offenders, and others alike.

What Are the Arguments for Community Justice?

Community justice has gained public support because crime damages community life and traditional criminal justice does not address that damage. Citizens groups and justice system leaders are coming together to develop ways so that criminal justice resources can be used to address the damage that results from crime and crime fighting in high crime localities. The arguments for community justice can be illustrated by four common assertions of the community justice movement.

Crime and Crime Problems Are Local

As a philosophy of justice, community justice concerns itself with the quality of life in a community. Two deficits prevent a reasonable quality of life: lack of resources and lack of safety. In communities that have high concentrations of crime, these impediments to quality of life go hand in hand.

Ever since the landmark work of Clifford Shaw and Henry McKay[3] criminologists have known that crimes tend to concentrate in certain areas. These high-crime areas are also the areas with other social problems: poverty, broken families, unemployment, and other social maladies criminologists refer to as "social disorganization." The concentration of social problems, the most troublesome of which is crime, makes these areas the least desirable places to live. People who live there tend to do so because they have few other choices.

For people stuck in socially disorganized areas, life is dominated by problems of safety. Streets are not safe, and public space is dominated by those who welcome trouble. Lacking financial and personal resources to create safety, residents of high-crime places endure a life in which risk of harm is a permanent fixture.

These neighborhoods also tend to become the places where offenders live after release from prison or jail, or while they are under community supervision. Figure 22.1 is a map of the Red Hook section of Brooklyn, New York, with locations of offenders released from incarceration in 1996 plotted on the map. This is an extraordinary concentration of

Figure 22.1   Residents of Red Hook, New York, Released from Jail or Prison in 1996

The data show the residence of only one year of people released from incarceration. What is the impact of such a high concentration of ex-offenders living in a neighborhood?

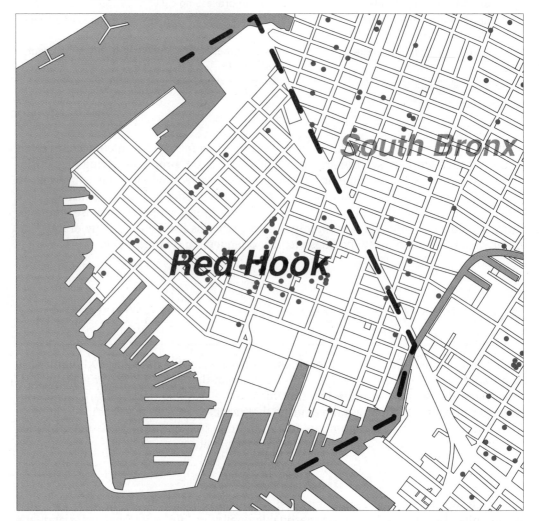

SOURCE: CASES, Community Justice Program, New York. Map generated at Pratt Institute Center for Community and Environmental Development, 1999.

residents involved in the criminal justice system—and yet it represents but one year's involvement. Stretched across the three to five years a typical offender is under correctional control, the picture emerges of a neighborhood of residents who are quite frequently under justice system supervision. Part of what makes high-crime residential areas different from other places is the high level of justice system clients who live there, and the impact this concentration has on life there.

Community justice is particularly concerned with these locations. Taking into account the families and associates, employers and neighbors of these many offenders, the distinction begins to fade between those formally under control of the state and those with whom their lives are directly intertwined. By focusing on quality of life in that neighborhood, Community justice accepts responsibility for services to those who are not targets of state coercive penal control. The rationale is that as so much of community life is affected by the large number of offenders living in these locations, correctional attention

A Vermont Reparative Sentencing Board meets with offenders and victims. They tailor penalties that they believe will serve the goals of restorative justice.

must be focused not only on the actual offenders under sentence, but also on the many people whose lives they affect.

Crime Fighting Improves the Quality of Life

What can be done in high-crime communities? There is reason to believe that the "trail-'em and nail-'em" approach of many correctional agencies works poorly for offenders and their families in these areas. The criminal justice system is designed as an adversarial attack on crime by identifying and accusing criminals, and removing them from the community on their conviction. Nationally, about 400,000 offenders are released back into the community, having served an average of just over two years in prison. Neighborhoods that contribute many residents to the prison system are the same ones who receive back large numbers of ex-offenders on their release. The usual correctional thinking about these offenders is "individualized case management": assessing each offender's risk and needs, and developing a supervision plan for re-entry.

Recently some researchers have begun to consider the impact of high incarceration rates on community life.[4] They point out that removing offenders from the community often disrupts families and, when it becomes pervasive in a neighborhood, leads to a sense of alienation from the law. Imagine, they say, living in a neighborhood where just about everyone has been arrested and almost every male has been to prison or jail. It is not hard to see that under those conditions, the legitimacy of the legal system itself comes into question and the impact of the threat of punishment erodes.

There is some evidence that problem communities in our cities have reached critical levels of justice system involvement in residents' lives. In several of our major cities, as noted earlier, one-fourth or more of all African-American adult males are under some form of justice system control.[5] In particularly hard-hit sections of some cities, as many as one-fourth of that group is behind bars.[6] This is not just a problem of the ghettos of large cities. A study of a medium-sized Southern city found one neighborhood that had 2 percent of all residents removed and placed in prison in one year alone.[7] If the community justice advocates are correct, such neighborhoods suffer repeated challenges absorbing the losses incurred as these residents are removed, while at the same time dealing with those who have returned from prison or jail.

By pursuing restorative justice, community justice seeks to ameliorate some costs of crime for these residents. By using a problem-solving, crime-prevention approach, community justice seeks to break the cycle of criminal behavior that has a grip on these communities.

Proactive Rather Than Reactive Strategies Are Needed

Restorative justice and problem solving-strategies illustrate some of the essential differences between the philosophies of traditional criminal justice and community justice: The latter is reactive, whereas the former is proactive. Reactive approaches begin only after a crime has occurred — and only after the costs of crime have already been imposed on victims and communities. Proactive approaches seek to prevent crimes from occurring in the first place.

The proactive approach is based on the assumption that preventing crimes is the most efficient aim of justice. Crime prevention not only represents a savings in costs to the justice system for processing the offender, but also avoids costs to the victim and the community. Because the costs to victims alone of felony crimes have been estimated to be $450 billion annually, the savings for each crime prevented can be considerable indeed.[8]

Advocates of traditional criminal justice often point out that one way to prevent crimes is to incapacitate the active offender by incarceration. Proponents of community justice respond that because most of those who go to prison eventually return to society, and many are less capable of making it after having been to prison, incapacitation effects on the crime rate are overstated.

Proactive strategies for environmental crime prevention are becoming increasingly popular. These approaches seek to identify the factors in a community that lead to crimes and overcome them: Vacant lots that attract idle youth groups are turned into appealing playgrounds that attract children and their parents; corner liquor stores are turned into corner grocery stores; dark alleyways are cordoned off and made available to residents as backyards; drug thoroughfares have their traffic patterns rerouted to enable residents to feel safer.

Individual problem-solving strategies can also be proactive. Ex-offenders who have trouble finding a job may work on community reclamation projects for pay, and children who have limited adult supervision are encouraged to attend after-school programs that are fun, strengthen skills, and provide adult contact outside of school settings.

The common thread in all this is to move away from an offender-based, reactive, retributive criminal justice system toward a community-based, proactive, restorative justice strategy. Community justice seeks to build a greater experience of justice by those communities hardest hit by crime.

What Are the Problems of Community Justice?

The image of community justice presented by its advocates is attractive. This is one reason why the concept of community justice has become more popular in recent years. Yet community justice is a new idea, and observers have raised a number of important questions about its prospects. Three central questions have been raised concerning individual rights, social inequality, and increased costs. Any attempt to embrace community justice will inevitably be forced to face these issues.

Community Justice and Individual Rights

In a community justice model, different communities will vary in the ways they pursue public safety and improved quality of life. For example, if localities are allowed to determine justice (and crime) priorities, then it follows that services such as policing and

Neighborhoods differ not only in their crime control priorities, but they differ in their capacities, resources, and resilience in meeting crime problems. Poor communities lack resources to deal with their crime problems. More prosperous communities are better at organizing to protect neighborhood members. Will community justice perpetuate these social inequalities?

prosecution may operate with differences in resource allocation and even practical action, even though they operate under identical criminal codes. How far may these differences go before they violate our belief in equality under the law? To what extent may a locality exert its unique vision of social control without infringing on freedoms of "deviant" members who are in the minority? Will a neighborhood justice movement take some characteristics of vigilantism; if not, what will stop that trend?

As citizens become more active in various aspects of the justice process, the state's role in presiding over that process is undercut. The adversarial ideal assumes that the state accuses a citizen and brings to bear evidence that supports the accusation. The dispute is between the state and the accused. Inserting other citizens—neighbors and residents—into that arrangement muddies the water by creating a third party to the dispute. It is unclear precisely what ought to be the role of the third party—observational, participatory, advisory, or even advocacy? Whichever, the presence of that party means that the state and its adversary can no longer be concerned only about each other. The concern for rights protections extend beyond those of the accused to the rights of victims and, indirectly, to affected community members. The question is, What does the growth of interest in the community mean for the rights of criminal suspects?

We must be uneasy about the implications of any developments that undermine the protection of rights. Perhaps the finest contribution of Western civilization to modern life is the idea of the sanctity and dignity of the individual. This idea is given life in the form of legal rights, in which citizens stand equal to one another as well as to the state.

Any movement toward community justice taken at the expense of this priceless heritage would impose a cultural cost of profound dimensions. Community justice ideals *will* alter established practices of substantive and procedural criminal law. The test will be to devise the changes that protect precious civil liberties.

Community Justice and Social Inequality

Neighborhoods differ not only in their crime control priorities, but they differ in their capacities, resources, and resilience in meeting crime problems. The same inequality that characterizes America at the individual level plays out as a community dynamic. The justice system really operates as two different systems, one for people with financial resources and another for the poor. Is there any assurance that the same kind of inequality will not come to characterize community justice?

This is not a small concern. Research shows that poor communities, particularly those hit hard by crime, also tend to lack resources to regulate neighborhood problems and pursue social control.[9] These communities do not come together to solve problems, and they have low rates of citizen participation in official business. One lesson of community policing has been that in troubled neighborhoods, it is often difficult to get citizens to take responsible action in response to their crime problems.

More prosperous localities will also have disproportionate political influence in many city and county governments. They will be better at organizing to influence the crime priorities, directing the funding decisions, and protecting their residents from negative impacts of change. A community justice model that enables localities to pursue interests and preferences will inevitably raise the potential for these more successful communities to strengthen their position in relation to other localities. Community justice cannot treat all communities as of equal importance or as independent from one another. Communities exist within larger social and political systems and local problems and public policies to address them must be understood within this broader context.

Inequality breeds crime. It would be a dismal irony if community justice, advanced to help places deal more effectively with their crime problems, contributed to the very dynamics that make those problems worse. If the problem of inequality is to be avoided, some local areas will likely require differential resource investment to take advantage of the promise of community justice.

Community Justice and Increasing Criminal Justice Costs

We spend nearly $100 billion on the criminal justice system every year. The cost of justice is increasing, and the burden it places on local areas through taxes interferes with the capacity to fund schools, provide child health care, and maintain basic services. A community justice model calls for criminal justice organizations to augment current services. How will these be paid for?

The disparity between community resources and crime rates means that local revenues cannot be the basis for funding community justice. As indicated, the very communities that most suffer from crime are least able to pay to combat it. Some mechanism for shifting financial resources from affluent communities to impoverished ones will be needed. This will obviously raise sensitive political issues because taxpayers are leery of spending for services from which they do not directly benefit.

In addition, some way of shifting costs *within* the existing justice budget will be needed. New money for new programs is scarce, and a proposal to greatly increase funding of justice work will be met with skepticism. Instead, community justice needs to be based on a shifting of resources within existing justice functions. The overall dollar costs of justice cannot be expected to rise too much; what can occur is a change in the allocation of justice dollars to provide support for new activities in place of previous functions. Community justice calls for collaboration between criminal justice agencies and other governmental and community social welfare agencies and services. Coordinated efforts will enhance effectiveness by combining the resources of different agencies using similar strategies to obtain different ends. For example, while one agency's objective may be increasing employment within a neighborhood, this goal may also reduce criminal activity.

The Future Prospects of Community Justice

Community justice is a new idea. It has proven very popular, but the important question of any new idea in correctional work is whether it has staying power. We might wonder whether the community justice movement will be a brief aspect of today's justice politics or, as it advocates intend, a long-term force in the reform of the justice system.

The popularity of community justice derives in part from deep dissatisfactions with contemporary justice politics. Many have become alarmed by the trends described in earlier chapters, such as the increased use of surveillance and the ever-growing size of correctional populations. Because it embraces community safety without the emphasis on "toughness" or surveillance, community justice provides an attractive alternative for many who are disillusioned with existing strategies.

In some ways, community justice is a throwback. Those who promote more local, informal, and citizen-supported responses to crime seem to have an image of the way communities traditionally dealt with misbehavior in the past—by collective effort to overcome it. If community justice is desirable because it calls us to a nostalgic past, it is likely to be short-lived. Modern problems call for modern solutions, not fuzzy history. The way we dealt with deviance in the past was often harsh, and far too frequently dehumanizing of fellow-citizens. If the call for community justice is not much more than a call for return to the past, it will not last long.

But if the community justice movement is successful in developing and demonstrating a true alternative to traditional criminal justice—with local, problem-solving, restorative solutions to crime problems—then it will be traditional bureaucratic justice that will someday be a thing of the past.

Summary

The term *community justice* refers to innovative neighborhood-based approaches for reducing crime and increasing public safety. As a philosophy of community safety, community justice includes strategies of community policing, situational crime prevention, and restorative justice. The central aim of this approach is to implement more effective justice programs in the local residential areas hardest hit by crime. To achieve this aim, community justice differs from traditional criminal justice in that it is neighborhood based, problem solving, and restorative, rather than jurisdiction based, case processing, and adversarial. The main arguments in favor of community justice rest in the way crime is a local social problem that affects quality of life immensely in high-crime areas, requiring innovative strategies to be effective. Problems with community justice include the need to protect individual rights, the problem of social inequality, and the immense cost of the justice system. The future of community justice will lie in the degree to which its programs can deliver a safer community without exacerbating the problems of the justice system. ∎

For Discussion

1. Would you rather live in a place that practiced traditional criminal justice or in one that practiced community justice?

2. Why do you think the community justice movement is so popular? Will it be long lasting, or will it be over soon, as a movement? Why?

3. What impediments block greater cooperation between correctional agencies, such as probation, and other governmental services such as the police or social welfare? How can these be overcome?

4. Do you think citizens want to get involved in their own crime prevention problems? Why or why not?

For Further Reading

Todd R. Clear and David R. Karp. *The Community Justice Ideal: Promoting Safety and Achieving Justice.* Boulder, CO: Westview, 1999. Provides an argument for community justice as a philosophy and strategy.

David R. Karp, ed. *Community Justice.* Boulder, CO: Westview, 1999. Describes the major tenets underlying community justice and describes some of the more prominent examples of the approach.

Wesley Skogan. *Disorder and Decline: Crime and the Spiral of Decay in American Neighborhoods.* New York: The Free Press, 1993. Develops the relationship between crime and other aspects of disorder, and describes how both affect the quality of community life.

Notes

1. These and other community justice projects are described in Todd R. Clear and David R. Karp, *The Community Justice Ideal: Preventing Crime and Achieving Justice* (Boulder, CO: Westview Press, 1999).

2. Felton Earles, "Linking Community Factors and Individual Development, *NIJ Research Preview* (Washington, DC: U.S. Department of Justice, September 1998).

3. Clifford R. Shaw and Henry D. McKay, *Juvenile Delinquency and Urban Areas* (Chicago: University of Chicago Press, 1942).

4. Dina R. Rose and Todd R. Clear, "Incarceration, Social Capital, and Crime: Implications for Social Disorganization Theory," *Criminology,* 23, August 1998, pp. 441–480.

5. Marc Mauer, "Young Black Men and the Criminal Justice System—1997" (Washington, DC: The Sentencing Project, February 1998).

6. James P. Lynch and William J. Sabol, *Did Getting Tougher on Crime Pay?* Crime Policy Report, The Urban Institute State Policy Center, Washington, DC, August 1997.

7. Todd R. Clear and Dina R. Rose, "Incarceration, Mobility, and Social Disorganization," paper presented to the American Society of Criminology, Washington, DC, November 14, 1998.

8. Ted R. Miller, Mark A. Cohen, and Brian Wiersema, *Victim Costs and Consequences: A New Look* (Washington, DC: National Institute of Justice, February 1996).

9. Robert J., Bursick, Jr. and Harold G. Grasmick, *Neighborhoods and Crime: The Dimensions of Effective Community Control* (New York: Lexington Books, 1993).

American Corrections Today and Tomorrow

Five Correctional Dilemmas
Mission

Methods

Structure

Personnel

Costs

Changing Corrections: A Final View

Since the mid-1970s the American corrections system appears to have embarked on something of a social experiment. The main tenet of the experiment was described in Chapter 18: the inexorable increase in the reach of the corrections system.

By every measure the penal system has grown by unprecedented amounts. Since 1973 the incarceration rate has increased from under 100 persons per 100,000 citizens to over 445 per 100,000. Including probation, parole, and jails, the number of people under correctional control also has more than quadrupled in that same time, from under a million to over 5 million.

This growth has disproportionately affected minority group members. For example, over one in three African-American males in their twenties is currently under correctional control—more than are in colleges and universities. Some observers estimate that in Los Angeles about one in three African-American youths will be arrested each year, though far fewer will be prosecuted. It is not hard to see why many residents in these communities believe that the criminal justice system is designed to oppress them and that the corrections system is intended to remove men from their neighborhoods. Consider the situation in New York State. Of the over 70,000 inmates in the state's prison system, an estimated three-fourths come from just seven neighborhoods in New York City—all of them minority neighborhoods.

It is hard to imagine that in the past twenty-five years we have deliberately created the corrections system we most want. To the contrary, most of those in charge of today's corrections system would argue that what we are doing is self-destructive and that an overhaul of the corrections system is long overdue. But there is little agreement about the fitting aims of reform.

This lack of agreement is one reason why it is not really accurate to refer to the unprecedented growth in corrections since the early 1970s as an "experiment." Experiments must be planned, and some hypotheses about how and why they might work must be advanced. The surge in correctional populations has resulted from disjointed, incremental policy shifts in sentencing and law enforcement practices. For example, the population of drug offenders in U.S. prisons has increased by 700 percent since 1980, more than five times the rate of increase in other offenders, and this was largely the result of the "drug war" of the 1980s and 1990s.

If we had conducted a deliberate experiment, we would also expect to see clear "results." But in the case of the twenty-five years of correctional growth, the results are obscure. Depending on the type of offense and the way it is measured, crime rates over that period have either grown, remained about the same, or fallen—though some claim the rates would have been even higher had we not expanded the corrections system. State correctional budgets have more than doubled in the past decade, whereas state budget allocations for education, transportation, and the like have declined.

If we could go back to the year 1970 and begin again to build a corrections system with an eye toward the year 2000, would we envision the costly, cumbersome behemoth we have today? Most people would say no.

Of course, we cannot re-create history. But we can examine today's corrections system in light of what we want it to become. We can identify—and begin to confront—the dilemmas and issues that must be faced to create a corrections system that reflects our nation's most cherished values.

Five Correctional Dilemmas

A dilemma is a situation that forces one to choose among unsatisfactory alternatives. Corrections faces many dilemmas, a fact to which any worker in the field will attest. We have selected five dilemmas as particularly important because they are what we consider orienting dilemmas for corrections. That is, not only must each corrections system confront them as it moves into the twenty-first century, but the resolution of most other issues—from daily problems in offender management to larger considerations— will be profoundly influenced by the manner in which these dilemmas are faced. Indeed, today's difficulties and tomorrow's potential solutions are very much bound up in how these five dilemmas were faced in the past.

Unlike much of the material in this book, our description of the dilemmas is not an objective restatement of facts and studies; rather, it is a subjective interpretation of many facts, studies, and observations. We return to the systems perspective as we identify five core concerns: mission, methods, structure, personnel, and costs.

Mission

Corrections lacks a clear mission. One reason for this is that it has so many different clients—offenders, the general public, other government agencies—each of which has

different expectations of corrections. In simplistic terms, we recognize tha
want fairness, leniency, and assistance; the public wants protection from an
ment of criminals; government agencies want cooperation and coordination. (
the expectations often come into conflict. Thus one goal of corrections ultimat
be to disentangle the expectations and establish a set of priorities for handling tl

At the same time, none of these competing expectations can be ignored. H
courts respond when corrections fails to provide rehabilitative services to offer
How does the public respond to instances of brutal recidivism? How do govern
agencies manage balky corrections officials?

One of the common solutions in corrections is to attempt to meet all expectatio
provide the services that are requested, take actions to protect citizens when public sat
becomes an issue, cooperate with agencies when asked to do so. The advantage of th
approach is that corrections can avoid the strains that accompany goal conflict because
is easier not to make hard choices about priorities. Of course, this supposed advantage
does not really materialize. The conflicts between attempts to serve clients and to protect
the community, or between attempts to coordinate government practices and to provide
assistance or protection, are real. When corrections tries to meet all these competing expectations equally, correctional workers must resolve the conflicts informally.

It is important for corrections to confront the problems created by ambiguity of mission. Doing so requires that choices be made. In the early 1960s most people agreed
that the primary mission of corrections was the rehabilitation of offenders, but the devaluation of treatment and the movement toward harsh, mandatory sentences left a
void in this area. Some observers have suggested that corrections must take on the role
of offender management; others have argued that the role of corrections is risk control;
still others have suggested punishment as corrections' mission. Whatever the choice of
mission, correctional leaders must articulate their philosophy of corrections and establish a clearer policy to guide its implementation. Both staff members and persons outside the system must be aware of what corrections does and what they should expect
from its efforts.

Methods

Obviously, if the correctional mission is unclear, the best correctional strategies and techniques will be ambiguous as well. When goals are in conflict, staff members have difficulty choosing among competing methods to perform their work: surveillance or service,
custody or treatment. But this is not the only problem with correctional methods; much
more significant is the fact that correctional techniques often don't seem to work.

We have discussed technical uncertainty and its implications for corrections; chronic
uncertainty has other consequences as well. A debilitating lack of confidence results when
apparently promising strategies, upon evaluation, turn out to lack merit. The list of failed
correctional methods includes reduced caseloads, offender counseling, family counseling,
group treatment, restitution, and offender classification. All these and many more methods have been promoted as the answer to a given pressing problem. Each time another
correctional strategy proves ineffective, the failure feeds an already pervasive feeling
among workers that corrections is incapable of performing its basic functions well.

This is one reason why the short-term history of corrections seems dominated by
fads. As each "innovative" technique or program is implemented, corrections is confronted by the method's limited ability immediately to solve the technical problems it
was intended to solve, and so it is replaced by something newer still.

The consequences of these frequent changes in approach are largely negative. No
firm, central technical process is allowed to develop and mature. Because corrections
works with people, the central technologies seemingly should involve interpersonal communication and influence, but the parade of new programs subtly shifts the emphasis
from process to procedures. The dynamic work of corrections is stalled by the static and
routinized activities that ebb and flow with each new program. Bureaucratic approaches
to offender management and warehousing come to dominate the technical approach to

the job. Workers become cynical about changes and about the potential of the work itself. And who can blame them? The most experienced correctional workers have seen many highly praised programs come and go, having failed to produce the expected results.

Another issue associated with correctional methods is fairness. In recent years the concept of just deserts has dominated the definition of fairness, and much effort has been devoted to ways to achieve it. Although the just deserts model of criminal justice is quite elaborate, it boils down to a single generalization: Offenders should be punished equally in accordance with the severity of their offenses. This seems to be a straightforward assignment.

Yet something is wanting in the doctrine of just deserts. The fact is that the more stringent correctional methods apply in practice almost exclusively to the poor and predominantly to minorities. One is left with the feeling that merely to be "equal" in our application of state power under these circumstances is not really to be fair in the broadest sense of the term. Genuine fairness must enhance the lives and the life potential of those we bring under correctional control. But if the history of corrections has taught us anything, it is that we often injure the people we try to help. We know very little about how to assist offenders effectively, but it is certainly not enough just to punish them equally. The dilemma of methods is complex. Can we overcome the tradition of faddism in corrections without becoming stodgily bureaucratic in method? Can we improve the life chances of correctional clients without injuring them further, despite good intentions?

Structure

Corrections is simply not in a position significantly to influence its own fate, and much of this inability has to do with its structure — internal and external. Internally, corrections is a process divided against itself. Jails, prisons, probation, and parole all struggle with one another; the practices of each become contingencies for the others. Externally, corrections represents the culmination of the criminal justice process, and it has little formal capacity to control the demand for its services. Thus correctional leaders face two structural dilemmas. First, their colleagues are often the ones who put the most immediate obstacles in the way of their attempts to manage their operations effectively. Second, the corrections system depends on significant factors outside of its control.

The practical consequences of corrections' structural dilemma are sometimes quite startling. In many jurisdictions, for example, large amounts of money have been spent renovating old jails or building new ones because the existing facilities are substandard, overcrowded, or both. Too often the new version is soon just as overcrowded as the old one was, or is deemed legally substandard. The fault rests with the inability of corrections to coordinate architectural planning with the programmatic needs of such nonjail agencies as the courts and probation. What initially seemed to be a problem of how much space is available really reflects a problem of how available space is used, which, in turn, is influenced by people other than jail administrators. The courts (through sentencing and pretrial release), law enforcement (through arrest), and probation/parole (through revocation) all use jail space for their own purposes. The lack of agencies to ameliorate the effects on corrections of population growth can eliminate the benefits of opening a new prison. This is only one of the deficiencies that repeatedly occur in correctional planning.

Formally the problem of structure in corrections is one of interdependence and coordination. The ability of corrections to function effectively in some ways depends on external processes that it must either respond to, influence, or at least understand. If corrections is to do so, its own processes must be better coordinated with those of the external agencies that produce the dependence — and the dissension.

The problem is that there is really no easy way to coordinate these processes. Separation of powers is both a constitutional and a traditional bulwark of our government. Each agency is jealous of its own power and reluctant to reduce it by coordination or planning. Thus, when a new jail is being designed, the approval of the municipal engineering bureau is seen as a hurdle to be cleared rather than a potential resource to be tapped. Each time an interagency control is put into place, it becomes an obstacle rather than a coordinating mechanism.

Most correctional administrators find that their greatest frustrations lie in getting other agencies to avoid actions that severely constrain their ability to function. A recent trend has been the formation of high-level commissions and task forces composed of heads of correctional, justice system, judicial, and executive branch agencies whose job it is to improve coordination. This is a promising step, but a small one.

Personnel

Because corrections is a people-processing operation, its personnel are its major resource. The two essential goals in regard to staff are (1) attracting the right kinds of people to work in corrections and (2) motivating them to remain once they are employed. Corrections traditionally has not done well in either area.

The initial recruitment problem frequently stems from the low starting salaries. Salaries vary widely from place to place, but correctional employees often earn less than workers in comparable positions elsewhere. For example, correctional officers frequently begin at wages lower than those of local law enforcement officers. Likewise, the starting salaries of probation and parole officers, who normally are required to have a college degree, often are not competitive with those offered to social workers and teachers.

For this reason correctional positions may be regarded as a good entry to the work world. A person new to the job market can obtain stable employment for a year or two while seeking alternative employment. The most qualified individuals find it relatively easy to move on to other occupations; less qualified people often stay longer, some for their entire careers.

Further, as a result of collective bargaining most correctional employees receive equal pay raises regardless of performance. Inevitably a system of equality becomes a disincentive to employees whose work efforts surpass those of others. Too frequently significant personnel decisions, such as promotions, raises, and increased responsibilities, are completely out of the hands of correctional administrators.

In times of fiscal abundance, salary is not so great a problem, but a decade of salary crunches in government employment combined with a constricted job market embitters many correctional employees. The organizational culture of many correctional operations is dominated by animosity toward management and cynicism toward the job. Too often correctional employees feel unappreciated, manipulated, and alienated. Under these conditions it is exceedingly difficult for a corrections system to perform its people-work function effectively because its most valued resource — the staff — is demoralized.

On the surface the solution to the personnel problem seems simple: Measure the performance of staff, reward those who are productive, and get rid of those who are not. Unfortunately this approach does not work in government employment (and may not work very well in the private sector either). For one thing, correctional performance is exceedingly difficult to assess. Although the general yardsticks of recidivism, institutional security, and so forth provide useful measures of corrections' performance, they are inadequate indicators of an individual's performance. Who can say that a parolee's failure was the parole officer's fault? Indeed, a case can be made that it represents an officer's successful surveillance. Too often secondary performance measures, such as contacts with clients, paperwork, and training, are substituted for primary measures of job success. These secondary measures are fairer because they fall within the staff's control. But for a secondary measure of performance to be useful, it must be clearly related to organizational success. In this respect most secondary measures in corrections are inadequate. In another vein, government employment is often sought because of its purported job security; altering the personnel picture to overcome lethargy is likely to cause extreme strain among the staff.

The correctional leader's choices in the personnel area, unhappily, involve no short-term solutions. The answer, if there is one, lies in long-term staff development. A sound staff is built by innovative selection and promotion methods; professional growth on the job is encouraged by education and training incentives; and "human resource" management approaches are taken to involve staff in the operations of the organization. However, turnover at the top of the correctional hierarchy may be so great that the administrator who undertakes to address personnel issues may not be on the job to reap the rewards of the efforts.

Costs

One of the most notable aspects of corrections is that it is expensive. The cost of building a prison runs upward of $100,000 per cell, excluding financing. Each personnel position represents expenditures equal to twice the total annual salary when fringe benefits, retirement costs, and office supplies are taken into consideration. The processing of an offender through the corrections system can run as high as $20,000 in direct costs and nearly half that much again in indirect costs (such as defaulted debts, welfare to families, and lost wages and taxes). The decision to punish an offender is a decision to allocate precious public resources, often irretrievably. Correctional administrators understand all this now more than ever. Allocating correctional resources wisely is a real challenge.

Institutional crowding, combined with fiscal restraint, has produced an unprecedented concern about correctional costs. The public is beginning to question the advisability of correctional growth. One might say that the public is exhibiting a form of political schizophrenia: The desire to punish criminals is not backed up by a willingness to pay for the punishment.

The ambivalence about punishment and funding has left correctional leaders in a bind. The arguments for expansion of large, secure facilities must be weighed against equally strong arguments for increased emphasis on community-based corrections. These arguments are in some ways easy to understand. Crime continues to be a matter of great public concern, and prisons may never have been so crowded as they are today.

Most correctional officials recognize that a focus on prisons is a regressive rather than a progressive approach. Many of our existing secure facilities are decrepit and need to be replaced, but the evidence is very strong that (1) prison construction does not alleviate crowding and (2) the incapacitation strategy for crime control is both imperfect and highly prone to error. Officials also know that once a prison is built, it represents a continuing management focus for as long as it is used—in contrast to field services, which are much more responsive to change and innovation.

To this puzzle must be added the recent trend toward privatization of corrections. Only time will tell if this trend is to become a lasting force; meanwhile, privatization is a potential threat to administrators' ability to manage the system. Most privatization plans call for skimming off the best of the worst—the nonserious offenders who can be efficiently processed. Thus the government-run part of the corrections system faces the possibility of having to manage only the most costly, most intractable offenders on a reduced budget.

Changing Corrections: A Final View

Throughout this book we have portrayed the corrections system as buffeted by its environment, changing yet unchanging. External pressures arise to move correctional leadership in one direction, only to be replaced by counterpressures in the opposite direction. One state abolishes parole release; another reinstates early release mechanisms. One prison reduces its treatment programs; another adds professional counseling staff. The image is one of an unplanned, reactive management style rather than a planned, proactive attempt to lead corrections down a path of gradual improvement.

To a great extent this image is accurate, but it, too, is changing, in part because corrections itself is in fact developing. Several forces contribute to this change, but predominant among them are professional associations and government agencies.

Perhaps the greatest influence is exercised by the National Institute of Corrections (NIC), a division of the Federal Bureau of Prisons in the Department of Justice. The NIC has served as (1) a national clearinghouse of information about correctional practices, (2) a source of technical assistance to local and state correctional agencies that wish to upgrade their practices, and (3) a training operation on both basic and advanced levels open to any correctional employee. The NIC has become to corrections what the FBI is to law enforcement: a strong force for professional standards, policy and procedural improvement, and general development of the field.

Similarly the American Correctional Association (ACA) has become an active lobbyist for the field. Over a decade ago it promulgated a set of national standards for correctional practices in jails, prisons, and field services. Correctional agencies that meet these standards may be accredited, much as universities are accredited by outside agencies. Although the ACA has not gone uncriticized, its work is indicative of the kind of ground-level upgrading that is going on in corrections today.

The American Probation and Parole Association (APPA) serves a function similar to that of the ACA but is focused on field services. It has only recently begun a high-visibility national campaign to organize the profession and to develop an improved professional consciousness of the importance of field services in probation and parole.

As important as these forces for change are, a new force for steady correctional growth and development is likely to outstrip all of them. That force is represented by the person who is reading this book: you, the student of corrections. For most of its history, the field has been the domain of amateurs, part-time reformers who were moved by a zeal to help prisoners, and local workers who took the jobs because nothing else was available. In recent years corrections has become a field of study for people interested in long-term professional careers, perhaps people like you. This is a dramatic change because it indicates a growing employee constituency with an interest in corrections to sustain the field's growth and development. This, more than any other influence, may be a stabilizing force for corrections in the years to come.

Career Opportunities in Corrections

The correctional job market is expanding, which is not surprising given the fact that the corrections system has quadrupled in size over the past twenty-five years. Since 1971, according to the Bureau of Justice Statistics, correctional budgets have grown 990 percent. In addition to the traditional functions of probation, prisons, and parole, the corrections system operates an array of programs, mostly intermediate sanctions but also diversionary programs. This appendix provides a brief description of some of the more common job titles in the correctional system. For more information, students should discuss their career plans with college and university placement officers, criminal justice faculty, and persons in the field. Organizations such as the American Corrections Association, 8025 Laurel Lakes Court, Laurel, Maryland 20707–5075, can be helpful.

Institutional Corrections

Correctional Officer

Job Description:
The term *correctional officer* is relatively new in the field; for most of the history of corrections, the term was guard. This reflects a change in thinking about the functions of the role. The older term gives the impression that the job's main duties are watching inmates to prevent escapes and fights. The new title depicts the worker as more integral to the corrective functions of the system. It reflects the fact that the correctional officer has responsibility for overseeing the offenders' adjustment to prison or jail and for assisting offenders in finding ways to turn away from crime.

Duties:
The institution requires security twenty-four hours a day. The typical correctional officer works an eight-hour shift and has an assignment that pertains to a cell range or housing unit within the facility. Normally the shifts rotate so that the correctional officer sometimes works days and other times works nights.

Requirements:
The basic educational requirement is a high school degree, but college graduates increasingly are being recruited to the job. Good physical condition is required.

Pay:
Starting pay averages $18,000–$20,000.

Correctional Counselor

Description:
The professional responsibilities are threefold: (1) to support the inmate's adjustment to incarceration, (2) to determine the best work and program assignments for the inmate during the incarceration, and (3) to help the inmate prepare for release.

Duties:
Correctional counselors are given a caseload to manage. They meet with these inmates when they first arrive in the facility to learn about their special needs, and they see them on a regular basis during their incarceration to monitor their progress. Correctional counselors also serve as a contact between inmates and their families.

Requirements:
A college degree generally is required, and frequently additional training in counseling psychology is required as well.

Pay:
Starting pay averages $23,000–$33,000.

Correctional Teacher

Description:
A correctional teacher provides classroom education to inmates who want to complete their high school education. The institutional school can be a challenging environment in which to work. Inmate motivation often is not very strong, and teaching frequently is made more difficult by inmate learning problems and histories of school failure.

Duties:
The correctional teacher evaluates student progress in the same way as any schoolteacher.

Requirements:
The correctional teacher is required to have the same credentials as a regular public schoolteacher.

Pay:
Starting pay averages $23,000–$29,000.

Vocational Program Staff

Description:
Vocational program staff are involved in the facility's rehabilitation process. They teach inmates job skills and basic job disciplines, such as punctuality, teamwork, and responsible behavior.

Duties:
Vocational program staff set up and run vocational training programs (woodworking, furniture repair, auto repair, and so on) and evaluate inmate progress in learning the vocational skills.

Requirements:
Vocational program staff are required to have a license and demonstrated skill in a vocational area, as well as experience in vocational training.

Pay:
Starting pay averages $24,000–$34,000.

Community Corrections

Probation/Parole Officer

Description:
Probation/parole officers supervise offenders who are living in the community. They help offenders become successful citizens, but they must be concerned about community safety. This balancing of "help" and "control" gives the probation/parole officer job satisfaction but also represents the source of the greatest job stress. To balance the needs of the offender and the interests of the community is not an easy task.

Duties:
Probation officers routinely carry one hundred cases or more, and parole officers almost that many. The officer monitors community adjustment by meeting with these offenders in the office and in their homes. Because it is difficult to have meaningful contact with the entire caseload, officer must choose the cases on which to concentrate their efforts.

Requirements:
Probation/parole officers usually are required to have a college degree; some states require more advanced education.

Pay:
Starting pay averages $21,000–$32,000.

Intensive Supervision Officer

Description:
Intensive supervision officers provide much more comprehensive supervision of offenders than regular probation/parole officers are able to provide. They work closely with the offender in employment and family matters in order to help ensure a better adjustment to the community.

Duties:
The intensive model calls for an emphasis on surveillance, and it augments that responsibility by providing much smaller caseloads than is typical—usually thirty or fewer clients.

Requirements:
Intensive supervision officers are normally the elite of their peers. They are specially selected from among regular probation/parole officers and represent the best of their profession.

Pay:
Intensive supervision officers usually are paid somewhat more than regular probation/parole officers.

Residential Workers

Description:
Residential staff work in facilities that provide residential placements for offenders: halfway houses, group homes, work release centers, and day treatment centers.

Duties:
Residential workers are somewhat like corrections officers, with responsibility for the security of the residential facility. But they are also like probation or parole officers, helping offenders learn how to adjust to the community and supporting the treatment, education, and vocational efforts of their clients.

Requirements:
Educational requirements vary widely, ranging from a minimum of a high school degree for basic positions to college and even advanced degrees for positions that include counseling responsibility.

Pay:
Starting pay averages $24,000–$30,000.

Treatment Specialists

Description:
Three main types of this specialized treatment are offered: substance abuse treatment, sex offender treatment, and anger control. These treatments are the cornerstone of many correctional programs, because they deal with problems that are central to the criminality of many correctional clients.

Duties:
Treatment personnel use a variety of techniques — group and individual counseling, structured intervention — to reduce the chances of return to substance abuse.

Requirements:
Advanced education and training in the area of the treatment specialty is required for these positions.

Pay:
Starting pay averages $30,000–$45,000.

Management and Administration

Supervisor

Description:
The supervisor's primary role is to facilitate staff creativity and effectiveness by providing support in the form of advice and consultation. A secondary function is staff control, which is carried out by ensuring that the standard organizational policies and procedures are followed by line staff.

Duties:
Supervisors review and evaluate the effectiveness of line staff. They serve as conduits of information between line staff and administration, and they conduct audits of staff performance.

Requirements:
In addition to the education requirements placed on line staff, supervisors are required to have a minimum number of years of experience in line staff positions.

Pay:
Starting pay averages $29,000–$41,000.

Administrator

Description:
Administrators manage the organization and determine its mission and policy. Large organizations often have several administrators, some of whom manage divisions and report to a chief executive officer.

Duties:
The professional life expectancy of the administrator is based on how well he or she keeps the political sources of support pleased with the management of the agency. The result is a natural tendency to be conservative in setting organizational policy and procedure.

Requirements:
A person becomes an administrator after years of service in various roles in the organization. The top administrator is appointed by some outside authority.

Pay:
Starting pay averages $55,000–$75,000.

Glossary

Age of Reason *See* Enlightenment.

alcohol abuser A person whose use of alcohol is difficult to control, disrupting normal living patterns and frequently leading to violations of the law while under the influence of alcohol or in attempting to secure it.

Antabuse A drug that, when combined with alcohol, causes violent nausea; it is used to control a person's drinking.

authority The ability to influence a person's actions in a desired direction without resorting to force.

bail An amount of money specified by a judge to be posted as a condition for pretrial release for the purpose of ensuring the appearance of the accused in court as required.

Beccaria, Cesare (1738–1794) Italian scholar who applied the rationalist philosophy of the Enlightenment to the criminal justice system.

behavior therapy Treatment that induces new behaviors through reinforcements (rewards and punishments), role modeling, and other active forms of teaching.

benefit of clergy The right to be tried in an ecclesiastical court, where punishments were less severe than those meted out by civil courts, given the religious focus on penance and salvation.

Bentham, Jeremy (1748–1832) English advocate of utilitarianism in prison management and discipline. Argued for the treatment and reform of prisoners.

bondsman An independent businessperson who provides bail money for a fee, usually 5–10 percent of the total.

boot camp A physically rigorous, disciplined, and demanding regimen emphasizing conditioning, education, and job training. Designed for young offenders.

campus style An architectural design by which the functional units of a prison are individually housed in a complex of buildings surrounded by a fence.

career criminal A person who sees crime as a way of earning a living, who has numerous contacts with the criminal justice system over time, and who may view the criminal sanction as a normal part of life.

case law Legal rules produced by judges' decisions.

chain of command A series of organizational positions in order of authority, with each person receiving orders from the one immediately above and issuing orders to the one immediately below.

civil disabilities Legal restrictions that prevent released felons from voting and holding elective office, engaging in certain professions and occupations, and associating with known offenders.

civil liability Responsibility for the provision of monetary or other compensation awarded to a plaintiff in a civil action.

classification A process by which prisoners are assigned to types of custody and treatment.

classification systems Specific sets of objective criteria, such as offense history, previous experience in the justice system, and substance abuse patterns, applied to all inmates to determine an appropriate classification.

"clear and present danger" Any threat to security or to the safety of individuals that is so obvious and compelling that the need to counter it overrides the guarantees of the First Amendment.

client-specific planning Process by which private investigative firms contract with convicted offenders to conduct comprehensive background checks and suggest to judges creative sentencing options as alternatives to incarceration.

coercive power The ability to obtain compliance by the application or threat of physical force.

coercive therapy Treatment in which the therapist determines the need for and the goals of treatment processes, whether or not the client agrees.

cognitive skill building A form of behavior therapy that focuses on changing the thinking and reasoning patterns that accompany criminal behavior.

community correctional center A small group-living facility for offenders, especially those who recently have been released from prison.

community corrections A model of corrections based on the assumption that reintegrating the offender into the community should be the goal of the criminal justice system.

community justice A model of justice that emphasizes reparation to the victim and the community, approaching crime from a problem-solving perspective, and citizen involvement in crime prevention.

community service Compensating for injury to society by performing service in the community.

compelling state interest An interest of the state that must take precedence over rights guaranteed by the First Amendment.

compliance Obedience to an order or request.

conditions of release Restrictions on parolees' conduct that must be obeyed as a legally binding requirement of being released.

confrontation therapy A treatment technique, usually done in a group, that vividly brings the offender face to face with the consequences of the crimes for the victim and society.

congregate system A penitentiary system developed in Auburn, New York, in which inmates were held in isolation at night but worked with fellow prisoners during the day under a rule of silence.

constitution Fundamental law contained in state or federal document that provides a design of government and lists basic rights for individuals.

continuum of sanctions A range of correctional management strategies based on the degree of intrusiveness and control over the offender, along which an offender

is moved based on his or her response to correctional programs.

contract labor system A system under which inmates' labor was sold on a contractual basis to private employers, who provided the machinery and raw materials with which they made salable products in the institution.

corporal punishment Punishment inflicted on the offender's body with whips or other devices that cause pain.

corrections The variety of programs, services, facilities, and organizations responsible for the management of individuals who have been accused or convicted of criminal offenses.

courtyard style An architectural design by which the functional units of a prison are housed in separate buildings constructed on four sides of an open square.

crime control model of corrections A model of corrections based on the assumption that criminal behavior can be controlled by more use of incarceration and other forms of strict supervision.

custodial model A model of a correctional institution that emphasizes security, discipline, and order.

day fine A criminal penalty based on the amount of income an offender earns in a day's work.

day reporting center Facility where probation violators attend day-long intervention and treatment sessions.

deinstitutionalization The release of mental patients from mental hospitals and their return to the community.

Depo-Provera A "chemical castration" drug that eliminates sexual response among males.

determinate sentence A fixed period of incarceration imposed by a court; associated with the concept of retribution or deserved punishment.

direct supervision A method of correctional supervision in which staff members have direct physical interaction with inmates throughout the day.

discretionary release The release of an inmate from prison to conditional supervision at the discretion of the parole board within the boundaries set by the sentence and the penal law.

drug abuser A person whose use of illegal chemical substances disrupts normal living patterns to the extent that social problems develop, often leading to criminal behavior.

electronic monitoring Probation supervision technique, ordinarily combined with home confinement, that uses electronic devices to maintain surveillance on offenders.

The Enlightenment, or The Age of Reason The 1700s in England and France, when concepts of liberalism, rationality, equality, and individualism dominated social and political thinking.

equal protection clause The constitutional guarantee that the law will be applied equally to all persons, without regard for such individual characteristics as gender, race, and religion.

exchange A mutual transfer of resources based on decisions as to the costs and benefits of alternative actions.

expungement A legal process that results in the removal of a conviction from official records.

federalism A system of government in which power and responsibilities are divided between a national government and state governments.

fee system A system by which jail operations are funded by a set amount paid for each prisoner held per day.

forfeiture Seizure by the government of property and other assets derived from or used in criminal activity.

formal organization A structure established for influencing behavior to achieve particular ends.

galley slavery Forced rowing of large ships or galleys.

general deterrence Punishment of criminals that is intended to be an example to the general public and to discourage the commission of offenses by others.

good time A reduction of an inmate's prison sentence, at the discretion of the prison administrator, for good behavior or for participation in vocational, educational, and treatment programs.

habeas corpus A writ (judicial order) requesting that a person holding another person produce the prisoner and give reasons to justify continued confinement.

hands-off policy A judicial policy of noninterference in the internal administration of prisons.

home confinement Terms of incarceration that offenders serve in their own homes.

house of correction Detention facility that combined the major elements of a workhouse, poorhouse, and penal industry by both disciplining inmates and setting them to work.

Howard, John (1726–1790) English prison reformer whose book, *The State of the Prisons in England and Wales,* was a major force in passage of the Penitentiary Act of 1779 by the House of Commons.

hulks Abandoned ships the English converted to hold convicts during a period of prison crowding between 1776 and 1790.

incapacitation Depriving an offender of the ability to commit crimes against society, usually by detaining the offender in prison.

indeterminate sentence A period of incarceration with minimum and maximum terms stipulated, so that parole eligibility depends on the time necessary for treatment; closely associated with the rehabilitation concept.

inmate code A set of rules of conduct that reflect the values and norms of the prison social system and help define for inmates the image of the model prisoner.

intermediate sanctions A variety of punishments that are more restrictive than traditional probation but less severe and costly than incarceration.

jail A facility authorized to hold pretrial detainees and sentenced misdemeanants for periods longer than forty-eight hours. Most jails are administered by county governments; sometimes they are part of the state government. Until the 1800s a jail was a facility authorized to hold primarily pretrial detainees, debtors, and vagrants.

judicial reprieve A practice under English common law whereby a judge might suspend imposition or execution of a sentence on condition of good behavior on the part of the offender.

lease system A variation on the piece price system in which the contractor provided prisoners with food and clothing as well as raw materials. In some southern states prisoners were leased to agricultural producers to perform field labor.

least restrictive methods Means of ensuring a legitimate state interest (such as security) that imposes fewer limits to prisoners' rights than alternative means of securing that end.

lex talionis Law of retaliation; the principle that punishment should correspond in degree and kind to the offense ("an eye for an eye and a tooth for a tooth").

line personnel Employees who are directly concerned with furthering the institution's goals; workers in direct contact with clients.

lockup A facility authorized to hold persons prior to court appearance for periods of up to forty-eight hours. Most lockups (also referred to as drunk tanks or holding tanks) are administered by local police agencies.

mandatory release The required release of an inmate from incarceration to community supervision on the expiration of a certain time period, as stipulated by a determinate sentencing law or parole guidelines.

mandatory sentence A sentence stipulating that some minimum period of incarceration must be served by people convicted of selected crimes, regardless of background or circumstances.

mark system A system in which offenders are assessed a certain number of points at the time of sentencing based on the severity of their crime. Prisoners could reduce their term and gain release by earning marks through labor, good behavior, and educational achievement.

maximum-security prison A prison designed and organized to minimize the possibility of escapes and violence; to that end it imposes strict limitations on the freedom of inmates and visitors.

mediation Intervention in a dispute by a third party to whom the parties in conflict submit their differences for resolution and whose decision (in the correctional setting) is binding on both parties.

medical model A model of corrections based on the assumption that criminal behavior is caused by social, psychological, or biological deficiencies that require treatment.

medium-security prison A prison designed and organized to prevent escapes and violence, but in which restrictions on inmates and visitors are less rigid than in maximum-security facilities.

mentally handicapped offender A person whose limited mental development prevents adjustment to the rules of society.

mentally ill offender A "disturbed" person whose criminal behavior may be traced to diminished or otherwise abnormal capacity to think or reason as a result of psychological or neurological disturbance.

methadone A drug that reduces the craving for heroin; it is used to spare addicts from painful withdrawal symptoms.

minimum-security prison A prison designed and organized to permit inmates and visitors as much freedom as is consistent with the concept of incarceration.

new-generation jail A facility of podular architectural design and management policies that emphasizes interaction of inmates and staff and provision of services.

normative power The ability to obtain compliance by manipulating symbolic rewards.

ombudsman A public official who investigates complaints against government officials and recommends corrective measures.

pardon An action of the executive branch of the state or federal government excusing an offense and absolving the offender from the consequences of the crime.

parole The conditional release of an inmate from incarceration under supervision after part of the prison sentence has been served.

penitentiary An institution intended to isolate prisoners from society and from one another so that they can reflect on their past misdeeds, repent, and thus undergo reformation.

piece price system A labor system under which a contractor provided raw materials and agreed to purchase goods made by prison inmates at a set price.

podular unit Self-contained living areas, for twelve to twenty-four inmates, composed of individual cells for privacy and open areas for social interaction. "New-generation jails" are made up of two or more pods.

positivist school An approach to criminology and other social sciences based on the assumption that human behavior is a product of biological, economic, psychological, and social factors, and that the scientific method can be applied to ascertain the causes of individual behavior.

power The ability to force a person to do something he or she does not want to do.

precedent Legal rules created in judges' decisions that serve to guide the decisions of other judges in subsequent similar cases.

presentence investigation (PSI) An investigation and summary report of the background of a convicted offender, prepared to help the judge decide on an appropriate sentence.

presentence report Report prepared by a probation officer, who investigates a convicted offender's background to help the judge select an appropriate sentence.

presumptive parole date The presumed release date stipulated by parole guidelines if the offender serves time without disciplinary or other incidents.

presumptive sentence A sentence for which the legislature or a commission sets a minimum and maximum range of months or years. Judges are to fix the length of the sentence within that range, allowing for special circumstances.

pretrial diversion An alternative to adjudication in which the defendant agrees to conditions set by the prosecutor (for example, counseling or drug rehabilitation) in exchange for withdrawal of charges.

preventive detention Detention of an accused person in jail for the purpose of protecting the community from crimes the accused is considered likely to commit if set free pending trial.

principle of interchangeability The idea that different forms of intermediate sanctions can be calibrated to make them equivalent as punishments despite their differences in approach.

principle of least eligibility The doctrine that prisoners ought to receive no goods or services in excess of those available to people who have lived within the law.

prison An institution for the incarceration of persons convicted of serious crimes, usually felonies.

prison program Any formal, structured activity that takes prisoners out of their cells and sets them to instrumental tasks.

prisonization The process by which a new inmate absorbs the customs of prison society and learns to adapt to the environment.

probation A sentence allowing the offender to serve the sanctions imposed by the court while living in the community under supervision.

probation center Residential facility where persistent probation violators are sent for short periods.

procedural due process clause The constitutional guarantee that no agent or instrumentality of government will use any procedures to arrest, prosecute, try, or punish any person other than those procedures prescribed by law.

Prozac A drug used to decrease the negative emotions associated with depression.

psychotherapy In generic terms, all forms of "treatment of the mind"; in the prison setting, coercive in nature.

public account system A labor system under which a prison bought machinery and raw materials with which inmates manufactured a salable product.

public works and ways system A labor system under which prison inmates work on public construction and maintenance projects.

punitive conditions Constraints imposed on some probationers to increase the restrictiveness or painfulness of probation, including fines, community service, and restitution.

radial design An architectural plan by which a prison is constructed in the form of a wheel, with "spokes" radiating from a central core.

rational basis test Requires that a regulation provide a reasonable, rational method of advancing a legitimate institutional goal.

reality therapy Treatment that emphasizes personal responsibility for actions and their consequences.

recognizance A formally recorded obligation to perform some act (such as keep the peace, pay a debt, or appear in court when called) entered by a judge to permit an offender to live in the community, often on posting a sum of money as surety, which is forfeited by nonperformance.

reformatory An institution for young offenders emphasizing training, a mark system of classification, indeterminate sentences, and parole.

regional jail Facility operated under a joint agreement by two or more governmental units, with a jail board drawn from representatives of the participating jurisdictions and having varying authority over policy, budget, operations, and personnel.

regulation Legal rules, usually set by an agency of the executive branch, designed to implement in detail policies of that agency.

rehabilitation The goal of restoring a convicted offender to a constructive place in society through some form of vocational or educational training or therapy.

rehabilitation model A model of a correctional institution that emphasizes the provision of treatment programs designed to reform the offender.

reintegration model A model of a correctional institution that emphasizes maintenance of the offender's ties to family and the community as a method of reform, in recognition of the fact that the offender will be returning to the community.

release on recognizance (ROR) Pretrial release granted on the defendant's promise to appear in court because the judge believes that the defendant's ties in the community are sufficient to guarantee the required appearance.

remunerative power The ability to obtain compliance in exchange for material resources.

restitution Compensation for financial, physical, or emotional loss caused by an offender, in the form of either payment of money to the victim or work at a service project in the community, as stipulated by the court.

restitution center Facility where probationers who fall behind in restitution are sent to make payments on their debt.

restoration Punishment designed to repair the damage done to the victim and community by an offender's criminal act.

retribution Punishment inflicted on a person who has infringed the rights of others and so deserves to be penalized. The severity of the sanction should fit the seriousness of the crime.

secular law The law of the civil society as distinguished from church law.

selective incapacitation Making the best use of expensive and limited prison space by targeting for incarceration those offenders whose incapacity will do the most to reduce crime in society.

sentence disparity Divergence in the lengths and types of sentences imposed for the same crime or for crimes of comparable seriousness when no reasonable justification can be discerned.

sentencing guidelines An instrument developed for judges that indicates the usual sanctions given previously to particular offenses.

separate confinement A penitentiary system developed in Pennsylvania in which each inmate was held in isolation from other inmates, with all activities, including craftwork, carried on in the cells.

sex offender A person who has committed a sexual act prohibited by law, such as rape, child molestation, or prostitution, for economic, psychological, and even situational reasons.

shock incarceration A short period of incarceration (the "shock"), followed by a sentence reduction.

shock probation A sentence in which the offender is released after a short incarceration and resentenced to probation.

situational offender A person who in a particular set of circumstances has violated the law but who is not given to criminal behavior in normal circumstances and is unlikely to repeat the offense.

social control Actions and practices of individuals and institutions designed to induce conformity with the norms and rules of society.

social therapy Treatment that attempts to make the institutional environment supportive of prosocial attitudes and behaviors.

span of control A management principle holding that a supervisor can effectively oversee only a limited number of subordinates.

special deterrence (specific or individual deterrence) Punishment inflicted on criminals to discourage them from committing any future crimes.

staff personnel Employees who provide services in support of line personnel (for example, training officers, accountant).

stakes The potential losses to victims and to the system if offenders fail; stakes include injury from violent crimes and public pressure resulting from negative publicity.

standard conditions Constraints imposed on all probationers, including reporting to the probation office, reporting any change of address, remaining employed, and not leaving the jurisdiction without permission.

state use system A labor system under which goods produced by prison industries are purchased by state institutions and agencies exclusively and never enter the free market.

statute Law created by the people's elected representatives in legislatures.

street-level bureaucrats Public service workers who interact directly with citizens in the course of their work, granting access to government programs and providing services within them.

system A complex whole consisting of interdependent parts whose operations are directed toward common goals and influenced by the environment in which they function.

technical violation The probationer's failure to abide by the rules and conditions of probation (specified by the judge), resulting in revocation probation.

technology A method of applying scientific knowledge to practical purposes in a particular field.

telephone-pole design An architectural plan for a prison calling for a long central corridor crossed at regular intervals by structures containing the prison's functional areas.

Thorazine A drug used to control violent or aggressive behavior caused by psychiatric problems.

to stand bail The practice, by a private citizen, of posting bail for a defendant and promising to make certain that the defendant will appear for trial.

token economy A type of behavior therapy that uses payments (such as tokens) to reinforce desirable behaviors in an institutional environment.

totality of conditions The aggregate of circumstances in a correctional facility that, when considered as a whole, may violate the protections guaranteed by the Eighth Amendment, even though such guarantees are not violated by any single condition in the institution.

transactional analysis Treatment that focuses on how a person interacts with others, especially on patterns of interaction that indicate personal problems.

transportation The practice of transplanting offenders from the community to another region or land, often a penal colony.

treatment conditions Constraints imposed on some probationers to force them to deal with a significant problem or need, such as substance abuse.

unconditional release The release of an inmate from incarceration without any further correctional supervision; the inmate cannot be returned to prison for any remaining portion of the sentence for the current offense.

unit management Tactic for reducing prison violence by dividing facilities into a number of small, self-contained, semiautonomous "institutions."

unity of command A management principle holding that a subordinate should report to only one supervisor.

urinalysis Technique used to determine whether someone is using drugs.

utilitarianism The doctrine that the aim of all action should be the greatest possible balance of pleasure over pain; hence the belief that a punishment inflicted on an offender must achieve enough good to outweigh the pain inflicted.

victim impact statements Descriptions in PSIs of the costs of the crime for the victim, including emotional and financial losses.

vocational rehabilitation Prison programming designed to teach inmates cognitive and vocational skills to help them find employment on release.

wergild "Man money"; money paid to relatives of a murdered person or to the victim of a crime to compensate them and to prevent a blood feud.

widening the net Increasing the scope of corrections by applying a diversion program to persons charged with offenses less serious than those of the persons the program was originally intended to serve.

work release center A facility that allows offenders to work in the community during the day while residing in the center during nonwork hours.

Index

Boldface numbers in this index refer to the page on which the term is defined.

Michigan
    Dunes Correctional Facility (Holland), 293
    Felony Firearms Statute, 66
    House of Shelter (Detroit), 272
    Michigan Reformatory, 293
    rules of general conduct, Michigan
        Department of Corrections, 297
    State Prison of Southern Michigan
        (Jackson), 255, 293
    Wayne County (Detroit), 204
    Western House of Refuge (Albion), 272
Middle Ages, corrections during, 24–29
Miethe, Terance, 78
Millbank Penitentiary (England), 38
Minimum-security prisons, **238**
Minnesota
    community corrections legislation, 217
    Comprehensive Community Corrections
        Act (1973), 217
    incarceration vs. crime rate, 217
    intermediate sanctions for
        overcrowding, 429
    Minneapolis judges' sentencing patterns,
        74, 76
    public account system, 335
    restitution centers, 207
    Sentencing Guideline Commission, 429
    sentencing guidelines, 77–78
    Supreme Court, cocaine sentence
        disparity, 79
Minorities. *See also* Race
    capital punishment inmates, 461–462
    as correctional officers, 307–308
    differential criminality, 439–441
    ethnic succession, 113, 260
    gangs and, 260
    race, ethnicity, and corrections, 436–447
    sentence disparity, 78–79
    War on Drugs, 445
Minors. *See* Children; Juvenile corrections
Minton, Mark, 388
Misdemeanor court, 72, 74
Mississippi
    capital punishment, racism and, 463
    female correctional officers, 307
    parole board composition, 351
Missouri
    executions (1976–1998), 461
    operating expense appropriations, growth
        of, 14
    Turner v. Safley, 91, 92
    Wilkins v. Missouri, 459
"The mix," 280
Modus operandi, 115–116
*Monell v. Department of Social Services for
    the City of New York*, 106
Money. *See also* Funding
    cigarettes as currency, 255, 256–257
    inmate savings accounts, 334
Montana
    operating expense appropriations, growth
        of, 14
    parole board, requirements for, 351
Montesquieu, Charles-Louis de, 29
Moody, Carlisle, 66
Moore, Charles, 78

Morash, Merry, 282
Morning Cloud, Denise, 274
Morocco, Oukacha, prison violence in, 229
Morris, Norval, 57, 60, 62, 67
Morrissey v. Brewer, 104–105
Motor vehicle theft
    actual time served, risk assessment, and
        parole, 358
    arrest and incarceration rates for, 112
    arrest rate, women vs. men, 270
    arrest vs. incarceration rates
        (1980–1994), 425
    committed supporting drug habit, 122
    juvenile arrests for, 369
Moyer, Imogene, 279
Murder
    actual time served, risk assessment, and
        parole, 358
    arrest and incarceration rates for, 112
    arrest rate, women vs. men, 270
    arrest vs. incarceration rates
        (1980–1994), 425
    committed supporting drug habit, 122
    estimated time served, 359
    juvenile, 415
    juvenile arrests for, 404
    prison term after parole revocation, 369
    sentences vs. time served, 67
    sentencing guidelines for, 77
    state court sentences, 75
Murderers, as parolees, 353

National Academy of Sciences (NAS),
    National Research Council, 442
National Advisory Commission on Criminal
    Justice Standards and Goals, 336
National Association for the Advancement
    of Colored People (NAACP), Legal
    Defense and Education Fund, 90
National Center on Addiction and Substance
    Abuse, 119
National Commission on the Causes and
    Prevention of Violence, 124
National Council on Crime and
    Delinquency, 278
National Crime Victimization Survey,
    offenders, race of (1992), 443
National Institute of Corrections, 159, 332, 503
National Institute of Justice, 130, 431
National Jail Census, 143
National Legal Aid and Defender
    Association, 79
National Prison Association, 43, 272, 347
Native Americans. *See also* Minorities
    history of, 438
    Okimaw Ohci Healing Lodge (Canada), 274
    religion, 93
    religious programs, 331
    tribal punishment, 27
Nebraska, 284
    *Greenholtz v. Inmates of the Nebraska
        Penal and Correction Complex*, 103
    housing of HIV/AIDS offenders, 130
Neglected, **398**
Neighborhoods, community justice and, 487

Neto, Virginia, 282, 284
Nevada
    housing of HIV/AIDS offenders, 130
    incarceration vs. crime rate, 215, 217
New generation jail, **160**–162
New Hampshire, housing of HIV/AIDS
    offenders, 130
New Jersey
    conditions of release, 365
    housing of HIV/AIDS offenders, 130
    New Jersey State Prison, 298, 312
    Rahway prison, 234, 356
    separate confinement, 39
    sex offender notification laws, 386–387
    strikes, by correctional officers, 312
    Trenton State Prison, 224, 234
New Mexico
    incarceration vs. crime rate, 215, 217
    riots at Santa Fe, 255, 258
New South Wales, 28
New York
    Attica prison, 224–225, 237
    Brooklyn, localization of crime in, 489–491
    capital punishment, cost of, 467
    corrections system in, 13–14
    cost of probation/parole violations, 213
    day fines, 206
    day reporting centers, 207
    Department of Correctional Services, 268
    Elmira Reformatory, 347
    expenses on criminal justice, per capita, 17
    hard labor in, 38
    House of Refuge, 396
    incarceration vs. crime rate, 215
    intensive supervision probation (ISP), 208
    New York City, 14
    New York City, federal detention facility
        in, 144
    New York City Probation Department, 167
    New York State Governor's Special
        Committee of Crime Offenders, 50
    New York State Lunatic Asylum for
        Insane Convicts, 126
    Newgate Prison (Auburn), 40
    Operation Pressure Point, 445
    parole board, requirements for, 351
    racism in sentencing, 442
    revocation of parole, 366
    Sing Sing (Ossining), 42, 237, 271, 347
    strikes, by correctional officers, 312
    Supreme Court, 37
    "three-strikes" law, 66
    Women's Correctional Institution
        (Bedford Hills), 267–268, 284
Newgate Prison (Auburn, NY), 40
Newgate Prison (London), 271
Newman, Charles, 184
News media and publicity, 6, 399, 452
    executions, live coverage of, 452
Newton, Sir Isaac, 29
Nichol, Fred, 337
NIMBY ("Not in My Backyard") syndrome,
    235, 376
Nixon, Richard M., 336
Normative power, **291**
Norms, inmate code of, **249**–252

Photo Credits

Part 1 Opener p. 2 © Martin J. Dain/Magnum Photos; p. 6 © John Gaps III/AP/Wide World Photos, Inc.; p. 8 © Jean-Claude Lejeune/Stock, Boston; p. 10 © Frank Fournier/Contact Press Images; p. 16 © Don Edgar/AP/Wide World Photos, Inc.; p. 19 © Frank Fournier/Contact Press Images; p. 25 Private Collection; p. 27 © Corbis/Bettmann/Hulton Deutsch Collection; p. 28 Drawing by R. Caton Woodville, 1903/Corbis/Bettmann; p. 32 Historical Pictures Stock Montage; p. 37 © American Stock/Archive Photos; p. 38 American Correctional Association; p. 39 Lithographer, P. S. Duval/The Library Company of Philadelphia; p. 41 Reproduced from Warden Cassidy on Prisons and Convicts, Michael J. Cassidy. Used with permission of the ACA; p. 43 Courtesy of New York Department of Correction. Used with permission of the American Correctional Association. Published in ACA, *The American Prison, A Pictoral History*, published by the ACA, 1983, p. 80, Machine Class, Elmira, 1898; p. 56 © Damian Dovarganes/AP/Wide World Photos, Inc.; p. 58 © Nick Ut/AP/Wide World Photos, Inc.; p. 59 © Steve Rasmussen/Sygma; p. 67 © Andrew Lichtenstien/Impact Visuals; p. 69 © Corbis/Bettmann; p. 72 © Pool/The Seattle Times/The Gamma Liaison Network; p. 78 © Mark Cowan/AP/Wide World Photos, Inc.; p. 84 © Eric Risberg/AP/Wide World Photos, Inc.; p. 86 © Ken Heinen/AP/Wide World Photos, Inc.; p. 92 © Ethan Hoffman/Picture Project; p. 97 © Robert McElroy/Woodfin Camp & Associates; p. 102 © Mark Sultz/AP/Wide World Photos, Inc.; p. 104 © Craig Murray/The Brockton Enterprise/AP/Wide World Photos, Inc.; p. 115 © AP/Wide World Photos, Inc.; p. 119 © Jan Halaska/Photo Researchers, Inc.; p. 124 William Lopez/NYT Pictures; p. 131 Alan S. Weiner/NYT Pictures; p. 134 © Orlin Wagner/AP/Wide World Photos, Inc.; Part 2 Opener p. 138 © Lionel Delevingne/Stock, Boston; p. 143 © Philip Taft/Black Star; p. 147 © Ahmad Terry/Rocky Mountain News/Sygma; p. 152 © A. Lichtenstein/Sygma; p. 155 James Hill/NYT Pictures; p. 157 © AP/Wide World Photos, Inc.; p. 160 © Louis Sohn/Chattanooga Times/AP/Wide World Photos, Inc.; p. 162 © Rick Friedman/Black Star; p. 168 Courtesy of the Bostonian Society Old State House; p. 174 © John Neubauer/PhotoEdit; p. 184 © John Boykin/PhotoEdit; p. 191 © A. Ramey/Woodfin Camp & Associates; p. 199 © Monty Davis/AP/Wide World Photos, Inc.; p. 206 © Ed Andrieski/AP/Wide World Photos, Inc.; p. 209 © Jack Kurtz/Impact Visuals; p. 211 © Joseph Rodriquez/Black Star; p. 215 © George Cohen/Impact Visuals; p. 226 © Barry Halkin; p. 233 © Tom Carroll/FPG International; p. 234 © Lizzie Himmel/Sygma; p. 237 © P. F. Bentley/Black Star; p. 242 © Donna Binder/Impact Visuals; p. 247 © Chris Cozzone/Sipa Press; p. 252 © The Gamma Liaison Network; p. 253 © Andrew Lichtenstein/Sygma; p. 258 © Mike Derer/AP/Wide World Photos, Inc.; p. 259 © Vincent Dewitt/Stock, Boston; p. 269 © Kathy Willens/AP/Wide World Photos, Inc.; p. 271 © Archive Photos; p. 273 © A. Ramey/Stock, Boston; p. 275 Courtesy of Okimaw Ohci Healing Lodge; p. 279 © A. Ramey/PhotoEdit; p. 282 © A. Ramey/PhotoEdit; p. 283 © Jane Evelyn Atwood/Contact Press Images; p. 290 © Susan Meiselas/Magnum Photos; p. 291 © 1992 Robert Harbison/The Christian Science Monitor; p. 298 © Joe Jines/Southern Illinoisan/AP/Wide World Photos, Inc.; p. 301 © Ben Klaffke; p. 307 © Joel Gordon; p. 318 © Andrew Lichtenstein/Impact Visuals; p. 322 © Bob Daemmrich/Stock, Boston; p. 331 © Michael S. Green/AP/Wide World Photos, Inc.; p. 333 Giovanni Chidini; p. 339

Elizabeth Gurney Fry
*Observations in Visiting,
Superintendence and
Government of Female
Prisons*
1827

Declaration of Principles,
Cincinnati, Ohio;
creation of National
Prison Association
1870

Cesare Lombrosco
Criminal Man
1876

Alexis de Tocqueville
and Gustave de Beaumont
*On the Penitentiary System
in the United States*
1833

N. Y. House
of Refuge
1825

Alexander Maconochie
and Walter Crofton
develop the concept
of parole
1840

Halfway house for women,
Boston
1864

Law establishes
first juvenile
court, Cook
County (Chicago)
1899

House of Shelter, a reformatory for
women run by Zebulon Brockway,
Detroit
1865

Western State
Penitentiary,
Pittsburgh
1825

John Augustus
develops the concept
of probation
1841

Ind. State Reformatory, first
independent, female-run prison
for women
1873

Eastern
Penitentiary,
Cherry Hill, Pa.
1829

N.Y. State
Lunatic Asylum
for Insane Convicts,
Auburn, N.Y.
1859

Elmira Reformatory,
Elmira, N.Y.
1876

Mass. Reformatory Prison
for Women, Framingham
1877

Amendment 14 to the Constitution
guarantees due process of law
and equal protection of the law
1868

N.Y. Good Time Law
1817

Ill. Juvenile
Court Act
1899

Civil Rights Act
1871

Ruffin v. Commonwealth
Upholds judicial "hands
off" policy
1871

Mass.
Probation Act
1878

First automobile patent
1895

Beginning of
Calif. Gold
Rush
1848

Wright
brothers'
flight
1903

American
Civil–War
1860–1865

Spanish-American
War
1898

War of 1812

Mexican War
1846–1848

1800

1900